MARGINALITY & CONDEMNATION

MARGINALITY & CONDEMNATION

A CRITICAL INTRODUCTION TO CRIMINOLOGY

Third Edition

edited by

Carolyn Brooks
& Bernard Schissel

Fernwood Publishing • Halifax and Winnipeg

Editing: Curran Faris
Cover artwork: April Doepker
Cover Design: John van der Woude
Text Design: Brenda Conroy
Printed and bound in Canada

Published by Fernwood Publishing
32 Oceanvista Lane, Black Point, Nova Scotia, B0J 1B0
and 748 Broadway Avenue, Winnipeg, Manitoba, R3G 0X3
www.fernwoodpublishing.ca

Fernwood Publishing Company Limited gratefully acknowledges the financial support of the Government of Canada through the Canada Book Fund and the Canada Council for the Arts, the Nova Scotia Department of Communities, Culture and Heritage, the Manitoba Department of Culture, Heritage and Tourism under the Manitoba Publishers Marketing Assistance Program and the Province of Manitoba, through the Book Publishing Tax Credit, for our publishing program.

Library and Archives Canada Cataloguing in Publication

 Marginality and condemnation: a critical introduction to criminology
/ edited by Carolyn Brooks & Bernard Schissel. -- 3rd edition.

Includes bibliographical references and index.
ISBN 978-1-55266-734-7 (pbk.)

1. Criminology. 2. Crime. 3. Marginality, Social. I. Brooks, Carolyn,
author, editor II. Schissel, Bernard, 1950-, author, editor

HV6025.M37 2015   364   C2015-900677-5

CONTENTS

ACKNOWLEDGEMENTS

Our aim for this third edition is to develop a text that introduces students to the rich and diverse nature of criminology, as well as engage them with thought-provoking research that links academic analysis to current social issues, crime control, criminal justice policy and practice. One of our intentions is always for students to see the value of sociological and criminological writing and to get a sense that a social critique also offers practical alternatives to injustice. In our quest to do this, we are indebted to the authors in this book, and in the previous two editions, for their insightful contributions, their inspiring research and knowledge and their devotion to their disciplines and to social justice work.

We are indebted to many people for their direct encouragement and assistance with this book. We have benefited tremendously from the diverse and thought-inspiring faculty, sessionals and other colleagues at or affiliated with the University of Saskatchewan and Royal Roads University. We have been influenced and inspired by their insights, research and many conversations. We are also indebted to the students who are impassioned by a search for justice, who have shared themselves with us in the classroom, and whose wisdom and enthusiasm are part of this book. We also acknowledge and thank all those who used our first and second editions in their classrooms and to those who made invaluable comments towards this new edition.

Thank you to Joanne Butler, Keely Kinar, Harpreet Aulakh, Glenn Andre and Marg Gauley who assisted in the development of the first and second editions of the book. Thanks to James Popham for his invaluable work on the test bank, index and extra pedagogical features in this new edition. Also, thanks to Cory Schewaga for his administrative and photographic work of the cover art, and especially to the artist April Doepker for her powerful artwork, which also shows viewers how art and social commentary may be embedded within graffiti. Her striking innovative rendition heartens our work. We gratefully acknowledge SCYAP (Saskatoon Community Youth Arts Programming), which is dedicated to arts-skill acquisition for at risk youth and community revitalization and worked with the artists who produced the front covers for every edition of this book: Chris Moffat, Crystal Kishayinew and April Doepker. Our gratitude to the University of Saskatchewan, the Office of Research Services Publication Fund, the skills and dedication of the staff in the Department of Sociology, the University of Saskatchewan and the Office of Research Professional Development Fund at Royal Roads University.

We continue to be indebted to everyone at Fernwood Publishing for their work and support for each edition, for their tireless efforts in working with us on improving our collection and, more generally, for their continued commitment to providing a Canadian publishing context in which social justice and critical thinking is paramount. We remain deeply thankful to Wayne Antony, in particular, for his thorough editing, for his skills as a sociologist, and his creative mindfulness, and to Errol Sharpe for his vision and dedication. Special thanks to Curran Faris for his copy-edit of the manuscript, to

Beverley Rach and Brenda Conroy for their work in design and production, to Debbie Mathers for making the final manuscript corrections, and to John van der Woude for the cover design.

Lastly, we thank our friends and families for providing the context in which we feel both inspired and fulfilled, especially to Sean, Rob, Ben, Declan and Delaney — from Carolyn — and to Wendy, Nathan and Matthew — from Bernard.

Finally we thank each other for a continuing productive, memorable and important collaboration.

CONTRIBUTORS

SHAHID ALVI is a professor of criminology and social science in the Faculty of Social Science and Humanities at the University of Ontario Institute of Technology, where he teaches graduate and undergraduate courses in criminology. He is the author or co-author of six books, including the recently released *Youth Criminal Justice Policy in Canada: A Critical Perspective* and the forthcoming MOOCs *for Sale: Informational Capitalism and the Edu-Factory.*

CAROLYN BROOKS is an associate professor of sociology at the University of Saskatchewan. Her research and publications focus on youth resilience, the politics of punishment, violence, and visual and community based participatory research methods.

WENDY CHAN is a professor of sociology at Simon Fraser University and has published widely on issues of race and crime, including *Racialization, Crime and Criminal Justice in Canada, Criminalizing Race, Criminalizing Poverty* and *Crimes of Colour: Racialization and the Criminal Justice System in Canada.*

HONGMING CHENG is an associate professor in the Department of Sociology at the University of Saskatchewan and an Edmond J. Safra Network Fellow in Ethics at Harvard University. His research and teaching cover various areas including white-collar crime, business ethics, corporate governance, commercial law, food safety, social control, policing and transnational crime.

ELIZABETH COMACK is a professor of sociology at the University of Manitoba. Over the past three decades she has written and conducted research on a variety of social justice topics. Her recent books include *"Indians Wear Red": Colonialism, Resistance, and Aboriginal Street Gangs* (co-authored with Lawrence Deane, Larry Morrissette and Jim Silver) and *Racialized Policing: Aboriginal People's Encounters with the Police.*

LAWRENCE DEANE is an associate professor in the Faculty of Social Work at the University of Manitoba, where he teaches in the Inner City Social Work Program. Lawrence has worked in community economic development for over twenty years, first in India and then in Winnipeg's inner city. He is author of *Under One Roof: Community Economic Development and Housing in the Inner City.*

ROBERT DIAB is an assistant professor in the Faculty of Law at Thompson Rivers University and the author of *The Harbinger Theory: How the Post 9/11 Emergency Became Permanent and the Case for Reform* and *Guantanamo North: Terrorism and the Administration of Justice in Canada.* His research focuses on national security, constitutional and criminal law and human rights.

DEBORAH DRAKE is a senior lecturer in criminology in the Faculty of Social Sciecnces at the Open University. She is author of *Prisons, Punishment and the Pursuit of Security* and co-editor, with J. Muncie and L. Westmarland, of *Crime and Justice: Local and Global* and co-editor, with R. Earle and J. Sloan, of *The Palgrave Handbook of Prison Ethnography*.

ROD EARLE is a lecturer in youth justice in the Faculty of Health and Social Care at the Open University. He has written and published mainly around the topics of men in prison, race and ethnicity, masculinity and gender. He helped to establish British Convict Criminology, a group mainly composed of, and that supports, ex-prisoners working as criminologists.

LAUREN EISLER is an associate professor in the Department of Criminology at Wilfrid Laurier University. She teaches courses in youth justice and advanced theory at both the undergraduate and graduate level and, with Carrie Sanders, developed the first pubic criminology course offered at a North American University in the fall of 2012. The course continues to be offered. Lauren is currently the inter-faculty associate dean of academic development and is located at the Brantford Campus.

KARLENE FAITH is professor emerita in criminology at Simon Fraser University in British Columbia. She is also a community activist and prisoners' rights advocate. Her publications include: *Unruly Women*; *The Long Prison Journey of Leslie Van Houten*; and *13 Women: Parables from Prison*.

KEARNEY HEALY, a lawyer, works for the Saskatchewan Legal Aid Commission, Saskatoon Office. For several years his work has focused mainly on young people. As a volunteer, he helped build a townhouse housing co-op, enabled people to obtain telephone service and drafted a proposed law that would allow children sexually abused by pimps and johns to sue them. He was given the C. Willy Hodgson Award by the Law Society of Saskatchewan in 2013 and was appointed Queen's Counsel in 2014.

BRYAN HOGEVEEN is an associate professor of sociology at the University of Alberta. He has published widely on justice, violence, epistemology, youth crime, martial arts in/and society, continental philosophy and the sociology of sport. He is co-editor (with Joanne Minaker) of *Criminalized Mothers, Criminalizing Mothering*; co-author (with Joanne Minaker) of *Youth, Crime and Society: Issues of Power and Justice*; and co-author (with AndrewWoolford) of *Cold Cities: Care and Control in the Inner City* (forthcoming). His Social Sciences and Humanities Research Council of Canada–funded research project examines the impact of governmental economic restructuring on the marginalized inner-city residents of Edmonton and Winnipeg.

YASMIN JIWANI is a professor of communication studies at Concordia University. She is the author of *Discourse of Denial: Mediations of Race, Gender and Violence*, as well as co-editor of *Girlhood, Redefining the Limits* and *Faces of Violence in the Lives of Girls*. Her research interests include mediations of race, gender and violence in the context of war stories, reporting of sexual violence and femicides in the press.

JOANNE MINAKER is an associate professor of sociology at MacEwan University. She is co-author (with Bryan Hogeveen) of *Youth, Crime and Society: Issues of Power and Justice* and numerous articles that identify the processes through which marginalized women and criminalized youth are excluded, silenced and dehumanized. She is co-editor (with Bryan Hogeveen) of *Criminalized Mothers, Criminalizing Mothering* and engaged in a research project about care and marginalized, young mothering. In 2013, Joanne founded Cared Humanity, a care-based education resource and community dedicated to the fundamental human work of self-care and practising care for others.

LARRY MORRISSETTE is the executive director of Ogijiita Pimatiswin Kinamatwin, an organization that works with Aboriginal street gang members. He also teaches in the Inner-City Social Work Program at the University of Manitoba.

JANET E. MOSHER is an associate professor at Osgoode Hall Law School, York University. Her research interests include legal interventions impacting women abused in their intimate relationship, access to justice for marginalized populations, welfare policy (welfare fraud and the criminalization of poverty in particular), poverty law, homelessness, legal aid and clinical legal education. She is co-editor (with Joan Brockman) of *Constructing Crime: Contemporary Processes of Criminalization* and (with Joe Hermer) *Disorderly People: Law and the Politics of Exclusion in Ontario*. She is the co-author of a number of reports, including *Take the Story, Take the Needs, and DO Something: Grassroots Women's Priorities for Community-Based Participatory Research and Action on Homelessness* (with Emily Paradis); and *No Cherries Grow On Our Trees:* A Brief by the Take Action Project, a Public Policy Initiative to Address Women's Poverty and Violence Against Women (with Nora Currie and METRAC).

BERNARD SCHISSEL is a professor of social sciences and program head of the Doctor of Social Sciences Program, Faculty of Applied and Social Sciences, Royal Roads University. His most recent books are *About Canada: Children & Youth*; *Still Blaming Children: Youth Conduct and the Politics of Hate*; and *The Legacy of School for Aboriginal People: Education, Oppression, and Emancipation* (with Terry Wotherspoon).

JIM SILVER is a professor in and chair of the Department of Urban and Inner-City Studies, University of Winnipeg. His research interests are in inner-city, poverty-related and community development issues. Jim is a member of the Manitoba Research Alliance and the leader of the Housing and Neighbourhood Revitalization stream of its SSHRC Partnership project, "Partnering for Change: Community-Based Solutions for Aboriginal and Inner-City Poverty."

WEI WANG graduated from the School of Criminology at Simon Fraser University. Her research interests include white-collar crime, drug trafficking, criminal careers and juvenile delinquency. She is an assistant professor in the National Police University of China.

1

CRIME, CRIMINOLOGY AND JUSTICE

Carolyn Brooks and Bernard Schissel

KEY FACTS

> The origin of criminology can be traced to the late 18th century Europe and the United States, where crime research was done as part of other occupations, such as running lunatic asylums or collecting prison and court statistics.

> The first phase of criminology is represented by the work of Benjamin Rush (1786/1815), a Philadelphian physicist interested in moral insanity and Cesare Lombroso (1835-1909), an Italian physician and criminologist infamous for his ideas of born criminality and criminal atavism.

> There is a renewed interest in Public and news making criminology—and for criminologists to help shape the representation of newsworthy criminal justice issues, such as increases in prison populations, youth crime, terrorism, racial profiling, missing and murdered Aboriginal women, and much more.

> Cultural criminology seeks to understand the use of crime in the media and social media as a source of news, entertainment and a partner in crime stoppers, blurring the boundaries between fiction and reality. This "CSI Effect "creates an illusion that all crime scenes yield foolproof forensic evidence, constructing false images of crime and criminal justice processes.

> Comparative criminology aims to learn from the experience of different societies, explaining how and why crime rates and criminal justice approaches vary: for example, clusters of societies who have very high versus very low prison rates, known as "penal excess" (in for example, England, Canada and the U.S.) versus "penal exceptionalism" (in Finland, Denmark and Norway).

Sources: Rafter 2011; Loader and Sparks 2011; Pratt and Eriksson 2013; Schissel 2011.

This book is an introduction to and an overview of the rich and diverse nature of criminology and the thought-provoking research that often links academic analysis to criminal justice policy and practice. It examines theoretical approaches to explaining crime, the public construction of crime (through media and law), the historical and contemporary shape of crime and punishment and future directions of theory and crime control. Many of the chapters and the main arguments developed throughout are shaped by critical criminology; they examine how some individuals and groups come to be defined as "criminals" — as immoral or abnormal or simply "bad" — and conclude that this stigma is often not because of what such individuals have done but because of who they are and where they fit into Canada's social and economic system.

Before we explore the complexity of issues that form the discipline of criminology, we need to think through what criminology actually is. At a very simplistic level we can say that criminology is the study of crime. But, what is it about crime that we wish to know: Do we want to know the gory details of crime? Do we want to know what a criminal is like? Or, do we want to know how the police solve crimes? These questions stem directly from our exposure to popular culture and these are the issues that make crime fiction so compelling and popular. Clearly, much of the common sense discourse about crime and popular culture focuses on the mostly superficial "details" of crime and whimsical circumstances, and somehow we assume that if we know these apparent details, we understand the crime and the criminal. The problem is the idiom "if it bleeds it leads" remains true. Fear-based news stories grab viewer attention but presents anecdotal, rather than scientific, evidence and portrays isolated criminal incidents as trends. In addition, reporting that doesn't go beyond merely telling a crime story may be good for sensationalism and ratings, but this practice creates a misunderstanding about actual crime and its control in our society. The obvious questions posed above form only a small piece of the criminology puzzle.

As a starting point for assembling the very diverse pieces of the crime puzzle, we must acknowledge that what constitutes good and bad behaviour is not always clear — that is, crime is contested territory. Taking someone's life in peacetime is a much different act from doing so in wartime. Against the grain of commonsensical cultural perception, we must acknowledge that not all criminals are "bad" people. What informs our "knowledge" of crime is the almost daily rendering of crime in popular media, especially television and movies; crime "stories" feed our curiosity and our prurience. To understand crime and criminology, however, we need to remove ourselves from popular culture and invest our curiosity in reflecting on the fundamentals about crime: crime does indeed cause harm; there is at least some social agreement about what is a crime; and there are laws that guide society in how to respond to crime. A more complex understanding of crime and justice demands that we think of both as contested domains, that many crimes are not easy to define as immoral and harmful, that there can be little social agreement about some crimes (or that social agreement varies from context to context) and that the justice system, and the laws that guide the system, are not always fair and just. This, then, provides the gateway to a critical, social-sciences approach to crime that forms the framework for this book.

WHAT IS CRIME?

Conventional criminology was necessarily predicated on the principle that we know what crime is. And, while this may seem like a commonsensical statement, the definition of crime is highly variable and is based on many contexts including history, geography, culture and political regime, to name a few.

Mostly, we know crime as a type of behaviour that breaks the law — crime is an intentional act by an individual that is in violation of criminal law (Michael and Adler 1933; Sutherland and Cressey 1970). But if we use this legalistic definition alone in determining offence, then we give over to "the law" an incredible amount of power to define morality. Issues of good and evil become embedded in the legal code as moral dimensions/moral universals that stand above social processes. The problem with moral universals is that the law changes over time and varies depending on context. At certain points in time, new behaviours become criminalized while others become decriminalized. Today, crimes including "association with terrorist organizations," child pornography, cyber vandalism/terrorism and environmental pollution have become central criminal legal issues while behaviours and acts involving sexual preference, some forms of drug use and euthanasia are *not* now part of our conception of crime, though such behaviours and acts were prosecuted in the past. In the end, the definitions of criminality are based on who has the power to implement new laws and reform existing ones.

A critical criminological approach to crime and justice focuses on who defines crime, why they do so and what the process is through which these definitions changes. The focus from this perspective is on the social and political development of crime, a focus very much different than a criminogenic focus on why individuals engage in bad behaviour. A criminogenic focus aims to understand what individual, relational and environmental factors may produce criminal behaviour. Forensic science and some consensus theories have a criminogenic focus. Critical criminology, by contrast, aims to challenge traditional and legal understandings about crime and criminal justice.

The critical perspectives understand crime and criminal justice as social constructs that uphold social, political, racial and economic inequalities. The injurious behaviours of the poor and racial minorities are more likely to be defined as criminal than the injurious actions of the rich and powerful. For example, the sale of a defective product or the exposure to workplace hazards are less likely to be defined as criminal than adolescent theft, street gang violence and/or welfare fraud. In Chapter 7 of this edition, Janet Mosher demonstrates the difference between taxpayers and welfare recipients who defraud the same " public purse." She shows how taxpayers, often men, who have significant assets "are often regarded indulgently while welfare recipients who defraud that same purse, more likely to be women and invariably poor, are harshly condemned." Wei Wang and Hongming Cheng (in Chapter 8) demonstrate the seriousness and growing international problem of environmental crimes effecting climate change, biodiversity and pollution, yet they show how laws have little power to tackle such harmful and criminal activities against the environment.

If we take the legalistic definition of crime as sacrosanct — if we assume that the criminal code is fundamentally correct — we restrict the work of criminologists to a focus on those who get caught and prosecuted. Arguably, the law cannot define or identify all forms of criminality. Crime becomes somewhat of an ambiguous notion as we try to blend the legal definition of crime with our individual and collective conceptions of moral violations (e.g., degrading pornography, prostitution and the sex trade), human rights violations (e.g., abuse of child labour), social violations (e.g., online abuse) and political and economic deviance (eg. insider trading, price-fixing, environmental degradation and tax violations). Consider for a moment current debates on criminalization and decriminalization related to the sex trade in Canada.

A landmark case (*Bedford v. Canada* 2010) *may* decriminalize the sex trade. In Canada, it remains illegal to communicate in a public arena for the purpose of prostitution and to use a certain place (bawdy house) for prostitution activity. Sex workers have argued that this violates section 7 of the *Canadian Charter of Rights and Freedoms*, and in December 2013, the Supreme Court of Canada ruled that current legislation did violate sex workers' right to protect themselves. In response, the Federal Government has put forward Bill C-36, which names johns and pimps as the exploiters, criminalizes the purchase of sex and decriminalizes sex work. While this decision by the Supreme Court is suspended until Dec 19, 2014, these reforms are based on an idea that criminalization is not a human rights–based response to sex work. This "third way model" (criminalizing johns and pimps and decriminalizing the sex trade) has been criticized as being a "moral high ground approach"— for naming all clients as perpetrators and for assuming all sex workers are victims. And these current debates show the political and contested nature of what acts are criminalized and decriminalized and how this changes overtime.

Crime then is an ambiguous notion fraught with legal, moral, social and economic claims. From a critical criminological point of view, crime is a political, not a value-free concept.

WHAT IS CRIMINOLOGY?

Criminology and the Enlightenment

Criminology, like most other disciplines in the academic/research world, was born of the Enlightenment period. The Age of Enlightenment began in the seventeenth century in Europe and was a cultural and intellectual movement that emphasized reason and individualism rather than tradition or historically significant beliefs. The enlightenment, in its adoption of the principles of science, stood against religion as the framework for understanding nature, especially with respect to how nature could be controlled. The social sciences grew from the positivist principles of natural science and their focus on social problems and the need to resolve such problems. Positivism was based on the principles that science could measure phenomena, make universal explanations about a particular phenomenon and ultimately correct anomalies in physical and social abnormalities. Criminological positivism became a powerful force in the social sciences crusade to understand good and bad behaviour and, of course, to correct bad behaviour. To correct such behaviour, one needed merely to understand the origins of anomalous behaviour.

This scientific approach to crime and criminals was epitomized in the early, rather seminal work of Cesare Lombroso in Italy in the late nineteenth century. The science of crime embedded in his work and subsequent works, was based on the principles of evolution that grew from the works of Charles Darwin. Simply put, Lombroso and his adherents believed that criminals were innately different from "normal people" and their difference could be observed in their physicality. While we do discuss Lombroso and the legacy of his work in several places in this book, suffice it to say for now that even today we have not abandoned the search for the evolutionary/genetic origins of badness, especially given that we now can, in theory, map genetic-based behaviour on the human genome (Kayser and Schneider 2009; Carter 2007). Sociological positivism merely extended biological positivism by incorporating the idea that the social anomaly, the marginalized social position, was a fundamental identifier of the bad individual.

Much of modern criminology grew out of the anxieties that were part of the development of North American society during the early twentieth century. The two world wars and the depression created considerable social and economic upheaval in North America. The intellectual work of universities, exemplified by the Chicago School of Sociology, focused on trying to understand and correct the maladies connected with rapid social change, maladies that included increasing inner-city crime and the growth of "delinquent cultures." The focus of much of this intellectual work was on "mapping" society to try to figure out where crime and deviance were most predominant and then linking these maps of deviance to other social characteristics such as how disorganized the society was, what the social and economic characteristics and the demographic profile of the communities were and how people adapted to social and economic change.

From the 1960s onward, police and justice movements drew on the principles of sociological positivism to establish law and order programs that focused on "wars on crime" that were really wars on certain types of communities, communities that had high rates of visible "street crime." The policy programs involved increasing police forces, building jails, building more courts and other administrative enhancements that were based, in part, on finding criminal/anti-social individuals and removing them from decent society. In part, such efforts ensured that criminals were caught and punished in order to discourage further criminal behaviour. Such wars on crime were premised on the principles of criminology that we discuss in Chapter 2 as consensus theories and the sociology of crime.

In such a strict, conventional, sociology of crime approach, the focus is most often on a set of foundational issues as they relate to the "causes of crime":

- *the extent and nature of crime* (premise: crime statistics are the most significant measure of crime — if we can find out where crime is, we can deal with it)
- *punishment as a deterrent to crime* (premise: criminals who are punished harshly will be unlikely to engage in future criminality and the general public will be discouraged from committing crime)
- *the nature of the offender* (premise: criminals are either flawed individuals or they are flawed by membership in dysfunctional communities)
- *communities as sources of crime* (premise: bad communities generate bad people and bad conduct)
- *crime detection and punishment: police, courts and prisons* (premise: the primary function of the justice system is to detect, judge and imprison offenders in a fair and impartial manner)
- *crime and its effect on victims* (premise: victims' rights are paramount and criminology has a commitment to understanding the effect of crime on victims and the effect of fear of crime on the general public)
- *public attitudes to crime and social policy* (premise: the public has the right to be informed about crime in the community and criminal justice policy must reflect the will of the community)
- *forensic assessments of current and potential criminals including genetic and psychological predispositions to criminality* (premise: forensic and psychological sciences have a fundamental role in detecting and explaining criminal behaviour)
- *cultural influences on crime, including a focus on gangs, "imported" criminality and criminal subcultures* (premise: some subcultures have higher rates of crime and deviance than others and the crime control system needs to focus on criminality, in part, as a subcultural characteristic)
- *jurisprudence and due process as the framework for detection and punishment:* (premise: the principle of due process is the cornerstone of the justice system and the courts use due process to determine guilt or innocence in a fair and impartial way)
- *crime prevention and community well-being* (premise: communities are safe when they are protected by the police and the courts and by community vigilance—safety is the result of a strong crime control system and active community members).

THE ANTIDOTE TO CONVENTIONAL CRIMINOLOGY: CRIME AND LAW AS POLITICAL ISSUES

The system of justice and punishment in our society is based on the rather conventional assumption that the law is correct both because it reflects the will of the majority and because the practice of law (jurisprudence) is an objective, impartial mechanism for protecting the rights of all citizens. Interestingly, the philosophy that frames such conventional approaches is the same one that frames the way in which we think about science and its ability to detect and treat deviance. As we consider the origins of modern science, we find that our conventional understanding of crime and punishment has, embedded in it, a strong forensic element, which assumes that the commission of crime represents a pathology, either social or biological, that can be diagnosed and treated. For example, forensic psychiatrists now use a well-established method of detecting psychopathology (the psychopathy checklist) to determine and treat what they define as psychopaths or dangerous offenders. The implications for law are that psychiatrists get to decide what constitutes the traits of a psychopath and who gets defined as dangerous.

A critical counterargument is that this mode of definition is, in part, a political act, for in the end the traits that constitute psychopathology are much the same traits that also appear, for example, in a modern, large business — aggression, self-indulgence, lack of empathy. Also, most of the individuals who end up in forensic psychiatric facilities, and who get defined as dangerous, come from the lower strata of society. This is not to say that they are not a danger to themselves or others; it is to say that their identification has much to do with where they come from, how they dress, or how articulate they are, and less to do with the actual science of identification. The science of conventional criminology, then, becomes largely a political mechanism that often works to define and "morally evaluate" the activities of only certain kinds of people, to the exclusion of others.

A criminal is not necessarily immoral, and the immoral is not necessarily criminal. Rather, who is defined as criminal is often someone who is disadvantaged socially or economically, or even perhaps physically. The disadvantaged position of the typical offender often enhances the image and the position of privilege of the non-offender who is socially unlike the offender; the offender is typically detected, defined, condemned and punished, not for bad behaviour necessarily, but for occupying a low, stigmatized position in the socio-economic hierarchy. The person's poverty in itself becomes a crime, and in the end, the crime control system identifies and punishes poverty as the only immorality. Jails are full of poor people. The critical criminological position identifies imprisonment as a political act — an act that constructs and reconstructs the criminal in the eyes of the world. Brooks (Chapter 9) demonstrates that while poverty and homelessness are at very high levels many very rich countries, such as Canada and the U.S., many have downsized social programs and housing initiatives and increased prison populations. As Brooks points out, what is defined as "crime" is often against underemployed, unemployed and poor people: "In labelling the addict or the woman working in the sex trade, for instance, as "criminal," society forgoes the obligation of dealing with the underlying social inequalities that lead people into these desperate living conditions."

Many traditional criminology books concentrate on philosophies and studies that focus on the characteristics, origins and effects of abnormal or non-conventional behaviour. We do not take that orthodox approach to crime in our book. Our focus, on the contrary, is primarily on the connections between socio-economic power, political power and social control. We look at how the morals, values and welfare of socio-economic elites are translated into the morality of the law and how power generates privilege through the courts. This means, for example, that the actions of corporations and the more powerful and rich may not be criminalized even when they pose a danger or threat, such as emitting pollution or tax evasion. We critique conventional criminology as a "scientific discipline," as a force that is an integral part of a particular worldview. Working within the boundaries of that worldview, the law exonerates and legitimates the powerful and indicts the poor for their poverty. We explore, in essence, the politics of morality and the morality of crime control.

Our approach, broadly framed, argues that it is difficult to define acceptable behavioural norms and appropriate penalties for violations of those norms. Definitions of, and prohibitions for, crime change over time and across social groups and societies, with little consensus around just what criminal behaviour is. As a result, our critical criminology is informed, in part, by historical studies that track changing modes of crime control. Historically, definitions of deviance and crime have been based on explanations ranging from sin to sickness to questionable lifestyle — explanations coinciding with the influences of religion, science and the law, respectively. In our approach, we assume that laws and norms are not necessarily unchangeable or correct or even shared by most people. In effect, socially and economically powerful individuals have more access and ways to influence those who define and construct the codes of conduct. And, generally, these criminal codes are used to control the behaviours and cultures of people who are on the social and economic margins, outside the mainstream or somehow disadvantaged. The sensitivity and objectivity that criminologists struggle to maintain in studying deviance must be based on the realization that research in the areas of crime and deviance, however important, can be misused and misrepresented to the detriment of certain people. As several writers in this book point out, today the definitions and control of crime are connected to the workings of global capitalism, which in most respects, is creating an ever-increasing global underclass of marginalized people. For example, of the largest one hundred economies in the world, fifty-one are not countries but transnational corporations, and *they employ less than 1 percent of the world's workforce* (see Chapter 9). Their mandate is to reduce reliance on labour, which is often the most costly (or uncontrollable) factor of production; ultimately they work to secure more and more of the world's resources while driving a greater proportion of the world's population into poverty. As global capitalism progresses and more people become disenfranchised, more people are also labelled as criminal. Rather than addressing the roots of increasing marginality, we are told we have to cut back on social provisions and add more police, courts and prison cells. These trends help to explain the high rate of imprisonment.

So, if we take this broad, critical approach to crime and punishment, we focus our attention on the same issues as those of conventional criminology, but our foundational questions are different. The crime concerns listed earlier is somewhat altered using a critical perspective:

- *what is defined as criminal:* What behaviours are criminalized? What is the connection between class, race, gender, sexuality, age and behavours and people who become criminalized? How is crime understood in the news, media, law, policy and social media and more? What is the connection between what we call crime and social harm? What isn't defined as crime and why?
- *the extent and nature of crime:* What is the connection between poverty and other forms of disadvantage and high crime rates? Are certain communities policed more

heavily than others? Are certain people policed more heavily than others? Do the police and the courts focus on certain types of crimes and ignore others?

- *punishment as a deterrent to crime:* Does punishment really deter crime or is it more an act of vengeance against people who commit certain types of crime? Why are the majority of people who come before the criminal courts and who go to jail, from disadvantaged sectors of the society (often poor, often racial minorities, often young and unemployed)? Does punishment actually increase the tendency to criminality?
- *the nature of the offender:* What are the factors in the life of an offender that generate a disposition to commit crime? Has the offender suffered personal and social disadvantage that makes a conventional career path difficult?
- *communities as sources of crime:* What is it about the community that makes crime a viable (or the only real) life choice?
- *crime detection and punishment — police, courts and prison system:* What is the reason for the social skew in the courts and in prison — in other words, why do marginalized people get arrested, convicted and sentenced the most? Is justice delivered fairly and without prejudice?
- *crime and its effect on victims:* Are victims used as political pawns in the politics of crime? Why do victims tend to want to punish their offenders? What is the relationship between victims and offenders — are victims threatened primarily by strangers or are victims most often known by offenders? What is the public perception about personal vulnerability and victimization, and how does fear of crime generate attitudes towards crime?
- *public attitudes to crime and social policy:* Does the general public have an impact on public policy or does politics manipulate public attitudes? Where does the general public receive its information about crime? Do public attitudes reflect the reality of crime?
- *psychological assessments of current and potential criminals (including genetic predispositions to criminality):* Why is there a disproportionately large number of people with mental health issues in prison? Does the way we pathologize crime through genetics and psychiatry/psychology disadvantage those who are targeted as "born criminals"? Does the pathology of crime discourse determine the way the general public understands criminality?
- *cultural influences on crime (including a focus on gangs, "imported" criminality, and criminal subcultures):* As we focus on gang related crimes, do we target certain racial and ethnic groups for increased scrutiny, and do we use a language of gang criminality that is racially derived? Do the police and the courts target certain racial groups for excessive scrutiny? Why does racial profiling exist, what is its effect and who are its targets?
- *jurisprudence and due process as the framework for detection and punishment:* Do the courts and the legal system actually determine fair outcomes? How does the principle of due process advantage some and disadvantage others? Do the courts merely process people bureaucratically with little regard for social justice?
- *crime prevention and community well-being:* How can public policy enhance community well-being to provide the conditions under which crime cannot thrive? How can the police adapt the criminal justice system to account for the variations in advantage and disadvantage across communities? Can the police and the courts be part of a model of community enhancement and sustainability?

INTERDISCIPLINARITY, MULTIDISCIPLINARITY AND CRIMINOLOGY

One of the things that becomes evident to us as authors as we put together such an array of the writings of critical criminologists and the complexity of criminology and justice studies is that the individual disciplines or methods that attempt to explain crime can rarely do so independently. The presumption is that a singular discipline is often unwilling or incapable of seeing alternative views of reality, especially views that involve the socio-political complexity. Psychology tends to look at personality disorder, the law focuses on fairness in the courts, police studies look at police efficiency and safety and anthropologists look at how laws are formed within certain cultures. All of these disciplines have something to offer, but their views of crime are incomplete. We turn then to a very current approach to social sciences work variously labelled as interdisciplinarity or transdisciplinarity. Although these labels are often used interchangeably, they do represent approaches to social inquiry based on a common framework that social phenomena are best understood from a variety of disciplines simultaneously. For example, a human geographer might use global information systems (GIS) to map areas with different crime rates. A sociologist would likely gather information on the social and economic well-being of community members based on personal interviews in the context of victimization. A political scientist might focus on voting patterns within areas in relation to police resource allocation based on Elections Canada data. And a health care specialist might conduct family studies that look at victimization and its effect on access to healthy food and adequate medical care. The team of interdisciplinary researchers would work, then, to create a common research framework that would facilitate the types of information they require as a combined team.

Such an interdisciplinary approach facilitates a critical perspective because it forces investigators to think outside their disciplines and to approach the act of crime from many perspectives, including that of the offender. Most importantly, it compels people to think about the political, social and economic contexts of crime, to see that the definition and the modes and degree of crime control are contested issues that are not written in stone.

These interdisciplinary and critical theorists not only help to emphasize the importance of drawing on diverse disciplines but also capture the importance of using multiple methods to understand crime.

A good deal is learned about patterns of crime and criminalization from a variety of statistical and methodological tools. Victim surveys (such as the Canadian Urban Victimization Survey), self-reports of delinquency and official reports (such as the Uniform Crime Reporting Survey (UCR)) all provide a partial picture, a picture only from the perspective of those who compile these reports. Interdisciplinary and critical criminologists do not limit themselves to these survey tools; they participate in qualitative, quantitative and visual and/or other creative research methods to learn more about crime and crime control.

Official crime statistics are based on the aggregate records of offences and offenders and on court, police and correctional agencies documentation. The UCR reports crimes known to the police but omits the dark figure of crime: the unreported or undiscovered crime. A simple critique is that this data represents only crime known to official agencies and law enforcement and that it relies on a legal definition of crime.

Victim surveys and self-reports ask individuals about experiences — and these are in response to the partiality of official crime statistics. The General Social Survey (GSS) samples the general public every five years about criminal offences and victimization, but this is limited to incidents that are categorized as theft of property, household victimization or violent victimization. One of the problems with victimization data is the limited nature of crimes, often excluding crimes such as computer hacking, crimes against the public order (driving under the influence of alcohol or drugs) and corporate or environmental crimes.

Critical criminology and interdisciplinary work does not limit investigation to official sources of statistics by government bodies; rather, critical criminologists have an arsenal of techniques available to them, including quantitative (counting, mapping, surveys, statistics) and qualitative (focus groups, in-depth interviewing, visual, ethnographic) methods. Criminological research has incorporated ways for individuals directly involved in crime (victims, offenders, young offenders, justice officials, Elders, lawyers and more) to share their stories and have their voices meaningfully heard. This has included the use of visual methods such as photovoice (the use of photography to tell one's story), art-based methods (creative use of drawing, art, video and cartooning to share lived realities), oral-narrative, ethnographic research, life histories and case studies. The ethnographer researcher, for example, affords the researcher to enter into the natural setting and become more directly exposed to the realities of respondents' lives. As Rod Earle states, "Prison ethnographers in the United Kingdom have offered rich and diverse accounts of penal interiors, and prisoners' views and experiences have been, for the most part, reported with sensitivity, creativity, and insight" (2014: 429). Rod Earle and Deb Drake draw on some of their own experiences with prison ethnographies in Chapter 15.

The critical perspective is, in the end, a social justice perspective because it aims, through multiple methods and interdisciplinary approaches, to understand crime in its social context. It accounts for the politics of crime, and crime control is always a hot-button political issue. It accounts for the reality that those who come under the scrutiny of the crime control system the most often are the most disadvantaged people in society. It accounts for the likelihood that people in positions of power benefit the most from a conception of crime that is based on personal fault. Finally, it accounts for the possibility that harsh crime control is unproductive in repairing human behaviour and that it is, in fact, responsible for increased criminality.

This last point takes us to a focus on the law. A critical criminological perspective argues that the conventional criminal justice system is only one means of responding to societal conflict and harm and that it may not be the best means to do so. The com-monsensical rationales for criminal justice are retribution, crime control, due process and rehabilitation (correction). The problem with such rationales is that injustice is often embedded in them, especially in practice. Retribution is a non-productive, emotional response to criminality that can only damage those already damaged. Crime control is often based on the visibility of the offender (as evidenced in racial profiling). Due process often gives way to economic and social advantage. Rehabilitation, while a laudable goal, is most often replaced by incarceration devoid of healing. Alternative principles of justice such as mediation and healing arise because they work within certain contexts; they are not judicial programs — they are restorative programs. The complexity of justice as a general principle is shown by the following litany of formal and informal justice types: criminal justice; civic justice; regulatory justice; informal justice; restorative justice; Indigenous justice; populist justice; social justice; global justice; and environmental justice. At present in Canada, we see all of these forms of justice at work, and they are borne out of necessity largely because the criminal justice system cannot be the place where all forms of justice are delivered adequately and fairly.

THE CONTENT OF THE BOOK

The book as a whole explores the diversity and importance of critical perspectives in criminology, but we do not ignore mainstream, traditional inquiry. Part I, "Explaining Crime," begins with a discussion of the theoretical underpinnings of the debates in criminology and the sociology of crime and justice. Chapter 2 presents the conventional, consensus-based theories of crime as a point of departure for the discussions that follow in that chapter. Chapter 3 provides a survey of the theories that form a paradigm labelled pluralist theory. This chapter describes how a theoretical and pragmatic accommodation can occur between the apparently polarized theories of consensus and conflict. Chapter 4 then builds a critical orientation through a survey of current and former critical theories. Chapter 5 provides an important contemporary dimension to criminology; it includes an historical overview of the development of feminist theory in crime and justice and shows how the incorporation of feminist and gender issues have made a significant contribution to crime and justice theory and policy. Chapter 6 reiterates the complexities within competing theories of crime by applying these to analyze contemporary crime problems by using the examples of gang and sex trade involvement. Whatever theoretical perspective we choose to study crime and justice, a primary, unforgettable factor is that some rules are just while others are unfair, some rules are applied without prejudice while others discriminate against the underprivileged and certain types of crime are more prevalent amongst certain categories of people than others.

The chapters that follow Part I bring to life both contemporary and critical criminological theoretical perspectives by linking them to the analysis of and explanations for crime and delinquency within Canadian communities. They suggest how different subgroups in society come to terms with being the victims or the agents of social control.

In Part II, "Crime and Class," the contributions examine the mechanisms through which we come to see certain types of people as criminal and how criminal justice is unjustly applied. The authors outline the forces that historically have relegated certain people to the economic margins of society and then condemned them for acts related to that marginality; the authors suggest that today those same forces are allowing corporate and environmental crime to flourish at the expense of criminalized women, children in the sex trade, Third World citizens and so on. A key element of this section is how economic power and privilege work in the process of defining how injurious behaviour of economically marginalized is defined as criminal while harmful behaviour of economic privileged is not. This section reveals much about how our common conceptions of crime are based on contemporary stereotypes of how people should act and how a typical criminal looks and behaves. This section also examines the process of punishment, and documents how punishment meted out relates to conditions of privilege and power. Indeed, as we will come to see, punishment has little to do with the commission of crime, and much to do with the degree of discretion that occurs at various levels of the system: when crime is defined, when the police decide to arrest, when the courts decide to indict, when the judges and juries decide to punish and when the prison institution takes on the management of inmates.

In Part III, "Crime and Race," the chapters focus on the historical and current connections between racial oppression and crime. The authors here focus on racially oppressed groups, including Aboriginal people who become criminalized, racial profiling, the racialization of violence in media and criminal justice and the construction of terrorism as a super-crime. These chapters include descriptions of historical and current colonization processes in Canada. For example, experiences of cultural genocide are linked to experiences of Aboriginal people who become involved in gangs and how they may understand their place in Euro-Canadian and Aboriginal societies. Contributors here show the connections between the experiences of colonialism, cultural genocide and neo-colonialism, the over-involvement of Aboriginal peoples in the criminal justice system and the racial skew in the criminal justice system more generally. This final chapter includes a discussion of the political discourse that shaped the legal response to terrorism and introduces how laws and policies post 9/11 have had consequences against the human rights of minority populations. Measures used against racial minorities are shown in all of the chapters in this section to engage colonialist, racist and imperialist assumptions.

Part IV, "Crime and Gender," links social constructions of gender — femininity and masculinity — to crime and its treatment in formal institutions such as the media, law and criminal justice. Chapters in this section focus on the public misconceptions about women and crime and the increased dangerousness of women in our society. This misperception of crime is often based on popular crime TV series and glorified news coverage, which continue to follow the old adage of "if it bleeds, it leads." These chapters show the importance for criminology to account for the gendered nature of crime and crime control. In particular, criminology has not been attentive to an issue that has been well-known to criminologists: the pre-eminence of men in crime statistics and criminology. As well, the authors in this section deal with the interactions between gender, class and race.

Part V, "Crime and Young People," focuses on several dimensions of youth crime, including media representations, public misperceptions, the extent of youth crime and violence and the criminal justice reaction. These chapters include discussions about the politics of youth crime and its control, demonstrating that criminal justice policies are often antithetical to youths' healing and may increase crime. In the end, these chapters offer a contextual understanding of youth marginalization and victimization and illustrate how poverty, racism and violence against youth is linked to offending. Explored are the underlying reasons why youth come into conflict with the criminal justice system, while putting forward restorative and transformative initiatives that are shown to be more successful at creating healthier youth and communities where youth may thrive.

By focusing on explaining crime as well as treating it, this book brings together broader issues of "criminality" as related primarily to inequality in Canadian society. The substantive sections of the book are designed around the discussion of specific crimes placed within a structural context — a context that includes the socio-economic and cultural forces that produce not only unconventional behaviour but also biases in crime control. The substantive chapters are more specific in their content than are most discussions in introductions to criminology. They contain both theoretical and substantive issues and illustrate the best that social research offers; they remind us that social analysis is at its very best when it is circumscribed by a sound theoretical position. We believe that discussing specifics will allow readers to "sink their teeth" into both the sociological problems that underlie what we call crime and the immorality (and consequent societal devastation) of the differential and discriminatory treatment practised within Canada's criminal justice system.

Many of the chapters are based on composites of several theories. They employ a type of theory raiding, which is also a compelling component of contemporary research, especially as framed in what has come to be known as a postmodern perspective, which states that the world is complex and multidimensional and that many of the issues that arise, in our case, for example, in the study of crime and justice are best explained by drawing on an array of related theories. This complexity, though perhaps daunting, can help us avoid the trap of theoretical nihilism, which argues that nothing works. When certain parts of a theory appear to be untenable, the social analyst can proceed not by rejecting or redrafting the theory, but by augmenting it with other insights. This rethinking of the use of theory can allow researchers to be social advocates and to shape social policies that are both just and practical.

Our intent is to introduce a critical analysis of crime to readers by presenting a concrete critique of the current and past treatment of offenders in Canada. Most importantly, we hope readers will share our passion — a passion developed in a long quest to have criminology recognize and support tangible alternatives in restorative justice and community development. Much of that passion emerges from investigations informed, again, by postmodern sensibilities, which remind us to be cognizant of the individual biographies and stories of offenders and their experiences with the Canadian criminal justice system. We hope too that readers will discover the richness of a critical perspective that builds on the necessary, solid alternatives to a system that now treats people with contempt, anger and vengeance.

The critical social analyst is thus impassioned to discover changes that, ultimately, can help the people who are most oppressed by discriminatory justice. This critical passion goes hand in hand with a desire to help bring fundamental change to the system of crime control. We hope that the readers will be similarly impassioned by a sense that there are concrete social justice alternatives to the "crime problem." For this reason, we believe that courses in crime and delinquency, and books that are pertinent to a profound and sensitive understanding of oppression and crime, must incorporate literature that investigates the roles of the "actors of crime" in more depth than is usual in conventional introductory books. The various analysts here examine crime and punishment as the embodiment of ideologically based institutions that operate within a larger structural context. To that end, the discussions address the role of poverty and inequality not only in criminal conduct, but also in how we define and punish bad conduct. This general theoretical and methodological focus must necessarily deal with the inequities of race, class, gender, age and geography in Canadian criminal justice.

By offering an analysis of the often prejudicial treatment of women, youth and men of marginalized racial and class backgrounds in the criminal justice system, we hope to demonstrate the importance of a critical understanding of crime. Such discussions are most poignant and relevant when they include the promise of alternative justice, restorative justice and community models of social justice. Using current critical theory, we also aim to provide a thought-provoking pedagogical study that demonstrates how criminology links up not only with social and criminal policy but also with possible alternatives to the punitive treatment of offenders.

GLOSSARY

Conventional Criminology: sometimes called mainstream criminology, conventional criminology focuses on understanding the nature of rule-breaking (its form, causes, and consequences). These theories rely on legalistic definitions of crime and include consensus theories such as the classical school, biological, functionalist, strain, subcultural, social control and interactive theories.

Crime: the most common definition of crime is behavior that violates the criminal law. For sociologists and criminologists, crime is a social construct and its definition changes depending on the historical time and place.

Criminogenic: aims to understand what individual, relational and environmental factors may produce criminal behaviour.

Criminology: in its most simple terms, criminology is the scientific study of crime, criminality and the societal and institutional response to this through the criminal justice system, media and more. Criminology is often interdisciplinary, including sociology, psychology, law, history, psychiatry and anthropology. Subcategories of criminology are penology and corrections, forensics and psychological analysis as well as victimology.

Critical Criminology: a theoretical paradigm that challenges traditional understandings about criminology, bringing into view decisions about what acts are defined as crime and ways in which different groups (races, classes, genders) of people are processes differently through the criminal justice system. A sizeable body of theory is defined under the umbrella of critical criminology including neo-Marxist theory, Left realism, peacemaking, postmodernism, poststructuralism, anti-racism, postcolonial theory, abolitionism and more.

Ethnographic Research: the researcher enters into the natural setting and becomes more directly exposed to the realities of respondents' lives.

Interdisciplinarity: represents approaches to social inquiry based on a common framework that social phenomena are best understood from a variety of disciplines simultaneously.

Legalistic Definition of Crime: an intentional act by an individual that is in violation of criminal law.

Positivism: based on the principles that science could measure phenomena, make universal explanations about a particular phenomenon, and ultimately find a solution.

Victim Surveys: the objective of these surveys is to provide estimates of personal experiences of victimization. Statistics Canada, for example, has a victimization cycle of the General Social Survey which estimates personal experiences relating to eight offence types, examines rates of reporting to police, nature of spousal violence, fear of crime, and public perceptions of crime.

SUGGESTED READINGS

Mary Bosworth and Carolyn Hoyle, *What Is Criminology?* New York: Oxford University Press (2011).

Walter Dekeseredy and Molly Dragiewicz (eds.), *Routledge Handbook of Critical Criminology*, New York: Routledge (2012).

Mike Maguire, Rod Morgan and Robert Reiner (eds.), *The Oxford Handbook of Criminology*, Oxford University Press (2012).

John Muncie and David Wilson (eds.), *Student Handbook of Criminal Justice and Criminology*, London: Cavendish Publishing (2013).

REFERENCES

Carter, Robert. 2007. "Genes, Genomes and Genealogies: The Return of Scientific Racism?" *Ethnic and Racial Studies* 30, 4.

Earle, Rod. 2014. "Insider and Out: Making Sense of a Prison Experience and a Research Experience." *Qualitative Inquiry* 20, 4: 429–38.

Kayser, M., and P. Schneider. 2009. "DNA-Based Prediction of Human Externally Visible Characteristics in Forensics: Motivations, Scientific Challenges, and Ethical Considerations." *Forensic Science International: Genetics* 3, 3.

Loader, Ian, and Richard Sparks. 2011. "Criminology's Public Roles: A Drama in Six Acts." In Mary Bosworth and Carolyn Hoyle (eds.) *What is Criminology?* Oxford: Oxford University Press.

Michael, J., and M.J. Adler. 1933. *Crime, Law and Social Science.* London: K. Paul, Trench, Trubner & Co.

Pratt, John, and Anna Eriksson. 2013. "Penal Policy and Social Democratic Image of Society." In Kerry Carrington, Matthew Ball, Erin O'Brien and Juan Tauri (eds.). *Crime, Justice and Social Democtracy: International Perspectives.* Hampshire, UK: Palgrave MacMillan.

Rafter, Nicole. 2011. "Origins of Criminology." In Mary Bosworth and Carolyn Hoyle (eds.) *What Is Criminology?* Oxford: Oxford University Press.

Schissel, Bernard. 2011. *About Canada: Children and Youth.* Halifax and Winnipeg: Fernwood Publishing.

Sutherland, E., and D. Cressey. 1970. *Principles of Criminology,* sixth edition. Philadelphia: J. Lippincott.

PART I

EXPLAINING CRIME

We begin Part I by examining the general explanations — the theories, perspectives and paradigms — about "crime" as offered by criminologists. An understanding or explanation of crime cannot focus merely on rule-breakers, on people violating laws. While the causes of violations and the individual motivations that lie behind those violations are important, they are not the only aspects of crime that call for explication: far from it. Whatever the approach, all explanations of crime must, in one way or another, explicitly or by assumption, address a number of key issues. All theories must consider how and why rules — laws — are made. Do the laws created by politicians and legislators reflect the actual harms inflicted by various forms of anti-social behaviour? Do laws reflect what all, or even most, of us believe are harmful behaviours that need to be controlled? Once laws and rules are made, they are meant to be enforced; to understand the full process of crime we must consider the actions of police, prosecutors and judges; and criminologists must ask questions about their work. Do these agents of crime control apply laws fairly? Is justice impartial?

Other areas of interest for criminologists include issues related to the sanctions applied to people convicted of violating laws. We need to not only know whether or not the "punishments" meted out are fair to individuals, befitting their behaviour, but also consider the effectiveness of particular punishments, or even punishment itself, in achieving the goals of justice. In other words, all theories have policy implications that must be openly and squarely discussed, and not all theories adequately answer the questions that need to be asked.

Chapter 2 provides an overview of "traditional/consensus" criminological theories — the classical schools and the biological, functionalist, social control and interactive approaches — and examines their contributions to the discipline of criminology as well as their policy implications. Other chapters throughout the book implicitly or explicitly incorporate and critique these theories by focusing on the relative failure of the consensus paradigm to acknowledge the substantive inequalities of class, race and gender. They also consider that paradigm's failure to understand the social construction of crime categories as they relate to systemic discrimination in the application of criminal law.

Consensus theories tend to focus on individuals and their relation to social organization in an attempt to understand the nature of rule-breaking (its form, causes and consequences) rather than engaging with how society produces marginalized or criminalized people and/or considering laws and other control mechanisms that privilege some and discriminate against others. Traditional theories, then, are part of mainstream ideology and, as a result, contribute to the labelling of offenders, the depoliticization of inequality and discrimination, and conditions that enhance crime rather than decrease it. By searching for the "cause" of someone's criminal activity, these theories have only asked why offenders have not upheld their responsibilities to the community and not whether the community has upheld its responsibility to the offenders. For example, conventional wisdom would suggest that jails are populated primarily by poor people because the poor commit the most crimes. A critical approach would contend, in contradiction, that when the state constructs the *Criminal Code*, it does so either deliberately or inadvertently in a way that primarily targets the activities of poor people. In addition, when the state applies the rules of law, it does so to the disadvantage of those who cannot "afford justice."

In Chapter 3 Lauren Eisler provides a description of those theories that blend consensus and conflict theories in an attempt to bridge the philosophical and practical gap between those theories that advocate for law and order and those that advocate for human rights. Several theories bring the critical and conventional orientations together in an attempt to understand how power operates in concert with individual human motivations and personal conditions. These bridging paradigms are provocative. They are not easily categorized as consensus or critical, and in the end they may both apologize for the status quo and advocate for it. Such "apologist theories" may be just another version of orthodox status quo criminology.

In general, pluralistic conflict theorists suggest that crime results from the use and abuse of power, from inequality. Pluralists, however, see conflict and accommodation as stemming from more than economic inequality. Max Weber gave the name "status groups" to groups that gain power and privilege because of wealth, status, political power or occupational authority. On the bases of power and inequality, privileged groups try to influence the content and application of our systems of laws. The drama that is played out is one of constant struggle for influence.

As you will see, some of the theories in this chapter overlap somewhat with the theories provided in chapters 2 and 4. This overlap is intentional as it provokes the reader to think of applied social theory in a more complex way than is suggested in the first two chapters. While the dichotomous paradigm of consensus-conflict is an important heuristic device for understanding the social world, it is somewhat lacking at the applied level. In the end, the world is not built on complete consensus or enduring conflict.

The critical paradigm, described in Chapter 4 and applied throughout the book, is an antidote to conventional consensus criminological theory. The theories making up the critical paradigm offer uncommon but profound insights into understanding criminal behaviour and the moral and practical contradictions in the criminal justice system. We know that in the absence of such an understanding we will continue to condemn and punish those already condemned by society.

Chapter 4 also provides a theoretical foundation for what follows, outlining the theories of Marxism (instrumentalist and structuralist), critical race theory and post-colonial theory, abolitionism, peacemaking, postmodernism, post-structuralism, governmentality and critical green criminology. The discussions focus on how various theories approach the study of crime; their focus is not on crime as the result of bad people behaving badly, but rather as a condition rooted in politics, in the inequalities of power in our society. Critical theories explore, in general, how the mechanisms for both defining and controlling the criminal — the lawmakers, courts, jails and law reformers — tend to differentiate people on the bases of socio-economic characteristics. Such theories, as a result, provide explanations of justice and punishment that account for a basic contradiction: while the systems of policing, courtroom justice and corrections are based on principles of equality and fairness, they exist in a socio-economic context of inequality and unfairness. In these "paradigms of injustice," equal and fair treatment of criminal behaviour is a fiction — but it is a fiction that has provided many believers with a good deal of influence in defining the connections between evil/badness and the poor or otherwise marginalized. Importantly, many of the critical theories support restorative justice and preventative approaches, but they do acknowledge that such policy approaches, while effective and truly just, are impotent as long as injustice and inequality in class, race, age, gender and geography flourish.

In Chapter 5, Elizabeth Comack provides a comprehensive overview of feminist theories and their application to crime and justice. Comack includes a feminist critique of mainstream criminology, while also showing why it is important to understand both women and men in gendered terms. The author takes us through the theoretical paradigms presented in the first theory chapters but provides a gender framework and critique. We see how criminology has been largely constructed from a patriarchal paradigm that was about men, with women interjected when convenient. Women (and the larger issue of gender) historically have been an afterthought in criminology until recently. As the author describes, the new gender, feminist paradigm of criminology does more than just add women to the mix; in their various incarnations, feminist criminology and gender theory sees gender as a fundamental reality in issues of crime and justice. In effect, these theories have opened our eyes to the reality that men and women may inhabit different worlds of crime and victimization and that a blanket paradigm of crime and justice is both inappropriate and doubly victimizing to women.

The final chapter in this section provides an example of the application of criminological theory. Carolyn Brooks and Bernard Schissel's chapter, "Critical Criminology and Contemporary 'Crime' Issues," applies both consensus and critical paradigms towards an analysis of gang involvement and prostitution. The authors demonstrate how consensus-based theories are more popular in public-policy decision making and with the voting public. Deterrence theories and modern classical theories, for example support criminal justice measures and incarceration, including imprisoning youth involved in gangs and exploited through the sex trade. More progressive programs are also drawn from consensus theories such as strain theory, social control and sub-cultural theory, which aim to rebuild social and economic support for street involved youth. Programs such as *Urban Aboriginal Youth: An Action Plan for Change* provide recreational, educational and cultural support for youth involved in gangs. *Operation Help* aims to help young women and women leave the sex trade by increasing societal and cultural supports. Feminist, critical and postmodern theories also challenge justice systems that ask for retribution and advocate for solutions to crime that focus on social and economic inequality. For some critical theorists this means advocating for restorative social-justice solutions — solutions that restore communities and people to states of wellness and well-being. Others advocate for transformative justice with a focus on the civil rights of vulnerable people. For the sex trade and gang involvement, this means asking why those most marginalized are also the most condemned. Critical theorists draw attention to the privilege of class, race, and gender and criticize restorative and restitution-based measures of justice for not doing so.

2

CONSENSUS THEORIES OF CRIME

Bernard Schissel

KEY FACTS

> Prison populations are increasing worldwide with the highest rate of incarceration in the United States.

> Law enforcement agencies compare DNA evidence gathered in crimes that have no suspect to DNA files stored in the COI and the CSI: the Convicted Offender Index and the Crime Scene Index. If a match is made between a sample and a stored profile, COI and/or CSI can identify a suspect.

> In Canada, the percentage of prisoners with mental illnesses doubled in the first decade of the 21st century. In 2012, 13 percent of male inmates and 29 percent of female inmates in federal institutions presenting mental health problems on admission; 30 percent of women offenders and 14.5 percent of male offenders had been hospitalized for mental health issues. And, four of five prisoners have substance abuse problems.

> The majority of homeless youth in Canada come from families that are economically strained and which exhibit, as a consequence, dysfunctional parenting styles.

> The Psychopathy Checklist-Revised (PCL-R) is a clinical rating scale of twenty items based on characteristics such as glib and superficial charm, grandiosity, need for stimulation, pathological lying, conning and manipulating, lack of remorse, callousness, poor behavioural controls, impulsivity, irresponsibility, and failure to accept responsibility for one's own actions. The PCL-R is used to predict criminal reoffending and the likelihood of rehabilitation.

> Low school grades, school failure and school drop-out are associated with the experiences of child abuse and/or victimization,poor health and lowe self-esteem, and ultimately with adolescent involvement in the criminal justice system.

Sources: Hare 2003, 1998; RCMP nd; Canada 2013.

Acts that society defines as criminal or deviant change over time and place. For example, until several decades ago vagrancy was considered a criminal act. If someone was found on the street without money or any visible means of support, that person could be arrested under vagrancy laws. Today vagrancy is not a grievance offence, although some urban governments in Canada are attempting to outlaw panhandling. Similarly, Canada once had an active trade in opium, which was even available in over-the-counter medicines such as children's cough syrup. Then, in 1908, the Canadian Government introduced a criminal law prohibiting its importation, manufacture and sale, a move largely based on racial prejudice against Asian immigrants rather than on any accepted scientific rationale. Since then, opium (especially in the form of heroin) has been an illegal substance. The penalties for possession are often severe, including incarceration. Prior to 1983 in Canada, a husband could not be charged for raping his wife. With the sexual assault legislation of 1983, this became no longer the case; in the eyes of the law, there is no immunity for offenders based on the relationship between offender and victim.

As we observe these changing laws and the changing definitions of crime, we are left with a number of fundamental questions. Why do laws and the definitions of crime change? Are there certain immutable acts that we consider universally criminal? Or is all crime "relative"? What do these changes reflect about the relationship between power and control?

The traditional and contemporary consensus theories of criminology, which form a large part of criminological work in North America, rarely discuss structural power — power that exists through the economy, politics and other forms of privilege. Instead, they assume that morality and the rules proscribing behaviour are natural, universal and unchanging. The general social policy response to such a belief system is that the individual rule-breaker can be changed into a law-abiding citizen or can be dissuaded from committing crimes. The criminal justice system, in a world based on consensus, assumes that bad behaviour can be identified and corrected or punished, a philosophical approach that tends to psychologize crime as something living within the individual.

The types of research based on traditional and consensus theories remain widely used today, not only in the academic community but also in government and other social policy organizations. As betokens their popularity, the theories are highly touted, and financially backed, as the basis of the "science of criminology." Indeed, their very popularity stems, in part, from their claim to scientific support — that empirical and objective research methodologies will uncover the "facts" of crime — and, in part, from the belief that they are intuitively logical: good people do good things and bad people do bad things. But the theories are also popular because they focus on a certain type of crime that is largely individual and highly visible because it occurs "on the street." Because of that focus, they appeal to people in positions of power and influence. The theories tend to isolate and condemn those who are relatively powerless and thus unable to object to, much less oppose, the cultural definitions of crime. Statistics show, for instance, that most of those in jail in the United States are poor, visible minority males, people who are poorly educated and minimally employed, and many of them are convicted of drug offences. In Canada, we lock up more young offenders per capita than we do adults. This is a somewhat odd finding, given that in terms of loss of life and loss of property, corporate crime and corporate wrongdoing cause much greater damage than do individual crimes.

CLASSICAL THEORY AND THE MODERN EXTENSIONS

The classical period embraced the scientific principles that started with Francis Bacon (1561–1626) and formed the philosophical framework for the Enlightenment. Prior to this historical period, knowledge was religion-based: bad behaviour was the result of the devil at work, and heretics and criminals were exterminated in the belief that the devil could be literally burned out of existence. The only morality was that defined by "God," and to understand the world believers needed only to discover what God wanted. During the Enlightenment, when knowledge came to be based upon the principles of science and objectivity, matters of immorality became objective and observable. Crime, while still envisioned as something absolute, was now understood as a result of natural tendencies towards hedonism or of human tendencies towards self-preservation. These "classical" approaches to criminology formed what amounted to the first modern approaches.

BECCARIA AND BENTHAM AND CLASSICAL CRIMINOLOGY

Classical theorists envisioned crime as the result of rational, calculated decisions by human beings, who are by nature predisposed to maximize pleasure and minimize pain. Several principles guide this perspective: (a) people are basically hedonistic; (b) people have free will; (c) people form a social contract with society (by birthright) whereby they agree to forgo selfish pursuits to partake of and foster the greater good of the society; and (d) punishment is an appropriate form of social control because it changes the pleasure-pain calculus, thus keeping criminals and crime under control. The Italian Enlightenment philosopher Cesare Beccaria (1738–94), who cautioned that punishment was only justified if it deterred hedonistic pursuits, articulated these principles in the late eighteenth century. He believed, furthermore, that punishment, as a means of social control, had to be minimized — that there should be just enough punishment to prevent further crime. In a very "enlightened way," classical theorists such as Beccaria abhorred punishment, especially execution, and recommended the prison as the appropriate form of minimal punishment.

Jeremy Bentham (1748–1832), whose work provided the blueprint for the modern prison system, again used the calculus of pleasure and pain as the starting point for social reform. Bentham used mathematical models to understand and evaluate the compelling nature of crime and the deterrent effect of punishment. He argued that money and other societal resources should be used in proportion to the degree of seriousness of the crime. Like Beccaria, he maintained that punishment should never exceed the degree necessary to prevent unacceptable behaviour.

Bentham's major contribution to modern systems of justice was his principle of the panopticon. For classical theorists, prison was an ideal form of punishment: the length of sentence could be determined in days and years proportionate to the seriousness of the crime. A state could also use the prison as a place in which the prisoner could re-evaluate the social contract and embrace a new belief in the value of conformity. The panopticon architecture was based on a circular design in which prison officials occupy a central observation tower surrounded by cells situated in a circular pattern around the tower and opening into the centre. The panopticon allowed prison officials to watch over inmates and staff without being seen. Both inmates and staff would conduct themselves properly — conforming to the rules — because of the certainty of being seen. They would be unlikely to go astray because of the high probability of detection. The panopticon became the architectural plan for many prison systems throughout the world. Ironically, social philosophers such as Michel Foucault (1979) used the concept of the panopticon in a metaphorical way to represent the omnipresent forces of social control in modern society.

MODERN CLASSICAL THEORY

Modern classical, or neo-classical, theories extended the approaches of Beccaria and Bentham to include some of the principles of law that we see in present-day society. For example, the justice system today takes mitigating circumstances into account when judging "culpability" for criminal action. If someone commits a criminal act in self-defence, we no longer assume that person is a criminal, simply by virtue of the act. When we calculate punishment, we now consider the record of the offender and adjust the punishment on this basis. While classical theory decried all forms of unequal punishment as unjust and unnecessary, neo-classical thought maintains that free will is not uniform and that the law must account for disparities in the will to commit criminal or deviant acts. For example, the law now acknowledges that some violators may suffer from insanity or that some criminal acts occur under duress. Violators are not seen as having free will in such cases.

The basis of neo-classical theory is that it is better to prevent crime than to punish it and that punishment is unsavoury no matter how it is administered. The modern extension of this philosophy is variously subsumed under deterrence theory (containment theory) or rationality theory. In effect, deterrence theory is one branch of social control theory that studies the various types of positive and negative sanctions that encourage normal behaviour and discourage or deter abnormal behaviour. People who commit deviant acts, then, not only lose social rewards such as job promotion and peer respect but may also suffer fines or imprisonment. Deterrence theory attempts to assess the effectiveness of official, state-administered punishment in inhibiting (a) the individual violator (specific deterrence) and (b) the general public (general deterrence) from engaging in a targeted act. Individuals, aware that they can be punished, take this information into account when they consciously choose to commit or refrain from deviant activity. One of the basic premises of our system of law and punishment is the principle of deterrence and cost-benefit. Of course, we need to ask why in certain instances we punish more than necessary — why drug users are put in prison rather than dealt with through medical facilities, for instance — and why certain categories of individuals are targeted for more severe forms of punishment (either formal or informal) than others, even when the deviant acts committed are similar.

The interest in neo-classical criminology increased in the early 1970s in North America and Europe with a rapidly growing body of literature that focused on criminals as rational actors. James Q. Wilson, a conservative U.S. political scientist, in a popular book entitled *Thinking about Crime* (1975), argued against the position that crime was a function of poverty and lack of privilege that could be changed or corrected by investing in government programs. He, and others like him, described the typical criminal as basically wicked and untamed by convention. His argument was that the primary purpose of the justice system was to make sure that anti-social individuals face the consequences of their actions. The state's mandate, then, is to deter through harsh punishment and to incapacitate through imprisonment. Some two decades later Wilson turned his conservative criminology into the study of and advocacy for biosocial research, which explained aggressiveness and criminality on the bases of the innate hormonal composition of the individual (Wilson 1975). His later position was related to his earlier arguments that crime tendencies are part of an individual's makeup.

Although neo-classical theory approaches to crime and punishment seem to have an intuitive logic — punishment should deter bad behaviour — they do leave unanswered some fundamental socio-legal questions. For example, the decision to offend may not be the result of a rational choice. Also, the distribution of crime is unequal across social groups — the bulk of offending rests among those with low incomes. Laws are written by powerful people and tend to give privilege to those in positions of power and authority.

BIOLOGICAL AND PSYCHOLOGICAL POSITIVISM: THE PATHOLOGY OF CRIMINALITY

Classical theory does not — and cannot — explain certain types of deviant or abnormal behaviour. Acts that seem to stem from truly evil sources, such as the crimes of serial killers or child molesters, defy logical social explanations. Rather than using criminological theory, we tend to explain such behaviours by invoking medical concepts of pathology or sickness. Biological or genetic explanations for human actions have persisted for hundreds of years, and while notions about discovering and treating biological sources of behaviour have changed, the basic premise remains: deviant behaviour is a condition lodged within the individual. Some people follow deviant paths not for rational reasons but because of a disease or defect of the body or mind.

These theories advocate correcting the mal-condition and use a medical model of cure or rehabilitation. They are based on a positivist model of understanding the world — a model founded on principles of science and evidence-gathering to uncover the secrets of both the natural and social worlds. This line of thought explains crime by studying the biology and/or the psychology of the individual and linking the differences between people to biological or psychological factors.

THE LOMBROSAN LEGACY AND SOCIAL DARWINISM

The earliest biological theories linked evil or abnormal behaviour with the idea of human evolution, making the assumption that evil humans were evolutionarily regressive or atavistic. The English natural historian and geologist Charles Darwin (1809–82) laid the groundwork for this theorizing, and his followers applied his concept of "survival of the fittest" in nature to the interpretation and management of human existence. Social Darwinists maintained that the marginalized and the unacceptable were less fit than the more privileged people in the society. For them, the criminals and deviants were proliferating because society was interfering with natural selection by artificially sustaining less fit and less deserving people.

Cesare Lombroso (1836–1909), an Italian physician working in the late nineteenth century, argued that criminal behaviour was a symptom of a lower position on the evolutionary scale (Lombroso 1911). Based on a comparison of a sample of inmates and Italian soldiers, Lombroso found that, relative to the soldiers, inmates were characterized by physical aberrations, such as high cheekbones, protruding foreheads, eye defects, poor teeth and malformed arms and legs. Deviants, he argued, could thus be distinguished from normal people because of their atavistic body characteristics. His logic had obvious and fundamental flaws: just being in prison, for instance, can have marked effects on the physical body; and the physiological traits identified in inmates may well be socially stigmatized traits that prevented the individuals involved from leading normal, productive lives and eventually landed them in jail. Poverty and malnutrition, moreover, can produce both physical abnormalities and the need to engage in criminal activity. Lombroso's faulty logic and poor research design, coupled with future research that failed to support his findings, discredited these particular types of biotheories, and his work is only of historical interest today. But the implications of his work and the connections to Social Darwinism have led to altered, and still flourishing, versions of the biological approach.

CONTEMPORARY BIOSOCIAL RESEARCH

The work of William Sheldon (1949) is one of the most noteworthy extensions of biological theories. Working in the 1940s, Sheldon attempted to link body type to criminal and deviant behaviour. He argued that certain body types — the ectomorph, who is skinny and fragile, the mesomorph, who is muscular, stocky and athletic, and the endomorph, who is soft, round and fat — each have associated temperaments and behaviours. Sheldon found an excessively high percentage of criminals, especially juvenile gang members, to be mesomorphs, which led him to argue for a cause and effect relationship between physiology and behaviour. Again, the argument shows a dubious logic because rather than being a matter of cause and effect, it may well be that mesomorphs are more likely to be recruited to delinquent gangs or that judges see strong athletic boys as more of a threat than other types. Like Lombroso's theories, Sheldon's theory was based on weak supporting evidence.

The findings of later research that deviants were more characterized by genetic abnormalities than were non-deviants created excitement in the medical and crime-control communities. With the discovery of Klinefelter's syndrome (men with an XYY genetic makeup instead of the "normal" XY) in males who were aggressive, had large (excessively tall) body types and had mental deficiencies, researchers concluded that the extra Y chromosome was the genetic marker for violent criminality (Shah and Roth 1974). Once again, subsequent evidence has suggested that faulty research and causal logic underpinned these studies. Even if we accept the association between chromosome composition and deviant tendencies, this finding does not suggest how or why the abnormality leads to crime. It could be that the physical difference isolates individuals and restricts them from conventional society. If XYY individuals have lower mental capacities, for example, it may be that they find it impossible to engage in conventional social and economic activities and are "driven" into the world of crime. The stigmatizing effects of an intolerant world may force deviant behaviour.

Despite the flaws in earlier biostudies, biological research has gained a new life in recent decades. Current sociobiological research on alcoholism concentrates on identifying the neurological or genetic traits of individuals with high-risk propensities to alcoholism (Pollock et al. 1986; Goodwin 1986). Recent studies comparing identical and non-identical twins also show an interest in biological phenomena. The basic research question in these studies is the degree to which twins of different types share criminal or deviant tendencies (Mednick and Volavka 1980). The general findings suggest a greater similarity in deviant behaviour for identical compared to non-identical twins. As well, recent work on male predispositions to violence attempts to link evolutionary concepts, such as reproductive competition — which is characteristic of our lower primate ancestors — and status competition with homicidal behaviour in male gangs, again based on a "survival of the fittest logic" (Wilson and Daly 1985). As practised, this popular evolutionary approach is strongly class-biased and sexist. When we strip away the language and the logic, such approaches are, arguably, amusing and fictitious.

The premise of one evolutionary approach, "cheater theory," is that in society there is a subpopulation of men who have evolved with genes that predispose them to low parental involvement:

> Sexually aggressive, they use their cunning to gain sexual conquests with as many females as possible. Because females would not willingly choose them as mates, they use stealth to gain sexual access, including such tactics as mimicking the behaviour of more stable males. They use devious and illegal means to acquire resources they need for sexual domination. Their deceptive reproductive tactics spill over into other endeavours, where their talent for irresponsible, opportunistic behaviour supports their anti-social activities. Deception in reproductive strategies is thus linked to a deceitful lifestyle.
>
> Psychologist Byron Roth notes that cheater males may be especially attractive to those younger, less intelligent women who begin having children at an early age. State-sponsored welfare, claims Roth, removes the need for potential mates to have the resources needed to be stable providers and family caretakers. With the state meeting their financial needs, these less-intelligent women are attracted to men who are physically attractive and flamboyant. Their fleeting courtship process produces children with low IQs, aggressive personalities, and little chance of proper socialization in father-absent families. Because the criminal justice system treats them leniently, argues Roth, sexually irresponsible men are free to prey on young girls. Over time, their offspring will supply an ever-expanding supply of cheaters who are both anti-social and sexually aggressive. (Siegel and McCormick 1999: 157)

This remarkable passage illustrates how, despite its seemingly absurd premise, such a theory works to draw on the public's trust of science to make its heavily laden biological assumptions legitimate. Most importantly, biosocial theories like this one condemn people for their "lack of intelligence," their lower-class (welfare) origins, their regressive evolutionary conduct, their inability to maintain a mother–father nuclear family (a subtle way of blaming single mothers for deviant children) and their dependence on the state. All of these features are linked to biological (animal-like) traits. Interestingly, "cheater theory" also engages in politics by blaming the state, in part, for being too lenient on predatory males. While these kinds of theories are blatant in their attacks on class, gender, race and culture, and while their logic appears to be somewhat absurd, they are powerful tools for advocating a certain position: that bad people are out there, that they are unlike you and me and that their biology, their psychology and their environment combine to make them monsters. Such theories have considerable ideological power. The potency of scientific approaches to crime appears to be on the increase, and the overall orientation will no doubt continue to gain credibility as the Human Genome Project comes to fruition.

The Human Genome Project began in 1990 and was completed in 2003. It is funded by the U.S. departments of Energy and Health, which committed billions of dollars to a project that would fundamentally alter how we view human wellness and human potential. The purpose of the project is to identify and map all of the 20,000–25,000 genes in human DNA and eventually to turn the massive database over to the private sector. It provides a gateway not only to understand the complete genetic makeup of a person, but also to alter the genetic code either before or after birth to "correct" genetic anomalies. The implications for medicine, including cancer, are astounding. Gene therapy has the potential to eliminate cancer, generate new organs and blood vessels, detect genetic diseases at the embryonic stage and even alter the genetic code that causes cells to age. Similarly, for forensic science, gene-mapping carries the almost foolproof potential for identifying suspects using evidence from crime scenes, absolving those wrongly accused, establishing paternity and tracking criminals based on their DNA identity.

In relation to crime and punishment, however, contemporary genetic research has a dark side. The discovery of a genetic basis for various disorders raises the possibility of identifying genes connected to criminal behaviour. The implications of this development are staggering. We will have the potential of giving someone, at a very early age, a DNA-based identity that has a moral definition attached to it. If we have the ability to detect and prove that a person has a genetic predisposition to crime, will we create a new taxonomy that will link genetic makeup to criminality? The fundamental legal question will be whether the person with the genetic flaw had a guilty mind (*mens rea*) when he or she committed the act. At present the law is premised on crime as a product of deliberate wrongdoing. Will crime-control agencies (including medicine and the law) become more proactive as they try to alter the "criminal design" of those we detect as genetically impaired (Hodgson 2000)? Will genetic engineering become part of crime control once the technology to alter genetic makeup becomes practical?

While biological studies are compelling and persistent, they have gained little favour in sociological research for two reasons. First, the research has failed to control for psychological and social factors that interact with biology. Second, the implications of such research appear to be frightening. For instance, potential policy implications affecting genetic engineering and selective abortions of defective fetuses involve a kind of tampering with human life that would be carried out with scientific fervour but without moral ballast. At the end of the day, however, the most important issue that frames these debates is who gets to say what is a good and bad gene/organism/person, just as critical legal scholars ask who gets to decide what is moral and immoral.

PSYCHOLOGICAL THEORIES

Like biological theories, psychological explanations of deviant behaviour adopt a scientific approach and focus on the causes of crime as originating within the individual. Psychological theories argue, though, that character and personality are acquired traits and not just inherited. For example, the psychoanalytical theories of Sigmund Freud (1856–1939) concentrated on the improper development of conscience. Freud maintained that personality is comprised of the id, the ego and the superego. The id, the mostly animalistic part of the personality that leads us to aggressive, self-destructive and antisocial tendencies, stands in conflict with the ego (the social self) and the superego (the conscience). Criminals or deviants, then, are those whose ego and superego are poorly developed, and they are thus inadequately equipped to hold the id in check. For Freud, this impairment starts at the earliest stages of infant development and is influenced by the degree and type of parental training.

As an extension of Freudian psychoanalysis, the frustration-aggression hypothesis (Berkowitz 1969) suggests that frustration, a result of unmet needs, leads to aggressive behaviour that may be manifested in anti-social or self-destructive behaviour. Albert Bandura and Richard H. Walters (1963) use such an explanation of aggression in their theory of social learning. They suggest that people come to behave aggressively through a process called modelling: when individuals who observe the deviant/criminal behaviour of others being rewarded are prone to internalize the rewarded behaviour as acceptable. Much of this research focuses on the influence that violence on television has on deviant behaviour. Simply put, if the viewer is exposed to depictions of crime and deviance that are socially acceptable, then that person may become insensitive to the crime and deviance and may no longer see acts of violence as negative.

The types of vicarious conditioning discussed by social learning theorists are fundamental to the theory of behaviourism. Beginning with the work of B.F. Skinner (1953), behaviourism assumed that behaviour was instilled through reward and punishment and that, because behaviour is learned, bad behaviour can be unlearned. H.J. Eysenck (1977) argued that immoral behaviour is the result of improper conditioning; children never learn to associate fear and pain with bad conduct. Eysenck considered this conditioned fear as the basis of conscience. In this general arena of psychological research stressing the effect of fear and punishment on moral development, the theory of cognitive development focused on how moral development coincides with stages of psychological and physical maturity. For psychologists such as Jean Piaget (1932) and Lawrence Kohlberg (1969), the individual is the source of "badness," and, as in psychoanalytic theories, deviants are characterized by deficits in moral reasoning. These deficits occur at certain stages of psychic development, and redirecting the individual through the appropriate stages of development can rectify deviant tendencies.

Psychological theories have maintained their appeal in the study and control of crime primarily because the emphasis on the individual permits the development of a treatment program based on psychotherapy. Therapies such as behaviour modification are still used in prison to establish conformist behaviour. The main criticism of psychological theories, however, is that they ignore the relative nature of crime: definitions and reactions to criminal behaviour depend on social power and social context. As well, psychological theories ignore major forms of criminal behaviour, including violations committed by organizations (corporate crime), political crimes and certain types of rational individual crimes such as credit-card fraud. Lastly, they study deviant and criminal acts "out of context" — they isolate the individual primarily as an independent organism.

The psychopathy checklist, a tool developed by Robert Hare and colleagues (Hare 1998) illustrates this approach. The development of the psychopathy checklist was considered to be a significant improvement over earlier methods of evaluating psychopathy, primarily because it uses objective information taken from official personal records and is based on a carefully structured interview. Because it is a psychometric instrument, it has stood the scrutiny of scientific testing over time. However, many of the characteristics that the instrument isolates are based on issues such as a high sense of self-worth, tendency to boredom, pathological lying, lack of remorse, impulsiveness and callousness. These traits, while not attractive, are common to many people in highly competitive occupations in which aggressiveness and self-interest are admired characteristics. In the end, the psychopathy checklist allowed the psychiatric profession to expand its mandate into the non-criminal world. As Steve Keyes (2001) points out:

> There are many psychopaths in society that we know virtually nothing about. These are the psychopaths who don't necessarily commit homicide, commit serious violence, or even come to the attention of the police. They may be successful businessmen, successful politicians, successful academics, successful priests; they exist in all areas of society. There is a growing awareness that psychopathic behaviour is around us in all walks of life. There are telltale signs in road rage

incidents and in the violence that surrounds sport. But it's in the cut and thrust of the business world, an arena where traditionally ruthlessness verges on a virtue that it's becoming increasingly worrying. (Keyes 2001: 1)

This brief passage illustrates a phenomenon common in the psychiatric profession: that psychiatry is in a constant search to expand its purview and its patient base (Szasz 1970). Most importantly, it illustrates how definitions of crime and criminality are constructed to the benefit of those in the practice of crime detection. Theorists and practitioners tend to have little regard for the context in which people act and little regard for the unfairness of labelling a person as potentially criminal on the bases of assessment instruments that do not account for factors such as culture, race, class, gender or age. They are, like other mechanisms of biological and psychological assessment, vehicles through which highly educated, well-heeled individuals and professions define morality and themselves on their own terms.

CONSENSUS THEORIES AND THE SOCIOLOGY OF CRIME

Sociological theories that are based on a consensus model make prior assumptions about social behaviour. The basic assumptions are that the rules and norms by which we conduct ourselves are shared and, therefore, correct. Morality is a given. The basic problem facing society then is that certain people fail to conform. For example, there is a largely indisputable argument that a person who kills someone in an act of vengeance does not belong in mainstream society. We also believe that someone who steals from someone also breaks the law — even if the thief is in need of food, clothing or shelter. These two examples are almost polar opposites with respect to the gravity of the offence and the motives for committing crime. Yet both are considered criminal violations, and very often both result in time in prison for the offenders. Both acts violate norms of conduct that prohibit murder and stealing despite the motives.

Functionalism, Anomie and Strain

Structural-functionalist theories can be traced to the work of Emile Durkheim (1858–1917), a French thinker known as one of the founders of modern sociology. For Durkheim and subsequent functionalists, the basic determinant of abnormality is a lack of social cohesion; societies with low levels of social cohesion are typified by high rates of crime and deviance (Durkheim 1964). When societies change rapidly, people are less likely to experience integration and regulation, and such societies will, as a consequence, experience high rates of unconventional behaviour. The psychological state experienced by people in such societies is called *anomie* or normlessness. Anomie exists when very few values and norms are shared and, thus, formal mechanisms of social control fail. For example, in his book, *The Dispossessed*, Geoffrey York (1992) describes how the rapid industrialization of Canada's Northern areas and the expropriation of Aboriginal lands and communities in the 1950s and 1960s resulted in the erosion of Aboriginal communities. The rapid change — the influx of money and Southern culture, alcohol and drugs, geographical displacement, new forms of exchange — resulted in a blurring of cultural values and expectations. The end result was that many communities that had previously experienced almost negligible violence and rates of substance abuse became characterized by overwhelming substance abuse, family violence and sexual abuse. Structural functionalists would suggest that the problems resulted from the lack of integration of local people into the community and the lack of regulation. The citizens are anomic — they lack shared values and commitments.[1]

Durkheim also suggested that because criminal and deviant behaviours are endemic to all societies, they have a positive or functional role to play in the stability of the society. He and his functionalist successors argued that deviance and crime serve to establish the boundaries of morality. They strengthen community and group ties through the presence of a common enemy (criminals and deviants), provide opportunities for the release of tension determined by rigid social norms and provide alternative norms that could engender adaptability to new values. Two classical studies that illustrate the positive functions of crime are Kingsley Davis's (1937) study of prostitution and Kai Erikson's (1966) study of puritan society. Davis views prostitution as functioning as a safety valve, protecting the family by providing a sexual outlet for men who might otherwise choose to abandon their spouses for different sexual experiences. Erikson argues that public deviancy and public displays of shame and punishment provide cohesiveness by redefining morality and illustrating the consequences of violating the moral code.

Robert Merton (1938) drew upon the Durkheimian paradigm by studying the social and economic forces that influence relatively vulnerable people. This contemporary body of research, labelled anomie, strain or blocked opportunity theory, proposes that anomic societies do not provide adequate acceptable avenues for people to achieve conventional life goals. The discrepancy between goals and the actual means of achieving those goals creates strain, and this strain, in turn, leads some people to find various non-legitimate ways of circumventing blocked opportunity. Merton categorized five types of responses to the strain of blocked opportunity: conformity, innovation, ritualism, retreatism and rebellion. Conformity is the only non-deviant response. Innovation involves the acceptance of shared goals but not the acceptance of the legitimate means of achieving them. For example, an unsuccessful student may cheat on an exam, or a corporate executive may decide to defraud his company or the shareholders. Most types of criminal behaviour fall into the category of innovation. Ritualism identifies activity wherein the means are accepted and the goals are rejected or altered. For example, Merton considered individuals to be deviant if they simply show up for work but do not accomplish as much as they should be able to or are expected to. This type of goal de-escalation, considered somewhat harmless, has received little attention in research on crime. Retreatism, as a response to blocked opportunity, has received more attention. Retreatists reject the goals and the means of achieving them by "dropping out" of society. Mental illness, substance abuse and compulsive gambling may all be forms of retreatist behaviour and are highly visible in studies on social control and crime, despite the likelihood of being primarily victimless activities. Lastly, rebellion signifies a form of deviance much like retreatism in that it rejects the goals and means. Rebellion, however, constitutes behaviour that advocates new forms of achievement. Merton might argue that political rebellion, for example, is born of blocked opportunity and that actions such as revolutionary activity on university campuses in response to funding cuts or political protests of First Nations peoples in North America typify forms of rebellion in response to lack of opportunity.

Merton's theory explained the class-based nature of crime by positing that lower-class individuals most frequently innovate in response to blocked opportunity because they are less likely than their higher-class counterparts to be socialized against the use of illegitimate means of pursuing success. Higher-class individuals, on the other hand, because they are socialized to conformity, are reluctant to break the law and tend to reduce their aspirations (ritualism) if they suffer the strain of blocked opportunity. In the end, the propensity for criminal behaviour is highest amongst the lower classes, in large part, because they suffer the greatest levels of blocked opportunity and adapt by engaging in illegitimate opportunities.

Various subsequent theories provided nuance to the general theory of strain/blocked opportunity. Albert Cohen (1955) modified Merton's theory by suggesting that lower-class delinquency is a sub-cultural adaptation to the predominance of middle-class culture in society. His theory of status frustration proposed that the place in which middle-class cultural values are most predominant and influential is education and that lower-class youths often do not meet the standards of attitude and achievement that are demanded of them. The frustration that results for lower-class youths is manifested in considerable frustration as they struggle to achieve in an essentially foreign culture. This status frustration results in a cultural adaptation in which lower-class youths form their own system of hierarchy and achievement that is based on criteria of success antithetical to middle-class values. The resulting cultural norms, in the words of Cohen, include "non-utilitarian, malicious, and negativistic" values, performed out of the pursuit of status and not out of need. Clearly, present-day public opinion about youth gangs would incorporate a sense that such gangs are typified by non-utilitarian and violent pursuits.

Cloward and Ohlin (1960) provide a further extension to Merton's theory by positing the theory of differential illegitimate opportunity, the essence of which is that many lower-class people are denied access to both legitimate and illegitimate opportunities. Simply put, not all lower-class individuals who suffer a discrepancy between "ends" and "means" know how to commit crime. Those who do commit crime obviously have been in a position to learn the skills of criminality and are able to survive in the criminal subculture; those who do not commit crime live in what Cloward and Ohlin describe as conflict subcultures and become "double failures." They neither partake of criminal activity nor violence-based status attainment activities and, as a result, "retreat" into the world of drugs and alcohol. In the end, Cloward and Ohlin provide a more complex framework for understanding the world of those who are denied access to legitimate means to attain the goals of a middle-class world.

Despite the intuitive logic embedded in the functionalist theories of anomie and strain, they, like most of the theories in this chapter, are biased in favour of middle-class values and structures. It is arguable that lower-class people are no more deviant than people from the middle and upper classes, especially when we consider issues of white collar and organizational crime. The theories are based on interpreting official crimes rates, and we will see throughout this book that official crime rates most often measure the extent and the nature of crime and punishment and not necessarily the amount of crime committed. By dwelling on the crimes of the lower classes, the theories tend to mask the wide range of crimes committed by well-heeled members of the society, which are often ignored by mechanisms of social control. Further, the theories tend to depict lower-class cultures as characterized by frustration and misery, and this is certainly open to question. As a related issue, blocked opportunity can occur at all levels of class and status; feelings of deprivation are relative to group and class expectations. For example, business people who have all the resources they need to lead the affluent lifestyle often struggle for more in the "game" of making money. Their personal sense of frustration and social angst should fit within the paradigm of blocked opportunity although the theories ignore high status crime. Lastly, the notion of value consensus — that all people share a set of common values, especially in relation to material success — is questionable. In highly complex societies like Canada in which difference and plurality are the cornerstones of the society, to contend that everyone aspires to the same goals is naïve and culturally insensitive.

Social Control Theory

Deterrence theory, and its parent, social control theory, are typically functionalist in their assumption that norms are generally shared, and, as a result, the appropriate areas of study are the mechanisms that compel some people to violate norms and others to resist the temptations to deviate. Unlike most other consensus theories, however, social control theory assumes that norm violations are attractive and that most people are motivated to engage in criminal or deviant behaviour. Simply put, we humans are rational, self-interested beings, and we will thus choose to violate society's norms if there is an advantage in doing so. This theory concentrates on the legal, social and personal reasons behind why so few people engage in illegal or criminal behaviour, given that such behaviour can be highly advantageous.

Early control theorists were concerned with the influences that prevented an individual from engaging in crime given the "classical" criminology assumption that crime is rational and an easy and attractive means to an end. The answer to this dilemma for social-control, containment theory (Nye 1958; Reckless 1973) rested with the concepts of inner and outer control. Inner control addresses the notions of guilt and remorse that result when people who adhere to and believe in the rules and norms of the society violate those rules. People who consciously choose to deviate, then, do so because they lack moral socialization; they lack conscience. The psychopathology of a serial killer, for example, may result from a complete lack of morality or conscience — the psychopath is neither moral nor immoral, but rather amoral in the sense of not being able to empathize with or even understand the trauma or pain of a victim. Outer control involves the sanctions that discourage anti-social and criminal behaviour. Quite clearly, the most common and accepted form of sanction for criminal behaviour is the use of prison — and, ultimately, capital punishment in some jurisdictions — to discourage criminal behaviour. As mentioned in the introduction to this chapter, the notion of outer control, encapsulated in deterrence theory, is the cornerstone of our criminal control system. Although we pose prisons as places of "correction," the predominant public thinking on prison is that it is a place of punishment and deterrence, a place in which the pain and suffering of criminal sanction becomes known to both the criminal and the general public.

For some social-control theorists, deviant behaviour is not so much controlled by fear of punishment as by an internal logic or "morality," the "natural" result of internalizing the rules and norms shared and valued by most people in society. The acceptance of such rules controls behaviour because people experience guilt and remorse as a matter of course when they act in a deviant manner. Crime results from a lack of moral socialization, a lack of conscience. Psychopaths represent the typical anomaly: they have no morality or conscience; they are not immoral, but rather amoral.

Travis Hirschi's social bonding theory (1969) focused on morality and inner control. Hirschi's interest was in the degree of bonding to conventional society as a general determinant of inner control and moral conduct. He introduced the dimensions of attachment, involvement, commitment and belief as components of bonding as they relate to family, education and peer groups. His theoretical model suggests that bonding is made up of attitudes and behaviours. Bonding involves both inner control, tapping the strength of conscience or morality, and outer control, the degree to which individuals respond to social pressure and proscription. The model defines attachment as an attraction to parents, school and peers. Commitment involves an attitude of aspiring to conventional goals in occupation and education. Involvement means participation in conventional goal-oriented activities. The belief component involves attitudes towards moral values, which are generated by society as a whole — in essence, as a measure of morality or conscience. For Hirschi, the greater the bond between an individual and society — attached to school, committed to a good job, involved with family, believing in social values — the less likely is that individual to engage in criminal or deviant behaviour.

More recent incarnations of Hirschi's work have tried to link the conservative tendencies of social control theory to obvious differences in power in society. Power-control theory focuses on how families reproduce power differences between gender and class. For power-control theorists, children are more likely to be deviant if their parents are less involved in their lives. Patriarchal family practices and structures influence how boys and girls approach risk-taking behaviour. Patriarchal, traditional families tend to produce boys who are aggressive and goal-oriented (and risk-takers) and girls who are passive and aspire to domestic life (non risk-takers). More modern, egalitarian families tend to produce girls who are relatively high risk-takers and have, according to the theory, a greater propensity to engage in deviant behaviour. The theory, then, attempts to explain how the relationships of power, social class and parental influence can lead to the creation of deviant children (Hagan, Simpson, and Gillis 1995). (See Chapter 3 for a more in-depth overview of power-control theory.)

One of the attractive qualities of social-control theories is that they are open to empirical verification. Empirical (survey research) on youth crime often shows that how attached a young person is to family, school and the community, among others, is indeed correlated with levels of criminal involvement. On the other hand, the general theoretical framework is suspect in that it fails to question how power operates for some and against others in institutions like education and the law. It also fails to question the efficacy of such institutions — do schools provide conventional space for only certain kinds of students to succeed? Schools are, in fact, middle-class establishments that are highly rigid and mostly unable to adapt to non-middle-class students who might require different methods of education, different methods for evaluating success and different priorities regarding life skills versus routine, formal knowledge. In fact, a failure to become attached and involved in education might be a failure of education and not of the individual or culture. Lastly, control theory simply cannot explain high-status criminality or why society comes to see crime only as a street activity and not an organizational activity.

SOCIAL DISORGANIZATION, SOCIO-CULTURAL THEORY AND HUMAN ECOLOGY

Socio-cultural theories of crime and deviance focus on the context in which individuals learn criminal behaviour and how they learn it. Cultures and subcultures are targeted as the "transmitters" of deviant values. Beginning with work in the sociology department at the University of Chicago in the 1930s (The Chicago School), a substantial body of research has focused on the relationships between environmental or spatial patterns and deviant cultures. This body of research was based on a natural science paradigm that focused on plants and animals and their relationships to one another and to the physical world around them. The central premise was that like the natural world, human groups, based on race, class and other group identifiers, affect one another's daily lives and that these groups are affected by the physical urban environment. Shaw and McKay (1969) were the foundational proponents of this "ecological" paradigm which contended that certain areas of cities had disproportionately high crime rates and that crime declined as one moved outward (concentric zone theory). This geographical approach coincided very well with the average citizen's commonsensical perception of the location of crime in urban areas, and in fact, these largely socio-cultural theories arose in response to the "objective" study of deviant and criminal groups in time and space. Urban settlement patterns were shown to be associated with pockets of crime. Shaw and McKay observed, for example, that inner-city urban areas inhabited by the poor, by recent immigrants and by visible minorities had relatively high rates of non-conformity. Their work, which came to be known as disorganization theory, rested on the assumption that geographic and cultural pockets of crime, which they described as transitional zones, were highly disorganized and lacked the community infrastructure that was needed in functional societies. The more functional societies were situated far from the core of the city, at the suburban edges. In fact, disorganization theory draws on Durkheimian functionalism in its contention that such high crime communities often have a transient population which results in disruptions of the social order.

While ecological theories of crime shift the attention on criminality away from the individual to the society and address geographic patterning of crime, they are flawed with respect to the nature and permanence of inner-city communities. In fact, many inner-core, marginal communities are highly organized despite socio-economic disadvantage. Furthermore, to assume that the values of a delinquent or criminal group are the values of a community is highly contentious. Most importantly, the theories fail to take into account how power is wielded throughout the society and how disadvantage in one sector of the society fosters advantage for other sectors. This is a critique that is fundamental to all of the theories in this chapter and is central to the critical focus of this book.

Cultural transmission theory was a natural extension to theories of social disorganization as it extended the paradigm to suggest that crime is indeed concentrated in identifiable urban areas, such as the inner city. For this theory, abnormal behaviour is a part of the culture of certain urban areas, as are unconventional values, which are attributed primarily to inner-city subcultures and passed on from generation to generation. Walter Miller (1958), for example, said that the propensity to be involved in delinquent (gang-related) behaviour is relatively high in lower-class areas and that a delinquent subculture that exists in such communities passes on the tradition of crime and delinquency to future generations. Values such as toughness, trouble, smartness, fatalism and autonomy were, for Miller, the traits that made lower-class boys and men more likely to be involved in crime than their higher-class counterparts. Miller's theories, like many of the functionalist theories in this chapter, make several basic assumptions that are highly suspect — the most important of those is the suggestion that lower-class communities have different sets of values than wealthier communities. In fact, lower-class youths, including those who are involved in the justice system, often share values with the greater society and have aspirations that are much like those of their more advantaged counterparts (Eisler 2004).

Differential association theory was influenced by social-disorganization and cultural-transmission theories to explain the mechanisms through which values become part of certain subcultures and how and why crime is transmitted from one generation to the next. This more micro-level (socio-psychological) approach to crime and environment focused on the person-to-person dynamics of becoming criminal. Edwin Sutherland (1939), for example, argued that people learned deviant behaviour in close association with intimates and friends. Deviant behaviour is probable if an individual is exposed to a relatively high number of deviant influences. This theory focuses on the process of socialization into crime and concentrates on the learning and evaluating of moral and immoral definitions of what constitutes values such as masculinity, bravery, honour and loyalty in a deviant subculture. In the end, differential association theory argued that some communities have pro-social norms and some have anti-social or pro-criminal norms and that such norms are transmitted from generation to generation, a paradigm that came to be known as cultural transmission theory.

For example, street drug trafficking is common in many inner cities in North America due to the drug-trafficking culture, which, because of the need to escape police scrutiny, is transient out of necessity. Drug dealers move in and out of communities and not only cause the social pathology of the drug trade but also raise fear and anger among the citizens. According to disorganization theory, such disruptions ultimately contribute to unstable cultural values and poorly defined mechanisms of inner and outer control. Community members, especially the young, may decide out of desperation or necessity to partake in the criminal lifestyle and will become socialized to the anti-social norms and values of life in the drug trade. Their exposure to drug dealers and customers orients them to what an outsider would consider a criminal culture. Their reasons for becoming part of the drug culture, however, are complex, having little to do with a criminal orientation and much to do with fitting in and learning to become part of the "deviant" community. According to this group of socio-cultural theories, the socially disorganized community, most likely located in the inner city, passes on the drug trade from generation to generation.

While it is difficult to reject the notion that criminal behaviour is learned in concert with others, the core of the theory is suspect for several reasons. Like many other functionalist theories, the primary flaw of disorganization theory is that it does not focus on how non-cultural factors like economic disparity and inequalities in power across communities influence street crime. And, like many other orthodox theories, it does not address high status crimes and especially how high status people become involved in criminality despite their conventional associations and "non-criminogenic" communities.

CONSENSUS CRIMINOLOGY IN THE 21ST CENTURY: THE RENEWAL OF CRIME CONTROL

While the philosophical, ideological bases for conservative criminology have persisted over decades, the twenty-first century is faced with global/political realities that have renewed and increased the focus of conventional criminology on surveillance and the administration of crime control. Despite the reality that crime has, in many jurisdictions, gone down rather steadily in the last few decades, academic and policy initiatives, from a conservative perspective, have increased the focus on issues of global crime and international trade, cybercrime as political crime, international corporate espionage, terrorism, the geography or mapping of crime and, as always, street crime. In short, conservative criminology has been rekindled by a new type of forensics focus including the scientific study of crime at the individual level — exemplified by DNA testing — to the scientific study of crime at the collective level — exemplified by GIS mapping of crime within and across countries.

Administrative criminology is the term that describes policy-directed criminology that has the rather narrow focus on the crime and the immediate, visible context in which crime occurs. The assumption that we have seen before in various types of consensus criminology is that the criminal is a rational actor who assesses the costs/benefits of crime. The administrative criminology response is to focus on what can be done to prevent crime based on the detection/punishment principle of deterrence. Because of the political nature of crime and the public's concern over safety and security, many academic and policy researchers feel compelled to engage in research devoted to detection and control. For example, recently, the criminology program at Simon Fraser University in British Columbia received funding for a supercomputer that will analyze crime at the network level as it focuses on mapping crime patterns within the province of B.C. The work of the computer has been heralded as similar to computers that map the human genome or global weather patterns. Clearly, such criminological work has a very scientific framework and its purpose is to build predictive models of the social structures of crime that will allow crime control agencies to focus on certain geographical areas, and of course, certain types of people, for intensive crime control activity. This type of criminological research is typical of the administrative criminology that advises governments on crime control policy and criminologists working with such a paradigm feel obligated and compelled to provide research and advice.

From a critical criminology perspective, and arguably from an academic perspective in general, administrative criminology, with its singular focus on crime control, and its atheoretical nature, has very little to say about crime as a phenomenon that is fundamentally connected to issues of poverty and lack of privilege and to issues of power and law. In short, administrative criminology stands against academic criminology, which tends to focus on structural issues related to crime, law and disadvantage — the philosophical framework for this book.

SUMMARY

Consensus theories of crime are based on several presumptions: our morality and the rules that control immoral behaviour are natural, universal and unchanging; through "correction" and punishment the individual rule-breaker can be changed into a law-abiding citizen; and the criminal justice system can identify and deal with criminal behaviour. In the end, though, conventional explorations of crime ignore fundamental issues. They leave out the relationships between social and political power and the construction or definition of abnormal behaviour. They also disregard the relationship between sociopolitical power and the official control of crime. Power is a type of currency or wealth, and its ownership makes certain peoples privileged over others. Those who have power are more able than those without power to define what constitutes immoral behaviour, and they are more able to influence the lawmakers. Their definitions of badness and goodness and the methods of justice and punishment become legitimate. Justice and punishment, then, comprise a social institution that becomes essential to social control and justice, and punishment can be applied in discriminatory and preferential ways.

DISCUSSION QUESTIONS

1. What are the basic presumptions of a consensus model of crime and justice?

2. How do scientific approaches to crime and deviance — typified by the Human Genome Project — support conventional or consensus views of crime and justice?

3. How is classical criminology incorporated into our justice system? Describe the principles involved in a classical, deterrence model of justice and punishment and discuss whether these principles are valid in modern society.

4. How do theories of human ecology incorporate the theory of differential association?

5. Why is it so easy for society and its members to adopt and endorse a consensus model of crime, justice, and punishment?

GLOSSARY

Anomie: a social condition that comes about when formal mechanisms of social control break down and, consequently, people's shared values and norms disappear. When this state exists, people lack guidelines for behaviour and experience a high degree of confusion about basic social norms. In this uncertain and frustrating atmosphere, some people respond in criminal and deviant ways.

Classical Theory: based on the view that it is better to prevent crime than to punish it and that punishment, although necessary to deter criminal behaviour, is unsavoury no matter how it is administered. Various types of negative sanctions discourage or deter criminal behaviour.

Consensus Theory: a general body of theories based on the overarching assumption that morality and the rules that proscribe behaviour are natural, universal and unchanging. Crimes are behaviours that are repugnant to all elements of the society.

Differential Association Theory: argues that people learn deviant behaviour in close association with intimates and friends. Deviant behaviour is probable if an individual is exposed to a relatively high number of deviant influences.

Human Genome Project: an international genetics program funded primarily by the U.S. departments of Energy and Health and dedicated to identifying and mapping all of the human genes that constitute an individual human being.

Social Control Theory: presumes that individuals will engage in crime unless they have the moral compass (inner control) to avoid criminal behaviour or if they are deterred from committing crime due to fear of being punished (outer control).

Socio-Cultural Theories: focuses, in the field of crime and deviance, on the context in which and the processes by which individuals learn criminal behaviour. Cultures and subcultures are targeted as the "transmitters" of deviant values.

Status Frustration Theory: proposes that lower-class youths often do not meet the standards of attitude and achievement that are demanded by middle-class culture. Status frustration results in a cultural adaptation, in which lower-class youths form their own system of hierarchy and achievement that is based on criteria of success antithetical to middle-class values.

Strain or Blocked Opportunity Theory: proposes that anomic societies do not provide adequate acceptable avenues for people to achieve conventional life goals. The discrepancy between goals and the actual means of achieving those goals creates strain, and this strain, in turn, leads some people to find various non-legitimate ways of circumventing blocked opportunity.

SUGGESTED READINGS

Werner Einstadter and Stuart Henry, *Criminological Theory: An Analysis of Its Underlying Assumptions,* Fort Worth, TX: Harcourt Brace College Publishers, (1995).

George Vold and Thomas Bernard, *Theoretical Criminology,* New York: Oxford University Press (1998).

Rob White and Fiona Haines, *Crime and Criminology,* Melbourne: Oxford University Press (2000).

Frank P. Williams and Marilyn D. McShane (eds.), *Criminological Theory: Selected Classical Readings,* Cincinnati, OH: Anderson Publishing Co. (1993).

NOTE

1. There are, of course, other ways of viewing the history of the development of Northern Canada, and York, himself, would not share the structural-functionalist theoretical understanding. His work focuses much more on economic oppression and marginality (1992: 29–30).

REFERENCES

Bandura, A., and R.H. Walters. 1963. *Social Learning and Personality Development.* New York: Holt, Rinehart and Winston.

Berkowitz, L. 1969. *Roots of Aggression: A Re-Examination of the Frustration-Aggression Hypothesis.* New York: Atherton Press..

Canada. 2013. Current Issues in Mental Health in Canada: Mental Health and the Criminal Justice System. Publication No. 2013-88-E. Legal and Social Affairs Division. Ottawa: Parliamentary Information and Research Service. At: parl.gc.ca/content/lop/researchpublications/2013-88-e.pdf

Cloward, R., and L. Ohlin. 1960. *Delinquency and Opportunity.* New York: Free Press.

Cohen, Albert. 1955. *Delinquent Boys: The Culture of the Gang.* New York: Free Press.

Davis, Kingsley. 1937. "The Sociology of Prostitution." *American Sociological Review* 2: 744–55.

Durkheim, Emile. 1964 [1897]. *Suicide.* Glencoe, IL: Free Press.

Eisler, Lauren. 2004. "Youth in Custody: A Foucauldian Analysis of Norm Internalization." Saskatoon, SK: University of Saskatchewan Doctoral Thesis.

Erikson, Kai. 1966. *Wayward Puritans: A Study in the Sociology of Deviance.* New York: John Wiley.

Eysenck, H.J. 1977. *Crime and Personality.* London: Routledge and Kegan Paul

Foucault, Michel. 1979. *Discipline and Punish: The Birth of the Prison.* New York: Vintage Books.

Goodwin, Donald W. 1986. "Studies of Familial Alcoholism: A Growth Industry." In Donald W. Goodwin, Katherin Teilman Van Dusen, and Sarnoff A. Mednick (eds.), *Longitudinal Research in Alcoholism.* Boston: Kluwer Academic Publishing Group.

Hagan, John, John Simpson, and A.R. Gillis. 1995. "A Power-Control Theory of Gender and Delinquency." In Robert Silverman and James Creechan (eds.), *Canadian Delinquency.* Scarborough, ON: Prentice-Hall.

Hare, R.D. 2003. Hare PCL-R, 2nd edition. Toronto: Multi-Health Systems.

___. 1998. "The PCL-R Assessment of Psychopathy: Some Issues and Concerns." *Legal and Criminal Psychology* 3: 101–22.

Hirschi, Travis. 1969. *Causes of Delinquency*. Los Angeles: University of California Press

Hodgson, D. 2000. "Guilty Mind or Guilty Brain? Criminal Responsibility in the Age of Neuroscience." *Australia Law Journal* 74: 661.

Keyes, Steve. 2001. "Are You Working with an Industrial Psychopath?" At <http://www.ignite-me.com/articles_viewcategory.cfm?ArticleCategoryID=13>.

Kohlberg, Lawrence. 1969. "Stage and Sequence: The Cognitive-Developmental Approach." In David A. Goslin (ed.), *Handbook of Socialization Theory and Research*. Chicago: Rand McNally.

Lombroso, Cesare. 1911. *Crime: Its Causes and Remedies*. Boston: Little, Brown.

Mednick, S.A., and J. Volavka. 1980. "Biology and Crime." In N. Morris and N. Tonry (eds.), *Crime and Justice: An Annual Review of Research*. Chicago: University of Chicago Press.

Merton, Robert K. 1938. "Social Structure and Anomie." *American Sociological Review* 3: 672–82.

Miller, Walter. 1958. "Lower Class Culture as a Generating Milieu of Gang Delinquency." *Journal of Social Issues* 14.

Nye, F.I. 1958. *Family Relationships and Delinquent Behaviour*. New York: John Wiley.

Piaget, Jean. 1932. *The Moral Judgement of the Child*. New York: Harcourt.

Pollock, V.E., T.W. Teasdale, W.F. Gabrielli and J. Knop. 1986 "Subjective and Objective Measures of Response to Alcohol among Young Men at Risk for Alcoholism." *Journal of Studies on Alcohol* 47: 297–304.

Reckless, W.C. 1973. *The Crime Problem*. Third edition. New York: Appleton Century Crofts.

Royal Canadian Mounted Police (RCMP). nd. National DNA Data Bank. At: rcmp-grc.gc.ca/nddb-bndg/index-accueil-eng.htm

Shah, Saleem A., and Loren H. Roth. 1974. "Biological and Psychophysiological Factors in Criminology." In Danial Glaser (ed.), *Handbook of Criminology*. Chicago: Rand McNally.

Shaw, C., and H.D. McKay. 1969. *Juvenile Delinquency and Urban Areas*. Chicago: University of Chicago Press.

Sheldon, William. 1949. *Varieties of Delinquent Youth: An Introduction to Constitutional Psychiatry*. New York: Harper and Row.

Siegel, Larry, and Chris McCormick. 1999. *Criminology in Canada: Theories, Patterns and Typologies*. Toronto: ITP Nelson.

Skinner, B.F. 1953. *Science and Human Behaviour*. New York: MacMillan.

Sutherland, Edwin. 1939. *Criminology*. Philadelphia: J.B. Lippincott.

Szasz, Thomas. 1970. *The Manufacture of Madness: A Comparative Study of the Inquisition and the Mental Health Movement*. New York: Harper and Row.

Wilson, James Q. 1975. *Thinking About Crime*. New York: Vintage Books.

Wilson, Margo, and Martin Daly. 1985. "Competitiveness, Risk Taking, and Violence: The Young Male Syndrome." *Ethology and Sociobiology* 6: 59–73.

York, Geoffrey. 1992. T*he Dispossessed: Life and Death in Native Canada*. Toronto: Little Brown and Company.

3

PLURALIST THEORIES OF CRIME

Lauren Eisler

KEY FACTS

> Between 1879 and 1996, tens of thousands of First Nations children were forced by the Canadian Government to attend residential schools.

> For nearly five decades, residents of Bountiful, British Columbia, exercised a fundamental tenet of their Mormon faith and practised polygamy. Little attention was paid to the community or its practices until the 1990s when allegations of polygamy resulted in an investigation by the Royal Canadian Mounted Police.

> The 60s Scoop is a term used to refer to the adoption of First Nation and Metis children in Canada between the years of 1960 and the mid-1980s. Department of Indian Affairs statistics record that a total of 11,132 status Indian children were adopted between the years of 1960 and 1990.

> The Victims Assistance Fund was created and implemented in 1987 by the Department of Justice. This fund allowed provinces and territories to create information, education, and training programs to improve the delivery of victim services and activities.

Sources: Annett 2001; Bramham 2008; Sobol and Daly 1993; White, Haines and Eisler 2013.

Pluralist theories emerged during the second half of the twenty-first century in an attempt to bridge the gap between conventional and critical perspectives around the issue of power. Conventional theories are based on two fundamental notions of society. First is the notion that a majority of members of society agree on what is morally right and wrong. The second is that the myriad of elements within society, including social institutions like schools, churches, business and government agencies, work cooperatively towards a common vision of the greater good. Pluralist theories, in an attempt to bridge the considerable gap between conventional and critical theories that argue the so-called common vision is the vision of particular social groups who have the power to dominate society, posit that power is held by a variety of groups that compete with each other for social dominance. Since no one group or class is able to dominate all other groups, a plurality of competing interest groups and political parties is seen to characterize democratic societies. Within this view, conflict is based upon the competitive interactions between different types of groups that are jockeying for power. From this perspective, conflict, compromise and accommodation result from the plural nature of society itself.

Key features of a pluralist paradigm include the premise that social power originates from a multiplicity of sources and is decentralized, fragmented and widely dispersed. This decentralization of power naturally occurs because society is comprised of many diverse groups that have dissimilar and often competing interests and struggle for control over resources. Pluralist theories and theorists posit that the variances found within society include differences in age, gender, sexual orientation, class, and/or ethnicity, and that they often provide the foundation for naturally occurring diversity. Such differences may unite individuals who have common interests that naturally set them apart from other groups in society. This multiplicity allows for a broadening of the variables to be considered when examining how and why conflict occurs within modern society — a fundamental way that pluralist theories attempt to bridge the divide between conventional and conflict explanations of delinquency and crime. It is also important to note that a pluralist perspective recognizes that some groups hold more power than others and, therefore, may have greater opportunity to set the agenda and exert control over the access to and distribution of resources. It is also a fundamental premise of pluralist theorists that power balances are in a constant state of flux between these competing groups and that no one social group dominates society over the long term.

An important point within this perspective is that while various social groups have different and often competing values, beliefs and interests, there is agreement on the usefulness of law as a value-neutral and formal means of dispute resolution. According to Schmalleger (2003: 74), from a pluralist perspective, the law, rather than reflecting common values, exists as a peace-keeping tool that allows officials and agencies within the government to settle disputes effectively between individuals and among groups. It also assumes that whatever settlement is reached will be acceptable to all parties because of their agreement on the fundamental role of law in dispute settlement.

In summation, pluralist theories essentially argue that conflict is a natural occurrence in societies characterized by multiplicity and its potential for competitiveness. However, this perspective also entails consensus on the role of law as a value-neutral mediator of the inevitable disputes that arise in modern pluralist societies.

Thorsten Sellin (1938), one of the first theorists to incorporate a pluralist perspective, focused on the impact of cultural diversity in modern, industrial society. Sellin argued that law reflected the values and interests held by the dominant cultural or ethnic group within that society. Criminal law defines what we may refer to as crime norms — those behaviours deemed socially inappropriate — and clearly establishes punishments considered acceptable by the dominant group. The conduct norms of other social groups reflect their values and belief systems and may contradict or come into conflict with the established crime norms. As a result, the everyday behaviours of individual members of competing and less powerful social groups may be defined as deviant and/or criminal. Sellin (1938) posited that as society became more heterogeneous, the probability of conflict between social, cultural, or ethnic groups would increase. This in turn would cause an increase in behaviours deemed deviant or criminal.

George Vold (1958) expanded upon Sellin's concepts when he suggested that instead of trying to explain crime as individual law violations, we needed to consider its social nature. Vold draws attention to crime as the by-product of group struggle and conflict. Competition arises as different groups struggle to maintain or increase the strength of their position in society concerning the control of resources: employment, money and education. The most successful group achieves the authority to create and pass legislation that limits the fulfilment of minority group needs. Vold thus furthers the pluralist contention that deviance and crime result from conflict and competition among groups struggling for social dominance, not from individual pathologies.

Ralf Dahrendorf further developed the analysis of power relations within society by shifting the focus from those who control the economics of society to those who control the social institutions present in modern society. Dahrendorf argued that in order to understand power one needs to focus on the competition for institutional authority (Liska 1987). Institutional authority is the power embedded in the structural relations found within specific societies that is often not directly related to the ownership of productive forces. Instead, power is located in the social institutions that govern everyday life. Authority is vested within groups that control central positions within educational, governmental and religious institutions (Liska 1987). A clear example of this can be seen in the residential school experience of Aboriginal people in Canada. Between 1879 and 1996, tens of thousands of First Nations children were forced by the Canadian Government to attend residential schools, allegedly designed to provide education, but in truth, the main goal was cultural genocide and to force Indian children to forget their language and culture. Reverend A.E. Caldwell, principal of the United Church school in Ahousat, B.C., clearly stated the true role of residential schools, and how Aboriginal people were viewed by those operating them:

> The problem with Indians is one of morality and religion ... They lack the fundamentals of civilized thought and spirit, which explains their childlike nature and behavior. At our school, we strive to turn them into mature Christians who will learn how to behave in the world and surrender their barbaric way of life and their treaty rights, which keep them trapped on their land and in a primitive existence. Only then will the Indian problem in our country be solved. (Reverend A.E. Caldwell to Indian Agent P.D. Ashbridge, November 12, 1938, in Annett, 2001.)

There is overwhelming evidence of the horrific treatment children received in these schools and the long term catastrophic effects the residential school experience had on not only individuals but on all First Nation people:

> They were always pitting us against each other, getting us to fight and molest one another. It was all designed to split us up and brainwash us so that we would forget that we were Keepers of the Land. The Creator gave our people the job of protecting the land, the fish, the forests. That was our purpose for being alive. But the whites wanted it all, and the residential schools were the way they got it. And it worked. We've forgotten our sacred task, and now the whites have most of the land and have taken all the fish and the trees. Most of us are in poverty, addictions, family violence. And it all started in the schools, where we were brainwashed to hate our own culture and to hate ourselves so that we would lose everything. That's why I say that the genocide is still going on. (Testimony of Harriett Nahanee to Kevin Annett, North Vancouver, BC, December 11, 1995, in Annett, 2001.)

On behalf of Canadians, Prime Minister Stephen Harper made a formal apology in 2008 to Canada's Aboriginal Peoples for the residential school experience and launched the Truth and Reconciliation Commission of Canada. The mandate of the Commission is to inform all Canadians of the abuse suffered by Aboriginal people in residential schools and to document the truth of survivors, families, communities and anyone personally affected by the Indian residential school experience.

Austin Turk builds on Dahrendorf's analysis and turns the focus to legal conflict and criminalization when he explores the conditions under which certain types of social, behavioural and cultural conflicts are redefined and reclassified into legal conflicts and the conditions under which people that violate the law become criminalized. In essence, Turk is asking, "Under what circumstances are laws enforced?" (Liska 1987: 178). For Turk, the law, far from being a neutral arbitrator of disputes, is in fact a mechanism for the expression of power and influence (1969).

The 1930s also saw the emergence of a new way of examining the nature of deviant and/or criminal behaviour. Radical shifts in criminological thought occurred when the Chicago School of Sociology began to challenge the Lombrosian idea that some individuals were born criminals. These shifts, combined with an emergence of critical assessment of social institutions — including government — established to control crime, influenced the emergence of this new school of thought. The idea of individual pathologies as an explanation for deviance and criminal behaviours began to lose support during the 1930s, and a new understanding of conflict as social reaction emerged.

THEORIES OF INTERACTION

By 1938, a new theoretical perspective known as "symbolic interactionism" emerged. In contrast to structural theories, which focused both on the characteristics of the deviant and the social structure that leads to deviance, interactionist explanations focus on the relationship between individuals and groups when defining and labelling certain acts as deviant (Rubington and Weinburg 1987). Interactionist theories challenge the structural argument that social consensus on norms and values ensures that deviant behaviour is easily recognized and that the punishment of deviant acts or actors is a necessary and functional reaffirmation of social norms and values. Instead, interactionist theories argue that all members and groups within a society use symbols, and place meanings on these symbols, through communication and that labels of deviance are best understood as symbols that identify and marginalize those so labelled. Because people act on the basis of these socially constructed definitions and labels of individuals and/or groups, the reaction of those labelled and those who create and implement the label are important (Rubington and Weinburg 1987).

Symbolic interactionism was greatly influenced by the work of George Herbert Mead and Charles Horton Cooley and focused on individual levels of interaction. Cooley is best known for his concept of the "looking-glass self" (Schur 1971). He postulated that our understanding of ourselves is, in essence, a reflection of our perception of how others perceive and react to us. Mead further develops this concept by drawing attention to the interaction between an emerging self and the perceptions of others' reactions to that self. According to Adler and Laufer (1993) Mead's concept of the "I and Me" represented attempts to describe the way in which the individual both affects and is affected by the social environment through the process of interpretation (Adler and Laufer 1993: 4).

LABELLING THEORY

Frank Tannenbaum's theoretical model (1938), known as the "dramatization of evil," has its roots in the work of Mead and Cooley and began to emerge in the mid- to late 1930s. Tannenbaum expanded the work of these two theorists by concentrating on what occurs after an individual is caught and identified as having engaged in a criminal act (Brown, Esbensen and Geis 2004). The term "dramatization of evil" refers to this process of social reaction to illegal behaviour and changes the focus from what is happening inside the individual who engages in criminal behaviour to what is occurring in the environment of the individual that creates the need for deviant behaviour. The causes of criminality, according to Tannenbaum, lie in society's inability to accept deviation from the socially constructed concepts of "normal." This concept of "normal" is the passing of judgments on the habits and ways of life of different groups. From this perspective, individuals or groups that engage in what is defined as deviant or criminal activity challenge the dominant groups' habits, values and beliefs. Those who challenge the dominant norms are excluded and branded "deviant" to ensure that the status quo is not threatened. The challenge, therefore, is to explore how a particular group ends up in conflict with mainstream society and how the individual is drawn into a criminal group.

An example of how individuals or groups outside of mainstream society can be labelled as deviant and how the state may criminalize their activities can be found in the case of Bountiful. For nearly five decades residents of Bountiful, British Columbia, exercised a fundamental tenet of their Mormon faith and practised polygamy. Little attention was paid to the community or its practices until the 1990s, when allegations of polygamy resulted in an investigation by the Royal Canadian Mounted Police. No charges were laid. In 2004, Bountiful again came under scrutiny when allegations of sexual exploitation, forced marriage and child abuse were leveled against residents (Bramham 2008). The subsequent investigation led to the 2009 arrest of Mormon leaders Winston Blackmore and James Oler. It became a constitutional issue when the matter was referred to the B.C. Supreme Court by the Provincial Government after polygamy charges laid against the two men were stayed in 2009. The British Columbia Attorney General asked the court to declare whether the prohibition on polygamy under s. 293 of the *Criminal Code* was consistent with the basic freedoms guaranteed by the *Charter of Rights and Freedoms*.

On 24 November 2011, the Chief Justice of the Supreme Court of British Columbia Robert Bauman released his decision in *Reference re: Section 293 of the Criminal Code of Canada*, otherwise known as the "Polygamy Reference." Chief Justice Robert Bauman ruled the ban against polygamy, while violating the religious freedoms of fundamentalist Mormons, is constitutional and is upheld because that the harm against children and woman by polygamy outweighs that concern. Justice Bauman did rule that 12- to 18-year-olds who violate the law should not be prosecuted, as the harm caused by the prosecution would outweigh the harm caused by polygamy. He also stated that Parliament should re-write the law to reflect this.

Melanie Heath's research on polygamy offers support for Tannenbaum's assertion that causes of criminality lie in society's inability to accept deviation from the socially constructed concepts of "normal":

> Majority religions tend to have the power to resist the influence of the state; the law gets involved only in the most conspicuous cases, such as the child sexual abuse scandals within the Catholic Church ... In criminalizing minority religious and/or cultural practices like polygamy, the domain of law provides the state the power to enforce strong moral claims. It is under these conditions that put "the constitutional protection of religious conscience and the substantive criminal law ... on a conceptual collision course. (Berger 2008: 515, in Heath, forthcoming)

Edwin Lemert continued to explore the results of labelling in his 1951 work "Social Pathology," in which he set out to show that deviance was the result of interactions between individuals and the social reactions to their behaviours. Lemert also used this work to outline his concept of primary and secondary deviance. For Lemert, primary deviance occurred when the individual engaged in actions that violate social norms but in which the individual does not view him or herself as engaging in a deviant role. In other words, the deviations "are rationalized or otherwise dealt with as functions of a socially acceptable role" (Lemert 1951: 75). In contrast, for Lemert, secondary deviance occurs:

> When a person begins to employ his deviant behaviour or a role based upon it as a means of defense, attack, or adjustment to the overt and covert problems created by the consequent societal reaction to him, his deviation is secondary. Objective evidences of this change will be found in the symbolic appurtenances of the new role, in clothes, speech, posture, and mannerisms, which in some cases heighten social visibility, and which in some cases serve as symbolic cues to professionalism. (1951: 76)

At this juncture, the individual undergoes a shift in self-identity and begins to internalize the deviant role. This internalization of the deviant self-identification is reinforced by the negative labels, which, in turn, are reinforced by the individual's continued engagement in deviant activities. Lemert also posited that the adoption of the deviant label occurred over time and that, for the most part, a single occurrence of deviant behaviour was not likely to generate a severe enough social reaction for secondary deviance to occur. Instead, for Lemert, there were stages to the development of secondary deviance, and he provides an example showing how negative social reactions can move the individual from primary to secondary deviation:

> As an illustration of this sequence the behaviour of an errant schoolboy can be cited. For one reason or another, let us say excessive energy, the schoolboy engages in a classroom prank. He is penalized for it by the teacher. Later, due to clumsiness, he creates another disturbance and, again he is reprimanded. Then, as sometimes happens, the boy is blamed for something he did not do. When the teacher used the tag "bad boy" or "mischief maker" or other invidious terms, hostility and resentment are excited in the boy, and he may feel that he is blocked in playing the role expected of him. Thereafter, there may be a strong temptation to assume his role in the class as defined by the teacher particularly when he discovers that there are rewards as well as penalties from such a role. (1951: 77)

To summarize, once an individual is labelled deviant, society will view and react to the individual based on the label. This encourages the individual to accept the label and continue in the deviant role. Such acceptance leads to a change in the individual's self-concept and results in secondary deviance. For Lemert, "deviance is established in social roles and is perpetuated by the very forces directed to its elimination or control (1967: v).

The work of Edwin Lemert brings into focus the role of societal reactions in the creation and adoption of labels for and on the individual. According to Lemert (1974), the term "societal reaction" refers to the process by which societies respond to deviant behaviours and includes informal and formal reactions through agents of social control (i.e., police, courts, corrections). He claims that the term "societal reaction" is a "very general term summarizing both the expressive reaction of others ... and the action directed to its control" (1967: 41–42). While societal reaction may not be a causal factor in primary deviation, once the labelling takes place, the deviant behaviour is encouraged and perpetuated through a self-fulfilling prophecy.

Howard Becker continued to explore and expand on labelling theory in his 1963 work "Outsiders: Studies in the Sociology of Deviance." Becker argued that deviance was not a naturally occurring phenomenon but was socially constructed to reflect the interests, beliefs, values and norms of those in positions of power. For Becker, it was important to study not the individual acts of deviance but how rules, as the reflection of social norms held by the majority of society, were enforced both formally and informally. Becker argued that enforced rules were applied differentially to individuals and groups and that these rules tended to facilitate favourable consequences for those who implement the label.

Becker also contributed to the development of labelling theory through the creation of a number of terms. One term — "outsiders" — is used to describe rule-breakers who are labelled and who internalize and accept the label and come to view themselves as different, or outside mainstream society (Becker 1963). Becker also builds on Lemert's (1951) work on primary and secondary deviance through his exploration of how an individual comes to accept deviance as his or her "master status." Master status refers to the primary role by which an individual internalizes and defines him or herself. For Becker, primary deviance, as defined by Lemert, is the first step in the adoption of a master status and may be taken intentionally or unintentionally. The process of being caught and labelled as deviant acts as a stepping stone to secondary deviance. If individuals accept the label "deviant" as a master status, they become outsiders and either reject or are denied opportunities to succeed in a socially acceptable manner. Once this occurs, the individual moves into secondary deviance and turns to illegitimate means to succeed or survive. The final step in this transformation occurs when the rule-breaker enters or joins a deviant subculture. This affiliation provides the individual with support and allows them to rationalize and justify their behaviour and activity.

Becker (1963) also explores how rules are created and enforced within society. He examines how individuals in positions of power and authority make rules, and he uses the term "moral entrepreneur" to describe these individuals. For Becker, a moral entrepreneur is a person who takes the lead role in crusading for a rule, or rules, to deal with a perceived social evil. The creation, implementation and enforcement of the rule occurs when the moral entrepreneur brings the rule infraction to the attention of the general public. According to Becker (1963), the success of each new moral crusade creates a new group of outsiders and new responsibilities for enforcement agencies. Therefore, according to Becker, it is less important to study the behaviour of the individual than to examine how and why rules are created and enforced and who becomes an outsider in the process. Comments made by a Toronto police officer in January 2011 while he was presenting safety pointers during a campus safety information session to a group of students at York University provide an example of how the behaviours of individuals may be labelled and contribute to our understanding of personal responsibility and victimization:

> "Don't dress like a slut." That's the safety tip for how women can avoid sexual assault, reportedly offered by a Toronto police officer speaking at a campus safety information session at Osgoode Hall Law School on January 24, 2011. At the session, university security and two male officers from the Toronto Police Service gave advice for how to stay safe on campus. "One of the safety tips was for

women not to dress like 'sluts.' He said something like, 'I've been told I shouldn't say this,' and then he uttered the words," Ronda Bessner, Osgoode assistant dean of the Juris Doctor Program, told York University's newspaper the *Excalibur*. "I was shocked and appalled." After the meeting, she called the police service to demand an apology and followed up with a letter.

The officer apologized for the statement, and according to a spokesperson for the Police Service he was also disciplined. However, because it was handled internally, the public was not informed of the discipline taken. "The comments were entirely inappropriate and should not have been made," said Mark Pugash, the director of communications.

Ms. Bessner suggested that the officer's comments might make it difficult for victims to go the police. "I think the problem with the constable's conduct was that he was blaming the victim," she said. "It's quite astounding that in 2011 that you hear comments like that from a professional." (*Globe and Mail* 2011, and Kwan 2011)

John Braithwaite (1989), in "Crime, Shame, and Reintegration," sets out to explore the process of social control that he calls "shaming." Braithwaite begins by defining two forms of shaming: reintegrative and disintegrative. When reintegrative shaming is utilized, the individual is brought back into society after making amends for deviant or criminal behaviours. Just the opposite occurs when disintegrative shaming is employed. In this case, the offender is permanently shunned by mainstream society. Braithwaite, in keeping with labelling theory claims, argues that disintegrative shaming creates a special class of outcasts who are prevented from reconnecting with society and are forced to re-engage in criminal activities to survive. Perhaps here we may consider the impact on an individual released from prison upon completion of their sentence when a police service issues a bulletin to the community announcing the name and address of the individual released along with a description of their past offence and their likelihood to reoffend. How might this announcement affect the individual's ability to successfully reintegrate into society? Braithwaite also argues that reintegrative shaming is possible when social rituals of forgiveness take place but that there are few such rituals available to the deviant. Instead there is an overabundance of disintegrative ceremonies used to confer deviant status on individuals, through formal agents of social control, such as the criminal justice system, as well as through informal social sanctions.

Labelling theories have helped to explain how internalizing socially constructed labels may increase the likelihood of criminal behaviours among individuals in society. However, labelling theories tend to be deterministic and view individuals as passive entities who are led to behave in predictable ways through the simple acceptance of the label. They also fail to explore how crime is socially constructed and how justice is applied.

PHENOMENOLOGY AND ETHNOMETHODOLOGY

Phenomenological theory emerged in the 1960s with the work of Alfred Schütz and posits that reality is a socially constructed and shared phenomenon. People act on the meaning that events and others have for them. Schütz suggested that subjective experience is a shared reality that draws upon a common stock of knowledge comprised of typifications and formulas for accomplishing particular tasks, and also utilizes common-sense understanding and theories shared by members of a group. Through the processes of socialization, these typifications and understandings are internalized by members of society (Berger and Luckmann 1967).

Although the primary focus of ethnomethodology differs from that of phenomenology, both are centred on describing the emergence of order from the shared experience of members of particular societies (Zimmerman and Wieder 1970: 286–90). This focus on order as a practical accomplishment of the everyday interaction of members of a group produces ethnomethodology's distinctive perspective on deviance. Simply put, deviance in and of itself is not a concern for ethnomethodological analysis. Deviance, as a social construct, is viewed as an organizing concept that emerges through social interactions. These ongoing constructions produce a sense of order within the world of everyday life. Within the context of these interactional constructions, which distinguish the normal and ordinary from the abnormal and strange, ethnomethodological interest is raised. Goth subculture may provide an opportunity to consider the concept of deviance as a social construct. The goth subculture has its roots in the 1980s in the United Kingdom as a gothic rock scene and has grown to incorporate a number of music genres, clothing styles and a distinct makeup style. It is interesting to note that the cultural representation found within the goth subculture lead to the impression that goths are violent and deviant individuals or groups. This, in fact, is not true as one of the strongest ideologies found in goth culture is tolerance and belonging. This sense of belonging is clearly articulated in a goth blog post:

> My interests were always different from other people's and the things I like to do, the music I liked to listen to and the stuff I liked to talk about seems to go way over their heads ... I felt like I was judged by other teenagers for being different. I always wished I could find friends who understood what I was going through ... One day I met a new girl at school ... I don't know why but I was drawn toward her style, her behavior ... I started going with her to see bands and she introduced me to all her Goth friends ... I slowly converted and became a Goth myself. That is when my life became so much better. After I embraced the Goth lifestyle, if finally felt like I belonged somewhere ... I know now that what was missing all those years was a true sense of belonging. (Gothus.com 2013)

While mainstream society may view the goth subculture and those who participate in it as deviant, for the participant, the subculture provides them a sense of belonging, a sense of normalcy they had not found elsewhere.

For the ethnomethodologist, there is no shared set of understanding and meaning that members of a society attach to the world around them. There is no shared sense of deviance that can be called upon to order the strange and unusual behaviours of others. What members of a group share are methods for making sense of their experiences and the world. Schütz's common stock of knowledge is re-conceptualized as a shared set of interpretive procedures — in essence, these are "making-sense activities," which are invoked and employed continually in human interactions. These procedures allow members to produce practical accounts of specific individuals engaged in specific activities in the context of specific situations. Deviance and deviants emerge as particular designations that provide practical understandings of everyday situations. By constructing a sense that particular people and specific behaviours are "outside" the norm, members produce a shared understanding of the reality of the norm.

The construction of deviance is always from a particular point of view. The meaning of being a criminal is not contained within the act one commits but emerges from the context through which one's act is interpreted.

Through this process, organizations emerge as definers and controllers of deviance; individuals come to be "understood" as deviant, and they often come to see themselves as deviant. The important component here is what we typically fail to see, or at least forget: that it is through our "work" that reality and our sense of self is constructed. These accounts develop a natural, taken-for-granted character that shapes the social response, which, in turn, generates new contexts — and the process continues (Phofl 1994).

Once we arrive at a particular account (explanation) of a situation or person, we reflexively reconstruct our understanding of the process so that our decision or definition, appear to us as normal, natural and "real."

The power of these constructions when they are couched in an assumption of deviant behaviour can be so overwhelming as to shape an actor's identity and lead to his or her immersion within a world of deviance. The former identity, at best, receives the accent of mere appearance — what he is now is what "after all, he was all along." (Garfinkel 1965: 422)

The construction of the deviant is a process that occurs at several levels. At the interpersonal level, the construction of deviance allows individuals to examine and define behaviours as problematic and to use these definitions as a measuring tool to examine and compare their own behaviours. At a formal level, the identification and control of activities and individuals labelled deviant becomes a practical activity embedded within the routines of organizational life (Sudnow 1965). Therefore, accounts of deviance provided by official agencies of social control (crime rates, prevalence of illicit drug use, etc.) are not viewed by the ethnomethodologist as the reality of deviant behaviour "but as indicators and reflections or organizational properties and routines" (Liska and Messner 1999: 154).

Ethnomethodology suggests that definitions of deviance and the deviant are socially constructed and are given meaning within the situational context of everyday life. This perspective forms a foundation for understanding how deviant labels and categories are created and applied through the social processes of interpretation, typification and negotiation. As Liska and Messner state:

> The qualities and attributes of a particular individual become lost or distorted as she or he is located within the context of a particular category of deviance. His or her behaviour, and identity, comes to represent the category of deviance, and the category of deviance, in turn, becomes an explanation for the behaviour or identity in question. (1999: 173)

Like labelling theories, however, ethnomethodology fails to explain how laws are constructed and differently applied to individual members of society.

INTEGRATED THEORIES

Integrated theories began to appear in the 1940s but gained strength and credibility during the 1970s. Criminologists began to combine existing theories to explore the causes of crime more fully. Traditional theories did not adequately account for the myriad of variations in crime rates, including differences in gender, race, social class and criminal activity. This new perspective recognized that there may be multiple issues involved in trying to determine the causes of crime. According to Brown, Esbensen and Geis, another reason for increased interest in integrated theories is the development of more sophisticated statistical methods in the social sciences during the 1950s. They argue:

> Early theories were usually limited to the examination of relationships between two variables, the connection, for example, between social class and crime. On occasion a third, or controlling variable, would be introduced to see if there were different patterns of association. This did not permit criminologists to talk about causes of crime, only correlates. (2004: 429)

The most common attempts at integration have involved social control and social learning theories. Less common has been the integration of social control and strain theories, and even less common have been attempts to integrate all three of the major perspectives. Still other attempts at integration have included the labelling approach, social disorganization, conflict and deterrence theories.

Clifford Shaw and Henry McKay (1942) provided an early attempt at integrating social disorganization and social learning theories. They posit that the organization and physical structure of the community were of major importance in affecting behaviour and interaction patterns. It was the diversity of values and behaviours in communities, however, that was instrumental in exposing youth to deviant alternatives. Attatwapiskat, an Aboriginal community, exemplifies the struggle with social organization and physical isolation that can influence both behaviours and reactions to these behaviors.

"Attawapiskat Resident Reveals History of Abuse"

While Attawapiskat has been thrust into the national spotlight because of a long-running housing problem, the attention is also exposing another major crisis in the impoverished community. Jocelyn Iahtail, a former resident of Attawaptiskat, is now coming forward with personal recollections of abuse. Iahtail says the sexual abuse and incest is an epidemic that spans generations; a scourge that plagues the community in a way that is impossible to ignore any longer. "The most frightening part is people know," Iahtail told CTV's Daniele Hamamdijiian. Iahtail says the abuse began when she was only four, and continued until she was 13. She says the abusers were people that she trusted, including relatives of some council members. Iahtail says the abuse in communities like hers is cyclical and systemic.

Iahtail's mother, Mary Lou, says she was abused while attending residential schools and on the reserve, victimized by family and the clergy. "My relatives, the priest, the nuns and the brothers," Mary Lou recalls. Recalling her childhood, Iahtail also says the abuse affected every portion of her young life. "I would be so overcome with nausea and vomiting. Just the simple act of brushing my teeth, because of the oral sex that I was forced to perform."

Iahtail and her mother decided to speak out this week because the pain continues to be pervasive in their community. They say they also want to break the cycle of abuse that has scarred her and many others.

The scars on the community are obvious, Iahtail says: suicide, alcohol and drug abuse, gas sniffing and violence are mere symptoms. Indeed, while abuse may be less visible than squalid shacks and poor housing, it is insidious and destructive. But because of familial ties and the tight-knit nature of many Aboriginal communities, exposing the abuse remains difficult. The subject is also considered taboo and off-limits, given the shame and pain it illicits. "You have a lot of individuals who say it is bad medicine to speak about the extent of sexual abuse in our communities," she said. "I can't even give you a number because there's so many ... male and female. (CTVNews.com 2011)

Cloward and Ohlin's differential association theory (1960) incorporates elements of traditional strain theory with social learning theory. Societal goals can be attained through the use of legitimate or illegitimate means, depending in part on a person's access to different opportunity structures. According to strain theory, when legitimate opportunities for success are unavailable and illegitimate means are present, a criminal subculture may develop. Cloward and Ohlin merge this perspective with a fundamental element of social learning theory when they posit that delinquency is a learned behaviour requiring social support and confirmation. Exposure to strain alone will not cause delinquent behaviours, but strain combined with exposure to delinquent subcultures and the presence of illegitimate opportunity may cause an individual to turn to illegitimate means of goal attainment.

Elliott, Ageton and Canter combine elements of strain, social learning and social control theories to create a theoretical model that "avoids the class bias inherent in traditional perspectives and takes into account multiple causal paths to sustained patterns of delinquent behaviour" (1979: 3). They argue that it is not only possible but also preferable to be able to identify individuals who are engaged in habitual criminal activity through the examination of early socialization experiences as resulting in weak or strong bonds (Brown, Esbesnson and Geis 2004). The behavioural patterns developed through early socialization processes are challenged as children enter early adolescence. They begin to experience an increased exposure to social institutions — school, work, athletics — and situations that may either challenge or support the early socialization outcomes. The peer group also begins to take on a more significant role in the life of the adolescent and the types of peer groups the youth associates with. Thus, there is no dominant theory to explain why some youth move towards delinquency while others avoid such behaviours. A combination of explanations is needed to do justice to the complexity of such behaviours. Again, we can turn to the treatment of Aboriginal people in Canada to highlight the complexity of attempting to link strain, social learning and social control theories to understand and explore causes of deviance and criminality.

The 60s Scoop is a term used to refer to the adoption of First Nation and Metis children in Canada between the years of 1960 and the mid-1980s, mostly to non-Aboriginal homes and families. Department of Indian Affairs statistics record that a total of 11,132 status Indian children were adopted during this time (Sobol and Daly 1993). However, it is believed that the numbers are significantly higher (20,000) due to the number of children not registered as "Status Indians" in either foster care or adoption records. Records also show that seventy of these children were adopted into non-native homes. Many of the children were literally scooped up from families and communities without the knowledge or consent of family and bands (Kimelman 1985). The negative results of this government policy have been significant on generations of Aboriginal peoples. Alston-O'Connor states:

Unfamiliar with extended family child-rearing practices and communal values, government social service workers attempted to "rescue" children from their Aboriginal families and communities, devastating children's lives and furthering the destitution of many families. Culture and ethnicity were not taken into consideration as it was assumed that the child, being pliable, would take on the heritage and culture of the foster/adoptive parents. The forced removal of children and youth from their Native communities has been linked with social problems such as "high suicide rates, sexual exploitation, substance use and abuse, poverty, low educational achievement and chronic unemployment." (2010: 54)

This government policy was discontinued in the mid-1980s in response to a resolution passed against it by Ontario Chiefs and the harsh findings of a Manitoba Judicial Inquiry outlined in the *Report of the Review Committee on Indian and Metis Adoptions and Placements*, also known as the "Kimelman Report." Two class action lawsuits have been since been filed by survivors, one in Ontario in 2010 and one in British Columbia in 2011. The latter alleges that "between 1962 and 1996, Canada negligently delegated Indian child welfare services to the Province of British Columbia. Ignoring its obligations to Aboriginal children, Canada took no steps to prevent them from losing their Aboriginal identity and the opportunity to exercise their Aboriginal and treaty rights when they were placed in foster homes and adopted by non-Aboriginals" (press release from Klein Lyons, Barristers and Solicitors, May 30, 2011).

On September 27, 2013, the Honourable Justice Edward Belobaba of the Ontario Superior Court of Justice certified The 60s Scoop as being a case of cultural genocide as a class action under Ontario's Class Proceedings Act. Belobaba rejected the argument of the Attorney General of Canada, who stated that what happened is not worthy of a legal-wrong case.

The 60s Scoop allows us to think about the need to move beyond individual pathology as an explanation for the high number of Aboriginal peoples who come into contact with the criminal justice system. This example encourages us to consider the social and environmental impact the removal of Aboriginal children from their families and communities had on not only the individuals who were removed but also the families and communities they were removed from. In addition, the resulting class-action lawsuits filed against the government provide a strong example of how individuals and groups may use the law to represent their interests, which are often in conflict with the status quo.

Colvin and Pauly (1983) challenge traditional theories of juvenile delinquency for focusing too heavily upon microsociological levels of explanations. These theories focus on behaviours or conditions that tend to occur prior to delinquent behaviours, but they do not attempt to address how these variables are distributed in social systems. In order to address this theoretical weakness, Colvin and Pauly developed a structural-Marxist theory that integrates elements of social control theory and maintains that capitalism, and its accompanying social relations to the means of production, produce different attitudes and responses to authority. Based upon the type of social control found within the workplace, workers develop respect and comply with the power structures, or they develop hostility and alienation. The stronger and more coercive the control, the greater the levels of alienation and resistance. Workplace experiences are recreated in the home and affect children's socialization experiences within the family, school and peer groups.

Power-control theory is an attempt to incorporate gender into social control theories of crime and deviance. The basic premise resembles other social control theories in assuming that delinquency and criminality are forms of risk-taking behaviour. The goal of this theory, however, is to explore sex differences in delinquency and criminality by examining the influence of variations in parenting styles on delinquent behaviours of young males and females (Hagan et al. 1979; Hagan et al. 1990). In particular, power-control theory posits that parental control and youth attitudes towards risk-taking behaviours are affected by family relations. Two distinctive ideal-family types are considered. First there is the patriarchal family, in which the husband is employed in a position of authority and the wife in not employed outside the home. The second ideal type is the egalitarian family, in which both husband and wife are employed in authority positions outside the home. Power-control theory argues that in the patriarchal family a traditional division of labour will exist. Fathers and, more importantly, mothers are expected to control their daughters more than their sons. Daughters will be socialized to concentrate on domestic labour, while sons will be socialized to prepare for their eventual participation in the outside workforce. In an egalitarian family type, both sons and daughters will experience the same types of parental control: "In other words, in egalitarian families, as mothers gain power relative to husbands, daughters gain power relative to sons" (Hagan et al. 1987: 792). Based on these assumptions, Hagan et al. predict, "patriarchal families will be characterized by large gender differences in common delinquent behaviours, while egalitarian families will be characterized by smaller gender differences in delinquency" (1987: 793).

Left realism is a relatively new orientation in criminology developed in Britain in the 1980s during the era of Thatcherism. Lea and Young (1984) argue that there were four fundamental reasons for the development of Left realist criminology. These were (1) the crisis of causality, represented by increasing crime rates; (2) the crisis of penality, represented by the failure of the prison system and methods of rehabilitation; (3) the growing public awareness of crimes that had been invisible and the effects on the victims; and (4) an increasingly critical public that demanded efficiency and accountability from the criminal justice system and agents of social control.

Left realist theorists argued that there was a need to "take crime seriously," which meant that while they acknowledged the structural conditions that exist within society and contribute to the unequal distribution of advantage and resources, they felt that short-term policies needed to be developed and implemented to protect those most at risk of criminal victimization and condemnation. They also argued that most crime was intra-class located — that is, crime committed against others in the same class. But they also noted that those who suffered the most from any crime were those who were economically and socially marginalized. This acknowledgement brings into consideration the impact of crime and gender, and of race and class, and may be the most important contribution of the theory. Left realists also acknowledged and drew attention to the impact that crime and the fear of crime has on victims and argued that risk statistics should be replaced by impact statistics (Lea and Young 1984).

Left realists were also highly critical of traditional approaches to criminology that focused on either structural conditions (Marxist theories) or the individual in society (functionalist theories) as causal explanations for crime. Instead of a primary focus on the crime causation, Left realists focused on crime control. To do so, they argued that crime must be examined within its social context. With this in mind, Left-realist criminologists posited that crime occurs at the intersections of the "square of crime." The square of crime includes the victim, the offender, the state (formal social control) and the public (informal social control), and all these elements must be considered when examining issues of crime. This emphasis on controlling crime, rather than on dealing with the causes of crime, could be seen clearly in the contribution Left realist writers made in response to the riots experienced in Britain in 1981. These riots occurred in areas of poverty and high levels of unemployment, such as Brixton, but it was not this unemployment and deprivation per se that captured the imagination of the Left realists who argued that while poverty and deprivation were a precondition of riots, and more generally of increases in crime, they were not a sufficient cause. Poverty and unemployment could be associated with fatalism and the acceptance of adversity as much as with rebellion and violence (Lea and Young 1982). Left realists posited the riots had their origins in three facets: West Indian counterculture, the political marginalization of the inner city and, significantly, police methods of interacting with people who lived in deprived neighbourhoods (White, Haines and Eisler 2013).

As illustrated by their work on the 1981 British riots, the fundamental points of Left realism include the need to examine crime in its "natural state." By this, they mean that one must examine the form of the crime, its social context, its location and its trajectory through time and space (Lea and Young 1994). The form of crime includes two dyads: the victim and the offender, and the state and the public. In this sense, Left realists were the first to consider the role of public opinion within the study of criminology. They also argue for the principle of multi-causality. It is not enough to look for structural explanations for crime, nor can one simply concentrate on the role of the individual. Instead, we need to examine a number of elements that contribute to the occurrence of crime if we hope to develop comprehensive anti-crime strategies.

Left realists also acknowledge that crime occurs within specific contexts and that findings cannot be generalized. As well, they draw upon social surveys to collect information that can be used to develop a clearer understanding of the issues. They argue that victimization surveys are also important because one should consider the fear of victimization as well as the impact of crime on victims. They are, however, suspicious of crime statistics, which do not necessarily reveal the true nature of crime. They argue that the "dark side of crime" remains unexplored through the use of crime statistics.

Left-realist criminology has successfully drawn attention to the complicated relationships among victim, offender, state and public in its analysis of crime and victimization. The use of social surveys, the focus on the multiple causal factors for criminal behaviour and the incorporation of the voices of victims of crime has opened new doors of exploration, including abuse against women, the elderly and the young. A Canadian example of how social surveys can be used to increase services for victims is the development and delivery of the 1982 Canadian Urban Victimization Survey by the Ministry of the Attorney General. The mandate of this survey — the first major survey of this nature taken in an urban setting — was to collect data on the nature and scope of victimization over eight categories of personal and property crime. Additionally, the Victims Assistance Fund was created and implemented in 1987 by the Department of Justice. This fund allowed provinces and territories to create information, education and training programs to improve the delivery of victim services and activities (White, Haines, and Eisler 2013).

In summation, integrative theories, while present in the work of theorists in the 1940s, gained strength and credibility in the 1970s and 1980s as theorists began to challenge traditional one-dimensional theories of crime and punishment. Integrative theorists continue to push the boundaries of explanation when examining issues of crime, criminal behaviour and justice. These theories have pursued a more complex and complete exploration of the variances between race, gender and class in relation to both crime and the social responses to crime, and they have offered more detailed and complex analyses of causal variables and criminal behaviour.

POSTMODERNISM AND POSTMODERN THEORIES

Postmodern theories, which emerged from European intellectual endeavours during the twenty-first century, are highly critical of traditional theories that use scientific methods to discover universal truths and explanations for social phenomena. Post-modernists argue that universal truths, or grand theories, do not exist and that there is a need for the recognition and acceptance of multiple, and often competing, truths. Michel Foucault (1975, 1979, 1980b) offers what may be considered a postmodern analysis of the ability of individuals to offer resistance and instigate social change.[1] Foucault claimed that the determining characteristic of modern society has been the expansion of domination over both human and non-human nature. Despite the promise of progress, the development of science and scientific discourse operates as a form of social control over both the actions and body of the individual. Indeed, according to Foucault, scientific discourse, with its promise of universal truths, objectivity and rational organization, replaced religion as the bearer of authority and control in modern society. As Schissel argues:

> [Foucault] extends the theme that as we become more "civilized" and knowledgeable, we increase our ability to define, detect, and control an increasing number of marginalized (deviantized) individuals. In effect, Foucault argues that we are creating an increasing number of "docile bodies" through scientific knowledge-based disciplines, such as criminology, that continually define and redefine unacceptable behaviour and enforce discipline (Schissel and Brooks 2002: 26).

The concept of power is central to the work of Foucault, who argued that power is not a binary force to be administered from the top down or from the dominant to the repressed. Nor does power exist explicitly in social institutions such as medicine or education, or in rules or laws. Instead, power exists in the everyday transactions between social institutions and individuals. It is "the multiplicity of force relations immanent in the sphere in which they operate and which constitutes their own organizations" (Foucault, cited in Fillingham 1993: 140). This means that power relations are not static but rather in a continual state of flux, being redefined and reinvented through the interactions of individuals and patterns of power within social institutions. For Foucault the existence of power relations depends on a multiplicity of points of resistance:

> These play the role of adversary, target, support, or handle the power relations ... They [resistance] are the odd term in relations of power; they are inscribed in the latter as an irreducible opposite. Hence they too are distributed in irregular fashion: the points, knots, or focuses of resistance are spread over time and space at varying densities, at times mobilizing groups or individuals in a definitive way, inflaming certain points or the body, certain moments in life, certain types of behavior. (1980a: 96)

Or, as Garland explains:

> The chains of interaction along with power flows are made up of a dense entanglement of freedoms and coercions, choices and constraints, the exercise of "voluntary choice" is itself entangled in calculations of interest, patterns of habits, and emotions of love, fear and obligation. (1997: 197)

Therefore, any analysis of power relations within society cannot be reduced to the study of a series of institutions but must be considered as rooted in the system of social networks.

Within his power/knowledge paradigm, Foucault conceptualized bio-power as a system of non-physical forces created and implemented in order to exert power and control over individual bodies. Bio-power consists of two elements: disciplinary technology and regularizing technologies. Disciplinary technology is aimed at the individual and is used to monitor movements, gestures and locations. Foucault (1979) cited Bentham's panopticon as an example of disciplinary technology at its best. The structure of the panopticon, with its central observation tower and cells with open fronts facing the tower, ensured that prisoners could be under constant surveillance without ever being sure when, and if, they were being watched. This uncertainty resulted in prisoners learning to monitor their own actions and the creation of what Foucault termed the "docile body" — individuals who participated in self-surveillance and modified their behaviours accordingly. For Foucault, the function of the panoptic prison is to arrange things so that the surveillance is permanent in its effects:

> The perfection of power should tend to render its actual exercise unnecessary; that this architectural apparatus should be a machine for creating and sustaining a power relation independent of the person who exercises it; in short, that the inmates should be caught up in a power situation of which they are themselves the bearers. (1979: 201)

The individual subject continues to be the focal point of concern, as the "target of power and knowledge techniques and the locus upon which docility is based" (Disano 2003). For Foucault, the concept of power must be examined through an analysis of the way knowledge is created and how it provides the base for the creation and deployment of power relationships (Eisler 2007). An example of the deployment of social control can be found within the education system. Children who experience difficulty emotionally, behaviorally or academically, are subjected to the scrutiny of specialists within the education system. Their task is to identify the factors responsible for the disruptive behaviors exhibited by the child and to prescribe the actions deemed necessary to rectify the situation. The goal of this course of action is to have the child return to the classroom docile and ready to learn in the manner deemed appropriate. Children who do not, or cannot, integrate into the traditional classroom run the risk of being classified as having learning difficulties or as being trouble-makers. Increasingly, parents and educators rely on medications, such as Ritalin, as a viable treatment for children who are experiencing difficulties in school. In the most extreme scenarios, children are expelled from the school system as unmanageable if they fail to behave in an acceptable manner (Eisler 2007: 104). Furthermore, youth who engage in delinquent or criminal behavior are subjected to additional scrutiny from the representatives of state-sponsored institutions such as social services and the criminal justice system. The purpose of this increased surveillance is to develop a deeper understanding of the youth in order to help him or her gain the self-knowledge needed to integrate and succeed in society (Eisler 2007: 104).

Regularizing technologies incorporate technologies of normalization and confession, are aimed at the "species" and rely on examination instead of force to achieve control under the guise of welfare and compassion. Here we see the development of techniques such as actuarial tables and census taking in order to gather information about various factions of society. Technologies of normalization involve the creation and presentation of social reality by experts. Here, individuals are encouraged to believe that they can gain a deeper understanding of themselves with the help of experts. The individual can both know and become known through this process and can learn to effect changes. It is here that we see the development of experts who hold specific knowledge over a particular element of the body and utilize this knowledge as power over the individual. Language is created and utilized by the expert as a means of exerting power and control over the individual.

According to Sawicki, "Foucault claims that deviance is controlled and norms are established through the very process of identifying the deviant as such, then observing it, further classifying it, monitoring and treating it" (1991: 39). Normalizing technologies establish common definitions of goals and procedures that become accepted examples of how a well-ordered domain of human activity should be organized.

In conjunction with technologies of normalization, Foucault explores what he refers to as the "technologies of the confessional." The technologies of the confessional have their roots in the nineteenth-century medical examination in which, as in other forms of confession, individuals exposed to authorities their deepest sexual fantasies and hidden practices. Equally important, and closely related to normalization, was the idea that individuals were convinced that through their participation in the confession it was possible to gain greater self-knowledge (Rabinow 1984). Foucault saw the confession, especially about sexuality, as a central component in the expanding technologies for the discipline and the control of bodies, populations and society itself. From this perspective, the individual equals a body of knowledge, both to him/herself and to others. Disciplinary and regularizing technologies are tied to scientific discourse in the technologies of the self and work towards the creation of the "docile body."

Foucault's work has been criticized for its perceived neglect of the state and for its tendency to characterize individuals as "docile bodies" instead of active subjects (Garland 1997). Foucault's work on governmentality addressed both these issues. His 1982 essay, "The Subject and Power," presented a reconceptualized concept of power that stressed the fundamental role of the active subject as the entity through which power is exercised. Here governmental power constructs individuals who are capable of choice and action, shapes them as active subjects and seeks to align their choices with the objectives of governing authority (Garland 1997). Within this context, government is not the suppression of individual subjectivity but rather the cultivation of that subjectivity in specific forms, aligned to specific governmental aims. Subjects of government are to be seen as participating in the process over which they exert no control.

It is important to note that while Foucault's analysis of government does not focus primarily on a substantive or institutional account of the "state," it does, at times adopt this broad perspective. However, for the most part Foucault focuses on particular practices of governing that are located in a variety of sites. This emphasis on practices, together with an extended conception of "governmental authorities" (one that embraces families, churches, professional experts and all the many powers that engage in what Garland (1997) refers to as the "conduct of conduct") dissolves any rigid line of demarcation between the private and the public, or between state and civil society. So while the state is without doubt a point from which a variety of projects of government emerge, and a location from which numerous private powers derive support for their authority, it is by no means the focus of all governmental activity. For Foucault, then, power is much more insidious and surrounds the individual with an invisible web of constraints from which they are powerless to escape. In fact, through the technologies of normalizing, the individual becomes a willing participant in subjectification.

There have been criticisms of Foucault's work, and the postmodernist/poststructuralist perspective in general, for ignoring issues of class, gender and race. As Schissel states:

> Foucault's writing as a whole tends to ignore the larger, structural sources of power, instead focusing on how power operates at the individual level. For example, if we, as Foucault did, want to study how new prisoners come to understand and conform to the rule and demands of prisons, we may certainly uncover the formal and informal mechanisms of social control. The prisoner code, the discretion of the guards, the diagnoses of social workers, and the prison rules all create an identified and disciplined prisoner. But as we study this "microphysics of power" we could easily ignore the larger structural issues that brought mostly marginalized people into prison — issues such as poverty, exploitation, discriminatory policing, and prejudicial legal treatment. (in Schissel and Brooks 2002: 26)

However, this body of work has made significant contributions to the study of the connections between power, knowledge and social control, and we are encouraged to study the ulterior motives found within language and knowledge systems that are created and controlled by a privileged few (Schissel 2002).

CONCLUSION

Pluralist theories have not been without criticism for their perceived failure to acknowledge power structures that operate within societies to limit choices for individual behaviours. There appears to be an inherent assumption in pluralist theories that groups within society have equal opportunities to influence change and to gain power and dominance in society. Critics of this theoretical perspective would argue that while pluralist theories acknowledge conflict between social groups competing for social dominance, they fail to explore how social structures and institutions develop and work to maintain power imbalances within society that tip the scales in favour of certain individuals or groups. Pluralist theories are also accused of being unconcerned with, or unable to explain, how different groups are processed through the criminal justice system or why laws are applied in different ways to different groups. According to Brooks, there is a need to focus on issues such as patriarchy, capitalism and colonization to begin to understand how structural inequalities may impede a group's ability to compete for social power and dominance (2002).

However, pluralist theories have attempted to bridge the gap between conventional and critical theories in order to develop and further our understanding of how power operates in tandem with human motivation and personal conditions. Conflict is not necessarily based on economic conditions but instead on the competitive interactions between different types of groups that jockey for power and control over resources. Pluralist theories have contributed to the development of criminology as a discipline by arguing that the variances found within society include differences in age, gender, sexual orientation, class and race. In this way, pluralist theories, including labelling theories, ethnomethodology theories, integrated theories and postmodern/poststructuralist theories, have encouraged criminological research and researchers to look beyond a single-cause exploration of criminal behaviour to a multi-variable exploration of deviance, crime and criminality.

DISCUSSION QUESTIONS

1. How do structural pluralist theories attempt to our advance our understanding of deviance, crime and criminality? How well do they succeed?

2. What role do negative social reactions play in the formation of secondary deviance?

3. What key insights does labelling theory provide to illuminate our understanding of deviance?

4. What is distinctive about the ethnomethodological approach to deviance that distinguishes it from other interactive and structural approaches?

5. Compare the different integrated theories detailed in the chapter.

6. What is central to Foucault's perspective on deviance and criminality that distinguishes it from "modern" approaches?

GLOSSARY

Bio-Power: a term developed by Michel Foucault that describes modern societies as characterized by systems of non-physical forces created and implemented in order to exert power and control over individual bodies. Bio-power consists of two elements: disciplinary technology and regularizing technologies. Disciplinary technology is aimed at the individual and is used to monitor movements, gestures, and locations. Regularizing technologies incorporate technologies of normalization and confession, are aimed at the "species" and rely on examination instead of force to achieve control under the guise of welfare and compassion.

Differential Association: developed by Edwin Sutherland in the 1930s, this phrase means that people experience different social situations and learn new things. It argues that crime, like any other social behavior, is learned in association with others.

Labelling Theory: sometimes called societal reaction theory, labelling theory is an extension of symbolic interactionism. Labelling theory entails analysis of social processes involved in the social attribution of positive or (more usually) negative char-

acteristics to acts, individuals or groups. It asks not only "who gets labelled" but "who does the labelling."

Looking-Glass Self: a term coined by Charles H. Cooley (1864–1929) that describes the relationship between the individual and society and the individual's sense of self as derived from how others perceive us.

Master Status: a status that holds the highest perceived importance. The individual is primarily judged by this status regardless of other personal or social attributes they possess.

Moral Entrepreneur: a term used by Howard Becker to describe people who take the lead role in crusading for a rule or rules to deal with a perceived social evil. The creation, implementation and enforcement of the rule occur when the moral entrepreneur brings the rule infraction to the attention of the general public. Becker argues that the success of each new moral crusade creates a new group of outsiders and new responsibilities for enforcement agencies.

Outsiders: a term used by Howard Becker to describe rule-breakers who are labelled and who internalize and accept the label and come to view themselves as different or outside mainstream society

Pluralist Theories: a theoretical approach that attempts to bridge the gap between conventional and critical theories by positing that power is dispersed among a variety of groups that compete with each other for social dominance. Since no one group or class is able to dominate all other groups, a "plurality" of competing interest groups and political parties is seen to characterize democratic societies. For pluralists, conflict is a natural occurrence in societies comprised of many different groups with different and often competing values and beliefs. This perspective also holds that there is consensus on the role of law as a value-neutral mediator of the inevitable disputes that arise in modern pluralist societies.

Power: the ability of individuals, groups or institutions to achieve their goals or impose their will on others, even when facing opposition.

Power-Control Theory: an attempt by Hagan and associates to expand pluralist theory by incorporating gender and family type into social control theories of crime and deviance.

Primary Deviance: according to Edwin Lemert, primary deviance occurs when the individual engages in actions that violate social norms but does not view him or herself as engaging in a deviant role. Rather, such deviations are rationalized or otherwise dealt with as functions of a socially acceptable role.

Secondary Deviance: Edwin Lemert argues that when a person begins to employ his deviant behaviour or a role based upon it as a means of defence, attack or adjustment to the overt and covert problems created by the consequent societal reaction to him/her, his/her deviation is secondary. In other words, secondary deviance involves a shift in self-identity in which an individual begins to internalize the deviant role. This internalization of the deviant self-identification is reinforced by the negative labels, which in turn are reinforced by the individual's continued engagement in deviant activities.

Societal Reaction Theory: refers to the process by which societies respond to deviant behaviours. It includes informal reactions and formal reactions through agents of social control (i.e., police, courts, corrections).

Strain Theory: argues that societal goals can be attained through the use of legitimate or illegitimate means, depending in part on a person's access to different opportunity structures. According to strain theory, when legitimate opportunities for success are blocked or otherwise unavailable, and illegitimate means are present, a criminal subculture may develop.

Symbolic Interactionism: a theoretical approach that focuses on the relationship between individuals and groups in the defining and labelling of certain acts as deviant, rather than focusing on social structural conditions. Interactionist theories argue that all members and groups within a society use symbols and place meanings on these symbols through the communication process. They maintain that deviant labels can best be understood as symbols that identify and marginalize those who are labelled as deviant. Since people act on the basis of these socially constructed definitions and labels of individuals and/or groups, the reaction of those labelled and those who create and implement the label are important.

SUGGESTED READINGS

Becker, H. 1963. *Outsiders: Studies in the Sociology of Deviance*. New York: Free Press.

Braithwaite, J. 1989. *Crime, Shame and Reintegration*. Cambridge: Cambridge University Press.

Foucault, M. 1979. *Discipline and Punish: The Birth of the Prison*. New York: Vintage Books.

Garfinkel, H. 1967. *Studies in Ethnomethodology*. Englewood Cliffs, NJ: Prentice- Hall.

Lemert, E.M. 1967. *Human Deviance: Social Problems and Social Control*. Englewood Cliffs, NJ: Prentice Hall.

Schur, E.M. 1971. *Labeling Deviant Behavior: Its Sociological Implications*. New York: Harper & Row.

Shaw, C., and H.D. McKay. 1942. *Juvenile Delinquency and Urban Areas*. Chicago: University of Chicago Press.

Tannenbaum, F. 1938. *Crime and the Community*. Boston: Ginn.

SUGGESTED WEBSITES

Attawapiskat's problems go beyond housing crisis <http://www.ctvnews.ca/attawapiskat-resident-reveals-history-of-abuse-1.740028>.

Department of Justice Canada background and information on the Federal Victims Strategy <http://www.justice.gc.ca/eng/news-nouv/nr-cp/2012/doc_32764.html>.

Reconciliation Canada: Community support organization <http://reconciliationcanada.ca/welcome/history/>.

Residential Schools: Calls to destroy evidence from residential school survivors <http://www.surreyleader.com/national/263898341.html>.

University of British Columbia Indigenous studies resource with information on the 60s Scoop <http://indigenousfoundations.arts.ubc.ca/home/government-policy/sixties-scoop.html>.

NOTE

1. It is important to note that Michel Foucault has been considered many different things by many people. His work may be considered as critical, functional, or postmodern, depending on who is discussing his work and depending on what piece of work is being analyzed.

REFERENCES

Adler, F., and W.S. Laufer (eds.). 1993. *New Directions in Criminological Theory*. New Brunswick: Transaction Publishers.

Alston-O'Connor, E. 2010. "The Sixties Scoop: Implications for Social Workers and Social Work Education." *Critical Social Work* 11, 1: 53–61.

Annett, Rev. Kevin D. 2001. "Hidden from History: The Canadian Holocaust." The Truth Commission into Genocide in Canada.

Becker, H. 1963. *Outsiders: Studies in the Sociology of Deviance*. New York: Free Press.

Berger, B.L. 2008. "Moral Judgment, Criminal Law and the Constitutional Protection of Religion." *Supreme Court Law Review* 40: 513–52.

Berger, P., and T. Luckmann. 1967. *The Social Construction of Reality*. Garden City, NY: Anchor Books.

Braithwaite, J. 1989. *Crime, Shame and Reintegration*. Cambridge: Cambridge University Press.

Bramham, D. 2008. *The Secret Lives of Saints: Child Brides and Lost Boys in a Polygynous Mormon Sect*. Toronto: Random House.

Brooks, C. 2002. "New Directions in Critical Criminology." In Bernard Schissel and Carolyn Brooks (eds.), *Marginality and Condemnation: An Introduction to Critical Criminology*. Nova Scotia: Fernwood Publishing.

Brown, S.E., F. Esbensen and G. Geis. 2004. *Criminology: Explaining Crime and Its Context.* Cincinnati: Anderson Publishing.

Cloward, R., and L. Ohlin. 1960. *Delinquency and Opportunity: A Theory of Delinquent Gangs.* New York: Free Press.

Colvin, M., and J. Pauley. 1983. "A Critique of Criminology: Towards an Integrated Structural-Marxist Theory of Delinquency Production." *American Journal of Sociology* 89: 513–51.

CTVNews.com staff. 2011. "Attawapiskat Resident Reveals History of Abuse." December 13. At <ctvnews.ca/attawapiskat-resident-reveals-history-of-abuse-1.740028>.

Disano, J.M. 2003. "Beyond Our Borders: A Foucauldian Analysis of 'At-Risk' Youth." Unpublished thesis, University of Saskatchewan.

Eisler, L. 2007. "An Application of Foucauldian Concepts to Youth in the Criminal Justice System: A Case Study." *Critical Criminology* 15: 101–22.

Elliott, D., S. Ageton and R. Cantor. 1979. "An Integrated Theoretical Perspective on Delinquent Behavior." *Journal of Research on Crime and Delinquency* 16: 3–27.

Fillingham, L.A. 1993. *Foucault for Beginners.* New York: Writers and Readers Publishing Inc.

Foucault, M. 1969. *Madness and Civilization.* New York: Mentor.

___. 1975. *The Birth of the Clinic: An Archeology of Medical Perception.* New York: Vintage Books.

___. 1979. *Discipline and Punish: The Birth of the Prison.* New York: Vintage Books.

___. 1980a. *Power/Knowledge: Selected Interviews and Other Writings 1972–1977.* New York: Pantheon Books.

___. 1980b. *The History of Sexuality, Vol. 1: An Introduction.* New York: Vintage Books.

___. 1967. *Studies in Ethnomethodology.* Englewood Cliffs, NJ: Prentice-Hall.

Garland, David. 1997. *Punishment and Modern Society: A Study in Social Theory.* Chicago: University of Chicago Press.

Gothus. 2013. <www.gothus.com>.

Hagan, J., A.R. Gillis and J. Simpson. 1979. "The Sexual Stratification of Social Control: A Gender-Based Perspective on Crime and Deviance." *British Journal of Sociology* 30: 25–38.

___. 1990. "Clarifying and Extending Power-Control Theory." *American Journal of Sociology* 95, 4 (January): 1024–37.

Hagan, J., and B. McCarthy. 1987. *Mean Streets: Youth Crime and Homelessness.* Cambridge, UK: Cambridge University Press.

Heath, M. Forthcoming. *Declaring Religious Belief or Harming Self, Marriage, and Society: An Analysis of the Polygamy Reference Case in Canada.*

Kimelman, Judge E.C. 1985. *No Quiet Place: Review Committee on Indian and Metis Adoption and Placements.* Manitoba Community Services.

Klein Lyons. 2011. "Aboriginal British Columbians Files Class Action Suit Against Federal Government." May 30. At <www.bcafn.ca/files/breaking-news-2011-05-31>.

Kwan, R. 2011. "Don't Dress Like a Slut: Toronto Cop." *Excalibur.* At <www.excal.on.ca/news/don't-dress-like-a-slut-toronto-cop>.

Lea, J., and J. Young. 1982. "The Riots in Britain 1981: Urban Violence and Political Marginalization." In D. Cowell, T. Jones and J. Young (eds.). *Policing the Riots.* London, UK: Junction Books.

___. 1984. *What Can Be Done About Law and Order?* New York: Penguin.

Lemert, E.M. 1951. *Social Pathology: Systemic Approaches to the Study of Sociopathic Behavior.* New York: McGraw-Hill.

___. 1967. *Human Deviance: Social Problems and Social Control.* Englewood Cliffs, NJ: Prentice Hall.

___. 1974. "Beyond Mead: The Societal Reaction to Deviance." *Social Problems* 21, 4: 457–68.

Liska, A. 1987. *Perspectives on Deviance.* Second edition. Englewood Cliffs, NJ: Prentice-Hall.

Liska, A., and S. Messner. 1999. *Perspectives on Deviance.* Third edition. Englewood Cliffs, NJ: Prentice Hall.

Phofl, S. 1994. *Images of Deviance and Social Control: A Sociological History.* Second edition. New York: McGraw Hill.

Rabinow, P. 1984. *The Foucault Reader.* Pantheon Books: New York.

Rubington, E., and Martin S. Weinberg. 1987. *Deviance: The Interactionist Perspective.* New York:

Macmillan Publishing Company.

Sawicki, J. 1991. *Disciplining Foucault: Feminism, Power, and the Body*. New York: Routledge.

Schissel, B. 2002. "Orthodox Criminology: The Limits of Consensus Theories of Crime." In Bernard Schissel and Carolyn Brooks (eds.), *Marginality and Condemnation: An Introduction to Critical Criminology*. Nova Scotia: Fernwood Publishing.

Schissel, B., and C. Brooks (eds.). 2002. *Marginality and Condemnation: An Introduction to Critical Criminology*. Nova Scotia: Fernwood Publishing.

Schmalleger, F. 2003. *Criminology Today: An Introduction*. Third edition. Upper Saddle River, NJ: Prentice-Hall.

Schur, E.M. 1971. *Labeling Deviant Behavior: Its Sociological Implications*. New York: Harper & Row.

Sellin. T. 1938. *Culture and Conflict in Crime*. New York: Social Science Research Council.

Shaw, C., and H.D. McKay. 1942. *Juvenile Delinquency and Urban Areas*. Chicago: University of Chicago Press.

Sobol, M., and K. Daly. 1993. "Adoption in Canada: Final Report." National Adoption Study, University of Guelph, Guelph, Ontario.

Sudnow, D. 1965. "Abnormal Crimes." *Social Problems* 12, Winter: 255–76.

Tannenbaum, F. 1938. *Crime and the Community*. Boston: Ginn.

Turk. A. 1969. *Crime and Legal Order*. Chicago: Rand McNally.

Vold. G. 1958. *Theoretical Criminology*. New York: Oxford University Press.

White, R., F. Haines and L. Eisler. 2013. *Crime and Criminology: An Introduction*. Second edition. Toronto: Oxford University Press.

Zimmerman, D.H., and D.L. Wieder. 1970. "Ethnomethodology and the Problem of Order: Comment on Dentin." In Jack Douglas (ed.), *Understanding Everyday Life*. Chicago: Aldine Publishing.

4

CRITICAL CRIMINOLOGY

Carolyn Brooks

KEY FACTS

> Canada's crime rate has been steadily dropping for the past two decades. In 2013, the police-reported crime rate was 5,191 incidents per 100,000 people — slightly lower than the crime rates reported in 1971.

> Despite the crime rate falling, most Canadians polled in a recent General Social Survey stated that they believed crime rates in their community had either remained the same or increased over the past five years.

> An Australian study found that news media sources used "highly emotive and dramatic language" to spur on a tough-on-crime campaign in response to slight changes in crime rates.

> Media presentations of crime also impact the public's perception of who criminals are. A U.S. study found that people living in areas with a relatively low population of Black Americans were more likely to make connections between race and criminality and that these connections were most often informed by the local news.

> U.S. incarceration data from 2011 suggests that a third of all police encounters are with Black Americans who make up 12 percent of the population. Further, data predictions suggest that 1 in 3 Black males will go to prison in their lifetime.

> Approximately 23 percent of the offender population in Canada identifies as Aboriginal; in contrast, approximately 4 percent of the general Canadian population identifies as Aboriginal.

> Poor people are more likely to be arrested. Once arrested, the poor are more likely to be charged, convicted and serve time in prison — with longer prison sentences — than the middle or upper classes.

> In one study of 180 white 15- to 17-year-old males from diverse socio-economic backgrounds, it was found that "virtually all respondents reported having committed not one but a variety of different offences ... those from the middle classes constituted 55 percent of the group, [yet admitted to] 67 percent of the instances of breaking and entering, 70 percent ... of property destruction, and an astounding 87 percent of all the armed robberies."

Sources: Juristat 2011, 2014; Schindeler and Ewart 2014; Gilliam,.Valentino and Beckmann 2002; Sentencing Project 2013; Canada 2012; Brooks 2008.

How often I think neither I know, nor any (one) knows, aught of them, May-be seeming to me what they are (as doubtless they indeed but seem) as from my present point of view, and might prove (as of course they would) nought of what they appear, or nought anyhow, from entirely changed points of view. — Walt Whitman, "Calamus," Leaves of Grass (1965)

From the time of the discipline's emergence in the late 1960s and early 1970s, the advocates of critical criminology have based their approach on an intensive critique not just of mainstream criminology, but also of the state institutions that surround the discipline — institutions such as law, media, schools and the criminal justice system. Critical criminology sprang from Marxist theory and the protest movements of its early years but has since broadened to include analyses from feminism, Left realism, peace-making, postmodernism, poststructuralism, anti-racism, green criminology and more. As Don Gibbons (1994: 60) points out, "A sizable body of theorizing, in the broad sense, has accumulated in recent years and can be identified as critical criminology." Many of these perspectives draw on a common theory and methodology, but as Gibbons argues, "This work does not form a coherent whole, that is, a shared body of broad propositions or generalizations and supporting evidence. Indeed, critical criminology is an intellectual posture around which a variety of criminological endeavors have been pursued."

Not surprisingly, those postures offer a diversity of solutions to problems of crime, from arguments for redefining what constitutes "crime," to proposals for the abolition of prisons; from challenging the state institutions that frame public understanding of crime and political responses, to calls for restorative justice or transformative justice. In general, though, the critical perspectives do have commonalities. They share a desire to look not at individual flaws as a means of explaining criminal behaviour, but at societal problems that create, breed and sustain criminals. Critical criminology rejects tougher laws and incarceration as short-term solutions and instead advocates fundamental socio-economic and cultural change — complete structural transformation. Critical theories bring into view decisions around what acts are called "crimes" and the ways in which different groups of people are processed differently through the criminal justice system. For example, the justice system tends to define poor people and "street" crimes (theft, assault and homicide, trafficking offences, aggressive panhandling) as "criminal" and punishes these offences more readily than it does the "suite" crimes of corporations and the elite (environmental pollution, exploitation of human and natural resources, formation of illegal monopolies, illegal use of child labour, unsafe work conditions), even though the corporate and elite actions may well cause greater human suffering and devastation. From the perspective of critical criminology, power and the inequalities of class, race and gender play a central role in any understanding of crime and criminal justice.

THE "BOOM" OF CRITICAL CRIMINOLOGY

Emerging partially in response to the labelling and social interactionist perspectives, the critical perspective grew mostly out of the political protests of the post-war period. Following the Second World War, struggles for social equality intensified, largely because of rising expectations. Blacks in the United States, for example, gained the sense that they could now venture into typically white domains. Although the wages of Blacks saw a significant increase between 1939 and 1947, the "modest gains in the post-war years were soon reversed as white males reassumed their positions in the peacetime economy"

(Pfohl 1985: 335). The continuing inequality fuelled the anger that led to the civil rights protests of the 1960s. Glaring police brutality and obvious injustice also spurred violent protests and rioting in the Black ghettos.

This same political energy was felt within U.S. prisons, which were disproportionately filled with Black inmates. Prisoners began to see themselves as victims of racism, interpreting their confinement as part of the political manipulation of an oppressive state (Cleaver 1968). The prisoners began to educate themselves and organize to challenge the criminal justice system. The response by prison administrators and parole boards was harsh. Many of those who participated in or supported the struggle died, including "over forty inmates and guards slaughtered by state police in quelling the rebellion at New York's Attica State Prison" (Pfohl 1985: 336). In part, prisoners and their supporters became feared. Their rebellion risked uncovering that they were more than just "individual bad guys" and symbolized what was wrong with the unequal, racist and class-based economy.

The struggles behind bars, as well as the police brutality and general struggles of Blacks in the United States, gave impetus to nascent critical criminological perspectives. Critical criminologists began to identify the lack of secure jobs, victimization, racism and classism as the real sources of criminal activity. They saw prisons as a means of ensuring that the political hierarchy remained unchallenged and a way to hide the injustices facing marginalized people.

MARXIST CRIMINOLOGY

Marxism and Crime Causation: Induced Selfishness and Greed

> *We shall show that, as a consequence of the present [capitalist economic system], man [sic] has become very egoistic and hence more capable of crime than if the environment had developed the germs of altruism.* — Bonger 1969: 40–41, cited in Akers 1997: 168

Even though Karl Marx (1818–83) wrote very little about criminal justice and crime, the critical perspective in criminology and its formations of crime causation are based on Marxist frameworks: they focus attention on the political, social and economic structures of capitalism. Marxists argue that the fundamental inequality in capitalist society, with a small percentage of haves and a majority of have-nots, gives rise to individualistic and competitive struggles for material gains. Crime is partly a rational response to the competitive and individualistic struggle for material wealth in a society that encourages conflict between the rich and poor or among the ranks of the wealthy or the poor themselves. Thus, for Marxist criminologists poverty is not the only factor that causes crime; the alienating and exploitative nature of capitalism itself also leads to crime. In other words, the link between poverty and crime is not only that those in dire need are driven to anti-social acts, but also that the influence of a consumer culture perpetuates an ideology of individualism and competition. Similarly, violent crime arises out of the brutal conditions that many poor people are forced to live in. "It is not that man behaves as an animal because of his 'nature' [under capitalism]: it is that he is not fundamentally allowed by virtue of the social arrangements of capitalism to do otherwise" (Taylor, Walton and Young 1975, quoted in Bohm 1997: 125). Capitalist society is *criminogenic*, that is, fundamentally structured to encourage all members of the society to take up anti-social behaviour. Capitalist institutions foster greed, selfishness and unlimited desires. Results are all that count. Even the well off are encouraged to find ways to acquire more material goods. Obviously, in such a scheme many people will lose out.

Willem Bonger (1876–1940), a Dutch criminologist, was the first to apply Marxism to criminology. Bonger argued that the profit motive inherent in capitalism induces greed and selfishness, creating what he called egoistic tendencies. He suggested that under different conditions an environment of altruistic tendencies could just as easily have developed. But under capitalism everyone was necessarily subjected to the workings of greed and egoism. With the law controlled by the ruling class, the actions most likely to be defined as crimes are those of the working class, and given the inequality characteristic of capitalist societies the most obvious crimes will occur among marginalized people.

Although Bonger's theory of crime received little acceptance in its day, during the boom period of Marxist theory in the 1970s a similar explanation was to surface again. Ian Taylor, Paul Walton and Jock Young (1973, 1975) argued that crime was a logical response to the oppression and exploitation of working-class marginalized people under capitalism. Crimes of accommodation (individual crimes), they argued, are signs of survival in the class struggle. Individual crimes, such as theft, organized crime and prostitution, are often a means of survival in the competitive capitalist system, with the aim of achieving material wealth or status. The authors also point to crimes of rebellion, which are responses to the inequality of the capitalist system. Such crimes are political acts against an often-oppressive state. Richard Quinney (1980) added that violent crimes are accommodation crimes by individuals in response to the brutality of capitalism. Others pointed out that ruling-class crimes, corporate crimes or crimes of domination and repression (for example, environmental pollution, marketing of defective products, illegal and unsafe working environments) are also a result of capitalism — acts by capitalists protecting economic privilege and domination (Quinney 1980; Lynch and Groves 1986).

Radical Marxist criminologists challenge the traditional definition of criminal behaviour as conduct that violates a criminal code. Marxist criminologists see this view as serving the interests of the elite — for Marxists the real crime is behaviour that violates human rights, including some actions that violate criminal codes, such as murder or robbery. Tony Platt (1975), for example, argues that behaviour infringing on the rights to decent shelter, food, human dignity and self-determination is in fact criminal. This means racism, classism, sexism, human exploitation and the infliction of human misery and deprivation can be defined as crime.

Marxism and the Criminal Justice System as Ideology

> Just 'cause they're poor and m'norities, It's them the p'lice mistrust —
> And then you think they're Sons of Sam,
> And make a great big fuss!
> — from a song inspired by working with offenders, in Morris 2000: 99

Marxism does not focus as much on crime causation as consensus theories do. It is more concerned with the role of criminal justice as a means of controlling marginalized people in society. The criminal justice system functions in part as an idea that society must fear the poor and marginalized as the dangerous class. North American prisons are highly overpopulated by poor, Native and Black people. This reality is presented in the media and by criminal justice officials as evidence that certain classes and races are to be feared. For the Marxist theorist, however, this state of affairs signifies the workings of a classist and racist system. That poor, marginalized people fill our jails does not mean that they are the people who cause the most harm to society, or that they are the most pathological, or that they above all others lack social conscience. On the contrary, dispossessed people are as generous and loyal as anyone else — especially to each other (see, for example, Schissel 1997). What their overrepresentation in the criminal justice system means is that the law works to define the behaviour of the marginalized as criminal and to weed out the rich at every step of the way (Morris 2000; Reiman 1998, 2007; Reiman and Leighton 2012; Mathiesen 1974).

The weeding out of the rich begins long before law enforcement starts. Defining "crime" is a creative act in itself — an act that is subjective, political and based on decisions made by state-appointed officials. For example, Canadians are six times more likely to die from unsafe working conditions on the job than to be murdered on the street (see Gordon and Coneybeer 1999). On-the-job death rates are thirty times higher than the homicide rates in Canada and the United States. Yet the state does not define employer negligence as murder. Jeffrey Reiman graphically demonstrates that workers may be safer in the underworld than the working world:

> Lest we falter in the struggle against crime, the FBI includes in its annual *Uniform Crime Reports* several "crime clocks," which illustrate graphically the extent of the criminal menace. For 2003, the crime clock shows a murder occurring every 31.8 minutes. If a similar clock were constructed for occupational deaths … this clock would show [for the workforce] an occupational death about every 10 minutes! In other words, in about the time it takes for two murders on the crime clock, more than six workers have died *just from trying to make a living*. (2007: 85)

Not only has criminal law failed to emphasize dangerous corporate actions as "criminal," but governments are also deregulating corporate misbehaviour. Karstedt (2010: 338) asks if white collar crimes are "legally crimes at all," arguing that these crimes indicate "unprecedented levels of recklessness, exploitation and greed." Laureen Snider (2008) demonstrates these contradictions in the current legal system. Many of the activities of corporations and the elite pose grave threats to our community and individual well-being, much more so than those of the "typical" street criminals; yet the individuals and organizations responsible for corporate misbehaviour are not dealt with through our criminal justice system. In fact, these individuals may be promoted for contributing to increased corporate profit by reducing expenditures on workers or environment safety. There is current research that suggests that public perspectives about corporate and white-collar crimes are beginning to be viewed as more serious than some street crime, suggesting public perceptions may be slightly changing (Dodge, Bosick and Antwerp 2013). Despite the public's willingness to recognize corporate crime and to put more resources towards its intervention and prevention, it remains an area often neglected within the criminal justice system (Dodge, Bosick and Antwerp 2013). Two variants of neo-Marxism — instrumentalist Marxism and structuralist Marxism — try to explain these contradictions.

Beginning with a similar starting point in political economy, both instrumentalist and structuralist positions argue that state institutions, including the law and criminal justice, protect the long-term interests of the capitalist class. The two variants differ only in the particulars of this process.

Instrumentalist Marxism: In Bed with the Elite

Instrumentalist Marxists argue that the elite class is directly involved in the activity of the state, including the criminal justice system (Miliband 1969; Quinney 1974). From this perspective, society's elite controls not only the economy, but also all state institutions, including law, criminal justice and education. The criminal justice system — the law, courts, police and definitions of "crime" — contains mechanisms to ensure the power of the dominant class. The elite and the rich have the power to impose morality on the rest of society, often in the form of what they define as illegal or criminal behaviour; and what they consider criminal are actions that could threaten the status quo or interfere with the quest for profit.

Instrumentalists say that the people who work in the system are directly supporting their own class. Those in government and justice decision-making positions have class backgrounds, education, financial goals and attitudes that are similar to the corporate elite (Miliband 1969; Quinney 1974). Because the government and business elites are part of the dominant class, when they violate the law the state seldom enforces laws against them. Some instrumentalists even say that the elite class is immune from criminal sanction of any kind (Chambliss 1975; Quinney 1975). Whether or not the poor commit more crimes than the rich is not the question; the fact is that the poor are arrested more and punished more (Chambliss 1975; Quinney 1975; Pearce 1976; Goff and Reasons 1978). This perspective sensitizes us to the class bias in the workings of criminal justice.

When we combine the instrumentalist investigation of the state and law with crime causation, what emerges is a story of manipulation and social control. The Marxist position (shared by instrumentalists) maintains that crime occurs as a result of class conflict. The working class is alienated from and develops hostility for the system that encloses them and prevents them from shaping or fully participating in the social order or even benefiting from the fruits of their labour. Eventually they find this situation intolerable and they take action, often through minor acts of rebellion, though sometimes with more serious acts. Those acts become defined as criminal, and the capitalist system, in its formation of law, creates a scapegoat. The working class and the marginalized are blamed for the problems of the system they are rebelling against. Their defined pathology and criminality deflects attention away from the structural injustices and the makeup of the system itself.

The most obvious difficulty with instrumentalist Marxism is that it cannot account for the legal and legislative limits on the elite class, such as human rights legislation, health and safety legislation and employment standards. For that reason, many neo-Marxists have instead adopted the structuralist Marxist position.

Structuralist Marxism

Structuralist Marxists emphasize that although state institutions, including the criminal justice system, benefit the elite class, to appear fair and just these institutions must still maintain a degree of relative autonomy from all classes (Althusser 1971; Poulantzas 1973; Balbus 1977; Chambliss and Seidman 1982; Quinney 1980). Structuralists argue that the state has two main functions: accumulation and legitimation. The accumulation function requires that the state ensure that appropriate conditions are in place for generating wealth and profit. The legitimation functions ensure that most citizens believe that the state is fair and just and has the loyalty of its citizens (O'Connor 1973). Thus the state may work in the short-term interests of working-class and marginalized people as long as it does not interfere with the hierarchy of power relations. At times, then, the organized resistance of the working class creates political movements that force the law to work in the interests of all people. This theory helps to explain why the law and the state can transcend the particular interests of capitalists.

A structuralist position extends the instrumentalist position that law and the criminal justice system are coercive to include a more in-depth discussion of ideology. The criminal justice system functions as an ideological tool, maintaining the status quo over the long term and helping to maintain the domination of the elite class. Structuralist Marxists see this as hegemony, a concept initially introduced by Antonio Gramsci (1971). Hegemony is the process by which the elite try to make their ideas, knowledge and values appear to be legitimate or natural, as something that everyone in society should want for themselves and their communities. Gramsci (1971) examines the creation of hegemonic ideologies that perpetuate capitalist order. He writes that those with power in capitalist societies rule not only through the state's legal apparatuses, but also by educating the "consent of the governed." This refers to the state's ability to control ideological production and secure hegemonic powers. This universalization of ruling-class ideas takes place in the law, criminal justice system and media, and it partly explains why many working-class and marginalized people support tougher crime control laws.

Hegemony and the Media: A Structuralist Marxist Critique

The criminal justice system and the media function as powerful tools to manipulate most of the population into believing that it is the poor and marginalized that must be feared as the dangerous class (Reiman 2007; Reiman and Leighton 2012; Clarke 2000; Schissel 1997, 2007; Collins 2013, 2014a, 2014b). Critical criminology appropriates the tasks of cultural analysis, attempting to penetrate the ideologies that mask interests of capitalist exploitation "that deflect attention away from capitalist society's real interests, naked oppressions and structural inequalities" (Pavlich 2000: 51). This approach emerges in several writings, including Hall et al. 1978, Ratner and McMullan 1985 and contemporary research on the media, law and criminal justice, including Schissel 1997, 2007; Wortley 2002; Faith 1993, 2002; Reiman 1998, 2001, 2007; Reiman and Leighton 2012; and Collins, 2013, 2014a, 2014b.

A very influential radical criminological writing that draws on Gramsci's ideas of ideological hegemony is Hall et al. in *Policing the Crisis* (1978). Hall attempts to apply neo-Marxist analysis to mugging and moral panics in England in the 1970s. He examines the connections between the media, ideological production and the elite, without which media may be interpreted as acting in isolation from economic and political roots. Hall suggests that moral panic is created by ruling elites to divert attention from political and economic problems. The British industrial state in England in the 1970s was in social and fiscal distress; stirring up a moral panic over mugging and street crime deflected attention from British capitalism (rising unemployment and poverty). In a destabilized society, blaming a scapegoat or "folk devil" creates the illusion of providing political solutions, thus deflecting attention from severe political, economic and ideological crisis. Constructing an ideologically driven moral panic drawing on stereotypes of black men and a dangerous "soft" criminal justice system helped the British state secure the consent of those it governed.

Bernard Schissel (1997, 2006) similarly writes that the state encourages moral panic at times of hegemonic crisis to secure the consent of the governed. His focus is on youth in Canada. He argues that most kids inside Canadian youth facilities are marginalized youth, forced to live on the fringes of society, and that they are often there for relatively minor crimes. Most sensationalistic media articles focus on the violent acts of the youth, creating a myth that violent youth crime is out of control, unpredictable and committed by pathological or nihilistic children (a whole generation of them). Typical headlines are, "Killer Girls" (*Alberta Report*, July 31, 1995), "Junior Gone Wild: An Aging Do-Your-Own-Thing Generation Lashes Out at Its Savage Offspring" (*Alberta Report*, May 9, 1994), and "Teen Violence: Murder, Mayhem Have their Roots in Boredom" (*Calgary Herald*, April 18, 1995). These headlines suggest a generation gone wild, yet the stories themselves are about rare isolated incidences of violent crime. Schissel (1997, 2006) explains that articles about teens who commit murder seldom refer to the rare occurrence of the acts; instead they provide testimonial to the "naturalness of youth violence." Articles about youth violence focus on gang membership, individual pathology or wickedness, family pathology, single parenting and poverty. These overgeneralized, stereotypical and inaccurate descriptions of youth criminals give media consumers the impression that an entire class of people, those who live on the margins, is out of control. They create a false sense of fear regarding poor and marginalized youth and their families. The misinformation and sensationalistic view of criminality — which is not supported by statistics from government and police — helps to shape public opinion and demands for harsher measures against all young offenders. The result of fear mongering and stereotyping young offenders is a probable increase in crime.

This critical criminological literature on hegemony and the media is also powerful in its depiction of gender and race (see, for example, Scott Wortley 2008; and Rachael Collins, 2014a, 2014b). For example, the majority of women in conflict with the law are not a danger to society. They are generally young and Aboriginal; these women have no job experience and low levels of education, and they have often been emotionally, physically or sexually abused (Boritch 2002, 1997; Adelberg and Currie 1993; DeKeseredy 2000). In Canada, most women's crimes are property offences (Mohony 2011). Yet as Karlene Faith's work (1993, 2002, 2011) demonstrates, decades of films have portrayed the female "villain" as a nihilistic and pathological "lesbian butch predatory killer maniac" — a complete contrast to the real woman in conflict. The films of the 1990s amplify the woman offender as a super-bitch killer beauty — beautiful on the outside but "evil" by nature. These films present inaccurate descriptions of women in prison, yet they shape an ideology that forms public opinion.

Critical media research consistently finds that violent crimes are dramatically over-represented on fictional crime shows as well as on TV news programs. As has been well documented, "if it bleeds it leads" (Matusow January, 1988: 102, cited in Reiman 1998: 62). Debra Seaqgal states:

> By the time our 9 million viewers flip on their tubes, we've reduced fifty or sixty hours of mundane and compromising video into short, action-packed segments of tantalizing, crack-filled, dope-dealing, junkie-busting cop culture. How easily we downplay the pathos of the suspect; how cleverly we breeze past the complexities that cast doubt on the very system that has produced the criminal activity in the first place. (cited in Reiman 2007: 175)

Hegemony and Prison: A Structuralist Marxist Critique

According to the early works of Thomas Mathiesen and Ian Taylor, and current writing by John McMurtry, Nils Christie and Jeffrey Reiman, prison is part of the same hegemonic control mechanism as the media, which hides capitalist inequalities and reinforces the poor as criminal, This position is also argued by infamous prisoners such as George Jackson.

George Jackson (1970), a prisoner and activist, writes that the idea that prisons contain "dangerous people" is a complex political act. Jackson, who was subject to racism and struggling to get a job, was arrested for a $70 theft, imprisoned and, while incarcerated, labelled dangerous. He argues that this process makes scapegoats out of individuals and depoliticizes inequalities such as classism and racism in the larger social structure. Mathiesen (1974) similarly argues that the ideological function of prison is to blame individuals for acts that are stimulated by capitalism's economic and social inequality. Taylor (1981) adds that prison's high walls and towers reinforce the image of the criminal as dangerous and (dichotomously) different from the "respectable, conforming" population.

More contemporary criticisms of the prison and the criminal justice system reiterate these earlier themes, as well as enlarging the idea that defining "crime" is a creative act; this draws into question corporate crime versus street crime. Critical theorists write that although poor people are overrepresented in prisons, this is not because they are committing the greatest social injustices or lack a conscience. Rather the poor are overrepresented in the criminal justice system because we weed out the actions of the rich at every step in the criminal system, including what we define as "criminal." We ensure that the individual in prison is going to be a member of the lowest social status (Reiman 2001; Reiman and Leighton 2012; Schissel 1997; Morris 2000). This has two results. First, it creates an image of the "typical criminal" — one who is involved in one-on-one harm, is usually young, lower-class and a member of a racial minority (Reiman 2001). Second, associating criminal behaviour with the individual has the powerful effect of undercutting efforts (class struggles) to address divisions between the rich and the poor and causing systemic abuses of human rights, which Marxist criminologists see as responsible for crime (Snider 1999; Currie 1998; Reiman 2001). The resultant ideological message is that the poor are morally defective and therefore poverty and crime is their own fault — not a symptom of economic or social injustice (Reiman 1998; Reiman and Leighton 2012). Research and writing by Marxists criminologists questions the extent to which definitions of crime and the processes of criminal justice protect the interest of the most powerful economic class. Their studies demonstrate how actions that are not defined as criminal (corporate crime) often cause the most social harm (see, for example, Snider 2002; Reiman, and Leighton 2012).

Hegemony and the Official Version of the Law: A Structuralist Marxist Critique

Key to how effectively the law and the criminal justice system manipulate the public is the so-called official version of the law. This dominant discourse posits that the law is fair, just and equal for everyone. Elizabeth Comack asks us to remember the image of the young "maiden" who holds the scales to dispense justice — demonstrating the supposed "impartiality," "neutrality," and "objectivity" of the legal system to date:

> A "maiden" is a virginal young (white?) woman — presumably untouched, untainted, or uncorrupted. That she is blindfolded suggests she is not swayed

or influenced by the characteristics of those who stand before her — she sees no class, no race, no gender distinctions. The scales she is holding connote the measured and precise nature of the decisions produced. But the Official Version of Law is reflected in elements other than the symbol of the blindfolded maiden. In both its form and its method, law asserts its claim to be impartial, neutral, and objective. (1999: 21–22)

This claim to objectivity and neutrality makes the law a powerful ideological tool. The law tells us that everyone — rich and marginalized alike — is subject to its rule and that everyone is treated alike. Anatole France's famous quotation is instructive: "The law in all its majestic impartiality forbids both rich and poor alike to sleep under bridges, to beg in the streets and to steal bread" (France, quoted in Hunt 1976: 184). The problem is that when we are substantially unequal in a society, formal equality before the law is a moot point.

Structuralists are criticized for emphasizing "the system" to the detriment of the individuals involved in daily struggles. Ronald Hinch (1992), for example, argues that structuralists lack an understanding of the real people who live with and create the social order and laws. As Comack says, "While instrumentalism was criticized for its overemphasis on capitalist class input into, and control over, the state, it could be argued that the structuralist account went too far in the other direction: it is the constraints and limitations of the structure — not human agency — that determine the direction of society" (1999: 42).

MARXIST CRIMINOLOGY: POLICY AND REFORM

The policy implications of Marxist criminology, including instrumentalism and structuralism, are obvious. First, it challenges what is defined as crime. The position argues that victimless offences must be decriminalized and violations of real human rights (through racism, classism, sexism, human exploitation, the infliction of human misery and more) must be defined and controlled as criminal. In other words, the consequences of uncontrolled pollution and the destruction of species, or the consumption of non-renewable resources (by-products of corporate activity), are, from this perspective, more criminal than the activities of the aggressive panhandler or squeegee kid, both of whom may now, in Ontario, receive a $500 fine or incarceration for activities so obviously connected to their poverty.

This perspective comes under severe attack, however, because no reform of existing institutions could eradicate the problem of crime without a movement towards a socialist economy and system of justice. As David Gordon states:

First, capitalism depends quite substantially on the preservation of the conditions of competition and inequality. Those conditions ... will tend to lead almost inevitably to relatively pervasive criminal behaviour; without those conditions, the capitalist system would scarcely work at all. Second, as many have argued, the general presence of racism in this country, though capitalists may not in fact have created it, tends to support and maintain the power of the capitalists as a class by providing cheap labour and dividing the working class. (Gordon 1976: 206, quoted in Bohm 1997: 127)

In the end, Marxist criminology argues that since conditions under capitalism create crime, the solution is socialism (see, for example, Quinney 1980; Bonger 1916; Lynch and Groves 1986), seemingly an unlikely prospect in today's modern, global world.

Critical race theory, postcolonial, abolitionism, peacemaking and critical green criminology draw on the Marxist understanding of the link between inequalities and "criminality." Critical green criminology attends to the role of transnational and global businesses and their roles in environmental crime and global environmental catastrophes. Critical race and postcolonial theorists recognize multiple oppressions and make central the socially constructed reality of "race" and racism. Abolitionists and peacemaking criminologists draw attention to the harm and violence against humanity evident in the criminal justice system and call for peaceful resolutions, including an eventual abolition of prisons and other crime control measures.

CRITICAL GREEN CRIMINOLOGY

Isn't one of the brief's of critical criminology to extend our understandings of what is harmful beyond that of the formally "criminal"? ... and what can be more harmful than global warming? Indeed, climate change is the greatest challenge facing planet Earth. — White 2013: 102

The study of environmental harms was neglected within criminology (Lynch and Stretesky 2003) until recently with a boom in scholarship in green criminology (South and Brisman 2014). Green criminologists address different types of crimes related to direct forms of environmental destruction as well as behavior that affects ecosystems. Victims include humans, non-human species and entire countries, whereby the exploitation of their plants, wildlife and minerals have been destroyed by global commerce (South and Brisman 2014).

The concerns of rural critical criminologists resonate with the concerns of green theorists. The reality of agricultural crime, for example, challenges farmers' misuse of the land (Dekeseredy and Donnermeyer 2013). Authors such as Donnermeyer (2012) and Walters (2006) have written about how farmers over use chemicals and genetic modification and pollute wetlands and water in order to enhance efficiency and generate higher profits.

Critical criminologists studying green and rural crimes also address legal biases, which often fail to realize environmental harms as criminal. A common position is that definitions of crime and law enforcement must include actions against the environment towards developing policy to reduce green crimes (Lynch and Stretesky 2012; White 2013). In addition, critical green criminologists draw attention to the common interest of fighting global environmental catastrophes and the importance of realizing how this is often in conflict with the quite specific interests of business classes and transnational corporations. White (2013), for example, argues that business- and corporate-class interests include ways to strategize and enact policies that may help rather than hinder the planet.

CRITICAL RACE THEORY: A CULTURE OF RACISM AND INEQUALITY

Our Aboriginal youth want what all other young persons in Canada want — hope. —Ms. Jamie Gallant, Youth and Labour Market Intern, Congress of Aboriginal Peoples

Marxist criminologists have documented the "whiteness" and "maleness" of the criminal justice system. This is well established. Critical race and postcolonial theorists teach that the social construction of "race" creates segments of the population who are subordinate.

Critical race theorists posit that racial minorities are not equally served by the law because of their race and that the condition is structural, not simply a product of jurists' individual racism. "Critical race theorists have demonstrated that law is structurally racist: the racialization of crime, criminalization of race, and/or the discriminatory sentencing and lack of serious legal response to attacks on the persons and property of minority citizens, are structural" (Schur 2002, cited in Hudson 2006).

Postcolonial theory stems from a dialogue with critical race theory. The focus on postcolonial theory is a concern of colonialism, neo-colonialism and its continued impact on people's lives (Brooks, Henry and Daschuk 2015). Neo-colonialism is less overt than colonialism, sustained by everyday assumptions, processes and structures and refers to current control measures of indigenous peoples (Ashcroft, Giffiths and Tiffin 1998).

Jaccoud and Brassard (2003: 143), for example, write that the "marginalization of Aboriginal people in an urban environment begins in childhood and is rooted in the consequence of colonization — poverty, violence, alcohol, homelessness, reliance on shelters and food banks." Statistics Canada (2003) notes that Aboriginal peoples continue to suffer disenfranchisement. Aboriginal peoples continue to lack adequate housing and childcare facilities; their likelihood of finishing school is less than the national average — 48 percent of Aboriginal youth do not complete secondary school. The effects of racism include much shorter life expectancy and lower educational levels and employment rates (Statistics Canada 2003). The present generation of Aboriginal youth is very vulnerable to poverty, social alienation, racism, high suicide rates (estimated to be five to six times higher for Aboriginal youth) and criminal activity (Assembly of First Nations Proceedings, June 2002).

Both critical race theory and postcolonial theories identify lower levels of education, high unemployment, dysfunctional families and low levels of support, high levels of substance abuse, lack of housing, and the experience of racism, poverty, loss, alienation and isolation as pressure points for criminal activity. There is no direct correlation between incarceration, crimes committed and these legacies — factors of discrimination within the criminal justice system are also a central explanatory factor. Aboriginal people are over policed, less likely to receive bail and more likely to be charged with multiple offences. Furthermore, they receive less preparation time for trials with lawyers and spend more time in pre-trial detention (Manitoba Justice Inquiry, cited in Waldrum 1997). Green and Healey (2003) concur with regards specifically to Aboriginal youth:

> The causes of Aboriginal over-representation are wide-ranging and complex ... and include: the poor socio-economic circumstances of many Aboriginals ... the level of policing in Aboriginal communities, the "snowball" effect of a prior criminal record, a greater likelihood of an Aboriginal accused being denied bail, and the lack of sentencing alternatives available.

Mary Ellen Turpel/Aki-kwe writes that Canada has violated the international human rights standards with its treatment of Aboriginal people. The overrepresentation of Aboriginal peoples and youth is one legacy of European colonialism, and the oppression, cultural destruction and dislocation of Indigenous people can only be understood in this social, political and economic context (Samuelson 2000). Critical Marxist criminology, critical race and postcolonial theorists assert that addressing these deeper structural issues is key to reducing Aboriginal peoples' involvement in criminal activities.

Criminal activity, trouble in school, family violence, inequality, racism and poverty are indicators of misery and signs of serious problems in the status quo. Criminalization of race and poverty contributes to the social construction of ethnic minorities and marginalized youth as "the other," and misrepresents the social problems of race and class discrimination as individual pathologies.

Green (2005) argues that the process of privilege and subsequent racism is normalized and therefore not visible. This creates anger against those who are privileged and at the same time deny that their privilege is a result of racism. Lawrence (2004: 39) defines the practice of racism and colonialism as "extreme discursive warfare," existent in media, legislation and government. The language of the media normalizes the white model, reinforcing racist assumptions. When Aboriginal people are written about, stereotypes are reproduced as the social pathologies of those who participate in violence, gangs and crime. This is paralleled by stories of criminal involvement focusing on harsh events and decontextualizing the individual, familial, social and political realities that largely account for Aboriginal peoples' overrepresentation in prison populations.

Critical race theory and postcolonial theory define the construction of "identity" as key to understanding how Aboriginal people are "othered" (Hudson 2006). Narratives that define the otherness are necessary to the self-identity of the "western subject's idea of himself" (Hudson 2006: 33). The criminal justice system and the law do not take racialized harm seriously (Hudson 2006; Comack and Balfour 2004). Criminal activity among Aboriginal people and Aboriginal youth is seen as linked to the material consequences of racism, yet the youth are defined in the law, media and many government reports as a racialized "other," obviating the need to deal with the material consequences of racism. High rates of social pathology disturb the public but are not put into political and social context. The statistics used in media and government reports seldom have accompanying theoretical and political analyses, which may explain why certain groups and communities systematically suffer from unaddressed social problems.

In sum, critical race and postcolonial theories realize interconnections between class, culture, racialization, historical subjugation and gender. These theories emphasize the importance of including the voices of more oppressed peoples towards an appreciation of colonized histories.

ABOLITIONISM AND PEACEMAKING CRIMINOLOGY: "PUNISHMENT AND REPRESSION NEVER SOLVE PROBLEMS"

There are guards and officials who find pleasure
To see your mind and manhood wilt with pressure.
But if your mind and beliefs remain strong,
You will surely overcome all inflicted wrong.
— The poetry of an inmate named Mike, in Morris 2000: 89

The founders of abolitionism in criminology are Thomas Mathiesen and Nils Christie (both Norwegians), as well as Dutch scholars Louk Hulsman and Herman Bianchi. Drawing on the labelling, Marxist and Left-realist approaches, the abolitionist perspective declares that the criminal justice system (more often referred to as the "criminal (in) justice system"), not only fails morally but also fails to meet its own stated objectives. Abolitionists advocate against a state that inflicts pain under the guise of reducing criminal activity; they seek the abolition of prisons, capital punishment, slavery, racism, sexism and classism. The abolitionist struggles take many faces, yet the essential philosophy is always the same — that punishment and repression never solve problems.

Peacemaking has its roots in Marxist criminology, abolitionism, ideals of transformative and restorative justice and religious traditions (Pepinsky 1991). Like abolitionism, peacemaking criminology seeks to uncover the violent and warlike characteristics of the criminal justice system. The peacemaking criminologists argue fervently that we cannot eradicate violence or human suffering with more human suffering and more violence: "Crime is suffering and crime can only therefore be eliminated by ending suffering" (Pepinsky and Quinney 1991). The criminal justice system is a failure because it perpetuates the same violence that it seeks to eliminate. As such, the peacemaking adherents endorse humanistic and restorative principles both at the level of dealing with the offender and in the larger society.

Like Marxists, prison abolitionists and peacemaking criminologists point out that prisons are really warehouses for the poor. Many of the people who fall into the criminal justice system are victims first of classism, racism and sexism, and only by addressing the issue of an unequal society will we effectively respond to crime. In other words, rather than acting for social and economic justice, society hides the problems of the economy by focusing on people labelled as "bad." The blame for social problems falls on certain races and classes, letting larger structural inequities off the hook.

For example, Claire Culhane (1991), a prison abolitionist, said Canada is in breach of the International Convention on the Rights of the Child. Throughout the country there are children whose mental, physical, moral and spiritual development is impaired because of their standard of living. But rather than dealing with this national crisis, the government cuts social programs designed to assist the poor and increases spending on criminal justice. Culhane points to the contradictions involved in waiting until the laws are broken to deal with poverty and then putting our poor in jails. She asserts that at least 1 percent of the billion dollars that Canada spends on police, courts and prison should instead go into social programs to help the poor get off the treadmill.

Abolitionists and peacemaking criminologists have exposed the dysfunctional and dangerous features of the criminal (in)justice system. The criminal law symbolizes values gone wrong in our society, especially the lack of concern for crime victims, inequities in criminal trials and the unethical treatment of our disenfranchised, whom we throw into cages. The theorists and activists have documented the physical and psychological problems of imprisonment and demonstrated the abuses in the system: solitary confinement, forced transfer, inadequate health care, overcrowding and excessive sentences.

Abolitionists and peacemakers declare that prisons foster recidivism because of their stigmatization and social exclusion. They argue for a less stigmatizing and more inclusive mechanism of social control. When punishment is needed, we should use only a minimum level of isolation. For abolitionists, crime is no different than other social problems, and the responses to crime should spring from within the community in which the crime was committed. As McLaughlin (2011: 51) reminds us, "Abolitionism insists that events and behaviours that are criminalized have nothing in common other than the fact that they have been usurped by the criminal justice system. Hence, crime has no ontological reality independent of the definitional processes and enforcement practices of the criminal law and criminal justice system." Abolitionists call for measures of restorative and transformative justice as well as the abolishment (dismantling) of the prison system. They advocate models of participatory justice in which offenders and victims must redefine their conflicts and their needs for healing (Culhane 1991; Morris 2000; McLaughlin 2011). Examples of participatory justice include mediation, reconciliation, alternative dispute resolution, sentencing circles and other non-penal measures to create safety within our society. For many peacemaking criminologists, this means addressing not only the semblance of conflict but also its essence. Nils Christie (1977) argues, for example, that individuals must take ownership of their own conflicts rather than give them away to the state as we do presently. Within our criminal justice model, the state provides a decision, voice and resolution. The offenders have no power to speak on their own behalf or to decide on the best means of resolution. The state decides what kind of punishment and compensation (if any) will be handed out to the offender and victim, respectively. Christie argues that our conflicts are an important part of being human and that through human interaction we must deal with the essence of the problems and conflicts, digging below the surface. As it is now, only legally pertinent parts of a conflict — those deemed important by the courts — are allowed into the courtroom. The criminal justice system thus blocks out key elements of life experience, excluding the people involved from full participation. The result is what Christie (1977) calls double victimization, which is doubly damaging because the person involved is denied the right to complete participation in an important symbolic event. The criminal justice system is, in essence, engaged in appropriating conflict because the political, economic and legal systems are designed to offer little chance for the participation and influence of either victims or offenders.

However, these theorists also insist that restorative measures will fail unless the system addresses the roots of injustice. In this regard, the true emphasis of abolitionism and peacemaking criminology is transformative justice, which insists that we cannot solve the problem of crime or rebuilding communities unless we challenge the true impact of capitalist inequalities, globalization, patriarchy and colonialization.

Some critics argue that abolitionism and peacemaking offer no concrete solutions (Braithwaite 1989), mainly because prison abolitionists not only call for the implementation of restorative measures, but also demand the eventual closure of all prisons. As a critical criminological approach, then, it may be more utopian than realistic. Don Gibbons (1994) asserts that peacemaking criminologists offer little that is new and do not show how to achieve the large-scale structural changes necessary in a movement working for non-violence and peace.

Postmodernism and poststructuralism provide a critique of the modern conceptions of "truth" and argue that "crime," "crime control" and criminology are modernist ideas that lay claim to a scientific truth that is philosophically problematic. Governmentality theory (as a critical theory in criminology) demonstrates the multiplicity of social controls, and, many argue, deepens the postmodern analysis.

POSTSTRUCTURALISM AND POSTMODERNISM

Only themselves understand themselves and the like of themselves,
as souls only understand souls.
— *Whitman 1965*

Poststructuralism and postmodernism are critical of all of the previous theories, which are all modernist. With its beginning in the Enlightenment, modernism is characterized by the use of the scientific method to uncover certain truths. Postmodernism points to a number of assumptions characteristic of modernism. For one thing, modernists believe in the possibility of human progress and emancipation through uncovering "truths" about human behaviour by means of science. Carol Smart states that modernism entails a search for "meta-narratives," or grand theories (Smart 1990: 194; Comack 2000: 62). Postmodernists and poststructuralists argue that we must abandon the modernist search for some kind of universal "truth" and instead accept the existence of a number of often competing truths.

Although postmodernism and poststructuralism take inspiration from Marxism, they ultimately reject it. Reaching beyond neo-Marxism, these theories investigate the dominant modes of expression (dominant discourse/accepted truths) in a society. Postmodernism and poststructuralism are critical theories; like the Marxist notion of hegemony, they view dominant discourses as being linked to the major power holders in society. They assert that these discourses attempt to create a public that conforms to the visions of the prevailing political economy. Discourse theorists point out, for example, how, from the fifteenth century on, people were compelled to believe in a dominant discourse that insisted on hard work as the source of success and goodness. They also assert that emancipatory discourse cannot provide alternatives to the status quo; the dominant discourses of our day, they argue, have marginalized and silenced such alternative views.

The methodology of discourse theories involves highlighting discourses and deconstructing them. Deconstruction is a "method of analysis that takes apart socially constructed categories in order to determine the makeup of a particular world view" (Ristock and Pennell, quoted in Comack 1999: 62). This process entails not only demonstrating how communication is formed but also how the dominant power holders of the political economy are supported by the discourse.

Poststructuralism

Poststructuralists (such as Michel Foucault, Pierre Bourdieu and Mikhail Bakhtin) reject the mainstream assumption that discourses are constructed simply as a means for communication. They assert that communication and language are tools of social control that create conformity. Language is constructed according to the needs of the powerful. As Bernard Schissel (1997) points out, poststructuralism uncovers the motives that lie behind the language and systems of knowledge that belong to the privileged.

Foucault (1977), for example, draws attention to the power and oppression of language, especially the language created by criminal justice and academic professionals under the guise of scientific objectivity. In this light, definitions of criminal behaviour are created as discourse according to the privileged — those with the power to control the knowledge. Mainstream discourse about crime in general is restricted to individual explanations and pathology, with almost no consideration of structural inequalities or the suffering of people on the margins. For example, an article in *Alberta Report* (July 31, 1995: 1) states: "Girls, it used to be said, were made of sugar and spice. Not anymore. The latest crop of teenage girls can be as violent, malicious and downright evil as the boys." The voices of experts back up these claims with professional knowledge and jargon. As Schissel emphasizes with regards to youth:

> This contemporary medical/psychological discourse of goodness and badness
> sets youth crime in a context of orthodox criminology: individuals gone wrong,
> either inherently or culturally. The underlying ideological position is that society
> is structured correctly and that individuals who offend are individually or socially
> pathological and identifiable. (1997: 105)

The dominant discourse is a powerful tool of social control precisely because it hides structural and societal problems and is written under the guise of expert knowledge and "scientific" objectivity.

Postmodernism

The theories of postmodernism and poststructuralism often come from the same authors, in similar writings. In fact, some critics argue that there is no difference between the two theories. Postmodernists analyzing crime and criminal justice focus on the position of the privileged in the creation of theories of crime and law (see, for example, Ferrell 1993; Henry and Milovanovic 1991; Pfohl and Gordon 1986). Like poststructuralists, postmodernists argue that we must abandon any search for "truth" and deconstruct the discourses of our day that lay claim to this knowledge. Many postmodernists are cynical about the world, seeing people as caught in consumeristic images representing a "hyperreal fantasy" in our ways of knowing. They seek to overturn the "dominant narratives" often characteristic of middle-class, white, male-dominant claims to information (Smart 1995).

Once discourse is deconstructed, the goal of postmodernism is to highlight less linear ways of thinking (see, for example, Smart 1990; Denzin 1990; Einstadter and Henry 1995). Here, postmodernists say that the redefinition of our truths must come from the words of those who experience oppression. Left theorists have often tried to speak for the oppressed; postmodernists allow the oppressed to speak for themselves. Postmodernists aim at including biographies, stories and personal experiences of crime and involvement with the criminal justice system (Smart 1990). An excellent example is the work of criminologists, historians and others that incorporate the opinions of individuals who have been in conflict with the law (see, for instance, Sangster 2002). Comack, for instance, gives voice to many women's different experiences, as in the following passage:

> Some people are violent, some people take it out in other ways, but that was my only
> way to release it. It was like, it's almost orgasmic, you know, you'd write the cheques,
> and you'd get home and you'd go through all these things and it's like "there's so much
> there. I have all these new things to keep my mind off of. I don't have to deal with the old
> issues." And so you do it. And it becomes an escape. You don't know what else to do ...
> I've tried other things like drugs. All it did was give me track marks, 'cause I was using
> drugs intravenously. And ... what more can you do? (Comack 1996: 86)

This perspective helps lay the groundwork for a postmodern legality challenging traditional definitions of crime and criminal justice. The practice supports and develops forms of dispute resolution that empower minority groups to define their own problems (Einstadter and Henry 1995). Postmodernism embraces the same forms of restorative justice and transformative justice that seek to have the offender, victim and community come to their own resolutions. It therefore supports the movement towards sentencing circles, family group conferencing, mediation and other practices that give the conflict back to those directly involved. In the end, restorative justice is based on believing the stories (accounts) of the oppressed.

GOVERNMENTALITY AND RISK THEORIES:
THE CRISIS OF CRITICAL CRIMINOLOGY AND THE DEMISE OF GRAND NARRATIVES

Critical criminology has been identified as in crisis since the end of the 1980s, especially because of the judgmental critique. "Whether one wanted to blame 'the end of history', the demise of grand narratives of progress and emancipation, the bankruptcy of socialism or the victory of individualistic consumerism, the project of critical criminology does not really seem to fit any more in the post-1984 world," write van Swaaningen and Taylor (1994: 183). There is no question that the radical challenges to the structures of justice are powerful. However, this level of critique privileges "authoritative judgment" above other discursive techniques, and times have changed, raising "important questions for the plight of such criticism in truth regimes that problematise the authority of expert or critical judgment" (Lyotard 1984, cited in Pavlich 2000: 60). Let's examine the specifics.

Zygmunt Bauman (1995) defines postmodernity as the declining role of the state and the recognition that the market manages the coordination of society. Citizens follow rules not because we are citizens of the state but because of the seductive promise of consumerism. Pettigrew (1996) describes this as a process of regulation that is based on envy, self-interest, competition, consumerism and endless production. What feeds the new global market, therefore, is abstraction, not human need. A shift in thinking towards the embrace of neo-liberal ideas accompanies these institutional changes. Citizens are viewed as autonomous individuals responsible for their own actions and fate. Economic opportunity is recast as an individual responsibility that is not connected to social structural conditions. Under these conditions, individuals are responsible for their own successes as well as their failures, leading to the importance of understanding the analysis of a risk society. A number of provisions have arisen to deal with managing risk (Rose 2000; Ericson, Barry and Doyle 2000), though most are beyond the confines of the state and state institutions (rendering an analysis of state institutions not irrelevant but only a small piece in a large puzzle). The power of the state is decentred (Garland 1997), with diverse risk-management strategies within "a black hole" of new market conditions controlling consumer identities (Bauman 1997).

Let's examine what this means in relation to crime control. In postmodern times, the state is no longer responsible for our protection; increasingly, managing our risks is considered our own responsibility. Managing risk includes buying better security systems, alarms and insurance, living in gated communities and more. Important to note here is that very few of society's have-nots can afford these risk-management measures, again leaving the poor more susceptible to crime.

The promise of critical and radical criminology can be assessed under this new terrain of risk management and extended forms of governmentality (Pavlich 2000). Although it is important to outline the state's role in managing the fallout of global market changes (see Chapter 13 for examples of the most desperate and most vulnerable sections of the population) and in reinforcing its authority by imposing tougher sentencing legislation (White 2002: 388), the state is only one means of upholding the postmodern social terrain and must be understood as such. The grammar of authoritative judgment is not capable of challenging fragmented, state-imposed, risk-based, diverse political technologies directed at new images of deviance and crime. Attention must be paid to the changing epistemological horizons where "judgmental grammar" no longer can thrive (Bauman 1997; Lyotard 1984; Vattimo 1997) and to recovering a critique that does not serve the technocratic demands of "advanced liberal" governmentalities that are dominant today

(Osborne 1996; Rose 1996). Further, the diversity acknowledged within literature on governmentality — the fractured social identities of postmodern conditions and life choices (in class, race, gender, age, sexual orientations) — nullifies the meta-narrative towards emancipation. Can we realistically say there is a universal vision broad enough to address all of the oppressions of our time? Yet this is often what radical criminology assumes (Butler 1992). Derrida points out that "nothing seems to be less outdated than the classical emancipatory idea" (1992: 28).

This critique applies to the movement in critical criminology that aims to find real, pragmatic solutions. This is especially relevant to critical criminologists who may blur boundaries between socialist pragmatism and "administrative" criminology. There is an acceptance of these neo-liberal agendas as well as neo-conservative solutions to the crime problem. Contemporary critical and radical criminologists' work often advocates (although cautiously) for restorative and communitarian justice (as we see throughout the book), such as family group conferences, sentencing circles, alternative models of education and community policing. As Pavlich (2000: 67) argues, "What strikes one in these debates is not so much the acceptance of several neo-conservative and neo-liberal foundations (which are there), but the sheer absence of any attempt to think beyond the ambit of techno-administrative rationales." Debates over restorative justice, zero tolerance and police-community relations are all part of a struggle that is political and part of a regulatory practice — the responsibilization of citizens. Thus, governmentality theorists recognize a blend of Keynesian and neo-liberal strategies, both acting as social control in a risk-based society, and criminology that supports this as simply a distraction. Rock (1994) argues that radical criminology remains vulnerable to administrative pressures to be co-opted by a wider institutional demand for a "normal science." The question becomes whether a radical criminology can embrace a technocratic logic that assumes the necessity of the reality it is are also trying to critique. Pavlich (2000) argues that critical criminology must continue to challenge administrative criminology and discourse in a way that does not support the advanced neo-liberal governmentalities. If critical criminology supports crime control measures (even restorative and progressive-looking measures), then it becomes part of social control and simply engages in a debate over existing policy. Governmentality theory argues that the role of criminology should remain at the level of understanding new forms of governmentality and continue to critique. This critique may include the question of why criminology has shifted to become more administrative in our global world.

The spirit of the Marxist critique remains relevant — but it needs to be expanded to understand modern times. Human beings are rendered knowable, shapeable and incapable of freedom within governmentality forces. Although governmentality recognizes diverse and decentred forms of social control, each of these can be examined not with the intent of developing technical solutions to things such as the crime problem but with the spirit of a critique that acknowledges human potential loss:

> A lesson to be drawn from critical thinking is this: the needed revisions to a grammar of (modern) judgmental critique cannot be achieved by accepting the dictates of a postmodern performance-based knowledge-producing ethos. Perhaps, an alternative grammar of critique could seek legitimacy by contesting this ethos, and developing alternative strategies to question the realties encompassing contemporary political subjects. (Pavlich 2000: 74)

Derrida (1992) calls for critical and radical texts to include the Marxist emphasis on change and escaping life limits. Governmental critiques can continue to embrace the spirit of Marxism and concepts of justice and democracy as promises that are ongoing, not endpoints that are achievable (Pavlich 2000). There cannot be an emancipatory goal, but we may embrace ongoing critique.

CONCLUSION

> *The priority research areas for Critical Criminology remain highlighting: the injustices associated with the relentless expansion of the crisis-prone criminal justice system; state violence; and the crimes committed by the powerful elites.*
> — McLaughlin 2011: 53

The sociological imagination (Mills 1959) must feed critical criminology — that is, the sociological imagination that understands the links between individual life chances and larger structural and historical forces. The critical perspectives ask not only whether individuals have maintained their responsibility to the community, but also whether the community has maintained its responsibility to individuals. The approach does not focus on individual flaws; rather, it questions societal structures and the role of those structures in breeding and sustaining criminals. Inequality and disenfranchisement, abuse and victimization, classism, racism and sexism produce criminal and anti-social behaviour. The approach looks at both criminal behaviour and the workings of the criminal justice system at the structural level. The issue in all critical criminology is whether it is a criminal justice system or an (in)justice system. Critical criminology raises questions about what is defined as criminal and how laws are enforced to work in the interests of powerful groups (men, professional and capitalist classes). It also questions how society responds to criminal behaviour. Does the criminal justice system help to reduce crime and recidivism, or does it instead work to reinforce criminogenic conditions? Jeffrey Reiman provides a clear answer. The current criminal justice system, he says, is the best model for the creation of crime that anyone could possibly think of: the system labels someone as an "offender," expects criminal tendencies from that individual, fails to deal with social issues that create criminogenic conditions, lowers self-esteem, criminalizes victimless and consensual acts, lumps disenfranchised individuals together in demeaning condition, and in general creates a breeding ground for dangerous and criminal behaviour.

Critical criminology rejects short-term solutions and "get-tougher" law-and-order responses to crime. The diverse proposals of critical criminology share a philosophy of healing, rebuilding, restoring and transforming — a movement away from punishment. The diversity is often found in the extent to which critical theorists are willing to embrace short-term restorative measures. Peacemaking, abolitionism, Left realism and postmodernism all call for restorative and transformative justice for offenders as well as the need to restructure society towards less violence and more justice. Each position continues to support the argument of Stanley Cohen (1985: 135): "It still makes sense today that mutual aid, good neighbourliness and real community are preferable to the solutions of bureaucracies, professionals and the centralized state."

Yet many neo-Marxist theorists remain extremely cautious about these community solutions. Their position is that restorative programs are often co-opted by the state to further control marginalized people. Some suggest that the projects could have a net widening effect, that judges could use restorative measures such as mediation, community services and restitution for "offenders" who might otherwise have been let go. Furthermore, restorative measures do not address the root causes of injustice. By implementing reforms that appear to be more humanitarian, measures that could actually alleviate suffering may well be forgotten. Neo-Marxism tends to demand a redefinition of what we define as criminal behaviour as well as a wake-up call for true equality (and, for many, socialism). Further, theories of structural Marxism and governmentality demonstrate how restorative measures fit within a neo-liberal ideology and thereby continue to control consumers to accept the status quo (and their own responsibilization to be consumers and law-abiding citizens) and to critique those who cannot succeed within this paradigm as "unfit" or compel them to become responsibilized (which may be through restorative justice or correctional paradigms). Either way, the global and numerous inequalities and social control measures remain unchallenged.

Transformative justice and the other long-term solutions of critical criminology are often criticized as being unattainable and, for recent governmentality theorists, no longer applicable in a world of complex and multiple social controls. For example, postmodernism is criticized for simply raising nagging theoretical questions about discourse. Even one of the leading peacemaking criminologists, Hal Pepinsky (1992), admitted that peacemaking strategies will not be replacing "law-and-order" initiatives any time soon. Some critics see abolitionism as seeking an idealist utopia. Some declare that the best critical criminology can offer is a rethinking of conservative political responses. The hope is that an enlightening of individual beliefs may then travel to the larger community through grassroots organizations. Police, media, public, politicians and criminologists may also be alerted by critical insights into the contradictions in our legal system, the benefits of healing and peace and the idea that things do not have to be the way they are. Still, many neo-Marxists claim that long-term structural changes can only be made slowly through law and other measures. This means we must continue to challenge globalization, the growing inequalities between the rich and the poor, downsizing, the dismantling of the social welfare system, the increased funding of the criminal justice system, the destruction of the environment in the pursuit of more profit, the deregulation of corporate crime and structural racism.

There are a significant number of authors who claim that a critical approach within criminology continues to be more relevant today than ever before, especially given the post-9/11 global war on terror (McLaughlin 2011). In the end, the continued goals of critical criminology are to critique the misuse of power and challenge evaluations of policy initiatives, which are sponsored by the state (Scraton 2004; McLaughlin 2011), as well as to continue to problematize state definitions of crime. These issues are addressed by all of the authors in this edition. This also leads some critical criminologists to talk about the importance of a public critical criminology and a continued critique of administrative managerialist criminology.

Critical criminologists continue to provide a critique of managerialist criminology and to work hard to separate themselves from the criminological enterprise of the state's agenda (McLaughlin 2011; Loader and Sparks 2011). Critical criminology, then, prioritizes policies related to social, rather than criminal, justice and a confrontation of power. In addition, the task of a public critical criminologist is to bring to light worrisome political trends and warn against "illiberal directions" that appear under a guise of crime control or control of terrorism. Loader and Sparks (2011: 30) remind the academy about the importance of critical criminologists speaking out publicly:

The more we can illuminate these dangers for our students, practitioners, and co-citizens, the more they may be mobilized to act against them.

DISCUSSION QUESTIONS

1. You have been invited to a prison abolition conference in Toronto to hear a presentation by a prison abolitionist and peacemaking criminologist entitled If Prison Is the Answer, then What Is the Question? In preparing for your trip you research the central assumptions of both perspectives on prison and develop a preliminary idea of what will be presented. What do you find?

2. Describe the difference between consensus theories that attempt to explain criminal behaviour as an event and critical criminological theories that examine the role of power in the creation and maintenance of "criminality."

3. Do you agree with critical criminologists who argue that criminology needs to shift the focus from personal harms and take green harm more seriously?

4. Marxist criminologists assert that although the poor and racial minorities are the people who fill prisons, this does not mean that they are the most dangerous or lacking in social consciousness. Rather, the overrepresentation means that the actions of the marginalized are defined as criminal and the rich are weeded out at each step of the criminal justice process. Explain.

5. Postmodernism, poststructuralism, and governmentality theories are said to both provide a critique and/or an extension of Marxist-based criminology. Explain.

6. Scan the newspapers for a crime article that cites a criminologist or sociologist as one of their sources. What did they say? Is this an example of public critical criminology? If not, what would you add to the news story.

GLOSSARY

Abolitionism: a movement that organizes individuals with the goal of reducing or eliminating prisons, capital punishment, slavery, racism, classism and sexism. Abolitionists maintain that (severe) punishment never solves problems.

Colonization: in a sociological context, colonization refers to the forceful imposition of one social group's cultural beliefs, values and moralities onto another group through symbolic and actual violence. In Canada, this term is often used to describe the actions undertaken by European colonizers against Aboriginal inhabitants (e.g., residential schools).

Criminogenic: a contemporary Marxist-criminological concept that explains that existing capitalist modes of production encourage criminality by design. The principal goal of material acquisition combined with unequal opportunity encourages individuals to find alternative means of fulfilling their material needs.

Critical Race Theory: a progressive movement that views race as a social construction and law as sustaining white supremacy.

Discourse: refers to the interchange of ideas or concepts through signs and symbols (e.g., language). Critical theorists argue that all individuals seek to manipulate discourse to their advantage and that the imbalance of power in society means certain actors will have more influence over discursive interchange than others.

Disenfranchisement: this Marxist term refers to the marginalization and deprivation of power for the working class under capitalist modes of production. Social values attest power to material items and define "legitimate" employment as the means of accessing them. Workers espousing these values focus on maintaining their income, and in doing so they cede their control of the mode of production to the bourgeoisie.

Governmentality: an emergent poststructuralist explanation of modern governance strategies. As the state distances itself from its traditional role of protecting from risk, it manipulates practices, discourses and ideologies to shift these responsibilities onto citizens.

Green Criminology: also titled eco-global criminology or environmental criminology, green criminology is the study of the harms that affect the planet, environmental injustice, the impact on both non-human and human life and matters related to speciesism.

Hegemony: originally denoting the predominance of one military over others, cultural hegemony was redefined by Antonio Gramsci in a critical context to describe the manipulation of morality and values wherein elite classes make use of their power to subvert the citizenry.

Hyperreal: this term describes the blurred lines between fiction and reality as well as the cultural impacts of this confusion. This concept is a useful tool for considering Marxist arguments about value and power. For instance, a consumer might choose one mobile phone over another because of the social capital (power) that it represents. A hyperrealist would argue that the phone's true power is its communication abilities

and that any other sense of power is in the realm of hyperreality.

Moral Panics: this term was popularized in a criminological context by Cohen (1972) to describe occurrences where "a condition, episode, person or group of persons emerges to become defined as a threat to societal values and interests." Critical theorists often attribute the creation of moral panics to media and state collusion within the context of hegemonic praxis.

Official Version of the Law: a method through which the legal world defines itself, to the effect that the law is a neutral, impartial and objective system designed for the resolving of social conflict. This is the principle tenet of the consensus approach to crime and criminality.

Peacemaking: seeks to uncover the warlike characteristics of the criminal justice system, prison and punishment. Peacemakers maintain we can end crime and suffering only by eliminating suffering.

Postmodernism: suggests we must reject the search for universal truth and knowledge. Postmodernist theorists point out that dominant discourses reflect the interests of the powerful and tend to silence alternative views and voices. In criminological analysis, these alternative voices are most often marginalized and labelled "criminal."

Restorative Justice: a critical approach to justice that focuses on repairing harms and restoring the relationship and relations between victims, offenders and their community. This movement eschews traditional forms of punishment, believing that carceral incapacitation further harms communities.

Risk Society: the preponderance of modern societies to seek and identify risks as a means of legitimizing themselves, regardless of whether or not said risks are rational.

Socialism: an approach to society and economics that seeks the redistribution and equalization of wealth through shared ownership of the means of production. Socialist theory also calls for the creation, maintenance and expansion of broad social support networks within society.

Sociological Imagination: originally penned by C. Wright Mills, this term describes the insights and perspectives that can be offered through a sociological lens.

Structural Marxism: proponents of structural Marxism argue that the criminal justice system and the "official version of the law" through claims to objectivity and neutrality legitimate capitalism. The law tells us that the rich and the marginalized are to be treated alike — but because our society is substantially unequal, such formal equality before the law perpetuates marginalization and class inequality.

Suite Crimes: an informal classification of deviant acts perpetrated by the elite strata of social classes, which have not been criminalized or are under-policed. Suite crimes are generally attested to the upper socio-economic classes in relation to the privileged access to related tools and protections (e.g., large-scale financial fraud).

SUGGESTED READINGS

Ronald L. Akers and Christine S. Sellers, *Criminological Theories: Introduction, Evaluation, and Application,* sixth edition, New York: Oxford University Press (2013).

Mary Bosworth and Carolyn Hoyle, *What Is Criminology?* Oxford: Oxford University Press (2011).

Angela Davis, *Are Prisons Obsolete?* Seven Stories Press, Open Media Series (2003).

Karlene Faith, *Unruly Women: The Politics of Confinement & Resistance,* second edition, Seven Stories Press (2011).

Michel Foucault, *Discipline and Punish: The Birth of the Prison,* New York: Pantheon (1977).

Harold E. Pepinsky and Richard Quinney (eds.), *Criminology as Peacemaking,* Bloomington: Indiana University Press (1991).

Ian Taylor, Paul Walton and Jock Young. *Critical Criminology.* Boston: Routledge and Kegan Paul (1975.)

Matthew Thomas James, *The New Abolitionists: (Neo)slave Narratives and Contemporary Prison Writings,* SUNY Press (2005).

R. White (ed.), *Climate Change from a Criminological Perspective,* New York: Springer (2012).

REFERENCES

Adelberg, Ellen, and Claudia Currie (eds.). 1993. *In Conflict with the Law: Women and the Canadian Justice System.* Vancouver: Press Gang Publishers.

Akers, Ronald L. 1997. *Criminological Theories: Introduction and Evaluation.* Second edition. Los Angeles: Roxbury.

Alberta Report. 1994. "Junior Gone Wild." May 9.

___. 1995. "Killer Girls." July 31.

Althusser, L. 1971. *Lenin and Philosophy and Other Essays.* New York: New Left Books.

Ashcroft, B., G. Griffiths and H. Tiffin. 1998. *Key Concepts in Post-colonial Studies.* New York: Routledge.

Assembly of First Nations. 2002. *Proceedings.* June 11. Matthew Coon Come, National Chief. At <turtleisland.org/news/absenyouth2.htm>.

Balbus, I. 1977. "Commodity Form and Legal Form: An Essay on the 'Relative Autonomy' of the Law." *Law and Society Review* 11: 571–88.

Bauman, Z. 1995. "From Welfare State into Prison." Unpublished paper for the International Conference on Prison Growth, Oslo. April.

___. 1997. *Postmodernity and Its Discontents.* New York: New York University Press.

Bohm, Robert M. 1997. *A Primer on Crime and Delinquency.* Wadsworth Publishing Company: An International Thomson Publishing Company.

Bonger, Willem. 1916. *Criminology and Economic Conditions.* Boston: Little, Brown.

Boritch, Helen. 1997. *Fallen Women.* Toronto: Nelson.

___. 2002. "Women in Prison in Canada." In B. Schissel and C. Brooks (eds.), *Marginality and Condemnation: An Introduction to Critical Criminology.* Halifax: Fernwood Publishing.

Braithwaite, J. 1989. *Crime, Shame and Reintegration.* New York: Cambridge University Press.

Brisman, A., and N. South. 2014. *Green Cultural Criminology: Constructions of Environmental Harms, Consumerism and Resistance to Ecocide.* London: Routledge.

Brooks, C. 2008. "Critical Criminology: Rejecting Short-term Solutions to Crime." In C. Brooks and B. Schissel, eds. *Marginality and Condemnation,* 2nd edition. Halifax: Fernwood.

Brooks, C., R. Henry and M. Daschuk. 2015. "Aboriginal Youth Gang Involvement: Decolonizing and Multi-Causal Perspectives Towards Community Strategies and Social Justice." In R. Corrado, A. Leschied and P. Lussier (eds.), *Serious and Violent Young Offenders and Youth Criminal Justice: A Canadian Perspective.* Burnaby, BC: Simon Fraser University Press.

Butler, J. 1992. "Feminism and the Question of Postmodernism." In J. Butler and J.W. Scott (eds.), *Feminist Theorize the Political.* London: Routledge.

Calgary Herald. 1995. "Teen Violence." April 18.

Canada, Office of the Correctional Investigator. 2012. *Bakgrounder: Aboriginal Offenders — A Critical Situation.*

Chambliss, William J. 1975. "A Sociological Analysis of the Law of Vagrancy." In W. Carson and P. Wiles (eds.), *The Sociology of Crime and Delinquency in Britain,* Volume 1. Oxford, UK: Martin Robertson.

Chambliss, W.J., and R.B. Seidman. 1982. *Law and Order, and Power.* Second edition. Reading, MA: Addison Wesley Publishing.

Christie, Nils. 1977. "Conflicts as Property." *The British Journal of Criminology* January.

Clarke, J. 2000. "Serve the Rich and Punish the Poor." In Gordon West and Ruth Morris (eds.), *The Case for Penal Abolition.* Toronto: Canadian Scholars Press.

Cleaver, Eldridge. 1968. *Soul on Ice.* New York: Dell Publishing.

Cohen, Leonard. 1994. "There Is a War." *Cohen Live.* Stranger Music (BMI).

Cohen, Stanley. 1985. *Visions of Social Control.* Cambridge: Polity Press.

Collins, Rachael. 2013. "The Construction of Race and Crime in Canadian Print Media: A 30-Year Analysis." *Criminology and Criminal Justice* 14, 1: 77 – 99.

___. 2014a. "'Beauty and Bullets': A Content Analysis of Female Offenders and Victims in Four Canadian Newspapers." *Journal of Sociology* April.

___. 2014b. "'Meet the Devil ... He'll Chill You to the Bone': Fear, Marginalization, and the Color of Crime: A 30 Year Analysis of Four Canadian newspapers." University of Saskatchewan dissertation.

Comack, Elizabeth. 1996. *Women in Trouble.* Halifax: Fernwood Publishing.

___. (ed.). 1999. *Locating Law: Race/Class/Gender Connections.* Halifax: Fernwood Publishing.

___. 2000. "The Prisoning of Women: Meeting Women's Needs." In K. Hannah-Moffat and M. Shaw (eds.), *An Ideal Prison? Critical Essays on Women's Imprisonment in Canada.* Halifax: Fernwood Publishing.

Comack, Elizabeth, and Gillian Balfour. 2004. *The Power to Criminalize: Violence, Inequality, and the Law.* Halifax: Fernwood Publishing.

Culhane, Claire. 1991. "Prison Abolition." In L. Samuelson and B. Schissel (eds.), *Criminal Justice: Sentencing Issues and Reform.* Toronto: Garamond Press.

Currie, Dawn. 1998. "The Criminalization of Violence Against Women: Feminist Demands and Patriarchal Accommodation." In Kevin Bonnycastle and George Rigakos (eds.), *Unsettling Truths: Battered Women, Policy, Politics, and Contemporary Research in Canada.* Vancouver:

Collective Press.

DeKeseredy, Walter S. 2000. *Women, Crime and the Canadian Criminal Justice System.* Cincinnati: Anderson Publishing Company.

DeKeseredy, Walter S., and Joseph F. Donnermeyer. 2013. "Thinking Critically about Rural Crime: Toward the Development of a New Left Realist Perspective." In S. Winlow and R. Atkinson (eds.), *New Directions in Crime and Deviancy.* London: Routledge

Denzin, N. 1990. "Presidential Address on the Sociological Imagination Revisited." *The Sociological Quarterly* 31, 1.

Derrida, J. 1992. "Force of Law: The 'Mystical Foundation of Authority.'" In D. Cornell, M. Rosenfeld and D.G. Carlson (eds.), *Deconstruction and the Possibility of Justice.* New York: Routledge.

Dodge, Mary, Stacey J. Bosick and Victoria Van Antwerp. 2013. "Do Men and Women Perceive White-Collar and Street Crime Differently? Exploring Gender Differences in the Perception of Seriousness, Motives, and Punishment." *Journal of Contemporary Criminal Justice* 29, 3 (August).

Donnermeyer, Joseph F. 2012. "Rural Crime and Critical Criminology." In W. DeKeseredy and M. Dragiewicz (eds.), *Routledge Handbook of Critical Criminology.* London: Routledge.

Einstadter, Werner, and Stuart Henry. 1995. *Criminological Theory: An Analysis of Its Underlying Assumptions.* Fort Worth, TX: Harcourt Brace.

Ericson, R., D. Barry and A. Doyle. 2000. "The Moral Hazards of Neo-liberalism: Lessons from the Private Insurance Industry." *Economy and Society* 29: 532–58.

Faith, K. 1993. *Unruly Women: The Politics of Confinement and Resistance.* Vancouver: Press Gang Publishers.

___. 2011. *"Unruly Women: The Politics of Confinement and Resistance.* Second edition. Vancouver: Press Gang Publishers

___. 2002. "The Social Construction of 'Dangerous' Girls and Women." In B. Schissel and C. Brooks (eds.), *Marginality and Condemnation: An Introduction to Critical Criminology.* Halifax: Fernwood Publishing.

Ferrell, Jeff. 1993. *Crimes of Style: Urban Graffiti and the Politics of Criminality.* New York: Garland.

Foucault, Michel. 1977. *Discipline and Punish: The Birth of the Prison.* New York: Pantheon.

Garland, D. 1997. "Governmentality and the Problem of Crime: Foucault, Criminology, Sociology." *Theoretical Criminology* 1: 173–214.

Gibbons, Don C. 1994. *Talking About Crime and Criminals: Problems and Issues in Theory Development in Criminology.* Englewood Cliffs, NJ: Prentice Hall.

Gilliam, F.D. , N.A. Valentino and M.N. Beckmann. 2002. "Where You Live and What You Watch: The Impact of Racial Proximity and Local Television News on Attitudes about Race and Crime." *Political Research Quarterly* 55, 4.

Goff, C., and C. Reasons. 1978. *Corporate Crime in Canada.* Scarborough, ON: Prentice-Hall.

Gordon, David. 1976. "Class and the Economics of Crime." In W.J. Chambliss and M. Mankoff (eds.), *Whose Law, What Order?* New York: Wiley.

Gordon, Robert, and Ian Coneybeer. 1999. "Corporate Crime." In N.Larson and B. Burtch (eds.), *Law in Society: Canadian Readings.* Toronto: Harcourt Brace Canada.

Gramsci, A. 1971. *Selections from the Prison Notebooks of Antonio Gramsci.* New York: International Publishers.

Green, Joyce. 2005. "Self-Determination, Citizenship, and Federalism: Indigenous and Canadian Palimpsest." In Michael Murphy (ed.), *State of the Federation: Reconfiguring Aboriginal-State Relations.* Institute of Intergovernmental Relations, School of Policy Studies, Queen's University, McGill-Queen's University Press.

Green, Ross Gordon, and Kearney Healey. 2003. *Tough on Kids: Rethinking Approaches to Youth Justice.* Saskatoon: Purich Publishing.

Hall, S., C. Critcher, T. Jefferson, J. Clarke and B. Roberts. 1978. *Policing the Crisis: Mugging, the State, and Law and Order.* London: Macmillan.

Henry, Stuart, and Dragan Milovanovic. 1991. "Constitutive Criminology: The Maturation of Critical Theory." *Criminology* 29.

Hinch, R. 1992. "Conflict and Marxist Theories." In R. Linden (ed.), *Criminology: A Canadian Perspective*. Toronto: Harcourt Brace Jovanovich, Canada.

Hudson, Barbara. 2006. "Beyond White Man's Justice: Race, Gender and Justice in late Modernity." *Theoretical Criminology* 10, 1: 29–47.

Hunt, Alan. 1976. "Law, State and Class Struggle." *Marxism Today* 20, 6)

Jaccoud, Mylene, and Renee Brassard. 2003. "The Marginalization of Aboriginal Women in Montreal." In David Newhouse and Evelyn Peters (eds.), *Not Strangers in These Parts: Urban Aboriginal Peoples*. Ottawa: Policy Research Initiative.

Jackson, George. 1970. *Soledad Brother: The Prison Letters of George Jackson. Introduction by Jean Genet*. New York: Coward-McCann.

Karstedt, Susanne. 2010. "Roundtable on the Phantom Capitalists by Michael Levi: The Phantom Capitalists: A Classic. *Global Crime* 11, 3: 336.

Juristat 2014. *Police-Reported Crime Statistics in Canada, 2013*.

___. 2011.*Canadians' Perceptions of Personal Safety and Crime, 2009*.

Lawrence, Bonita. 2004. *"Real" Indians and Others: Mixed-Blood Urban Native Peoples and Nationhood*. Vancouver: UBC Press.

Loader, I., and R. Sparks. 2011. "Criminology's Public Roles: A Drama in Six Acts." In M. Bosworth and C. Hoyle (eds.), *What Is Criminology?* Oxford: Oxford University Press.

Lynch, M., and W. Groves. 1986. *A Primer in Radical Criminology*. New York: Harrow and Heston.

___. 1989. *A Primer in Radical Criminology*. Second edition. New York: Harrow and Heston.

Lynch, M., and P.B. Stretesky. 2003. "Green Criminology." In F.T. Cullen and P. Wilcox (eds.), *The Oxford Handbook of Criminological Theory*. Oxford Handbooks Online. <oxfordhandbooks.com/view/10.1093/oxfordhb/9780199747238.001.0001/oxfordhb-9780199747238-e-32>.

Lynch, M.J., and P.B. Stretesky. 2012. "Green Criminology." In F.T. Cullen and P. Wilcox (eds.), *The Oxford Handbook of Criminological Theory*. Oxford: Oxford University Press.

Lyotard, J.F. 1984. *The Postmodern Condition: A Report on Knowledge*. Minneapolis: University of Minnesota Press.

Mathiesen, T. 1974. *The Politics of Abolition: Essays in Political Action Theory*. London: Martin Robertson.

McLaughlin, Eugene. 2011. "Critical Criminology: The Renewal of Theory, Politics, and Practice." In M. Bosworth and Carolyn Hoyle (eds.), *What Is Criminology?* Oxford: Oxford University Press.

Miliband, R. 1969. *The State in Capitalist Society: The Analysis of the Western System of Power*. London: Quartet.

Mills, C. Wright. 1959. *The Sociological Imagination*. New York: Oxford University Press.

Mohony, T. Hotton. 2011. "Women and the Criminal Justice System." Component of Statistics Canada Catalogue no. 89-503-X *Women in Canada: A Gender-based Statistical Report*. Statistics Canada. <statcan.gc.ca/pub/89-503-x/2010001/article/11416-eng.pdf>.

Morris, Ruth. 2000. *Stories of Transformative Justice*. Toronto: Canadian Scholars' Press.

O'Connor, J. 1973. *The Fiscal Crisis of the State*. New York: St. Martin's Press.

Osborne, P. (ed.). 1996. *A Critical Sense: Interviews with Intellectuals*. London: Routledge.

Pavlich, George. 2000. *Critique and Radical Discourses on Crime*. Burlington, Great Britain: Dartmouth Publishing Company.

Pearce, F. 1976. *Crimes of the Powerful: Marxism, Crime and Deviance*. London: Pluto Press.

Pepinsky, Harold. 1991. *The Geometry of Violence and Democracy*. Bloomington: Indiana University Press.

___. 1992. "Abolishing Prisons." In M. Schwartz, L. Travis and T. Clear (eds.), *Corrections: An Issues Approach*. Third edition. Cincinnati: Anderson.

Pepinsky, Harold E., and Richard Quinney (eds.). 1991. *Criminology as Peacemaking*. Bloomington: Indiana University Press.

Pettigrew, P. 1996. "Notes from Speech to a Conference on 'Accelerating Rural Development in Africa.'" Airlie, Virginia, September 23.

Pfohl, Stephen. 1985. *Images of Deviance and Social Control: A Sociological History*. New York: McGraw-Hill.

Pfohl, Stephen, and Avery Gordon. 1986. "Criminological Displacements: A Sociological Decon-struction." *Social Problems* 33.

Platt, Tony. 1975. "Prospects for a Radical Criminology in the USA." In I. Taylor, P. Walton, and J. Young (eds.), *Critical Criminology.* Boston: Routledge and Kegan Paul.

Poulantzas, N. 1973. *Political Power and Social Class.* Atlantic Fields, NJ: Humanities Press.

Quinney, Richard. 1974. *Critique of Legal Order: Crime Control in Capitalist Society.* Boston: Little, Brown.

___. 1975. "Crime Control in Capitalist Society: A Critical Philosophy." In I. Taylor, P. Walton, and J. Young (eds.), *Critical Criminology.* London: Routledge and Kegan Paul.

___. 1980. *Class, State and Crime.* New York: Longman.

Ratner, R.S., and J.L. McMullan. 1985. "Social Control and the Rise of the 'Exceptional State' in Britain, the United States, and Canada." In T. Fleming (ed.), *The New Criminologies in Canada: State, Crime, and Control.* Toronto: Oxford University Press.

Reiman, Jeffrey. 1998. *The Rich Get Richer and the Poor Get Prison: Ideology, Class and Criminal Justice.* Boston: Allyn and Bacon.

___. 2001. *The Rich Get Richer and the Poor Get Prison: Ideology, Class and Criminal Justice.* Boston: Allyn and Bacon.

___. 2007. *The Rich Get Richer and the Poor Get Prison: Ideology, Class and Criminal Justice.* Boston: Pearson Press.

Reiman, Jeffrey, and Paul Leighton. 2012. *The Rich Get Richer and the Poor Get Prison: Ideology, Class and Criminal Justice.* Boston: Pearson Press.

Rock, P. 1994. *History of Criminology.* Aldershot: Dartmouth Publishing Company.

Rose, N. 1996. "Governing 'Advanced' Liberal Democracies." In A. Barry, T. Osborne and N. Rose (eds.), *Foucault and Political Reason: Liberalism, Neo-liberalism, and Rationalities of Government.* Chicago: University of Chicago Press.

___. 2000. *Government and Control.* Oxford; New York: Oxford University Press.

Samuelson, Les. 2000. "Indigenized Urban 'Community' Policing in Canada and Australia: A Comparative Study of Aboriginal Perspectives." *Police Practice and Research* 2, 4.

Sangster, Joan. 2002. *Girl Trouble: Female Delinquency in English Canada.* Toronto: Between the Lines.

Schindeler,E., and J. Ewart. 2014. "Manufacturing a Crime Wave: The Gold Coast Saga." *Media International Australia* 151 (June).

Schissel, Bernard. 1997. *Blaming Children: Youth Crime, Moral Panics and the Politics of Hate.* Second edition. Halifax: Fernwood Publishing.

___. 2006. *Still Blaming Children: Youth Conduct and the Politics of Child Hating.* Halifax: Fernwood Publishing.

Scraton, P. 2004. "Defining 'Power' and Challenging 'Knowledge': Critical Analysis and Resistance in the UK." In R. Hogg and K. Carrington (eds), *Critical Criminology: Issues, Debates and Challenges.* Cullompton: Willan.

Sentencing Project. 2013. *Report of the Sentencing Project to the United Nations Human Rights Committee Regarding Racial Disparities in the United States Criminal Justice System.*

Smart, Carol. 1990. "Feminist Approaches to Criminology or Postmodern Woman Meets Atavistic Man." In L. Gelshthorpe and A. Morris (eds.), *Feminist Perspectives in Criminology.* Bristol, England: Open University Press.

___. 1995. *Law, Crime and Sexuality: Essays in Feminism.* London; Thousand Oaks: Sage Publications.

Snider, Laureen. 1999. "Relocating Law: Making Corporate Crime Disappear." In Elizabeth Comack (ed.), *Locating Law: Race/Class/Gender Connections.* Halifax: Fernwood Publishing.

___. 2002. "The Sociology of Corporate Crime: An Obituary." *Theoretical Criminology* 4, 2.

___. 2008. "But They're Not Real Criminals: Downsizing Corporate Crime." In C. Books and B. Schissel (eds.), *Marginality and Condemnation: An Introduction to Criminology.* Halifax: Fernwood Publications.

South, N., and A. Brisman. 2014. "Critical Green Criminology, Environmental Rights and Crimes of Exploitation." In S. Winlow and R. Atkinson (eds.), *New Directions in Crime and Deviance.* London: Routledge.

Statistics Canada. 2003. "Aboriginal Peoples Survey: Well-Being of the Non-Reserve Aboriginal Population." *The Daily.* September 24. <statcan.ca/Daily/English/030924/d030924b.htm>.

Taylor, I. 1981. *Law and Order: Arguments for Socialism.* London: Macmillan.

___. 1999. *Crime in Context: A Critical Criminology of Market Societies.* Boulder: Westview.

Taylor, I., P. Walton and J. Young. 1973. *The New Criminology: For a Social Theory of Deviance.* New York: Harper and Row.

___. 1975. *Critical Criminology.* Boston: Routledge and Kegan Paul.

Van Swaaningen, R., and I. Taylor. 1994. "Rethinking Critical Criminology: A Panel Discussion." *Crime Law and Social Change* 21: 183–90.

Vattimo, G. 1997. *Beyond Interpretation: The Meaning of Hermeneutics for Philosophy.* London: Polity Press.

Waldram, James B. 1997. *The Way of the Pipe.* Peterborough: Broadview Press.

Walters, R. 2006. "Crime, Agriculture, and the Exploitation of Hunger." *British Journal of Criminology* 46: 26–45.

White, R. 2002. "Restorative Justice and Social Inequality." In B. Schissel and C. Brooks (eds.), *Marginality and Condemnation: An Introduction to Critical Criminology.* Halifax: Fernwood Publishing.

___. 2013. "But Is It Criminology?" In S. Winlow and R. Atkinson (eds.), *New Directions in Crime and Deviance.* London: Routledge.

Whitman, Walt. 1965. *Leaves of Grass.* New York: Norton New York.

Wortley, Scott. 2008. "The Depiction of Race and Crime in the Toronto Print Media." In B. Schissel and C. Brooks (eds.), *Marginality and Condemnation: An Introduction to Critical Criminology.* Halifax: Fernwood Publishing.

Wortley, Scott. 2002. "The Depiction of Race and Crime in the Toronto Print Media." In B. Schissel and C. Brooks (eds.), *Marginality and Condemnation: An Introduction to Critical Criminology.* Halifax: Fernwood Publications.

5

THE SEX QUESTION IN CRIMINOLOGY

Elizabeth Comack

KEY FACTS

> Men commit higher rates of crime than women and men's crimes tend to be more violent. While this fact is often undisputed in criminology, feminist criminology has made this "gender gap" a key focus of research.

> In 2011/2012, men made up the majority (85 percent) of those admitted to correctional services.

> In 2009, approximately 233,000 women were accused of violating the criminal code. The vast majority (41 percent) were property crimes, followed by minor assault (13 percent). While the media commonly typifies the female offender as one involved in the sex trade, only 1,351 prostitution charges were laid — less than half of one percent of all encounters.

> Physical strength, power, assertiveness and being in control are stereotypical masculine traits glamorized and reinforced throughout the media.

> Of police-reported physical assaults, females more commonly victimized by former or current intimate partners whereas males are more commonly victimized by a non-family member or a stranger.

Sources: Heidensohn and Gelsthorpe 2012; Perreault 2013; Mahony 2011; Heitmeyer, Bockler and Seeger 2013; Newman 2013; Vaillancourt 2008.

Even a cursory look at crime statistics tells us that males make up the vast majority of persons who come into conflict with the law and an even greater proportion of those who are sent to prison. In 2011, for example, 79 percent of adults charged with Criminal Code offences in Canada were men (Brennan 2012). In 2008/9, men represented 94 percent of admissions to federal custody, 89 percent of provincial/territorial sentenced admissions and 87 percent of remand admissions in Canada (Mahony 2011). Criminologists have long known this correlation between sex and crime. Yet until recently the maleness of their subject matter has escaped close scrutiny. It was the feminist critique of criminology that put the "sex question" front and centre on the criminological agenda. Initially, this critique took the form of documenting the invisibility of women in criminological accounts, but it soon broadened to include a more concerted focus on the discipline's ability to explain male patterns of criminal activity. As a result, the past decade has seen a veritable explosion of work in the area of men, masculinity and crime.

The purpose of this chapter is to explore the sex question — or the placement of men and women — in criminological theorizing. As Judith Allen (1990: 21) has noted, the capacity to explain the correlation between sex and crime and the sexed character of many criminal activities could be considered "a litmus test for the viability of the discipline." As we will discover, theorists more often than not have premised their work on some notion of "difference," both between men and between women and men. While some theorists have located the sources of this difference in *sex* (the physical and sexual differences between males and females), others have located its sources in *gender* (the cultural constructions of man and woman). Still others have argued that we need to abandon this sex/gender distinction altogether and focus on *sexed bodies* (the meanings that different sexes carry at the cultural level).

MAINSTREAM CRIMINOLOGY: BIOLOGY AS DESTINY?

Early criminologists understood "difference" as rooted in biology. Cesare Lombroso's (1912) biological determinist approach, for instance, sought to uncover those constitutional predisposing factors that drove some men to criminality. In the process, a clear demarcation was made between the criminal male and the law abiding male. In sharp contrast to his opposite, the criminal man was pathological, "an atavistic being who reproduces in his person the ferocious instincts of primary humanity and the inferior animals" (Lombroso, cited in Wolfgang 1972). While Lombroso posited clear differences between criminal versus non-criminal men, he also saw women as being "naturally" different from men. Following his evolutionary premise that criminals were a biological throwback to an earlier, more primitive form of man, Lombroso reasoned that women had lower crime rates than men because of their natural inferiority; women simply had not progressed as far along the evolutionary continuum and so could not degenerate as far. Given that women were relatively "primitive," the criminals among them would not be highly visible. As well, Lombroso held that women were by nature deceitful, vengeful and jealous, but these negative traits were supposedly neutralized by their maternal instinct, piety and inherent weakness, thereby producing greater conformity in women.

As more sociologically informed work emerged throughout the twentieth century, the search for the causes of crime — criminology's leitmotif — broadened to include factors in the social environment that produced criminality. These factors were variously located in terms of anomie (Merton 1938), differential associations (Sutherland 1949), subcultures (Cohen 1955) and illegitimate opportunity structures (Cloward and Ohlin 1960). Although endeavouring to distance themselves from the biologically based formulations of their predecessors, these more sociologically oriented criminologists continued the focus on the individual offender and the distinction made between the offending (criminal) man and the non-offending (conformist) man. Biology also surfaced in their efforts to account for the sex differentials in criminal activity. In this regard, one theorist to have a profound influence on criminological theorizing in the mid-twentieth century was sociologist Talcott Parsons.

In the 1940s, Parsons coined the term "sex roles," which Allen (1990: 27) describes for us as "socially ascribed behaviours, attributes and capacities assigned to be appropriate for each sex." Parsons saw women and men playing two different roles in the family that help to integrate the overall social system: an *expressive* role that involves integration and an *instrumental* role that involves goal attainment. According to Parsons, women's biological capacity to reproduce naturally disposed them to the expressive role of child rearing in the private domain of the family, while men were considered better suited to the instrumental role of providing financial support by performing work outside the home:

> In our opinion the fundamental explanation of the allocation of the roles between the biological sexes lies in the fact that the bearing and early rearing of children established a strong presumptive primacy of the mother to the small child and this in turn establishes a presumption that the man who is exempted from these biological functions should specialize in the alternative instrumental direction. (Parsons and Bales 1955: 23)

In turn, Parsons maintained that the family unit prepared children for adequate participation in society by socializing them into their appropriate sex roles: masculine (instrumental) for males and feminine (expressive) for females. While boys were raised to be assertive, competitive and achievement-oriented, girls were expected to be passive, nurturing and compliant.

Parsons, then, located the differences between men and women in relation to the social roles they occupied in society. However, these roles — and the resulting forms of masculinity and femininity attached to them — had a distinctly biological basis. In Parsonian terms, it was "functional" for women to be confined to the home as their reproductive capacities and inherent nature (the maternal instinct) made them better suited to the roles of motherhood and acting as the emotional mainstay to their husbands. Similarly, men's more assertive, outgoing and independent nature made them better suited to the rough and tumble of the work world in the public sphere and the provision of economic support for their wives and children.

This particular conception of "difference" between men and women found its way into mainstream criminological theorizing. Edwin Sutherland's differential association theory, for instance, was intended as a general, non-sex-specific theory of crime that focused on the learning and transmission of criminal patterns of behaviour. As Ngaire Naffine (1987: 30) notes, Sutherland's first mention of females comes late in his work, where he comments on the fact that the male crime rate is "greatly in excess" of the crime rate for females: "Sex status is of greater statistical significance in differentiating criminals from non-criminals than other traits" (Sutherland and Cressey 1966: 138). Sutherland accounts for this discrepancy in terms of the differential socialization of boys and girls: "From infancy, girls are taught that they must be nice, while boys are taught that they must be rough and tough" (Sutherland and Cressey 1966: 142). According to Sutherland, females are more conforming than males because they are supervised more closely in the home and positively schooled in anti-criminal behaviour patterns.

Similarly, Albert Cohen's (1955) subcultural theory of delinquency drew heavily on the Parsonian conception of sex roles and their corresponding traits of masculinity and femininity. The delinquency of lower-class boys, according to Cohen, represented not only a reaction to the demands of the middle-class value system, but also an effort to distance themselves from the feminine persona represented by their mothers:

> Because his mother is the object of the feminine identification which he feels is the threat to his status as a male, he tends to react negativistically to those conduct norms which have been associated with mother and therefore have acquired feminine significance. Since mother has been the principal agent of indoctrination of "good," respectable behaviour, "goodness" comes to symbolize femininity, and engaging in

"bad" behavior acquires the function of denying his femininity and therefore asserting his masculinity. This is the motivation to juvenile delinquency. (Cohen 1955: 164)

Delinquency, then, is represented in Cohen's theory as a means by which boys can assert their masculinity; it is a male solution to a male problem. On the other hand, destined to become wives and mothers, girls were preoccupied with establishing relationships with the opposite sex. According to Cohen (1955: 142, 147) while "boys collect stamps," "girls collect boys." Given their domestication, the delinquency of girls was less frequent than that of boys, and when it did occur it was most likely to involve sexual promiscuity. Even so, Cohen (1955: 46) claimed that males' illicit heterosexual relations were "richer" and "more varied" than that of females.

These explanations for the sex differentials in crime that draw upon sex role theory have been critiqued from a number of angles. Allen (1990: 28) has commented that in relying on differential socialization, Sutherland failed to consider *why* it is the case that females are treated differently than males. In other words, his remarks may describe, but they do not explain. Naffine (1987: 31) observes that Sutherland effectively transforms females into the anomaly or exception to his supposedly general theory of crime; "He describes as general what he later reveals to be limited to the male case." In a similar fashion, Cohen's subcultural theory basically amounts to the tautological or circular claim that "men commit crimes because crime is masculine and women do not because crime is masculine" (Allen 1990: 32). Even more problematic than these critiques, however, is that Parsonian functionalism had the political effect of reaffirming a particular sexual division of labour — and the relations of power between men and women that flowed from it — as "functional" for society. This rationalization for women's inequality came under heavy criticism with the advent of the second wave of the women's movement in the 1970s.

FEMINIST CRIMINOLOGY: FROM SEX TO GENDER

Intent on challenging the functionalist assumption that women "naturally" belonged in the home and were "naturally" inferior to men, second-wave feminists shifted the discourse from sex to gender in their theorizing. While sex was used to describe the sexual and physical differences between men and women, gender was understood as a cultural construction; it referenced the socially produced differences that arose from the ways in which boys and girls were socialized and the limited nature of the social roles assigned to men and women. This shift had the political effect of drawing attention to the power relations between men and women, thereby enabling an interrogation of the social basis of women's inequality in society. For feminists, in other words, the problem was not rooted in women's biology (sex) but in the way in which femininity and the roles assigned to women in a patriarchal or male-dominated society had been socially constructed (gender).

In criminology, this feminist attention to gender led to a far-reaching critique of the discipline. According to feminist criminologists (see, for example, Smart 1976; Naffine 1987; Gelsthorpe and Morris 1988; Daly and Chesney-Lind 1988; Comack 1992), mainstream theories were really "malestream" as they were decidedly premised on the criminal as male, with females positioned as an afterthought. Despite the use of generic terms — such as "criminal," "defendant," or "delinquent" — criminology has historically been about men. More often than not, mainstream criminologists simply gave no consideration to women. Robert Merton's (1938) anomie theory, for example, was offered as a general theory explaining crime in relation to the strain that results from the disjunction between culture goals (like monetary success) and institutionalized means (education, jobs). While Merton's theory reflected a sensitivity to the class inequalities that exist in society, the same could not be said of his awareness of gender inequalities. If lower-class individuals were more likely to engage in crime because of a lack of access to the institutionalized means for achieving monetary success, then it follows that women — who as a group experience a similar lack of access — should also be found to commit their share of crime as a consequence of this strain. But the statistics tell us that this is not the case.

Travis Hirschi's (1969) control theory was likewise characterized by a neglect of the female. While other criminologists focused their attention on explaining deviance, Hirschi turned the tables and set out to explain conformity. Since women appear to be more conformist than men (given, for example, their underrepresentation in crime statistics), it would have made sense for Hirschi to treat women as central to his analysis. Nevertheless, despite having collected data on females, he simply set these data aside and — like his colleagues — concentrated on males.

When women did come into view in criminological theories, they were understood in relation to a male standard or measuring rod and were typically judged to be lacking. Naffine (1987: 12), for instance, notes that Cohen's subcultural theory is premised on a male-centred conception of American society. Cohen singles out values such as ambition, autonomy, individualism, achievement, rationality and emotional restraint as constituting "the American way of life." In effect, what he describes are those traits associated with the male role. Women, who are described by Cohen as "inactive, unambitious, uncreative, and lazy," are simply relegated to the sidelines. Feminist criminologists, then, took issue with the sexism of criminological theories — socially undesirable characteristics were attributed to women and assumed to be intrinsic characteristics of their sex.

As a consequence of this feminist critique, increasing attention was devoted to the sex question in criminology throughout the 1970s and 1980s. Why are women less likely than men to be involved in crime? What explains the sex differences in rates of arrest and in the variable types of criminal activity between men and women? Numerous studies were conducted to address these questions (see, for example, Scutt 1979; Kruttschnitt 1980–81, 1982; Steffensmeier and Kramer 1982; Zingraff and Thomson 1984; Daly 1987, 1989). The main issue that guided this research was one of chivalry: were women being treated more leniently by the criminal justice system than men? The results, however, were mixed. Research that supported this chivalry hypothesis indicated that when it does exist, chivalry benefits some women more than others — in particular, the few white, middle-class or upper-class women who come into conflict with the law. It also appears to apply only to those female suspects who behave according to a stereotypical female script, that is, "crying, pleading for release for the sake of their children, claiming men have led them astray" (Rafter and Natalazia 1981: 92). In this regard, Nicole Rafter and Elena Natalizia argued that chivalrous behaviour should be seen as a means of preserving women's subordinate position in society, not as a benign effort to treat women with some special kindness. Naffine (1997: 36), however, pointed to a larger problem with this research. By turning on the question of whether women were treated in the same way as men, or differently, the chivalry thesis (and its rebuttal) took men to be the norm: "Men were thus granted the status of universal subjects, the population of people with whom the rest of the world (women) were compared."

Another variation on the sex question that attracted considerable attention in the 1970s and 1980s was the women's liberation thesis. This thesis posited that women's involvement in crime would come to resemble men's more closely as differences between men and women were diminished by women's greater participation and equality in society. As reflected in the work of Rita Simon (1975) and Freda Adler (1975), the women's liberation thesis suggested that changes in women's gender roles would be reflected in their rates of criminal involvement. Simon argued that the increased employment opportunities that accompanied the women's movement would also bring an increase in opportunities to commit crime (such as embezzlement from employers). Adler linked the apparent increase in women's crime statistics to the influence of the women's movement and suggested that a "new female criminal" was emerging: women were becoming more violent and aggressive, just like their male counterparts.

The women's liberation thesis "captured the imagination of the media and practitioners" (Morris and Gelsthorpe 1981: 53, cited in Gavigan 1993: 221). While law enforcement officials were quick to confirm its tenets, charging that the women's movement was responsible for triggering a massive crime wave, the media had a heyday with its claims, featuring headlines such as "Lib takes the lid off the gun moll" (*Toronto Star* 15 May 1975, cited in Gavigan 1993: 222). Nevertheless, representations of emancipated women running amok in the streets and workplaces did not hold up to closer scrutiny (see, for example, Chesney-Lind 1978; Weiss 1976; Steffensmeier 1980; Naffine 1987; Gavigan 1993). Carol Smart (1976), for one, noted that the women's liberation thesis was premised on a "statistical illusion" in that the supposed increases in women's crime were being reported as percentages. Given the small base number of women charged with criminal offences, it did not take much of a change to show a large percentage increase. Holly Johnson and Karen Rodgers (1993: 104) provided an example of this problem using Canadian data. Between 1970 and 1991, charges against women for homicide increased by 45 percent, but that figure reflected a real increase of only fifteen women charged with that offence. As well, while the women's movement was primarily geared toward privileged white women, poor women and racialized women were most likely to appear in police and prison data. These women were not inclined to think of themselves as "liberated" and — far from considering themselves as feminists — were quite conventional in their ideas and beliefs about women's role in society. For many feminist criminologists, the main difficulty with the women's liberation thesis — similar to the chivalry thesis — was that it posed a question that took males to be the norm: were women becoming more liberated and thus more like men, even in their involvement in crime?

Given the difficulties encountered in efforts to explain the sex differentials in crime — in particular, the tendency to take men as the standard or measuring rod — many feminist criminologists saw the need to "bracket" these issues for the time being in order to understand better the social worlds of women and girls (Daly and Chesney-Lind 1988: 121). Maureen Cain (1990) took this suggestion further. She noted that while feminist criminologists needed to understand women's experiences, existing criminological theory offered no tools for doing this. Therefore, feminists needed to transgress the traditional boundaries of criminology, to start from outside the confines of criminological discourse. In carrying out this project, feminist criminologists drew inspiration from the violence against women movement.

Transgressing Criminology: The Issue of Male Violence Against Women

At the same time as feminists were fashioning their critiques of criminology, the women's movement in Canada and other Western countries was breaking the silence around the issue of male violence against women. This violence was understood as a manifestation of patriarchy — the systemic and individual power that men exercise over women (Brown-miller 1975; Kelly 1988) — and various reports and surveys revealed it to be a widespread and pervasive phenomenon. The Canadian Advisory Council on the Status of Women (CACSW), for instance, estimated that one in every five Canadian women will be sexually assaulted at some point in her life, and one in every seventeen will be a victim of forced sexual intercourse. In 1981, CACSW released a report, *Wife Battering in Canada: The Vicious Circle* (MacLeod 1980), which estimated that, every year, one out of every ten Canadian women who is married or in a relationship with a live-in partner is battered. In 1993, Statistics Canada released the findings of the Violence Against Women (VAW) Survey. The first survey of its kind anywhere in the world, the VAW Survey included responses from 12,300 women (see Johnson 1996). Using definitions of physical and sexual assault consistent with the Canadian Criminal Code, the survey found that one-half (51 percent) of Canadian women had experienced at least one incident of physical or sexual violence since the age of sixteen. The survey also found that 29 percent of ever-married women had been assaulted by a spouse.

The violence against women movement had a number of implications for the work of feminist criminologists. For one, the movement allowed feminists to break away from the confines of mainstream criminology, which had been complicit in the social silencing around the issue of male violence against women. Official statistics suggested that crimes like rape were relatively infrequent in their occurrence. Victim surveys — which asked respondents whether they had been victimized by crime — indicated that the group most at risk of victimization was young men, not women. Most mainstream criminologists took these data sources at face value. They seldom questioned whether (and why) acts like rape might be under-reported, undercharged or under-prosecuted or the extent to which victim surveys had been constructed in ways that excluded the behaviours women feared most. When criminologists did turn their attention to crimes like rape, the focus was on the small group of men who had been convicted and incarcerated for the offence, and these men were typically understood as an abnormal and pathological group. Much of traditional criminology also tended to mirror widely held cultural myths and misconceptions about male violence against women (such as women "ask for it" by their dress or behaviour; see Morris 1987; Busby 2014). In these terms, the issue of violence against women pointed to significant knowledge gaps in mainstream criminology and encouraged a host of studies by feminist criminologists intent on rectifying this omission (see Dobash and Dobash 1979; Klein 1982; Stanko 1985; Gunn and Minch 1988; Kelly 1988).

For another, pointing to the widespread and pervasive nature of male violence against women, the movement raised the issue of the impact that experiences of violence have had on women who come into conflict with the law. Several quantitative studies in the 1990s began to expose the extent of abuse experienced by women caught up in the criminal justice system. In interviewing women serving federal sentences, Margaret Shaw and her colleagues (1991) found that 68 percent had been physically abused as children or adults, and 53 percent were sexually abused at some point in their lives. Among Aboriginal women, the figures were considerably higher: 90 percent said that they had been physically abused, and 61 percent reported sexual abuse (Shaw et al. 1991: vii, 31). Another study in a provincial jail (Comack 1993) found that 78 percent of the women admitted for over a six-year period reported histories of physical and sexual abuse.

Influenced by these findings, as well as Cain's call to transgress the boundaries of criminology and discover more about the lives of women who come into conflict with the law, feminist criminologists began to engage in qualitative research.

Women in Trouble

One of the primary tasks of feminist scholarship has been to produce knowledge that is "women-centred" — knowledge that is about and for women. This has involved placing women as knowers at the centre of the inquiry in order to produce better understandings of women and the world (Naffine 1997: 46). In criminology, this undertaking took the form of interviewing women who were caught up in the criminal justice system to find out more about their lives. Central to much of this research were the links between women's victimization and their criminal involvement.

In the United States, Mary Gilfus (1992) conducted life-history interviews with twenty incarcerated women to understand their entry into street crime. Most of these women had grown up with violence, and violence was a common feature in their relationships with men. Repeated victimization experiences, drug addiction, involvement in the sex trade, relationships with men involved in street crime and the demands of mothering: these themes marked the women's transitions from childhood to adulthood.

Beth Richie's (1996) study focused on African-American battered women in prison. Richie (1996: 4) developed a theory of "gender entrapment" to explain the "contradictions and complications of the lives of African-American battered women who commit crimes." Gender entrapment involves understanding the connections between violence against women in their intimate relationships, culturally constructed gender-identity development and women's participation in illegal activities. In these terms, Black women were "trapped" in criminal activity in the same way that they were trapped in abusive relationships.

Working in Canada, Ellen Adelberg and Claudia Currie (1987) reported on the lives of seven women convicted of indictable offences and sentenced to federal terms of imprisonment. Regularly occurring themes in these women's lives included "poverty, child and wife battering, sexual assault, women's conditioning to accept positions of submissiveness and dependency upon men," which led Adelberg and Currie to conclude that "the problems suffered by women offenders are similar to the problems suffered by many women in our society, only perhaps more acutely" (Adelberg and Currie 1987: 68, 98).

My own work, *Women in Trouble* (Comack 1996), was built around the stories of twenty-four incarcerated women. The women's stories revealed complex connections between a woman's law violations and her history of abuse. Sometimes the connections are direct, as in the case of women sent to prison for resisting their abusers. Janice, for instance, was serving a sentence for manslaughter. She talked about how the offence occurred at a party:

> I was at a party, and this guy, older guy, came, came on to me. He tried telling me, "Why don't you go to bed with me. I'm getting some money, you know." And I said, "No." And then he started hitting me. And then he raped me. And then [pause] I lost it. Like, I just, I went, I got very angry and I snapped. And I started hitting him. I threw a coffee table on top of his head and then I stabbed him. (Janice, cited in Comack 1996: 96)

Sometimes the connections only become discernible after a woman's law violations are located in the context of her struggle to cope with the abuse and its effects. Merideth, for example, had a long history of abuse that began with her father sexually assaulting her as a young child, and the abuse extended to several violent relationships with the men in her life. She was imprisoned for bouncing cheques — she said she was writing the cheques to purchase new things to keep her mind off the abuse:

> I've never had any kind of conflict with the law. [long pause] When I started dealing with all these different things, then I started having problems. And then I took it out in the form of fraud. (Merideth, cited in Comack 1996: 86)

Sometimes the connections are even more entangled, as in the case of women who end up on the street, where abuse and law violation become enmeshed in their ongoing, everyday struggle to survive. Another woman in prison, Brenda, described her life on the street:

> Street life is a, it's a power game, you know? Street life? You have to show you're tough. You have to beat up this broad or you have to shank this person, or, you know, you're always carrying guns, you always have blow on you, you always have drugs on you, and you're always working the streets with the pimps and the bikers, you know? That, that alone, you know, it has so much fucking abuse, it has more abuse than what you were brought up with!... I find living on the street I went through more abuse than I did at home. (Brenda, cited in Comack 1996: 105–106)

Overall, these efforts to draw out the connections between women's victimization experiences and their lawbreaking activities had the benefit of locating law violations by women in a broader social context characterized by inequalities of class, gender and race.

Intersectionality

While gender was the starting point for analyzing criminalized women's lives, it soon became apparent to feminist criminologists that they needed to somehow capture the multiple, fluid and complex nature of women's identities and their social relations. Much of the impetus for this recognition came from the critiques offered by racialized women of the tendency for white feminists to theorize "Woman" as a unitary and homogeneous group. As Marcia Rice (1990: 57) notes, while feminist criminologists had succeeded in challenging stereotypical representations of female offenders, Black women and women from developing countries were "noticeably absent in this discourse," and when attempts were made to incorporate Black women's experiences into feminist writings there were few attempts "to develop perspectives which take into account race, gender and class simultaneously."

In response to this critique, feminist criminologists embraced "intersectionality," a concept first highlighted by Kimberlé Crenshaw (1989), to theorize the multiple and complex social relations and the diversity of subject positions involved. Crenshaw argues that the experience of oppression is not singular or fixed but derives from the relationship between interlocking systems of power. With regard to the oppression of Black women, Crenshaw explains that, "because the intersectional experience is greater than the sum of racism and sexism, any analysis that does not take intersectionality into account cannot sufficiently address the particular manner in which Black women are subordinated" (1989: 140). Adopting the notion of intersectionality, then, means that rather than viewing race, gender and class as additives (that is, class + gender + race), these concepts — and the relations and identities they represent — need to be considered as simultaneous forces (that is, class X gender X race) (Brewer 1997).

In contrast to the women's liberation thesis, which argued that women's involvement in crime was a consequence of their "emancipation," feminist criminologists adopted an intersectionality approach to connect women's involvement in crime to poverty. In recent decades, poverty has increasingly taken on a "female face" — especially in terms of the number of single-parent families headed by women (Little 2003; Chunn and Gavigan 2014; Mosher 2014). As more and more women are confronted with the task of making ends meet under dire circumstances, it is argued, the link between poverty and women's lawbreaking becomes more obvious. But so too has the move by the state to criminalize those who must rely on social assistance to get by. Using an intersectionality approach, Kiran Mirchandani and Wendy Chan (2007) document the move in British Columbia and Ontario to criminalize welfare recipients through the pursuit of "fraudulent" claimants. In the process, they argue that this "criminalization of poverty" is also racialized and gendered in that women of colour have borne the brunt of this attack.

Attending to the intersections of class, gender and race also assisted in explaining some forms of prostitution or sex-trade work (Brock 1998; Phoenix 1999). According to Johnson and Rodgers (1993: 101), women's involvement in prostitution is a reflection of their subordinate social and economic position in society: "Prostitution thrives in a society which values women more for their sexuality than for their skilled labour, and which puts women in a class of commodity to be bought and sold. Research has shown one of the major causes of prostitution to be the economic plight of women, particularly young, poorly educated women who have limited *legitimate* employment records." Maya Seshia's (2005) research on street sexual exploitation in Winnipeg revealed that poverty and homelessness, gender discrimination and generational sexual exploitation, and colonialism and the legacy of residential schools all combined to lead women and transgenders to become involved in the sex trade.

In learning more about the lives of women and the "miles of problems" (Comack 1996: 134) that brought them into conflict with the law — problems with drugs and alcohol use, histories of violence and abuse, lack of education and job skills and struggles to provide and care for their children — feminist criminologists took pains to distance their work from formulations that located the source of women's problems in individual pathologies or personality disturbances. Instead, the intersecting structural inequalities in society — of class, gender and race — that contour and constrain the lives of women provided the backdrop for understanding women's involvement in crime. As British criminologist Pat Carlen (1988: 14) phrased it, "Women set about making their lives within conditions that have certainly not been of their own choosing."

GENDERING CRIME

The feminist critique of mainstream criminology and the effort to draw attention to the gendered nature of women's lives soon led to a call to "gender" crime more broadly. Women, it was held, were not the only ones with a gender; men's lives too needed to be understood in gendered terms. In this regard, while mainstream criminology had been characterized by its neglect of the female, critics pointed out that the discipline's aptitude for explaining male patterns of criminal activity was just as troublesome. As Elizabeth Gosz (1987: 6, cited in Allen 1990: 39) framed it, there was a need to question "what is it about men, not as working class, not as migrant, not as underprivileged individual, but *as men* that induces them to commit crime?" During the 1990s, various criminologists responded to this challenge by initiating studies of men, masculinity and crime.

Men, Masculinity and Crime

One criminologist to take up this project was James Messerschmidt. In his book, *Masculinities and Crime: A Critique and Reconceptualization of Theory*, Messerschmidt directly addressed the sex question in criminology by posing the question "Why do men engage in more and different types of crime than women and in differing amounts and forms amongst themselves?" (Messerschmidt 1993: 77). In the course of framing his answer to this question, he offered a number of criticisms of sex role theory, which can be summarized as follows:

- Sex role theory presumes "natural" traits in men and women. For instance, men are "naturally" aggressive and women are "naturally" compliant or passive. As Janet Katz and William Chambliss have noted, however, "An individual learns to be aggressive in the same manner that he or she learns to inhibit aggression. One is not a natural state, and the other culturally imposed; both are within our biological potential" (Katz and Chambliss 1991: 270, cited in Messerschmidt 1993: 25).
- "Sex" is itself a cultural construction. Assuming that there are only two sexes — male and female — is a culturally specific move. Messerschmidt cites a number of examples of cultures where sex is not assigned on the basis of genitalia (as is the practice in Western cultures) but social activities, and where more than two dichotomous sexes are recognized.
- In concentrating on the differences *between* men and women, sex role theory ignores variability not only across but also *within* cultures, for example, in terms of the variations in the construction of masculinity among boys and men.
- Sex role theory tends to reduce individuals' capacities for action; it is the sex roles into which we are socialized that are "determining." In this respect, sex role theory "obscures the work that is involved in producing gender in everyday activities" (West and Zimmerman 1987: 127, cited in Messerschmidt 1993: 28).
- Sex role theory fails to situate sex roles within a structural explanation of their origin. Its referent is more biology and the focus is more on gender differences than on gender relations (and the tensions, conflicts and power dynamics attendant to these relations). It also neglects power relations *between* men.

In his endeavour to move criminological theorizing beyond the limitations of sex role theory — as well as to contribute to a "feminist theory of gendered crime" (1993: 62) — Messerschmidt has designed a theory that situates men's involvement in crime in the context of "doing" masculinity.

"Doing" Masculinity

In developing his theory, Messerschmidt adopts sociologist Anthony Giddens' (1976) concept of "structured action" to resolve an issue that continues to haunt social thinkers: how to theorize the seeming disconnect between social structures (such as capitalism, patriarchy and colonialism) and individual agency (the location and wilful activity of individuals within those structures). Following Giddens, Messerschmidt conceptualizes the relation between structure and action as reciprocal: "As we engage in social action, we simultaneously help create the social structures that facilitate/limit social practice" (1993: 62). Moreover, rather than conceptualizing structures of inequality as separate yet interconnected (as many feminist theorists have done), Messerschmidt suggests that divisions of labour based on class, gender and race are *simultaneously* produced in the everyday interactions of social actors (1993: 64).

Following on the work of ethnomethodologists Candace West and Don Zimmerman (1987; see also Fenstermaker, West and Zimmerman 1991), gender is viewed as a "situated accomplishment." While sex is the social identification of individuals as man or woman, gender is the accomplishment of that identification in social interaction: "we coordinate our activities to 'do' gender in situational ways" (Messerschmidt 1993: 79). In the process, individuals realize that their behaviour is accountable to others and, as such, "they construct their actions in relation to how they might be interpreted by others in the particular social context in which they occur" (Messerschmidt 1993: 79). In a culture that believes there are but two sexes — male and female — this accountability will involve living up to the gender ideals that have been tied to each sex; that is, behaving "as a man" or "as a woman" would in a given social situation. Moreover, because we accomplish masculinity and femininity in specific social situations (although not necessarily in circumstances of our own choosing), these are never static or finished products.

From the work of R.W. Connell (1987, 1995, 2000) Messerschmidt borrows the concept of "hegemonic masculinity." Connell was interested in theorizing how a particular gender order — a "historically constructed pattern of power relations between men and women and definitions of femininity and masculinity" (Connell 1987: 98–99) — comes to be reproduced in society. He suggested that male dominance in the gender order is achieved by the ascendancy of a particular idealized form of masculinity that is culturally glorified, honoured and exalted. Hegemonic masculinity references not just a set of role expectations or an identity; it is a "pattern of practice" (Connell and Messerschmidt 2005: 832). Different from a male sex role, this cultural ideal may not correspond with the actual personalities of the majority of men and may well not be "normal" in a statistical sense as only a minority of men may enact it. In these terms, exemplars such as sports heroes, movie starts and even fantasy figures (such as Rambo or the Terminator) offer representations of masculinity that come to be normative in the sense that they embody "the currently most honored way of being a man" and require all other men to position themselves in relation to these representations (Connell and Messerschmidt 2005: 832).

Hegemonic masculinity is constructed in relation to women and what Connell (1987: 188) refers to as "emphasized femininity," a femininity organized as an adaptation to men's power and emphasizing compliance, nurturance and empathy as womanly virtues. As well, because men will "do" masculinity according to the social situation in which they find themselves, different types of masculinity — complicit, subordinated and oppositional — exist in relation to the hegemonic form. For example, while hegemonic masculinity valourizes heterosexuality, a key form of subordinated masculinity is homosexuality. In these terms, it makes more sense to speak of masculinity in the plural — as *masculinities*.

Messerschmidt argues that it is in the process of "doing" masculinity that men simultaneously construct forms of criminality. He explains: "Because types of criminality are possible only when particular social conditions present themselves, when other masculine resources are unavailable, particular types of crime can provide an alternative resource for accomplishing gender and, therefore, affirming a particular type of masculinity" (1993: 84).

Messerschmidt subsequently put his theory to work to understand varieties of youth crime, street crime, corporate crime, sexual harassment in the workplace, wife beating and rape (Messerschmidt 1993) as well as the lynching of Black men in the American South in the late nineteenth century, the life of Malcom X, violence among working-class girls in gangs and the decision to launch the space shuttle *Challenger* in 1986 (Messerschmidt 1997). Key to his analysis is the thesis that gendered power is central to understanding why men commit more crimes and more serious crimes than women: crime is one practice in which and through which men's power over women can be established and the different types of crime men may commit are determined by the power relations among them (1993: 84).

Messerschmidt's theorizing, then, marked an important advance in thinking about the relation between men and crime. As an antidote to sex role theory and its limitations, his formulation called attention to the ways in which men's crime is connected to broader structural features and power relations and tied to culturally dominant and contested constructions of what it means to be a male in modern industrialized societies. As Kathleen Daly (1997: 37) has noted, rather than seeing crime as an attribute of a person, this "doing gender" approach has the benefit of putting the focus on "how situations and social practices produce qualities and identities associated with membership in particular social categories." Nevertheless, Messerschmidt's work — especially his use of the concept of "hegemonic masculinity" — has been subject to criticism by other criminologists interested in the sex question in criminology.

Masculine Subjectivity: The Case of Mike Tyson

Tony Jefferson (1994, 1996a, 1996b), for one, notes that pressures on men to live up to the "patriarchal masculine ideal," to be a "man's man," can create considerable feelings of insecurity and vulnerability. He cites the example of falling in love: "Here the need for and dependence on another is posed most starkly, in direct contradiction to the notions of self-sufficiency and independence central to hegemonic masculinity. It is almost as if to succeed in love one has to fail as a man" (1994: 12). This recognition of the difficulties men may experience in relating to dominant models of masculinity, according to Jefferson, points to the need for a theory of masculine subjectivity, one capable of connecting social and psychic processes.

Jefferson demonstrates his point through an analysis of the biography of Mike Tyson, who transformed himself "first from a pudgy, passive, lisping schoolboy — the butt of local bullies — to a feared neighbourhood bully and thief, and then to a boxing prodigy who went on to become the youngest-ever [at the age of 20] world heavy-weight champion" (Jefferson 1996b: 153). He argues that Tyson cannot be explained solely by reference to his structural location as a poor Black boy from the American ghetto and aims to show "how subjectivity can be both a product of various social discourses, and of unique personal biography" (Jefferson 1996b: 158).

Jefferson understands Tyson's transformation as connected to his adoption of the "tough guy" discourse, wherein toughness connotes "one's ability to survive on the streets" as well as "the ability to meet and resist physical challenges" (1996b: 160). Identifying with a "bad boy" image enabled Tyson to socially succeed in the world of boxing, with its "hypermasculine ethos." But Tyson's identification with boxing was not just about winning, money or power, it was also a way of suppressing feelings of powerlessness and anxiety. In relation to Tyson's statement "I'm 'Mike Tyson,' everyone likes me now," made before the 1982 Junior Olympics, Jefferson suggests:

> Tyson desperately wanted it to be true that "everyone," but especially those close to him, liked him as a person; but the response of "everyone" close to him, in teaching him to control and surmount this fear in the ring, only convinced

him that the "truth" of his identity lay only in the boxing ring, as the "compleat destroyer." Then, and possibly only then, in the act of destroying another man, the psychic anxiety underpinning the feared passivity could be (if temporarily) assuaged, and the delight of all those close to him, and his fans, could be "good enough" testimony of love. (Jefferson 1996b: 164)

While boxing may have provided a socially acceptable (and decidedly masculine) venue for Tyson to resolve his contradictory feelings (passive quitter/compleat destroyer; gentle/vicious; needy/needing no one), things were far less straightforward outside the ring. As Jefferson notes, Tyson was particularly ill-equipped to deal with the fame and fortune that accompanies heavyweight championships, and his troubles eventually extended to include a conviction and six-year prison sentence for rape.

Jefferson's work has the advantage of highlighting the complex and variable nature of men's experiences and emotions. Men (as with women) can be assertive or timid, hateful or loving, confident or unsure. While not denying the social costs of men's actions (violence against women being one prominent example), it bears remembering that men too have their troubles and uncertainties. His insights also showcase the kinds of pressures, contradictions and tensions that boys and men encounter in their struggles to live up to the "patriarchal masculine ideal." Without an appreciation of this complexity, we are confined to a view of men as "always already empowered" (Collier 1998: 295).

Critiquing the "Masculinity Turn"

Richard Collier (1996, 1998, 2004) has taken Messerschmidt to task for his tendency to over-emphasize the negative or undesirable traits associated with "doing" masculinity. Messerschmidt, for instance, tells us that hegemonic masculinity "emphasizes practices toward authority, control, competitive individualism, independence, aggressiveness, and the capacity for violence." As Collier (1998: 22) notes, what men are not seen as "doing" is a masculinity that might in any sense be interpreted as positive. In these terms, understanding masculinity primarily in relation to a set of negative traits could easily lead to a kind of essentialist position that views "real men" as inherently oppressive, dominating and violent. It may well be, for instance, that for some boys and men (especially those marginalized by their race and class position) a search for independence constitutes a positive trait that emanates from their desire to escape the oppressive conditions of their existence. It is important, therefore, to resist demonizing *all* men simply *because* they are men. This means being continually mindful of the particular social contexts in which boys and men find themselves as they endeavour to "accomplish" masculinity.

Criminologists have also been critical of Messerschmidt's use of hegemonic masculinity to explain the causes of crime. John Hood-Williams (2001: 43) makes the point that crime is a highly generalized notion "which puts together disparate practices and invites us to treat them as if they were similar." Men are seen as "doing" masculinity through engaging in such varied practices as the rape of women, property theft, corporate crime, violence toward other men and even football hooliganism. As Collier notes, "To account for such diversity in terms of men 'accomplishing' a gender identity is asking a great deal of the concept of masculinity" (Collier 2004: 292).

In addition to these concerns, there are other difficulties encountered with Messerschmidt's treatment of the category "crime." In his 1993 book, he makes the following statement three times in the space of two pages: "Crime is a resource that may be summoned when men lack other resources to accomplish gender" (Messerschmidt 1993: 84–85). Here he seems to be suggesting that crime is like the default button on your computer — an option taken when other resources are inoperable. In the process, Messerschmidt sets up a dualism whereby law-abiding behaviour is taken to be the norm while criminal behaviour is the exception. Such a dualism operates to obscure the similarities between so-called "law abiding" and "criminal" behaviours — especially in relation to "doing" masculinity. In short, what actually constitutes "crime" is never made problematic in Messerschmidt's theorizing. Even in his later works (Messerschmidt 1997, 2004), he entertains no theoretical discussion of crime as a category of analysis, but only situates it as a "resource" for enacting gender.

Collier (1998) locates Messerschmidt's work as a key component of what he calls "the masculinity turn" in criminology, the recent body of work that explores the relationship between men and crime by means of an explicit foregrounding of the concept of masculinity. Skeptical of this turn, Collier (2004: 297) maintains that, "it is open to question, ultimately, just how adequate the concept of masculinity is when seeking to explain, understand, or otherwise account for the crimes of men." Instead of "gendering crime," he argues, what is required is a "sexing of the criminal."

SEXED BODIES AND THE ISSUE OF "EMBODIMENT"

As Messerschmidt (1993) pointed out in his critique of sex role theory, "sex" is actually a cultural construction. Assuming that there are only two sexes — male and female — is a culturally specific move. To make a distinction between sex and gender, then, as feminist philosopher Judith Butler (1990) has argued, does nothing but reproduce as gender (man/woman) the assumption of a prediscursive sexual difference (male/female). In other words, "the distinction between sex and gender turns out to be no distinction at all" since the use of the term "gender" commonly refers to "sex," that is, the cultural meanings ascribed to bodies sexed as male or female (Butler 1990: 7). For Butler, gender is merely a "performance" of the cultural significance of sex. Theorists who adopt a "sexed bodies" approach (Daly 1997), therefore, have argued that we need to begin with the concept of sex; it is sex — more specifically, the "sexed body" — and not gender that should be the focus of our investigation.

To focus on bodies as "sexed" does not signal a return to the kind of biologically based formulations found in earlier criminological theories. Instead, it represents an effort to transcend the sex-gender distinction altogether. The aim is to showcase how our bodies are more than just markers of difference (as male or female). In these terms, *embodiment* is considered central to our sense of self; it is our way of "being in the world" and therefore an essential part of our subjectivity or identity. Feminist theorists such as Iris Marion Young (1990) and Moira Gatens (1996) have pointed out that the way we experience our bodies is not direct or unmediated; how we experience our bodies as male or female is a reflection of both our personal histories and the culturally shared notions of certain bodily forms. For instance, Young suggests that many of the ways in which females relate to their bodies comes from the experience of living in a patriarchal society where women are continually under threat (especially in terms of their sexual safety) and constantly exposed to the male gaze (whereby women come to see themselves and their bodies as they think men see them). In these terms, femininity and masculinity are ways of living in differently shaped bodies and our identities as women and men are formed as ways of giving significance to different bodily forms.

Despite Collier's harsh verdict as to the limits of "masculinity" as a theoretically useful concept, Messerschmidt has gone on to revise his theorizing on masculinity and crime in his later writing, especially in relation to this issue of "embodiment." For instance, in *Flesh and Blood: Adolescent Gender Diversity and Violence* (2004; see also Messerschmidt 2012), he proposes to "bring the body back in" to criminology — not by "sexing the criminal" but by "embodying gender"; that is, by concentrating on embodiment as a lived aspect of gender, on the way in which our bodies constrain and facilitate social action and therefore mediate and influence social practices. As Connell (1995: 52) has noted, masculinity involves "a certain feel to the skin, certain muscular shapes and tensions, certain postures and ways of moving, certain possibilities of sex." In these terms, the physical sense of "maleness" is central to the social interpretation of gender.

Messerschmidt's revised theory, then, conceptualizes "doing gender" as both mindful and physical: "the body is a participant in the shaping and generating of social practice. Consequently, it is impossible to consider human agency — and therefore crime and violence — without taking gendered embodiment into account" (Messerschmidt 2004: 49). Utilizing case studies of two white working-class boys and two white working-class girls involved in assaultive violence, Messerschmidt (2004) applies his revised theory of gendered embodiment to understand how motivations for violence (and non-violence) emerge in three different sites — the home, the school and the street — in the life histories of these youth. In the process, he is able to show "how gender difference is not simply constructed between boys and girls (as most criminologists contend), but it is also prominent among boys and among girls as well as individually *across* the three settings" (Messerschmidt 2004: 131).

GENDER MATTERS

Attention to the "sex question" in criminology has generated a corpus of thought-provoking literature. Earlier formulations of mainstream criminologists that rested on biologically based notions of "difference" between men and women — and women's "natural" inferiority to men — have been challenged by feminist criminologists intent on developing distinctly women-centred theory and research that exposes how the gendered nature of women's lives in a patriarchal society affects both their risk of victimization at the hands of violent men and their involvement in crime. Responding to the call to "gender" crime more broadly, criminologists initiated a "masculinity turn" that sought to understand the connections between men, masculinity and crime. One realization that has emerged from this corpus of literature is that *gender matters*. Criminologists can no longer afford to ignore the ways in which the gendered nature of women's and men's lives brings them into conflict with the law. Addressing the tendency of mainstream criminologists to neglect women in their theories, Lorraine Gelsthorpe and Allison Morris have noted:

> Theories are weak if they do not apply to half of the potential criminal population; women, after all, experience the same deprivations, family structures, and so on that men do. Theories of crime should be able to take account of *both* men's and women's behaviour and to highlight those factors which operate differently on men and women. Whether or not a particular theory helps us to understand women's crime is of *fundamental*, not marginal importance for criminology. (Gelsthorpe and Morris 1988: 103, emphasis added)

This attention to the sex question in criminology has had the benefit of drawing attention to how gender matters in another way: in terms of how the criminal justice system responds to those who are caught in its reach. In this respect — and as various chapters in this book will testify — masculinity and femininity are cultural constructions that not only give contour to the lives of men and women, they also infuse the ways in which law operates to categorize and criminalize particular behaviours and particular individuals. For instance, to the extent that aggression comes to be understood as "masculine" behaviour, criminal justice actors (police officers, defence lawyers, Crown prosecutors, and judges) will come to define violence by men as "normal" or expected and violence by women as an anomaly, a breach of expected gender scripts (see, for example, Comack and Balfour 2004: ch 3).

But while it is important to address the gendered experiences of men and women and the particular ways in which criminal justice processes may work to "gender" crime, it is also the case that other factors — race and class in particular — have a bearing on people's lives. To the extent that approaches such as "doing" gender or "sexed bodies" take gender/sex as a priority in their theorizing, then these other factors are given secondary status. The challenge, therefore, is to fashion an intersectional approach that recognizes the importance of gender in the construction of identities or subjectivities as well as how gender practices inform and constrain people's lives while at the same time not losing sight of these other important factors.

Theorizing is never a static process. Theories are continually subject to revision and reformulation as their creators endeavour to respond to critiques from their colleagues and — just as significant — to the changing and dynamic nature of the social world that they are trying to understand (see, for example Messerschmidt 2012, 2013). In this regard, the effort to grapple with the "sex question" is sure to be an ongoing — and vital — project in criminology.

DISCUSSION QUESTIONS

1. Why do you think mainstream criminology traditionally ignored or neglected to consider women?

2. What are some of the limitations of relying upon "sex roles" to answer the sex question in criminology?

3. In what ways do you see "hegemonic masculinity" operating in our culture? What about "emphasized femininity"?

4. Why should gender matter for criminologists?

GLOSSARY

Biological Determinism: the belief that human behaviour is fundamentally directed by innate, inborn or "essential" factors.

Embodiment: embodiment connotes the idea that the body is an entity that both derives meaning from and gives meaning to social and cultural processes.

Emphasized Femininity: a concept referring to a cultural ideal that is celebrated for women (for instance, that women should be nurturing, passive, sociable, receptive to male desire). Because it is constructed in a subordinated relation to hegemonic masculinity, women's adherence to this ideal reinforces male power and privilege.

Gender: the cultural constructions of what it means to be a man or woman.

Hegemonic Masculinity: a concept used to refer to the ways in which culturally idealized forms of masculinity (for example, risk taking, aggression, independence, competitiveness) become dominant in society. These forms set out "scripts" for males that are acted out differently depending upon the social situations and social locations (class and race) of the participants.

Patriarchy: a system of male domination; a structure and an ideology that privileges men over women.

Sex: the physical and sexual differences that are thought to exist between males and females.

The Sex Question in Criminology: focuses on the placement of men and women in criminological theorizing, especially in terms of the ability of the discipline to explain both male and female patterns of criminal activity.

Sexed Bodies: refers to the meanings that different sexes carry at the cultural level. Rather than assuming a dualism between "sex" and "gender," the sexed bodies approach views the differences that are thought to exist between the sexes (male and female) as culturally inscribed.

SUGGESTED READINGS

Gillian Balfour and Elizabeth Comack (eds.), *Criminalizing Women: Gender and (In)justice in Neo-Liberal Times,* second edition, Halifax and Winnipeg: Fernwood Publishing (2014).

Gary T. Barker, *Dying to Be Men: Youth, Masculinity and Social Exclusion,* London: Routledge (2005).

Richard Collier, *Masculinities, Crime and Criminology: Men, Heterosexuality and the Criminal(ised) Other,* London: Sage (1998).

James Messerschmidt, *Crime as Structured Action: Doing Masculinity, Race, Class, Sexuality and Crime,* second edition, Landham, MD: Rowman and Littlefield (2013).

Ngaire Naffine, *Feminism and Criminology*, Sydney: Allen and Unwin (1997).

REFERENCES

Adelberg, Ellen, and Claudia Currie. 1987. "In Their Own Words: Seven Women's Stories." In E. Adelberg and C. Currie (eds.), *Too Few to Count: Canadian Women in Conflict with the Law.* Vancouver: Press Gang.

Adler, Freda. 1975. *Sisters in Crime.* New York: McGraw-Hill.

Allen, Judith. 1990. "'The Wild Ones' The Disavowal of Men in Criminology." In R. Graycar (ed.), *Dissenting Opinions: Feminist Explorations in Law and Society.* Sydney: Allen and Unwin.

Brennan, Shannon. 2012. "Police-Reported Crime Statistics in Canada, 2011." *Juristat* July 24.

Brewer, Rose. 1997. "Theorizing Race, Class, and Gender: The New Scholarship of Black Feminist Intellectuals and Black Women's Labour." In R. Hennessy and C. Ingraham (eds.), *Materialist Feminism.* London: Routledge.

Brock, Deborah. 1998. *Making Work, Making Trouble: Prostitution as a Social Problem.* Toronto: University of Toronto Press.

Brownmiller, Susan. 1975. *Against Our Will: Men, Women and Rape.* New York: Bantam Books.

Busby, Karen. 2014. "'Sex Was in the Air': Pernicious Myths and Other Problems with Sexual Violence Prosecutions." In E. Comack (ed.), *Locating Law: Essays on the Race/Class/Gender Connections.* Third edition. Halifax and Winnipeg: Fernwood Publishing.

Butler, Judith. 1990. *Gender Trouble: Feminism and the Subversion of Identity.* New York: Routledge.

Cain, Maureen. 1990. "Towards Transgression: New Directions in Feminist Criminology." *International Journal of the Sociology of Law* 18: 1–18.

Carlen, Pat. 1988. *Women, Crime and Poverty.* Milton Keynes: Open University Press.

Chesney-Lind, Meda. 1978. "Chivalry Re-Examined." In Lee Bowker (ed.), *Women, Crime and the Criminal Justice System.* Lexington, MA: Lexington Books.

Chunn, Dorothy E., and Shelley A.M. Gavigan. 2014. "From Welfare Fraud to Welfare As Fraud: The Criminalization of Poverty." In G. Balfour and E. Comack (eds.), *Criminalizing Women: Gender and (In)justice in Neo-Liberal Times.* Second edition. Halifax and Winnipeg: Fernwood Publishing.

Cloward, Richard, and Lloyd Ohlin. 1960. *Delinquency and Opportunity: A Theory of Delinquency Gangs.* New York: Free Press.

Cohen, Albert. 1955. *Delinquent Boys: The Culture of the Gang.* New York: Free Press.

Collier, Richard. 1996. "'Just (More) Boys Own Stories'? Gender, Sex and the 'Masculinity Turn' in Criminology." *Social & Legal Studies* 5, 2: 271–78.

___. 1998. *Masculinities, Crime and Criminology: Men, Heterosexuality and the Criminal(ised) Other.* London: Sage.

___. 2004. "Masculinities and Crime: Rethinking the 'Man Question'?" In C. Sumner (ed.), *The Blackwell Companion to Criminology.* Oxford: Blackwell Publishing.

Comack, Elizabeth. 1992. "Women and Crime." In R. Linden (general editor), *Criminology: A Canadian Perspective.* Second edition. Toronto: Harcourt Brace Jovanovich.

___. 1993. "Women Offenders' Experiences with Physical and Sexual Abuse: A Preliminary Report." Criminology Research Centre, University of Manitoba.

___. 1996. *Women in Trouble: Connecting Women's Law Violations to Their Histories of Abuse.* Halifax: Fernwood Publishing.

Comack, Elizabeth, and Gillian Balfour. 2004. *The Power to Criminalize: Violence, Inequality and the Law.* Halifax: Fernwood Publishing.

Connell, R.W. 1987. *Gender and Power.* Cambridge: Polity Press.

___. 1995. *Masculinities.* Cambridge: Polity Press.

___. 2000. *The Men and the Boys.* Berkley: University of California Press.

Connell, R.W., and James Messerschmidt. 2005. "Hegemonic Masculinity: Rethinking the Concept." *Gender & Society* 19, 6: 829–59.

Crenshaw, Kimberlé. 1989. "Demarginalizing the Intersection of Race and Sex: A Black Feminist Critique of Antidiscrimination Doctrine, Feminist Theory and Antiracist Politics." *University of Chicago Legal Forum* 140.

Daly, Kathleen. 1987. "Discrimination in the Criminal Courts: Family, Gender, and the Problem of Equal Treatment." Social Forces 66, 1: 152–75.

___. 1989. "Rethinking Judicial Paternalism: Gender, Work–Family Relations, and Sentencing." *Gender and Society* 3, 1: 9–36.

___. 1997. "Different Ways of Conceptualizing Sex/Gender in Feminist Theory and Their Implications for Criminology." *Theoretical Criminology* 1, 1: 25–51.

Daly, Kathleen, and Meda Chesney-Lind. 1988. "Feminism and Criminology." *Justice Quarterly* 5, 4: 101–43.

Dobash, R. Emerson, and Russell Dobash. 1979. *Violence Against Wives: A Case Against Patriarchy.* New York: Free Press.

Fenstermaker, Sarah, Candace West, and Don Zimmerman. 1991. "Gender Inequality: New Conceptual Terrain." In Rae Lesser Blumberg (ed.), *Gender, Family and Economy.* Newbury Park, CA: Sage.

Gatens, Moira. 1996. *Imaginary Bodies: Ethics, Power and Corporeality.* London and New York: Routledge.

Gavigan, Shelley A.M. 1993. "Women's Crime: New Perspectives and Old Theories." In E. Adelberg and C. Currie (eds.), *In Conflict with the Law: Women and the Canadian Justice System.* Vancouver: Press Gang.

Gelsthorpe, Lorraine, and Allison Morris. 1988. "Feminism and Criminology in Britain." *British*

Journal of Criminology 23: 93–110.

Giddens, Anthony. 1976. *New Rules of the Sociological Method*. London: Hutchinson.

Gilfus, Mary. 1992. "From Victims to Survivors to Offenders: Women's Routes of Entry and Immersion into Street Crime." *Women and Criminal Justice* 4, 1: 63–89.

Gunn, Rita, and Candace Minch. 1988. *Sexual Assault: The Dilemma of Disclosure, The Question of Conviction*. Winnipeg: University of Manitoba Press.

Heidensohn, Frances, and Loraine Gelsthorpe. 2012. *Gender and Crime*. Oxford University Press.

Heitmeyer, W., N. Bockler and T. Seeger. 2013. "Social Disintegration, Loss of Control and School Shootings," in N. Bockler, P. Sitzer, T. Seeger and W. Heitmeyer (eds.), *School Shootings: International Research on Conflict and Violence*. New York, NY: Springer.

Hirschi, Travis. 1969. *Causes of Delinquency*. Berkeley: University of California Press.

Hood-Williams, John. 2001. "Gender, Masculinities and Crime: From Structures to Psyches." *Theoretical Criminology* 5, 1: 37–60.

Jefferson, Tony. 1994. "Theorising Masculine Subjectivity." In Tim Newburn and Elizabeth A. Stanko (eds.), *Just Boys Doing Business? Men, Masculinities and Crime*. London and New York: Routledge.

___. 1996a. "Introduction to Masculinities, Social Relations and Crime." Special issue of *The British Journal of Criminology* 36, 3: 337–47.

___. 1996b. "From 'Little Fairy Boy' to 'The Compleat Destroyer': Subjectivity and Transformation in the Biography of Mike Tyson." In Mairtin Mac an Ghaill (ed.), *Understanding Masculinities*. Buckingham: Open University Press.

Johnson, Holly. 1996. *Dangerous Domains*. Toronto: Nelson.

Johnson, Holly, and Karen Rodgers. 1993. "A Statistical Overview of Women in Crime in Canada." In Ellen Adelberg and Claudia Currie (eds.), *In Conflict with the Law: Women and the Canadian Justice System*. Vancouver: Press Gang.

Kelly, Liz. 1988. *Surviving Sexual Violence*. Minneapolis: University of Minnesota Press.

Klein, Dorie. 1982. "The Dark Side of Marriage: Battered Wives and the Domination of Women." In N. Rafter and E. Stanko (eds.), *Judge, Lawyer, Victim, Thief: Women, Gender Roles and Criminal Justice*. Boston: Northeastern University Press.

Kruttschnitt, Candace. 1980–81. "Social Status and Sentences of Female Offenders." *Law and Society Review* 15, 2: 247–65.

___. 1982. "Women, Crime and Dependency." *Criminology* 195: 495–513.

Little, Margaret. 2003. "The Leaner, Meaner Welfare Machine: The Ontario Conservative Government's Ideological and Material Attack on Single Mothers." In D. Brock (ed.), *Making Normal: Social Regulation in Canada*. Scarborough: Nelson Thompson Learning.

Lombroso, Cesare. 1912. *Crime: Its Causes and Remedies*. Boston: Little, Brown, and Company.

MacLeod, Linda. 1980. *Wife Battering in Canada: The Vicious Circle*. Ottawa: Canadian Advisory Council on the Status of Women.

Mahony, Tina. 2011. "Women and the Criminal Justice System," *Statistics Canada* <statcan.gc.ca/pub/89-503-x/2010001/article/11416-eng.pdf>.

Merton, Robert. 1938. "Social Structure and Anomie." *American Sociological Review* 3: 672–82.

Messerschmidt, James. 1993. *Masculinities and Crime: Critique and Reconceptualization of Theory*. Lanham, MD: Rowman and Littlefield.

___. 1997. *Crime as Structured Action: Gender, Race, Class, and Crime in the Making*. Thousand Oaks, CA: Sage.

___. 2004. *Flesh and Blood: Adolescent Gender Diversity and Violence*. Lanham, MD: Rowman and Littlefield.

___. 2012. *Gender, Heterosexuality, and Youth Violence: The Struggle for Recognition*. Lanham, MD: Rowman & Littlefield.

___. 2013. *Crime as Structured Action: Doing Masculinity, Race, Class, Sexuality and Crime*. Second edition. Landham, MD: Rowman and Littlefield.

Mirchandani, Kiran, and Wendy Chan. 2007. *Criminalizing Race, Criminalizing Poverty*. Halifax and Winnipeg: Fernwood Publishing.

Morris, Allison. 1987. Women, Crime and Criminal Justice. Oxford: Basil Blackwell.

Mosher, Janet E. 2014. "The Construction of 'Welfare Fraud' and the Wielding of the State's Iron Fist." In E. Comack (ed.), Locating Law: Race/Class/Gender/Sexuality Connections. Third edition. Halifax and Winnipeg: Fernwood Publishing.

Naffine, Ngaire. 1987. Female Crime: The Construction of Women in Criminology. Sydney: Allen and Unwin.

___. 1997. Feminism and Criminology. Sydney: Allen and Unwin.

Newman, K.S. 2013. "Adolescent Culture and the Tragedy of Rampage Shootings," In N. Bockler, P. Sitzer, T. Seeger and W. Heitmeyer (eds.), School Shootings: International Research on Conflict and Violence. New York, NY: Springer.

Parsons, Talcott, and Robert Bales. 1955. Family, Socialization and Interaction Process. Glencoe, IL: Free Press.

Perreault, Samuel. 2013. "Admissions to Adult Correctional Services in Canada, 2011/2012," Statistics Canada <statcan.gc.ca/pub/85-002-x/2014001/article/11918-eng.htm#a3>.

Phoenix, Joanna. 1999. Making Sense of Prostitution. New York: Palgrave.

Raftner, Nicole H., and Elena M. Natalazia. 1981. "Marxist Feminism: Implications for Criminal Justice." Crime and Delinquency 27 (January): 81–98.

Rice, Marcia. 1990. "Challenging Orthodoxies in Feminist Theory: A Black Feminist Critique." In L. Gelsthorpe and A. Morris (eds.), Feminist Perspectives in Criminology. Milton Keynes: Open University Press.

Ritchie, Beth. 1996. Compelled to Crime: The Gender Entrapment of Battered Black Women. New York: Routledge.

Scutt, Jocelyn. 1979. "The Myth of the 'Chivalry Factor' in Female Crime." Australian Journal of Social Issues 14, 1: 3–20.

Seshia, Maya. 2005. The Unheard Speak Out. Winnipeg: Canadian Centre for Policy Alternatives–Manitoba.

Shaw, Margaret, Karen Rogers, Johannes Blanchette, Tina Hattem, Lee Seto Thomas, and Lada Tamarack. 1991. Survey of Federally Sentenced Women: Report on the Task Force on Federally Sentenced Women: The Prison Survey. Ottawa: Ministry of the Solicitor General of Canada. User Report No. 1991-4.

Simon, Rita. 1975. Women and Crime. Lexington, MA: D.C. Heath.

Smart, Carol. 1976. Women, Crime and Criminology: A Feminist Critique. London: Routledge and Kegan Paul.

Stanko, Elizabeth. 1985. Intimate Intrusions: Women's Experience of Male Violence. London: Routledge and Kegan Paul.

Steffensmeier, Darryl. 1980. "Sex Differences in Patterns of Adult Crime, 1965–1977." Social Forces 58, 4 (June): 1080–09.

Steffensmeier, Darryl, and J. Kramer. 1982. "Sex-Based Differences in the Sentencing of Adult Criminal Defendants." Sociology and Social Research 663: 289–304.

Sutherland, Edwin. 1949. Principles of Criminology. Fourth edition. Philadelphia: Lippincott.

Sutherland, Edwin, and Donald Cressey. 1966. Principles of Criminology. Philadelphia: Lippincott.

Vaillancourt, Roxan. 2008. "Gender Differences in Police-Reported Violent Crime in Canada, 2008." Canadian Centre for Justice Statistics Profile Series <statcan.gc.ca/pub/85f0033m/85f0033m2010024-eng.htm>.

Weiss. Joseph. 1976. "Liberation and Crime: The Invention of the New Female Criminal." Crime and Social Justice 6 (Fall–Winter): 17–27.

West, Candace, and Don Zimmerman. 1987. " Doing Gender." Gender & Society 1, 2: 125–51.

Wolfgang, Marvin E. 1972. "Cesare Lombroso." In H. Mannheim (ed.), Pioneers in Criminology. Montclair, NJ: Patterson Smith.

Young, Iris Marion. 1990. "Throwing Like a Girl." In I.M. Young (ed.), Throwing Like a Girl and Other Essays in Feminist Philosophy and Social Theory. Bloomington: Indiana University Press.

Zingraff, M., and R. Thomson. 1984. "Differential Sentencing of Women and Men in the U.S.A." International Journal of the Sociology of Law 12: 401–13.

6

CRITICAL CRIMINOLOGY AND CONTEMPORARY "CRIME" ISSUES

Carolyn Brooks and Bernard Schissel

KEY FACTS

> The International labor Organization, ILO (2012) estimates that more than twenty million children and adults are sold into forced sexual servitude. UNICEF (2005) estimates that 2 million children are exploited in the sex trade each year and routinely face both physical and sexual violence against them.

> In Canada, common reasons for entry into the sex trade are financial need, abuse, recruitment, addictions, homelessness and poverty. Young men are said to enter the sex trade at a younger age than women. Young men involved in the sex trade have also commonly run away from physically and sexually abusive homes.

> Individuals involved in the sex trade experience violence against them at painfully high rates and are 15 to 20 times more likely to be killed than women in the same age category who are not involved.

> There are 1017 police reported Aboriginal female homicides and an additional 164 missing Aboriginal women between 1980 and 2012. 12 percent of these women were sex trade workers and these cases have received little news or investigation.

> Through the Royal Commission on Aboriginal Peoples (RCAP) (1993) and the recent Truth and Reconciliation panels (2011), Canada has acknowledged that the residential school era negatively impacted Aboriginal peoples, families, and their communities.

> According to a 2012 Report by the Criminal Investigator of Canada, the Aboriginal population of Canada makes up 4 percent of the general population but 21.3 percent of all federally incarcerated offenders. Since 2005–06, the Aboriginal offender population has increased by 43.5 percent compared to only 9.6 percent for non-Aboriginal offenders.

> STR8UP, a Saskatoon initiative, was founded in 1997 at the request of two Aboriginal gang members looking to escape their respective gangs. This program aspires to support gang-involved individuals to "provide support to one another" and "contribute to the education, information and prevention concerning addictions, criminal lifestyles, gangs and prostitution to the communities at large."

Sources: Cobbina and Oselin 2011; West 1993, 2010; Brooks, Henry and Daschuk 2015; STR8UP 2012.

Perceptions about "crime" are shaped by different sources — including law, media and criminology. This gives rise to diverse visions of how best to address crime. In the present chapter, we demonstrate the link between criminological theories and crime and crime and social policy. Two contemporary crime issues, youth gangs and the sex trade, show how different theoretical assumptions lead to very different questions and answers about crime and criminal justice. Different theoretical models advance both the theoretical and applied knowledge of criminality. Certain paradigms of explanation — primarily consensus-based — are more popular in public policy decision making and are certainly more popular with the voting public. Critical criminology and critical feminism provide an alterative explanation and call for socially transformative justice, not criminal justice.

THE CONSENSUS PARADIGM

There are multiple criminological theories under the rubric of consensus criminology that attempt to explain the sex trade and why youth become involved in gangs. The consensus paradigm contains both micro- and macro-level analyses that focus on the social structure as well as the individual. In terms of youth gangs, structure-based theories like social control, strain/anomie, and social disorganization (as described in Chapter 2) frame the general-consensus paradigm of crime and combine elements of social structure and individual choice.

UNDERSTANDING YOUTH GANGS: CONSENSUS MODELS

A good deal of sensationalism occurs in Western, industrial societies in the public sentiment and political discourse about youth gangs. Arguably, the media sensationalizes the "gang problem," especially the involvement of ethnic minorities, and more specifically the involvement of Aboriginal groups in gang activity, crime and violence. Commonplace examples include reporting on exceptional events, realized in these attention grabbing headlines: "Toronto Yorkdale mall killing likely gang-related 'ambush" (CBC News Toronto 2013), "More Gang Violence on the Way: Sources Blame Drug Trade for Volatile Situation" (McIntyre 2014). Media sources also often report the difficulty in attempting to explain the problem of gang activity:

> Theories of youth violence could fill a newspaper: family breakdown and poor parenting, poverty, violence in the home, the Internet, the decline of religion and morality, video games, the proliferation of guns, lenient laws and weak sentences, a lack of discipline in schools, and on and on. (*Toronto Sun* 2004)

Unfortunately, much of the talk about the causes of youth crime is misinformed, although, interestingly, it draws upon many of the beliefs about crime that we see in consensus theories in criminology. The demand for retribution and punishment is very much a part of the reasoning behind many of the orthodox theories that we describe — theories that presume crime can be dealt with by focusing our efforts on the individual offender.

So, how do criminological theories from the consensus model explain youth gangs, and how do such theories inform public policy? As we shall see, most formal justice policy is based on a rather traditional view of criminogenesis, which we label generically as consensus criminology.

Strain Theory

> The central concept of strain theory is that society sets universal goals for its populace and then offers the ability to achieve them to a limited number of people. (Wood and Alleyne 2010: 103)

Strain theory emphasizes cultural norms of "success," and links illegal and gang activity with the unequal distribution of the means to obtain this success. Bartollas (2005, 2007), for example, argues that with a decline in opportunity for minority youth, more youth are using drug trafficking within gangs as an economic opportunity. Fagan (1989), Esbensen and Huizinga (1993) add that drug use is becoming more widespread and normative as an economic response to the lack of legitimate opportunities. Quite clearly, this line of thinking resonates very well with researchers and policy-makers who are interested in the "economies of crime," but only at the street level. The preoccupation is with the inner workings of crime "syndicates." There is little focus on either the unfairness of the disadvantage under which many people live or the associated reality that crime at the organizational, upper-class, corporate level is much more economically and socially damaging than anything that occurs at the street level (Reiman 2007).

Many of the "research-based" studies that take a strain-theory approach emphasize the machinery of troubled communities and relate it to the embeddedness of disadvantage and blocked opportunity (Hagan and McCarthy 1998, for example). However, strain theory–based work does not tend to frame lack of opportunity in a large political-economic, structural context that consistently disadvantages a section of the population, who are often identified by race and ethnicity (a step that we will see is taken by critical criminology) (cf. Wilson 1996). Despite the critique, strain theory has been one of the most popular consensus theories to understand youth involvement in gangs (Sharkey, Shekhtmeyster, Chavez-Lopez, Norris and Sass 2011).

Social Disorganization, Cultural Transmission and Differential Association Theories

In a similar vein to strain theory, social disorganization and cultural transmission theories suggest crime varies according to area, neighbourhood and community characteristics For example:

> [Gang membership] becomes a satisfying alternative to unsatisfactory legitimate conventions. If family, school, church and government all fail to adequately provide for young people young people will form indigenous groups such as gangs which provide a social support system in socially disorganized communities. (Hill et al. 1999; Papachristos and Kirk 2006, cited in Wood and Alleyne 2010: 103)

These so-called "ecological theories" hearken back to the work of Shaw and McKay at the University of Chicago in the 1930s, in which they mapped cities and were able to identify areas that had persistently high crime rates. They extended their argument to suggest that certain areas, such as the inner-city core, were characterized by social disorganization and as such produced generations of delinquents that passed on their deviancy from one generation to another. They further argued that neighborhoods characterized by social disorganization culturally transmit traditions of "criminality" in a similar fashion to other cultural traditions. "Families in poor inner city areas have low levels of functional authority over children, who, once exposed to delinquent traditions, succumb to delinquent behavior" (Wood and Alleyne 2010: 102). Shaw and McKay argued that this happened because adults who adopt a deviant lifestyle — a gambler, pimp or drug dealer — are some of the most financially successful people in the neighbourhood, and when slum kids make a decision to pursue a particular lifestyle, the deviant lifestyle is highly attractive.

Theories of social disorganization and cultural transmission are evident in more recent work. Sullivan (1989), for example, in his ethnographic, ecological study of neighbourhoods and gangs, characterizes "criminogenic communities" as having low socio-economic status, high poverty rates, low labour-force participation and high unemployment. Other authors, such as Lane and Meeker (2004) and Papachristos and Kirk (2006) have linked gang activity to the need for youth to find social support systems where socially disorganized communities have social institutions (such as family, church and school) that fail to provide for them. Steenbeek and Hipp (2011) demonstrate the usefulness of longitudinal data through their research over ten years in the city of Utrecht in the Netherlands. Their research affirmed that neighborhoods with high social cohesion, high socio-economic status, low ethnic diversity and high stability of residents are able to exercise relatively high control and have low crime rates. Overall, their data, by incorporating time into the analysis, found that social disorder is stable over time; social disorder causes people to move out of a neighbourhood and the resultant high residential instability leads to fewer people willing or able to take action to ensure community stability and livability. Neighbourhood disorder, thus, has a cumulative effect.

Sullivan (1989) and others (including the recent examples) have had a great deal of influence with policy-makers and the public. As we think about stereotypes of typical gang activity, our imaginations turn to the "dangerous inner city." In practice, however, these stereotypes are imaginary, as police presence is dominant in poor, non-white urban areas and civic officials focus on the inner city in developing crime policies (James 2002; Tator and Henry 2006).

Social Control Theory

Social control theory links gang involvement to weakened social bonds with family, school or other social institutions (Thornberry 2006; Hirschi 1969; Vigil and Yun 1990; Klemp-North 2007). When bonds are broken, youths seek bonds with other groups, using gangs as one of the ways to meet their needs. For example, the lived reality for many young offenders is characterized by lack of success in schools and dysfunctional families. The easy conclusion from these empirical realities is a link between delinquency and lack of "bonding" to conventional institutions like family and education. Hirschi, in his original research, found that youth who were attached to their parents (who spent a good deal of time with family), who had strong peer group connections and who valued education (who did their homework regularly, for example) were much less likely to engage in delinquent activities than those of their age group who were disconnected from family, friends and school, despite the reality that delinquent and non-delinquent kids shared similar beliefs about society. It is important to note here that many young gang members are school dropouts and are so disaffected from their families that they search for security and nurturance in a gang family. The logic of the connection seems reasonable. However, as is typical of many orthodox theories, the causal logic is not always clearly explored. For example, schools may discriminate against students who have non-traditional abilities and learning styles, families who live on the margins of society may not have the resources to be functional families and gangs may be non-criminal and still fulfill valuable socio-economic functions.

Rational Choice Theory and Deterrence Theory

At the heart of social control theories is the classical criminological assumption that adolescent criminal behaviour is largely rational and that criminal actions can be prevented through discouraging crime.

Rational choice theory has been "one of the most influential and criticized criminological models to emerge in the latter quarter of the twentieth century" (Leclerc and Wortley 2013: 3). Rational choice models aim to understand why people engage in deviant or criminal acts, realizing the importance of rationality and choice within a paradigm of the need for status and money, previous experience and learning as well as blocked opportunities. Rational choice theorists also argue that calculations of punishments and rewards motivate people towards or away from criminal behavior. This is the foundation of deterrence theory.

Deterrence theory assumes that individuals will tend not to commit crime if the penalties for doing so outweigh the benefits of engaging in crime. As Akers (2012: 17) states: "The principles of certainty, severity and celerity of punishment, proportionality, and specific and general deterrence remain at the heart of modern deterrence theory." Interestingly, and not so unexpectedly, much of the original research on deterrence theory focused on the effect of capital punishment on homicide rates, in part, because execution is the ultimate and most severe form of punishment and should have the greatest deterrent effect. Importantly, much of this original research found little deterrent effect, and research to date is consistent with this finding (Akers 2013).

Our judicial and penal systems are based on these two presumptions of rational choice and deterrence — that punishment will deter the individual from committing another act of deviance ("specific deterrence") and that the act of punishment will deter individuals in the general population from committing a premeditated criminal act ("general deterrence"). In general, although rehabilitation is the official mandate of our justice system, punishment as a deterrent to crime is really the cornerstone of our system of justice and corrections (Akers 2013).

If we believe that deterrence works, then our approach to youth gangs would be to "get tough" and increase punishments. This is, in fact, a common strategy for dealing with young people, especially in the last few decades, during which political movements have used tough crime policies to score points with the voting public. The justice system response to youth gang panic in North America is to get tough on youth by increasing surveillance and punishment. For example, Canada's *Youth Criminal Justice Act* has provisions for longer and tougher sentences for repeat offenders (Tustin and Lutes 2007), plus there is a push for tougher sentences for youth involved in gang activities (Brooks, Henry and Daschuk 2015). In the U.S., there has been strong support for legislation such as the *Gang Deterrence and Community Protection Act* of 2005 (H.R. 1279), which created new gang offences and saw the transfer of youth to adult prisons and courts. This act also favours new mandatory minimum sentences and will expand the death penalty. In Canada, legislative and programmatic responses to the problem of youth gangs have traditionally centered around incarceration (Aboriginal Council of Winnipeg 2010) and have come to be recognized as ineffective and even counter-intuitive (Totten 2009).

Such deterrence-based responses are very popular with the general public, as there appears to be a fundamental belief that punishment stops criminal behaviour. Get-tough policies always seem to allow politicians to score political points, even in light of more evidence that punishing young people is not only ethically suspect and dangerous to the young person (Schiraldi and Zeidenberg 1997), but also counterproductive in reducing crime (Green and Healy 2003). As mentioned previously, deterrence has proven largely ineffective for many types of criminal behaviour, especially serious crime.

Forensics

Lastly, consensus theories lend themselves to a broad and very popular approach to youth crime, which, for want of a better term, is simply entitled "forensics." Forensic investigations focus on detecting the criminal before s/he acts or on ensuring an offender is detected and caught. The forensic paradigm is based on crime as emanating primarily from the individual. The power of this particular ideological explanation of "immorality" has incredible resonance with the general public, given the popularity and proliferation of television shows like CSI.

The public policy extension of forensics as applied to young offenders is to find ways to detect their delinquency before the fact — sometimes referred to as "pre-delinquency." For example, the Young Offender Level of Supervision Inventory (YO-LSI), a risk assessment tool used in one form or another in Canada and other countries, is a mechanism for determining whether a young person will break the law, and, if so, the degree, type and level of intervention that the young person should be given. Fundamentally, the measurement instrument assesses criminal history, education/employment, family/marital issues, leisure/recreation issues, companions, substance abuse, pro-criminal attitude/orientation and anti-social patterns (Girard and Wormith 2004). At a very basic level, young people who are characterized empirically with issues such poor school achievement, prior violence, lack of empathy, poor peer interaction and negative attitudes are in need of high levels of intervention. The scientific premise of such tools is that they are diagnostic mechanisms for detecting criminal potential, and for that they are efficient. They are, in effect, clinical tools that use "hard" data (both behavioural and attitudinal) to predetermine delinquent behavior.

The problem with such forensic tools is that the logical underpinning is tautological — using criminality to predict criminality, risk to predict risk. The YO-LSI can predict criminality, but so can any common-sense judgment made by a youth worker who understands the life of a marginalized or dispossessed youth. The power of the instrument is that it has the credibility of science, especially empirically based science, to condemn the already condemned. As with all forensic types of investigation, however, such detection instruments focus on deficiencies and are never able to focus on potential. They are scientific methods that confirm only the bad things in a person's life, an orientation that should be contradictory to philosophies of care and healing.

BEING IN THE SEX TRADE: CONSENSUS MODELS

A sizable body of theorizing on prostitution (the sex trade) has included many of the general theories that we discussed above. In general, the consensus models posit a social dynamics very similar to their explanations of youth involved in gangs, focusing on individual characteristics of the women. In contrast, feminist explanations tend to be more nuanced and certainly less condemnatory of women in the sex trade.

Commonly applied consensus-based theories include the pathological model (Lombroso and Ferrero 1895; Glueck and Glueck 1934; Benjamin and Masters 1964), the criminal subculture model (Gray 1973; Jarvinen 1993) and an orthodox functionalist and economic model (Kinsey, Pomeroy, and Martin 1948).

The Pathological Model

A very typical level of inquiry on prostitution historically has been the "pathological model," which attributes the cause of prostitution to individual pathology or abnormalities of the women involved:

> The physical and moral characteristics of the delinquent belong equally to the prostitute ... both phenomena spring from idleness, misery and especially alcoholism ... both are connected likewise with certain organic and hereditary tendencies. (Lombroso and Ferrero 1895: 186)

This model essentially creates the label of "prostitute" and tells us that prostitutes are different from other women (Phoenix 1999: 37). Lombroso and Ferrero (1895) saw prostitution as the equivalent to male forms of criminalization. They argued that women who were prostitutes exhibit more degenerative qualities (monstrosity, degeneracy, insanity, epilepsy) than other female offenders. They believed that women were less evolved generally than men because of their maternal functions, which produced a "retardation" of evolution. While they conceded that social conditions such as poverty and population density encouraged women's involvement in prostitution, the main cause, they argued, was evolutionary degeneracy.

Several decades later, Sheldon and Eleanor Glueck in *Five Hundred Delinquent Women* (1934) claimed that female prostitution (based on a study of 500 women sentenced to the Massachusetts Reformatory for Women) resulted from "feeblemindedness," which was the result of parents' low mentality, broken homes and unintelligent disciplinary practices. This, they argued, was the unfortunate psychological atmosphere that contributed to the development of women with psychopathic personalities who could not survive in legitimate ways.

Benjamin and Masters (1964), although working years later, similarly saw some prostitutes as "compulsive," with deep neurotic needs that compelled them into prostitution. These behaviours were attributed to the violence and trauma they experienced.

Although these models focused on the individual pathology of "prostitutes," they also allowed for feminist and other critical work by hinting at violence, trauma, poverty and other social factors that limit women's choices. Pathological theorizing, however, failed to break free from a problematic essentialism that prostitutes are fundamentally abnormal and in need of "correction." Interestingly, Benjamin's and Masters's position is actually a dual explanation: "compulsive prostitutes possess an individual psychological abnormality that predisposes them to involvement in prostitution, whilst voluntary prostitutes engage in prostitution because of the poverty they have experienced and the social environment in which they grew up" (Phoenix 1999: 40).

Although pathological models are no longer in academic favor (Reeve 2013), there are a number of authors who continue to understand the sex trade from this pathological perspective. Shutt et al. (2011) for example, have developed a biosocial explanation related to the behavior of johns. Using self-reports of sex-purchasing behavior, they argue that males in comparison to females have an instinctive biology, which underlies demand for prostitution. Other authors have linked post-traumatic stress disorder to women in the sex trade (Ramsey et al. 1993). In contrast to understanding individuals in the sex trade as pathological, the subcultural model defined the importance of the cultural context.

The Subcultural Model

> We are dealing with a class of people whose behaviour standards are utterly different from our own … a beating-up is of far less significance to the girl herself than others who hear about it imagine. (Wilkinson 1955: 122, cited in Phoenix 1999: 47)

This model examines what proponents call "the subculture of prostitution" (Wilkinson 1955; Gray 1973; Jarvinen 1993), identifying the extent to which women are segregated from legitimate relationships and therefore seek out alternative social connections that make prostitution inevitable. This theoretical model, which focuses on the cultural context in which prostitution occurs, is often intertwined with more micro-level, interactionist models that study the interpersonal dynamics of prostitution, including relationship formation (Gray 1973; Salomon 1989). Such research focuses on the macro-level structural conditions that determine prostitution, such as "rootlessness, drifting, and belongingness that lead some women to become involved in sex work" (Wilkinson 1955). Other studies describe the life of the "typical prostitute" at an interpersonal level.

Wilkinson's (1955) *Women in the Streets*, for example, saw prostitutes as being like other women in their need for social bonding, family and friends while also being different, mostly because of the nature of these bonds (cited in Phoenix 1999). The bonds and connections that are acceptable by society's standards were not available to prostitutes, either because of a deficiency or because of a circumstance (such as giving birth to an illegitimate child). The women thus developed alternative bonds and normative structures. These relationships were often characterized by violence and coercion, not acceptable to society but normal to the women in the sex trade as they established their own "livable culture."

Is it interesting that some researchers/theorists combine approaches; Jarvinen (1993), for example, blends a subcultural, interactionist and feminist approach in her study, which explores social relationships between prostitutes, pimps and clients as well as the control experienced by the women during their career in the sex trade. She argues that the factors that bind women to their subculture include interpersonal relationships and socializing with men (pimps and others) and other sex trade workers. The feminist part of this work argues, however, that subcultures are male and work to reinforce the interests of clients and pimps, who are primarily men. Jarvinen's work is based on her reading of other subcultural studies of prostitution, which are very structural-functionalist in nature. They are based on studying and defining fixed categories of subcultures. Davis's (1971) study, for example, suggests there are three main categories of subcultures to which prostitutes belong: hustler (women structure their lives around prostitution and live in an environment that includes drugs and alcohol), dual-world culture (conventional jobs and families are combined with the sex trade) and criminal (criminal activity, such as theft and drug offences, are combined with prostitution). Jarvinen's work is an attempt to reduce the conservative nature of strict subcultural studies by studying the patriarchal structures under which women develop subcultural attachments.

Subcultural analysis allows room to explore the similarities and differences between prostitutes and other women. Phoenix (1999) describes two other important theoretical spaces opened up from the subcultural analysis: reference to different "types of prostitutes" and the examination of "social" causes for entrance to and effects of prostitution. Wilkinson (1955), for example, asked questions regarding prostitutes' perceptions of their engagement in prostitution, as well as their identity and the ways that similar experiences for women (such as violence against them) may be experienced differently by women involved in prostitution. However, Wilkinson also argued that not all women who experience dislocation and participation in deviant subcultures become involved in prostitution. She explains this by discussing an individual pathology of a "disorganized personality" (Wilkinson 1955: 54–55) to women who enter prostitution. The idea of attributing a psychological pathology to explain deviant behaviour was dominant in literature on criminality during the time of Wilkinson's writings (Phoenix 1999).

In general, subcultural and related interactionist models, while interesting in an anthropological way, fail to consider the economic and social structures that frame the lives of many marginalized women and essentially prohibit them from alternatives to prostitution. The subcultural orientation also ignores the issue of human rights and the fundamental need to be safe and secure as is illustrated by the international prostitutes' rights movement that lobbies for prostitutes' rights as an antidote to discrimination against women in desperate life circumstances.

The Economic Model and Orthodox Functionalism: A Variation of Strain Theory

> You want to get across that we are ordinary women. (Sally in McLeod 1982, cited in Phoenix 1999: 57)

The economic model has a natural parallel with strain theory explanations for youth gangs. Strain theory focuses on gang activity as a viable economic alternative to living on the margins of society. The same claim has been made for prostitution. The essence of the economic model is that women engage in prostitution because their labour market chances are limited and that their "career" choices are driven by poverty (Roberts 1992; Overall 1992, cited in Phoenix 1999): women engage in prostitution because of a lack of other opportunities and/or because prostitution tends to be economically more beneficial than many economic options available. As Phoenix (1999) tells us, this model emphasizes prostitutes' similarities to other women in poverty and shifts away from the more orthodox consensus view of prostitution to a position that accounts for economic inequality and gender discrimination.

McLeod (1982), for example, examines prostitution as a profession, like other labour choices for women in the context of patriarchal capitalism. Women suffer economic, social and political oppression as well as disenfranchisement. Prostitution, therefore, is a rational choice as a means to survive economically. Women's individual choices are made within a gendered division of labour and their relatively low status in capitalist economies; prostitution, in effect, is a rational response to living on the margins of society.

Like prostitutes, married women often "barter sex for goods" (McLeod 1982: 28, cited in Phoenix 1999: 55). Emotional detachment during sexual encounters is a "part of a women's sexual repertoire in a day to day way" (McLeod 1982: 38, cited in Phoenix 1999: 55). Violence against women is also an experience that all women share and a manifestation of their position in society; spousal violence, in this paradigm, is no different than client perpetrated violence in the sex trade.

In the end, the economic model helps us understand the connections between poverty and "deviance." However, such analyses share an essentialist quality with consensus theories of crime, not for assuming a biological or psychological pathology, but rather for assuming that men and women are fixed categories with shared social locations. As Phoenix states:

> The difficulty that arises from this essentialism is that it prohibits questions and theorizing about (1) the differences between prostitutes and other women, (2) the differences between groups of prostitutes (for example, black prostitutes, "high-class call girls" and so on), and (3) how and under what conditions prostitutes can gain control over their own work and lives. (1999: 58)

In many ways, the economic model, however critical, sees the world of prostitution as a fixed reality, simple and understandable in terms of male and female sex. It is, on the other hand, a natural bridge to conflict/critical feminist theories on prostitution that take us beyond the world of sex into the realm of gender construction and socio-economic exploitation. Critical explanations are based on the presumption that economic and patriarchal power are the mechanisms through which women and children (and some men) are commodified and exploited for their sexuality.

THE CRITICAL PARADIGM

From critical perspectives, macro structures such as colonialism, global capitalism and patriarchy are part of the context of social, economic and political inequality that helps us understand gang activity and the sex trade — and these structures ultimately help us frame social justice policies that should reduce criminal injustice and ultimately reduce crime. These macro structures condition and limit choices individuals make as they go about their daily lives. Relevant critical theories are Marxist criminology, critical feminism, critical gang theories, postmodernism, anti-racism and postcolonial theories. In relation to the sex trade, most of the work has included different versions of feminism. Although there are some primarily Marxist works on prostitution, the most relevant critical work that has existed for decades is decidedly feminist and too extensive for a complete review (Smart 1978, 1989, 1992; Edwards 1987, 1988a, 1988b; Boritch 1997; Fedec 2002; Phoenix 1999; O'Neil 2001). In this section, we apply Marxist criminology and critical race theory to gang involvement and the sex trade (together). Feminism and postmodernism are applied to the issues separately — showing the diversity of these theories.

Understanding Youth Gangs and Sex Trade Involvement Through Critical Criminology

Recent Marxist theories argue that gangs and prostitution are quite a normal response to living marginally in the wider society. Communities and their families form multiple marginalities as part of the inequality in the larger society (cf. Sheldon, Tracy and Brown 2001; Gorkoff and Runner 2003). Involvement in both marginalizations results from social, political and racial inequality deeply integrated into the unequal distribution of power that define our current economic structures (cf. Sheldon, Tracy and Brown 2001). A number of authors working within critical paradigms link growing inequalities and globalization to crime (cf. Chapter 9 in this volume; Crocker and Johnson 2010; White 2002; Martin 2002; Gorkoff and Runner 2003).

The growing inequalities in Canadian society that result in part from globalization are accompanied by a downsizing of social programs and are justified by neo-liberal and neo-conservative ideologies that blame individuals for their own poverty and justify racist exclusion. Statistics on the poverty of children, for example, are discouraging — especially as child poverty is arguably a precursor to social problems such as prostitution (sexual exploitation by perpetrators and pimps), crime and gang involvement. A recent report by the United Nations Children's Fund (UNICEF 2012) highlights that 13.3 percent of Canadian children continue to live in poverty. This is higher than the 11 percent across thirty-five economically advanced countries. The reality for First Nations youth is even starker. The Canadian Center for Policy Alternatives and Save the Children Canada found that poverty rates among First Nations youth exceeded 50 percent (Macdonald and Wilson 2013). Macdonald and Wilson emphasize the harsh living reality for First Nations youth:

> Indigenous children trail the rest of Canada's children on practically every measure of wellbeing: family income, educational attainment, crowding and homelessness, poor water quality, infant mortality, health and suicide. Status First Nations children living in poverty are three times more likely to live in a house that requires major repairs compared to the non-Indigenous children of families with similar income levels and five times more likely to live in an overcrowded house. More than half of all water systems on First Nation reserves pose a risk to those using them. (2013: 19)

Neo-liberal governmental policies are largely based on economic principles of fiscal restraint; they often attack government spending on social programs and education, and they promote a shrinking in the social safety net. The deregulation of rents, the downsizing of social programs and the abolition of many social-housing projects contribute to increased homelessness and visible poverty (Martin 2002). Young people suffer much of the effect, especially Aboriginal youth. Disadvantaged children, especially those who have suffered deprivation and neglect, have historically been provided for somewhat, as wards of the state. Kids older than fourteen, however, have had fewer options — and since the mid-90s they have not been eligible for student welfare. As well, alternative educational programs to help children stay in school have been cut. As Martin argues:

> School funding formulas [mean that] dropouts become a liability who only receive funding based on students enrolled ... [and] sometimes leads to the death of flexible, part time programs that have kept some at least tenuously attached to the educational system. (2002: 94)

It is commonly argued that this lack of social-service support forces kids into crime, gangs and prostitution (Bittle 2002; Gorkoff and Waters 2003). Some of the most common reasons cited for entry into prostitution, for example, are financial need, previous abuse, homelessness, addictions and coercion (Cobbina and Oselin 2011; Farley, Lynne and Cotton 2005). In addition, the social and economic marginalization of Aboriginal youth fuels violence in gangs (Totten 2009). Gang life is said to be attractive because it offers income and employment (Totten 2009). There is a noted overrepresentation of marginalized and Aboriginal people who are involved in gangs and in the sex trade (Bittle 2002; Brooks, Henry and Daschuk 2015).

Marxist theories of political economy show that dramatic cutbacks in social spending guarantee that certain youth have nowhere to belong except on the street, especially when funding changes to education, for example, are combined with current zero-tolerance policies that ensure the expulsion of any student who engages in violence (cf. Martin 2002; Gorkoff and Waters 2003).

In this same way, critical gang theories examine unequal structures, which are tied to the political economy and show the connection to gang activity (Wacquant 2008; Comack et al. 2013). As outlined later in this book (Chapter 10), Comack, Deane, Morrissette and Silver show that critical gang studies researchers link increases in gangs to global restructuring, downsizing of social programs and the resulting impact on inner-city communities:

> According to critical gang studies researchers, street gangs are one of the by-products of these broader social and economic changes ... Contemporary street gangs are located, then, in intensified urban poverty that is a consequence of global economic forces and neoliberal; ideologies and forms of governing that lead to a loss of well-paid jobs and reduced public expenditures directed a the poor. This process is also racialized, in that those who are marginalized and become involved in street gangs are disproportionately youth of colour.

The critical criminology and critical gang studies response to gang activity would therefore be to attack the bases of inequality, to institute social programs that distribute wealth and opportunity, to uncover how institutions of criminal (in)justice perpetuate the link between inequality and crime through discriminatory programs such as racialized policing/racial profiling and to ensure that the fundamental institutions in society, like law, education and politics, give privilege to the poor as well as the wealthy. If gangs and prostitution are logical responses to economic and social deprivation, then programs to reduce that deprivation are also logical.

Critical Feminism

The critical dimension of feminist theorizing and feminist practice teaches that power differentials exist in race, class, age and gender. Even the terminology used by critical feminists indicates the shift in understanding - they refer to the sex trade rather than prostitution. The sex trade is built on the subordinate status of women and children. Fedec, for example, writes:

> Since women and children, in general, occupy subordinate economic positions in patriarchal, capitalist societies, the hierarchical structure of society defines and creates a certain type of criminality for women and children, often based on imputed sexual morality. For most prostitutes, then, selling sex is a survival mechanism. (2002: 256)

Critical feminists examine the structures of class discrimination, racism and sexism showing how they influence the choices of women to enter what is essentially street exploitation. This type of theory also debunks the idea that women and youth enter into the sex trade by choice. Lowman writes:

> Once we transcend a phenomenal level of analysis to consider the context of a youth's choice to sell sexual services, it becomes obvious that the choice must be located in the "wider origins of the deviant act," particularly the marginal position of youth in the labour force, and patriarchal power structures both inside and outside the family. (1987: 111, cited in Gorkoff and Runner 2003: 21)

Broad socio-structural factors, including poverty, marginalization, racism and violence create the circumstances in which some women are more vulnerable than others to choosing the sex trade and to being exploited by pimps and johns. When young women are in a situation of poverty, it is difficult to survive, and sometimes that means involvement in activities that society defines as illegal. It is certainly plausible that some consensus models (maybe all) know the conundrum for young women in poverty but choose to ignore it. They take inequality and discrimination for granted and focus on issues of individual choice, rarely focusing on the social structures that condition individual choice.

It is important to remember that social problems such as poverty, violence against women, lack of helping agencies and lack of employment for youth are not the result of individual choice. Rather, it is macro-level societal structures of socio-economic inequality that give rise to ideologies and practices that devalue women, engender violence against them, marginalize them because of their race and ethnicity and condemn them for their sexuality (especially homosexuality).

> Indeed ... some individuals such as gay and lesbian youth, Aboriginal and migrant/immigrant girls, and the poor are in positions where they are more vulnerable to choosing sex-trade work simply because of these characteristics. Homophobia, racism and cultural genocide, and lack of opportunities for the poor, impact on children's decisions to run away and seek approval from other sources. (Jiwani 1998, cited in Gorkoff and Runner 2003: 21)

As for gang involvement, critical feminist theory focuses on masculinity and violence as a social construct embedded in patriarchal culture. Male violence results in part from a society that constructs the dominant forms of masculinity around themes of domination and violence, created (in part) and reinforced through the celebration of male violence in war, sports and popular culture (Robinson 1998; Messner and Sabo 1994; McBride 1995; Brooks, Henry and Daschuk 2015). Girls and boys tend to adapt to a social script based on patriarchal norms of what constitutes masculine and feminine.

The myth of the "real man" is one that teaches boys that the dominant culture expects them to be tough and strong in ways that are not passive — these cultural norms feed dangerous stereotypes that encourage violence among young men (Katz 1999; Robinson 1998; Messner and Sabo 1994; McBride 1995). Importantly, masculine constructs may affect racial minorities more severely. In the powerful film *Tough Guise*, "social and economic structures deny [urban Black males] success ... one thing that has not been taken is their ability to pose as tough guys so they can get respect ... masculinity is a pose of culture ... men become real men through power and through control."

From this perspective, we can see the "maleness" of gangs as a stereo-typical gendered response to marginality. Gangs are not very different from sports teams or the military, in which violence and domination are the norm (Dunning 1999; Miedzian 1991). In effect, the violent and gendered nature of gangs has a template in the larger patriarchal world.

There is also recent research that speaks about hyper-masculine practices, allowing young racialized men a means of conforming with conceptions of what it means to be a real man (Henry 2013; Totten 2012). Young Aboriginal males, for example, arguably use the street gang as a social space where they may participate in masculine constructions of identity, constructions that are otherwise less available to them:

> Taking on a "protest masculine" identity ... allows those who are denied the optimal benefits of being "male" within a patriarchal society to adopt and em-

> body hyper-masculine practices in their attempt to reclaim some measure of the social power denied to them on the basis of their ethnicity or class standing ... it also ensures that marginalized men will attempt to broadcast their status by adopting practices based around stereotypical masculine traits ... epitomized in the emergence ... [of] street gangs. (Brooks, Henry and Daschuk 2015: 20)

Comack et al. and Earle and Drake's chapters in this edition both discuss the importance of understanding social constructions of masculinities and their impact on criminal involvement and identities of young men.

A logical social policy response from this critical feminist perspective would be to attack sources of economic and gender inequality. As with all the critical theories, the focus of social policy would include social-support programs for young people living on the margins of society, with awareness that girls and boys live in different worlds of security and vulnerability.

Critical Race Theory

Critical race theory attributes Aboriginal people's involvement in gangs and the sex trade, in part, to overt and institutional racism and economic exploitation. Yet racialized youth are defined in the law, media and many government reports as the "other," outside "normal society" and identified by race. The material consequences of racism and economic exploitation are vulnerability to poverty, social alienation, racism, high suicide rates (estimated to be five to six times higher for Aboriginal youth) and criminal activity (Assembly of First Nations Proceedings, June 2002; Minaker and Hogeveen 2009). Such high rates of social pathology (including gang and sex-trade involvement) disturb the public, who rarely hears the argument that such pathologies originate within a political and social context. Statistics in the media and in government reports seldom have coinciding theoretical and political analyses of why certain groups and communities have more social problems than others. Crime statistics that "prove" that members of visible minorities are more "criminal" than white citizens rarely have accompanying narratives that explain how racism, class discrimination and sexism foster criminal involvement.

In critical race theory, the public's construction of the "identity" of the racialized other is a precursor to racial discrimination. The belief system that attributes crime to individuals of a certain race results because the public sees social problems like gang involvement and sexual exploitation as the result of "bad people doing bad things." Furthermore, the harm that racism does to people is rarely considered in the justice system's decisions about guilt and punishment (Hudson 2006; Comack and Balfour 2004). In general, the language of media, politics and public policy normalizes whiteness and reinforces racist assumptions. Aboriginal people are stereotyped as people with social pathologies. Stories of gang involvement focus almost exclusively on incidents, not on the individual, familial, social and political realities that lead some Aboriginal youth to join gangs.

The role of the criminal justice system, government and public policy in the construction of normalized racism is of fundamental concern in a critical race theory paradigm. From this perspective, racial minorities suffer bigotry and social injustice in part because structural racism (especially institutional racism) is hard to identify, whereas the racist leanings of a jury, for example, are relatively obvious. Structural racism is subtle; it does not often appear as a day-to-day confrontation between races. It does exist, for example, in the geography of a city where certain areas are adjudged by the police and other agencies of control to be "problem areas." Urban communities in which Aboriginal people often live are defined by the police service as problem areas, so they look for crime in such areas by over-policing or by racial profiling. The police will stop young Aboriginal men as part of their standard operating procedures simply because, in the eyes of the police, they look like offenders. Critical race theorists demonstrate that there is a structural foundation to racism within the law: "the racialization of crime, criminalization of race, and/or the discriminatory sentencing and lack of serious legal response to attacks on the persons and property of minority citizens, are structural" (Schur 2002, cited in Hudson 2006).

When critical criminologists and critical race theorists talk about gangs and the sex trade, they often describe some of the most vulnerable people in society, many of whom have become the "raw material" for media stories. The fact is that societies mostly fail to address marginalization in employment, socio-economics, schooling, housing, neighbourhoods and gendered violence. Instead, the various mechanisms of social control and political influence focus on youth as "gang members" and "criminals" and by using strategies of traditional criminal justice (or even strategies of restorative community approaches) to control youth; these mechanisms contribute to the false ideology of Aboriginal and disenfranchised youths as primarily bad, dangerous or violent. In the language of the law, media and government, a person who is a visible minority is talked about as a racialized "other," someone who is different from the "average." As someone who is not average, the visible minority person and his or her community become the focus of intervention when, logically and morally, the focus should be on the racist structure of modern society.

There have been 1017 police reported Aboriginal female homicides and an additional 164 missing Aboriginal women between 1980 and 2012, yet until recently, these tragic events have demonstrated very little formal interest through legal response or media attention. The media portrayal of the Robert Pickton case and the murder of sex-trade workers from Vancouver's Downtown Eastside did little to acknowledge the value of their lives. The women were primarily identified as prostitutes. When Aboriginal sex workers are portrayed in the media they are often silenced and racialized, portrayed as though they are different from a "respectable rest" (Hugill 2010). Jiwani and Young state:

> Strategic silences contribute to representations of Aboriginal women who are sex workers as deserving of violence ... representation of Aboriginal women in Vancouver's Downtown eastside oscillate between invisibility and hyper visibility: invisible as victims of violence and hyper visible as deviant bodies. (2006: 3)

In trying to make sense of the relatively little interest in the devastating killings in Vancouver's Downtown Eastside and the disappearance of so many women, researchers have asked the obvious: "Do you think if 65 women went missing from Kerrisdale [an affluent Vancouver neighborhood] we'd have ignored it so long?" (Wood 2004, cited in Hugill 2010: 10).

In the end, critical race theorists focus on race as a social construction and on how society comes to make moral estimations of people based on their perceived primordial characteristics. We know that racial minorities and poor youth and adults are overrepresented in the sex trade, in gangs and in custodial institutions. These realities demand that we reflect on why there is a war on crime, sex trade and gang involvement, rather than a war on social disenfranchisement and structural disadvantage. Perhaps we focus on prostitution and gang involvement as individual "criminal activities" because it soothes the conscience of the middle class?

Finally, beginning with an understanding of the very real impact of racism and the importance of hearing multiple voices, anti-racist researchers also facilitate the voices of the marginalized, especially, some ague, through storytelling in racialized cultures whereby this has a long history (see, for example, Okolie 2005). This must be done in a way that is holistic and that emphasizes emancipation and the elimination of racism. Experiential accounts (and multiple tellings) are important. The reality of racism demands, however, that these accounts must not stay just at the level of the individual. Racism is experienced individually, relationally, societally and politically. The aim of the anti-racist researcher is to ensure the experiential account includes the political and structural problems inherent within racism and social construction of race (Okolie 2005). Comack et al.'s chapter in this edition demonstrates the impact of personal tellings of gang members' experiences.

POSTCOLONIAL INDIGENOUS THEORY AND POSTCOLONIAL FEMINISM

Colonization has taken its toll on all Native peoples, but perhaps it has taken its greatest toll on women. (LaRocque 1996: 11–12)

Key for postcolonial indigenous theory is colonialism, neo-colonialism and the continued impacts they have on people's lives. Neo-colonialism is less overt than colonialism, is sustained by everyday assumptions, processes and structures and refers to current control measures of Indigenous peoples such as the *Indian Act*, the system of treaties intended to manage Indigenous communities and the negotiations and expropriations of traditional lands for resource exploration and pipeline development for the "benefit" of local communities and Indigenous peoples (Ashcroft, Griffiths and Tiffin 1998).

Postcolonial Indigenous theory and anti-racism have as their goal transformative social change. If social policy is devoted to social transformation, it must be based on an acknowledgement that societies are heterogeneous, that contexts differ from place to place and that although people may have shared experiences, the result of those experiences depend on whether they are a member of a racial minority, whether they lives on the margins of the political economy and whether their marginalization has deep roots in history. Postcolonial theorists focus on the connections between class and race and acknowledge that both past and current colonialism affects current lives, choices and opportunities (Anderson 2000, 2004). The history of Indian residential schools in Canada is a poignant example of how extreme colonialist oppression destroyed not only the generation of kids who were sexually and physically abused, but also the future generations who felt the effects of the damage done to their parents and grandparents.

What postcolonial Indigenous theory adds to critical gang studies is an understanding of the ongoing reality of colonization on Aboriginal gang members' life situations and identities. As Comack et al. describe in greater detail in Chapter 10, colonialism is "A major factor in the production of Aboriginal street gangs." Here, we only begin to understand how street gang activities are a product of space, which is colonized and oppressed, as well as a form of resistance to marginalization and alienation.

Postcolonial-feminist theorizing aims to address social determinants of the sex trade, including historical determinants found through colonialism and neo-colonialist relations. Experiences in the sex trade are found through a critical gaze, informed by an understanding of women and girls experiences, contextualized in the wider political, social, economic and historical context. The 1876 *Indian Act*, for example, meant forced assimilation of Aboriginal peoples through appropriating lands, outlawing spiritual and cultural practices, forced indoctrination into dominant culture through residential schools and forced marginalization onto reserves. "Status" or "Registered" First Nations continue to be governed under the *Indian Act* — and Aboriginal women are argued to have fewer "fundamental rights than men" (Fiske 2006, cited in Browne, Smye and Varcoe 2007: 131). Under the *Indian Act,* and until the amendment of the controversial Bill C-31 (Monture Angus 1995; Cannon 2007, 2008), Aboriginal women lost their Status and rights/protection if they married non-Status Indian men or non-Indian men. This affected their ability to own property, for example, which has had an impact on their current rates of poverty and, therefore, is a direct cause of their poorer heath (Dion Stout, Kipling and Stout 2001) and heightened involvement in crime. Although these decisions were amended through Bill C-31, continued effects are felt (Monture-Angus 1995; Cannon 2007, 2008).

It is well known that Aboriginal women's socio-economic status is lower than non-Aboriginal peoples in Canada and that they suffer higher levels of poverty. Some scholars link colonized histories to levels of poverty and argue that this provides a context for understanding why women and girls enter or are forced into the sex trade. In fact, Sikka (2009) has argued that Aboriginal women and girls have been recruited into the sex trade under such exploitative circumstance that it should be defined as trafficking. Canada's definition of "trafficking in persons" (introduced into the *Criminal Code* in 2005) includes recruiting, harbouring and transporting persons for exploitation, as well as threatening those individuals. Sikka (2009) argues that this applies to Aboriginal youth, who often are prayed upon, have their vulnerabilities exploited and are moved into the cities for prostitution.

Postcolonial feminists also agree (similar to anti-racist theorists above and postmodern theorists below) that the perspectives of marginalized peoples must be the starting point towards the development of knowledge about and deconstruction of the social construction of race, culture and the other. Postcolonial feminists ask why Aboriginal people are more susceptible to certain "risk." Yet this perspective also warns that assumptions about class, cultural and racialized identities that inform criminal justice and mainstream theories of "risk," create/reinforce difference, othering and culturalism. Bringing forward voices that are often not heard provides insight into the workings of the criminal justice system. For example, the words of one Aboriginal woman show the difference in power between individuals on the stroll and the police:

> If you're on the stroll they look at you like you're lower than them [police] ... They can do whatever they want. Cops come up to you say, "I'm gonna stick you in jail for seventy-two hours just because I can!" (cited in Nixon and Tutty 2003: 77).

The process of othering means that stereotypical (and often racialized) assumptions of identity, culture and difference are placed onto certain groups, which are not reflective of actual identities. Bringing forward the voices of individuals provides a perspective generally not heard.

The problem of culturalism and othering is also true when interpreting justice and police statistics and indicators. Profiles of crime and statistics alert communities to important trends regarding criminal activity, but they also may indicate the behaviors of police and other justice professionals. There are important risks in reporting trends without contextualizing this within social, economical and historical determinants. The wider determinants of crime evident in the intersecting of class, culture, racialization, historical subjugation and gender are easily overlooked in favour of blaming individuals and groups of people/cultures for lifestyles associated with these activities.

In sum, postcolonial indigenous and feminist theorists provide an understanding of how crime and life chances are affected by the intersection of class, culture, racialization, historical subjugation and gender. These theories emphasize critical and inclusive analysis and the inclusion of marginalized voices, especially those who have suffered effects of colonized histories.

POSTMODERNISM AND CRITICAL CRIMINOLOGY: DISCOURSE ANALYSIS AND GANGS

One of the issues that frames critical race and postcolonial theorizing is the connection between living on the margins of the society and the way that crime is constructed in the media. One branch of postmodern theory shows that we come to speak and think about issues in a particular, rather rigid way and that people who "produce" knowledge have a great deal of ideological power (see Chapter 3 in this book, especially the discussions on Foucault). Discourse analysis, as a methodology for studying images and beliefs, is based on uncovering the hidden messages in public discourse.

For youth gangs, discourse analysis would focus on how youth are portrayed in all sorts of public venues, including television and film, newspapers and political talk, showing that such portrayals so often lead to inequality and injustice. The concern is how stereotypes of badness and criminality become equated with racial, ethnic, gender, class and age traits. Media portraits of youth-gang members are often fraught with fear-invoking statements and images of minority group members.

Sensational reporting of exceptional events — e.g., "A Quiet Killing: Murder Conviction Sheds Light on 'Cult of Indian Secrecy'" (*Saskatoon Star Phoenix* 2011); "Gang Attacks Becoming More Violent" (*Petaluma Argus Courier* 2006); "The Immigrant Gang Plague" (*City Journal* 2005) — are commonplace and raise public fear, as noted earlier. Furthermore, law enforcement, government and some academic agencies extend the biased discourse by focusing on statistics, events and media reports that often ignore the context within which gang involvement arises and are based on ambiguous, unclear definitions of what a gang actually is (Sullivan 2005). The Criminal Intelligence Services Saskatchewan (CISS 2005), for example, highlights gang activity, especially among Aboriginal youth, as a serious problem, estimating 1,315 young gang members in the Province of Saskatchewan — more per capita than anywhere else in Canada. The agency argues that Native gang activity is "associated with violent crimes, drug trafficking, prostitution, and cross-border smuggling," and there is heightened concern about Aboriginal youth as "prime recruits" (CISS 2005). The public in Saskatchewan hears of youth gangs identified as the Crips, Junior Mixed Blood, Indian Mafia Crips and North Central Rough Riderz. Accompanying the statistics is a narrative about a continual increase in the numbers of gangs and increase in violence. In its 2010 *Report on Organized Crime*, Criminal Intelligence Service of Canada (CISC) focused on street gang activity and said that there has been an overall increase in these groups in Canada. It is important to realize, though, that for what they represent, statistics do not lie, but they do not tell the whole truth. They do present a version of the truth that is non-contextual — a truth that is present only in numbers and not in the day-to-day reality of ordinary people, including the reality of being a gang member.

One of the ways that such a narrow form of public discourse maintains its legitimacy is by drawing upon the "knowledge of experts." A *Toronto Sun* article from December 12, 2004, quotes a psychologist and researcher at Central Toronto Youth Services as saying, "Kids are fed a steady diet of aggression in all forms of popular culture ... if you need scripts to teach you how to act out violently, they're everywhere." Similarly, the Canadian Press (December 7, 2003) cites the testimony of Ray Corrado (a criminologist at Simon Fraser University), who "speculated": "I've argued it might reflect the cultural norms of the last 15, 20 years, where video games and movies and music, even television, portray a level of violence that is really extraordinary." When experts speak "through" the media, they are given a few lines of commentary at most which often dictates that what they say is taken as definitive when most commentary is certainly not. Discourse analysis explores the under-meanings of public commentary, the covert messages that distort the ways we view others, especially those who live on the margins of society. For example, the commentary above speaks to the already presumed conclusion that kids' violence is on the rise; the commentary is preordained to support the argument.

This research on public discourse is important in that it tends to concentrate on how people with knowledge, or with the ability to produce and disseminate knowledge, use that power to their advantage. So, for example, we might ask whether newspapers have a particular vested interest, attracting advertisers for example, in attaching images of crime to the young and the poor in order to divert attention from crimes of the wealthy. Or we might investigate how public discourse draws on the work of medical/forensic experts to talk about crime only as a phenomenon of the individual rather than a product of class, race and gender inequality. When experts speak, they do so only from their body of expertise. They are, in fact, isolated from other issues that are so important. In the end, whether intentional or not, the prevailing method of talking about goodness and badness as individual pathology, within a context of street crime and official justice, ascribes immorality to the least privileged in the society, and the "gang talk" that we discuss above is typical of how public discourse condemns the already condemned.

TRANSFORMATIVE JUSTICE INITIATIVES AND CRITICAL PERSPECTIVES: RETHINKING STRATEGIES OF JUSTICE FOR YOUTH GANGS AND FOR THE SEX TRADE

The worldview of critical criminology is more than just "tilting at windmills." It can shape transformative social policy — policy that takes aim at the social inequalities at the root of crime. The basic premise is that current attempts to address the sexual exploitation of youth and/or women in the sex trade or measures to alleviate involvement in gangs are, basically, band-aid solutions that rarely focus on the fundamental problems of social inequality, marginalization and exploitation. A critical orientation, at a general level, focuses not only on individuals in the sex trade or youth in gangs, but also on the structural and material conditions that give rise to the sex trade and to an individual's "choice" to be involved in illegal gang activities. This is the essence of transformative policy, and it is substantially different from the existing justice system.

CONSENSUS THEORY IMPLICATIONS: GET TOUGH ON CRIME

Within criminology, theories such as deterrence theory and modern classical theories support "get tough" measures, ones essentially designed to punish individuals, such as, for example, the increasing use of incarceration. By contrast, there are also programs, drawn from subcultural theory, strain theory and economic theory, which emphasize rehabilitation and restorative initiatives.

Following principles of deterrence, we now have legislation designed to imprison youth who are involved in youth gangs, and we continue to imprison women and youth involved in the sex trade. We also have devised innovative measures to help youth exit the sex trade (such as the *Protection of Sexually Exploited Children Act* in Alberta), but they too continue to permit the arrest and detainment of young women and men on the streets, as does the Canadian Youth Gang strategy, which is lobbying for tougher sentences for gang-involved youth. In dealing with problems of gangs and the sex trade, traditional rehabilitation (corrections) or retribution (punishment) approaches are not only costly, but they also fail to prevent recidivism, damage offenders' life chances, fail to deter crime and largely ignore the needs of victims (White 2002; Cunneen and White 1995).

Other programs drawn from consensus theories such as subcultural theory, strain theory and economic theory, by contrast, focus on rehabilitation and restorative initiatives by supporting measures that rebuild social supports and economic opportunities. Two Saskatchewan-based anti-gang initiatives in Regina and in Prince Albert, for example, aspire to equip gang-involved youth with skills for employment, reduce participation in violent crime and promote education. Regina's Anti-Gang Services (RAGS) offered a seventy-seven week intensive service that helped youth develop relationships with positive adult role models and engage in programming related to life skills. Participants were encouraged to build healthy relationships as well as work on healthy parenting. Prince Albert's Warrior Spirit Walking program similarly implemented a neighborhood-based service, which promoted completion of high school and offered alternatives to standard public education (through Won Ska Cultural School). This program also offered counselling and a center for youth activity. The National Crime Prevention Centre (2012) provided evaluations of both programs and found success in reducing the risk of gang involvement. Also in Saskatoon, a program entitled Operation Help employs a multi-agency approach to help women and young women leave the sex trade. Operation Help aims to provide immediate support at the time of arrest from a variety of agencies that can help individuals change their lifestyle. Individuals that are involved in the sex trade are given the opportunity to develop their own case plan with an established support system and provided a sixty-day agreement with a support team towards lifestyle change. There is also follow up support after the charges are dropped.

Importantly, programs such as RAGS, the Warrior Spirit Walking program and Operation Help do seem to address some of the social problems underlying gangs and the sex trade. They do not, however, fundamentally alter society in a way that reduces inequality and exploitation.

RESTORATIVE JUSTICE

Restorative justice, as an alternative to punishment, emphasizes repairing harm, rebuilding relationships, reintegrating offenders into the society and establishing social inclusion. The restorative justice approach to law and crime is not adversarial; in other words, it does not focus on guilt or innocence and the associated combative arguments. It focuses, rather, on ensuring that the community that was harmed by the crime is restored, that reparation is part of the solution, that offenders need to take responsibility for the harm they have done and that the community brings the offender back into the fold. With this focus, the victim, or victims, are a fundamental part of the healing process not only as those who receive reparation but also as those who are active in the establishment of a healed community.

The drawback of restorative justice, however, is that it tends to ignore structural inequality by focusing on street crime, targeting lower-class people and defining crime as an individual action. Consequently, restorative justice initiatives may serve to reinforce the ideology that is the cornerstone of the criminal justice system, a system that punishes and imprisons (Walgrave and Bazemore 1999; Woolford 2009). The heart of restorative justice is similar in philosophy to harsh measures of social control — to control crime we need to change the offender and not communities or the structural conditions of inequality (White 2000; Woolford 2009).

Restorative justice is therefore not really a radical shift but a policy shift to deal with working- and lower-class people. As such, it does not involve substantial change; it fails to include consciousness-raising or political mobilization, and it ignores questions of social injustice and inequality. Like most other crime and justice paradigms, restorative justice may undermine, or at least overshadow, other types of political struggle that are aimed at poverty and the abuse of human rights. In the end, even for restorative justice, the real problem is crime and not class divisions and global inequalities.

For gang involvement and the sex trade, what this means is that although community supports, alternative educational programs and employment opportunities are important, the need for a fundamental change in people's civil rights remains unanswered (Brooks, Henry and Daschuk 2015). We are still left with a system that privileges people on the bases of race, gender and class. The overrepresentation of racial minorities and the poor in youth gangs, in youth custody and in the sex trade is a clear indication that privilege exists. Transformative justice demands an answer to justice-based wars on youth on the street and women and children in the sex trade. Advocates for transformative justice define these troubles as the result of social disenfranchisement rather than "deviance." Transformative justice is about the civil rights of vulnerable people. The fundamental problems these people face are poor or no employment, socio-economic inequality, poor and ineffective schooling, poor housing, unlivable neighbourhoods and gendered violence (all which contribute to choices to become street-involved). A transformative, justice-based society would contain provisions for a minimum standard of living, adequate and comfortable housing, universal day care, educational institutions that account for all types of learners, employment programs that focus a living wage and decent mentorship and neighborhood enhancement programs that focus on community integration for all citizens.

By focusing on deviance and crime rather than structure, social control institutions like the police, the courts and the prisons contribute to the false ideology that people break the law because they are immoral or amoral. This masks the reality of colonization, racism and discrimination and keeps such fundamental structural issues off the political radar screen. To go beyond orthodox justice requires that the social control institutions come to understand that the decision to engage in sex work or gang involvement goes beyond issues of victimization into issues of social and economic marginalization. To date, the strategies to eradicate youth involvement in the sex trade or gang involvement have not addressed a social-change perspective; they are only temporary solutions and most certainly are not transformative. Transformative policing, for example, would recreate the mandate of the police from that of a crime control officer to a frontline social worker.

Interestingly, a few successful police officers already do this in their role as peace officers in a community-policing context. Instead of arresting a drug user, such a police officer would find the avenue for a drug user to become healthy. This does happen in Vancouver's Downtown Eastside, for example, where police officers can direct street drug users to safe injection clinics as the starting point for their role as police.

MARGINALITY AND CONDEMNATION

We have explored the social phenomena of gangs and prostitution to give you a sense of how two very different issues of crime and justice can be seen from various theoretical perspectives. We have not been able to discuss all the possible theories, but we have tried to show how the general paradigms of consensus and critical criminology are quite different in their understandings of deviance and crime, although in some ways their understandings are quite complementary.

In the end, most social and justice (crime-control) policies are based on a consensus-theory view of the world where the moral guidelines of the society are correct and "consensual" and violations must be dealt with. Critical criminology and critical feminist theory challenge this view. In his critique of retributive justice and imprisonment, Garland (2001: 10–11), for example, proposes, "The background effect of policy is now more frequently a collective anger and a righteous demand for retribution rather than a commitment to a just, socially engineered solution." Critical theorists advocate for transformative social policy, which strikes at the heart of privilege, class, race and gender and critiques restitutive and restorative programs for not doing so.

The prevalence of racial minorities and poor people in youth gangs, in youth custody and in the sex trade demands an answer as to why there is a war on marginalized people rather than a war against social disenfranchisement and inequality. Critical criminology asks why those most marginalized are also the most condemned.

DISCUSSION QUESTIONS

1. Critical and consensus theories are quite different in their understanding of crime, yet they are also quite complementary. Please explain.

2. Search the local newspapers in your communities or the Criminal Intelligence Service Canada website for information on street gangs. Provide a discussion on what you learn about gang involvement through these sources and, more importantly, what may be missing.

3. Define the key differences between retributive, restorative and transformative justice. Which of these crime control strategies does a critical criminological approach propose to be the most effective and why?

4. Levels of explanation in criminology concerning gang and sex-trade involvement range from biological pathologies, to understanding gendered prescriptions (masculinities and femininities), to problems of structural inequalities. Which perspective or combination of perspectives resonates best with your understanding of these issues? Explain.

5. Critical criminology asks why those most marginalized are also the most condemned. Explain this theoretical question, drawing on central themes developed throughout this book.

GLOSSARY

Condemnation: refers to pronouncing blame or condemning as wrong. This may include judicial condemning.

Deterrence Theory: this theory shifts attention to the criminal act and asks what can/should be done to prevent it or to make it less attractive to the individual. The aim is to develop crime policies that persuade individuals not to engage in criminal activity. Strategies include legal deterrents such as mandatory sentencing, three-strikes laws and the death penalty.

Discourse Analysis: a deconstructive interpretation of text or reality (which is itself socially constructed text, in postmodern theories). Discourse analysis does not provide absolute answers but examines conditions and assumptions behind a socially constructed reality. It aims to make assumptions and epistemologies explicit and therefore to gain a "higher," more comprehensive view.

Forensic Science: the application of science to legal questions. This may include scientific searches for physical traces, indicated as useful to establish an association between a suspect and a victim or the scene of a crime.

Institutional Racism: refers to the systematic practices and policies within organizations/institutions that disadvantage certain racial and ethnic groups. Examples include systematic profiling of certain races by law-enforcement and security workers as well as stereotyped representations and mis/representations of racial groups in the media.

Marginalized/Marginality: these terms refer to groups of people who are treated differently or unequally. Marginalization is a form of collective discrimination, in which certain groups are excluded and ostracized by the wider society.

Neo-Colonialism: less overt than colonialism, neo-colonialism is sustained by everyday assumptions, processes and structures, and it refers to current control measures of indigenous peoples.

Postcolonial Feminism: provides an understanding of how crime and life chances are affected by the intersection of class, culture, racialization, historical subjugation and gender. This theory emphasizes critical and inclusive analysis, marginalized voices, especially those who have suffered effects of colonized histories.

Postcolonial Indigenous Theory: focuses on colonialism, neo-colonialism and the continued impact of these social forces on people's lives.

Postmodern Feminism: this theory rejects claims of scientific objectivity and truths. The analytical central task is to unpack gender thereby revealing the reality of womens' lives by collaborating with women in research and documenting their oral histories.

Postmodernism: postmodernist theories say we must reject the search for universal truth and knowledge. These theories point out that dominant discourses reflect the interests of the powerful and tend to silence alternative views and voices. In criminological analysis, these alternative voices are most often the marginalized and those labelled "criminal."

Social Control Theory: this theory focuses on formal and informal control mechanisms (external to the individual) that regulate human conformity/compliance to society's rules, including morals, beliefs, families, school, and more. Social control theory may be macro-social, focusing on formal control systems including legal, economic, educational and government institutions, or micro-social, focusing on informal controls that help individuals conform.

Social Disorganization Theory: this theory has its origin in ecological studies and refers to the failure of social organizations and institutions (including schools, policing, real estate and more) in certain neighbourhoods and communities to maintain public order. Modern social disorganization theorists have introduced the terms "collective efficacy" and "social capital" to criminology, demonstrating the community's ability to maintain order and the informal networks that assist in this process.

Transformative Justice: a philosophical approach concerned with root causes of social and criminal problems. Criminal offences are treated as transformative opportunities to deal with societal inequalities, community problems such as poverty, housing, employment, and more.

SUGGESTED READINGS

Ronald L. Akers, *Criminological Theories: Introduction and Evaluation,* New York: Routledge (2012).

Elizabeth Comack, Lawrence Deane, Larry Morrissette and Jim Silver, *Indians Wear Red: Colonialism, Resistance, and Aboriginal Street Gangs,* Halifax: Fernwood Publishing (2013).

Jeff Karabanow, Alexa Carson and Philip Clement, *Leaving the Streets: Stories of Canadian Youth,* Halifax: Fernwood Publishing (2010).

Kelly Gorkoff and Jane Runners, *Being Heard: The Experiences of Young Women in Prostitution,* Halifax: Fernwood Publishing and RESOLVE (2003).

Bernard Schissel, *STILL Blaming Children: Youth Conduct and the Politics of Child Hating,* Halifax: Fernwood Publishing (2007).

Andrew Woolford, *The Politics of Restorative Justice: A Critical Introduction,* Halifax: Fernwood Publishing (2009).

REFERENCES

Aboriginal Council of Winnipeg. 2010. Urban Gang Initiatives in the City of Winnipeg. *Abcouncil. org* <abcouncil.org/PDF/ACWI%20Gang%20Prevention%20Programs%20Community%20 Resource%20Guide.pdf>.

Akers, Ronald L. 2012. *Criminological Theories: Introduction and Evaluation.* New York: Routledge.

Anderson, J.M. 2000. "Gender, Race, Poverty, Health and Discourses of Health Reform in the Context of Globalization: A Postcolonial Feminist Perspective in Policy Research." *Nursing Inquiry,* 7, 220–29.

___. 2004. "The Conundrums of Binary Categories: Critical Inquiry Through the Lens of Postcolonial Feminist Humanism." *Canadian Journal of Nursing Research* 36, 4: 11–16.

Ashcroft, B., G. Griffiths and H. Tiffin. 1998. *Key Concepts in Post-Colonial Studies.* New York: Routledge.

Assembly of First Nations. 2002. "Assembly of First Nations Proceedings." June 11. At <www. turtleisland.org/news/absenyouth2.htm> accessed Feb. 1, 2006.

Bartollas, Clemens. 2005. *Juvenile Delinquency.* Addison-Wesley.

___. 2007. *Juvenile Delinquency,* Seventh edition. Boston: Allyn and Bacon.

Benjamin, H., and R. Masters. 1964. *Prostitution and Morality: A Definitive Report on the Prostitute in Contemporary Society and an Analysis of the Causes and Effects of the Suppression of Prostitution.* London: Souvenir Press.

Bittle, Steven. 2002. "Youth Involvement in Prostitution: A Literature Review and Annotated Bibliography." Department of Justice, Canada. At <justice.gc.ca/eng/rp-pr/cj-jp/yj-jj/rr01_13/

toc-tdm.html>.

Boritch, Helen. 1997. *Fallen Women: Female Crime and Criminal Justice in Canada.* Scarborough, ON: ITP Nelson.

Brooks, Carolyn, Robert Henry and Mitch Daschuk. 2015, forthcoming. "Aboriginal Youth Gang Involvement: Decolonizing and Multi-Causal Perspectives towards Community Strategies and Social Justice." In Ray Corrado, Alan Leschied and Patrick Lussier (eds.), *Serious and Violent Young Offenders and Youth Criminal Justice: A Canadian Perspective.* Burnaby, BC: Simon Fraser University Press.

Browne, A.J., V.L. Smye and C. Varcoe. 2007. "Postcolonial-Feminist Theoretical Perspectives and Women's Health." In M. Morrow, O. Hankivsky and C. Varcoe (eds.), *Women's Health in Canada: Critical Perspectives on Theory and Policy.* Toronto: University of Toronto Press.

Canadian Press. 2003. "Viciousness of Youth Attacks Increases While Numbers Remain Static." December 7. Violent Crime Statistics, Canada. At <http://www.fradical.com/Violent_crime_statistics_Canada.htm> accessed February 20, 2006.

Cannon, M. 2007. "Revisiting Histories of Legal Assimilation, Racialized Injustice, and the Future of Indian Status in Canada." In Jerry P. White, Erik Anderson, Wendy Cornet and Dan Beavon (eds.), *Aboriginal Policy Research: Moving Forward, Making a Difference,* Volume V. Toronto: Thompson Educational Publishing.

____. 2008. "Revisiting Histories of Gender-Based Exclusion and the New Politics of Indian Identity." Research paper for the National Centre for First Nations Governance. May.

CBC News. 2013. "Toronto Yorkdale Mall Killing Likely Gang Related." *CBC News.* April 3. At <cbc.ca/news/canada/toronto/toronto-yorkdale-mall-killing-likely-gang-related-ambush-1.1336761>.

CISS (Criminal Intelligence Service Saskatchewan). 2005. "2005 Intelligence Trends: Aboriginal-based Gangs in Saskatchewan." At <http://ciss.sasktelwebhosting.com/PDF/Public-gang-report.pdf> accessed July 2007.

City Journal. 2005. "The Immigrant Gang Plague." Summer. At <www.city-journal.org/html/14_3_immigrant_gang.html> accessed February 20, 2006.

Cobbina, J.E., and S.S. Oselin. 2011. "It's Not Only for the Money: An Analysis of Adolescent Versus Adult Entry into Street Prostitution." *Sociological Inquiry* 81, 3: 310–32.

Comack, Elizabeth, and Gillian Balfour. 2000. "The Prisoning of Women: Meeting Women's Needs?" In K. Hannah-Moffat and M. Shaw (eds.), *An Ideal Prison? Critical Essays on Women's Imprisonment in Canada.* Halifax: Fernwood Publishing.

Comack, Eliabeth, Lawrence Deane, Larry Morrisssette and Jim Silver. 2013. *"Indians Wear Red": Colonialism, Resistance, and Aboriginal Street Gangs.* Halifax and Winnipeg: Fernwood Publishing.

Crocker, Diane, and Val Marie Johnson. 2010. *Poverty, Regulation and Social Justice: Readings in the Criminalization of Poverty.* Halifax and Winnipeg: Fernwood Publishing.

Cunneen, C., and R. White. 1995. *Juvenile Justice: An Australian Perspective.* Melbourne: Oxford University Press.

Davis, N. 1971. "The Prostitute: Developing a Deviant Identity." In J. Henslin (ed.), *Studies in the Sociology of Sex.* Englewood Cliffs, NJ: Prentice-Hall.

Dunning, Eric. 1999. *Sport Matters: Sociological Studies of Sport, Violence, and Civilization.* London: New York: Routledge.

Edwards, W. (ed.). 1987. *Gender, Sex and the Law.* London: Croom Helm.

____. 1988a. "Policing Street Prostitution: The Street Offences Squad in London." *Police Journal* 61, 3: 209–19.

____. 1988b. "Prostitution, Policing, Employment and the Welfare of Young Women." Report prepared for the Nuffield Foundation.

Esbensen, F., and D. Huizinga. 1993. "Gangs, Drugs, and Delinquency in a Survey of Urban Youth." *Criminology* 31: 565–89.

Fagan, J. 1989. "The Social Organization of Drug Use and Drug Dealing Among Urban Gangs." *Criminology* 27: 663–67.

Farley, Melissa, Jacqueline Lynn and Ann J. Cotton, 2005. "Prostitution in Vancouver: Violence and the Colonization of First Nations Women." *Transcultural Psychiatry* 42: 242–71.

Fedec, Kari. 2002. "Women and Children in Canada's Sex Trade: The Discriminatory Policing of the Marginalized." In B. Schissel and C. Brooks (eds.), *Marginality and Condemnation: An Introduction to Critical Criminology.* Halifax: Fernwood Publishing.

Garland, David. 2001. *The Culture of Control: Crime and Social Order in Contemporary Society.* Chicago: University of Chicago Press.

Girard, Lina, and Steve Wormith. 2004 "The Predictive Validity of the Level of Service Inventory — Ontario Revision on General and Violent Recidivism Among Various Offender Groups." *Criminal Justice and Behaviour* 31, 2: 150–81.

Glueck, Sheldon, and Eleanor Glueck. 1934. *Five Hundred Delinquent Women.* New York: Knopf.

Gorkoff, Kelly, and Jane Runner (eds.). 2003. *Being Heard: The Experiences of Young Women in Prostitution.* Halifax: Fernwood Publishing and RESOLVE.

Gorkoff, Kelly, and Meghan Waters. 2003. "Balancing Safety, Respect and Choice in Programs for Young Women Involved in Prostitution." In Kelly Gorkoff and Jane Runners (eds.), *Being Heard: The Experiences of Young Women in Prostitution.* Halifax: Fernwood Publishing and RESOLVE.

Gray, D. 1973. "'Turning Out': A Study of Teenage Prostitution." *Urban Life and Culture* 4: 401–25.

Green, Ross Gordon, and Kearney Healey. 2003. *Tough on Kids: Rethinking Approaches to Youth Justice.* Saskatoon: Purich Publishing.

H.R. 1279 [109]: "Gang Deterrence and Community Protection Act of 2005." Legislation: 109 U.S. Congress (2005–2006). GovTrack.US. At <www.govtrack.us/congress/bill.xpd?bill=h109-1279> accessed July 3, 2007.

Hagan, John, and Bill McCarthy. 1998. *Mean Streets: Youth Crime and Homelessness.* Cambridge: Cambridge University Press.

Henry, R. 2013. "Social Spaces of Maleness: The Role of Street Gangs in Practicing Indigenous Masculinities." In K. Anderson and R. Innes (eds.), *Indigenous Masculinities in a Global Context.* Winnipeg, MB: University of Manitoba Press.

Hill, K.G., J.C. Howell, J.D. Hawkins and S.R. Battin-Pearson. 1999. "Childhood Risk Factors for Adolescent Gang Membership: Results from the Seattle Social Development Project." *Journal of Research in Crime and Delinquency* 36: 300–22.

Hirshi, T. 1969. *Causes of Delinquency.* Berkeley: University of California Press.

Hudson, Barbara. 2006. "Beyond White Man's Justice: Race, Gender and Justice in Late Modernity." *Theoretical Criminology* 10, 1: 29–47.

Hugill, David. 2010. *Missing Women, Missing News: Covering Crisis in Vancouver's Downtown Eastside.* Halifax and Winnipeg: Fernwood Publications.

James, Carl. 2002. "Armed and Dangerous: Racializing Suspects, Suspecting Race." In B. Schissel and C. Brooks (eds.), *Marginality and Condemnation: An Introduction to Critical Criminology.* Halifax: Fernwood Publishing.

Jarvinen, M. 1993. *Of Vice and Women: Shades of Prostitution.* Scandinavian Studies in Prostitution. Oslo: Scandinavian University Press.

Jiwani, Yasmin, and Mary Lynn Young. 2006. "Missing and Murdered Women: Reproducing Marginality in News Discourse." *Canadian Journal of Communication* 31: 895–917.

Katz, Jackson. 1999. *Tough Guise: Violence, Media, and the Crisis in Masculinity.* Media Education Foundation.

Kinsey, A.C., W.B. Pomeroy and C.E. Martin. 1948. *Sexual Behaviour in the Human Male.* London: W.B. Saunders.

Klemp-North, M. 2007. "Theoretical Foundations for Gang Membership." *Journal of Gang Research* 14: 11–25.

Lane, J., and J.W. Meeker. 2004. "Social Disorganization Perceptions, Fear of Gang Crime, and Behavioral Precautions among Whites, Latinos, and Vietnamese." *Journal of Criminal Justice* 32, 1: 49–62.

LaRocque, E.D. 1996. "The Colonization of a Native Woman Scholar." In C. Miller and P. Chuchryk (eds.), *Women of First Nations: Power, Wisdom and Strength.* Winnipeg: University of Manitoba Press.

Leclerc, J.B., and R. Wortley. 2013. *Cognition and Crime: Offender Decision Making and Script Analysis.* London: Routledge.

Lombroso, Cesare, and William Ferrero. 1895. *The Female Offender.* New York: Philosophical Library.

Lowman, John. 1987. "Taking Young Prostitutes Seriously." *Canadian Review of Sociology and Anthropology* 24, 1.

MacDonald, David, and Dan Wilson. 2013. "Poverty or Prosperity: Indigenous Children in Canada." Canadian Center for Policy Alternatives. June. At <savethechildren.ca/document.doc?id=361>.

Martin, Dianne. 2002. "Demonizing Youth, Marketing Fear: The New Politics of Crime." In Joe Hermer and Janet Mosher (eds.), *Disorderly People: Law and the Politics of Exclusion in Ontario.* Halifax: Fernwood Publishing.

McBride, J. 1995. *War, Battering, and Other Sports: The Gulf Between American Men and Women.* Atlantic Highlands, NJ: Humanities Press.

McIntyre, Mike. 2014. "More Gang Violence on Way: Sources Blame Drug Trade for Volatile Situation." *Winnipeg Free Press,* May 6. At <thecarillon.com/provincial/more-gang-violence-on-way-258065071.html>.

McLeod, E. 1982. *Women Working: Prostitution Now.* London: Croom Helm.

Messner, M., and D. Sabo. 1994. *Sex, Violence and Power in Sports: Rethinking Masculinity.* Freedom, CA: Crossing Press.

Miedzian, Miriam 1991. *Boys Will Be Boys: Breaking the Links Between Masculinity and Violence.* Toronto: Doubleday.

Minaker, J.C., and B. Hogeveen. 2009. *Youth, Crime, and Society: Issues of Power and Justice.* Toronto, ON: Pearson Education.

Monture-Angus, P. 1995. *Thunder in My Soul: A Mohawk Woman Speaks.* Halifax: Fernwood Publishing.

National Crime Prevention Center. 2012a. "Regina Anti-Gang Services." National Crime Prevention Center Website. At <http://www.publicsafety.gc.ca/res/cp/res/_fl/2012-es-26-eng.pdf>. Accessed April 2013.

___. 2012b. "Youth Alliance Against Gang Violence." National Crime Prevention Center Website. At <http://www.publicsafety.gc.ca/res/cp/res/_fl/yth-llnc-eng.pdf>. Accessed April 2013.

Nixon, Kendra, and Leslie M. Tutty. 2003 "'That Was My Prayer Every Night—Just to Get Home Safe': Violence in the Lives of Girls Exploited through Prostitution." In Kelly Gorkoff and Jane Runners (eds.), *Being Heard: The Experiences of Young Women in Prostitution.* Halifax: Fernwood Publishing and RESOLVE.

O'Neill, Maggie. 2001. *Prostitution and Feminism: Towards a Politics of Feeling.* Cambridge: Polity Press.

Okolie, A. 2005. "Toward an Anti-Racist Research Framework: The Case for Indepth Interviewing." In G.J. Sefa Dei and G.S. Johal (eds.), *Critical Issues in Anti-Racist Research Methodologies.* New York: P. Lang.

Papachristos, Andrew, and David Kirk. 2006. "Neighborhood Effects on Street Gang Behavior." *Studying Youth Gangs* 12: 63.

Petaluma Argus Courier. 2006. "Gang Attacks Becoming More Violent." February 15. At <www.arguscourier.com/news/news/gangactivity060215.html> accessed August 2007.

Phoenix, Joanna. 1999. *Making Sense of Prostitution.* London: MacMillan Press.

Ramsay, R., C. Gorst-Unsworth and S. Turner. 1993. "Psychiatric Morbidity in Survivors of Organized State Violence Including Torture: A Retrospective Series." *British Journal of Psychiatry* 162: 55–59.

Reeve, Karla. 2013. "The Morality of the 'Immoral': The Case of Drug-Using Street Prostitutes. *Deviant Behaviour* 34, 10: 824–40.

Reiman, Jeffrey. 2007. *The Rich Get Richer and the Poor Get Prison: Ideology, Class and Criminal Justice.* Eighth edition. Boston: Pearson.

Roberts, N. 1992. *Whores in History.* London: Harper Collins.

Robinson, L. 1998. *Crossing the Line: Violence and Sexual Assault in Canada's National Sport.*

Toronto: McClelland and Stewart.

Salomon, E. 1989. "The Homosexual Escort Agency: Deviance Disavowal." *British Journal of Sociology* 40, 1–21.

Schiraldi, V., and J. Zeidenberg. 1997. *The Risks Juveniles Face when They Are Incarcerated with Adults.* Washington, DC: The Justice Policy Institute.

Schur, Richard. 2002. "Critical Race Theory and the Limits of Auto/Biography: Reading Patricia Williams's The Alchemy of Race and Rights Through/Against Postcolonial Theory." *Biography* 25, 3 (Summer).

Sharkey, J.D., Z. Shekhtmeyster, L. Chavez-Lopez, E. Norris and L. Sass. 2011. "The Protective Influences of Gangs: Can Schools Compensate?" *Aggression and Violent Behavior* 16, 1: 45–54.

Sheldon, Randall G., Sharon K. Tracy and William B. Brown. 2001. *Youth Gangs in American Society,* Second edition. Belmont, CA: Wadsworth and Thompson Learning.

Shutt, J. Eagle, J.C. Barnes, Kevin M. Beaver, George E. Higgins and Richard Tewksbury. 2011. "Does Biology Underlie the Oldest Profession? Prostitution and Sex Disparities in John Behavior." *Biodemography and Social Biology* 57, 2: 155–70.

Sikka, Anette. 2009. "Trafficking of Aboriginal Women and Girls in Canada. Institute on Governance. At <iog.ca/publications/trafficking-of-aboriginal-women-and-girls-in-canada/>.

Smart, C. 1978. *Women, Crime and Criminology.* London: Macmillan.

___. 1989. *Feminism and the Power of Law.* London: Routledge.

___. 1992. *Regulating Womanhood: Historical Essays on Marriage, Motherhood and Sexuality.* London: Routledge.

Steenbeek, Wouter, and John R. Hipp. 2011. "A Longitudinal Test of Social Disorganization Theory: Feedback Effects between Cohesion, Social Control and Disorder." *Criminology* 49, 3: 833–71.

STR8UP. (2012). *STR8UP and Gangs: The Untold Stories.* Saskatoon, SK: Hear My Heart Books.

Sullivan, Mercer L. 1989. *Getting Paid: Youth Crime and Work in the Inner City.* Ithaca, NY: Cornell University Press.

___. 2005. "Maybe We Shouldn't Study 'Gangs': Does Reification Obscure Youth Violence?" *Journal of Contemporary Criminal Justice* 21, 2: 170–90.

Tator, Carol, and Frances Henry. 2006. *Racial Profiling in Canada: Challenging the Myth of a Few Bad Apples.* Toronto: University of Toronto Press.

Thornberry, T. 2006. "Toward an Interactional Theory of Delinquency." In F.T. Cullen R. Agnew (eds.), *Criminological Theory: Past to Present (Essential Readings),* third edition. Los Angeles, CA: Roxbury Publishing.

Toronto Sun. 2004. "Violent Youth Crime Rising." December 12. Violent Crime Statistics—Canada. At <http://www.fradical.com/Violent_crime_statistics_Canada.htm> accessed February 20th, 2006.

Totten, M. 2009. "Aboriginal Youth and Violent Gang Involvement in Canada: Quality Prevention Strategies." *IPC Review* 3: 135–56.

___. 2012. *Nasty, Brutish, and Short: The Lives of Gang Members in Canada.* Toronton, ON: James Lorimer.

Tustin, Lee, and Robert E. Lutes. 2007. *Guide to the Youth Criminal Justice Act.* Butterworths Canada Ltd.

UNICEF. 2012. "New League Tables of Child Poverty in the World's Rich Countries." Innocenti Report Card 10, written by Peter Adamson.

Vigil, J.D., and S.C. Yun. 1990. "Vietnamese Youth Gangs in Southern California." In C. Ronald Huff (ed.), *Gangs in America.* Newbury Park, CA: Sage.

Wacquant, Loïc. 2008. *Urban Outcasts: A Comparative Sociology of Advanced Marginality.* Cambridge, UK: Polity Press.

Walgrave, L., and G. Bazemore. 1999. *Restorative Juvenile Justice: Repairing the Harm of Youth Crime.* Monsey, NY: Criminal Justice Press.

West, Donald J. 1993; 2010. *Male Prostitution.* Binghamton: Hawthorn Press.

White, R. 2000. "Social Justice, Community Building and Restorative Strategies." *Contemporary Justice Review* 3, 1.

___. 2002. "Restorative Justice and Social Inequality." In B. Schissel and C. Brooks (eds.), *Marginality and Condemnation: An Introduction to Critical Criminology.* Halifax: Fernwood Publishing.

Wilkinson, R. 1955. *Women of the Streets: A Sociological Study of the Common Prostitute.* London: British Social and Biology Council.

Wilson, William Julius. 1996. *When Work Disappears: The World of the New Urban Poor.* New York: Random House.

Wood, J., and E. Alleyne. 2010. "Street Gang Theory and Research: Where Are We Now and Where Do We Go from Here?" *Aggression and Violent Behavior* 15,: 100–111. At <http://www.goccp.maryland.gov/msac/documents/gang-studies/gang-involvement-theory/Wood-Alleyne-2010.pdf>.

Woolford, A. 2009. *The Politics of Restorative Justice.* Halifax: Fernwood Publishing.

PART II

CRIME AND CLASS

The consensus approaches within criminology assume that the state and the criminal justice system are democratic institutions. They presume that the morality we share and the ways in which we understand crime and punishment are matters of collective agreement — hence, consensus. The general abhorrence of people who kill others is testament to a consensus about what constitutes murder. The consensus paradigm does not, however, question what is defined as murder or as "crime" generally, or whether certain classes or races are criminalized more often than others. For example, the killing of someone during wartime — especially someone in another country and of a different racial/ethnic background — is considered an act of courage and patriotism with no regard to how easy, one-sided or premeditated the killing might have been. Similarly, if the executive of a car company and various colleagues make a conscious decision to forgo safety measures to increase profits, they deliberately endanger (and perhaps ultimately murder) people. Those acts, however, are rarely considered to be acts of violence or murder. As acts that presumably do not immediately threaten the average citizen, they are somehow construed as acts of necessity or chance occurrences. That they are not part of people's fear of crime is an important consideration in understanding how average people come to understand good and evil behaviour.

As for the question of who tends to get punished for acts of murder, and as the chapters in this part of the book make clear, it is poor people, in general, who populate the prisons. The fundamental question is, then, whether the poor and disaffiliated people who are so numerous in prison are there because they are truly bad, or are they there because of their life circumstances. Are the types of crimes they commit the crimes that preoccupy the public consciousness — drug trafficking, shoplifting, assaults, robbery and theft? Are the poor more visible and vulnerable to police scrutiny than the average citizens because of where they live, their race or ethnicity, the way they dress, where they drink and how they speak? Perhaps they are highly vulnerable to conviction and punishment for other reasons: they cannot afford private lawyers; they and their families cannot provide alternatives to incarceration; they lack a permanent address or visible means of support; they are stereotypic reoffenders in the eyes of the police and judicial officials; or they cannot or do not speak the "language of justice."

These are fundamental questions that we must ask as we attempt to understand, through a critical lens, how the law works. At the end of the day, the common sense and legal/philosophical justification for the justice system and the system of punishment is that they are fair and objective. In jurisprudence, all individuals have the same opportunity in court to accuse their accusers, to have access to counsel and to have fair hearings before a judge and/or jury. The fairness of justice is based on the juridical principle that only the "facts" of the case are important in determining guilt or innocence. Extralegal considerations, such as race, class and gender, should not, in theory, influence seemingly impartial judgments in law. They may influence judges' decisions about lenient punishment, but, ironically, the leniency that judges display usually disadvantages the poor, powerless, "address-less," recidivist offender.

In response to these fundamental questions, critical criminologists question the role of human decisions in the creation of what is defined as "crime" and who is criminalized. These social categories are shaped by human decisions, which themselves are shaped by the needs of the social system. One inescapable conclusion here is that the criminal justice system helps to create the reality that we see; it does not reflect the reality of crime. It is true that people who live on the margins of society commit certain crimes more often than other people, and this reality is the focus of conventional criminology and of political and social policy. Poor people from the inner city do have relatively higher rates of shoplifting, street-drug use, soliciting and theft. But other considerations also must play a part: invisible theft and robbery occur at a corporate level — insider trading is theft of great magnitude; cocaine and marijuana use and alcohol abuse are very much middle-class activities, although they are rarely detected or admonished; and certain forms of prostitution serve a wealthy clientele and do not come under the purview of the police. It is relatively easy for academics, legal scholars and social policy administrators to focus on crimes that occur on the street. That focus is an act of politics, and it is a part of an ideology suggesting that we are most likely to be harmed by "individuals" who are dispossessed in our socio-economic hierarchy. Importantly, the perpetrators of these crimes become embedded in the public consciousness as the people we need to fear the most, the people who will create the most harm to a society.

The criminal justice system helps construct our morality, and it also determines who should be condemned and punished on the basis of socio-economic power. The critical criminology position, in response, focuses on the system of justice as a political body that is not impartial or unbiased. That the poor and racial minorities fill our prisons in contemporary Canadian society does not necessarily mean that they are the most likely to engage in socially harmful behaviour. On the contrary, critical criminology draws attention to how we excuse the rich at every stage of the criminal justice process, from the very definition of a criminal act to the sanctions of the police and judiciary. For example, the actions of corporations and the elite are often overlooked even when their actions pose a threat to social well-being. Yet the actions of the unemployed and poor are quite typically criminalized. They are more often incarcerated than wealthier lawbreakers, even when their behaviours are less damaging. Our definitions and understandings of violence and harm, then, are at once ideological and political. The law and criminal justice system, as well as journalistic and academic accounts of "criminality," are instruments of social control because they stigmatize and scapegoat some of the most disenfranchised people in our society.

The title of Part II, "Crime and Class," emphasizes that "crime" is not a universal concept but rather a social creation; moreover, punishment is highly discretionary and is served up not only to those who are easiest to punish but also to those who are most damaged by it. For example, fining an unemployed, penniless person living on the street makes little sense, because the punishment contributes to further impoverishment. Being sent to jail eventually stigmatizes the convicted person as an "ex-con" and takes the person out of the job market, both of which damage his/her chances for social advancement. The well-heeled corporate executive does not experience any similar damage to career or finances.

In Chapter 7, "Social Class and Invoking Criminality," Janet Mosher shows the link between marginality and condemnation by comparing "fraud" and tax "evasion." Tax evasion costs the taxpayer dramatically more money than welfare fraud, yet is not defined by the public as fraudulent (by contrast there seems to be an acceptance of this type of evasion) or a serious social problem. If tax evasion is detected, it is often seen as a minor transgression and gains only a solicitous response from the state. By contrast, welfare fraud is depicted as a crime against "the needy," and extreme public (and private) scrutiny (including the welfare snitch line) is encouraged. Any failure to abide by the (quite extreme) rules may result in severe penalties — including imprisonment. Mosher reminds readers that welfare fraud and tax evasion are similarly non-violent acts that defraud the state money, yet perpetrators are both judged and punished extremely differently. As Mosher states:

> Tax evaders benefit from the positive attributes commonly ascribed to the "taxpayer": employed, entrepreneurial, independent, hard-working, and self-reliant ... By contrast, welfare recipients, while occasionally evoking sympathy, are depicted as lazy, dependent, and untrustworthy free-riders.

Mosher's chapter demonstrates crime control as a political activity, one that "criminalizes" poverty and deregulates crimes of the more powerful in society.

In Chapter 8, "Corporations and Environmental Crime," Wei Wang and Hongming Cheng focus on why behavior that degrades the physical environment should be viewed as crime. The authors put forward the extent of social and environmental harm committed by corporations, providing a global portrait of a devastating situation affecting climate change, biodiversity, pollution, environmental and human health. They point out that the justice system does not often define harmful acts by corporations as being wrong, even though those acts may cause more death, injury, and environmental and financial ruin, than does street crime. We have evidenced the deregulation of the harmful acts of corporations and socio-economic elites. For example, although the environment is in a state of severe damage, over the last decade regulatory agencies have continued to have their budgets slashed. Cheng and Wang provide examples of the devastation involved. The cornerstone of this corporate motivation is the "new citizen," defined by consumerism and individualistic pursuits. The focus on the individual as the target of environmental responsibility directs public focus away from any sense of collective responsibility. The authors offer some hope that the power of corporate capitalism is becoming increasingly questioned and introduce the ideas of critical green criminology, a branch of criminology which advocates for regulatory measures in government intervention, market and non-market solutions, control regulation, recognition of environmental achievements, educational tools and economic incentives such as green funds.

In Chapter 9, "Imprisonment and Economic Marginality," Brooks describes the criminal justice system as an expensive mess, examining the link between contemporary forms of punishment and current economic and social conditions. Brooks explores the increase in poverty, homelessness and inequality that goes hand in hand with increasing globalization. Alongside growing inequalities we are witnessing a trend away from social welfare provisions towards social repression and the increase of policing and prisons, including measures such as Three-Strikes legislation, chain gangs and building maxi-maxi and high security prisons. Prison populations are increasing at a time when crime is declining. Brooks draws on Gramsci's notion of hegemony and Nils Christie's discussion of the prison industrial complex, to describe the ideological, structural and economic function of incarceration. By putting mostly poor and marginalized people in prison and taking up neo-liberal policies that focus on the individual offender in their approaches to rehabilitation or punishment, the state and the justice system leave the impression that the members of a certain class of people are more immoral or criminal than the average citizen. The media also reinforce individual or familial explanations of crime and suffering. When judges and other legal officials condemn the poor through their judicial decisions, they tell us, very covertly, that the poor are "morally defective," and, by implication, official legal messages to us are devoid of any consideration of how their crimes and their poverty could be symptomatic of socio-economic inequality. Brooks concludes that the so-called "dangerous classes" are "threatening" because they have the potential for revealing the fundamental injustices within the global economy. This chapter includes a discussion on why comparative criminology is important, briefly introducing comparisons of crime control measures in Nordic and other countries.

As the chapters in this part indicate, the people who are financially, socially and politically secure are rarely a part of the equation that links certain forms of bad behaviour to crime, immorality and punishment. Those who suffer the most from crime, those who are exploited because of their imputed criminal behaviour and those who are most severely punished by the criminal justice system all live on the margins of the social and economic hierarchy. If you strip away all the rhetoric of immorality and deviance, privation and marginalization are the ultimate crimes.

7

SOCIAL CLASS AND INVOKING CRIMINALITY

Janet Mosher

KEY FACTS

> Recent estimates of the underground economy range from 2.3 percent to 15.7 percent of GDP (the latter equaling an annual tax loss of $81.2 billion).

> Taxpayer segmentation data indicates that 13 percent of those surveyed fit the category of "outlaws," a group very likely to "cheat on their taxes," while a further 12 percent, the "rationalizers," are at moderate risk.

> Canada Revenue Agency data for 2012–13 show well over 300,000 audits out of some 43 million returns filed, generating billions of dollars in unpaid taxes. Only 71 files were referred for prosecution.

> The Criminal Code offence of fraud over $5,000 is an indictable offence carrying a maximum sentence of 14 years imprisonment. By comparison, the offence of tax evasion, if prosecuted by indictment (an approach reserved for serious cases involving, for example, the evasion of more that $250,000) carries a maximum term of imprisonment of five years.

> Taxpayers who have not reported all their income can avoid penalties and prosecution by making a voluntary disclosure.

> The wide public acceptance of tax evasion stands in sharp contrast to public sentiments regarding welfare fraud.

Sources: Schneider, Buehn and Montenegro 2010; CRA 2014; CRA 2015a, 2015b; *Criminal Code of Canada; Income Tax Act;* Mosher and Hermer 2010

A comparison between welfare fraud and tax evasion reveals striking differences in attributions of blameworthiness, the scope and intrusiveness of surveillance, the processing of suspected violations and sentencing patterns. Taxpayers who defraud the public purse, largely men with significant assets, are often regarded indulgently, while welfare recipients who defraud that same purse, more likely to be women and invariably poor, are harshly condemned. Tax evaders benefit from the positive attributes commonly ascribed to the "taxpayer": employed, responsible, independent, hard working and self-reliant. In short, the taxpayer epitomizes the good neo-liberal citizen. From this perspective, tax evaders invite not scrutiny of their actions, and punishment for their transgressions, but understanding, forgiveness and, in the minds of some, even respect. By contrast, welfare recipients, while occasionally evoking sympathy, are depicted as lazy, dependent and untrustworthy free-riders. Indeed, they are often explicitly positioned as the very antithesis of the taxpayer (obscuring the fact that they too pay taxes). This depiction builds upon and sustains a pervasive stereotype that caricatures welfare recipients as potential criminals, poised to defraud the state. To contain the threat posed by this class of undeserving, "failed" neo-liberal citizens, sweeping surveillance measures and harsh treatment seem not only reasonable, but also essential. While this stereotype of welfare recipients has deep historical roots, over the past two decades in Canada and a number of other countries (the United Kingdom and Australia for example) the stereotype has been reinvigorated and deployed to fundamentally transform welfare regimes.

The comparison between welfare fraud and tax evasion illustrates some of critical criminology's central insights. The intrusive and punitive regime that governs welfare recipients, by contrast to the relatively lax and forgiving treatment given taxpayers, together with the variations in the invocation of criminal law and criminal processes to deal with those who defraud the public purse, reveal the socially constructed and contingent nature of criminal misconduct. The comparison also shows how criminal law is engaged in a political project; the state's selective invocation of criminal law in relation to frauds upon the public purse serves to create and maintain categories of deserving and undeserving citizens that in turn, reproduce neo-liberal norms. Welfare recipients, as a class, are punished because they are not the self-reliant, independent citizens required by neo-liberalism. They are defined as criminals not because of what they have done, but rather because of who they are. Tax evaders, as good neo-liberal citizens, largely escape attributions of criminality and criminal justice processing.

WELFARE FRAUD: THE CONSTRUCTION OF A PROBLEM

In Ontario, sweeping reforms were introduced in the mid-1990s with the enactment of the *Ontario Works Act, 1997* (welfare benefits) and the *Ontario Disability Support Program Act, 1997* (disability benefits). For recipients without statutorily recognized disabilities the reforms included the introduction of "workfare" (benefits made conditional on participation in employment or employment readiness activities), the reduction of benefit levels by 21.6 percent, a new definition of "spouse" (resulting in some 8,000 single mothers being cut off assistance) and a host of measures to fight welfare fraud. Indeed, the government identified fighting welfare fraud, ensuring individual responsibility and addressing the needs of persons with disabilities as the three key objectives of the legislative reforms. Since 1997, only a handful of modest legislative changes have been introduced, and benefit levels as of 2012 (at $599 per month for a single person) were, in real terms, $225 less than immediately following the 21.6 percent cut (Stapleton 2012).

As in many other jurisdictions, "fighting" welfare fraud was — and continues to be — strategically deployed to diminish the role of the state in the provision of social welfare and to enforce individual responsibility through labour market participation (Henman and Marston 2008; Marston and Walsh 2008; Prenzler 2010, 2011; McKeever 2012). Central to this strategy has been the construction of welfare fraud as a problem spinning out of control, requiring aggressive new measures to tackle it. In seeking to convince the public that the problem was real and urgent, a number of tactics common to claims-makers were deployed (Parnaby 2003). At critical junctures welfare fraud has been depicted as a significant problem, with rhetorical claims about its magnitude and harms abounding. The invocation by the state of explicitly criminal terms — "fraud," "cheats," "liars," "theft," "zero tolerance" and "crackdowns," or in Australia and the United Kingdom, "dole bludgers," "scroungers" and "dole cheats" — has aided in the construction of the problem as a criminal menace and thus all the more serious and threatening.

During the period of significant reforms in Ontario in the mid-late 1990s, welfare fraud "cheat sheets" were posted on the government's website, and accounts of complex frauds involving multiple fabricated identities appeared in local media, further contributing to the sense of serious criminality. Capitalizing upon the lack of definitional clarity and precision as to just what constitutes welfare fraud, the "official statistics" widely circulated by the government included all errors giving rise to an overpayment (but tellingly not an underpayment) of welfare benefits, dramatically increasing the depth of the problem. McKeever (2012: 474) describes a similar strategy currently underway in the United Kingdom.

The government's *Welfare Fraud Control Report 2001–2002* exemplifies this collapsing of fraud and error (Ontario, Ministry of Community, Family and Children's Services 2003). The report is permeated with the language of "fraud"; reference is made to the Welfare Fraud Hotline, to the fraud control database to track fraud investigations, to "anti-fraud measures [that] help catch welfare cheats and deter others from thinking about cheating" and to welfare fraud as a crime that the government is cracking down on through the introduction of a zero-tolerance policy. The report claims that "over $49 million was identified in social assistance payments that people were not entitled to receive and an estimated $12 million in avoided future costs" (1). Given the general thrust of the report and its title, the message conveyed is that these dollars are directly attributable to welfare fraud. But a close examination reveals a different picture; in 2001–2 there were 38,452 fraud investigations, resulting in only 393 convictions for welfare fraud (representing approximately 0.1 percent of the caseload) and 12,816 cases where assistance was reduced or terminated as a result of the Ministry reassessing the recipient's case. In more than 12,000 cases, fraud had not been established, no crime had been proven and any dollars saved were not the result of fraud detection. While some of the 12,000 cases may represent a modest number of instances where prosecution was not recommended even though there existed a strong case to support a conviction for fraud, the vast majority are likely to be instances where an administrative rule had been broken, but without the requisite intent to constitute criminal fraud — in other words, they were the result of client misunderstanding, oversight or error. But the report, by collapsing all errors into fraud and through its use of terms such as "cheats," "cracking down on crime" and "zero tolerance," portrays a picture of criminal fraud as rampant and, correspondingly, of recipients as actual or potential criminals. To understand both how readily this collapsing occurs and how problematic it is, a fuller exploration of the crime of "fraud" and its interface with the welfare regime is essential.

WHAT IS FRAUD?

Fraud is governed by section 380 of Canada's *Criminal Code*.[1] As with other criminal offences, fraud has two components: the *actus reus* (the guilty act) and the *mens rea* (the guilty mind). The *actus reus* of fraud contains two elements: the prohibited act (of "deceit, falsehood or other fraudulent means") and the deprivation that is caused by the prohibited act. While "deceit, falsehood and fraudulent means" are three separate heads, the courts have held that the real core of the offence of fraud is dishonesty (Ewart 1986).

Whether an act is appropriately characterized as dishonest is to be determined not by reference to the accused's subjective mental state (whether the accused subjectively believed the act in question to be dishonest) but by whether a reasonable person would stigmatize the act in question as dishonest. The Supreme Court of Canada, in *R. v. Olan* (1978), noted that while "dishonesty" was difficult to define with precision, it connotes an underhanded design, is discreditable, or even unscrupulous.

The *mens rea* of fraud also contains two elements: subjective knowledge of the prohibited act (the act which, based upon a reasonableness standard, is appropriately stigmatized as dishonest) and subjective knowledge that the prohibited act could have as a consequence the deprivation of another. With regard to the second of these elements, the accused must have a subjective awareness that undertaking the prohibited act (of deceit, falsehood or other dishonest means) could cause deprivation. In his concurring judgment in *R. v. Théroux* (1993), Justice Sopinka (with whom then Chief Justice Lamer joined), took care to point out the necessity of distinguishing between the conclusion that an accused's belief that his act is honest will not prevail if objectively the act is dishonest and his belief in facts that would deprive the act of its dishonest character. This distinction is a crucial one, yet while it seems to be dutifully drawn in the tax context, it is regularly obscured in the context of welfare.

The case of *R. v. Maldonado* (1998) illustrates the importance of the distinction. Mr. Maldonado was in receipt of General Welfare Assistance, the precursor to what is now Ontario Works (ow). He had been told that he must report any change in income to social services. When his wife obtained part-time employment, it was dutifully reported. But when he began attending school and obtained a student loan he did not report it. When the Ministry learned that Mr. Maldonado had received the loan, he was charged with fraud. His evidence was that he had not considered a loan to be income, since it had to be repaid, so he had not contemplated that it needed to be reported. He did not know that the Ontario Works Regulations defined "income" to include loans. Nor did he know that had the loan been reported, his benefits would have been reduced. Based on Supreme Court jurisprudence, it will not matter if Mr. Maldonado subjectively believed his actions to be honest. The question is whether his actions are appropriately stigmatized as dishonest — not merely negligent, but as discreditable, underhanded or unscrupulous. Or to invoke Justice Sopinka's query, is there a belief by the accused in a set of facts (here, that a loan is not income and need not be reported) that would deprive the act of its dishonest character? Surely the answer here is affirmative; applying an objective standard, Mr. Maldonado's belief that a loan was not income and thus not reportable suggests that his actions ought not to be characterized as "dishonest." Moreover, given his belief in this set of facts, he lacked the subjective knowledge that the non-reporting could have as a consequence the deprivation of another. Justice Weagant, the trial judge hearing Mr. Maldonado's case, concluded the trial by stating the following:

> Not only do I have a doubt that Mr. Maldonado did not have the subjective knowledge of the possibility of deprivation, I am quite sure he did not ... I would not be surprised if Mr. Maldonado, even if given a copy of the Regulations to read for himself, were unable to glean the true meaning of "income" or "change of circumstances." The Regulations are extremely complicated and difficult to read ... my own experience of wading through the Regulations leads me to believe their inaccessibility plays a major role in the scenario under consideration. The Regulations governing the question of entitlement are fiendishly difficult to

understand ... the sense or structure of the policy which might help a person on welfare to determine when he or she is breaking the law, is not apparent on the face of the Regulation. (*R. v. Maldonado* 1998: para. 29, 40, 41, 43)

It is important to appreciate how complex the welfare system is (Matthews 2004). Governed by some 800 rules that determine eligibility, it is, as Justice Weagant observed, "fiendishly difficult" to comprehend. Many of the rules are counter-intuitive, others incomprehensible, and it is extremely difficult to access accurate and timely information about the governing rules. Not uncommonly, recipients find themselves in situations in which a "fraud" allegation hangs in the air, if not formally charged, where they had no idea that the rule they had allegedly violated existed at all: that many loans are treated as income and must be reported (as in the case of Mr. Maldonado); that gifts and "voluntary payments of small value" are also treated as income and reportable (although a recent reform exempts up to $6000 over 12 months); or that details about intimate relationships are expected to be disclosed (and just what level of detail is far from clear) (Mosher 2010). Given the number of rules, their complexity and their impenetrability, it is hardly surprising that inadvertent rule violations are an endemic feature of the welfare system. Indeed, a government report prepared by the Honourable Deb Matthews concludes that the complexity of the system and the difficulties of adequately communicating the rules make client error — and indeed significant system error — unavoidable (Matthews 2004). Problematically, however, the careful reasoning of Justice Weagant is not characteristic of the approach of officials within the social assistance system, nor even within the criminal justice system. Rather, recipients' lack of knowledge of the complex, voluminous and "fiendishly difficult" requirements of welfare law and regulations is routinely, and wrongly, assumed to be irrelevant to the question of whether fraud has been committed. When virtually all rule breaches are characterized as fraud, every recipient who breaches a rule — whether through inadvertence, lack of knowledge/information, mental or cognitive disability or misunderstanding — is tainted with the moral brush of criminality. The routine categorization of such rule violations as criminal fraud is the sleight of hand that has rendered welfare fraud a serious problem and welfare recipients a dangerous class. It also, of course, renders all welfare recipients less deserving of public support and thus helps to facilitate the state's retreat from the provision of support to its citizens and a corresponding reinvigoration of the enforcement of private obligations.

TAMING WELFARE FRAUD

To respond to the serious problem that welfare fraud was constructed to be, a broad array of measures was introduced in the mid-1990s, and since then, they have been continuously refined. In turn, the extent, breadth and severity of these measures have served to solidify the construction of welfare fraud as a serious problem. These various measures are best understood as tools of surveillance (Maki 2011), defined by Lyon as "the collection and processing of personal data, whether identifiable or not, for the purposes of influencing or managing those whose data have been garnered" (cited in Henman and Marston 2008: 191). As Henman and Marston maintain, surveillance occurs in the context of relationships characterized by inequalities of power (2008: 188). The intensity of surveillance signals not only the depth of those inequalities, but also the social value ascribed to those who are the objects of its gaze (Mulzer 2005, Dee 2013).

VERIFICATION MEASURES

In a succession of reports, the provincial Auditor General has noted modest improvements in verification systems, but has consistently called for yet further steps to ensure only those truly eligible are receiving benefits, and in the correct amount (Auditor General Ontario 2009, 2011). Responding to these concerns, various new technologies and practices have been introduced over the past two decades, beginning with "enhanced verification," shifting to "consolidated verification" and, most recently, in 2012, to a new "eligibility verification model" (EVM). Developed by Equifax, the EVM employs a risk-based model to identify "cases in which there is a high likelihood that there has been a change in the recipient's financial eligibility" (Ontario, Policy Directive 9.1, 2013). It promises new and better risk flags (Commission for Review of Social Assistance 2012: 102–03). Each month, the entire Ontario Works caseload is run through the EVM to rank the highest risk cases, with the top three percent of high-risk cases distributed to delivery agents for review (Daley 2011; Commission for Review of Social Assistance 2012: 102–03).

As is clear from the above, measures to gather information and verify eligibility occur not only at the time of application but in an on-going manner. The amount of information required to be provided at the time of applying for assistance and during regular or risk-determined reviews is sweeping, as is the scope of the consent to the collection and release of information that must be signed as a precondition to receiving benefits. The extensive and ongoing reporting requirements, together with a host of information-sharing agreements negotiated with a range of provincial and federal departments, permit the ministry to gather and share vast amounts of information about social assistance recipients. Third-party checks to verify eligibility are conducted through the Ministry of Transportation (vehicle ownership), Equifax Canada (asset verification), the Family Responsibility Office (child and support obligations), Canada Revenue Agency (income verification) and Employment Insurance (employment history) (Ontario, Policy Directive 2.1, 2013). These networks of communication serve not only to verify information, but also to trigger the surveillance technologies embedded within other ministries and departments. This "convergence of what were once discrete surveillance systems" operates to from what Haggerty and Ericson have termed a "surveillant assemblage" (2000).

THE WELFARE SNITCH LINE

The public is charged with a responsibility — a civic duty — to engage in the surveillance of welfare recipients. As noted above, the public is told that welfare fraud is rampant, that people not genuinely in need are taking money from the pockets of the hard-working taxpayer. One way to discharge this civic duty is to call a toll-free welfare fraud hotline (6,527 people did in 2001–2, down from 9,348 in 2000–1). Introducing the welfare fraud hotline on October 2, 1995, then minister of community and social services David Tsubouchi proclaimed in the House, "Welfare fraud is a problem that hurts the most vulnerable people in our society. Every cent that is paid to the wrong person through fraud is help taken from the needy." He noted that experience had shown hotlines to be an effective device to ensure this does not happen, projected savings of $25 million per year and invited the people of Ontario to call 1-800-394-STOP to help "stop fraud and to protect the system for people who really need help" (Ontario Legislative Assembly, *Hansard* October 2, 1995). The current website of the Ministry of Community and Social Services notes that there are "some who take unfair advantage of assistance programs" and undertakes that "if you want to report welfare fraud we will take you very seriously" and "every case will be investigated."

As the number of calls to the snitch line suggest, recipients' lives are scrutinized intensely by non-state actors. Present or current abusive boyfriends or spouses, landlords and neighbours have all taken up the government's invitation to participate in the surveillance project (Mosher and Hermer 2005). There is no doubt that class, gender and race stereotypes play a role in shaping who is scrutinized and reported as "suspicious," creating differential impacts on particular groups of recipients: racialized peoples, single women and, most pervasively, racialized women (Mirchandani and Chan 2005). This solicitation of the public into the role of "watchers" is helpfully understood as a form of public participatory surveillance in which "responsible citizens" are enlisted to report suspicious activity. As Larsen and Piché argue, drawing the public into this role creates both "new forms of responsibilized citizenship and novel opportunities for exclusion and othering" (2009: 197).

In addition, the snitch line is not uncommonly used for purposes completely extraneous to preventing or detecting fraud. Abusive men make false reports to further their power and control over women, landlords make false reports to facilitate the eviction of a tenant and vindictive neighbours or other acquaintances make false or misleading reports simply out of spite (Mosher, Evans and Little 2004; Mosher and Hermer 2005)

FRAUD INVESTIGATIONS

Significant numbers of fraud allegations are made annually; over 35,000 in 2001–2 and over 52,000 in 2000–1. While recent provincial data are not publicly available, the City of Toronto (one of 48 regions for the administration of ow) carried out more than 9,000 reviews in 2007 in response to allegations of fraud or abuse (identifying 700 overpayments and resulting in 15 criminal proceedings) (City Auditor General 2008).

After an initial review of an allegation of fraud, if a determination is made that a more thorough review is required, the matter is referred to an Eligibility Review Officer (ERO). After a comprehensive review, the ERO makes a determination as to whether eligibility will continue and whether to make a referral to police (Ontario, Policy Directive 9.1, 2013). If there is sufficient evidence to suspect intent to commit fraud, the Policy Directive provides that the case *must* be referred to the police for investigation under the *Criminal Code*. Notwithstanding this Directive, the provincial Auditor General has expressed concern that tips from the fraud hotline are being ignored or inadequately investigated and that the numbers of referrals to police are extremely low (reflecting approximately one percent of all tips across the three service municipalities audited) (2009:266). In response, the Ministry has reiterated that where sufficient evidence exists staff is directed to refer all cases of suspected welfare fraud to police and has promised to further improve fraud investigation practices "through the development of additional tools that support effective program management and oversight" (Auditor General Ontario 2009: 267).

The owa and regulations grant significant powers to EROs to undertake their investigations of fraud allegations, including to enter any place other than a dwelling if there exist reasonable grounds to believe that evidence relevant to eligibility may be found there and to require the production of records. EROs have the right to obtain "information or material from a person who is the subject of an investigation … or from any person who the officer has reason to believe can provide information or material relevant to the investigation" (Ontario Regulation 134/98, s.65). These powers are reinforced by subsection 79(3) of the Act, which makes it an offence to obstruct or knowingly give false information to a person engaged in an investigation.

In the course of their investigations, EROs will often seek information from landlords, neighbours, teachers and others who may know something of the circumstances of the recipient under investigation. Additionally, an investigation will often include a meeting with the person who is the subject of the investigation. While practices may have changed subsequently, research conducted in 2004 found that Charter cautions were not routinely provided during these meetings, even though the evidence gathered was regularly used against recipients in the event of subsequent criminal prosecutions (Mosher and Hermer 2005). Certainly one characterization of these meetings is that they are solely for the purpose of determining eligibility and are thus integrally connected to the enforcement of a regulatory regime. But a competing and compelling characterization is that they often take the form of *de facto* criminal investigations and, as such, require Charter warnings and limitations on the use of evidence so gathered. While the issue of when a regulatory investigation becomes a *de facto* criminal investigation has received significant attention in the context of income tax, it has received very little critical interrogation in the realm of welfare (*R. v. Jarvis* 2002). This omission is disconcerting because it appears to be not uncommon for police and Crown Attorneys to rely upon the investigations undertaken by EROs in their prosecution of persons accused of welfare fraud. Given the number of fraud investigations and given the statutory power of EROs to compel information, there is a strong concern that the Charter rights of recipients are being violated.

A related concern is that recipients under investigation who are called in for a meeting with an ERO frequently do not fully understand the import of the interview or that the statements given may subsequently be used against them in a fraud prosecution. Moreover, fearing a possible criminal charge, and within a broad context in which fraud language is pervasive and recipients are constantly dehumanized, those accused of fraud (even inferentially) may agree all too readily to administrative sanctions such as terminations or overpayments (Mosher and Hermer 2005). Recipients are also understandably reluctant to complain about mistreatment during investigations. They are, after all, in a position of extreme vulnerability in their interactions with agents of the administrative regime who have the power to cut them off benefits, assess overpayments and refer matters to the police. Rocking the boat almost always promises to be more trouble than it is worth.

A HOME VISIT

An additional tool for verification, and in some circumstances investigative, purposes is euphemistically called "the home visit." OW workers, with consent of the applicant or recipient, may enter the home to verify information that is "in plain view." A "visit," which may occur with or without notice, may be refused, but absent a valid reason for the refusal, denial or cancellation of benefits may be the consequence. Additionally, an ERO may, with consent of the applicant or acting under the authority of a search warrant, enter the home for the purposes of a fraud investigation (Ontario, Policy Directive 2.8, 2013).

LIVING UNDER A MICROSCOPE

Recipients variously describe the experience of being on ow as "living under a microscope" or "having one's life gone through with a fine-tooth comb," where virtually everything you do is everyone's business (Mosher and Hermer 2005). The climate around recipients' interactions with the system is permeated with suspicion and hostility, and constant fear is part of their everyday reality: fear of not being able to meet the basic needs of their children, fear of losing custody, fear of declining health, fear — especially for their children — of the impacts of social ostracism, stigmatization and discrimination and fear of breaching a rule or of someone calling the snitch line and becoming the target of a hostile investigation. Front-line workers sometimes encourage this latter fear. Recipients report being told by their workers that they know they must be up to something because it is just not possible to survive on their welfare cheques and that it will only be a matter of time before they figure out exactly what they are up to (Herd and Mitchell 2002).

Verification procedures perform functions well beyond that of verifying entitlement (Maki 2011; Mulzer 2005). Rather where, as here, such procedures create a dense web of surveillance, they perform an essential role in signaling deservedness and disciplining populations:

> stringent and invasive verification procedures stigmatize the receipt of benefits and express these concerns to claimants. At the same time, these procedures serve as a sign to the public that their concerns are well-founded ... Verification procedures both assuage public fears — seemingly guaranteeing that only the "deserving" are given aid — and reaffirm the assumptions upon which they fears are based. (Mulzer 2005: 683)

HARSH PENALTIES FOR CONVICTION: THE LIFETIME BAN AND INCARCERATION

Perhaps the most punitive measure introduced in the new welfare fraud control regime was an additional penalty upon conviction. The Ontario Government first introduced a three-month ban on receipt of welfare for a first conviction (six months for subsequent convictions) and later a lifetime ban (for crimes committed after April 1, 2000). Thus, upon conviction for welfare fraud, one was automatically banned for life from receiving welfare benefits. The constitutionality of the lifetime ban was under challenge when the Liberal Government announced its repeal in December 2003, while at the same time introducing a revised Policy Directive making referral of cases by welfare administrators to the police mandatory in all cases where there is sufficient evidence to suspect intent to commit fraud (*R. v. Broomer* 2002; Ontario, Policy Directive 45, 2004). The potential for a return to a lifetime ban re-emerged during the 2011 Ontario provincial election in the "Changebook" of the Progressive Conservative Party, promising that "the worst repeat offenders of welfare fraud will face tough penalties, up to a lifetime ban." In British Columbia, a lifetime ban on receipt of income assistance continues in effect. Although a hardship allowance is potentially available, it must be applied for on a monthly basis.

Notwithstanding that both the owa and the *Ontario Disability Support Program Act, 1997* (odspa) contain offence provisions that prohibit knowingly obtaining assistance to which one is not entitled, these provisions are never utilized. Rather, it is the policy of the Ministry to deal with such matters as criminal, rather than as provincial, offences.

SENTENCING: "THE MOST DESPICABLE FORM OF THEFT"

Significantly, conviction for welfare fraud has long attracted disproportionately harsh punishments (Mosher and Hermer 2005; Martin 1992).

The primacy accorded the principle of general deterrence and the characterization of welfare fraud as a serious crime involving a breach of trust have supported a *de facto* presumption of imprisonment as the appropriate sentence. *R. v. Thurrott* (1971), a decision of the Ontario Court of Appeal, has long been regarded as a leading case on this matter. In *Thurrott* the court observed,

> although this case is pitiful in many respects, this Court is unanimously of the opinion that the paramount consideration in determining the sentence is the element of deterrence. Welfare authorities have enough difficulties without having to put up with persons who set out to defraud them. This is one such instance, and others who are similarly minded must be warned that these offences will not be treated lightly. (461)

The trial court had ordered five months imprisonment for a fraud of $1,700 and the Court of Appeal affirmed that anywhere up to five months would be an appropriate sentence. Subsequent cases have confirmed that absent unusual or exceptional mitigating circumstances, a period of incarceration is presumptively warranted.

The British Columbia Court of Appeal's decision in *R. v. Friesen* (1994), another influential precedent, not only affirmed general deterrence as the paramount concern, but also characterized welfare fraud as a "crime in respect of which there is a real chance that substantial penal consequences will deter." A sentence of nine months of incarceration and restitution of $12,000 was imposed.

Of the fifty cases reviewed by Dianne Martin in the early 1990s, a jail sentence was ordered in 80 percent (Martin 1992). A review of fifty-eight welfare fraud sentencing decisions covering the period 1989–2002, revealed that custodial sentences were ordered in thirty-three, conditional sentences (house arrest) in fifteen, suspended sentences in eight, a conditional discharge in one and a fine in another. Given that a conditional sentence can only be imposed if the circumstances warrant a period of incarceration, the fifteen cases of conditional sentences are appropriately grouped together with those where a jail term was imposed to generate an incarceration rate of 83 percent. In thirty of the cases, sentences also included a restitution or compensation order, and in thirteen cases, community service orders ranging from 100 to 300 hours (Mosher and Hermer 2005). In a recent review of sentencing patterns in Australia, Marston and Walsh come to a similar conclusion: while most cases reviewed involved small debts and complex underlying causes, imprisonment was taken as the starting point in sentencing (Marston and Walsh 2008: 292).

JUSTIFICATORY FRAMEWORK

Several common tropes invoked by Crown prosecutors and judges provide the justificatory framework to support imprisonment as the appropriate sentence in cases of welfare fraud. One of the most common tropes personalizes the state; judges are at pains to point out that a crime has been committed not against some faceless, amorphous entity but against every citizen of the community. Welfare fraud is described as, "depriving all citizens of the province" or as a "crime against every member of the community" (*R. v. McIsaac* (1998), *R. v. Gallagher* (1996), *R. v. Reid* (1995)). It is rendered a crime of colossal proportions; unlike a simple theft from a single individual, the pocketbooks of every citizen have been pinched.

It is not uncommon for judges to admonish the accused for having taken from those genuinely in need, inferring that the accused is herself not genuinely in need and obscuring the reality that while there are indeed some instances of complex schemes to defraud the state, in the overwhelming majority of cases, need and desperation motivate the actions. This trope is often elaborated to render the accused responsible for the difficult circumstances of others on welfare; judges will suggest that every extra penny the accused has received has caused a corresponding diminution of money available for those "genuinely in need." Moreover, recipients who "abuse" the system by stealing from those "genuinely in need" are blamed for eroding taxpayers' willingness to fund the system. Consider, for example, the case of *R. v. McGillivray* (1992), in which the accused was sentenced to six months' incarceration and one year of probation for a fraud of $23,263. The accused had not disclosed her common-law relationship with a man whose only income was a student loan and from whom she received no financial benefit (note that the court does not query whether on the facts the state had been deprived, an essential — and one would have thought contested — issue in this case given their potential eligibility for benefits as a couple). Although Justice Daniel found that by all accounts the accused was "an emotionally abused, battered wife who is very much manipulated by her boyfriend," he went on to characterize her actions as criminal insofar as her living arrangements were concerned. Justice Daniel, in sentencing the accused, quoted favourably from another case in which welfare fraud was described as the "most despicable form of theft," and its impact explained as follows:

> There is only a certain amount of money available for people in need. And as the fund is abused by people who are not entitled to it, there is less money to go around, and others who possibly need more help simply don't receive it ... So theft of this nature is, when you analyze it, really a theft from the poorest people of the community. And that is one of the major reasons that this type of offence must be treated very, very seriously by the Courts. (p3)

Similarly, in *R. v. Friesen* (1994) discussed earlier, the British Columbia Court of Appeal highlighted the strain on taxpayers of providing for the "truly needy" and characterized the welfare system as a "fragile system, easily invaded by those such as the accused."

Judges are also given to characterizing welfare fraud as a violation of trust, and thus a serious matter (and an aggravating factor for sentencing purposes). One way of understanding the nature of the trust at issue is that the welfare system, as judges are prone to point out, depends upon self-reporting. The system's functioning and integrity are portrayed as entirely dependent upon recipients' candour and honesty (a characterization which neatly obscures the depth of surveillance described earlier), and in this sense, recipients are being trusted to make full disclosure. But one also has a sense that the nature of the trust and of the violation at issue may well be something quite different. Cases in which the offence is characterized as a violation of trust are frequently marked by a tone of self-righteousness and outrage that the accused has taken advantage of the taxpayer, whose largesse and compassion have not been dutifully respected and gratefully appreciated.

Both explicitly in their remarks, and more commonly implicit in their failure to acknowledge the circumstances of those who commit these "crimes," judges project a particular view about the welfare state: that it provides a finely woven web of protection, ensuring that no one goes without adequate shelter or food. These assumptions about the extent of welfare assistance are profoundly out of step with the realities of life on welfare. Most recipients struggle to survive, often depleting their monthly benefits to secure accommodation. But the mistaken assumption that the welfare state provides adequately for all lends itself to a characterization of those who are accused of fraud as greedy, rather than needy, and of the taxpayer as righteously indignant that his generosity has been exploited. Thus, the strongly articulated sense of a violation of trust seems to flow more directly from a view that taxpayer generosity and largesse have been exploited, than from welfare recipients' failure to make full disclosure within a system whose integrity depends on the candour of its beneficiaries.

At least on occasion, courts have been prepared to depart from a strict adherence to the principles of deterrence and denunciation to grant a conditional discharge. In *R. v. Wilson* (2005), the accused had failed to report the receipt of student loans and income from part-time employment, under-reported child support and over-reported the amount paid for rent. The amounts were significant: $20,000 in social assistance and $44,000 in rent subsidies. Ms. Wilson, at the time of sentencing, had obtained two bachelor degrees, was working full time and pursuing a master's degree. Although the Crown sought a conditional sentence (house arrest) of four to six months, Justice Lampkin ordered a conditional discharge. While agreeing with the Crown's characterization of welfare fraud as a serious crime, Justice Lampkin reasoned that a conviction would result in the loss of the accused's employment, the "community would lose her specialized training in child welfare" and she "would no longer be a contributing member of society" (2005: para.18). Certainly one way of understanding this case is that Ms. Wilson, now well educated and self-supporting had, in the eyes of Justice Lampkin, transformed herself into a proper neo-liberal citizen.

The courts have also granted discharges in cases where mental illness contributed significantly to the offending and have prioritized the principle of rehabilitation in sentencing the accused in such cases (*R. v. Fayemi* 2009). In *R. v. Dennis* (2013), the British Columbia Court of Appeal was persuaded by a range of factors — the accused was an Aboriginal woman with fetal alcohol spectrum disorder who had been in an abusive relationship and as a result of a fraud conviction involving $1,382 was subject to a life-time ban on receipt of income assistance (a consequence that her defence lawyer was unaware of at the time her guilty plea was entered) — to substitute a one-year conditional sentence, three years of probation and full restitution with a conditional discharge and three years of probation.

Yet in *R. v. McCloy* (2008), the court insisted that notwithstanding the accused was employed and supporting his family, his wife's disability prevented her from working and together with their four young children the couple resided in a campground, "society's abhorrence" of his crime in failing to disclose $11,000 in employment income warranted a period of incarceration of sixty days. He was ordered to serve his time on weekends, so that he might preserve his weekday employment. No restitution order was made, as it was understood that the funds would be recovered through deductions from the government benefits to which his wife was entitled.

In sentencing, judges consistently emphasize what the accused has taken from her community (or from "the taxpayer"). Unlike the tax evader, rarely are her contributions acknowledged. This is starkly evident in the 2001 case of Kimberly Rogers, who tragically died, eight months pregnant while serving a six-month conditional sentence for welfare fraud — a sentence that permitted her to leave her sweltering apartment for three hours one day each week. In sentencing Ms. Rogers for her failure to disclose the student loans she had received, Justice Rodgers admonished her in the following terms: "This is how serious the matter is, Ms. Rogers. There is a jail term that is going to be involved, it just happens to be a jail term that will be served in your home, and not at the expense of the community. You have taken enough from the community." In Justice Rodgers' view, Kimberly Rogers was so dehumanized that even jail was too good for her; she was to fund her own incarceration and to do so without access to welfare benefits (she was subject to a three-month ban, which was subsequently lifted through an injunction obtained as part of a constitutional challenge; but even then she had only $18/month to live on).

Restitution orders also create incredible burdens for low-income people. Many of those convicted of welfare fraud are receiving social assistance at the time of sentencing. Their benefits will be reduced by 5 to 10 percent to collect the monies owing as a result of the overpayment. Given that existing benefit levels are already below what is required for subsistence, taking more money away means further reducing people's ability to meet basic needs. Moreover, because in most instances it was need that led to the "crime" in the first place, further decreasing recipients' income serves to tighten the knot of the moral double bind they are forced to confront. Complete candour about money or food received from friends or family, or small amounts of earned income may prevent allegations of fraud, but full disclosure commonly results in a dollar-for-dollar deduction from one's welfare cheque, leaving recipients unable to meet their basic needs and those of their children.

Thus, in many of the reported cases decision-makers do not try to understand the realities of life on welfare; rather they construct, demean and devalue the "other" as all that they are not. While some aspects of the life of the accused may be described in the decision, that context is quickly discarded as irrelevant, rather than mitigating. So too, the accused's circumstances, while considered "pitiful," are often seen as her own fault — ignoring the ways in which social structures, institutions and ideologies construct and limit choices. This juxtaposition of the welfare recipient and the taxpayer, and the values and attributes ascribed to each, underlies the starkly different treatment of welfare fraud and tax evasion.

INCOME TAX EVASION

While income tax evasion will usually meet the *Criminal Code* test for fraud, it is most commonly prosecuted under subsection 239(1)(d) of the *Income Tax Act*. This subsection defines income tax evasion as conduct that "wilfully, in any manner, evaded or attempted to evade compliance with this Act or payment of taxes imposed by this Act." While the offence has been characterized by the Supreme Court of Canada as criminal in nature and as such requiring full *mens rea* for conviction, the terminology of "evasion" and the avoidance of explicitly criminal terms soften the image of the tax evader and render the harms of tax evasion less obvious and troubling.

The proper functioning of the income tax system is largely dependent upon the candour of taxpayers in the full and honest disclosure of income. While for many taxpayers taxes are deducted at source, leaving little room for hiding income, it is often those with larger incomes and/or who are self-employed who have the greatest opportunities to evade taxes (Giles and Tedds 2002; CRA 2005). The precise amount of income not disclosed to the Canada Revenue Agency (CRA), either as a result of taxpayer error (similar to welfare, the rules governing tax are extremely complex, and errors are likely to be common) or due to wilful evasion, is unknown and estimates vary significantly. Recent estimates of the underground economy (a significant, but only one, source of wilful evasion), for example range from 2.3 percent of GDP in 2009 (Statistics Canada 2012) to 15.7 percent (equaling a tax loss of $81.2 billion) (Tax Justice Network 2011). A 2010 report of the CRA concludes that while the extent of fraud/evasion is unknown, various indicators suggest that it is a serious problem (CRA 2010).

While attitudes regarding evasion are not directly correlated with actual behaviour, data from CRA tax compliance surveys consistently reveal that a significant percentage of those surveyed believe tax cheating to be minimally harmful and justifiable in certain situations. Taxpayer attitudinal segmentation research commissioned by the CRA categorized 49 percent of Canada's population as "law abiders" or "altruistic compliers" and who are at low risk of tax evasion. Thirteen percent, however, fit the category of "outlaws," a group very likely to "cheat on their taxes," while a further 12 percent, the "rationalizers," are at moderate risk. While the final two categories, the "underground economists" and the "over-taxed opportunists," are thought less likely to cheat, they may well do so in particular circumstances (CRA 2011). Rationalizations for evasion offered by respondents are consistent with those found in other research: the system is too complex; tax administration is unreasonable; no real harm comes of it/there is no victim; the tax burden is too heavy; government mismanages its spending of tax dollars; others are doing it; there is little risk of being caught; and penalties are minimal (CRA 2011).

The line between tax "avoidance" — which is not merely condoned but celebrated and heavily supported through the professional assistance of lawyers, accountants and other experts — and tax "evasion" is a blurry one, making it easy to regard tax evasion not as criminal conduct but as a minor technical breach by a hard-working, contributing citizen. Moreover, the norms and values of neo-liberalism — individualism, self-reliance, entrepreneurial spirit and material consumption — cut against the values underpinning a collective and redistributive taxation system and help to valourize tax avoidance.

As observed by Canada's Auditor General some time ago, the public attitude that regards non-compliance as a victimless and not particularly serious crime has "shaped low rates of enforcement coverage and the relatively lenient treatment of tax evaders" (Auditor General 1990). The converse may be equally true: low rates of enforcement and lenient treatment may shape public attitudes regarding compliance.

MONITORING COMPLIANCE

Surveillance and detection methods employed to catch tax "evaders" differ significantly from those used to detect against welfare "fraudsters." Under the ITA the audit is the primary tool used to detect failure to comply with the Act (CRA 2013; Van Der Hout et al. 2000). Files to be audited are selected based on high-risk factors, and specific audits are targeted towards small and medium businesses, international and large businesses, aggressive tax planners and the underground economy. CRA data for 2012–13 show well over 300,000 audits out of some 43 million returns filed, generating billions of dollars in unpaid taxes (CRA 2013).

By contrast, given informational reporting demands within the EVM environment, virtually every social assistant recipient is under the equivalent of a constant audit. The Social Assistance Review Committee's (SARC) observation in 1988 that the *Income Tax Act* operates in a different and less intrusive way than the social assistance system is even more apt today, given the dramatic increase in surveillance and scrutiny under the social assistance system without corresponding changes on the income tax side (Social Assistance Review Committee 1988). Importantly, within both the social assistance and tax systems, various investigative and monitoring tools are justified by citing the need to maintain public confidence in the integrity of the respective systems, both of which depend (though to varying degrees) upon self-reporting. However, substantially more extensive scrutiny (and accompanying incursions upon individual privacy) is deemed necessary to maintain confidence in the welfare system than in the tax system.

As well, those with money can draw upon an army of expert resources to protect and guard their privacy as taxpayers. There has been a significant amount of litigation challenging the powers of the CRA to investigate the taxpayer, especially on the question noted earlier of when a regulatory investigation (audit) becomes a *de facto* criminal investigation. The argument made by Van Der Haut et al. that "even in a self-assessing system, where fair disclosure is critical, there must be clear limits to and tangible protections for taxpayers, their advisors and other third parties in the course of the audit or investigation, even where that exercise is not criminal in nature" is widely accepted (Van Der Haut et al. 2000: 89). Taxpayers, and those advising them, are encouraged to know the permissible limits of the CRA's powers, to invoke solicitor-client privilege to protect information against disclosure, to realize the potential to sue if an audit is conducted with malice and to understand the Charter remedies available to protect the "target" of an audit (Van Der Haut et al. 2000). The point here is not to suggest that the advice is ill founded but rather to note just how very different the context is from that of welfare fraud. On the income tax side, the arguments proceed on the assumption that the taxpayer is a full citizen, worthy of respect, whose interests (privacy, liberty, autonomy) ought to be zealously guarded from incursions by the state. By contrast, the starting assumption for the welfare recipient is that she is undeserving and unworthy of respect; her privacy is scarcely acknowledged, let alone respected (Gilman 2012; Mosher 2002). Moreover, no body of accumulated expert resources exists that she or her counsel, should she be lucky enough to have representation, can draw upon.

Advice and guidance are also available to the taxpayer/evader from the CRA itself, through its voluntary disclosure program (VDP). The program seeks to encourage taxpayers to correct inaccurate or incomplete information by foregoing the pursuit of penalties or prosecution (and sometimes full interest owing) in exchange for voluntary disclosure (that is, disclosure made before the taxpayer is subject to an enforcement action). More broadly the CRA reflects an understanding that "sometimes non-compliance is the result of unintended errors, misunderstandings, or a lack of information" and a desire to address non-compliance "in the least intrusive way" to minimize "the risk of taxpayers paying penalties and interest" (CRA 2013: 38, 21). This framing of errors and misunderstandings stands in marked contrast to the welfare system.

The taxpayer can choose to "remain nameless" in the early stages of the VDP process, discuss the situation with a VDP officer, and secure an understanding of the CRA's position on the potential availability of relief. Moreover, if the taxpayer proceeds with the disclosure and disagrees with a decision made under the Program, he may request a second review of his file. In 2012–13, 15,133 voluntary disclosures resulted in approximately $1.2 billion in tax revenues, an increase of over 40 percent from 2011–12 (CRA 2013: 51). Significant amounts are waived in penalties and interest through this and other programs (CRA 2013).

Recent phone surveys and focus groups undertaken by the CRA revealed widespread public support for the VDP. While some participants in the focus groups "felt the program might be oriented more towards those who deliberately underpaid their taxes and were therefore aware of an underpayment, rather than those who had made an honest error," 85 percent of respondents in the phone survey said they supported the VDP. Some 93 percent agreed with statements describing the VDP as a program meant to provide a break to people who have made honest mistakes on their taxes, a program designed to encourage those who have not fully disclosed their tax information to do so (90 percent), and also that the VDP is a good way for the government to collect unpaid taxes it might otherwise not know about (83 percent). However, 54 percent agreed with the statement that the VDP "allows cheaters to avoid penalties they should be paying" (CRA 2012).

While the CRA has what may be described as a very low-key snitching program — the Informant Leads Program — it has not been advertised and trumpeted in the manner that Ontario's welfare snitch line has been. There were approximately 22,000 leads received during fiscal years 2006–7 and 2007–8 (compared to over 32,000 calls to Ontario's welfare snitch line in 2001–2 and 52,000 in 2000–1) (CRA 2010). More recently, in a targeted effort at offshore tax havens, rewards have been offered for tips leading to the assessment or collection of $100,000 or more in outstanding taxes.

If, in the course of an audit, evasion is suspected, the matter can be referred to the "criminal investigations program," which is mandated to investigate suspected cases of tax evasion, fraud and other serious violations of tax laws. In 2012–13 a total of 164 files were referred for prosecution (CRA 2013). Prosecution under the ITA may be either by summary conviction or indictment. Upon summary conviction, the accused is liable to a mandatory fine of not less than 50 percent and not greater than 200 percent of the amount of the tax that was being evaded, or to a fine and imprisonment for not more than two years. At the discretion of the Attorney General of Canada (with advice from the CRA), evasion may be prosecuted by indictment. If convicted of an indictable offence, the accused is liable to a mandatory fine of not less than 100 percent and not more than 200 percent of the amount of tax that was sought to be evaded and imprisonment for a term not exceeding five years. Current policy indicates that "it would normally be appropriate to proceed by indictment" where the accused has previously been convicted of tax evasion, has entered a conspiracy to evade tax, or engaged in comparable criminal behaviour, *or* where the tax evaded exceeds $250,000 *and* at least one of several additional circumstances exists (including the scheme was sophisticated, the accused counselled others to evade taxes and/or an innocent third party suffered significant losses) (Federal Prosecutors Service Deskbook). As the Auditor General observed in 1990, when the dollar threshold for prosecution by indictment for tax evasion was $100,000 and the breakpoint for indictment for fraud over in the *Criminal Code* was $1,000 (now $5,000) with imprisonment of up to ten years as a potential outcome (now fourteen years): "Setting a $100,000 threshold for prosecutions by indictment in tax evasion cases means that most tax evaders face a much lower chance of being incarcerated than those convicted of other types of frauds" (Auditor General 1990). Moreover, it is important to reiterate that frequently tax evaders avoid prosecution entirely, and the matter is addressed through civil penalties also available under the ITA.

The Auditor General's observation regarding the lowered risk of incarceration for tax evaders is certainly borne out by a review of sentencing decisions. Whether prosecuted summarily or by indictment under the ITA (a maximum of two years and five years re-spectively), unlike the welfare fraud context, a jail term is not the starting presumption. Rather, punishment of jail time for tax evasion is usually reserved for cases where the accused is, for example, a person who prepares tax returns for others and has facilitated the evasion of taxes by multiple taxpayers (often several hundred), or where, in addition to the charge of tax evasion, the accused has also been charged with fraud upon a public-benefits program. Interestingly, in *R. v. Silvestri*, a 2001 decision, the court observed that neither the Crown nor defence counsel were able to point to a case of first offence tax evasion in the range of $50,000 where incarceration was ordered in addition to the fine required by the Act.

A review of convictions for Ontario between October 2012 and October 2013 posted on the CRA website shows that of forty-nine convictions, fourteen resulted in incarcera-tion (of these five were conditional sentences). Of the fourteen, eight of the cases result-ing in incarceration included charges of counseling others to commit fraud, and of the forty-nine, only seven were prosecuted under the *Criminal Code* fraud provisions where maximum liability for imprisonment is fourteen years rather than five (these involved very significant amounts of money and usually the creation of false documents such as charitable receipts and/or the counselling of others to evade tax). A 2010 CRA report concludes that the average number of convictions resulting in a custodial disposition for tax cases falls "well below the average for other tax administrations and of white collar crime cases prosecuted in Canada" (CRA 2010). Interestingly, while one might assume that the publication of convictions on the CRA website is intended to deter others, each case summary also includes information about the avoidance of prosecution and penal-ties through voluntary disclosure:

> Taxpayers who have not filed returns for previous years, or who have not reported all of their income, can still voluntarily correct their tax affairs. They may not be penalized or prosecuted if they make a valid disclosure before they become aware of any compliance action being initiated by the CRA against them. These taxpayers may only have to pay the taxes owing, plus interest.

Several authors and the Auditor General (on multiple occasions) have commented on the relatively insignificant penalties imposed for tax evasion. Sossin, for example, has argued that tax evasion is treated as a "minor regulatory infraction rather than as a viola-tion of any esteemed social values" (Sossin 1999: 1). While the Auditor General's office has explicitly refrained from suggesting that the penalties for tax evasion are inadequate, successive Auditor Generals have invited the government to consider the value judgment reflected by weak enforcement and light penalties and to consider sending a message to Canadians that tax cheating is unacceptable (Auditor General 1999). Indeed, the repeated advice of successive Auditor Generals has been that tax evasion ought to be considered a serious crime. The 1994 report, for example, observed that, "Tax evasion is a serious criminal offence. It results in a loss of revenue; it shifts the tax burden from dishonest taxpayers to honest taxpayers; and it creates unfair competition between businesses that abide by the law and those that don't" (Auditor General 1994).

SENTENCING TAX EVADERS

In comparing the judicial decisions on welfare fraud to those for income tax evasion, two significant differences appear: the attention given to *mens rea* and the justifications invoked to support sentencing outcomes. In the tax evasion cases — both within the CRA and throughout the criminal prosecution — the slippage from rule violation to guilt, so pervasive in the welfare system, does not occur. To the contrary, it is accepted as a matter of course that ignorance of the admittedly complex tax rules applicable to the situation in issue will negate *mens rea*. Indeed, even sophisticated businessmen with an advanced grasp of tax law and able to obtain expert assistance have successfully invoked ignorance of the ITA to negate *mens rea*. Consider, for example, the following two cases.

In *R. v. Chusid* (2002) the accused was charged with wilful evasion and the making of false or deceptive statements. Mr. Chusid had failed to disclose a $1 million commission in the year it was received (when it ought to have been disclosed), but did disclose it later (when he knew he was under investigation). The court stressed that mere carelessness or inattention is not enough to establish guilt, rather there must be proof beyond a reasonable doubt that his actions were deliberately undertaken to evade taxes. Likewise, it was not enough that the accused was an experienced businessman, with an advanced grasp of taxation, who should have known of his obligation to report the commission. Additionally, the court noted that he was careless in his bookkeeping and his failure to disclose could have resulted from simple carelessness, thus raising in the judge's mind the benefit of a doubt. Mr. Chusid was acquitted.

In *R. v. McGuigan* (2002) the accused was similarly charged with wilfully evading taxes and making a false or deceptive statement. The case turned on whether Mr. Mc-Guigan honestly believed that the stock options taxable in 1996, and not disclosed by him, were taxable not in 1996 but in 1997 and that he intended to disclose them then. The court noted that the law is complex, the treatment of stock options in this regard perhaps counter-intuitive and that the law had changed. And while Mr. McGuigan had been the president of a company with sales of $500 million and vice president of a company with sales of $5 billion, there was, to quote the trial judge, "no evidence of any financial sophistication or knowledge outside his sphere" (para 64). The court further observed that Mr. McGuigan had recently lost his job and no doubt experienced shock and disorientation as a result, that apart from his actions there was no evidence to infer *mens rea* (the court mentions debts, gambling problems, living beyond his means) and that his character evidence provided by witnesses was strong (including that given by a former assistant deputy minister of National Defence). The trial judge concluded, "during Mr. McGuigan's testimony there was something that made me believe him. There was a genuineness in his testimony, even when he was stumbling on difficult points" (para 89). Mr. McGuigan was acquitted.

Yet welfare recipients — those with very limited, if any, access to expert advice and assistance — are commonly imputed with knowledge of the complex rules and regulations surrounding OW. The complexity of the regulatory regime has meant little in defending against an allegation of welfare fraud, in contrast to the outcome of income tax cases.

In justifying sentences, while judges will sometimes observe that the income tax system is dependent upon taxpayer candour and honesty, tax evasion is far less commonly characterized as a breach of trust than is welfare fraud. Recall that this characterization is pervasive in welfare fraud cases, and is employed — together with the characterization of the crime as one against the public purse — to support a presumption of incarceration.

The income tax system is, in fact, more dependent upon candour and honesty than is the welfare system (in large measure because taxpayers are assumed to be honest and welfare recipients are not — a troublesome assumption in light of the data regarding acknowledged evasion). Although evading taxes is also a fraud upon the public purse, this breach of trust rarely generates a presumption of incarceration in tax evasion cases. This difference reinforces the view that the real issue in welfare fraud cases is the perceived exploitation of the largesse of the hardworking taxpayer.

Consistent with the views regarding tax evasion solicited through compliance surveys, judges tend to regard tax evasion as a victimless crime — not as a crime against every member of the community, nor a crime against those most in need of state support. Finally, one also observes in income tax cases that the fall from a position of elevated social status is used as a mitigating factor in sentencing. While there are exceptions, the status the accused has enjoyed in the community and his good character and reputation — all now tarnished by the prosecution — are considered relevant to sentencing. The stigma, sometimes personal bankruptcy and more generally the loss of status, are regarded as dimensions of punishment already inflicted upon the accused. The welfare recipient, by contrast, is unable to invoke these badges of social esteem that are soiled by the criminal prosecution.

In *R. v. Kutum* (2013) the accused, a chartered accountant, prepared 487 false returns over a six-year period, resulting in lost tax revenue of over a million dollars. In sentencing Mr. Kutum, the court emphasized that he had left the scheme prior to being charged, had made voluntary post-charge statements to the CRA and had set aside money for restitution. In addition, his wife and four adult children have, the court observed, "all felt the shame of [the] crime" and the "shame he has suffered within his family has extended to his professional and community lives." Note is also made of his contributions to the community over time, providing volunteer placements for students and assisting new Canadians (in contrast to the contributions to community made by welfare recipients which are virtually never acknowledged). "Significant collateral effects including shame, loss of professional status, and loss of economic opportunity pending the outcome of the case" were all mitigating factors. Importantly the court does frame the accused's behaviour as a breach of trust and draws upon a line of cases for the proposition that a penitentiary sentence is warranted for significant breaches of trust (cases involving, for example, theft over a million dollars). Noting that "large frauds perpetrated "by professional criminals a grave scourge on society," Justice Schwarzl sentenced Mr. Kumar to two years, plus a fine representing his illegal profits. Presumably none of the hundreds of taxpayers who knowingly filed the fraudulent returns prepared by Mr. Kumar were charged. Contrast this outcome with that of *R. v. Dennis* (2013) discussed earlier, where at first instance the accused was sentenced to a one-year conditional sentence for frauds totaling $1,382 or *R. v. McGillivray* (1992), where six months incarceration for a fraud of $23,000 was the outcome notwithstanding she was in an abusive relationship and receiving no income from her abusive spouse.

CRIMINALITY AND CATEGORIES OF DESERVEDNESS

The taxpayer, constructed as a homogeneous category, is assumed to be employed, productive and deserving; should he evade the payment of his taxes — absent his participation in an elaborate scheme to enable the complicity of others in fraud — he is likely to enjoy considerable compassion from his fellow citizens who empathize with his desire to hold onto his hard-earned dollars and leniency from state authorities. He can resort to a range of justificatory frameworks to rationalize his transgression, notwithstanding that its consequence is the diminishment of public resources and the redistribution of the tax burden. The welfare recipient, yet another homogeneous category, is portrayed as the virtual antithesis of the taxpayer: lazy, undisciplined, dependent and undeserving. Her poverty is often cast as of her own making, and her need often misrepresented as greed by those who have infinitely more resources than she. Regarded with intense suspicion she is positioned as a threat to the honest, hard-working taxpayer.

To contain the threat posed by welfare recipients, intensive surveillance is understood as both desirable and necessary. As Henman and Marston have argued, surveillance is differentially applied, with marginalized populations bearing its heaviest burdens. In its differential application to those persons in receipt of welfare and those obligated to pay taxes, surveillance operates to "categorise and divide populations, thereby reinforcing social fissures and inequalities" (2008: 188). Their conclusion in comparing three domains in which forms of social welfare are distributed (welfare benefits, taxation and employment) is that differences in the intensity of surveillance align not with the need for surveillance to detect and punish crime, but rather to mark out the deserving and undeserving, and this conclusion captures well the comparison here of welfare fraud and tax evasion in Canada (Henman and Marston 2008).

The wide public acceptance of tax evasion stands in sharp contrast to public sentiments regarding welfare fraud and welfare recipients (Marriott 2013, 2012). The rationalizations that are regularly invoked to justify tax evasion have no traction in relation to welfare fraud. Rather, the amorphous state is transformed into millions of innocent victims, all recipients are expected to know, understand and comply with the admittedly complex rules and the inadequacy of benefit levels in no way mitigates the crime. And while much of the conduct of welfare recipients is mischaracterized as "fraudulent" — as criminal in nature — precisely the opposite holds true for taxpayers, whose criminal misconduct is largely ignored, condoned and excused.

Notwithstanding the many similarities between the conduct of welfare fraud and tax evasion — both are non-violent acts in which the state is deprived of money — assumptions about the perpetrators of these crimes and their moral worth vary dramatically. Survey data repeatedly find that welfare fraud is regarded as a more serious offence than tax fraud; indeed, in Gupta's research, tax evasion ranks just ahead of running a red light (Gupta 2009).

The language of criminality, the imagery of "the criminal" and the deployment of criminal processes and sanctions have been invoked by the state to construct a problem of welfare fraud and to scrutinize, diminish and punish welfare recipients. By contrast, tax evaders are not regarded as criminals, nor is tax evasion constructed as a serious social problem. Rather, the tax evader is first and foremost a taxpayer; he is a good neo-liberal citizen, worthy of a solicitous response from the state to his minor transgression, should it ever be detected. The very selective invocation of criminality by the state simultaneously draws upon and enlarges the moral worthiness of taxpayers and the moral failings of welfare recipients. In so doing, it entrenches categories of deservedness — categories that valourize competitive individualism and erode collective obligation.

DISCUSSION QUESTIONS

1. How should the motivation for engaging in conduct inform our views (and laws) as to whether or not that conduct is "criminal" in nature? Or should it be a matter relevant to sentencing, or not at all relevant? For example, if a young mother defrauds welfare by failing to disclose small amounts of money received from the father of her children she knows she is required to disclose and her motivation in so doing is so that she may feed her children, should this be considered a crime? Or considered relevant to sentencing? Would your views change if you knew that should she fail to adequately feed her children she may be blamed for failing to provide adequately for their needs and possibly lose custody of her children to the state? How would your answers to these questions vary if you were to adopt consensus theories or critical theories?

2. What do we mean by "need"? What do we really need: the means necessary to survive, the means to live with dignity, the means to belong? What part should government have in providing for the needs of citizens? Or should society encourage more self-reliance? Does the criminal law have a place in determining whether social responsibility or individualism should be emphasized?

3. Try an experiment. Ask your friends and/or family if they have ever failed to report income to Revenue Canada or paid cash to avoid paying taxes, and ask why they did this? Then try asking about their views regarding welfare fraud and compare the answers.

4. What does this case study reveal about the claim of traditional approaches to criminology that the rules proscribing behaviour are neutral, universal and unchanging?

5. What alternative approaches to welfare fraud and tax evasion might a critical criminologist argue in favour of?

GLOSSARY

Conditional Sentence: a sentence that may be ordered provided three preconditions are satisfied: the offence does not have a minimum prison term; a custodial sentence of less than two years is imposed; and serving the sentence in the community would not endanger community safety. The court may order that the offender serve the sentence in the community. Most commonly, a conditional sentence takes the form of house arrest, with several conditions attached. As a result of the passage of the new *Safe* Streets and Communities Act: conditional sentences, as of November, 2012, are no longer available for the offence of fraud over $5,000.

Indictable Offences: these are more serious offences, wherein the maximum penalties will be higher than those for summary conviction offences (see below). The procedures for prosecuting indictable offences are more involved than for summary conviction. Many offences are "hybrid" offences, wherein the Crown elects whether to proceed by indictment or by summary conviction.

Neo-Liberalism: a term used to describe the dominant international political economy in place today. It is a way of thinking that stresses the shrinking of state responsibility for the needs of citizens, with a corresponding emphasis upon the importance of private obligation and self-sufficiency. This theory of government and the state is tied to a belief that open markets, rather than a strong welfare state, will provide the greatest good in society.

Ontario Works: income support benefits governed by the *Ontario Works Act, 1997*. Eligibility depends upon the assessment of the financial needs of the "benefit unit," which includes "spouses" (as defined by the OWA and not pursuant to family law) and dependent children. With few exceptions, all adult beneficiaries are required to engage in work or work readiness activities as a precondition to receiving benefits and children are required to attend school.

Ontario Disability Support Program: this program creates a separate benefit regime, with higher benefit levels and no work requirements, for persons with a "disability" as defined by the *Ontario Disability Support Program Act*.

Social Assistance: social assistance refers to residual, means-tested government financial assistance programs. In Ontario, Ontario Works and the Ontario Disability Support Program are both forms of social assistance. Social assistance is often commonly referred to as "welfare," although sometimes Ontario Works is referred to as "welfare" and Ontario Disability Support Program benefits as "disability benefits."

Summary Conviction Offences: generally less serious offences wherein unless a different penalty is specified in the offence section, the maximum sentence for summary conviction offences are $2,000 and/or six months' imprisonment. The procedures for charging and prosecuting differ from indictable offences.

SUGGESTED READINGS

Paul Henman and Greg Marston, "The Social Division of Welfare Surveillance," *Journal of Social Policy* 37, 2 (2008): 187–205.

Mike Larsen and Justin Piché, "Public Vigilance Campaigns and Participatory Surveillance after 11 September 2001," in Sean P. Hier and Josh Greenberg (eds.), *Surveillance: Power, Problems, and Politics*, Vancouver: UBC Press (2009).

Janet Mosher, "Intimate Intrusions — Welfare Regulation and Women's Personal Lives," in Dorothy Chunn and Shelley Gavigan (eds.), *The Legal Tender of Gender*, London: Hart, Onati Law & Society Series (2010).

Amy Mulzer, "The Doorkeeper and the Grand Inquisitor: The Central Role of Verification Procedures in Means-Tested Welfare Programs," *Columbia Human Rights Law Review* 36 (2005): 663–711.

SUGGESTED WEBSITES

Income Security Advocacy Clinic <http://www.incomesecurity.org/>

Ontario Coalition Against Poverty <http://www.ocap.ca/>

PovNet <http://www.povnet.org/>

HomelessHub <http://www.homelesshub.ca/about-homelessness/legal-justice-issues/criminalization-homelessness>

NOTES

This article draws upon research undertaken by the author and Professor Joe Hermer and funded by the Law Commission of the. Deep gratitude is owed to the Law Commission for its support of this work. I am also indebted to Nicole Veitch for her excellent research assistance.

1.   If the value is greater than $5,000 the Crown proceeds by way of indictment with the maximum

penalty being up to fourteen years of imprisonment; below $5,000 the Crown may elect to proceed by indictment (imprisonment of up to two years) or by summary conviction (fine of up to $2,000 and/or six months imprisonment).

REFERENCES

Auditor General of Canada. 1990. *1990 Report of the Auditor General of Canada*. Ottawa: Office of the Auditor General of Canada.

___. 1994. *Report of the Auditor General Canada*. Ottawa: Office of the Auditor General of Canada.

___. 1999. *Opening Statement to the Committee on Public Accounts: Revenue Canada - Underground Economy Initiative*.

Auditor General, City of Toronto. 2008. *Managing the Risk of Overpayments in the Administration of Overpayments of Social Assistance*. At <http://www.toronto.ca/audit/2008/managing_risk_social_assistance_audit_report_may2008.pdf> accessed Nov. 3, 2014.

Auditor General, Ontario. 2009. *Ministry of Community and Social Services: Ontario Works Program*, Chapter 3.11. At <http://www.auditor.on.ca/en/reports_en/en09/311en09.pdf> accessed Nov. 3, 2014.

___. 2011. *Ministry of Community and Social Services: Ontario Works Program*, Chapter 4.11. At <http://www.auditor.on.ca/en/reports_en/en11/411en11.pdf> accessed Nov. 3, 2014.

Broomer v. Ontario (Attorney General). June 5, 2002. Toronto 02-CV-229203CM3 (Ontario Superior Court of Justice).

Commission for the Review of Social Assistance in Ontario. 2012. *Brighter Prospects: Transforming Social Assistance in Ontario*. At <http://www.mcss.gov.on.ca/documents/en/mcss/social/publications/social_assistance_review_final_report.pdf> accessed Nov. 3, 2014.

CRA (Canada Revenue Agency). 2010. *Enforcement and Disclosures Programs Evaluation*. At <http://www.cra-arc.gc.ca/gncy/ntrnl/2011/nfrcmntdclsprgms2011-eng.html> accessed Nov. 3, 2014.

___. 2011. *Taxpayer Attitudinal Segmentation Research*. At <http://www.cra-arc.gc.ca/gncy/pr/txpyr-rsrch-eng.html> accessed Nov. 3, 2014.

___. 2012. *Voluntary Disclosures Program Research*. At <http://www.cra-arc.gc.ca/gncy/pr/vdpr-eng.html> accessed Nov.3, 2014.

___. 2013. *Annual Report to Parliament 2012–13*. Ottawa: Canada Revenue Agency. At <http://www.cra-arc.gc.ca/gncy/nnnl/2012-2013/images/ar-2012-13-eng.pdf> accessed Nov. 3, 2014.

___. 2014. *Annual Report to Parliament 2013-2014*. At: cra-arc.gc.ca/gncy/nnnl/2013-2014/ar-2013-14-eng.pdf

___. 2015a *Tax Alert: Criminal Investigations*. At: cra-arc.gc.ca/gncy/lrt/crmnl-eng.html

___. 2015b. *Voluntary Disclosures Program*. At: cra-arc.gc.ca/voluntarydisclosures/

Criminal Code of Canada, R.S., 1985, c.C-46.

Daley, Maxine. 2011. Memo to OW Administrators. At <www.adsab.on.ca> accessed Nov. 3, 2014.

Dee, Mike. 2013. "Welfare Surveillance, Income Management and New Paternalism in Australia." *Surveillance & Society* 11, 3: 272–86.

Ewart, Douglas J. 1986. *Criminal Fraud*. Toronto: Carswell Legal Publications.

Federal Prosecution Service Deskbook. At <http://www.ppsc-sppc.gc.ca/eng/pub/fpsd-sfpg/fps-sfp/fpd/ch19.html> accessed Nov. 3, 2014.

Gilles, David E.A., and Lindsay M. Tedds. 2002. *Taxes and the Canadian Underground Economy*. Toronto: Canadian Tax Foundation.

Gilman, Michele Estrin. 2012. "The Class Differential in Privacy Law." *Brooklyn Law Review* 77, 4: 1389–445.

Gupta, Ranjana. 2009. "An Empirical Study of Demographics of Perceptions of Tax Evasion in New Zealand." *Journal of Australian Taxation* 12, 1: 1–40.

Haggerty, Kevin D., and Richard V. Ericson. 2000. "The Surveillant Assemblage." *British Journal of Sociology* 51, 4: 605–22.

Henman, Paul, and Greg Marston. 2008. "The Social Division of Welfare Surveillance." *Journal of*

Social Policy 37, 2: 187–205.

Herd, Dean, and Andrew Mitchell. 2002. *Discouraged, Diverted and Disentitled: Ontario Works' New Service Delivery Model.* Toronto: Community Social Planning Council of Toronto & Ontario Social Safety Network.

Income Tax Act, R.S.C. 1985, c.1 (5th Supp.).

Larsen, Mike, and Justin Piché. 2009. "Public Vigilance Campaigns and Participatory Surveillance after 11 September 2001." In Sean P. Hier and Josh Greenberg (eds.), *Surveillance: Power, Problems, and Politics.* Vancouver: UBC Press.

Maki, Krystle. 2011. "Neoliberal Deviants and Surveillance: Welfare Recipients under the Watchful Eye of Ontario Works." *Surveillance & Society* 9, 1/2: 47–63.

Marriott, Lisa. 2012. "Justice and the Justice System: A Comparison of Tax Evasion and Welfare Fraud in Australasia." At <http://docs.business.auckland.ac.nz/Doc/40-Lisa-Marriott.pdf> accessed Nov. 3, 2014.

___. 2012. "Tax Crime and Punishment in New Zealand." At <http://sydney.edu.au/law/parsons/ATTA/docs_pdfs/conference_papers/Marriott.pdf> accessed Nov.3, 2014.

___. 2013. "Justice and the Justice System: A Comparison of Tax Evasion and Welfare Fraud in Australasia." *Griffith Law Review* 22, 2: 403–29.

Marston, Greg, and Tamara Walsh. 2008. "A Case of Misrepresentation: Social Security Fraud and the Criminal Justice System in Australia." *Griffith Law Review* 17, 1: 285–300.

Martin, Dianne L. 1992. "Passing the Buck: Prosecution of Welfare Fraud; Preservation of Stereotypes." *Windsor Year Book of Access to Justice* 12: 52–97.

Matthews, Deb. 2004. "Report to the Honourable Sandra Pupatello, Minister of Community and Social Services: Review of Employment Assistance Programs in Ontario Works and Ontario Disability Support Program." Toronto: Ministry of Community and Social Services.

McKeever, Grainne. 2012. "Social Citizenship and Social Security Fraud in the UK and Australia." *Social Policy & Administration* 46, 4: 465–82.

Mirchandani, Kiran, and Wendy Chan. 2005. "The Racialized Impact of Welfare Fraud Control in British Columbia and Ontario." Canadian Race Relations Foundation. At <http://www.crr.ca/divers-files/en/publications/reports/pubRacialized_Impact_Welfare.pdf> accessed Nov. 3, 2014.

Mosher, Janet. 2002. "The Shrinking of the Public and Private Spaces of the Poor." In J. Hermer and J. Mosher (eds.), *Disorderly People: Law and the Politics of Exclusion in Ontario.* Halifax: Fernwood Publishing.

___. 2010. "Intimate Intrusions — Welfare Regulation and Women's Personal Lives." In Dorothy Chunn and Shelley Gavigan (eds.), *The Legal Tender of Gender.* London: Hart, Onati Law & Society Series.

Mosher, Janet, Patricia Evans and Margaret Little. 2004. *Walking on Eggshells: Abused Women's Experiences of Ontario's Welfare System.* At <http://www.yorku.ca/yorkweb/special/Welfare_Report_walking_on_eggshells_final_report.pdf> accessed Nov. 3, 2014.

Mosher, Janet, and Joe Hermer. 2005. *Welfare Fraud: The Constitution of Social Assistance as Crime.* Ottawa: Law Commission of Canada.

___. 2010. "Welfare Fraud: The Constitution of Social Assistance as Crime." In J. Mosher and J. Brockman (eds) *Constructing Crime: Contemporary Process of Criminalization.* Vancouver: UBC Press.

Mulzer, Amy. 2005. "The Doorkeeper and the Grand Inquisitor: The Central Role of Verification Procedures in Means-Tested Welfare Programs." *Columbia Human Rights Law Review* 36: 663–711.

Ontario Disability Support Program Act, 1997, S.O. 1997, c. 25, Sch. B.

Ontario, Legislative Assembly. 1995. *Official Report of Debates (Hansard),* 1st Sess., 36th Leg., October 2.

Ontario, Ministry of Community, Family and Children's Services. 2003. *Welfare Fraud Control Report 2001–2002.* Toronto: Ministry of Community, Family and Children's Services.

Ontario, Ministry of Community and Social Services. 2004. *Ontario Works, Policy Directive 45.*

Toronto: Ministry of Community and Social Services.

___. 2013. *Ontario Works, Policy Directives 2.1, 2.8 and 9.1.* Toronto: Ministry of Community and Social Services.

Ontario Works Act, 1997, S.O. 1997, c. 25, Sch. A.

Ontario Works Act, 1997, O. Reg. 134/98.

Parnaby, Patrick. 2003. "Disaster Through Dirty Windshields Law, Order and Toronto Squeegee Kids." *Canadian Journal of Sociology* 28, 3: 281–307.

Prenzler, Tim. 2010. "Detecting and Preventing Welfare Fraud." *Trends & Issues in Crime and Criminal Justice* 418 (June).

___. 2011. "Welfare Fraud in Australia: Dimensions and Issues." *Trends & Issues in Crime and Criminal Justice* 421 (June).

R. v. Chusid. 2002. CanLII 29375 (Ontario Superior Court of Justice).

R. v. Dennis. 2013. CanLII 53 (British Columbia Court of Appeal).

R. v. Fayemi. 2009. CanLII 123 (British Columbia Provincial Court).

R. v. Friesen. 1994. CanLII 2011 (British Columbia Court of Appeal).

R. v. Gallagher. 1996. O.J. No. 4761 (Ontario Court of Justice, Provincial Division).

R. v. Jarvis. 2002. CanLII 73 (Supreme Court of Canada).

R. v. Kutum. 2013. CanLII 241 (Ontario Court of Justice).

R. v. Maldonado. 1998. O.J. No. 3209 (Ontario Court of Justice, Provincial Division).

R. v. McCloy. 2008. CanLII 212 (Alberta Provincial Court).

R. v. McGillivray. 1992. A.J. No. 886 (Alberta Provincial Court).

R. v. McGuigan. 2002. O.J. No. 3989 (Ontario Superior Court of Justice).

R. v. McIsaac. 1998. CanLII 4654 (British Columbia Supreme Court).

R. v. Olan. 1978. CanLII 9 (Supreme Court of Canada).

R. v. Reid. 1995. CanLII 4319 (Nova Scotia Court of Appeal).

R. v. Rogers. 2001. O.J. No. 5203 (Ontario Court of Justice).

R. v. Silvestri. 2001. O.J. No. 3694 (Ontario Superior Court of Justice).

R. v. Stapley. 1997 O.J. No. 3235 (Ontario Court of Justice, General Division).

R. v. Théroux. 1993. CanLII 134 (Supreme Court of Canada).

R. v. Thurrott. 1971. CanLII 381 (Ontario Court of Appeal).

R. v. Wilson. 2005. CanLII 21 (Ontario Court of Justice).

Schneider, F., Buehn, A., and Montenegro, C.E. 2010. *Shadow Economies all over the World: New Estimates for 162 Countries from 199 to 2007* (Policy Research Working Paper 5356, July). At: <openknowledge.worldbank.org/bitstream/handle/10986/3928/WPS5356.pdf?sequence=1>.

Social Assistance Review Committee. 1988. *Report of the Social Assistance Review Committee: Transitions.* Toronto: Queen's Printer.

Sossin, Lorne. 1999. "Welfare State Crime in Canada Revisited: The Politics of Tax Evasion in the 1980s and 1990s." *The Tax Forum* 1 (Autumn).

Stapleton, John. 2012. "Of the 1%, for the 1%, to the 1%?" At <http://openpolicyontario.com/of-the-1-for-the-1-to-the-1/> accessed Nov. 3, 2014).

Statistics Canada. 2012. "Estimating the Underground Economy in Canada, 1992–2009." At <http://www.cra-arc.gc.ca/nwsrm/fctshts/2012/m09/fs120927-eng.html> accessed Nov. 3, 2014.

Tax Justice Network. 2011. "The Cost of Tax Abuse: A Briefing Paper on the Cost of Tax Evasion Worldwide." At <http://www.taxjustice.net/wp-content/uploads/2014/04/Cost-of-Tax-Abuse-TJN-2011.pdf> accessed Nov. 3, 2014.

Van Der Hout, Susan, Robert Goldstein and Angelina Fisher. 2000. "Taxpayer Information: Administration and Enforcement Procedures Under the Income Tax Act (Canada)." *Advocates Quarterly* 23.

8

CORPORATIONS AND ENVIRONMENTAL CRIME

Wei Wang and Hongming Cheng

KEY FACTS

> Forests covered 46 percent of Canada's land area in a 2006 official report, but the percentage was reduced to 39 percent in 2013.

> The funding available for use by Environment Canada decreased by 18.4 million in fiscal year 2014–15 compared to the previous fiscal year.

> Approximately, 30 to 40 million tons hazardous waste is being trafficked across international borders each year, driven by the difference of dumping prices among countries (e.g., US$250 per ton in the U.S. vs. US$40 per ton in countries in Africa).

Sources: Canada Forest Service 2013; Environment Canada 2014; Liddick 2011.

In the early morning of August 4, 2014, the Mount Polley tailings dam in the Cariboo region of British Columbia, run by the Imperial Metals Corporation, burst and released 10 million cubic metres of water and 4.5 million cubic metres of slurry into Polley Lake and continued into the nearby Quesnel Lake. According to the company's disclosure document filed with Environment Canada in 2013, "there was 326 tonnes of nickel, over 400 tonnes of arsenic, 177 tonnes of lead and 18,400 tonnes of copper and its compounds" in the tailings pond. No matter how hard the company and the government are working to clean up the tailings in water, the heavy metals that swept down into the lakes are still there and may slowly be taken up into the food chain. The Mount Polley pond breach has been called one of the largest environmental disasters in modern Canadian history (Koven 2014). It is clear that insufficient efforts in dam designing and maintenance are at the centre of this crisis. Such environmental violation is one major dimension of corporate crime of our era.

Issues of environmental crime, such as air pollution, disposal of toxic wastes and illegal exploitation of forest and water resources, have frequently appeared in news headlines (White 2008, 2010). The powerful phrase "go green" has perfectly drawn the attention of a wide range of interested parties from the public to politicians and indicated the urgency of taking actions to protect our planet. Despite the optimism of this slogan, there are those who argue that the essential relationship between human activities and the well-being of the environment is toxic (White 2010). An increasing number of studies from a variety of perspectives, including sociology, geography, public health, economics, policy studies and law, have illustrated that environmental crime is a serious and growing international problem (Gibbs et al. 2010a; Shover and Routhe 2005; Wolf 2011; Zilney et al. 2006). In this view, environmental crime affects every person in society, for environmental problems such as loss of biodiversity, climate change and pollution have negative impacts on both human and environmental health. For instance, many studies find that climate change is adversely affecting millions of people and is associated with the increase of cardio-respiratory disease, susceptibility to pathogens and allergenicity potential (Noyes et al. 2009).

Environmental crime has long been associated with rapid industrialization, which has driven corporations and individuals toward minimizing costs and maximizing profits, rather than social and environmental responsibility. Globalization has also influenced patterns of other environmental crimes in the world and amplified the influence of those criminals who traditionally commit crimes in one country on other countries (White 2010). For instance, illegal exploitation and trade of wild flora and fauna is an example of transnational organized environmental crime that involves numerous criminals in the chain of exploitation in various countries. Toxic waste is also illegally transferred between countries under the name of recycling (White 2010). As a result, harms caused by environmental crime are no longer concentrated at single spots, but rather connect one nation to another.

Increased globalization and new industrialization launched by a number of Third World countries in the late twentieth century brought new opportunities for environmental crime in both developed and developing countries. In Canada, the immerse, multinational state–corporate project is currently under way in the northern part of Alberta to extract and refine naturally created, tar-bearing sand into exportable and consumable oil. While the tar sand project is undoubtedly benefiting Canada's economy, it has been criticized as "one of the world's most fantastic concentrations of toxic waste" (Nikiforuk 2008: 78), for the process of extracting tar sands is harming both ecological and human health (Smandych and Kueneman 2010). In developing economies such as China, where economic growth is rapid, waves of industry-produced toxic air pollution have attacked multiple cities, which started in the mega cities on the eastern coast and now seem to invade skies of the western part of the country. Welfare damage caused by air pollution is estimated over 110 billion US dollars in 2005 (Matus et al. 2012), and air pollutants are found associated with respiratory hospital admissions, which have more fundamental impacts on females and elderly (Tao et al. 2014).

Researchers from different disciplines have been increasingly concerned with many environmental issues and started to seek explanations and responses to environmental offences. Criminologists have not devoted much attention to environmental issues until recently, although the idea on developing a new branch of critical criminology, "green criminology," that incorporates perspectives of environmentalism, radicalism and humanism, has been introduced in the early 1990s (see Lynch 1990). Green criminology is a term typically used to describe, analyze and examine issues on environmental crime and environmental justice (Lynch 1990; South 1998). The basic assumption is that environmental crime is a distinctive subset of crime, and more efforts are advocated for conceptualizing environmental crime and environmental harm, providing responses to protect the environment from degradation, and so on. Research on environmental crime has also been envisioned under the category of white-collar crime, since such activities are mainly committed by corporations in order to maximize profits or avoid unexpected costs and violate their fiduciary responsibilities or trust obligations to the public (Friedrichs 2010).

Although recent criminological research has raised significant issues of environmental crime, such studies are still limited, and critical questions and unresolved issues remain (see Zilney et al. 2006). The goal of this chapter is to address some critical issues related to environmental crime and the discourse of regulation in Canadian society. We begin with a discussion of some core concepts related to the study of environmental crime as a subtype of corporate crime. We then examine various forms of environmental crime and historical patterns of environmental crime in Canada. Third, we analyze different types of organizational violators and their motivations for degrading the environment. This chapter concludes with a discussion on regulation as a response to environmental crime.

DEFINING ENVIRONMENTAL CRIME

In the early 1980s, environmental justice movements that occurred in the U.S. raised concerns on issues of environmental harm and policies. Environmental justice frequently refers to the implementation, development and improvement of environmental law by all kinds of people, regardless their race, nation and income, and emphasizes the equal protection of environmental harm (Lynch and Stretsky 2003; Wolf 2011). Since the early 1990s, the term "environmental crime" has been used by the news media to cover a wide range of issues such as illegal dumping of toxic waste, water pollution, wildlife abuse, endangered species smuggling and other violations of environmental laws and irresponsible corporate activities. Although journalists and policy makers frequently use this term to indicate "offenses against the environment" (Clifford and Edwards 1998: 8), "environmental crime" is unpopular among criminologists who study illegal or unethical activities that harm the environment. Part of the reason is that "environmental criminology" was coined decades ago to describe a subfield of criminology that examines the impact of social ecological factors on crimes and explores spatial and locational patterns of criminal activities (see Brantingham and Brantingham 1981). Crimes against the environment, however, had drawn little attention from criminologists at that early time, so no specific term had been created to describe the related problems. After sensing the conceptual gap and potential overlap in terminology across the two different subjects of criminology, since 1990, criminologists have attempted to clarify this confusion by using other terms, such as green crime (Lynch 1990; South 1998; South and Beirne 2006), conservation crime (Gibbs et al. 2010a; Herbig and Joubert 2006) and environmental harm (White 2010). However, some argue for reclaiming "environmental criminology" to denote crimes against the environment for two reasons. First, the word "green" may not be appropriate due to its political implications with the growth of green politics in the twentieth Century. Second, the nature of the research in this field is focusing on crimes against and activities that do serious harm to the environment and on environmental laws and regulations to prevent environmental harms (Clifford and Edwards 2012; White 2008).

Because of the debate on terminology and the fact that some scholars saw pollution as only a technical problem that could be resolved by scientists or technology alone (Burns and Lynch 2004), environmental crime did not have a definition until the late 1990s. Clifford and Edwards (1998) discussed two approaches to define environmental crime. From a philosophical perspective, they suggested that five elements should be taken into the consideration including the type of activity, the specific act, the actor(s), the social status of the actor(s) and the sanction applied. Several questions related to these elements needed to be addressed before a definition of environmental crime could be developed. For instance, in terms of the type of activity, should we only include activities that had already diminished the quality of the environment or those that had potential to harm the environment? Who should be the actors responsible for the environmental harm/crime, individuals or corporations? How could the status of the actors, such as the position of an executive or a lower-level employee, affect the responsibility or the punishment? Clifford and Edwards (1998) argued that an environmental crime could be defined as "an act committed with the intent to harm or with a potential to cause harm to ecological and/or biological system and for the purpose of securing business or personal advantage" (Clifford and Edwards 1998: 26). This definition not only covered a wide range of activities described in the news media, but also clarified the uncertainty of actual harm and potential harm. In addition, it also highlighted the intent to commit the crime as an important factor in determining culpability. Therefore, it has provided a meaningful category of crime for purposes of scientific analysis and has been espoused by most contemporary criminologists in this area.

An operational legal definition may serve the greatest purpose for the environmental enforcement purposes. Under a legal framework, environmental crime has been defined as any act that violates environmental laws and/or regulations and is subject to criminal and civil prosecution and sanctions (Clifford and Edwards 1998; Situ and Emmons 2000). The legal definition provides a general guideline for law enforcement and regulatory officers to detect and investigate offenders who violate environmental legislation and sets a particular direction for studying environmental crime under the perspective of criminal justice. Such a legalistic approach in defining environmental crime, however, also constrains analysis because it omits certain practices or behaviours that are not covered by any statutes but may or do harm the environment. For instance, the extraction and transportation of tar sands in Alberta are damaging ecological systems and endangering various flora and fauna in the related areas, but so far no certain laws or regulations have defined these activities as crimes.

In the Canadian *Criminal Code*, there is no clear definition of environmental crime. Perhaps the most relevant provision that could be used to prosecute offenders who commit crimes against the environment is criminal negligence, which applies to anyone who "shows wanton or reckless disregard for the lives or safety of other persons" (Section 219). However, criminal negligence is not directly concerned with either environmental offences, or the harms to the environment (Law Reform Commission of Canada 1985). To compensate this situation, the *Canadian Environmental Protection Act* (CEPA) that was originally enacted in 1988 covers a variety of activities that may cause damage to the environment. It is stated in the CEPA that a fine or imprisonment of less than five years can be imposed if a person "intentionally or recklessly causes a disaster that results in a loss of the use or the non-use value of the environment" (Section 274). This provision shows that that environmental issues finally became a major focus of Canadian law and a sanction has been stipulated for an environmental offence. However, by requiring "a disaster" as the necessary harm element, the CEPA definition has set an extremely high threshold for environmental crimes that makes it difficult for prosecuting environmental offenders. Some critical criminologists have also suggested that we should be careful in using the statutory definitions, because many times the state itself has actually colluded in the most serious environmental harms that cost millions of dollars (see Green et al. 2007) or cause injury to people. Therefore, in such a case, legal definitions are considered to contain potential bias due to the state's involvement in those activities.

The various attempts to resolve confusions in the terminology should be appreciated,

although the definitions provided are far from perfect. An accurate and adequate definition of environmental crime can be extremely difficult to achieve (Clifford and Edwards
1998). In studies, some have employed the term "environmental harm" in the analyses
(see White 2008), while others highlight that environmental crime refers to an act origi-
nated by human beings, which may or may not violate the current rules and regulations
but "has identifiable environmental damage outcomes" (Lynch and Stretsky 2003: 227).
The definition debate and underlying theoretical conflicts, however, might not be the
obstacles but, instead, could enhance the development of research on environmental
crime. A workable definition should incorporate issues such as the amount and seriousness of harm, laws and regulations, and the most important factor — the determination
of actors that is frequently missing in most definitions. Since corporations are frequently
involved in environmental crime and blamed by both the public and researchers for being
responsible for their activities, more attention should be drawn on clarifying the role that
corporate interests played in environmental crime. Although individuals can also cause
harm to nature and violate environmental law and regulations, such as hunting wildlife
out of season, illegal disposal of household waste or fishing without a license, they are
rarely appearing in environmental crime studies (Shover and Routhe 2005) as the harm
caused by individual activities is relatively small-scale and unverifiable compared to those
conducted by corporations. Therefore, in this chapter, environmental crime refers to the
acts committed by corporations or individuals on behalf of a corporation with direct or
potential intent to cause environment harm and/or violating environmental legal statutes.

CORPORATIONS AND CORPORATE CRIME

Since being founded in the early seventeenth century, the power and wealth of corporations have been frequently associated with their involvement in illegal activities, such as
bribery, fraud, stock manipulation and unsafe working conditions (Clinard and Yeager
2006; Friedrichs 2010). On the one hand, corporations are viewed as a fundamental
component of contemporary societies with many positive contributions, which not only
offer millions of job opportunities to ordinary citizens to raise their families, but also
play important roles in community service, charities, public events and even scientific
research. On the other hand, there is clearly a dark side to corporations. The very essence of the corporation is unlimited earnings for its shareholders and limited liability
for its shareholders. For instance, industrial enterprises have long been condemned for
maximizing profits while minimizing the preservation of human life (Friedrichs 2010).
A large number of corporations are found associated with a wide range of illegal and
socially harmful activities, such as illegally dumping toxic wastes, causing various forms
of pollution, operating unsafe working conditions, corrupting politicians and producing
unsafe products (Simon 2006).

Corporate crimes have been principally associated with Western, capitalist countries,
especially the United States, the United Kingdom, Canada, Australia and so forth. Globalization, however, has spread capitalism to almost every cranny of the world. Corporate
activities, therefore, occur throughout developed and developing countries. As such, the
corporation is a symbol and product of the capitalist system, and the pursuit of profits
is unchanged no matter where they operate. Unsurprisingly, corporate crime is also a
product of a capitalist society, where power and resources are unevenly distributed to
members in different classes.

Since Sutherland (1949) first explored issues of corporate crime in his book, *White Collar Crime*, corporate crime has drawn lots of attention from criminologists. Sutherland defined white-collar crime as "a crime committed by a person of respectability and high social status in the course of his occupation" (1949: 2). This initial foray into the field actually conflated the concepts employing white-collar/corporate crime as a very broad concept to include both occupational crime and corporate illegalities. Over time, and with some intellectual development, the two were differentiated, and corporate crime referred to any activities conducted by corporations or individuals on behalf of a corporation that were prohibited by laws or punishable by the state (Braithwaite 1982; Clinard and Yeager 2006). Some scholars emphasize corporate victimization and define corporate crime as the activities that cause harm to individuals, such as employees and customers, organizations or society in general (Croall 2007; Friedrichs 2010; Snider 2000). In this regard, some negative behaviours by corporations may not actually be criminal or illegal in a certain jurisdiction, yet they should still fall into the corporate crime category. Therefore, corporate crime includes a diversity of violations and harmful activities for researchers to investigate, from price gouging to tax evasion or strategic bankruptcy, although some activities may be legal at some times.

Hence, from a critical perspective, corporate crime refers to unlawful or unethical activities committed by executives or other employees for the purpose of pursuing corporate interests (Friedrichs 2010). The key phrase here is "pursuing corporate interests." It clearly points out the fundamental characteristics and aims of modern corporations and suggests that most corporate crimes are driven by the combination of the emphasis on short-term profit and ignorance of/disregard for long-term harm. For instance, the executives of oil extraction companies may turn a blind eye to issues of environmental degradation and global warming; instead, the profit of producing a barrel of oil is their primary consideration. Extracting oil from tar sands produces four times more CO_2 than those in the conventional oil industry (Milmo 2007). However, oil companies do not stop their investment because of these obvious and/or potential harms to the environment. Corporations, in order to increase profits and/or reduce costs of their products, intentionally or unintentionally, practise in a way that pollutes our air and waters, poisons lands and puts the ecological systems on Earth at risk. Furthermore, because of the great power and resources possessed by corporations, the government, the legal system and even the military are all involved in a complex network that enables corporations to have high-level freedom of seeking and obtaining their interests without being punished (Tenenbaum and Ross 2006). For instance, giant corporation owners are consistently opposing certain regulations on reducing environmental crime but supporting those that could fit their economic interests (Simon 2000). The shared interests within the powerful elite network lead many legislators and policy makers to ignore such problems.

Environment plays an important role in the initiation and development of modern corporations as numerous companies either directly trade raw natural materials such as oil, gas and mineral resources or conduct natural resource–based activities including agriculture, fishing, logging and hunting. Canada had a well-known record for exporting natural resources even before the country was founded, since the early explorers traded fish and fur at the time of first contact with the Indigenous people of the land. For centuries, Canada's economic development has largely been driven by natural resources. Today, many Canadians are enthusiastic for globalization that brings opportunities for increasing wealth and enhancing economic success through conducting business with more countries. Yet globalization has also exaggerated the exploitation and extraction of a variety of natural resources. Although there are attempts to shift the Canadian economy away from exporting resources to manufacturing and financial industries, the increase in international trade and intensified resource demand brought about by globalization restrains Canada from shedding its dependency upon resource extraction (Hessing 2002). Environmental deterioration and degradation are the hidden costs of economic globalization and the tremendous economic success it has offered (Hessing 2002). Although, for their long term interests, Canadian corporations seem more likely to support regulations on environmental protection compared to their counterparties in the U.S. (Buhr and Freedman 2001), the balance between maximizing profits and protecting the ecological system and geographic environment cannot easily be achieved. Therefore, in Canada, environmental crime is more prevalent in natural resource–related industries, including fishing, logging, hunting, mining and quarrying.

TYPES OF ENVIRONMENTAL DEGRADATION

Since most definitions of environmental crime are very broad, categorizing environmental degradation varies. For instance, Carrabine and his colleagues (2004) identified two types of environment crime based on the harm and damage: "primary green crimes" refer to criminal activities that directly lead to destruction of the environment and natural resources on earth, whereas crimes that are symbolic or dependent on environmental degradation are considered "secondary green crimes." According to this typology, primary green crimes include air pollution, deforestation, water pollution, species decline and acts against animal rights; state violence against oppositional groups and hazardous waste are considered secondary green crime (Carrabine et al. 2004).

Some scholars have suggested taking the consideration of the public when discussing types of environmental crime. For instance, White (2005, 2008) argued that with the consideration of public perceptions and public participation, three different types of environmental degradation could be distinguished. He categorizes them as colors:

- "Brown" issues refer to pollution and activities related to urban life, including air pollution, pollution of urban stormwater, pollution of beaches, pesticides, oil spills, pollution of water catchments and disposal of toxic/hazardous waste.
- "Green" issues include crimes that affect wildness areas and conservation matters, including acid rain, habitat destruction, loss of wildlife, logging of forests, depletion of the ozone layer, toxic algae and water pollution.
- "White" issues are defined as activities conducted in the scientific laboratories and influenced by new technologies, such as genetically modified organisms, genetic discrimination and animal testing and experimentation.

As the prevalence of environmental crime varies temporally and spatially (Shover and Routhe 2005), it can be assessed at different geographic levels. White (2008) highlighted that geographic considerations could contribute to the analysis of environmental crime, not only because laws were implemented in certain geographic territories, but also because of the unique and special characteristics of each country. We here undertake a review of a number of forms of environmental crime in Canada, some of the consequences of such crime for Canadian society and the evolution of the Canadian state. While it is not possible to review all of the different types of environmental crime in this country, we discuss some significant aspects of three of the most notable forms of environmental crime: illegal logging, disposing toxic wastes and environmental harm caused by the extraction of natural resources. In addition, transnational environmental crime is a relatively new category that affects Canadian society and requires more academic attention.

Illegal Logging

Logging has been a major economic activity in countries that are dependent on exporting natural resources. Canada is certainly one of those, and forestry activities have a significant influence on the state and people. The forests, however, have been declining continuously: forests were described as 46 percent of Canada's land area in a 2006 official report (Canada Forest Service 2006), but the percentage was reduced to 39 percent in the most recent report (Canada Forest Service 2013). Canada's forest products have played an important role in its national economy since the earliest days of colonization, and Canada is one of the major forest exporting countries in the world. The timber industry contributed 18 billion Canadian dollars to the national GDP in 2012 (Canada Forest Service 2013).

Today, illegal logging and over-exploitation of the forests have become one of the most damaging environmental crimes in Canada. In British Columbia alone, for example, the annual cut has "exceeded economic sustainability by 20 to 25 percent" (Hessing 2002: 32). Ambiguous legislation and lack of effective enforcement are the main reasons for illegal logging (Green et al. 2007), which is frequently mixed with legal logging. Timber harvesting is determined not by ecological considerations, but by social, economic and political criteria, and it is found that "overcutting is the norm, not the exception" (Marchak et al. 1999: 30). In addition, misuse and abuse of logging permits issued by the government is also typical in the industry (Green et al. 2007). Intensified global competition further stimulates logging corporations' extraction of timber in excess of their allowed harvesting rates.

Harms associated with illegal logging are obvious, including biodiversity loss and climate change. Numerous species have become endangered and threatened due to loss of their habit as a result of massive forest cutting. In terms of climate, forests are buffers that can consume and reduce the CO_2 in the atmosphere, and the decline of forests is fundamentally damaging the environment and living conditions for human beings. The hectares of harvested areas are reported to be decreasing after it peaked in 2005, and greenhouse gas emission related to the deforestation also represents an upward trend (Canada Forest Service 2013). However, this temporary change only coincides with the decline in demand for forest products associated with the global economic downturn and does not reflect the government and industry's willingness to protect the forests. Timber companies, with the support of the government, may arguably recover and increase their harvesting rates after the world demand for forest products comes back.

Toxic Waste

Producing waste is inevitable in almost every industry, as a social process (White 2008), and finding an effective way to deal with waste disposal is one of the major responsibilities of the corporate sector. Perhaps, simply dumping waste into the air, water and/or on land is most cost-effective, which satisfies the philosophy of reducing costs. However, several laws and regulations provide guidelines for companies to recycle, reuse and apply appropriate treatment before releasing toxic waste to the environment (Rebovich 1992). Legitimate means, nonetheless, usually lead to a huge increase in the cost of products. For instance, it took more than $30 million to build onsite facilities to dispose toxic waste, but dumping these wastes to a developing country had an extremely low cost for $20 per ton at times (Simon 2000). Therefore, it is not difficult to imagine the reasons for companies using "economical" disposal methods. Illegal toxic waste disposal was first described as "midnight dumping," and wastes were usually dumped at "the nearest isolated areas" (Rebovich 1992: 3). Now, the activity has been extended to illegally disposing harmful chemical materials to air, water and land.

Toxic waste is one of the most complex issues in terms of environmental harm and crime. First, little clarification has been achieved on what should be considered toxic waste (Snider 2000; Szasz 1986). In Canada, it is estimated that over 60,000 industrial chemical materials have been used by manufacturers and more than 1000 new chemical substances are introduced each year (Snider 2000). Clearly identifying toxic substance from these materials is an almost impossible mission. Then, when turning the inquiry to legal statutes, only 44 of the chemical substances are listed as priorities in the Domestic Substances List by Environment Canada and only five of them were examined in ten years (Snider 2000).

Second, because of the limited resources and continuous budget cuts of millions of dollars Environment Canada has been facing (Environment Canada 2013), many programs operated by the agency, including Substance and Waste Management, have been curtailed, and hence only a small numbers of toxic waste cases can be investigated. For example, the funding available for use by Environment Canada decreased by 18.4 million in fiscal year 2014–15 compared to the previous fiscal year. Funding for programs to "reduce threats to health and the environment posed by pollution and waste from human activities" will fall from $76 million to $44 million between now and 2016–17 (Environment Canada 2014). Numerous corporations are dumping their toxic wastes unwatched, and it is hard to determine whether these activities are legal or illegal (Simon 2000). The dark figure in the official database limits the collection of accurate qualified data, which increases the difficulty of researching toxic waste in Canada.

Third, the lenient legislation regulating toxic waste makes Canada an attractive destination of dumping hazardous substances (Jacott et al. 2004). Hence, an increasing number of corporations in the U.S. and Mexico have been allowed and "invited" to dispose their wastes, untreated and toxic, into Canada, where cheaper and easier dumping sites are offered. Quebec is the primary victim found in the Jacott et al.'s (2004) survey report of cross-border dumping in North America. These activities are not banned by the government, so both domestic and international companies keep poisoning the land and water of Canada, secretly and unexamined out of the public eye.

Natural Resource Extraction

Canada is rich in natural resources: oil reserves, including the tar sands, are the third largest in the world, and coal reserves rank the fourth largest compared to other nations. Even though Canada possesses these important natural resources and sells them as commodities, for huge profits, a major concern must be raised: how can we extract the resources without damaging the environment? The current extraction process in the coal and oil industries is always associated with different types of environmental destruction and degradation (Bell and York 2010; Long et al. 2012; Smandych and Kueneman 2010). In the coal mining industry, due to the appalling toll on workers' safety, underground mining has been abandoned. The most commonly used method today is called "mountaintop" or "surface mining," which removes the "overburden" (soil, rocks, gravel, forests, etc.) and then loads and transports the exposed coal to further processing. The consequences of this mountaintop removal mining are multi-level, including deforestation, threats to biodiversity and the increase of flooding because nothing has been left to stop the running rain waters (Bell and York 2010; Long et al. 2012). In addition, because raw coal must be cleaned in order to reduce sulfur and non-combustible materials before being sent to market, the waste (coal slurry) produced in this process, consisting of water, fine particles from coal and numerous chemical substances, is highly toxic and frequently stored on the flattened mountaintop or dumped at the abandoned coal mines (Bell and York 2010). The leak and collapse of slurry impoundment has caused water pollution, wildlife loss and deaths of humans. In 2013, the largest coal slurry spill in Canadian history occurred in Alberta, where one billion litres of waste water contaminated the Athabasca River (Lisenby 2013). It caused tremendous damage to habitat and risks to certain fish species.

The situation in the oil industry is similar. The majority of oil reserves in Canada are in the tar sands, known as the oil sands to its proponents, mostly in Alberta. It is reported that one in fourteen jobs in Alberta was related to energy industries and every dollar invested in oil sands creates eight dollars worth of economic activity (Government of Alberta 2011). Although the oil sands projects have provided job opportunities and created economic value, the techniques employed to extract the tar sands are extremely hazardous because they are destroying forests, producing toxic waste and polluting the Athabasca watershed (Smandych and Kueneman 2010). In addition, new pipelines stretching over one thousand kilometers in-length are proposed to move oil from Alberta to the west coast of British Columbia. These projects have received radical opposition from Indigenous communities and environmentalists, but the corporations ask the public to concentrate only on the job opportunities they have created and "safe" protection of the environment they have utilized.

TRANSNATIONAL ENVIRONMENTAL CRIME

Transnational environmental crime is a relatively new subfield of environmental crime, and little attention has been paid to it by both law enforcement experts and criminologists (White 2010; Wright 2011). Typically, understanding environmental crime emphasized the activities and regulations based on sole nations and governments from a perspective of natural resource management and conservation (Wright 2011). A lack of adequate legal and judicial support between countries is one of the reasons for the neglect of transnational environmental crime in the enforcement side. Transnational environmental crime is again difficult to define, but most agree that it includes (illegally) transporting natural resources, international trading in flora and fauna and cross-border dumping of toxic waste and e-waste such as computers, television, cell-phones and other types of electronics (Elliott 2012; Gibbs et al. 2010b; Meyer et al. 2006; White 2010; Wright 2011). Transnational environmental crime is global and organized in nature, and it can be categorized into four major types, exploiting nature (e.g., fishing and logging), illegally dumping waste (e.g., traditional garbage and e-waste), hazarding specific geographic regions (e.g., illegally hunting specific species) and threatening the worldwide society (e.g., climate change) (White 2010).

In addition, illegal fishing, logging and wildlife transporting all have negative a impact on biodiversity, which refers to the variance of all species living on earth (White 2011;

Wyler and Sheikh 2009). For instance, secret lobster poachers in the Atlantic provinces in Canada are busy selling their illegal catches to fishing companies, restaurants and hotels, which not only costs the government millions in lost taxes, but also causes the decline of the species (White 2009). These criminals are organized and professional in nature, and the crimes are typically carried out in complex and sophistic networks and routines (Elliott 2012). A diversity of flora and fauna are targets, such as snakes, black bears, birds, elephants and timber, and are smuggled from one country to another. Sometimes, it is not the animals themselves that are desired, but the products made from their organs and bodies, such as pieces of ivory and rhinoceros horn.

In addition to the threats to biodiversity, pollution and waste is another problem associated with transnational environmental crime. It is estimated that 30 to 40 million tons of hazardous waste is being trafficked cross international borders each year, driven by the difference of dumping prices among countries (e.g., US$250 per ton in the U.S. vs. US$40 per ton in countries in Africa) (Liddick 2011). The economic value and revenue lost worldwide may not be generated precisely, but it is estimated that environmental toxic waste crime is more than $10 billion each year in the U.S. (Wright 2011). The estimated profit of organized transportation of waste between the U.S. and Canada is around 2.48 million dollars per year (Elliott 2012). International transporting of hazardous waste is also an organized crime in nature, but the specific organizations involved in this type of environmental crime remains unclear. However, its consequences are not difficult to investigate: soil pollution, water pollution and deforestation (Liddick 2011; White 2011). E-waste, referring to used electronic equipment (e.g., television, computers, printers, cellphones, etc.), destined for disposal, reuse or recycling is a relatively new type of "goods" that are transported from one country to another (Gibbs et al. 2010b). Many of them are exported from the developed countries and imported by developing countries in the name of recycling. However, the factories in those developing countries do not have sufficient facilities and equipment to handle the e-waste they have brought in, which ends up being dumped in local areas (Gibbs et al. 2010b). Both human health and the environment are seriously threatened and harmed due to the toxic substances, such as mercury, contained in the e-waste.

PATTERNS OF ENVIRONMENTAL CRIME IN CANADA

It is difficult to describe the patterns of environmental crime in Canada because environmental change can hardly be tracked due to both technical difficulties and social, political and economic limitations (Hessing 2002). Several factors have contributed to the limited information on the patterns and rates of environmental crime. First, the economic interest in natural resource exploitation can easily blind politicians and corporate executives to ecological and environmental concerns. The sharp year-over-year budget cuts to Environmental Canada during the past two to three decades is a good example of such almost wilful ignorance. These budget cuts have substantially undermined the agency's capacity to pursue environmental offenders and manage its enforcement cases, leading to a significant under-enforcement of environmental laws and regulations.

Second, because of the confusions and conflicts of definitions and operational typologies of environmental crime, cases reported by the regulatory agencies may not reflect the real patterns of environmental crime in Canada. One result of this problem is the under-reporting of environmental harm and crime.

A third factor is the methodological issues in handling and collecting data and measuring the value of affected resources. Many criminologists are not familiar with examining environmental data, which could be at irregular time intervals (Gibbs and Simpson 2009). Inadequate assessment, funding cuts and economic and political pressures are all reasons for discontinuous data (Hessing 2002). In addition, although it is possible to assess the economic value of certain types of nature resources, the impact of exploiting those resources on the environment is extremely difficult to be measured accurately.

Finally, a lack of and several changes of legislation have played a role in the under-enforcement and under-reporting of environmental crime, which has in turn affected the reliability and validity of enforcement data (Shover and Routhe 2005). For instance, no clear description of environmental crime can be found in the Canadian *Criminal Code*. Although Environment Canada was established in 1971 to be responsible for protecting and enhancing the quality of the natural environment, the principle federal environmental statute, the CEPA, was not passed until 1988. The CEPA 1988 was criticized for ignoring its own strict compliance policy and was replaced by the CEPA 1999, which includes 250 recommendations on environmental issues. However, this legal change did not lead to a more extensive or proactive enforcement system. In addition, due to the unbalanced coverage between street crime and corporate crime by news media, the general public rarely realizes and reports themselves as victims of environmental crime, which has further limited the number of reported environmental crime cases. Therefore, little data is available from Environmental Canada to analyze the exact patterns of environmental crime in Canada. Most researchers have employed specific cases for their analyses.

Fortunately, we can have a general understanding of the issue of environmental crime by analyzing the CEPA annual reports (Environment Canada 2001–2012). Typically, the first stage of enforcement of the CEPA is inspection, and for cases with suspected violations, enforcement tools might be used, including tests and measures, investigation, warnings, injunctions and prosecutions. From 2001 to 2011, the total number of inspection cases was approximately 4,500 to 5,000 each year, but this number was around 2,500 in both 2006 and 2007. However, no clear pattern or trend of the inspection can be found according to these reports. Most efforts were conducted to inspect activities of exporting and importing hazardous wastes, pollutants release inventory, and tetrachloroethylene

Figure 1. Total Inspections and Inspections on Hazardous Wastes, 2001–2011

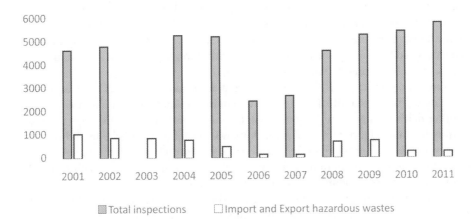

(used in dry cleaning and reporting requirements). Figure 1 shows the number of tons of imports and exports of hazardous wastes from 2001 to 2011.

Total imports of hazardous wastes have been slightly decreasing in recent years, whereas exports from Canada have increased a little. However, both imports and exports of hazardous waste are stable in general. Yet, the total number of inspections involving tetrachloroethylene increased annually from 40 cases of 4413 inspections in 2003 to 1640 cases of 5808 inspections in 2011.

Although the total numbers of inspection were high, the total numbers of investigation have been kept at a very low level. Environment Canada investigated 86 cases in 2011, which was the largest number in eleven years, up from 32 in 2003. So, the ration of investigations to inspections has been approximately 1 percent (e.g., 0.7 percent in 2003, 0.7 percent in 2008 and 1.4 percent in 2011). However, written warnings on the violations have been increasing. The number of written warnings was 517 in 2001 and 1810 in 2009, and in 2011, over 4,000 writing warnings were sent out to various corporations. Because of the low investigation rates, it is not surprising to find that the number of convictions have been even smaller. In the period of eleven years from 2001 to 2011, the total number of convictions was 70, whereas the total number of investigations was 526. In 2004 and 2007 each, only one conviction was recorded for committing environmental crime, whereas in 2003, there were 14 convictions in total.

In summary, it is difficult to explore the patterns of conducting environmental crime in Canada using a legal definition and using information from the government agency mandated to monitor environmental harm and to enforce environmental laws. Although, one pattern is very clear: the inspections remain at a relatively high level, and the total numbers of investigations and convictions remain extremely small. Furthermore, many inspections are for relatively minor environmental harms, rather than the huge environmental impact of resource extraction industries and projects.

TYPES OF ORGANIZATIONAL VIOLATORS

Individual white collar criminals are typically driven by personal economic interests, whereas corporate violators commit crimes on behalf of the organization to achieve corporate goals of maximizing profits. Several factors may impact corporate offenders on environmental degradation. For instance, company size plays an important role in pollution and other types of environmental crime (Grant et al. 2002; Simpson et al. 2007). It is found that larger companies are more likely to commit environmental crimes, pollution in particular, than their smaller counterparts (Grant et al. 2002; Simpson et al. 2007). Yeager argued that "a large firm that is consistently compliant with all legal requirements is little more likely than a crime-free city" (2007: 27).

Environmental crime is also more prevalent in certain industries. Corporations in the oil industry are found more likely to commit environmental crimes than those operating in other fields (Clinard and Yeager 2006). Chemical and petrochemical companies are leading in the illegal dumping of hazardous waste (Rebovich 1992). In addition, toxic waste is not just in one form produced by corporations "on land." Many cruise companies have also played a role in dumping hazardous waste, and numerous cruise ships have been fined because of polluting the oceans (Carmichael 2007).

Governments also play a role in hazarding the environment (Situ and Emmons 2000; Wolf 2011). The extreme reluctance to criminalize environmental harm is a central way that governments are complicit. As discussed in the previous section, none of activities that hazard the environment are criminalized in the Canadian *Criminal Code*. In addition, governments could easily affect the efforts of enforcing laws. For instance, when the Conservative Government launched its "Common Sense Revolution" in 1995, there was a huge decline of charges for environmental violations, from 1640 in 1994 to 724 in 1996; companies were fined two-third fewer (from 3.6 million in 1992 to 1.2 million in 1997) for pollution than they were five years ago (Girard et al. 2010).

The failure or insufficiency of effective regulations against environmental harm also illustrates the government as a quasi-offender of environmental crime. In addition, the denial of environmental harm makes the state a co-offender by encouraging corporations to ignore environmental problems. For instance, most toxic substances are not listed on the enforcement agenda by Environmental Canada, which could largely affect the environment. Many black lakes, or coal slurry, produced by the coal industries, are allowed to be left at the mining sites. Furthermore, disposal of toxic waste by militaries and energy projects is another significant type of environmental crime committed by the government (Situ and Emmons 2000). From time to time, the government is also directly involved in the criminal activities, such as pollution. For instance, in 2013, the City of Ottawa was fined $15,000 for violating the *Pollution Prevention Provisions of Fisheries Act* (Environmental Canada 2014). In the same year, the City of Red Deer, Alberta, was ordered to pay a penalty of $50,000 after pleading guilty under the CEPA due to the release of approximately 160 litres of polychlorinated biphenyl contaminated oil from a metal drum located at electrical substation (Environmental Canada 2014). Therefore, when examining the offenders of environmental crime, the federal and local governments are important players that cannot be ignored.

CORPORATE MOTIVATIONS FOR COMMITTING ENVIRONMENTAL CRIME

In a capitalist society, corporations are a fundamental part of the capitalist class that owns and controls the social surplus (the profits) created by workers, the direct producers, within the economy. The corporation exists to maximize profit — seeing profits as unlimited — for its owners. While the corporation must operate within society, its economic (profit) goals are not social; it exists to ignore that social context to the greatest extent possible. Thus, the corporate form is criminogenic in nature (White 2008) — it is not organized to pay attention to social harm. Coporations' connections to social elites and politicians assist them to avoid punishment by legal statutes, as many laws work on behalf of corporate goals, with the consideration of the economic and wealth interests of the capitalist class being a priority instead of dealing with environmental concerns. The public perception of environmental harm is also controlled by, or at least mediated by, those with power and resources. Therefore, the view that corporate crime is less harmful than "street crime" pervades the mass media (Friedrichs 2010; White 2008). Most people are convinced that economic development is the most important need in society and are taught that corporations are the key instrument to achieve economic success. Environmental degradation occurring in accelerated economic activities becomes almost invisible (Hessing 2002). Since corporations are driven by their fundamental characteristics of maximizing profits that demands the exploitation of human beings, nature and consumption markets, environmental harm is inevitable from corporate operations.

A critical strain theory can be used to explain the motivation of environmental criminals (Situ and Emmons 2000). Competitive markets and limited resources exaggerate the difficulty of surviving and succeeding for corporations. The goal of achieving financial success and the legitimate (unharmful) means are not always balanced and available for every corporation. For corporations that lack of legitimate means, they may not hesitate to seek for alternative illegitimate means to accomplish their tasks. Although the primary goals for executives vary from maximizing profits to expanding market share or sustaining rapid growth, the pressure on their shoulders motivates criminal activities. For instance, executives of logging companies may direct their employees to go over their legitimate allowance for more profits. For some chemical companies, exporting and dumping hazardous waste to other nations where environmental laws are missing or more lenient for a cheaper price is also a desired illegitimate means to lower their costs.

Another motivation for corporations to degrade the environment can be addressed by rational choice theory, which is commonly used in explaining corporate crimes (Shover and Routhe 2005). Corporate and white-collar offenders are considered more rational in decision making than street criminals. They are more likely to balance the benefits and risks before taking an action. For instance, General Motors issued several recalls about millions of small cars due to an ignition switch defect in 2014 and has accepted claims for more than 150 deaths (Anderson and Subramaniam 2014). There is evidence showing that the company has long been aware of the deadly defect since 2005 or even earlier. However, it took approximately ten years to make the recall. There is no doubt that the executives have chosen the most beneficial way for their company to deal with these defects, regardless of the possible death of their clients.

Similarly, the benefits that executives could gain from committing environmental crimes are significant and consistent with the ideology of maximizing profits and minimizing costs. On the other hand, the risk they are facing is at an extremely minimal level, as our earlier discussion of the enforcement of environmental regulation shows so clearly. In this view, if every environmental criminal were quickly and significantly punished, then potential rational criminals should be deterred or restrained from committing similar activities. However, in reality, few executives have been apprehended or sanctioned under the category of environmental crime. The typical punishment corporate executives face and receive is being fined a relatively small amount of money. In addition, "techniques of neutralization" (see Chapter 2) are also used by executives to deny the existence of victims, responsibilities and injury to any parties — hence they feel innocent of any misconduct. A typical tactic of "greenwashing" is commonly used to neutralize their activities, which helps corporations hide their harmful behaviour, mislead the public and deny their responsibilities for the damage of the environment (Holcomb 2008; Smandych and Kueneman 2010). The Internet has become a powerful tool to help them accomplish such a task. Public safety, environmental friendliness and the introduction of highly developed technology are the common themes found on corporations' websites, illustrating their carefulness on environmental issues.

REFORMING AND REGULATION

What should be the societal response to environmental crime? The question turns to how we could improve the situation and save the planet as habitable for human beings. Many argue that laws have little power to tackle criminal activities against the environment

(Hawke 1997). In Canada, since the CEPA 1999 has been implemented, only ninety-six convictions were made in the eleven years from 2001 to 2011 (Environmental Canada 2012). Part of the reason is the difficulty of determining responsibility: is it the executives or employees who should be responsible for the environmental harm? One solution is to focus prosecution and punishment to make the corporation liable and to control of the corporation, just as street criminals are made liable for their harmful behaviour. This would essentially involve criminalizing environmental crime. However, the nature of corporations hinders the process of prosecution. In Canadian law, determining whether a corporation has committed a prohibited act and whether a corporation has the requisite mental state is far more complicated than for an individual. Obviously, the only actors that may be held liable are corporate executives and employees, since corporations are not real beings. Due to the shared interests between economic elites and politicians, prosecution and conviction are hardly received by corporate executives and owners. Because of the failure of laws, some analysts have suggested a different approach to deal with environmental crime: "smart" regulation (Gibbs et al. 2010b; Gunningham and Graboshy 1998; White 2008).

The idea of regulation has been recommended by many criminologists. It includes not only government intervention, but also a range of combinations of market and non-market solutions, and it involves the public and other interested parties (Gunningham and Grabosky 1998; White 2008). It is argued that more effective and efficient policies handling environmental crises can be produced by the combination of these regulatory actors. According to White (2008), the model of smart regulation consists of several elements, such as command and control regulation (e.g., license and permits), voluntarism (e.g., public recognition of environmental achievements), education and information (e.g., corporation environmental report) and economic instruments (e.g., green funds). For instance, after more education on environmental crises and protection is provided to the public, customers may make purchasing decisions based on corporate environmental reports and choose the products from the companies with good records on environmental performance. Green funds or awards for environmental achievements may encourage the corporations to put more efforts towards improving their conditions on environmental issues. In addition to the positive reinforcement, the government should make more efforts to prohibit violations of legal statutes on the environment. A first step could be amending environmental crime into the *Criminal Code*. The incorporation of the regulatory actors at different levels, as mentioned above, might change the current situation on regulating environmental crimes. However, further examinations and efforts are required to illustrate the advantage of this model. More public awareness, contributions made by researchers in academy and enhanced government and self-regulation of corporations are all necessary to improve solutions of the environmental issues.

CONCLUSION

This chapter introduced several important issues of environmental crime in Canada. The definition of environmental crime from philosophical and legal perspectives is provided, and the difficulties of achieving an accurate and adequate definition are also discussed. In addition, environmental crimes, serious ones in particular, are linked to corporate crime due to the nature of corporations. We also analyzed several major types of environmental crime hazarding Canada. A clear pattern of environmental crime in Canada, however, is difficult to obtain. Types of violators and their motivations are discussed in detail. It is urgent that more efforts are needed to deal with these issues of environmental crime.

DISCUSSION QUESTIONS

1. We know that the oil sands projects operating in Alberta are a risk to our environment, but we cannot simply shut them down because they have an immense influence on the economics of both the province and Canada. Do you have any suggestion that helps balance economic development and prevention of environment?

2. Think about this statement: "Corporate profits are not more important than people's lives and health, and the laws need to reflect in such a way." Do you agree with this standpoint? Why or why not?

3. Discuss whether and how we should amend the Canadian Criminal Code to improve the legislation of environmental crime.

GLOSSARY

Environmental Crime: acts committed by corporations or individuals on behalf of a corporation with direct or potential intent to cause environment harm and/or violating environmental legal statutes.

E-waste: used electronic equipment (e.g., television, computers, printers, cellphones, etc.) destined for disposal, reuse or recycling.

Greenwashing: tactics that corporations use to ask the public to concentrate only on the job opportunities they have created and "safe" protection of the environment they have utilized.

Illegal Dumping: dumping of toxic wastes intentionally or unintentionally through runoffs, leakage of old underground tanks or pipes by individuals or organizations, which contributes to toxic waste pollution that threatens and destroys waterways and pollutes groundwater.

Primary Geen Crimes: criminal activities that directly lead to destruction of the environment and natural resources on earth.

Secondary Green Crimes: crimes that are symbolic or dependent on environmental degradation.

SUGGESTED READINGS

M. Clifford and T. Edwards (eds.), *Environmental Crime*, second edition, Burlington, MA: Jones and Bartlett Learning (2012).

R. White, *Crimes against Nature: Environmental Criminology and Ecological Justice*, Cullompton, UK: Willan Publishing (2008).

R. White (ed.), *Global Environmental Harm: Criminological Perspectives*, Cullompton, UK: Willan Publishing (2010).

SUGGESTED WEBSITES

Environmental Canada <http://www.ec.gc.ca/?lang=En>
United Nations Environment Programme <http://www.unep.org/>

REFERENCES

Anderson, S., and V. Subramaniam. 2014. "Transport Canada Aware of Deadly GM Defect 8 Months Before Recall." At <cbc.ca/news/business/transport-canada-aware-of-deadly-gm-defect-8-months-before-recall-1.2807674>.

Bell, S., and R. York. 2010. "Community Economic Identity: The Coal Industry and Ideology Construction in West Virginia." *Rural Sociology* 75, 111–43.

Braithwaite, J. 1982. "Enforced Self-Regulation: A New Strategy for Corporate Crime Control." *Michigan Law Review* 80, 1466–507.

Brantingham P., and P. Brantingham. 1981. *Environmental Criminology*. Newbury Park, CA: Sage.

Buhr, N., and M. Freedman. 2001. "Culture, Institutional Factors and Differences in Environmental Disclosure between Canada and the United States." *Critical Perspectives on Accounting* 12, 293–322.

Burns, R.G., and M.J. Lynch. 2004. *Environmental Crime: A Sourcebook*. New York: LFB Scholarly Publishing.

Canada Forest Service. 2013. *The State of Canada's Forests 2013*. Ottawa: Natural Resources Canada.

___. 2006. *The State of Canada's Forests 2006–2007*. Ottawa: Natural Resources Canada.

Carmichael, S.E. 2007. "Cruise Line Industry." In J. Gerber and E. Jensen (eds.), *Encyclopedia of White-Collar Crime*. Westport, CT: Greenwood Press.

Carrabine, E., P. Iganski, M. Lee, K. Plummer and N. South. 2004. *Criminology: A Sociological Introduction*. London: Routledge.

Clifford, M., and T. Edwards. 1998. "Defining Environmental Crime." In M. Clifford (ed.), *Environmental Crime: Enforcement, Policy and Social Responsibility*. Gaithersburg, MD: Aspen.

___. 2012. "Identifying Harm and Defining Crime: Exploring the Criminalization of Environmental Issues." In M. Clifford and T. Edwards (ed.), *Environmental Crime*, Second edition. Burlington, MA: Jones and Bartlett Learning.

Clinard, M.B., and P.T. Yeager. 2006. *Corporate Crime: With a New Introduction by Marshall B. Clinard*. New Brunswick, NJ: Transaction Publishers.

Croall, H. 2007. "Victims of White-collar and Corporate Crime." In P. Davies, P. Francis and C. Greer (eds.), *Victims, Crime and Society*. London: McMillan.

Elliott, L. 2012. "Fighting Transnational Environmental Crime." *Journal of International Affairs* 66: 87–104.

Environment Canada. 2001–2012. *Canadian Environmental Protection Act, 1999 Annual Report*. At <ec.gc.ca/lcpe-cepa/default.asp?lang=Enandn=477203E8-1#archived>.

___. 2012. *2012 Annual Report on Environment Canada's Use of the Law Enforcement Justification Provisions*. At <ec.gc.ca/alef-ewe/default.asp?lang=Enandn=2A4AB71A-1>.

___. 2013. *Environment Canada's Quarterly Financial Report*. At <ec.gc.ca/default.asp?lang=Enandn=658453E9-1>.

___. 2014. *Environmental Offenders Registry*. At <ec.gc.ca/alef-ewe/default.asp?lang=Enandn=1F014378-1andxsl=genericsearchrenderer%2Cresultandsearchoffset=1andsearchdisplaycount=50anddatabasematch=wsformsandfiltername=formtypeandformtype=6E11861D-0087-4DF6-B3B1-11E7377D6289andcorporation_name=andcorporation_province=D8E6567C-50D6-4A72-A076-06EBF8D810DCandoffence_province=andkeywords=andsubmit=Search#resulttop>.

Friedrichs, David O. 2010. *Trusted Criminals: White Collar Crime in Contemporary Society*, Fourth edition. Belmont, CA: Wadsworth Cengage Learning.

Gibbs, C., M.L. Gore, E.F.McGarrell and L. Rivers. 2010a. "Introducing Conservation Criminology: Towards Interdisciplinary Scholarship on Environmental Crimes and Risks." *British Journal of Criminology* 50: 124–44.

Gibbs, C., E.F. McGarrell and M. Axelrod. 2010b. "Transnational White-Collar Crime and Risk: Lesson from the Global Trade in Electronic Waste." *Criminology and Public Policy* 9: 543–60.

Gibbs, C, and S. Simspon. 2009. "Measuring Corporate Environmental Crime Rates: Progress and Problems." *Crime, Law and Social Change* 51: 87–107.

Girard, A.L., S. Day and L. Snider. 2010. "Tracking Environmental Crime through CEPA: Canada' Environment Cops or Industry's Best Friend?" *Canadian Journal of Sociology* 35: 219–41.

Government of Alberta. 2011. "Alberta's Oil Sands: Economic Activity in Alberta and Canada." At <oilsands.alberta.ca/FactSheets/Economic_Activity_in_Alberta_and_Canada.pdf>.

Grant, D.S., A.J. Bergesen and A.W. Jones. 2002. "Organizational Size and Pollution: The Case of the U.S. Chemical Industry." *American Sociological Review* 67: 389–407.

Green, P., T. Ward and K. McConnachie. 2007. "Logging and Legality: Environmental Crime, Civil Society, and the State." *Social Justice* 34: 94–110.

Gunningham, N., and P. Grabosky. 1998. *Smart Regulation: Designing Environmental Policy.* Oxford: Clarendon Press.

Hawke, N. 1997. "Corporate Environmental Crime: Why Shouldn't Directors Be Liable?" *The London Journal of Canadian Studies* 13: 12–24.

Herbig, F.J., and S.J. Joubert. 2006. "Criminological Semantics: Conservation Criminology — Vision or Vagary?" *Acta Criminologica* 19: 88–103.

Hessing, M. 2002. "Economic Globalization and Canadian Environmental Restricting: The Mill(ennium)-end Sale." In S.C. Boyd, D.E. Chunn and R. Menzies (ed.), *Toxic Criminology: Environment, Law and the State in Canada.* Halifax, NS: Fernwood Publishing.

Holcomb, J. 2008. "Environmentalism and the Internet: Corporate Greenwashers and Environmental Groups." *Contemporary Justice Review* 11: 203–11.

Jacott, M., C. Reed and M. Winfield. 2004. *The Generation and Management of Hazardous Wastes and Transboundary Hazardous Waste Shipments between Mexico, Canada and the United States since NAFTA: A 2004 Update.* Austin, TX: Texas Center for Policy Studies.

Koven, P. 2014. "Imperial Metals Plans Debenture Issue in Wake of Dam Breach." *National Post* August 16. At <thestarphoenix.com/business/Imperial+Metals+plans+debenture+issue+wa ke+breach/10124148/story.html>.

Law Reform Commission of Canada. 1985. *Crime against the Environment.* Ottawa, ON: Law Reform Commission of Canada.

Liddick, L.R. 2011. *Crimes Against Nature: Illegal Industries and the Global Environment.* Santa Barbara, CA: Praeger.

Lisenby, D. 2013. "Did Canada Just Have the Largest Coal Slurry Spill in Its History?" At <ecowatch. com/2013/11/08/canada-largest-coal-slurry-spill/>.

Long, M.A., P.B. Stretesky and M.J. Lynch. 2012. "Crime in the Coal Industry: Implications for Green Criminology and Treadmill of Production." *Organization and Environment* 25: 328–46.

Lynch, M.J. 1990. "The Greening of Criminology: A Perspective on the 1990s." *Critical Criminologist* 2: 1–5.

Lynch, M.J., and P.B. Stretsky. 2003. "The Meaning of Green: Contrasting Criminological Perspectives." *Theoretical Criminology* 7: 217–38.

Marchak, M., S.L. Patricia and D. Herbert. 1999. *Falldown: Forest Policy in British Columbia.* Vancouver: David Suzuki Foundation and Ecotrust Canada.

Matus, K., K. Nam, N.E. Selin, L.N. Lamsal, J.M. Reilly and S. Paltsev. 2012. "Health Damages from Air Pollution in China." *Global Environmental Change* 22: 55–66.

Meyers, G.D., G. McLeod, and M.A. Anbarci. 2006. "An International Waste Convention: Measures for Achieving Sustainable Development." *Waste Management and Research* 24: 505–13.

Milmo, C. 2007. "The Biggest Environmental Crime in History." *The Independent.* At <independent. co.uk/environment/the-biggest-environmental-crime-in-history-764102.html>.

Noyes, P.D., M.K. McElwee, H.D. Miller, B.W. Clark, L.A. Van Tiema, K.C. Walcott, K.N. Erwina and E.D. Levina. 2009. "The Toxicology of Climate Change: Environmental Contaminants in a Warming World." *Environment International* 35: 971–86.

Nikiforuk, A. 2008. *Tar Sands: Dirty Oil and the Future of the Continent.* Vancouver: Greystone Books.

Rebovich, D. 1992. *Dangerous Ground: The World of Hazardous Waste Crime.* New Brunswick: Transaction Publishers.

Shover, N., and A.S. Routhe. 2005. "Environmental Crime." *Crime and Justice* 32: 321–71.

Simon, D.R. 2000. "Corporate Environmental Crimes and Social Inequality: New Directions for Environmental Crime Research." *American Behavioral Scientist* 43: 633–45.

___. 2006. *Elite Deviance.* Eighth edition. Boston: Allyn and Bacon.

Simpson, S.S., J. Garner and C. Gibbs. 2007. *Why Do Corporations Obey Environmental Law? Assessing Punitive and Cooperative Strategies of Corporate Crime Control.* Washington, DC: National Institute of Justice.

Situ, Y., and D. Emmons. 2000. *Environmental Crime: The Criminal Justice System's Role in Protecting the Environment.* Thousand Oaks, CA: Sage.

Smandych, R., and R. Kueneman. 2010. "The Canadian-Alberta Tar Sands: A Case Study of State-Corporate Environmental Crime." In R. White (ed.), *Global Environmental Harm: Criminological Perspectives.* Cullompton, UK: Willan Publishing.

Snider, L. 2000. "The Sociology of Corporate Crime: An Obituary (or: Whose Knowledge Claims Have Legs?)" *Theoretical Criminology* 4: 169–206.

South, N. 1998. "A Green Field of Criminology? A Proposal for a Perspective." *Theoretical Criminology* 2: 211–33.

South, N., and P. Beirne (ed.). 2006. *Green Criminology.* Hampshire, UK: Ashgate Publishing.

Sutherland, E.H. 1949. *White Collar Crime.* New York: Dryden Press.

Szasz, A. 1986. "Corporations, Organized Crime, and the Disposal of Hazardous Waste: An Examination of the Making of a Criminogenic Regulatory Structure." *Criminology* 24: 1–27.

Tao, Y., S. Mi, S. Zhou, S. Wang and X. Xie. 2014. "Air Pollution and Hospital Admissions for Respiratory Diseases in Lanzhou, China." *Environmental Pollution* 185: 196–201.

Tenenbaum, S., and R.J.S. Ross. 2006. "Who Rules America?" *Teaching Sociology* 34: 389–97.

White, R. 2005. "Environmental Crime in Global Context: Exploring the Theoretical and Empirical Complexities." *Current Issues in Criminal Justice* 16: 271–85.

___. 2008. *Crimes Against Nature: Environmental Criminology and Ecological Justice.* Cullompton, UK: Willan Publishing.

___. 2010. "Globalisation and Environmental Harm." In R. White (ed.), *Global Environmental Harm: Criminological Perspectives.* Cullompton, UK: Willan Publishing.

___. 2011. *Transnational Environmental Crime: Toward an Eco-global Criminology.* New York: Routledge.

Wolf, B. 2011. "'Green-Collar Crime': Environmental Crime and Justice in the Sociological Perspective." *Sociology Compass* 5: 499–511.

Wright, G. 2011. "Conceptualising and Combating Transnational Environmental Crime." *Trends in Organized Crime* 14: 332–46.

Wyler, L.S., and P.A. Sheikh. 2009. *International Illegal Trade in Wildlife.* New York: Nova Science Publishers, Inc.

Yeager, P.C. 2007. "Understanding Corporate Lawbreaking: From Profit Seeking to Law Finding." In H.N. Pontell and G. Geis (ed.), *International Handbook of White-Collar and Corporate Crime.* New York: Singer.

Zilney, L., D. McGurrin and S. Zahran. 2006. "Environmental Justice and the Role of Criminology: An Analytical Review of 33 Years of Environmental Justice Research." *Criminal Justice Review* 31: 47–62.

9

IMPRISONMENT AND ECONOMIC MARGINALITY

Carolyn Brooks

KEY FACTS

> The United States of America has highest level of incarceration in the world, with more than 2 million people behind bars. That's an incarceration rate of 716 people per 100,000.

> Approximately 40,000 Canadians are imprisoned on any given day in Canada — an incarceration rate of 118 people per 100,000. This rate is lower than the U.S., but it is still more than double that reported by Japan, Finland and Iceland.

> In provinces where the information is collected, approximately 44 percent of all incarcerated people aged twenty-five or higher have not completed high school and have a low socio-economic status.

> The 2012 Ashley Smith inquiry acknowledged that the mental health of incarcerated persons, particularly women, is often overlooked by institutions. The report subsequently calls for easier access to mental health services for inmates.

> Recent statistics indicated that the Federal Government of Canada, as well as provincial and territorial governments, spent approximately $4.3 billion on the adult correctional system in 2011–12. That equates to more than $106,000 per offender.

> Between 2000–1 and 2008–9 the number of people remanded to custody in Canada rose from 7,392 to 13,600, a growth of 84 percent, while the number of people sentenced to custody remained somewhat stable. This means that more than half of all people behind bars in Canada have not been convicted of a crime.

> During the fortieth session of Canadian parliament, the Conservative Party of Canada passed Bill C-25 into legislation. This bill, given the populist title Truth in Sentencing Act, limits Judges' ability provide sentencing credit for time spent in remand. At the time of its passing, the Parliamentary Budget Officer estimated that implementation of this this new law would cost Canadians $6.5 to $7 billion for new facilities and an additional $5.3 billion per year due to increased incarceration numbers.

> Corrections Corporation of America, the largest private prison company in the United States, reported a $162 million net income for 2011. This corporation operates sixty-six correctional and detention facilities, representing more than 91,000 beds.

Sources: Juristat. 2011, 2012, 2014; Correctional Services of Canada 2013; Office of the Parliamentary Budget Officer 2010; U.S. Securities and Exchange Commission 2012.

Despite the lack of evidence that the prison successfully fulfills its supposed purposes, there persists a strong social and political attachment to it as a crime control tool and as a symbol of societal censure. —Drake 2012: 31

Today, prisons and the "corrections" system continue to be seen as the ultimate answer to crime. A trend of penal convergence with an increasing high reliance on imprisonment can be observed in North America, Australasia and Europe (Drake 2012). In 2011, there were reportedly 10.1 million people behind prison bars throughout the world (Walmsley 2012). The highest rate of imprisonment is in the United States at 730 per 100,000 people. Norway, Sweden and Finland are at the lower end with rates of 73, 70 and 59 per 100,000, respectively (Drake 2012).

Critical approaches to criminology explain (the increased use of) imprisonment as one of the ways dominant social groups maintain their hegemony over society. Some critical approaches see imprisonment as being essential to the functioning of capitalism, while others focus more on social regulation. These include books such as *Prison on Trial* (2005) by Thomas Mathiesen, *The Rich Get Richer and the Poor Get Prison* (2012) by Jeffrey Reiman and Paul Leighton, *Crime Control as Industry* (2000) by Nils Christie and *Prisons, Punishment and the Pursuit of Security* (2012) by Deborah Drake, to name but a few. Perhaps more poignantly, however, are the words of infamous prisoners who fought for freedom from "the larger social prison around them" (McMurtry 2000: 180), such as Mahatma Gandhi, Nelson Mandela, Antonio Gramsci, Angela Davis and George Jackson.

There is also growing interest in comparative penology and research focusing on countries that are exceptions to this general global move toward increasing imprisonment and tough crime control (see, for example, *Comparative Criminal Justice and Globalization* (2011) by David Nelken, and *Contrasts in Punishment: An Explanation of Anglophone Excess and Nordic Exceptionalism* (2013) by John Pratt and Anna Erikkson). Nordic countries such as Iceland, Norway and Sweden are said to show "exceptionalism" in penology, with lower imprisonment rates and prison settings that are described as being more humane (Pratt and Eriksson 2013).

This chapter presents a critical criminological analysis of the prison and the control of crime. We begin by detailing the current state of "corrections" in Canada and the United States, which both favour militaristic, harsh and deterrence-based models of exclusion (Garland 2001; Christie 2000; Moore and Hannah-Moffat 2002; Turney 2013). We then discuss the theories that allow us to better understand increases in the use of prisons, including a brief review of the consensus paradigm and a more thorough explanation of critical criminology approaches. We then move to a discussion of the politics of penality, including the role of neo-liberal globalization, mounting poverty and the shift from the welfare state to the repressive state as conditions leading to the increased use of prisons. The chapter ends with a brief discussion on how some jurisdictions, such as Nordic countries, are adopting more socially democratic approaches to penology as a result of the rise of neo-liberal communitarianism.

THE CURRENT STATE OF PENAL POPULISM

We want them to have self-worth...
so we destroy their self-worth.
We want them to be responsible...
so we take away all responsibility.

We want them to be part of our community...
so we isolate them from our community.
We want them to be positive and constructive...
so we degrade them and make them useless.

We want them to be trustworthy...
so we put them where there is no trust.
We want them to be non-violent...
so we put them where there is violence all around them.

We want them to quit hanging around 'losers'...
so we put all the 'losers' in the province under one roof.
We want them to quit exploiting us...
so we put them where they exploit each other.

We want them to take control of their lives, own their own problems
And quit being a parasite...
so we make them totally dependent on us.
—Judge Dennis Challeen, speaking about prison (quoted in Morris 2000)

Current trends toward increased incarceration and the costs associated with the justice system are not correlated to a growth in crime. In Canada and the United States, for example, crime has gone down for a number of years while the number of prisons has increased. It is also widely accepted that prison fails to satisfy its objectives and may, in fact, heighten the problem of crime (Reiman and Leighton 2010).

In the immediate post-World War II era, the prison, as one part of the penal system, was viewed as a problematic institution that was counterproductive, failing to meet its own correctionalist goals and reporting high levels of recidivism (Garland 2001). The aim of much government work was to expand other penalties such as probation, community supervision and fines. The last thirty-five years, however, have seen this tendency reversed, especially in the U.S. and the U.K. (Garland 2001; Christie 2000; Muller and Schrage 2014). Part of this reversal involves the increased use of the prison (Drake 2012; Muller and Schrage 2014). Garland states:

> In the last few decades, the prison has been reinvented as a means of incapacitative restraint, supposedly targeted upon violent offenders and dangerous recidivists, but also affecting masses of more minor offenders. Probation and parole have de-emphasized their social work functions and given renewed weight to their risk-monitoring functions. (2001: 14)

The current state of penal populism and the adoption of punitive penal policies and incarceration by most Western liberal democratic governments are of concern to many criminologists (Hogg 2013; Drake 2012; Reiman and Leighton 2012). Penal populism is a process (usually experienced as feelings or intuitions) where citizens believe criminals and prisoners are favored over the public who are not committing crime (Pratt 2007). A key question for criminologists is to try to understand penal populism and why prison continues to be used even more than in the past despite its apparent lack of success in solving problems of crime.

Canada: Higher Incarceration and Lower Crime?

Though Canadian law stipulates that prison sentences must be the last resort of the criminal justice system, Canada's level of incarceration is higher now than it has been in the past (Brosnahan 2013). Canada's rate of incarceration in 2011 was 117 per 100,000 people, and it is growing fast, with increasing numbers of visible minorities entering the prison population, especially visible minority women and Aboriginal people (Mac-Charles 2012). In fact, between March 2010 and March 2012, the numbers of federally incarcerated people increased by 6.8 percent or by almost 1,000 inmates; a large enough number to fill two large male prisons (MacCharles 2012).

The amount of spending in the justice system in Canada is also rising and, interestingly, at a time when crime rates are falling. The 2013 Annual Report of the Correctional Investigator, Howard Sapers, indicates that the crime rate fell 23 percent between 2003 and 2013, while spending in the Canadian justice system rose by exactly the same amount. He concludes that increases in incarceration are not driven by crime but by policy (Brosnahan 2013). Of the $11 billion a year that Canada spends on its criminal justice system, over $3.85 billion goes to corrections (Office of the Correctional Investigator 2012) and $1.4 billion and $512 million, respectively, to courts and legal aid. The costs of the prison system are high: the average cost for one prisoner in 2009–2010 was $113,000 a year for federal inmates. Keeping an inmate in the community, by comparison, costs approximately $29,500 per year. For women, the average cost of incarcerating an inmate is $578 per day, while for male prisoners, the cost is just over $300 per day (MacCharles 2012).

Despite the already high costs and the decreasing crime rates, many Canadians continue to demand increasingly severe penalties for criminal violations and increased expenditures on criminal justice, mainly due to a belief that this spending will help keep them safe from harm. The newly adopted Conservative crime bill demonstrates political support for increased incarceration in Canada. The Harper crime bill has imposed tougher sentences for a variety of offences, including firearms offences, smuggling and trafficking, robbery with a stolen weapon, first-time weapons offences and second-time and multiple offenders. The legislation also plans to eliminate house arrest for a number of offences and has implemented minimum mandatory sentences. Mandatory minimum jail sentences are in place now for a number of offences including some violent and sex crimes, drug trafficking and the sexual exploitation of children. Upon introducing the bill, former justice minister Vic Toews said in the House of Commons: "If criminals are to be held to account, they must face a punishment that matches the severity of their crime" (Deveau 2006). Among other criticisms, legislation such as mandatory minimums and lower numbers of conditional offences will lead to increases in prison overcrowding.[1]

In the last five years, the budget for Correctional Service of Canada (csc) has increased by 40 percent, with 2,700 new cells for inmates. Sapers' report warns that even with the creation of these new cells, over 20 percent of inmates are double-bunked (Sapers 2013). Today overcrowding in Canadian prisons defies common decency and is against international convention. Higher numbers of institutional charges and placements in segregation in Canadian prisons also point to current problems with overcrowding in penitentiaries. What's more, inmates are lacking time outside their cells, and there is a shortage of meaningful training, programs and prison work within the corrections system. Sapers writes:

The trend lines are clear — a greater percentage of offenders are spending longer and more of their sentence behind bars in increasingly volatile and hardening conditions of confinement. At a time when more offenders are remaining longer in custody, a renewed focus on Correctional Service Canada's rehabilitation obligations and a stronger commitment to community reintegration are as urgently required today as they were four decades ago. (2013)

Problems with segregation, institutional management and increased expenditures are of increased concern for offenders with complex needs, such as federally sentenced women, Aboriginal and other visible minority offenders, seniors and those labelled as mentally ill. In his 2013 annual report, Sapers calls attention to the complex demographics inside Canadian prisons, which now house increasing numbers of visible minority groups, including Aboriginal women, Black, Hispanic, East Indian and elderly prisoners. The 2013 annual findings report the following:

One-in-five inmates are over age 50.
The average level of education among inmates is grade 8.
80 percent of offenders have addiction or substance abuse problems.
80 percent of federally sentenced women have been sexually abused.
31 percent have Hepatitis C and 5 percent have HIV.
Nearly half of all offenders required mental health care in the past year.

Because of an increase in elderly inmates and those who have a mental illness or other special needs, health and mental health care costs are climbing. In 2012, CSC's health care spending was over $210 million (Brosnahan 2013).

Differences in incarceration rates between Canadian provinces are interesting. From 2010 to 2013, in-custody population of federal offenders increased in Canada by 1,214 prisoners, or over 8 percent. However, this increase was not evenly distributed across the five regions of the Correctional System of Canada. Ontario and the prairies lead the growth in prison population. In the 1990s, the Government of Québec suggested that by substituting incarceration and punishment for prevention and conflict resolution, it would save $16 million a year and decrease imprisonment by 7.5 percent annually. Even though Québec saw an increase in its prison population numbers in 2010–11 (Brennan 2012), Québec currently has the lowest incarceration rate and the second lowest crime rate in all of Canada. Québec's approach to crime and justice may be viewed as similar to that of Nordic countries, which are discussed below.

Although incarceration is increasing in Canada, especially among Aboriginal peoples, alternative measures such as restorative justice have also been embraced. Beginning with the report of the Sentencing and Corrections Review Group in 1995, the Federal Government has shown concern for the rise in prison populations. Alternatives to incarceration were devised with conditional sentencing provisions within the *Criminal Code*. Section 742.1 of the *Criminal Code* allowed offenders to serve sentences of two years or less in the community, as long as safety was not a concern.

"Law and order" politics in Ontario are comparable to that of the U.S., drawing on themes of punitiveness, victim centredness, exclusion and enhanced control. For instance, such politics call for the increased use of prisons, restrictions on parole release, austere prisons, super-max prisons and boot camps (Moore and Hannah-Moffat 2002). Privatized correctional facilities and "super-jails" were both envisioned and implemented by the

Ontario Correctional Renewal Project and are characterized by electronic surveillance, minimal staff, and reduced parole. Patterns of homicides, high-profile escapes and violations of the rights of prisoners have been observed in Ontario's super-max facilities, with investigations linking these problems directly to both the size of the facility and prison privatization (Office of the Corrections Trustee, cited in Moore and Hanna-Moffat 2002: 111).

The Canadian prison system has been expanding at the apparent expense of social systems such as education, health care and the social welfare of individuals. CSC reports cost-cutting in service delivery, prison libraries, prison chaplain contracts, lifer programs (such as Lifeline) and other correctional and employment programming, all which will make it more difficult for inmates to re-enter the outside world. In addition, it was announced in 2012 and 2013 that inmate charges for room and board and phone calls would be increased, and pay within prison industries would be decreased (Brosnahan 2013).

Anthony Doob, a criminologist at the University of Toronto, told the *Globe and Mail* that increased prison time alongside the elimination of programs is "not going to make me and you any safer ... this has nothing to do with making our streets safer and everything to do with politics" (Deveau 2006). Doob argued that filling prisons does not tackle the problem of crime and in fact takes away money that could prevent crime. There is "no evidence" he said, "to support the suggestion that heavier sentencing works as a deterrent against violent crime," especially when using the United States as the example.

"Get Tough/No Frills": The United States and Prison Growth

The United States increased its prison population five-fold between 1970 and 2010 (Muller and Schrage 2014), resulting in approximately 730 per 100,000 people imprisoned (Drake 2012). Today, the U.S. continues to have a larger per capita prison population than any other nation in the world (Zimring 2010). The U.S.'s over-reliance on incarceration is familiar and shocking when expressed in any number of ways:

> The U.S. has less than 5 percent of the world's population but over 25 percent of the world's incarcerated people; the incarceration rate in the U.S. is four times the average for Western European countries; the U.S. incarcerates more people than South America, Central America and the Caribbean combined; one in four African-American children in the U.S. has grown up with a parent incarcerated ... with 80,000 prisoners in solitary confinement, the U.S. holds more people in segregation than other countries have in their entire prison system. (Inter-American Commission on Human Rights 2013, cited in Ebenstein 2013)

In the last two years, the incarceration rate has decreased by 0.9 percent in the United States, which is believed to be a result of prisoner decline in California. However, federal prison numbers have increased by 3.1 percent, and 24 other states also show an increase (Carson and Sabol 2012). California's adult incarceration rate grew from 80/100,000 in 1977 to 483/100,000, for a total of 144,000 prisoners in 2011 (Grattet and Hayes 2013). The slight overall decrease in California is a historic realignment in imprisonment, which has transferred the authority for felony offenders who commit non-serious, non-sexual and non-violent crimes from the prisons to counties. Despite this slight reduction in numbers, African American men continue to be incarcerated at higher rates than any other group or race in California (Grattet and Hayes 2013).

Statistics fail to capture the treatment of many prisoners in the United States, who increasingly come from vulnerable populations such as racial minorities, the elderly, those with mental health problems and children. In March 2013, the Inter-American Commission on Human Rights (IACHR) held a human rights hearing on solitary confinement, describing inhumane conditions in U.S. prisons where some prisoners can be in isolation for months on end.

Like in Canada, the number of prisoners with special needs in the U.S. is growing, particularly among seniors and women. These shifting populations mean that additional medical care, appropriate housing and mental health services are required, which also increase costs. Older prisoners, for example, are estimated to cost three to nine times more than younger prisoners. Between 2007 and 2010, the Human Rights Watch (2012a) found that the population of U.S. prisoners aged 65 years or older grew by 94 percent compared to the rate of other prisoners. Part of the problem is that prisons are built for younger people. Prisoners are often expected to follow rules, which include walking distances to dining halls and climbing into their bunks. There are no specialized services for prisoners who suffer from dementia or incontinence, for example, leaving staff and prisoners to renegotiate long-standing practices on an ad hoc basis (Human Rights Watch 2012a).

The militaristic and punitive conditions of U.S. prisons are also difficult for younger prisoners. Human Rights Watch (2012b), for example, recently estimated that over 95,000 youth under 18 years of age were incarcerated in prisons and jails in the United States. Incarcerated youth often live through traumatic life experiences before entering prison, which they then re-experience through, for instance, time spent in solitary confinement. The Human Rights Watch warns that this negatively impacts youth rehabilitation as well as their physical and mental health. The words of the youth themselves are powerful. For example, one incarcerated youth from California wrote: "Being in isolation to me felt like I was on an island all alone ... dying a slow death from the inside out" (letter from Kyle B. (pseudonym) to Human Rights Watch 2012b: 1). Another young woman from Michigan stated: "It was concrete ... [I felt] doomed, like I was being banished ... like you have the plague or that you are the worst thing on earth. Like you are set apart [from] everything else. I guess [I wanted to] feel like I was part of the human race — not like some animal" (Ibid. 5).

In the United States, inmates in a number of federal and state prisons can be held in cell confinement twenty-three hours a day with no visitations. The *Los Angeles Times* described conditions in the Pelican Bay State Prison during the 1990s:

> Pelican Bay is entirely automated and designed so that inmates have virtually no face-to-face contact with guards or other inmates. For 22 hours a day, inmates are confined to their windowless cells, built of solid blocks of concrete and stainless steel so that they won't have access to materials they could fashion into weapons. They don't work in prison industries; they don't have access to recreation; they don't mingle with other inmates. They aren't even allowed to smoke ... the SHU (Secure Housing Unit) has its own infirmary ... inmates can spend years without stepping outside the unit. (Christie 2000: 101)

Pelican Bay was found to be in violation of the U.S. Constitution by Judge Henderson, who wrote, "Dry words on paper cannot adequately capture the senseless suffering and sometimes wretched misery [of the inmates]" (cited in Cayley 1998: 53). His account mentioned prisoners who were assaulted by having their heads bashed into floors and against walls while they were shackled; prisoners were kicked and knocked out, with their teeth and jaws fractured, and had their bodies burned and limbs broken. Conditions at Pelican Bay and several other high-tech/security prisons in America have been criticized by United Nations human rights reports as "inhuman and degrading" (Cayley 1998: 53).

On August 19, 2013, 30,000 inmates stopped eating at Pelican Bay State Prison in order to demand better treatment. This recent protest actually began in 2011, spreading to other facilities in the state. The goals of the protest were to appeal to the public's sense of human decency and to end long-term solitary confinement, collective punishment for individual violations, as well as to implement the recommendations of the 2006 U.S. Commission on Safety and Abuse in America's Prisons and other rights, such as providing adequate health care, food, programs, privileges, phone calls and mail (Dayan 2013).

Other examples are just as glaring. Florida State Prison at Starke has a windowless Q-Wing where inmates are not allowed to go outside. Some inmates are being held there for up to seven years. Closely managed inmates may be deprived of any form of exercise and may not be allowed outside for years at a time (Christie 2000: 102). In 1991, the *Sunday Oklahoma* reported that inmates in that state's high-max secure conditions could potentially be moved into a cell house where they would never see the outside again (Christie 2000: 101).

Public pressure to crack down on crime has led to the demand that politicians get tough on crime, many of whom have revived strategies and prison conditions used prior to the recognition of prisoners' civil rights in the 1970s. Mississippi, for example, reintroduced caning and "ordered that convicts once again wear striped uniforms — red and white for maximum-security offenders, black and white for medium, green and white for minimum — with the word 'convict' written on the back." Grants for post-secondary education in that state were also cut by the crime bill of 1994. In some jurisdictions, prisoners have been required to pay for their own incarceration: "In 1996, a Missouri circuit court judge ruled that Daryl Gilyard, who is serving a life sentence without parole, must reimburse the state for the cost of his imprisonment, beginning with a back payment of $97,724.61" (Cayley 1998: 47).

Arizona, Alabama and Florida have reinstated chain gangs — the shackling together of groups of uniformed convicts with leg irons and chains while on work detail. The philosophy behind chain gangs and their reintroduction in U.S. prisons proposes to remove any privilege from sentenced offenders as a measure of deterrence. They are not to receive any education, programming, benefits or special privilege in the hopes of eradicating the concept of entitlement to anything (Farndale 2012). Critics insist that such measures will deliver deeply dangerous and unreformed men who require more imprisonment in the future.

Harsher U.S. prison conditions are also exacerbated by the popular concept of "Three Strikes and You're Out." This legislation, introduced by President Bill Clinton in 1994 under the *Violent Crime Control and Law Enforcement Act*, authorizes mandatory life imprisonment for anyone convicted of violent felonies on two previous separate occasions. Revised statutes under accountability laws lessened the requirements for the life penalty. In California, a criminal convicted of a property crime or burglary may receive life imprisonment upon the third conviction. The following examples speak for themselves concerning the harshness of this approach:

> A drunken parolee who broke into an Orange County restaurant and stuffed his pockets with chocolate chip cookies was sentenced yesterday to 25 years to life under California's three strikes law ... [California] Superior Court judge said she

had no alternative after Kevin Weber, 32, was convicted of second-degree commercial burglary. Mr. Weber's first two strikes stemmed from separate burglaries in 1989 at a Huntington Beach apartment, which earned him two years after he pulled a gun on a surprised tenant. (*Globe and Mail* 1995)

One of the first ... three strike prosecutions was of a twenty-seven-year-old San Diego man subject to life in prison for stealing a piece of pizza because he previously had pleaded guilty to two felonies — robbery and attempted robbery ... The first prosecution of a woman under the law was for a $20 cocaine purchase she allegedly made nearly fourteen years after her second strike. (Reuben 1995)

The unconstitutional nature of the three strikes legislation is extremely controversial, meting out unusually cruel jail terms for non-violent crimes. The Campaign for an Effective Crime Policy has revealed that 85 percent of offences under this new law are non-violent (1995, cited in Cayley 1998). Some of the effects of three strikes are devastating: overcrowding in prison facilities, extremely high costs and further violence — often against police — when suspects are cornered and at risk of a twenty-five-year-to-life sentence.

Private prisons in the U.S. are also a booming industry. Privatizing prisons means that inmate labour is sold at subminimum wages, often to Fortune 500 companies such as AT&T, IBM or the Bank of America. Prison labour provides a reserve army of labour, with inmates making between 93 cents and $4.80 per day. Today, nearly a million prisoners do call center work, build furniture, reserve hotel rooms and manufacture clothing, shoes and other textiles (Fraser and Freeman 2012). On the one hand, some authors such as Minarovich (2013) talk of the potentially positive impact of prison labour for inmates, arguing that work means prisoners are not as likely to succumb to the ill effects of prison life. On the other hand, those who criticize the prison industry argue that because the prison population is made up of mostly Hispanic and Black marginalized people who work for a pittance, prisons create profit by exploiting the most vulnerable populations (Pelaez 2008).

DIFFERENT APPROACHES IN CRIMINOLOGY: UNDERSTANDING THE INCREASED USE OF PRISONS

Theoretical perspectives are essential for understanding the increased uses of and comparative trends in penality, as well as working toward meaningful crime prevention and intervention. Criticism of retributive justice and prison is levelled on ideological and ethical grounds by critical criminologists. We begin here with a brief overview of consensus theories, moving toward a criminology understanding of increased penality as part of the new politics of the repressive state.

Consensus Paradigm

As discussed in Chapter 2, the consensus paradigm involves macro-level analysis focusing on structural problems such as material strains, as well as microelements, which focus on agency and the individual. At their essence, these theories focus on deterrence effects and the social control potential of punishment as a response to criminal behaviour.

Deterrence Theory: Decreasing Crime through Increasing Punishment

Crime policy is all stick, no carrot. Tough on crime is what we get. — Blaikie 2011

Despite statistics and in the absence of common sense, Prime Minister Stephen Harper seems hell bent on creating Canada's Version of Springfield's Bear Patrol. — Kotarski 2011

The increased use of imprisonment is advocated through deterrence theory in criminology. Deterrence theory maintains that crime is prevented by deterring and discouraging it through extensive, certain and punitive use of the legal and criminal justice system. The underpinning of deterrence theory is that if the punishment outweighs the benefits of the crime, criminal activity will be discouraged in individuals and in society generally. Much media coverage and harsher law and order campaigns are built on the foundation of this type of theory, which tends to be the cornerstone of our criminal justice system. In fact, if we assume that the logic of deterrence is true, then prevention and intervention should focus on getting even tougher. This is specifically what the Conservative Government in Canada has done as of late although the rate of crime has been declining, we are witnessing a move away from rehabilitative models toward retribution.

Forensics: Detecting Crime Before it is Committed

Medicalized discourse does what the language of criminality has done for centuries: it identifies and indicts the perpetrator as flawed, biologically and/or culturally, and by consequence, morally flawed. — Schissel 2006: 80–81

Forensic discourse concentrates on crime as stemming from the individual and on detecting crime before it is committed. For these reasons, "risk assessment" tools are seen as extremely important and help to determine if an individual is more susceptible to breaking the law and which level of intervention and prevention should be offered. Measurement instruments vary in Canada and other countries, but often the instruments assess participation in both social and anti-social patterns: leisure, recreation, substance abuse, pro-criminal attitudes, education, employment, family issues and criminal history, among others (Girard and Wormith 2004). The power of the forensic model is that it is informed by the scientific premise and diagnostic mechanisms for detecting criminality. Top rated forensics crime television dramas such as *CSI: NY* and *CSI: Miami* portray the intermixing of policing, morality and science and often determine what the public knows of "forensics." Forensic psychology is the understanding of criminal behaviour through the application of psychological principles and a focus on the individual.

The problem is that risk assessments often measure categories in which marginalized individuals fare worse and then address the individual person as the problem, rather than the reasons why there may be pre-existing challenges with family, leisure, education, employment or anti-social behaviour. Lets take an example from a risk assessment tool, the Level of Service Inventory-Revised and the specific questions asked. Relating to their finances, the offenders are asked questions such as "Does the household sometimes receive welfare or other forms of assistance?"; "Do you have a bank account?"; "Do you have credit?"; "Do you have a personal budget?" Similarly, offenders are asked questions about their family: "Are you dissatisfied with your marital or equivalent situation?"; "Have you ever contemplated divorce?" The critique is that these questions assume a financial and/or family norm, that individuals are concerned about credit and finances. Also, the questions don't necessarily link to respondents' criminal activity, so why would they be a focus of increased risk or programming? Moffat, (2005: 37) states: "Questions guiding the assessment of dynamic risk/criminogenic need assume ideal types and construct risk and need based on moral assessments of values, lifestyles and experiences". The information gathered from these tools is used in pre-sentence reports and to determine the levels of security, programming and case planning. When the questions are examined in detail, however, the risk-assessment questions and scales reveal an evaluation of character based on middle-class values of what are normal and acceptable ways of living.

There are often social causes for difficult and criminal histories, but forensics commonly links these histories to pathological people. This is a theme shared by other consensus theories, as addressed in Chapter 2, which is also often drawn upon in our current system of justice.

Pluralist Theory: Secondary Deviance, Master Status and Shaming

Some pluralist criminological theories, discussed in Chapter 4, provide a critique of both the increased use of prison and of harsh prison conditions. Labelling theory draws attention to key aspects of the deviance process, such as secondary deviance, master status, and reintegrative and disintegrative shaming.

Secondary deviance is deviance that occurs after a prisoner is labelled and because of this label (see, for example, Becker 1963). Lemert (1951, 1967, 1974) emphasizes master status, or the ways in which individuals may internalize labels such as "deviant" and come to define themselves in accordance with these labels. Braithwaite (1989) explores how social control and shaming of those who have committed a crime may have positive or negative impacts. Negative labels that shun an individual from society constitute disintegrative shaming, but labelling can be reintegrative if that individual is given a chance to be socially forgiven by taking responsibility for their actions (e.g., through circle sentencing and other restorative measures, as discussed in Chapter 18).

Labelling theory has contributed to the criticism of the criminal justice system and to the move away from labelling individuals. Pluralist theories have also suggested that individuals may be more likely to offend again if they go through the criminal justice system providing a strong critique of prison as being contrary to its own ends. However, these theories are criticized for not being able to explain the persistence of the criminal justice system despite its failures.

Critical Criminology: Marginality and Condemnation

As discussed in Chapter 3, critical criminology focuses more on the macro structures of, for example, global capitalism, colonialism and patriarchy to help understand crime and punishment. These types of theories address issues that could be called "the criminalization of inequality." They argue that involvement in crime is a result of social, economic and racial inequality brought about through current economic situations and unequal power structures (Reiman 2009, 2012; Gorkoff and Runner 2003). Critical theories, then, draw attention to the problem of individualizing crime and of not recognizing the underlying inequalities that characterize criminogenic societies. By criminalizing the individual and focusing on pathological individuals through forensics and in the media, we deflect attention from the unequal distribution of wealth and real social problems.

As we saw in Chapter 3, there are many different critical criminological theories, including neo-Marxism and conflict theory, discourse theories (including poststructuralism, postmodernism and newer forms of governmentality), critical race theories, critical feminism and more. Here we will not distinguish between different critical theories; rather, we will discuss the types of questions about criminal justice and injustice that arise from these critical frameworks as a whole.

The Priority of Public Sentiment over Professional Judgment and Penological Experts

> Whoever speaks on behalf of victims speaks on behalf of us all — or so declares the new political wisdom of high crime societies. — Garland 2001

There is very little evidence to suggest that reintroducing super-max prisons, chain gangs, increased incarceration or other "get-tough" legislation reduces the incidence of crime or helps to rehabilitate offenders. Ironically, there is much research that shows the opposite is true: harsh law and order penalties and draconian measures have been found to increase crime (see, for example, Morris 2000; Clarke 2000; McMurtry 2000; Mathiesen 1974, 1990; Reiman 2001; Cayley 1998; Comack 1996). Yet many Canadians and most Americans support these get-tough policies (Cayley 1998; Hermer and Mosher 2002; Christie 2000; Reiman 2004). As stated by Garland, "punishment — in the sense of expressive punishment, conveying public sentiment — is once again a respectable, openly embraced penal purpose and has come to affect not just high-end sentences for the most heinous offences but even juvenile justice and community penalties" (2001: 9).

The language of condemning the offender appears to express the sentiment of the public, and this public discourse informs political platforms and becomes policy (Pratt 2007; Indermauer and Roberts 2009). Public sentiment takes priority over professional and expert opinion. Thus draconian measures are indicative of a public that fears both crime and strategies that are soft on crime (Garland 2001; Moore and Hannah-Moffat 2002; Hogg 2013). Hogg, essentially defines what could be called "penal populism": "The symbolism clustering around crime and punishment is a valuable political prize that parties seeking to connect with disaffected voters in an increasingly volatile political climate cannot afford to ignore" (Hogg 2013: 107). Those who defend this type of politics talk about reflecting the views of voters in law and policy as a strong symbol of a democratic society (Hogg 2013). Those who criticize this type of penal populism argue that public views do not occur naturally but rather are constructed through media outlets, which may misinform the public:

> Critics of penal populism ... argue that politicians are prone to talk up criminal threats and public fears in pursuit of partisan electoral advantage, nurturing the very climate in which harsh punitive measures are embraced by the public and adopted as solutions by governments and oppositions. This self-perpetuating cycle proceeds with little regard for the effectiveness of punitive policies or the evidence regarding crime and the sorts of policies that might actually work to combat it. (Hogg 2013: 108)

Feeding public sentiment is a return to the focus on victims — their protection, memory, fears and voices — which often means harsh treatment of offenders in the name of protecting and honouring victims' suffering. As Garland notes, "The interests and feelings of victims — actual victims, victims' families, potential victims, the projected figure of 'the victim' — are now routinely invoked in support of measures of punitive segregation" (2001: 11). Routinely, when political figures announce new laws, crime victims or family members will accompany them. Laws are often named for the victims, such as "Megan's law" or "Jenna's law." Victims represent the public, and victimization is seen as indicative of a society whose risk of crime is very high: "Publicized images of actual victims serve as the personalized, real-life, it-could-be-you metonym for a problem of security that has become a defining feature of contemporary culture" (Garland 2001: 11). This concept of victimization can be used as a powerful political tool, which feeds politics of law and order, instilling collective passions against a common enemy.

Law and order movements have used victims' rights rhetoric to seek punishment for offenders on behalf of the rights of all victims (Shah and Pryor 2005). The victims' rights movement flourished in the 1970s and was given legitimacy by the creation of the President's Task Force on Victims of Crime and the *Victims of Crime Act* (VOCA) in the U.S. in the 1980s. Today, the movement campaigns for victim services and often lobbies against defendants' rights (Shah and Pryor 2005). Victim impact statements are also commonly used and supported by victims' rights movements, especially during sentencing and at parole hearings. These are said to provide therapeutic experiences for the victim; however, they are criticized both for their lack of impact on proceedings and for biasing juries against defendants, infringing on rights of due process.

Another prominent theme within Western cultures is the fear of crime (Sacco 2005; Altheide 2009; Collins 2014). While very widespread, most statistical research shows that the fear is largely unfounded. For instance, crime is feared to be escalating at times when there is either no change or a decrease in crime rates (Schissel 2006; Garland 2001; Collins 2014), and fear is not related to actual victimization (Chockalingam and Srinivasan 2009). The media dramatizes crime, conjuring up images of "folk devils" — unruly, pathological, nihilistic career criminals who require harsher law and order measures (Gelb 2008; Schissel 2006; Collins 2014). Media images are often false and stereotypical, yet they inform the public, which in turn provides politicians with justification for tough law and order campaigns (Schissel 2006; Collins 2014).

Misinformed Policy and Ill-Informed Public Sentiment

Misinformed policy comes from ill-informed public sentiment (Garland 2001; Gelb 2008). Garland eloquently articulates the situation: "The background effect of policy is now more frequently a collective anger and a righteous demand for retribution rather than a commitment to a just, socially engineered solution" (2001: 10–11). Policy on crime and its control is no longer informed by experts and professionals, but it plays a prominent role in electoral campaigns. Criminological knowledge and research is replaced with the voice of "common sense":

> New initiatives are announced in political settings — the U.S. part convention, the British part conference, the televised interview — and are encapsulated in sound-bite statements: "Prison works," "Three-strikes and you're out," "Truth in sentencing," "No frills prisons," "Adult time for adult crime," "Zero-tolerance," "Tough on crime, tough on the causes of crime." (Pillsbury, cited in Garland 2001: 13)

Punitive attitudes are criticized as exploiting fears, rather than promoting effective policy (Gelb 2008). Critical research in this area also demonstrates that support of punitive measures declines as education levels increase. A recent survey of public attitudes in Saskatchewan, for example, indicates there are significant differences of opinion between education levels as education increases, support for increased punitive measures falls dramatically (McDowell et al. 2012). Implications of this type of research highlight the importance of a more informed public for rational foundations and better penal policy (Hogg 2013).

Penal Politics: From the Welfare State to the Repressive State

The critique of retributive justice is also levelled on ideological and ethical grounds by critical criminologists who detail the fit between criminal justice "reform" and global economic conditions. In recent years, industrialized countries have been changing state policy regarding criminal justice and welfare provisions. While poverty, homelessness and child poverty are at unthinkable levels in many of the richest countries in the world (Wilkinson and Pickett 2010), well-off countries, such as the United States and Canada, are downsizing social programs and housing initiatives as well as increasing their prison populations (Wilkinson and Pickett 2010; Pratt and Ericksson 2013). According to critical criminology, rather than addressing the problem of inequality (especially at a structural level), we are instead effectively blaming people for their own poverty and for their own criminality. Critical criminologists have defined this shift as moving from the welfare state toward the repressive state (White 2002; Clarke 2000; McMurtry 2000). This position suggests that the retributive (and the restorative) justice tag supports this political agenda. The role of the government is no longer to ensure the well-being of the population through full employment and social welfare. Instead, that role has shifted toward creating a favourable environment for transnational investment (Clarke 1997; Dobbin 1998). Governments are cutting funding for the poor, privatizing social services and spending more money on criminal justice (White 2002; Clarke 2000). It is within this social context that critical criminology contextualizes restitutive justice.

Globalization, Poverty and the New Underclass

Despite the complexity of neo-liberal globalization (see, for example, O'Loughlin, Staeheli and Greenberg 2004), its trends are said to be instructive (Routledge 2006; Anderson and Cavanagh 2000; Dobbin 2003). For most of us, the sheer size and power of transnational corporations are difficult to even imagine. Trivett (2011) released a story in the *Business Insider*, where he claims: "25 major American corporations [have] 2010 revenues that surpass the 2010 Gross Domestic Product of entire countries, often with a few billion to spare ... Even some major countries like Norway, Thailand, and New Zealand can be bested by certain U.S. firms." Wal-Mart, with a gross revenue greater than the gross domestic product (GDP) of 157 countries, is the twenty-fifth largest economy in the world . (Fortune/CNN, IMF, cited in Trivett 2011). On paper, Visa is larger than South Zimbabwe, Nike surpasses Paraguay and McDonald's is bigger than Latvia.[2] The 2007 Human Development Report (HDR) notes the poorest 40 percent of humanity has 5 percent of total income. Seventy-five percent of all income belongs to the richest 20 percent of people.

The rising power of transnational corporations works in tandem with the declining role of the state. The economic strategy as promoted, for example, by the Business Council on National Issues becomes creating jobs to support the needs of the business community. By following this strategy, both provincial and federal governments accommodate the demands of big business to the detriment of the social and economic rights of citizens, which means downsizing the public sector, deregulating corporate wrongdoing and crime (see Chapter 10) and slashing social spending and corporate taxes (see, for example, Dobbin 2003). Accompanying these trends is the dismantling of our welfare state and the abrogation of the social rights of Canadians.

The recent history of unemployment insurance helps to demonstrate how Canadian governments are abandoning those in need. Before four sets of reforms to the unemployment insurance program (now termed "employment insurance"), Canada was offering assistance to 87 percent of the unemployed. By 1996, and to this day, less than 40 percent of unemployed Canadians are eligible for benefits, and those benefits are also being paid out in lower amounts than before. Today, 1.3 million Canadians are without jobs, yet tougher policies around employment insurance criteria means only 37 percent of unemployed are eligible (Whittington 2013).

According to the U.N. Committee on Economic, Social and Cultural Rights report, minimum wage in every Canadian province was considered insufficient to allow workers a decent standard of living. The report stated that social assistance rates "bear no resemblance" to the cost of living in Canada (Goddard 2006). In 2013, the U.N. Right to Food envoy Olivier De Schutter stated that Canada's problems are not transient but systematic, indicative of "a broken social protection system and the failure of the state to meet its obligations to its people" (cited in Schmidt 2012: 3).

Cuts in social programs have both an ideological and an economic basis. The welfare state was initially seen as a route to freedom. Through social support, the state could increase the health of the population and therefore eventually make welfare largely unnecessary. The safety net allowed people to take more risks because, as Bauman (1995a) states, "they can exert themselves because there is always this safety provision if they fail" (quoted in Cayley 1998: 78). Under neo-liberal globalization, this idea of a safety net for those who have "unluckily fallen" has shifted to a perception that those who collect have given way to a "permanent crippling dependency." The idea of collective responsibility toward all citizens has thus been replaced with the idea of individual responsibility. The clamour for tax cuts speaks to a similar ideological belief in personal rather than collective responsibility.

Canadian census data and Canadian Council on Social Development analysis show increasing numbers of Canadians living in poverty and growing inequity (Wilkinson and Pickett 2010). The richest 10 percent of the population are making more than $81,000 per year (with the very rich making more than $272,000), while the median individual income is under $28,000 per year (Canadian Press 2013). The richest 1 percent are making over $380,000 per year, which is ten times the average income of Canadians (Canadian Press 2013). In addition, in 2010, 4.8 million Canadians were living in households considered to be low-income (Canadian Press 2013), and one in seven Canadian children were living in a low-income household (National Council of Welfare 2011). In the United States, some 37 million men, women and children live below the poverty line, with countless people unable to afford proper nutrition, education and health care (Reiman 2007). In 2004, the poorest 60 percent of families received 26.8 percent of the total income, whereas the richest 20 percent made 50.1 percent (Reiman 2007). In other words, "this means that the richest 5 percent — less than 4 million families — have more money to divide among themselves than the 30.4 million families who make up the bottom 40 percent" (Reiman 2007: 189).

With more poverty and homelessness, laws and other policies have the potential to unite people against a common enemy. The critical criminological position is that the attempt by the state to contain the most desperate and most vulnerable sections of the population (which includes Indigenous people), has led it to embrace law and order policies. As such, the state has been working to "reconfigure police-community relations (through zero-tolerance approaches and community policing initiatives), to expand surveillance and intervention into working-class communal life (through crime prevention and community safety projects), and to reinforce state authority (through tougher sentencing legislation)" (White 2002: 388).

Condemning the Marginalized: Crime and Punishment

Imprisonment thrives as a "psychological safety valve" in the unstable order of the market (Cayley 1998: 80). The global market sets the tone of personal responsibility and therefore has the dual effect of providing a person's chance for advancement and the possibility of failure (Bauman 1995a). Indeed, the unemployed and the poor threaten the internal functioning of market society because they are reminders of failure. Critical criminology authors, such as Christie (2000), Davis (2005), Reiman (2001, 2004), Clarke (2000) and Bauman (1995a), have developed a critique of the criminal justice system and the prison that sees each entity as an essential part of hegemony, hiding capitalist inequalities and reinforcing the poor as "criminal." They argue that an ideological function of the prison is to blame individuals for acts that are stimulated by capitalism's economic and social inequality, without asking whether society upheld its obligations toward the social rights of individuals.

What we call crime may not be the most dangerous or the most anti-social behaviour. The position of critical criminology is that crime is a social creation, satisfying the needs of the market economy. This means that, on the one hand, the actions of corporations and the well-off are often not criminalized even when they pose a grave threat to our social well-being (Snider 1999; West and Morris 2000; Reiman 2004). Meanwhile, on the other hand, the "redundant" or "disposable" people — the underemployed, unemployed and poor — become the "dangerous class" (West and Morris 2000; Clarke 2000; Martin 2002; Reiman 2004; Reiman and Leighton 2010).

Disorderliness begets fear, which in turn feeds a public appetite for imprisoning the disorderly. As global capitalism progresses, more and more poor and disenfranchised people are labelled criminal and are imprisoned. They become, as Bauman puts it, "The enemies who have laid siege to [society's] walls," the system's "own inner demons" (Bauman 1995, quoted in Cayley 1998: 76). In labelling the addict or the woman working in the sex trade, for instance, as "criminal," society forgoes the obligation of dealing with the underlying social inequalities that lead people into these desperate living conditions. Rather than addressing the roots of increasing homelessness, poverty and numbers of marginalized people, society uses the criminal justice system to squash the human manifestations of the problem. Approximately two-thirds of prisoners in Canada, or 80 percent of inmates in provincial facilities and 20 to 30 percent of federal prisoners, are incarcerated for offences deemed non-violent (Statistics Canada 2006). As anti-poverty activist John Clarke (2000: 82) puts it, the "balance between reluctant social provision and repression is being tilted" in favour of the latter. In its "social regulation of the poor," the state cuts back on income and housing programs and provides more and more police patrols, courtrooms and prison cells. For example, in 1999, 255 schools were shut down in Ontario, 1,700 schools needed repair and funding for both immigration and housing decreased — yet funding for prisons was up 17 percent (Hanson 2006).

The homelessness problem in larger cities, for instance, has led to more and more people sleeping in parks and begging on city streets. As homelessness becomes more and more visible in Canada, it interferes with commercial and residential development. The National Coalition on Housing and Homelessness (cited in CCPA 2006) shows us that more than 2 million Canadians "are still in desperate need of decent, affordable housing [yet] the federal government is poised to take billions of housing dollars out of housing." To solve these problems, residents and business people pressure politicians to act against the homeless. This problem escalates as housing is renovated and built for the more affluent while social housing initiatives decline, having fallen victim to policies that see low-income housing as an unnecessary expense. From the critical criminological point of view, criminalizing the poor is criticized as a way of cleansing the city, making it a supposedly safe and attractive environment for affluent people (Clarke 2000).

This drive against the dispossessed and marginalized is often disguised as an anti-crime movement: "Acts of survival like petty drug dealing or prostitution are focused on but the real agenda is the 'social cleansing' of the homeless" (Clarke 2000: 82). In Ontario, for instance, the *Ontario Safe Streets Act*, passed by the Conservative Government in 2000, makes it illegal to squeegee and to panhandle — acts most likely involving the homeless and the poor. Public safety is the official reason for this new act, as Ontario Attorney General Jim Flaherty proclaimed in a news conference: "*The Safe Streets Act* responds to the real life concerns the people of Ontario have about these activities that compromise our safety in our communities ... People must be able to carry out their daily activities without fear, without feeling afraid" (*Star-Phoenix*, Feb. 1, 2000: B7). But the Safe Streets legislation is in essence not about safety but about economic distress, unemployment and homelessness. Similarly, the City of Toronto has developed "community action policing," giving police permission to persecute the poor and homeless. Aggressive panhandlers and squeegee kids can receive a fine of up to $500, with the possibility of incarceration if they do not pay. There are an estimated 25,000 homeless people in Toronto. These initiatives ensure that many of the homeless and poor will end up behind bars.

Justice system statistics also provide a different picture than that of the news media. The average length of a prison sentence in Canada is thirty days (Statistics Canada, updated 2006), while one-quarter of admissions to custody are for two weeks or less, and 50 percent of those sentenced to jail get less than thirty days (Roberts 2000). In 2003, some 30 percent of people convicted in court received fines, not jail sentences, while 38 percent of convictions resulted in incarceration. It would seem, then, that our courts see most offenders as being of no great danger to society. Federal penitentiary time, or sentences of two years or longer, account for less than 3 percent of all sentences (Roberts 2000). In 2003, the offence of theft under $5,000 was the most frequently heard type of case in adult courts in Canada (Statistics Canada 2006). Violent crimes accounted for 11.8 percent of the cases heard. Assaults (from level one to level three) account for 9.1 percent of the 11.8 percent of violent crimes. The offences that would be considered most "dangerous" — abduction, sexual abuse, attempted murder, robbery and homicide — represented less than 1 percent of all of cases heard. Homicides accounted for .02 percent of the 11.8 percent, and attempted murder accounted for .023 percent (Statistics Canada 2006).

The statistics not only demonstrate that most offenders are not particularly dangerous, but they also raise questions about the very definition of "crime." The typical prisoner is poor, male, probably Aboriginal or Black, undereducated and unemployed. However, our idea of a typical criminal tends to fit certain stereotypes. Although we condemn offenders for not upholding their obligations to society and fulfilling their responsibilities as good citizens, we fail to ask whether society has upheld its responsibility to the offenders (Reiman 2004, 2007). This prevailing approach denies the reality that the acts of the poor are most often not nearly as dangerous as, for instance, the everyday activities of many corporations — activities that are often praised or acknowledged as simply being "good business." Even worse, in recent years corporate lobbies and neo-liberal governments have pushed to deregulate corporate activity and to dismantle government protection of environmental and human life.

Law and order politics is a key strategy in trying to forge alliances between the rich and the poor. The themes of criminal responsibility and dangerous social groups are ideological tools that try to manage the most vulnerable social classes. The criminal justice system functions as a powerful tool to manipulate the majority of the population into believing that it is the poor and marginalized that must be feared as the dangerous class (Reiman 2001; Clarke 2000). Critical criminology attempts to penetrate the ideologies that mask capitalist exploitation in order to "deflect attention away from capitalist society's real interests, naked oppressions and structural inequalities" (Pavlich 2000: 51). Harsh, militaristic, punitive law and order and super-max prisons reinforce the imagery of the criminal as dangerous and (dichotomously) different from the "respectable, conforming" population (Moore and Hannah-Moffat 2002; Garland 2001; Reiman 2004).

Nils Christie (2001) and Angela Y. Davis (2005) add a powerful critique of the prison industrial complex and demonstrate how these prisons are an integral part of a system that uses people to generate massive profits. The most vulnerable people are the "raw material" for the prison industrial complex. Imprisoning the poor and racial minorities is a complex political act, depoliticizing inequalities and yielding vast profits. This is evident in the pain market of the penal system, as profits are generated from the building of prisons and the push to privatize them and outfit them with expensive, cutting-edge technology. The people who live in super-max prisons (or any prison) are seen as society's problems. Yet they are often members of racial minorities who cannot find work. The war against crime is a war that strengthens control by the state over those who are "the least useful" part of the population — those who illustrate that the social fabric is not as it should be.

COMPARATIVE PENAL POLICY

Cavadino and Dignan (2006) argue that countries with the most imprisonment are economies defined by neo-liberal ideologies, such as the U.S., the U.K. and Australia. These authors and others (see Drake 2012; Pratt and Eriksson 2013; Lacey 2008) provide a comparison to social democratic countries such as the Nordic countries of Sweden, Norway, Denmark and Finland. These comparative analyses address levels of investment in education, training, literacy rates, social welfare and wealth distribution found in Nordic countries. These authors link investment in social and educational programs to lower incarceration rates. Lacey states: "Co-ordinated systems which favor long-term relationships through investment in education and training, generous welfare benefits, long term employment relationships have been able to resist the powerful excluding and stigmatizing aspects of punishment" (2008). Similarly, John Pratt (2008, 2011) correlates lower Scandinavian prison rates with strong welfare state solidarity, social democracy and a focus on equality, as well as prison conditions known for rehabilitation and humane conditions:

> Issues of security have not been allowed to dominate prison administration to anything like the same extent as in the Anglophone world. Even as concerns

about prison escapers were beginning to fundamentally change the administration of Anglophone prisons, Connery wrote of Sweden as follows: "I asked [the governor] what was done about escaping prisoners, since none of the guards had guns and the [prison] walls were not exactly formidable. He replied, 'it is better to let the man go than to put a hole in him ... we can always catch him later.'" (cited in Pratt 2011: 258)

Although conditions have changed slightly in Nordic countries recently, with security moderately tightened, Pratt assures his reader that conditions are still exceptional:

> Look in on Finland's penal institutions, whether those the system categorizes as "open" or "closed," and it is hard to tell when you've entered the world of custody ... [in one closed institution] there are linoleum-floored hallways lined with living spaces for inmates that resemble dormitory rooms more than lock ups in a slammer ... in some Norwegian and Swedish prisons, [there are] unsupervised contact visits, even in maximum security institutions, and car parks for prisoners in some open institutions. (2011: 259)

Notably, comparative literature also draws attention to the absence of media that would undermine experts in criminal justice. For example, the Finnish "Police-TV" is said to be about public information and education, using officials in criminal justice to explain what is happening. As a result, public pressure toward harsher sentences is virtually absent in the country (Pratt 2011; Pratt and Erikkson 2013).

Although a much longer conversation here is needed to put forward the complexity of the comparative analysis, the key point is that critical and comparative criminologists argue for the connection between penality and levels of social democracy and advocate for social reform based on sustainable social democratic reform. Neo-liberalism is criminogenic and punitive, and the prison may "obscure other social problems and conceal its own failings" (Drake 2012: 1).

CONCLUSION

The criminal justice system might seem to be unfair and ineffective, but it does not fail the status quo, and it successfully accomplishes what the elite groups see as being in their best interests (Reiman 2004, 2007). Those who have the power to change the system benefit, and they do not have the desire to change the system. Those without power suffer the costs of the failure within the criminal justice system. Reiman (2004, 2007) argues that the current criminal justice system is the best possible model for the creation of crime. What we have is a profound system for causing more crime: labelling certain individuals "offenders," the expectation of criminal tendencies, failing to deal with societal issues that create criminogenic conditions, lowering self-esteem, criminalizing victimless and consensual acts, lumping disenfranchised individuals together in demeaning conditions and creating a breeding ground for dangerous criminal behaviour. We continue to use this costly, and obviously ineffective, criminal justice system because it enhances and legitimizes the global economy and market, despite the human devastation created in the process.

In asking us to consider the benefits provided for the wealthy and powerful, Reiman (2007: 183) points to the ideological message that results from criminalizing the actions of the poor and marginalized: "The ultimate sanctions of criminal justice dramatically sanctify the present social and economic order, and the poverty of criminals makes poverty itself an individual moral crime!" Those from the middle and upper classes can easily justify the large disparities in wealth as they come to believe that the poor are at fault for their plight. "Thus by focusing on individual responsibility for crime, the criminal justice system effectively acquits the existing social order of any charge of injustice!" (Reiman 2004: 166). Public demands for more equality and an equal distribution of wealth are not part of the current political agenda. Morality and fairness do not appear to be part of the social justice picture in Canada:

> If we acknowledge the degree to which our economic and social institutions themselves breed poverty, we would have to recognize our own responsibilities toward the poor. If we can convince ourselves that the poor are poor because of their own shortcomings, particularly moral shortcomings like incontinence and indolence, then we need acknowledge no such responsibility to the poor. Indeed, we can go further and pat ourselves on the back for our generosity in handing out the little that we do — it is my view that this conception of the poor is subtly conveyed by the way our criminal justice system functions. (Reiman 2007: 182–83)

As Reiman points out, we know too much about the causes of poverty to assume that the rich are rich only because of skills and motivation or that the poor are poor because of laziness or incompetence. The global market is based on self-interest — creating never-satisfied consumers wanting more material goods and penalizing those who have little. Free-enterprise philosophy is based on the assumption that everyone has the potential to succeed as long as they possess the required skills and motivation. But with the restructuring of the market and decreased social programs, we are nowhere near offering everyone an equal opportunity for education or income or addressing the cycle of poverty and racism. We may not, in clear conscience, argue that income distribution is representative of what people deserve or have earned. That we have adopted a false ideology becomes abundantly clear when we consider the workings of law, crime, criminal justice and incarceration.

Clearly, social justice initiatives must resist simple criminal justice strategies and the urge to separate the problem of crime from other social problems such as poverty, homelessness, abuse and racism. We can begin not only with restorative measures that address the immediate needs of the convicted or incarcerated person, but also with community development. To work toward real justice means building strong social movements to counter the effect of globalization, deregulation of corporate wrongdoing and the criminalization of the poor. The development of a counter-hegemony that will work toward a democratization of criminal justice, law, media and the state requires active citizen groups demanding human rights. And it requires that people have access to education, full employment, fair wages, safe working environments and adequate, decent and affordable housing, as well as good nutrition and truly safe communities. As Reiman spells out:

> Every step toward reducing poverty and its debilitating effects, toward criminalization of the dangerous acts of the affluent and vigorous prosecution of "white-collar" crime, toward decriminalization of "illicit drugs" and "victimless

crimes" ... every step toward creating a correctional system that promotes human dignity, toward giving ex-offenders a real opportunity to go straight, toward making the exercise of power by police officers, prosecutors and judges more reasonable and more just, toward giving all individuals accused of crime equal access to high-quality legal expertise in their defence; and every step toward establishing economic and social justice is a step that moves us from a system of *criminal* justice to a system of criminal *justice*. The refusal to take those steps is a move in the opposite direction. (2007: 211)

DISCUSSION QUESTIONS

1. There is a growing interest in comparative criminology and focusing on countries that are exceptions to the general global move towards increasing imprisonment and tough crime control. Would you argue that a comparative criminology would be instructive to Canadian penal policy?

2. Current trends towards increased incarceration and cost do not correlate to a growth in crime. Drawing on a critical criminological approach, explain why the use of prison increases while crime is decreasing.

3. How does the concept of the prison industrial complex help demonstrate a changing mindset from rehabilitation of prisoners to profit maximization within corrections?

4. Media images about crime are said to inform the public, which in turn provides politicians with justification for tough law and order campaigns. Watch any television news or crime program and discuss how this may influence public perception (or your perception).

5. The consensus, pluralist and critical theories would explain some of the current trends in incarceration in the U.S. and in Canada quite differently. Drawing on themes such as justice spending, changing prison populations, minimum mandatory sentences, overcrowding and/or privatization, explain how the different criminological theories may view these trends.

GLOSSARY

Abrogation of Social Rights: abrogation refers to the diminishment or neutralization of statues. In the context of prison and social rights, certain concepts such as freedom from unlawful confinement and cruel or unusual punishment are being undermined by penal populism.

Alternatives to Incarceration: a number of potential responses to crime and wrongdoing exist within and external to the criminal justice system. Most criminologists acknowledge that incarceration is one of the least effective approaches within this spectrum.

Commission on Safety and Abuse in America's Prisons: an institutional review of United States prisons that sought to understand the preponderance of violence and abuse reported by inmates and workers. The corresponding report made thirty recommendations for improving the safety and effectiveness of U.S. prisons.

Comparative Penology: a consideration of criminal and prison regulations within the scope of external systems. For example, the practices of the Correctional Services of Canada are often compared to the Federal Bureau of Prisons in the United States.

Conflict Resolution: this approach to intervention uses conversation and negotiation to facilitate peaceful conclusions to interpersonal conflict.

Exceptionalism: when the practices of another jurisdiction, in the case corrections and penology, are identified as being contrary to common practices or trends.

Folk Devils: in times of moral panic, news media and other public outlets for information will focus on people who threaten the social order.

Incapacitation: an approach to punishment that aims to actively prevent future criminal activity by physically restraining individuals.

Inmate Labour: justice systems around the world have historically taken advantage of the manpower of inmates to produce goods and services for the state or paying contractors. This work ranges from extreme physical duress to menial tasks.

Institutional Charges: while in prison, incarcerated persons are expected to live according to the rules set out by the institution. When these rules are violated, prisoners are subjected to additional punishment. In some cases these rules are codified, but many times they are unofficial sanctions.

International Convention: a number of international agreements have been ratified by most European and American nations that set out a minimum standard of treatment for incarcerated persons. In principle, these treaties identify nature of just treatment for the imprisoned; however, their interpretation varies across different nations.

Models of Exclusion: in the context of this chapter, this term refers to the Canadian status quo approach to corrections, which attempts to infer punishment through near-total segregation.

Penal Convergence: observed similarities between differing jurisdictions' approaches to incapacitation at local, state/provincial, or national levels.

Penal Populism: a common approach to election campaigns in Western democracies is to develop policy proposals that are "tough on crime" in order to trump up public sentiment. This often entails harsher penalties and increased enforcement of certain laws.

Repressive State: this concept refers to political actions, whether conscious or subversive, that contribute toward the ongoing persecution of individuals or groups that pose a threat to the normative actions of a state and its mode of production.

Risk Assessments: Correctional Service Canada uses a series of measures to estimate the level of risk that a given offender poses to prison staff and fellow inmates, which is then used to justify the type of confinement applied to that offender.

Super-Max Facilities: super-maximum security prisons, or units within prisons, utilize extreme segregation to control the behaviours of prisoners that have been deemed dangerous. This approach to incarceration is best illustrated in this chapter's discussion of Pelican Bay.

Three Strikes Legislation: this approach to justice was pioneered in the United States as a response to "habitual offenders." People who have been convicted of three crimes face significantly longer-than-prescribed sentences on their third offence. This type of legislation originally targeted violent offenders, but has since been applied to property offenders.

SUGGESTED READINGS

Jeffrey Reiman and Paul Leighton, *The Rich Get Richer and the Poor Get Prison: Ideology, Class and Criminal Justice,* tenth Edition, Boston: Allyn and Bacon (2012).

Kerry Carrington, Matthew Ball, Erin O'Brien and Juan Tauri, *Crime, Justice and Social Democracy: International Perspectives,* London: Palgrave Macmillan (2013).

John Pratt and Anna Eriksson, *Contrasts in Punishment. An Explanation of Anglophone Excess and Nordic Exceptionalism,* Oxford: Routledge (2013).

Deborah Drake, *Prisons, Punishment and the Pursuit of Security,* England: Palgrave MacMillan (2012).

NOTES

1. For more details on the background of Bill C-10 and an overview of key changes, see "The State of Incarceration" or watch the CBC episode, both at <http://www.cbc.ca/doczone/features/backgrounder-bill-c-10>.

2. For a 2012 breakdown of Corporations that have larger economies than countries, see "The Corporation Bigger than Nations" at <http://makewealthhistory.org/2014/02/03/the-corporations-bigger-than-nations/>.

REFERENCES

Altheide, David L. 2009. "Moral Panic: From Sociological Concept to Public Discourse." *Crime, Media, Culture* 5, 1: 79–99.

American Civil Liberties Union. 2013. "Criminal Justice: Victims' Rights Amendment." At <aclu.org> accessed December 11, 2013,

Anderson, Sarah, and John Cavanagh. 2000. "Top 200: The Rise of Global Corporate Power." *Global Policy Forum.* At <global policy.org/socecon/tncs/top200.htm>.

Bauman, Zygmunt. 1995. *Life in Fragments: Essays in Post-Modern Morality.* Oxford: Blackwell.

Becker, Howard. 1963. *Outsiders: Studies in the Sociology of Crime.* New York: Free Press.

Blaikie, Peter. 2011. "Crime Policy Is All Stick, No Carrot." *Montreal Gazette.* At <http://canadianharmreduction.com/node/327>.

Braithwaite, J. 1989. *Crime, Shame and Reintegration.* Cambridge, UK: Cambridge University Press.

Brennan, S. 2012. "Police-Reported Crime Statistics in Canada, 2011." *Juristat.* Statistics Canada Catalogue no. 85-002-x.

Brosnahan, Maureen. 2013. "Canada's Prison Population at All-Time High: Number of Visible Minority Inmates Increased by 75% in Past Decade." *CBC News.* At <cbc.ca/news/canada-s-prison-population-at-all-time-high-1.2440039>.

Canadian Press. 2013. "Wealthiest 1% Earn 10 Times More than the Average Canadian." Canadian Press. At <cbc.ca/news/business/wealthiest-1-earn-10-times-more-than-average-canadian-1.1703017>.

Carson, E. Ann, and William J. Sabol. 2012. "Prisoners in 2011." *U.S. Department of Justice: Office of Justice Programs Bureau of Justice Statistics.* At <bjs.gov/content/pub/pdf/p11.pdf>.

Cavadino, Michael, and James Dignan. 2006. "Penal Policy and Political Economy." *Criminology and Criminal Justice* 6, 4: 435–56.

Cayley, David. 1998. *The Expanding Prison: The Crisis in Crime and Punishment and the Search for Alternatives.* Toronto: House of Anansi.

CCPA (Canadian Center for Policy Alternatives). 2006. "Report Card: Minority Report: A Report Card on the 2004-05 Minority Government." At <http://www.policyalternatives.ca/sites/default/files/uploads/publications/National_Office_Pubs/2006/AFB_Minority_Report.pdf>.

Chockalingam, Kumaravelu, and Murugesan Srinivasan. 2009. "Fear of Crime Victimization: A Study of University Students in India and Japan." *International Review of Victimology* 16: 89–117.

Christie, Nils. 2000. *Crime Control as Industry: Towards Gulags, Western Style.* New York: Routledge.

Clarke, John. 2000. "Serve the Rich and Punish the Poor." In Gordon West and Ruth Morris (eds.), *The Case for Penal Abolition.* Toronto: Canadian Scholars Press.

Clarke, Tony. 1997. *The Silent Coup: Confronting the Big Business Takeover of Canada.* Toronto: Canadian Centre for Policy Alternatives.

Collins. Racheal. 2014. "'Meet The Devil … He'll Chill You to the Bone' Fear, Marginalization, and the Colour of Crime: A Thirty-Year Analysis of Four Canadian Newspapers." At <ecommons. usask.ca/handle/10388/ETD-2014-03-1491>.

Comack, Elizabeth. 1996. *Women in Trouble.* Halifax: Fernwood Publishing.

Correctional Services of Canada. 2013. *Coroner's Inquest Touching the Death of Ashley Smith* (2013).

Davis, Angela Y. 2005. *Abolition, Democracy: Beyond Prison, Torture and Empire.* Toronto: Seven Stories Press.

Dayan, Colin. 2013. "Fear and Hunger at Pelican Bay." *Aljazeera America.* At <http://america. aljazeera.com/articles/2013/8/21/fear-and-hunger-inpelicanbay.html>.

Deveau, Scott. 2006. "Crime Bill Sets Mandatory Minimum Sentences." *Globe and Mail,* May 5, 2006.

Dobbin, Murray. 1998. *The Myth of the Good Corporate Citizen: Democracy Under the Rule of Big Business.* Toronto: Stoddart.

___. 2003. *Paul Martin: CEO for Canada?* Toronto: James Lorimer.

Drake, Deborah. 2012. *Prisons, Punishment and the Pursuit of Security.* London: Palgrave Macmillan.

Ebenstein, Julie. 2013. "The Sad State of Solitary in Florida: Is There Hope for This Human Rights Violation?" ACLU American Civil Liberties Union Blog of Rights March, 2013. At <aclu.org/ blog/prisoners-rights-human-rights/sad-state-solitary-florida-there-hope-human-rights-violation>.

Farndale, Nigel. 2012. "This British Reporter Lived Life on a Female Chain Gang in the Blazing Arizona Desert." *Business Insider Austrailia.* At <businessinsider.com.au/step-into-the-worlds-only-female-chain-gang-right-here-in-america-2012-11>.

Fraser, Steve, and Joshua B. Freeman. 2012. "21st Century Chain Gangs: The Rebirth of Prison Labor Foretells a Disturbing Future for America's "Free Market" Capitalism." *New York Times: Salon.* Thursday, April 19. At <salon.com/2012/04/19/21st_century_chain_gangs/>

Garland, E. 2001. *The Culture of Control: Crime and Social Order in Contemporary Society.* Chicago: Oxford University Press.

Gelb, K. 2008. "Myths and Misconceptions: Public Opinion versus Public Judgment about Sentencing." In Carrington et al. (eds.), *Crime, Justice and Social Democracy: International Perspectives.* London: Palgrave MacMillan.

Girard, Lina, and J.S. Wormith. 2004. "The Predictive Validity of the Level of Service Inventory — Ontario Revision on General and Violent Recidivism among Various Offender Groups." *Criminal Justice and Behavior* 31: 150–81.

Globe and Mail. 1995. "What's the Real Cost of Punishment?" March 31.

Goddard, John. 2006. "Canada's Poor Face 'Emergency': U.N." *Toronto Star.* At <lubicon.ca/pa/ negp/po06/po060523.htm>.

Gorkoff, Kelly, and Jane Runner. 2003. *Being Heard: The Experiences of Young Women in Prostitution.* Winnipeg: Fernwood Publishing.

Grattet, Ryken, and Joseph Hayes. 2013. "California's Changing Prison Population." *Public Policy Institute of California* June.

Hannah-Moffat, Kelly. 2005. "Criminogenic Needs and the Transformative Risk Subject: Hybridizations of Risk/Need in Penality." *Punishment & Society* 7: 29–51.

Hanson, Ann. 2006. "Brampton Prison Blues." *Independent Voice* 1, XV, 2 (March). Damian T. Lloyd, (ed.). Kingston, ON: PIC Press.

Hermer, Joe, and Janet Mosher. 2002. *Disorderly People: Law and the Politics of Exclusion in Ontario.* Halifax: Fernwood Publishing.

Hogg, Russell. 2013. "Criminology Beyond the Nation State: Global Conflicts, Human Rights and the 'New World Disorder.'" In Kerry Carrington and Russell Hogg (eds.), *Critical Criminology: Issues, Debates, Challenges.* Oregon: Willan Publishing.

Human Rights Watch. 2012a. "Old Behind Bars: The Aging Prison Population in the United States." At <hrw.org>.

___. 2012b. "Growing Up Locked Down." At <http://www.hrw.org/node/110545/section/6>.

Juristat. 2014. "Correctional Services Key Indicators, 2012/2013."

___. 2012. "Adult Correctional Statistics in Canada, 2010/2011."

___. 2011. "Trends in the Use of Remand in Canada."

Kotarski, Kris. 2011. "Animated Fear about Crime." *Calgary Herald*, Monday, July 25. At <canada.com/calgaryherald/news/theeditorialpage/story.html?id=824e0006-6b21-4083-9476-f06290ad57e3&p=2>.

Lacey, N. 2008. *The Prisoners Dilemma: Political Economy and Punishment in Contemporary Democracies.* Cambridge: Cambridge University Press.

Lermert, Edwin. 1951. *Social Pathology.* New York: McGraw-Hill.

___. 1967. *Human Deviance, Social Problems, and Social Control.* University of Michigan: Prentice-Hall.

___. 1974."Beyond Mead: The Societal Reaction to Deviance." *Social Problems* 21, 4 (April): 457–68.

MacCharles, Tonda. 2012. "Federal Prison Populations in Canada Growing." *Thestar.com* October 23. At <thestar.com/news/canada/2012/10/23/federal_prison_population_in_canada_growing.html>.

Martin, Dianne. 2002. "Demonizing Youth, Marketing Fear: The New Politics of Crime." In Joe Hermer and Janet Mosher (eds.), *Disorderly People: Law and the Politics of Exclusion in Ontario.* Halifax: Fernwood Publishing.

Mathieson, Thomas. 1974. *The Politics of Abolition: Essays in Political Action Theory.* London: Martin Robertson.

___. 1990. *Prison on Trial.* London: Sage Publications.

___. 2005. *Prison on Trial.* Hampshire: Waterside Press.

McDowell, M., K. Jones, T. Keatings, C. Brooks, H. Cheng, M. Olver and S. Wormith. 2012. "Taking the Pulse of Saskatchewan 2012: Crime and Public Safety in Saskatchewan." Saskatoon, SK: Social Sciences Research Laboratories, University of Saskatchewan.

McMurtry, John. 2000. "Caging the Poor: The Case Against the Prison System." In Gordon West and Ruth Morris (eds.), *The Case for Penal Abolition.* Toronto: Canadian Scholars Press.

Minarovich, Ryan. 2013. "The Modern Chain Gang: How Convict Leasing Can Help Repair the California Prison System." *Social Science Research Network.* At <papers.ssrn.com/sol3/papers.cfm?abstract_id=2324569>.

Moore, Dawn, and Kelly Hannah-Moffat. 2002. "Correctional Renewal Without the Frills: The Politics of 'Get-Tough' Punishment in Ontario." In Joe Hermer and Janet Mosher (eds.), *Disorderly People: Law and the Politics of Exclusion in Ontario.* Halifax: Fernwood Publishing.

Morris, Ruth. 2000. *Stories of Transformative Justice.* Toronto: Canadian Scholars' Press.

Muller, Christopher, and Daniel Schrage. 2014. "Mass Imprisonment and Trust in the Law." *The Annals of the American Academy of Political and Social Science* 651: 139. At <http://ann.sagepub.com/content/651/1/139.full.pdf+html>.

National Council of Welfare. 2011. "The Dollars and Sense of Solving Poverty." *National Council of Welfare Reports* 130 (Autumn). At <publications.gc.ca/collections/collection_2011/cnb-ncw/HS54-2-2011-eng.pdf>.

Nelkin, David. 2011. *Comparative Criminal Justice and Globalization.* Surrey: Ashgate Publishing.

O'Loughlin, John, Lynn Staeheli and Edward Greenberg (eds.). 2004. *Globalization and Its Outcomes.* New York: Guildford Press.

Office of the Correctional Investigator. 2012. " Report on Plans and Priorities." At <tbs-sct.gc.ca/rpp/2012-2013/inst/oci/oci-eng.pdf>.

Office of the Parliamentary Budget Officer. 2010. *The Funding Requirement and Impact of the "Truth in Sentencing Act" on the Correctional System in Canada.*

Pavlich, George. 2000. *Critique and Radical Discourses on Crime.* Burlington, Great Britain:

Dartmouth Publishing.

Pelaez Vicky. 2008. "The Prison Industry in the United States: Big Business or a New Form of Slavery?" *Global ResearchEl Diario-La Prensa, New York and Global Research* 10 March. <globalresearch.ca/the-prison-industry-in-the-united-states-big-business-or-a-new-form-of-slavery/8289>.

Pratt, John. 2007. *Penal Populism.* New York: Routledge.

___. 2008. "Scandinavian Exceptionalism in an Era of Penal Excess. Part I: The Nature and Roots of Scandinavian Exceptionalism." *British Journal of Criminology* 48: 119–37.

___. 2011. "The International Diffusion of Punitive Penality: Or, Penal Exceptionalism in the United States? Wacquant v. Whitman." *Australian and New Zealand Journal of Criminology* 44: 166–28.

Pratt, John, and Anna Eriksson. 2013. *Contrasts in Punishment: An Explanation of Anglophone Excess and Nordic Exceptionalism.* Oxford: Routledge.

Reiman, Jeffrey. 2001. *The Rich Get Richer and the Poor Get Prison: Ideology, Class and Criminal Justice.* Boston: Allyn and Bacon.

___. 2004. *The Rich Get Richer and the Poor Get Prison: Ideology, Class and Criminal Justice.* Seventh edition. Boston: Allyn and Bacon.

___. 2007. *The Rich Get Richer and the Poor Get Prison: Ideology, Class and Criminal Justice.* Eighth edition. Boston: Allyn and Bacon.

___. 2009. *The Rich Get Richer and the Poor Get Prison: Ideology, Class and Criminal Justice.* Ninth edition. Boston: Allyn and Bacon.

Reiman, Jeffrey, and Paul Leighton. 2012. *The Rich Get Richer and the Poor Get Prison: Ideology, Class and Criminal Justice.* Tenth edition. Boston: Allyn and Bacon

Reiman, Jeffrey, and Paul Leighton. 2010. *The "Rich Get Richer and the Poor Get Prison": A Reader.* Boston: Allyn and Bacon.

Reuben, Richard C. 1995. "Get-Tough Stance Draws Fiscal Criticism." *American Bar Association Journal* Jan.

Roberts, Julian. 2000. *Criminal Justice in Canada: A Reader.* Toronto: Harcourt Brace and Company.

Roberts, Lynn, and David Indermaur. 2009. "What Australians Think about Crime and Justice: Results from the 2007 Survey of Social Attitudes." *Research and Public Policy* series no. 101. Canberra: Australian Institute of Criminology.

Routledge, Paul. 2006. "Book Review: *Globalization and Its Outcomes.*" *Growth and Change* 37: 331.

Sacco, Vincent F. 2005. *When Crime Waves.* Sage Publications.

Sapers, Howard. 2013. "Annual Report of the Office of the Correctional Investigator 2012–2013." *Correctional Investigator.* At <oci-bec.gc.ca/cnt/rpt/annrpt/annrpt20122013-eng.aspx>.

Schissel, Bernard. 2006. *Still Blaming Children: Youth Conduct and the Politics of Child Hating.* Black Point, NS: Fernwood Publishing.

Schmidt, Sara. 2012. "U.N. Envoy Blasts Canada for 'Self-Righteous' Attitude over Hunger, Poverty." Post-media News. At <news.nationalpost.com/2012/05/15/un-envoy-blasts-canada-for-self-righteous-attitude-over-hunger-poverty/>.

Shah Palak, and Tom Pryor. 2005. "Conservative Agendas and Campaigns: Victim's Rights." In *An Activist Resource Kit: Political Research Associates.* At <publiceye.org/defendingjustice/pdfs/chapters/complete_intro.pdf >.

Snider, Laureen. 1999. "Relocating Law: Making Corporate Crime Disappear." In Elizabeth Comack (ed.), *Locating Law: Race/Class/Gender Connections.* Halifax: Fernwood Publishing.

Star Phoenix. 2000. "Squeegee Kids No Longer Welcome on Ontario Streets." February 1; B7.

Statistics Canada. 2006. "Sentenced Cases and Outcomes in Adult Criminal Court (Median Length of Prison Sentence)." 252-0021 and Catalogue no. 85-002-X. Last modified 2006-04-21.

Trivett, Vincent. 2011. "25 US Mega Corporations: Where They Rank if They Were Countries." *Business Insider.* At <businessinsider.com/25-corporations-bigger-tan-countries-2011-6?op=1>.

Turney, Kristin. 2013. "The Intergenerational Consequences of Mass Incarceration: Implications for Children's Contact with Grandparents." University of California. At <crcw.princeton.edu/workingpapers/WP13-07-FF.pdf>.

U.S. Securities and Exchange Commission. 2012. *sec Form 10-K: Corrections Corporation of America*.

West, W. Gordon, and Ruth Morris (eds.). 2000. *The Case For Penal Abolition.* Toronto: Canadian Scholars' Press.

White, R. 2002. "Restorative Justice and Social Inequality." In Bernard Schissel and Carolyn Brooks (eds.), *Marginality and Condemnation: An Introduction to Critical Criminology.* Halifax: Fernwood Publishing.

Whittington, L. 2013. "Conservatives Dismantling Social Programs Built Over Generations." *Toronto Star,* Dec. 9.

Walmsely, Roy. 2012. "World Prison Population List (ninth edition)." National Criminal Justice Reference Service. At <ncjrs.gov/App/Publications/abstract.aspx?ID=262857>.

Wilkinson, Richard, and Kate Pickett. 2010. *The Spirit Level: Why Equality Is Better for Everyone.* UK: Penguin.

Zimring, Franklin E. 2010. "The Scale of Imprisonment in the United States: Twenty-First Century Prospects." *The Journal of Criminal Law and Criminology* 100, 3: 1225–46.

PART III

CRIME AND RACE

Traditional historians argue that crime and crime control change according to the socio-demographic nature of a particular time period. Their analyses tend to focus on the characteristics of criminality in a historical epoch: what types of people are in prison; the types of punishment they experience; the nature of their crimes (especially high-profile individual cases); government policies directed at criminality; and the ability of the state and its citizens to counter "crime waves." D. Owen Carrigan, in *Crime and Punishment in Canada: A History* (1991), for example, paints an historical picture of crime based on crime rates over time, historical descriptions about the age, race and gender profile of criminals, the socio-economic conditions of the criminal class and historical accounts of forms of punishment. Such traditional histories are descriptive; they are "constructed" histories, much like fiction. They tell us a great deal about the norms and values of the society the authors live in, but they do little to help us understand how and why certain peoples are more damaged by society and by the justice system than others. Nor does Carrigan's history reveal how laws and social control benefit some to the disadvantage of others, or how crime and justice are related to socio-economic conditions at specific points in history.

Traditional criminological histories, as being primarily descriptive, then, tend to place changes in crime and punishment in an evolutionary framework premised on the assumption that society, as it develops technologically/scientifically, is becoming more civilized. Therefore, they suggest that our responses to crime are becoming more rational and civilized as well. This paradigm for understanding change tends not to place historical change in an analytical framework that helps explain oppression and marginalization or to indicate why some people are condemned primarily for their place in the socio-economic structure.

As an antidote to traditional history, the chapters in Part III concern the history of oppression of certain peoples in Canada and globally, and they reveal how historical forces, both specific and general, shape contemporary criminal justice and what we define as crime. They focus on how and why society inordinately condemns marginalized people and how this condemnation is tied to the politics and economics of a particular time. Most importantly, the discussions illustrate an often forgotten issue: that people who are economically, socially and spiritually oppressed over generations will be over-represented in the crime-control system. Unlike traditional criminological history, these works show, for example, how the phenomenon of Aboriginal people in conflict with the law is related to continuing but changing forms of colonization, how the current extraordinary measures designed to address terrorism have resulted in human rights violations with devastating effects (such as mass surveillance and detention without charges) on racialized minorities and how carding or street checks as a policing practice show continued evidence of racial bias.

The chapters in this section are all new chapters to this book, and they focus mainly on issues of race, criminalization, policing, terrorism and the criminal justice system. The authors question how we have, in Canada and elsewhere, constructed people of colour and other racial/ethnic minorities as troublemakers and lawbreakers and how the discourse of race and crime informs the behavior of citizens, police and criminal justice.

In Chapter 10, "'Colonialism, Resistance and Aboriginal Street Gangs," Elizabeth Comack, Lawrence Deane, Larry Morrissette and Jim Silver draw on their current research and extensive interviews with Aboriginal street gang leaders and other inner-city Aboriginal people in Winnipeg. The authors demonstrate how the current "get tough on crime" approaches result in high levels of policing of inner city areas, harsh prison terms and other excessively draconian legal provisions. They clearly argue that such punitive crime control activities cannot address the root causes of street gang issues and cannot address racialized and spacialized poverty. In their critical analysis of gangs, the authors acknowledge the impact of global economic change on inner-city communities in a Canadian context and argue that gang membership signifies resistance to colonialism.

Comack et al. elucidates how colonialism has been destructive and how street gang membership and activity is also destructive. Street gangs have devastating effects for those in contact with them, as well as for gang-involved individuals themselves, "most of whom end up with nothing, regretting their involvement and wanting out of life." Meaningful ways to address gang activities must attend, the authors argue, to the ongoing damages caused by the history and current realities of colonialism. This means decolonizaing measures, rebuilding communities and families and resistance.

In Chapter 11, "Criminalizing Race," Wendy Chan furthers the conversation about antagonisms between the criminal justice system and racialized people and argues against the claims that we live in a post-racial society. She points to dishonoring stereotypes such as "driving while black; flying while brown" that are reinforced through media and end up justifying harsh penal control and discriminatory treatment.

From a framework of race as a socially constructed category, Chan introduces different intellectual traditions, such as positivism and "race thinking" and demonstrates the problems with assuming certain racial or ethnic groups are prone to crime. In response to the problem of racialized conceptions of crime, she introduces critical criminology and the notion of racialization, including a thoughtful discussion on how racialized groups are more prone to being labelled criminal, policed, processed and sentenced more often than non-racialized people. Her work provides insight into how devastating the impact of racialized processes (such as racial profiling, over-policing, criminalizing immigrants and refugees) have been on individuals who end up criminalized, demonized and, ultimately, denied justice.

Wendy Chan's chapter also draws attention to the importance of an intersectional analysis — showing how gender, class and race intersect in individuals' lives and lead to differential life opportunities and differential treatment in the criminal justice system. For example, she talks about the research on the "blackening of prisons," and demonstrates how the numbers of Black inmates has not only increased but that most of the inmates are men. And, of course, there is a class dimension. She states. "While women are being funneled into part-time, precarious employment, unemployed, racialized men are increasingly being managed by the penal system." Thus, Chan's work helps elucidate the interconnections between the race/class/gender/age approaches in this book.

In the final chapter in this section, "Terrorism as Crime or War?", Robert Diab focuses on the political nature of what gets defined as terrorism and the relationship between terrorism, war and crime. His position is that terrorism became defined as a super-crime and dealt with in two ways: by adding offences within the criminal law and by conceiving of terrorism as war and, as a consequence, a public safety threat. The resulting efforts involved extraordinary measures evolved including increased surveillance, indefinite detention and targeted killing, violating the human rights of mostly racialized minorities.

Diab's chapter begins with an overview of the criminological assumptions of the U.N.'s 2001 call for an increase in counter-terror legislation and the provisions that have been added to Canada's *Criminal Code* in response, including the *Anti-Terrorism Act*. Soon after the events of September 11, 2001, the United Nations called upon member states to pass additional counter-terror laws and stiffer sentences for terrorism offences. In responding to this call, Canada, the U.S. and other Western nations acknowledged the act of terrorism as a criminal offence and the use of conventional tools of prosecution and punishment as appropriate means of response. Diab draws attention to the failure on the part of governments to uphold the rights to dignity and equality of Arab or Muslim populations within Western nations through practices of racial profiling and the perpetuation and dissemination of misinformation, all of which have lead to wrongful arrests, detention and/or torture. These same Western nations have resisted in offering redress or accountability to members of these marginal communities. In the end, Diab's chapter highlights laws unique to post-9/11 society and demonstrates the link between counter-terror policy and rhetoric-masking imperialist and racist assumptions.

All of the chapters in this section explore how Canadian policy and reform accommodate rather than challenge the status quo. The arguments are clear: criminal justice policy can only be called progressive it if challenges issues of social injustice that results from systemic racism and structural inequalities. The authors explore the urgency of addressing a system that currently punishes people as much for their race — in conjunction with other social categories — as their conduct.

10

COLONIALISM, RESISTANCE AND ABORIGINAL STREET GANGS

Elizabeth Comack, Lawrence Deane, Larry Morrissette and Jim Silver

KEY FACTS

> The Government of Canada's Department of Public Safety estimates that there are 434 youth gangs in Canada comprising approximately 7,000 members.

> Studies of youth gangs, particularly Aboriginal gangs, have indicated a relationship between poverty and membership. Most incarcerated Aboriginal youth suggested that they were involved in gangs; and 47 percent of these youth came from families that received social assistance.

> Gang membership and disputes follow members when they are incarcerated. A recent Correctional Services Canada report estimated that 16 percent of men and 12 percent of women in federal custody were involved in prison gangs.

> Most studies of urban youth street gangs found that female members were in the minority. Estimates range from 0 percent to 32 percent of membership. However, research has illustrated a growing trend of female gang membership since the mid 1990s, leading to a 500 percent change.

> When female gang members are incarcerated, they exhibit high levels of risk and social need. Over 30 percent are considered high-risk offenders (i.e., more likely to be a danger to themselves or others) compared to 6 percent in the general incarcerated population; and 43 percent had high-needs (i.e., histories of substance abuse; poor life attitudes) compared to 19 percent of the general population.

> The nature and typology of gangs in Canada vary greatly. For example, research on gangs in Montreal found that they were primarily made up of people with immigrant backgrounds from Caribbean and Latin American countries. Studies in Vancouver found that nearly half of all gang members (45 percent) had Asian heritage, while gang members in the Prairie Provinces are almost exclusively Aboriginal.

Sources: Public Safety Canada 2003; Canada, Department of Justice Canada 2004; Correctional Service Canada 2003; RCMP 2009.

At the age of twelve Tyler left a troubled home life in his Aboriginal community and made his way to Winnipeg. Landing in the North End, one of the city's large inner-city communities, he soon plugged into street gang life and its culture. As Tyler recalled, "a lot of parties" went on — "lots of parties. Like, I remember going party to party to party in the north side." Schooling seemed irrelevant — the main attraction was to just "stay in school so you could sell drugs." That particular business arose from necessity. "You're on your own, you know, you got rent to pay, you got to do something. I remember the first thing I did was I figured out the prices of marijuana and I saved up enough to buy myself a bag of marijuana and I sold that bag and I made myself a couple of dollars off of it. So I thought, well hey, I found something to support myself."

In his mid-teens Tyler joined an Aboriginal street gang and became a striker, which meant "You got to do whatever you're told, and even though you don't agree with it you just do it, a lot of violence and a lot of, you know, crime and stuff." As he became more senior in the gang he began hustling drugs and supervising the work of other street-level sellers, which involved a regular work routine: "In the morning I'd check my phone to see who called and check my text messages. I'd go and see who's on call on the lines — 'cause we had different drug lines and different houses happening — and then organize who's working where. And then I'd drive around and I'd go pick up money and then drop off more drugs."

Violence was a central part of Tyler's life. "A lot of fighting with other youth over gang colours and stuff and … then there's the violence of being an angry kid." His anger came "from an abusive father." It came from "not having anything for myself, just having to stand on my own two feet, yeah. So, you know, when you want to stand on your own two feet you're not going to let nobody push you around and that's pretty much how it was."

The result was a raft of criminal charges — for stealing cars, assaults, dealing drugs and armed robbery. "You know, you do an armed robbery with your friends, that's a fuckin' adrenaline rush right there." Doing crimes ended him up in a detention centre as a youth. "You're locked in that little cell and of course it's shitty and you want to get out of there. But at the same time you're so immersed in that lifestyle you know you're going to be back anyway so you make the most of it." Turning eighteen "just opened up the doors to all the other jails" for Tyler. Being sent to jail as an adult "was an ordinary life at the time, which I thought was an ordinary life, right. So you just graduate to the next institution."

Now, at twenty-seven years of age, Tyler reflected back on what it meant to grow up like that: "A large effect, huge, huge, you know. Where you come from is where you're going and it's hard to get off that track once you're on the track." Given his criminal record, it was especially hard getting off that track. Tyler has a sociological analysis of the street gang life he was drawn into: "I think the gangs, the drugs and the violence is just a byproduct of the poverty and desperation. That's what I think. If you really want to tackle issues that these youth are going through, then you really have to look at poverty."

The emergence and proliferation of street gangs such as the one that Tyler joined have become a global phenomenon (Hagedorn 2008; Klein 2007; Bourgois 2003). Even Canadian cities have witnessed the phenomena. In the mid-1990s, Winnipeg garnered a media reputation as the "gang capital of Canada," and the names of Aboriginal street gangs — Indian Posse, Manitoba Warriors, Native Syndicate — became part of the public discourse. Since then, Aboriginal street gangs have become equated with crime, violence and the illegal drug trade in Winnipeg's inner-city communities (Carlson 2009; Comack and Silver 2006, 2008). Cast as the epitome of the "Criminal Other," street gang members are vilified in the media as a "cancer" that "terrorizes the communities in which they live" (Procaylo 2012). Concerns about street gangs have also fuelled calls from conservatives to "get tough on crime" and impose "law and order" solutions that include heightened police surveillance of inner-city communities, more rigorous legal provisions that define street gangs as "criminal organizations" and harsher prison terms for street gang members (Report of the Standing Committee on Justice and Human Rights 2012; Mallea 2011; Helmer 2009). While these "get tough" strategies offer the promise of a quick and ready solution, they will not quell the tide of kids such as Tyler being swept into the gang life. This is because the roots of the street gang issue run deeper than these solutions can contemplate. As Tyler recognizes, "you really have to look at poverty."

Understanding the phenomena of the "street gang" requires not just looking at poverty, but also acknowledging the particular form of poverty — spatially concentrated and racialized —that has become entrenched in North American inner-city communities (see, for example, Wilson 1987; Wacquant 2008). There is a growing body of criminological research that helps us to understand street gangs. In particular, we highlight the work of "critical gang studies" researchers (Davis 2008: xv), who locate street gangs in their broader social, economic and political context by showcasing the impact of global economic restructuring on inner-city communities and the state's neo-liberal withdrawal from the provision of social benefits. Drawing on extensive interviews we conducted with Aboriginal street gang leaders and with other young inner-city Aboriginal men and women in Winnipeg, we add another significant factor that is specific to the Canadian context — colonialism and its present-day impact on the lives of Aboriginal people — and argue that Aboriginal street gangs represent a form of resistance to colonialism. Colonization is described by Justice Murray Sinclair, chair of the Truth and Reconciliation Commission, as an act of genocide against Aboriginal people that has left an indelible impact on Canadian society (Puxley 2012). This genocide caused deep and lasting damage — "cumulative waves of trauma" (Wesley-Esquimaux and Smoleski 2004: iii) — for generations of Aboriginal people and their families. Because of colonization, Aboriginal youth like Tyler have grown up in conditions in which troubles at home, at school and on the street, as well as troubles that emanate from being taken into custody by the state and placed into foster and group homes or in detention centres, have figured prominently in their lives. These troubles have prompted some young Aboriginal people to resist their colonial condition by acting collectively.

WHAT IS A "STREET GANG"?

Considerable attention has been devoted to defining a "street gang" (see, for example, Wortley 2010; Chatterjee 2006; Kelly and Caputo 2005; Jones et al. 2004; Gordon 2000). Some definitions are so broad and inclusive that they could encompass virtually any grouping of young people. The U.S. National Youth Gang Survey, for instance, advises law enforcement officials that a gang is "a group of youths or young adults in your jurisdiction that you or other responsible persons in your agency or community are willing to identify or classify as a gang" (Egley and Arjunan 2002). Others have singled out characteristics that are considered to be essential elements of the gang: having a name; displaying specific colours and insignia ("rags" and tattoos); using particular communication patterns (hand signs and graffiti); identifying with a certain geographical area (or turf); practising initiation rituals (such as "beating in" new members); having clearly identified leaders and followers; and engaging in violence and criminal activity (Wortley and Tanner 2007; Chettleburgh 2007).

For researchers in the Eurogang network, "A street gang is any durable, street-oriented youth group whose own identity includes involvement in illegal activity" (Weerman et al. 2009: 20). As Malcolm Klein and Cheryl Maxson (2006: 4) note, this definition accommodates how membership in a street gang may be relatively short-lived while the gang itself nevertheless continues despite turnover of its members. Much of the time of gang members is spent, quite literally, "on the street"; its members can include younger as well as older youth; the gang's activities often revolve around criminal activities; and the street gang members have a collective identity.

However, a significant factor is the political and economic context in which street gangs originate and flourish. Commenting on the Canadian experience, Jana Grekul and Patti LaBoucane-Benson (2008: 64) note, "Gang problems in Toronto are different from those in Winnipeg or Vancouver ... While there are similarities ... across the nation, the specific form the group takes depends in part on the region of the country in which it is located." What particularly distinguishes Aboriginal street gangs is their colonial context.

CRIMINOLOGICAL EXPLANATIONS FOR STREET GANGS

Criminologists have traditionally explained street gangs in cultural and ecological terms, as a subcultural response of male youth in socially disorganized, low-income urban areas. In his classic study of 1,313 gangs in 1920s Chicago, Frederic Thrasher (1927) proposed that the gangs were the result of the social disorganization of inner-city communities populated by poor, newly-arrived immigrants. Given the apparent disorganization of these communities — such as the disintegration of family life, inadequate schooling, unemployment and low wages, lack of recreational facilities and poor housing and sanitation — the gangs represented "the spontaneous effort of boys to create a society for themselves where none adequate to their needs exists" (Thrasher 1963: 33). This gang involvement, according to Thrasher, was temporary, usually lasting only a generation until the immigrant community managed to become more assimilated into the mainstream society. "As immigrant groups moved up into better working class jobs and out of the worst housing, the new immigrant groups who took their place spawned new youth gangs who warred with gangs in neighboring areas" (see Hagedorn 1988: 39). Other gang researchers, such as James Short (1964), Irving Spergel (1964), and Malcolm Klein (1971), continued in this tradition by focusing their studies on the social disorganization of inner-city communities and the corresponding "group processes" of adolescents (Hagedorn 2007a: 297).

Taking a decidedly subcultural approach that "othered" lower-class youth, Albert Cohen (1966: 106–07) focused on what he saw as the "non-utilitarian, malicious and negativistic" behaviour of some lower-class boys: they "steal for the hell of it"; they challenge and defy their teachers; and they are "just plain mean" and "ornery." According to Cohen, delinquent subcultures emerged as a reaction against the norms and values of the "respectable middle-class society" (1966: 116), such as deferred gratification, respect for property rights and desire for educational and occupational achievement. For Cohen, delinquent gangs represented a (male) solution to a (male) status problem: by engaging in delinquent activities, the boys take the norms and standards of the dominant culture and turn them on their heads.

Walter Miller (1966) offered a variation of the subcultural approach that explained street gangs as a result of a distinct "culture of poverty" (see also Lewis 1959). For Miller, the problem for lower-class boys was not their inability to conform to the middle-class value system, as Cohen had postulated, but the dominance of female-headed households in their communities. In response, young men escape to the streets and form into "one-sex peer groups" focused on "focal concerns" of trouble, toughness, smartness, excitement, fate and autonomy (Miller 1966: 139). For Miller, like other "culture of poverty" theorists, class was "a subjective variable, a reflection of the outlook of certain people, not a specific place within social structure" (Hagedorn 1988: 113). Hagedorn noted, "This analysis has been popular, particularly in today's government circles, in part because it attributes gang crime and violence to persisting individual cultural traits, instead of analyzing destructive behavior in terms of changing social and economic structures" (113).

Although still remaining within the subcultural tradition, Richard Cloward and Lloyd Ohlin (1960: 152) took an approach different from Cohen and Miller. Focused on explaining the causes of delinquency, they distinguished between "two opportunity structures — one legitimate, the other illegitimate" in U.S. society. Denied opportunities in the legitimate economy, some young men in urban ghettos pursue illegitimate means of reaching conventional economic goals. Like Cohen, Cloward and Ohlin were influenced by Robert Merton's (1938) "strain theory," which identified the tensions that occur when lower class youth, influenced by the American commitment to upward mobility and monetary success, have fewer opportunities to realize these goals and so develop adaptive subcultures that may include street gang involvement.

More recently, critical gang studies researchers have moved beyond these traditional approaches by linking urban processes and unequal opportunity structures to the political economy. These researchers situate the "astounding proliferation of U.S. street gangs" (Klein 1995: 205) in the context of the impacts of global economic restructuring on inner-city communities and the state's neo-liberal withdrawal from the provision of social benefits since the 1980s (Wacquant 2008).

Over the past three decades, the increasingly global or international nature of the capitalist economy has led to significant transformations within particular nations, including the United States and Canada. Corporate restructuring and downsizing have led to heightened levels of inequality (Kerstetter 2002; Yalnizan 2011) because employment has become more precarious given the move towards part-time, non-union jobs and outsourcing to developing countries that have considerably lower wages. In tandem with the widening gap between rich and poor has come a decided shift away from a professed commitment to social welfare on the part of governments towards an emphasis on enhancing economic efficiency and international competitiveness. Commentators have termed this new governmental rationality "neo-liberalism," as it is premised on the values of individualism, market predominance and minimal state involvement in the economy (Larner 2000; Rose 2000).

The impact of this shift has been profound. The social safety net — historically designed to assist those who were out of work or in need of assistance — has been unravelled, and more and more people are being left to fend for themselves. The increasing numbers of people living in poverty are stigmatized and — consistent with the individualism at the heart of neo-liberalism — personally blamed for their dire circumstances (Young 1999, 2007; Teeple 2000; Swanson 2001). The criminal justice system has been implicated in this process. Jonathon Simon (2007), for example, documents the increasing move in the U.S. to "govern through crime," as social problems ranging from welfare dependency to educational inequality have been reconfigured within a crime discourse, with an attendant focus on assigning individual fault and imposing punishment. In the Canadian context, commentators have noted the increasing criminalization of poverty, as everyone from welfare moms to squeegee kids is made subject to criminal sanctions (Crocker and Johnson 2010; Hermer and Mosher 2002).

According to critical gang studies researchers, street gangs are one of the byproducts of these broader social and economic changes. Mike Davis (2008: xvi) indicts "the impact of economic restructuring and post-liberal social policy" as processes that have marginalized growing numbers of urban youth. James Vigil (2002: 7) argues, "The street gang is an outcome of marginalization, that is, the relegation of certain persons or groups to the fringes of society, where social and economic conditions result in powerlessness." John Hagedorn (2001: 44) has observed, "In the 1980s, as the U.S. economy restructured, legitimate opportunities in poor neighbourhoods fatefully constricted. In these conditions, young men began to sell drugs on a never-before-seen scale. A sharp rise in violence accompanied the carving out of new crack markets." Contemporary street gangs are located, then, in intensified urban poverty that is a consequence of global economic forces and neo-liberal ideologies and forms of governing that lead to a loss of well-paid jobs and reduced public expenditures directed at the poor. This process is also racialized, in that those who are marginalized and become involved in street gangs are disproportionately youth of colour.

Recognition of the racialized character of street gang involvement has not always informed criminological understandings of gangs. As Hagedorn (2007b: 17) notes, because the project of Chicago School researchers such as Thrasher was "to dispel stereotypes and humanize immigrants for a sometimes hostile native-born public," they emphasized gangs, delinquency and crime as "products of areas, not ethnic groups." Meanwhile, subcultural theorists such as Cohen (1955), Miller (1966) and Cloward and Ohlin (1960) practised a "studied deemphasis on race and ethnicity" (Hagedorn 2008: 86). For these criminologists, it was delinquent subcultures that produced gang members' non-racial, antisocial and criminal acts. For Hagedorn, however, "This is, at best, extremely one-sided. Anyone who spends any time on the streets knows that for black, Hispanic, Asian, *and* white gang members, ethnicity and race are crucial aspects of their lives" (2008: 87). Critical gang studies researchers root street gang activities in racialized inner-city poverty. As Malcolm Klein (1995: 194) notes, "One of my favorite black gang members put it simply: 'Bein' poor's a mother-fucker.'" The facts speak for themselves: in U.S. ghettos and barrios it is primarily Black and Hispanic youth who form street gangs (Moore 1991; Rios 2011; Bourgois 2003; Hagedorn 2008); in Western Canadian urban centres it is primarily Aboriginal youth who form street gangs (Totten 2012; Chettleburgh 2007). Colonialism is a crucial factor in racialized poverty.

COLONIALISM

Colonialism in Canada has a long history of oppressing Aboriginal people. European settler society pushed Aboriginal peoples off their historic lands onto economically marginal reserves where they were subjected to the harsh terms of the *Indian Act* and the control of the Indian Agent. First Nations people were prohibited from engaging in a wide range of activities. For example, they needed a pass from the Indian Agent to leave the reserve, and many of their cultural and spiritual practices (such as the Potlatch and the Sun Dance) were outlawed. First Nations and Métis economic and political systems were undermined or destroyed, and their children were forcibly seized by the state and confined in residential schools, where they were forbidden to speak their languages and were taught to be ashamed of being Aboriginal (Milloy 1999; RCAP 1996; Hamilton and Sinclair 1991; Grant 1996). Bernard Schissel (2002: 120) points out, "Residential schools were run like modern day youth and adult prisons in Canada."

The incarceration of Aboriginal children in residential schools and the deliberate attempt by that means to destroy Aboriginal families and cultures has had devastating effects on Aboriginal families, exemplified by the astonishingly high numbers of Aboriginal children taken into care (Brownell 2012; Hamilton and Sinclair 1991; Kimelman 1985). Cindy Blackstock (2003) estimates that there now may be as many as three times more Aboriginal children in the care of child welfare authorities as were placed in residential schools at the height of those operations in the 1940s. As the Royal Commission on Aboriginal Peoples (1996: vol. 3 chap. 2) notes, most of the parents who have lost their children to the child welfare system were themselves the clients of that same system. Indeed, one can draw a direct line of descent from residential schools, to the 60s Scoop — the forcible removal of Aboriginal children from their own families to (typically non-Aboriginal) foster families detached from their communities that began in earnest in the 1960s — to the large numbers of Aboriginal children today who are in care and in youth detention centres of various kinds, and from there to the large numbers of Aboriginal adults in penal institutions. Colonialism is, among other things, a story of the institutionalization of Aboriginal people.

Contrary to popular discourse, colonialism is not simply a historical artifact. One of the effects of colonialism is the grinding, racialized poverty of Winnipeg's inner-city communities. Of major cities in Canada, Winnipeg has the highest number of Aboriginal people — 68,380 in 2006, representing 10 percent of the total population of the Winnipeg Census Metropolitan Area. Aboriginal people are overrepresented among the ranks of Winnipeg's poor; they are approximately three times as likely as their non-Aboriginal counterparts to have poverty incomes (Statistics Canada 2010: 13). While poverty is found in pockets throughout the city, it is spatially concentrated in Winnipeg's inner city, where 65 percent of Aboriginal households are poor (MacKinnon 2009: 30).

Colonialism has also been a major factor in the production of Aboriginal street gangs. As Aboriginal writer Nahanni Fontaine (2006: 116) argues, "Aboriginal gangs are a product of our colonized and oppressed space within Canada — a space fraught with inequity, racism, dislocation, marginalization, and cultural and spiritual alienation." Aboriginal street gangs are a form of resistance to colonialism — albeit one that has had negative consequences.

STREET GANGS, RESISTANCE IDENTITIES, AND HYPER-MASCULINITY

Resistance has become a key theme in critical gang studies research. In his ethnographic work in East Harlem, Philippe Bourgois (2003) describes the "street culture of resistance" that has emerged in opposition to the exclusion of young El Barrio youth from mainstream society. While not a "coherent, conscious universe of political opposition," this culture involves "a spontaneous set of rebellious practices that in the long term have emerged as an oppositional style" (2003: 8). Centered on drug dealing, violence and crime, El Barrio street culture has distinctly contradictory tendencies. Although it "emerges out of a personal search for dignity and a rejection of racism and subjugation, it ultimately becomes an active agent in personal degradation and community ruin" (2003: 9).

Victor Rios found that the forty young Black and Latino men he studied in depth over a three-year period in Oakland, California, engaged in "acts of survival and crimes of resistance." These young men "were clearly aware of, recognized, and had an analysis of the system that criminalized them" (2011: 103). More than just the search for respect and dignity, Rios maintains that the youth were acting "as a conscious revolt against a system of exclusion and punitive control that they clearly understand" (2011: 103). He goes on to elaborate: "Instead of remaining passive and allowing the system to shame, criminalize and exclude them, the boys continued to produce scattered acts of resistance. From stealing at the store to cussing out the police officers who had once brutalized them, the boys engaged themselves in deviant politics" (2011: 120).

In a similar fashion, Kathleen Buddle (2011: 173) describes Aboriginal street gang members in Winnipeg's inner city as being "unwilling to passively succumb to marginality," and engaging in a process of "defying exclusion by 'others.'" Echoing this unwillingness and defiance, one of the street gang leaders we interviewed described his now well-known gang coming into existence in Winnipeg's Youth Detention Centre: "You know, first it was just like, "What do you think it is, bro? Do you wear this one or this one, a red rag or a black rag?" "I fuckin' wear a red rag. Fuck. We're Indians. Indian wear red." ... And the next thing you know we're a fuckin' gang." The gang's choice of a red rag was not accidental. It symbolizes their resistance identity. The names they chose for their gangs — Indian Posse, Manitoba Warriors, Native Syndicate — also reflect their identity as "Indians."

Far from being passive victims of social forces largely beyond their control, then, racialized youth involved in street gang activities can be seen to be engaged in acts of resistance against the dominant society that has marginalized and oppressed them. These acts of resistance are deeply-rooted products of economic structures that offer no hope, and of racialized youth who, in the absence of conventional opportunities, carve out their own form of (often illegal) economic survival, taking on particular identities in the process. As Hagedorn (2008: 160) asserts, "The gangster identity ... this contested resistance identity is no longer a transient subculture of alienated youth but a permanent oppositional and racialized culture arising in the wake of the retreat of the state."

Many are the negative aspects of this resistance, not the least of which is "hyper-masculinity," an exaggerated form of masculinity that emphasizes toughness and male bravado and is performed, in part, through various acts of misogyny and sexual exploitation. Masculinity finds expression in different social contexts depending upon the resources available (Messerschmidt 2001). Corporate executives, for example, will practise a masculinity that does not require a resort to physical violence to exercise their power. In contrast, racialized and economically marginalized men may draw upon the resources that are available to them to perform a "street masculinity" that emphasizes toughness and violence.

In his exploration of "street masculinity," Christopher Mullins (2006: 102) found that one of the few resources available to impoverished Black men in Saint Louis, Missouri was their reputation on the streets. "This resource was constantly promoted and jealously guarded. The key way to earn and maintain reputation was to prove you were more violent and ruthless than your street associates." In addition to violence, the men used the proceeds of crime to enhance their masculine capital through conspicuous consumption — "blatantly displaying large amounts of money, wearing expensive, fashionable clothing, adding expensive features to a car (e.g., stereo systems, rims, curb feelers, etc.), and other flashy behavior. It also involved extravagant spending in a social context, primarily buying drugs and otherwise being involved in a culture of desperate partying" (2006: 69-70). Aboriginal street gang members in Winnipeg also subscribe to this "street masculinity." One of the ways of maintaining the reputation and status of the gang is through conspicuous consumption. As one gang member commented, "Every gangster wants to live better than everyone else, you know, the biggest chain or the biggest rings, stuff like that."

Given the hyper-masculine culture of the gang, relationships with women are decidedly secondary to the men's allegiance to their gang. As one gang member put it, "You always got to put your brothers first." Moreover, sexual exploitation and violence against women are common aspects of street gang life (see, for example, Bourgois 2003: chap. 8). Jody Miller (2001) suggests that girls involved with gangs strike a "patriarchal bargain" that allows them to reconcile the negative aspects of their gang affiliation with the perceived benefits. The lives of young girls growing up in inner-city neighbourhoods are complicated by contradictory messages that young women can gain status through their sexual appeal yet be denigrated for their sexual activity. As well, sexual victimization and exploitation of young women, both in their homes and on the streets, mean that "the world around gang girls is not a particularly safe place, physically or psychically" (Miller 2001: 193). As such, the gender hierarchy and inequality that Aboriginal girls encounter with street gangs is not unlike that in the larger world around them — as evidenced, for example, in the more than 1,100 missing and murdered Aboriginal women in Canada (RCMP 2014; Native Women's Association of Canada 2009; Amnesty International 2004). When young women in that social world are seen as such ready targets of violence and victimization, affiliation with a gang can offer at least a semblance of protection. Nevertheless, Miller found that "many young women's means of resisting gender oppression within gangs tended to be an individualized response based on constructing gendered gang identities as separate from and 'better than' those of the girls and women around them in their social environments. It meant internalizing and accepting masculine constructs of gang values" (Miller 2001: 197).

In her research involving Aboriginal girls in Winnipeg, Fontaine (2006) found that there were no female gang members or female gangs operating in the city. Rather, females were connected to street gangs by virtue of their relationships with male gang members as "old ladies," "bitches" and "hos." Old ladies are the "women or girls with whom male gang members have some semblance of a committed and loving relationship" (2006: 121). As such, they are accorded a certain status and respect by the gang members. Bitches and hos, on the other hand, were lower on the rung of the gender hierarchy. "These women and girls were not looked upon favourably and were always described in pejorative ways" (2006: 124). The women we interviewed were familiar with these categories. One woman told us that she hated being called an "old lady":

> I frickin' hated being called that 'cause I was only twenty-two, you know ... I was made to feel like I was old ... and I did, honestly, I felt old, you know, and when you feel that way you're kind of like on the backburner and, you know, you're the home and that's where they always return to, but that means' they're allowed to go do this and that. So you're kind of like that's the safe spot, right? And when you're old people want something that's new, right ... It's just, for me it's always been a bad situation. I always knew that my man was out fucking around and, you know, I wanted to be new, but it just didn't work out that way. Yeah. I hated that.

Not surprisingly, the hyper-masculinity of a street gang member's resistance identity is associated with difficulties in creating and maintaining healthy family lives. The family — especially single parent households — has been identified in conventional street gang research as a key risk factor in gang participation (Linden 2010; Wortley and Tanner 2007). Grekul and LaBoucane-Benson (2008: 67), for example, suggest that "Family problems can push young people into the gang lifestyle, while family members who are already gang-involved pull youth in the direction of gang involvement."

Resting explanations for street gangs on "dysfunctional" families, however, fails to acknowledge the broader socio-economic forces that bear down on those families. As Elliot Currie (1998: 141) notes, "The family's role is so important precisely because it is the place where the strains and pressures of the larger society converge to influence individual development." It is those broader socio-economic forces that combine to create the kind of spatially concentrated, racialized poverty in which good jobs are scarce. Elijah Anderson (1999: 147) argues, "The lack of family-sustaining jobs denies many young men the possibility of forming an economically self-reliant family, the traditional American mark of manhood." In the absence of decent jobs, they develop resistance identities. These resistance identities make it extremely difficult to find and hold jobs in the dominant economy. Bourgois (2003: 142) observes that "street culture is in direct contradiction to the humble, obedient modes of subservient social interaction that are essential for upward mobility" in the dominant economy. When such men are rejected by or themselves reject the dominant economy, they have little choice but to revert back to their street survival skills (Rios 2011: 99–100; Anderson 1999: 286–89), thus reinforcing their exclusion. Once their street gang activities lead to imprisonment, they are further marked for exclusion. As Devah Pager (2007: 4) notes, "The credential of a criminal record, like educational or professional credentials, constitutes a formal and enduring classification of social status, which can be used to regulate access and opportunity across numerous social, economic and political domains."

Street gang members are cycled from prison to community and back to prison, worsening their prospects for paid employment and contributing further to family breakdown. A vicious cycle is set in motion: young racialized men in impoverished spaces are excluded from the labour market; they develop resistance identities that include the performance of hyper-masculinity; this adversely affects the formation of healthy families; family disruption pushes some youth into street gang activity. A key component of that activity is the trade in illegal drugs.

STREET GANGS AS A BUSINESS

Hagedorn (1988: 185) argues, "The color of money has replaced gang colors as the underlying rationale for the behavior of adult gang members and the structure of their gangs … The gang is now mainly a way to 'make your money.'" A Chicago street gang member said about the 1986 arrival of crack cocaine: "It became all 'bout the money real quick, ain't nobody give a damn no more about nothing else" (Venkatesh and Levitt 2000: 441). This phenomenon is, according to Venkatesh and Levitt (2000: 430), the byproduct of economic restructuring and the ascension of the corporatist ideology in American society. It is also a by-product of the related ascension of greed as a driving economic force in this neo-liberal era, exemplified by the Wall Street crash of 2008.

Similarly, the sale of illegal drugs is the main focus and the primary source of income for Winnipeg street gang members:

> This is like our business, you know what I mean. Like, all this corruption and wickedness, it's like a business, man, we're turning this into a business ... This is our reality. You guys are making these drugs our reality ... So we're going to be like anyone else. We're going to be entrepreneurial.

Like other profit-seeking undertakings, the illegal trade in drugs relies upon a readily available market of consumers, an easily exploitable labour force to sell the product and the skills and ingenuity of the "owners" to manage the business to ensure profitability.

Crack — a mixture of cocaine and baking soda — appeared in the Winnipeg drug trade in the late 1990s. Given its highly addictive properties, crack is, from a business point of view, the perfect commodity. While powder cocaine (which is sniffed or injected) is absorbed more slowly into the body, the baking soda in crack enables the psychoactive ingredient to be released when smoked. The result is an exceptional rate of product turnover. As one of the gang members explained, doing a line of powder cocaine lasts "maybe half an hour, twenty minutes." Give the same person a hit of crack "and like ten seconds later" the customer wants another piece. "So which drug are you going to sell? Are you going to sell the one that takes them a half-hour to come back or are you going to sell them the one that takes them five minutes to come back? ... That's where the money's at ... Repeat customers. Crack is all about repetition."

The arrival of crack on the Winnipeg scene was also a catalyst for a change in technology of the street gangs' illegal drug business. One strategy involved setting up crack lines. Customers phone in their drug order to a particular cellphone number, and the product is delivered to the customer. Another strategy involved establishing "crack shacks" in rented houses in the inner city, which are frequented especially by women working in the street sex trade. If crack is the perfect commodity, then street sex workers are the perfect customers because they just keep coming back for more. It's a symbiotic relationship: the street sex workers need the drugs to dull the pain, and then need to do more work to earn the money to buy the drugs that dull the pain. The street gangs only need to sit in their crack houses and wait for these women, in full knowledge that they will come.

The labour force for street gangs is very young Aboriginal kids who grow up poor in the inner city. They are crucially important to the street gangs' illegal drug business. While popular discourse suggests that street gangs force young kids into joining, the street gang members we met with were adamant that no one was being strong armed. One of the guys said, "The gang I'm with they don't force you in." While it may have been the case "a long time ago," he said, "it's not like that anymore, really, 'cause nowadays if you force someone in they ain't going to really have no heart for your gang, right." Another gang member added: "They come to us. They always have.... What are you going to do, are you going to force somebody to be with you? Like, that doesn't make sense. They got to be loyal to you. And somebody that wants to be with you, that's loyalty."

Why, then, would young kids want to join a gang? One gang member explained that his familiarity with street gang life came from his family connections. As youth growing up in Winnipeg's North End, many of his older cousins were street gang members. "So I kinda tagged along, 'cause I'd grown up fast with them too, right." Another street gang member who had "packed his bags" and left home when he was fifteen said, "I wanted to be part of that, you know what I mean? Like, I never had a family when I was growing up. I was in foster homes most of my life. So I wanted to be part of something." Another gangster said: "A lot of people want to be part of something, right? I don't know what it is they're looking for but — like, you always want to be part of something, right, and if you're not good at home you're gonna want to belong." The breakdown of families — an ongoing legacy of colonization — drives Aboriginal youngsters onto the streets, where they are socialized by older friends and relatives already involved in crime and the street gang life. In this fashion, street gang activities are produced and reproduced in this colonized inner-city space.

For many — but certainly not most — young Aboriginal men in the inner city, then, joining a street gang has simply become part of their normal. For kids who have grown up with so little in the way of social supports, the promise of the gang lifestyle can have a strong appeal.

The young kids are a significant proportion of the front-line sales force of the illegal drug business. They deal directly with customers, consequently taking most of the risk. If they sell drugs on the street to an undercover cop, they take the fall. If the police raid a crack house and gain entry, the junior guys, the "soldiers," take the fall, because they are expected to do what they are told. Although they incur most of the risk, they push almost all of their sales revenue up the street gang hierarchy. Once a street gang member reaches a more senior position, his exposure to risk is reduced, his profits are increased. The young ones get very little of the profits that they generate. But what they do get is food and clothing and a place to sleep; they get access to parties and girls and booze and drugs. One of the gang leaders described taking a young crew member to a mall and buying him all the clothes he wanted.

> I take care of my boys. Like, if I'm in the mall shopping and I look at one of my kids and they've got ugly shoes or ugly pants on, fuck, I'll dress them right up. To them, that's gold, man. That's better than any fuckin' paycheque you give them, man ... That makes them loyal, shit like that.

For a kid who grew up in poverty, that experience may well be a good deal. From that point of view, the risk-taking makes a certain sense.

For an aspiring street gang member incarceration is not really a risk. Being sent to prison is the business equivalent to being sent to the company's head office. In prison, the young wannabe meets and gets to know the organization's higher-ups and soaks up its history and culture. He makes contacts and learns new criminal skills. He comes out of prison — he returns from the head office — not only with more contacts and skills, but also with more status and respect and street credibility. In the culture of the street gang, a stint in prison is a badge of honour, one that is literally marked on the body by tattoos.

The parallels between street gangs and businesses do not necessarily mean that street gangs are tightly organized and hierarchical organizations with the characteristics of large capitalist enterprises, although some writers (Sanchez-Jankowski 1991, for example) do argue otherwise. Klein (1995: 36) observed almost two decades ago that the street gang with several hundred members "is giving way to relatively autonomous, smaller, independent groups, poorly organized and less territorial than used to be the case." More recently, he noted that gangs were now "surprisingly loose knit collectivities" (Klein 2007: 54). Hagedorn (2008: 19) found that the Chicago street gangs were not "godfather-run, centralized, efficient crime syndicates" but rather "networks" or "loosely coupled systems." Similarly, the Criminal Intelligence Service of Canada (2004: 20–21) described Aboriginal street gangs as being "involved in opportunistic, spontaneous and disorganized street level criminal activities," adding that "gang structures and alliances remain fluid, resulting in short-lived splinter groups with affiliations and rivalries that regularly change and evolve."

In Winnipeg, street gang activity is somewhat episodic. Business activity may be exceptionally intensive for a certain time, followed by long periods when little or no business is done. On occasion, the work resembles the antics of the Keystone Cops — with street gang members failing to make drug deliveries because they got drunk or were beaten by a rival gang, or lost their car, and with sums of $5,000 simply going missing while tens of thousands of dollars are kept in shoeboxes. Much of the street gangs members' time is spent sitting around doing nothing, or talking with friends or watching TV. As such, describing street gangs' involvement with the illegal drug trade as a business, as a variety of entrepreneurial activities, is not intended to create the image of a business like those discussed in the business pages of the daily press.

Although some street gangs operate and think of themselves as businesses, most members of the gang — and junior members in particular — derive surprisingly little financial benefit from their activities. According to Venkatesh and Levitt (2000: 454; see also Levitt and Venkatesh 2000: 770–71): "Our finding affirms available research suggesting that gang members do not earn very high salaries.... 'Foot soldiers' earn menial wages compared to the few who have managed to attain leadership positions ... The typical foot-soldier earns less that $2000 per year ... [and] his hourly wage remains less than $6.00." The leaders of the Chicago gang they were studying did much better, earning between $50,000 and $130,000 per year at that time. Nevertheless, the members earn more than they would in the kinds of jobs now available to them elsewhere in the economy. It is not surprising that most Winnipeg Aboriginal street gang members are also making little from their illegal drug sales. One of the men we interviewed commented: "I don't know anybody in this lifestyle that's actually succeeded ... I don't know any retired drug dealers that have money. I don't know any. There's none ... There is no dental, there is no pension, there is nothing."

Nevertheless, many of the street gang leaders are intelligent and skilled. They have to be in order to run what are in some cases complicated and complex ventures. Had their early lives been different, had they not pursued a street gang lifestyle, these men might well have become productive members of their communities and positive contributors to a healthy neighbourhood. But more than that, as intelligent and energetic people in an impoverished, colonized space, and as men fully aware of their identity as Aboriginal people and at least partially aware of the harmful effects of colonization, it is likely that at least some of them would have directed their skills to the creative and political activities necessary to produce the progressive change that is so needed in their impoverished and racialized communities. However, the profit-seeking illegal path that they took has left destruction and wasted lives — their own included — in its wake, and has precluded their making positive contributions. This enormous waste of human talent, as well as the destruction that they have wrought upon their own people, is the legacy of Winnipeg's Aboriginal street gangs — and of colonialism.

STREET GANGS AND VIOLENCE

Violence is a day-to-day reality in many impoverished and racialized spaces. It is likely that much of it has its origins in the family violence experienced by street gang members as children, observing violence between the adults in their lives and having violence done to them. David Brotherton and Luis Barrios (2004: 239), for example, found that for New York street gang members, "Violence was endemic in their neighbourhoods, schools and families. Few could remember being raised in a violence-free environment." In Philadelphia, the "code of the street" is a constant "predisposition to violence" (Anderson 1999: 72). Alford Young (2004: 50) noted that for African-American men in Chicago's Near West Side, "The regularity with which violence was acknowledged in discussion of daily life was astounding" (see also Decker and Van Winkle 1996; Nafekh 2002: 10; Hagedorn 1988: 204).

Winnipeg street gang members were well aware of the potential for violence that is rising with the increasing availability of guns:

> There's guns, man. Like, everybody you run into now, you can get shot, you know. Like, back in the day where everybody you ran into, you know, maybe they had a knife. You could pick up a stick and fight them. Everybody you run into now could have a gun on them, man ... Twelve-year-old, three-foot-high kid walking on the street, you're telling him to get the fuck out of your way, he could turn around and shoot you in the back of the head.

The preponderance of guns is not peculiar to Winnipeg; it is now a global phenomenon (Decker and Pyrooz 2010).

What is more, violence is functional and is an essential component of street gangs' business, which has worsened with the arrival of crack cocaine (Anderson 1999: 271). Among El Barrio crack dealers, "Regular displays of violence are essential for preventing rip-offs by colleagues, customers, and professional hold-up artists. Indeed, upward mobility in the underground economy of the street-dealing world requires a systematic and effective use of violence" (Bourgois 2003: 24). According to Simon Hallsworth (2011:189), "The retail end of crack-cocaine and heroin markets" is an "incredibly violent space ... probably the most violent arena in the criminal underworld." For Hallsworth and Silverstone (2009, as quoted in Hallsworth 2011: 189), this space is "the zone of the outlaw":

> This is a zone where deeply internalized anger and rage among depoliticized and deeply alienated young men finds violent expression. The tragedy here is that the rage and anger they feel is not directed outwards and towards the world that marginalizes them. Instead it is directed inward and against each other. Guns have become a part of this logic of self-destruction as young men pointlessly die at each other's hands.

Such violence — and the illegal drug trade of which it is a necessary part — leads almost inevitably to arrest and time spent in prison.

STREET GANGS AND PRISONS

The barrio/ghetto/inner city and the prison are closely connected. Joan Moore (1978: 98) observed about Los Angeles, "Prison is an omnipresent reality in barrio life, and contact with it is continuous and drastic, affecting nearly everybody in the barrio," while "prison adaptations are seen by convicts themselves as variants of adaptations to street life." Young (2004: 95) found that for African-American men in Chicago's Near West Side, "jail formed a bigger part of their lives than did work" and that "detention was talked about as if it were a common event in their lives." When Rios (2011: 36) asked the forty

Oakland youth he studied to write the names of close friends and family members who were in prison, "all of them knew at least six people." All of the young men in his study "discussed prison as a familiar place."

Prison has become another part of the normal in the lives of many Aboriginal families. As one of the men we interviewed commented:

> It was always a normal thing to say, "Oh, my brother's locked up" or, "Oh man, your uncle's locked up" or "Oh, my cousin's locked up," you know. It was, you heard that every single day, "Oh, he got locked up today and I don't know how long he's going to be gone" or "Oh, he's gone for thirty-six months," "Oh, he's gone for nine years" or "Oh, he got twelve years." Like, it was always, there's not a day that goes by where, you know, someone's getting locked up or someone's getting out. When that someone gets out there's someone to take his place. It's just a revolving door.

For many of the young gangsters, making it to the penitentiary was a mark of status, a means of gaining respect and a reputation within their gang culture. As one of the men told us:

> When I was younger, all I looked up to was gang members, right, 'cause of my family and my older cousins and uncles. And I just wanted to be something, you know … so I thought that if I went [to the penitentiary] that it would help me, help out my record of, you know, gangsters, you know what I mean?

Prisons have become an important site for the production and reproduction of street gangs. While some gang researchers make a distinction between "street gangs" and "prison gangs" as if they were two completely separate phenomenon (Grekul and LaBoucane-Benson 2007; Skarbek 2012), our discussions with gang members make it clear that this is a false dualism: the barriers between the prison and the outside community are permeable. If you are not a street gang member when you are sentenced, you will become one for protection once you reach prison. And when you leave the prison, usually with no money in your pocket, the gang will be there to assist with the transition back to the street.

Street gang leaders continue to run gang activities even while incarcerated. Hagedorn (2008: 12), for example, observes, "Gang leaders in Chicago today are nearly all incarcerated, but most maintain control of key gang functions." The result was that "rather than prison being a place to send gang members in an attempt to break up the gang, gangs have adapted and have used prison to advance their interests." One of the Winnipeg gang leaders told us that "A lot of business on the street is run from the jails." Even while he was inside, this man continued to do the work of the general manager of his drug business. He was on the phone all day, issuing instructions in code, keeping track of money, and generally taking care of business. "We were investing our money in crack from jail for our people on the street to sell for us."

Further, illegal drugs are readily available in prisons. Indeed, street gangs "specialize in narcotics trafficking inside the prison" (Klein 1995: 23), where a lucrative market for their sale exists. One of the Winnipeg gangsters told us:

> What we really made a lot of money on was morphines. We'd buy them on the street for a dollar, two dollars a pill, and we'd buy at any given time anywhere

from a hundred here, a hundred there, and then we'd send them inside and they would get sold for $40 to $80 a pill.

Drugs appear to move easily into the prison, and through a variety of methods. One man told us, "Well, the guys would usually just bring the dope in through their girlfriends and visits." Another gang member described tennis balls being thrown over the fence surrounding the jail: "The packages are so tightly packed you can get an ounce, two ounces, into something smaller than this [he indicates the size of a tennis ball] of weed." Those on a temporary absence from the prison can also swallow drugs or stick the drugs up their rectums. A man who had recently been released from prison on parole was offered $10,000 "to breach myself and go back, 'cause I can load on four or five ounces of cocaine and a couple of packs of pills. There's a lot of money to be made."

The massive incarceration of African-Americans in the United States (Alexander 2010; Wacquant 2009) and of Aboriginal people in Canada (Perreault 2009; Samuelson and Monture-Angus 2002) is testament to how racialized poverty in inner cities spawns a steady stream of prospective prisoners. About one-third of all Black males in the United States will experience state prison in their lifetimes (Snider 2004: 229). In Canada, prison has become for many young Aboriginal people the contemporary equivalent of what the Indian residential school represented for their parents (Jackson 1989: 216). Aboriginal youth are almost eight times more likely to be in custody than their non-Aboriginal counterparts. In Manitoba, Aboriginal youth were sixteen times more likely to be incarcerated than non-Aboriginal youth (Latimer and Foss 2004). For street gang members, detention centres, jails and prisons are simply a part of their normal way of life — a racialized and excluded space in which street gang activities are carried on. They are not a way to eliminate gangs.

RESPONDING TO THE "PROBLEM" OF ABORIGINAL STREET GANGS

Aboriginal street gangs constitute a form of resistance to colonialism. But just as colonialism has been destructive, so too has street gang activity. It is destructive to those low-income, racialized communities in which street gang violence occurs, and from which so many scarce dollars are drained through the illegal drug business. It is destructive to the many people who come into contact with street gang members: addicted individuals who need illegal drugs; girlfriends who are subject to misogynist abuse; community members whose lives become more fearful and stressful. And the activity is destructive to street gang members themselves, most of whom end up with nothing, regretting their involvement and wanting out of the life.

Often it is easier to address the question of what can be done by asking what should *not* be done? We know that criminal justice strategies are expensive. What Angela Davis (2000) called the "prison industrial complex" involves huge financial costs for the state. As a key part of its law and order agenda, the Canadian Government pours considerable monies into shoring up and expanding its penitentiary system. Federal expenditure for prisons was $2.98 billion in 2013. When provincial expenditures are added, the annual cost is $4.4 billion and rising (Ormond 2014: 109). Evidence suggests that this is a fruitless path, that greater benefits would follow if the money was spent instead on meaningful employment, assistance with mental health and addiction issues, appropriate forms of education, adequate housing and supports to strengthen families (see, for example, CCPA–MB and The John Howard Society of Manitoba, Inc. 2012).

Certainly, some gang members must be imprisoned for the safety of the broader community. Street gang members themselves acknowledge this. As one of the men told us, "I'm a gang member. I do what I do. I am what I am. There has to be laws for people like me" (Comack et al. 2009: 3). These men are fully prepared to accept the consequences of their actions and to go to jail or prison for crimes they commit. But they are adamant that imprisoning ever more young Aboriginal people will not solve the street-gang-related violence in the inner city. As we concluded in another report, "We should continue to send violent offenders to prison. But we shouldn't fool ourselves into thinking that the problems [of street gangs] will be solved by this means" (Comack et al. 2009: 3).

Nor should we be fooled into thinking that there is a quick and easy fix that will resolve the problem of street gangs. Much writing about street gangs is devoted to the issue of "exiting," on developing programs that facilitate leaving gangs (Hastings, Dunbar and Bania 2011; MacRae-Krisa 2011; Spergel 2007). The difficulty with this approach is that it is entirely individualistic. It is premised on the notion that the problem is street gangs per se — and not the underlying systemic issues that have produced street gangs.

Moreover, anti-street gang programs will not, on their own, solve this complex issue. Many of these programs produce positive outcomes and deserve more financial support than they now receive. But programs focused on saving or assisting or altering the lives of street gang members are the equivalent of the proverbial tale of pulling some people to safety from the river, without going upstream to find out why people keep getting pushed into the river in the first place. The roots of the street gang problem run deep; they are systemic. Effective solutions must address that reality.

A meaningful response to the issue of Aboriginal street gangs must attend to the damage caused by colonialism. For far too long Aboriginal people have been expected — and often forced — to assimilate into the mainstream society. In the process, the dominant society has made concerted efforts to destroy Aboriginal cultures. These attempts at forced assimilation have taken their toll: many Aboriginal people do not know their histories and cultures; many do not know who they really are; many Aboriginal families have been shattered. But Aboriginal people have resisted these attempts at assimilation — and they continue to resist colonialism and to struggle to reclaim their Aboriginal culture and identity.

The pathway forward, therefore, is one of decolonization. At its core, decolonization involves resistance. But rather than the negative and destructive form of resistance epitomized by street gang activity, decolonization involves rebuilding Aboriginal communities, strengthening Aboriginal families and kinship ties and instilling hope for a better future in Aboriginal children. It also involves decolonizing spaces, including Winnipeg's inner city, home to so many Aboriginal people.

Aboriginal people must be at the centre of this decolonization process. Signs of this process can be seen in Winnipeg's inner-city communities, in the form of culturally based schools, adult education initiatives, day-care facilities and Aboriginal community-based organizations aimed at providing support to families (see, for example, Silver 2006, 2013; MacKinnon 2013). Decolonization also requires willingness on the part of governments and non-Aboriginal people — both of whom have benefited enormously from colonialism — to participate in the process. Governments need to commit to investing in the education, employment and family-strengthening measures that will rebuild the inner city and create a safe space there for Aboriginal people to live and work as Aboriginal people. This will require a shift away from government austerity strategies that starve those at the bottom of the income scale of the resources that they need to rebuild their communities and themselves (Yalnizyan 2007). Non-Aboriginal people have a role to play as allies, walking beside and not in front of or behind Aboriginal people in their quest for change (Silver 2006: 156).

Great injustices have been committed against Aboriginal people, and those injustices persist. Some Aboriginal people resist these many injustices by forming street gangs and engaging in illegal and often violent practices. This destructive process needs to be replaced by a form of resistance that involves decolonization. Street gang members should not be marginalized or othered in this process. Far too many of the residents of Winnipeg's inner city have been made "disposable people" by the immense poverty and racism that prevails there and by the trauma trails of many decades of colonization that so affect their lives. It is this racialized poverty in a colonized space that has to be defeated. Such a strategy is a massive undertaking, and is very much at odds with neo-liberal orthodoxy. But the result would be the creation of a space in which Aboriginal people could live full and productive lives, and could do so as Aboriginal people, proud of their identity and the communities they have built. That is how the problem of Aboriginal street gangs can be addressed effectively. It will not be an easy path, nor will it happen overnight. But there is no other path.

DISCUSSION QUESTIONS

1. Why is a chapter about street gangs titled "You Really Have to Look at Poverty"?

2. How useful are the different criminological approaches for understanding the emergence and proliferation of street gangs?

3. Why do the authors claim that street gang activity is a form of resistance?

4. What role does masculinity play in street gangs and their activities? How does this compare to other social contexts in which masculinity plays out?

5. What is your view of the "get tough on crime" approach to street gangs? Does prison offer a solution to the street gang problem?

6. What is decolonization and how would that address the phenomenon of Aboriginal street gangs?

GLOSSARY

Street Gang: "Any durable, street-oriented youth group whose own identity includes involvement in illegal activity" (Weerman et al. 2009: 20). The gang continues despite turnover of its members, much of the time of gang members is spent "on the street," members can include younger as well as older youth, the gang's activities often revolve around criminal activities, and the street gang members have a collective identity.

Colonization: an act of genocide against Aboriginal people that has caused deep and lasting damage for generations of Aboriginal people and their families.

Resistance Identity: a sense of self formed in response to conditions of marginalization and social exclusion.

Hyper-Masculinity: an exaggerated form of masculinity that emphasizes toughness and male bravado and is performed, in part, through various acts of misogyny and sexual exploitation.

Racialized Poverty: draws attention to the overrepresentation of racialized groups among the ranks of the poor, especially in inner-city communities.

Decolonization: a form of resistance to colonialism that involves rebuilding Aboriginal communities, strengthening Aboriginal families and kinship ties, and instilling hope for a better future in Aboriginal children.

SUGGESTED READINGS

John M. Hagedorn (ed.), *Gangs in the Global City: Alternatives to Traditional Criminology*, Chicago: University of Chicago Press (2007).

John Hagedorn, *A World of Gangs: Armed Young Men and Gangsta Culture*, Minneapolis and London: University of Minnesota Press (2008).

Christopher Mullins, *Holding Your Square: Masculinities, Streetlife and Violence*, Portland: Willan Publishing (2006).

Victor M. Rios, *Punished: Policing the Lives of Black and Latino Boys*, New York: New York University Press (2011).

James Diego Vigil *A Rainbow of Gangs*, Austin: University of Texas Press (2002).

SUGGESTED WEBSITES/ACTIVIST RESOURCES

Gang Action Interagency Network (GAIN) <http://gainmb.wordpress.com/>

NOTE

This chapter is drawn from our book, *"Indians Wear Red": Colonialism, Resistance, and Aboriginal Street Gangs* (2013).

REFERENCES

Alexander, Michelle. 2010. *The New Jim Crow: Mass Incarceration in the Age of Colorblindness.* New York and London: New Press.

Amnesty International. 2004. *Stolen Sisters: Discrimination and Violence against Indigenous Women in Canada.* London: Amnesty International.

Anderson, Elijah. 1999. *Code of the Street: Decency, Violence and the Moral Life of the Inner City.* New York and London: W.W. Norton.

Blackstock, Cindy. 2003. "First Nations Child and Family Services Restoring Peace and Harmony in First Nations Communities." In Kathleen Kufeldt and Brad McKenzie (eds.), *Child Welfare: Connecting Research, Policy, and Practice.* Waterloo: Wilfred Laurier University Press.

Bourgois, Philippe. 2003. *In Search of Respect: Selling Crack in El Barrio.* Second edition. New York: Cambridge University Press.

Brotherton, David C., and Luis Barrios. 2004. *The Almighty Latin King and Queen Nation: Street Politics and the Transformation of a New York City Gang.* New York: Columbia University Press.

Brownell, Marni. 2012. "Time to Treat Kids in Care Differently." *Winnipeg Free Press*, March 22.

Buddle, Kathleen. 2011. "Urban Aboriginal Gangs and Street Sociality in the Canadian West: Places, Performances and Predicaments of Transition." In Heather Howard and Craig Proulx (eds.), *Aboriginal Peoples in Canadian Cities: Transformation and Continuities.* Peterborough: Wilfred Laurier University Press.

Canada, Department of Justice. 2004. *A One-Day Snapshot of Aboriginal Youth in Custody across Canada: Phase II.*

Carlson, Kathryn Blaze. 2009. "Gangs Fuelling Violence in Winnipeg." *National Post*, September 25.

CCPA-MB (Canadian Centre for Policy Alternatives-Manitoba) and the John Howard Society of Manitoba, Inc. 2012. *Bill C-10: The Truth about Consequences.* Winnipeg: CCPA-MB.

Chatterjee, Jharna. 2006. *A Research Report on Youth Gangs: Problems, Perspective and Priorities.* Research and Evaluation Branch, Community, Contract and Aboriginal Policing Services Directorate. Ottawa: Royal Canadian Mounted Police.

Chettleburgh, Michael C. 2007. *Young Thugs: Inside the Dangerous World of Canadian Street Gangs.* Toronto: Harper Collins Publishers.

Cloward, Richard, and Lloyd Ohlin. 1960. *Delinquency and Opportunity.* New York: Free Press.

Cohen, Albert. 1955. *Delinquent Boys: The Culture of the Gang.* Glencoe: Free Press.

___. 1966. "The Delinquency Subculture." In R. Giallombardo (ed.), *Juvenile Delinquency: A Book of Readings.* New York: John Wiley and Sons.

Comack, Elizabeth, Lawrence Deane, Larry Morrissette and Jim Silver. 2009. *If You Want to Change Violence in the 'Hood, You Have to Change the 'Hood.* Winnipeg: Canadian Centre for Policy Alternatives-Manitoba.

___. 2013. *"Indians Wear Red": Colonialism, Resistance, and Aboriginal Street Gangs.* Halifax and Winnipeg: Fernwood Publishing.

Comack, Elizabeth, and Jim Silver. 2006. *Safety and Security Issues in Winnipeg Inner-City Neighbourhoods: Bridging the Community-Police Divide.* Winnipeg: Canadian Centre for Policy Alternatives-Manitoba.

___. 2008. "A Canadian Exception to the Punitive Turn? Community Responses to Policing Practices in Winnipeg's Inner City." *Canadian Journal of Sociology* 33, 4.

Correctional Service Canada. 2003. *A Profile of Women Gang Members in Canada.*

Criminal Intelligence Service of Canada. 2004. *Annual Report on Organized Crime in Canada.* Ottawa: Criminal Intelligence Service Canada. At <cisc.gc.ca/annual_reports/documents/2004_annual_report.pdf>.

Crocker, Diane, and Val Marie Johnson. 2010. *Poverty, Regulation and Social Justice: Readings in the Criminalization of Poverty.* Halifax and Winnipeg: Fernwood Publishing.

Currie, Elliott. 1998. *Crime and Punishment in America.* New York: Henry Holt and Company.

Davis, Angela. 2000. *The Prison Industrial Complex and Its Impact on Communities of Color.* Videocassette. Madison: University of Wisconsin.

Davis, Mike. 2008. "Reading John Hagedorn." Foreword by John M. Hagedorn. *A World of Gangs: Armed Young Men and Gangsta Culture.* Minneapolis: University of Minnesota Press.

Decker, Scott, and David Pyrooz. 2010. "Gang Violence Worldwide: Context, Culture, and Country." In Graduate Institute of International and Development Studies Geneva, *Small Arms Survey 2010: Gangs, Groups, and Guns.* Cambridge: Cambridge University Press.

Decker, Scott, and Barrik Van Winkle. 1996. *Life in the Gang: Family, Friends and Violence.* Cambridge, UK: Cambridge University Press.

Egley, Arlen, and Mehala Arjunan. 2002. "Highlights of the 2000 National Youth Gang Survey." OJJDP Fact Sheet. At <ncjrs.gov/pdffiles1/ojjdp/fs200204.pdf>.

Fontaine, Nahanni. 2006. "Surviving Colonization: Anishinaabe Ikwe Gang Participation." In Gillian Balfour and Elizabeth Comack (eds.), *Criminalizing Women: Gender and (In)justice in Neoliberal Times.* Halifax: Fernwood Publishing.

Gordon, Robert. 2000. "Criminal Business Organizations, Street Gangs and 'Wanna-Be' Groups: A Vancouver Perspective." *Canadian Journal of Criminology* 42, 1.

Grant, Agnes. 1996. *No End of Grief: Indian Residential Schools in Canada.* Winnipeg: Pemmican.

Grekul, Jana, and Patti LaBoucane-Benson. 2007. *An Investigation into the Formation and Recruitment Processes of Aboriginal Gangs in Western Canada.* Ottawa: Department of Public Safety Canada.

___. 2008. "Aboriginal Gangs and Their (Dis)placement: Contextualizing Recruitment, Membership and Status." *Canadian Journal of Criminology and Criminal Justice* 50, 1.

Hagedorn, John M. 1988. *People and Folks: Gangs, Crime and the Underclass in a Rustbelt City.* Chicago: Lakeview Press.

___. 2001. "Globalization, Gangs, and Collaborative Research." In Malcolm W. Klein, Hans-Jurgen Kerner, Cheryl L. Maxson, and Elmar Weitekamp (eds.), *The Eurogang Paradox: Street Gangs and Youth Groups in the U.S. and Europe.* The Netherlands: Kluwer.

___. 2007a. "Gangs in Late Modernity." In John M. Hagedorn (ed.), *Gangs in the Global City: Alternatives to Traditional Criminology.* Chicago: University of Chicago Press.

___. 2007b. "Gangs, Institutions, Race, and Space: The Chicago School Revisited." In John M. Hagedorn (ed.), *Gangs in the Global City: Alternatives to Traditional Criminology.* Chicago: University of Illinois Press.

___. 2008. *A World of Gangs: Armed Young Men and Gangsta Culture.* Minneapolis and London: University of Minnesota Press.

Hallsworth, Simon. 2011. "Gangland Britain? Realities, Fantasies and Industry." In Barry Goldson (ed.), *Youth in Crisis? 'Gangs,' Territoriality and Violence.* London: Routledge.

Hamilton, A.C., and Murray Sinclair. 1991. *Report of the Aboriginal Justice Inquiry of Manitoba. Volume I: The Justice System and Aboriginal People.* Winnipeg: Queen's Printer.

Hastings, Ross, Laura Dunbar and Melanie Bania. 2011. *Leaving Criminal Youth Gangs: Exit Strategies and Programs.* Institute for the Prevention of Crime, University of Ottawa. At <crimepreventionottawa.ca/uploads/files/initiative/final_report_-_leaving_criminal_youth_gangs_exit_strategies_and_programs.pdf>.

Helmer, Aedan. 2009. "Getting Tough on Street Gangs." *Sun Media*, February 27.

Hermer, Joe, and Janet Mosher. 2002. *Disorderly People: Law and the Politics of Exclusion in Ontario.* Halifax and Winnipeg: Fernwood Publishing.

Jackson, Michael. 1989. "Locking Up Natives in Canada." *University of British Columbia Law Review* 23.

Jones, Dean, Vince Roper, Yvonne Stys and Cathy Wilson. 2004. *A Review of Theory, Interventions, and Implications for Corrections.* Ottawa: Correctional Services of Canada.

Kelly, Katharine, and Tullio Caputo. 2005. "The Linkages Between Street Gangs and Organized Crime: The Canadian Experience." *Journal of Gang Research* 13, 1.

Kerstetter, Steve. 2002. "Top 50% of Canadians Hold 94.4% of Wealth, Bottom Half 5.6%." *The CCPA Monitor* 9, 6.

Kimelman, Associate Chief Judge Edwin C. 1985. *No Quiet Place.* Report of the Review Committee on Indian and Métis Adoptions and Placements (Final Report). Winnipeg: Manitoba Community Services.

Klein, Malcolm W. 1971. *Street Gangs and Street Workers.* Englewood Cliffs, NJ: Prentice Hall.

___. 1995. *The American Street Gang: Its Nature, Prevalence and Control.* New York and Oxford: Oxford University Press.

___. 2007. *Chasing after Street Gangs: A Forty-Year Journey.* Upper Saddle River, NJ: Pearson Education, Inc.

Klein, Malcolm, and Cheryl Maxson. 2006. *Street Gang Patterns and Policies.* New York: Oxford University Press.

Larner, Wendy. 2000. "Neo-Liberalism: Policy, Ideology, Governmentality." *Studies in Political Economy* 63 (Autumn).

Latimer, Jeff, and Laura Casey Foss. 2004. *A One-Day Snapshot of Aboriginal Youth in Custody Across Canada, Phase II.* Ottawa: Research and Statistics Division Department of Justice Canada.

Levitt, Steven, and Sudhir Venkatesh. 2000. "The Financial Activities of a Street Gang." *Quarterly Journal of Economics* 115, 3.

Lewis, Oscar. 1959. *Five Families: Mexican Case Studies in the Culture of* Poverty. New York: Basic Books.

Linden, Rick. 2010. *Comprehensive Approaches to Address Street Gangs in Canada.* Ottawa: Department of Public Safety Canada. At <publications.gc.ca/collections/collection_2012/sp-ps/PS4-113-2011-eng.pdf>.

MacKinnon, Shauna. 2009. "Tracking Poverty in Winnipeg's Inner City: 1996–2006." *State of the*

Inner City Report 2009. Winnipeg: CCPA–MB.

___. 2013. "Aboriginal/Second Chance Learners in Three Inner-City Programs." In Jim Silver (ed.), *Moving Forward, Giving Back: Transformative Aboriginal Adult Education.* Halifax: Fernwood Publishing.

MacRae-Krisa, Leslie. 2011. *Exiting Gangs: Toward an Understanding of Processes and Best Practice.* Mount Royal University Centre for Criminology and Justice Studies. At <mtroyal.ca/cs/groups/public/documents/pdf/pdf_exitinggangs.pdf>.

Mallea, Paula. 2011. *Fearmonger: Stephen Harper's Tough on Crime Agenda.* Toronto: Lorimer.

Merton, Robert. 1938. "Social Structure and Anomie." *American Sociological Review* 3.

Messerschmidt, James. 2001. "Masculinities, Crime and Prison." In Don Sabo, Terry A. Kupers, and Willie London (eds.), *Prison Masculinities.* Philadelphia: Temple University Press.

Miller, Jody. 2001. *One of the Guys: Girls, Gangs, and Gender.* New York: Oxford University Press.

Miller, Walter. 1966. "Lower Class Culture as a Generating Milieu of Gang Delinquency." In R. Giallombardo (ed.), *Juvenile Delinquency: A Book of Readings.* New York: John Wiley.

Milloy, John. 1999. *A National Crime: The Canadian Government and the Residential School System, 1879–1986.* Winnipeg: University of Manitoba Press.

Moore, Joan W. 1978. *Homeboys: Gangs, Drugs, and Prison in the Barrios of Los Angeles.* Philadelphia: Temple University Press.

___. 1991. *Going Down to the Barrio: Homeboys and Homegirls in Change.* Philadelphia: Temple University Press.

Mullins, Christopher. 2006. *Holding Your Square: Masculinities, Streetlife and Violence.* Portland: Willan Publishing.

Native Women's Association of Canada. 2009. *Voices of Our Sisters in Spirit: A Report to Families and Communities.* Second edition. Ottawa: Native Women's Association of Canada.

Nafekh, Mark. 2002. *An Examination of Youth and Gang Affiliation within the Federally Sentenced Aboriginal Population.* Ottawa: Research Branch, Correctional Service of Canada.

Ormond, Aiyana. 2014. "Jaywalking to Jail: Capitalism, Mass Incarceration and Social Control on the Streets of Vancouver." *Radical Criminology* 3.

Pager, Devah. 2007. *Marked: Race, Crime and Finding Work in an Era of Mass Incarceration.* Chicago: University of Chicago Press.

Perreault, Samuel. 2009. "The Incarceration of Aboriginal People in Adult Correctional Services." *Juristat* 29, 3.

Procaylo, Chris. 2012. "Treat Gangs like Cancer They Are." *Winnipeg Sun,* September 15.

Public Safety Canada. 2003. *Youth Gangs in Canada: What Do We Know?*

Puxley, Chinta. 2012. "Residential Schools Called a Form of Genocide." *Globe and Mail,* February 17.

RCAP (Royal Commission on Aboriginal Peoples). 1996. *Report of the Royal Commission on Aboriginal Peoples.* Ottawa: Indian and Northern Affairs Canada.

RCMP (Royal Canadian Mounted Police). 2014. *Missing and Murdered Aboriginal Women: A National Operational Overview.* At <rcmp-grc.gc.ca/pubs/mmaw-faapd-eng.pdf>.

___. 2009. *Proceeds of Crime Program* <http://www.rcmp-grc.gc.ca/poc-pdc/pro-crim-eng.htm>.

Report of the Standing Committee on Justice and Human Rights (Dave MacKenzie, M.P, Chair). 2012. *The State of Organized Crime* (March) 41st Parliament, 1st Session.

Rios, Victor M. 2011. *Punished: Policing the Lives of Black and Latino Boys.* New York: New York University Press.

Rose, Nikolas. 2000. "Government and Control." *British Journal of Criminology* 40, 2.

Samuelson, Les, and Patricia Monture-Angus. 2002. "Aboriginal People and Social Control: The State, Law and 'Policing." In Bernard Schissel and Carolyn Brooks (eds.), *Marginality and Condemnation: An Introduction to Critical Criminology.* Halifax: Fernwood Publishing.

Sanchez-Jankowski, Martin. 1991. *Islands in the Street: Gangs and American Urban Society.* Berkeley: University of California Press.

Schissel, Bernard. 2002. "Youth Crime, Youth Justice, and the Politics of Marginalization." In Bernard Schissel and Carolyn Brooks (eds.), *Marginality and Condemnation: An Introduction to Critical Criminology.* Halifax: Fernwood Publishing.

Short, James F. Jr. 1964. "Adult-Adolescent Relations and Gang Delinquency." *The Pacific Sociological Review* 7, 2.

Silver, Jim (ed.). 2013. *Moving Forward, Giving Back: Transformative Aboriginal Adult Education.* Halifax: Fernwood Publishing.

___. 2006. *In Their Own Voices: Building Urban Aboriginal Communities.* Halifax: Fernwood Publishing.

Simon, Jonathon. 2007. *Governing Through Crime: How the War on Crime Transformed American Democracy and Created a Culture of Fear.* New York: Oxford University Press.

Skarbek, David. 2012. "Prison Gangs, Norms, and Organization." *Journal of Economic Behaviour & Organization* 82, 1.

Snider, Laureen. 2004. "Female Punishment: From Patriarchy to Backlash?" In Colin Sumner (ed.), *The Blackwell Companion to Criminology.* Oxford: Blackwell.

Spergel, Irving. 1964. *Racketville Slumtown Haulberg.* Chicago: University of Chicago Press.

___. 2007. *Reducing Youth Gang Violence: The Little Village Gang Project in Chicago.* Lanham: AltaMira Press.

Statistics Canada. 2010. *2006 Aboriginal Population Profile for Winnipeg.* Ottawa: Statistics Canada. At <statcan.gc.ca/pub/89-638-x/2010003/article/11082-eng.pdf>.

Swanson, Jean. 2001. *Poor-Bashing: The Politics of Exclusion.* Toronto: Between the Lines.

Teeple, Gary. 2000. *Globalization and the Decline of Social Reform: Into the Twenty-First Century.* Toronto: Garamond Press.

Thrasher, Frederic L. 1927. *The Gang.* Chicago: University of Chicago Press.

___. 1963. *The Gang.* Abridged edition. Chicago: University of Chicago Press.

Totten, Mark. 2012. *Nasty, Brutish, and Short: The Lives of Gang Members in Canada.* Toronto: James Lorimer.

Venkatesh, Sudhir, and Stephen Levitt. 2000. "Are We a Family or a Business? History and Disjuncture in the Urban American Street Gang." *Theory and Society* 29, 4

Vigil, James Diego. 2002. *A Rainbow of Gangs.* Austin: University of Texas Press.

Wacquant, Loïc. 2008. *Urban Outcasts: A Comparative Sociology of Advanced Marginality.* Cambridge, UK: Polity Press.

___. 2009. *Punishing the Poor: The Neoliberal Government of Social Insecurity.* Durham and London: Duke University Press.

Weerman, Frank M., Cheryl L. Maxson, Finn-Aage Esbensen, Judith Aldridge, Juanjo Medina and Frank van Gemert. 2009. *Eurogang Program Manual: Background, Development, and Use of the Eurogang Instruments in Multi-Site, Multi-Method Comparative Research.* At <umsl.edu/ccj/eurogang/EurogangManual.pdf>.

Wesley-Esquimaux, Cynthia, and M. Smolewski. 2004. *Historic Trauma and Aboriginal Healing.* Ottawa: Aboriginal Healing Foundation.

Wilson, William J. 1987. *The Truly Disadvantaged: The Inner City, the Underclass, and Public Policy.* Chicago: University of Chicago Press.

Wortley, Scott. 2010. *Identifying Street Gangs: Definitional Dilemmas and Their Policy Implications.* Ottawa: Public Safety Canada.

Wortley, Scott, and Julian Tanner. 2007. *Criminal Organizations or Social Groups? An Exploration of the Myths and Realities of Youth Gangs in Toronto.* At <ceris.metropolis.net/Virtual%20Library/EResources/WortleyTanner2007.pdf >.

Yalnizan, Armine. 2011. "A Problem for Everyone." *National Post.* September 21.

___. 2007. *The Rich and the Rest of Us: Changing the Face of Canada's Growing Gap.* Ottawa: Canadian Centre for Policy Alternatives.

Young, Alford. 2004. *The Minds of Marginalized Black Men.* Princeton: Princeton University Press.

Young, Jock. 1999. *The Exclusive Society: Social Exclusion, Crime and Difference in Late Modernity.* London: Sage Publications.

___. 2007. "Globalization and Social Exclusions: The Sociology of Vindictiveness and the Criminology of Transgression." In John Hagedorn (ed.), *Gangs in the Global City: Alternatives to Traditional Criminology.* Chicago: University of Chicago Press.

11

CRIMINALIZING RACE

Wendy Chan

KEY FACTS

> Racial stereotypes continue to inform public and institutional understandings of crime and criminal justice.

> Punitive criminal justice policies have a greater impact on racialized individuals and communities.

> Post-9/11 racial profiling is routinely practised and accepted in many law enforcement contexts.

> There is a deep unwillingness to acknowledge that the problem of racism in Canadian society is systemic and structural. The problem of racism in Canada is caused by more than just a "few bad apples."

> Crime control policies have been, and continue to be, widely used to control racialized populations.

> Racialized individuals have been the primary targets in incidents involving police use of force in Canada.

Sources: Henry and Tator 2006; Chan and Chunn 2014; Comack 2012.

Recent efforts to monitor racial bias in the "carding" practices of the Toronto Police Force highlight the troubled history that racialized communities have with criminal justice institutions (Rankin and Winsa 2013). Carding or street checks is a police practice that involves stopping, questioning and documenting people in mostly non-criminal encounters. A study by the Toronto Star paper found that Black people in Toronto were more likely than white people to be carded in 2013, even though the overall number of people carded had dropped from previous years (Rankin and Winsa 2013). Critics contend that this is evidence of systemic discrimination. In response, the Toronto Police Force claims they are working hard to eliminate racial bias from police practices.

The above example highlights how the issue of race and criminal justice in Canada is a complex one, shaped to a large extent by historical policies and practices. In the present day, the issue of race and criminal justice simmers in the background, punctuated at times by well-publicized events such as the mistreatment of undocumented migrants to Canada or the tensions between Aboriginal communities and the state. Unlike the United States, Canada has not seen the same level of antagonism between racialized communities and the criminal justice system. However, this is not to say that the issue of racism and criminal justice in Canada is unproblematic. Perceptions and allegations of discriminatory treatment of racialized groups have been and continues to be commonplace, with problems of racial profiling, over-incarceration and inadequate responses to victimization, to name a few, receiving ongoing attention by policy-makers and critical scholars.

This chapter unpacks the complex relationship between race and criminal justice in Canada. My starting point is the recognition that race and racism in Canada are still very relevant. Contrary to claims that we now live in a post-racial society, there remains unresolved tensions between racialized minorities and the state. Within the criminal justice system, racialized Canadians, particularly black and Aboriginal Canadians, continue to experience higher levels of criminalization and incarceration. Stereotypes about who is more likely to commit crimes or engage in deviant behavior (e.g., "driving while Black," "shopping while Black," "flying while brown") remain strong reference points in shaping public perceptions about crime, dangerousness, fear and safety. Mainstream media have reinforced specific messages about race and criminality, making it easier to justify the punitive treatment of racialized minorities. Furthermore, there is a deep reluctance to acknowledge that these problems are structurally rooted, rather than the work of a "few bad apples" in the justice system. The legacy of colonization and racial discrimination in Canada has shaped contemporary processes of criminal justice, with racial injustices reflecting the differential power relations between white and non-white groups over time. Thus, the unequal treatment of racialized minorities in the criminal justice system is not accidental. It is the result of both conscious and unconscious practices, individual choice, institutional dynamics and systemic practices. As Omi and Winant (1994) observe, the state is inherently racial in that it does not stand above racial conflicts, but is thoroughly immersed in racial contests. Racial injustices in the criminal justice system are a reflection of the wider society. Therefore, recognizing how racial discrimination is structurally embedded in the justice system is the first step towards eradicating the harms and injustices that stand in the way of social and political equality for racialized minorities in Canada.

This chapter is organized around three key sections. In the first section, I examine contemporary debates on race and crime in Canada and the different intellectual approaches that have shaped the research in this area. For example, the positivist tradition, which uses the concept of race as a socio-demographic variable to describe victims and offenders in empirical research, has played a significant role in developing ideas about crime and criminals. I examine the limitations of this approach as well as the problems of conducting research on race and crime in Canada when there is limited access to statistical data on the racial and/or ethnic background of victims and offenders. I explore the problems associated with conceptualizing race as a fixed identity, and I situate the impact of these problems in the context of the criminal justice system. For example, the tendency to view some racial groups as more prone to criminal behaviour than others is one consequence to emerge from "race thinking." Critical approaches to race and crime emerged as a counter to the positivist tradition. I highlight the key issues critical criminologists have focused on in striving for racial equality and anti-racist practices in the criminal justice system. This section ends with a brief discussion of why many critical scholars have turned to the concept of racialization to frame discussions about racism and criminal justice in Canada.

Section two critically examines racialized constructions of crime in Canada. Drawing on a range of different examples, I demonstrate how the practice, discourse and policies of criminal justice have been shaped by racial stereotypes and myths or misperceptions about racialized groups. As many critical criminologists have pointed out, definitions of crime and criminal behaviour focus on street crimes or property crimes rather than corporate or white-collar crimes. Typically, racialized minorities are over-represented in so-called street crimes. This creates the perception that danger or threat is strongly associated with racialized individuals and groups. Increased police attention and harsher sentences are then justified in the name of crime control.

The final section of this chapter explores the other side of this dynamic — the ways in which processes of criminalization target racialized individuals and groups. While some scholars have highlighted how crime is racialized in Canada, other scholars add that racialized groups are also more likely to have their acts and behaviours labelled as deviant and/or criminal. As such, they are at greater risk of being policed, investigated and prosecuted. Practices of racial profiling, over-policing and increased detention have resulted in the disproportionate representation of Aboriginal people, racialized Canadians and non-citizens, migrants and refugees in the criminal justice system. The effects of criminalization on racialized people has been devastating — they are widely demonized as the cause of chaos and disorder, and they have been denied basic human rights. Paying attention to patterns of criminalization will expose how racism is embedded in criminal justice practices, how it influences decision making and reinforces stereotypes about racialized minorities.

Throughout this chapter, race is understood to be a socially constructed category where meanings are not fixed, but contested and transformed through political struggle. The concept of race has always been problematic, and many scholars use the term in inverted commas to highlight the complex, political and contested nature of is usage (Mason 2000). Some scholars have argued for the use of ethnicity instead. I believe that the term is still analytically relevant. When used as an analytical term rather than a descriptive one, it highlights the power relationships that have shaped contemporary social relations in Canada, even while still recognizing its problematic status.

Race also intersects with other social characteristics, such as gender, class and sexual orientation, to produce racialized positions. Where possible, I use an intersectional approach to raise awareness of the complexity in the lives of racialized minorities. For example, many Aboriginal women who have been battered choose not to call authorities for help because they do not want to further criminalize male Aboriginal members of their community. Their responses differ from many battered non-Aboriginal women due to the convergence of factors such as gender, race and social class. By taking a wider lens to the study of race and crime, I hope to capture the nuances of these convergences in influencing crime and victimization as well as criminal justice policy and practice.

THE CONSTRUCTION OF THE RACE-CRIME PROBLEM IN CANADA

Mainstream criminological research on race and crime conceptualizes race as a sociodemographic variable. Much of this research is positivist in orientation, with a focus on highlighting the crime patterns of different racial and ethnic groups and comparing them to other social groups to locate causative factors. One of the central claims of mainstream criminologists is that criminals are different from non-criminals and that it is these differences, "criminogenic properties," that compels them into crime. These differences can include having different biological or genetic features such as low IQ or testosterone levels, or they may be different social conditions such as poverty, education and age. Once these differences are identified, and an individual has gone through intervention, treatment and reform, that person can be steered away from deviant and criminal behavior. This body of scholarship typically relies on official statistics to provide victim and offender profiles or to establish the crime rates and incarceration rates of a particular racial group (Trevethan and Rastin 2004). In Canada, the most discussed racialized group in the criminal justice system is Aboriginal people (Wood and Griffiths 1996). This is likely attributed to their history of being overrepresented in the criminal justice system. Other racialized groups, such as Black Canadians and immigrants, have received sporadic attention from Canadian criminologists (Roberts and Doob 1997; Gordon and Nelson 1996).

There are many limitations to treating race as an independent variable in criminological research. While positivist criminology offers a detailed picture of who is involved in the criminal justice system, there are also fears that the research creates false pathologies that may be used to naturalize and reify racialized people as inherently criminal (Phillips and Bowling 2003). For example, official crime statistics have been heavily criticized for its overrepresentation of marginalized and vulnerable social groups. Furthermore, the racial categories found in official statistics are often adopted at face value, raising further questions about the role of these statistics in perpetuating racial inequalities. Seeing some racialized groups as more criminogenic than others not only reinforces negative racial stereotypes, but also leads to racialized groups being blamed for high levels of crime and delinquency. Methodologically, race scholars have pointed out how the classification of different racial groups is inconsistently defined (Mann 1993), and they question whether or not humankind can be divided according to skin colour. As geneticist James King (1981) explains, formulating a typology of races is an arbitrary exercise because there is no objective (biological) criteria for dividing humans in this way. Thus, attempts to develop a racial classification scheme cannot be easily divorced from the assumptions about human origins and group inferiority and superiority that inform these classification systems.

Efforts to move beyond crude and essentialist categorizations of racialized minorities have been taken up by critical criminologists who have adopted a different approach. Contrary to the positivist tradition, these criminologists regard race as the product of social interactions and argue that racial categories are not fixed and immutable, but fluid and subject to change. That is, race is a social idea where racial categories and meanings are constructed by the dominant group in society as one way to mark difference. Racial differences are used to justify discriminatory treatment and the differential allocation of rights and resources. Much of the work of critical criminologists centers on examining whether or not the treatment of offenders and victims by the criminal justice system is racially biased and highlighting differential trial outcomes and over or under-representation in the prisons, for example. Comack's (2012) study of policing of Aboriginal communities is exemplary. She highlights how the relationship between Aboriginal people and the justice system is shaped by colonization, decades of mistreatment and inequality. As a result, Aboriginal people do not trust the police and are reluctant to cooperate with the justice system, while police officers have been accused of over-criminalizing Aboriginal people. For critical scholars, then, racial prejudice and discrimination are key factors in explaining the differential criminal justice treatment and outcomes of non-white offenders and victims. Tanovich (2008: 656) questions whether or not fundamental justice is possible for Aboriginal and racialized communities given the limited impact of reforms on racial injustice in Canada.

Whether consciously or unconsciously, criminological research has reproduced racial hierarchies, but it has also been the site of resistance. For example, although historically there were criminal anthropologists such as Lombroso arguing that criminals were evolutionary throwbacks and the "white races [were] the triumph of the human species" (quoted in Miller 1996: 185), others such as Bonger were challenging the fascist movement and the superiority of Nordic peoples (Hawkins 1995: 23). Today, similar tensions within the study of race and crime persist, albeit in a more nuanced form. Positivist criminologists continue to analyze crime using official statistics and racial classification schemes, but they are cautious about claiming that racialized groups are more criminogenic as they recognize that unequal treatment affects the overrepresentation of racialized groups in the justice system. Critiques of biological determinism by critical criminologists also persist, with the added recognition that racial categories are unstable and that crime and definitions of crime are subject to change. Indeed, as they have pointed out, the socially constructed nature of both race and crime tells us more about systems of control and regulation and how the criminal justice system is used by the powerful to dominate and subordinate the powerless than it does about racial groups.

It is within this context of criminological scholarship that an ongoing debate has been taking place in Canada over whether or not the government should even be collecting data on race and crime. The Canadian Government has never systematically collected race-based data in the criminal justice system, and as a result, it has been more difficult to provide a detailed portrait of the relationship between race and crime in Canada. While there is a wealth of information in the U.K. and the U.S. on this topic, there is much less research available in Canada. The only data that is routinely collected in this area are federal imprisonment rates for Aboriginal people. During the 1990s, Canadian criminologists were engaged in a lively debate over whether or not statistics on race and crime should be collected. Scholars such as Thomas Gabor (1994) argued that restricting access to this information is both "alarmist" and "paternalistic" and that the public should not be denied access to information about their security and safety (Gabor 1994: 154). Furthermore, race-based crime statistics can be used to challenge racial inequality by invalidating biological explanations of crime, by identifying areas of criminal justice practices that are in need of reform and by identifying problems that disproportionately impact minority communities (Wortley 1999). Scholars who support the continued ban on collecting raced-based crime statistics state that racism in the justice system can be studied without the need for race-based crime statistics (Johnston 1994). They express a number of concerns, such as fears that the police would not be able to collect reliable and accurate data, that the accuracy of race-based crime statistics would be hampered by the changing definitions of race and crime, that the public will misinterpret the data and that racism and discrimination against minority groups will increase as a result of this data (Johnston 1994; Roberts 1994). Instead of an all-or-nothing approach, Wortley (1999) suggests several compromises such as restricting who would have access to the data and the type of analysis that would be permitted with the data.

Successive governments in Canada have not indicated any interest in changing the status quo. What has changed since the 1990s is that many minority groups are now calling for the collection of race-based crime statistics in order to redress racial discrimination in the justice system (Owusu-Bempah and Millar 2010) because they recognize that the lack of race-based crime data is a double-edge sword: while not collecting data may prevent further racism and discrimination from taking place, the absence of race-based data also makes understanding racial discrimination and mistreatment by criminal justice officials much more difficult. More recently, Paul Millar and Akwasi Owusu-Bempah (2011) have made a spirited called for change, arguing that race-based crime data is necessary to conduct quantitative anti-racism research. They attempt to put more pressure on policy-makers to revisit the ban on data collection by claiming that criminal justice institutions in Canada are deliberately suppressing race-based crime data and that this is an attempt to avoid accountability and to "whitewash" the criminal justice system. Indeed, in this post-September 11 context, where racism has reached new heights in many minority communities due to fears around national security, previous concerns that race-based crime data would exacerbate or act as a justification for discriminatory behavior appear moot. Racial profiling, for example, is now routinely practised by law enforcement agents, and many minority communities have suffered grave injustices (e.g., Arab and Muslim communities) without the ability to counter official claims and negative public perceptions due to the lack of data available.

Despite the absence of race-based crime statistics in Canada, criminologists have produced a small, but rich, body of qualitative scholarship examining topics such as racial profiling (Satzewich and Shaffir 2009), the criminal justice treatment of racialized Canadians (Anand 2000) and perceptions of crime and justice by minority communities (Oriola and Adeyanju 2011). Intellectual interest in this area of study remains strong, particularly by critical scholars carrying out research examining the treatment of racial minorities as an index of social control and how the criminal justice system is used to perpetuate racial inequality (Gordon 2006; Nelson 2011).

Yet critical researchers are increasingly wary of using the concepts "race" and "crime," with some scholars opting instead for terms like racialization and criminalization. As mentioned earlier, one significant consequence of this way of thinking has been the tendency to view entire communities as predisposed for criminal behavior by virtue of their racial identity. Furthermore, others suggest that race as an analytical concept in criminal justice is too limiting. Walsh and Yun (2011) argue that it would be more fruitful to consider race as both a biological reality *and* a social construction. Although there is no scientific basis to the category of race, the concept of race still exists and continues to be used in official and unofficial discourse. They state that "we cannot change the underlying reality, but we can certainly change our beliefs about the representation of that reality" (Walsh and Yun 2011: 1281).

An emphasis on racialization draws attention to the process in which racial understandings are formed and re-formed in the creation of racialized positions, thus recognizing that social understandings and the implications and consequences of race change over time. For example, southern and eastern Europeans have been de-racialized and assigned to the broad category of white. As Satzewich observes, "Many European groups that are now routinely thought of as white were far from being considered white as little as two or three generations ago ... Groups from the southern and eastern periphery of Europe were particularly prone to racialized othering" (2000: 277). Yet Omi and Winant (1994) are careful to point out that the creation and characterization of racial categories is a variable process that has played out differently for different groups. For example, Aboriginal people in Canada were subjected to harsh assimilation policies and Asian and Black people were excluded from Canada; more recently, Arab and Muslim Canadians are labelled as terrorists. Different processes of racialization have resulted in a racial hierarchy that sees whites on top and minorities, particularly Aboriginal and African/ Black Canadians, at the bottom (Omi and Winant 1994). In the context of criminal justice, decades of disproportionate representation of Aboriginal people in Canadian prisons is evidence that a certain type of "race thinking" makes this phenomenon possible. The state's capacity to wield such power over a certain segment of society demonstrates its ability to reproduce racial hierarchies and maintain racial hegemony. Thus, even if race has no essence, racism persists, and mapping out the complex manifestations of racism in the criminal justice system by highlighting the power differentials implicated in the practice of racism is a central feature of racialization.

Within Canadian society, racism is often either denied through claims that we live in a multicultural society and race no longer matters, or it is held to be an individual problem, rather than a structural or systemic issue. Where racial inequality occurs, it is often regarded as a problem "of the people who fail to take responsibility for their own lives" (Brown et al. 2005: vii) rather than an institutional problem. This view can be found across many social institutions in Canada, from police chiefs denying that racial profiling occurs (Satzewich and Shaffir 2009), to politicians labelling asylum seekers coming to Canada as illegitimate or illegal (Levine-Rasky 2012), to the mainstream media virtually ignoring the topic of racism altogether (Decoste 2013a). Yet, when you commit a crime, as Rachel Decoste (2013b) notes, your race matters. Compare the treatment of Rob Ford, ex-mayor of Toronto, or Mike Duffy, a Conservative senator, two public figures caught in crime-related scandals, to the treatment of racialized offenders, whom the previous minister of citizenship and immigration, Jason Kenny, would like to "deport without delay" from Canada (Decoste 2013b). In contrast, there has not been any discussion of a similarly punitive treatment for Rob Ford or Mike Duffy. For many race scholars in Canada, this double standard comes as no surprise. The multicultural discourse in Canada celebrates a tolerance of Aboriginal and racialized minorities while ignoring acts of colonial violence, genocide, residential schools and racist immigration policies. Respect for racial differences are based on white decisions and their definition of what are *allowable* differences (O'Connell 2010: 540). While ethnic food and cultural celebrations are welcomed, social and economic demands are not. As Bannerji (1997: 35) states, "Multiculturalism is itself a vehicle for racialization. It establishes Anglo-Canadian culture as the ethnic core culture while 'tolerating' and hierarchically arranging others around it as 'multiculture.'" Dua, Razack and Warner (2005) add that national mythologies operate to sustain Canada's vision of itself as a white nation, even though many urban centers like Vancouver and Toronto are increasingly moving towards a majority-minority population.

Problems of racial discrimination in Canada are more subtle today compared to historical practices, but they have not disappeared. The everyday racism found in body language or tone of voice is one that many racialized Canadians experience. As one Ontario community organizer noted, "Racism is prevalent, persisting and perpetually growing [in Canada]" (Douglas and Rosella 2013). In the criminal justice system, racial discrimination takes on many forms — from not being able to access services and programs, to harsher sentences and deaths in police custody. The paucity of research in Canada has allowed culturally produced images of crime and criminals, by mainstream media in particular, to reinforce racial stereotypes and myths about crime and victimization. Like many Western states, criminal justice in Canada is heavily racialized.

RACIALIZED CONSTRUCTIONS OF CRIME IN CANADA

In Ontario, allegations and counter-allegations of a race problem in the justice system led to a public inquiry into the issue of systemic racism in the criminal justice system in the mid-1990s. The Commission's key findings were that Black males in Ontario were significantly more likely to be stopped by the police, to receive harsher treatment by judges, to be refused bail or release before trial and to be given a prison sentence than whites or other racialized minorities (Commission on Systemic Racism in the Ontario Criminal Justice System 1995). Other studies show that close to one-quarter of those incarcerated in Canada are Aboriginal, even though they make up only 4 percent of the population. Black and Aboriginal inmates are dramatically overrepresented in Canada's maximum security federal penitentiaries and segregation placements — they are also more likely to have force used on them, to incur a disproportionate number of disciplinary charges, to be released later in their sentences and to have less access to day or full parole (Correctional Investigator of Canada 2013).

Despite these findings, the problem of crime has been, and continues to be, framed primarily as a problem of deviant, minority communities. Whether it is the suggestion that these groups are "innately criminal" or that they possess deviant cultural values, public anxieties about crime and chaos fuel the ongoing hostility about their presence and alleged criminal tendencies. Crime is racialized when individual behaviours are attached to the traits of a wider racial community or group such that "whole categories of phenotypically similar individuals are rendered pre-criminal and morally suspect" (Covington 1995: 547). In Canada, the pool of people that comprise the "dangerous classes" has been, and continues to be, drawn largely from racial and ethnic communities, thereby allowing for their over-policing and subsequent disproportionate representation in the criminal justice system (Roach 1996).

Monaghan documents how Aboriginal leaders at the end of the nineteenth century were subjected to a campaign of surveillance and labelled as "good" or "bad" characters, depending on their willingness to assimilate and promote the colonialist project of expansionism (2013: 499). Fears of Indigenous danger and backwardness led to Aboriginal activities being problematized as suspect and dangerous and to the construction of Aboriginal leaders as abnormal and deviant because they threatened the advancement of settler colonialism with their demands for rights and dignity (Monaghan 2013). Similarly, Mosher's (1996) historical study of Black offenders in Ontario at the turn of the twentieth century found that they were more likely to be imprisoned for public order offences such as prostitution or vagrancy and to receive harsher sentences than white offenders. D'Arcy's (2007) study shows that, in Toronto, the "Jamaican criminal" has become a taken-for-granted category of pathology who embodies a threat to public safety and from whom "we" need to be protected, a perception that has remained unchanged for decades (D'Arcy 2007).

Law and order campaigns targeting behaviours linked to racialized communities magnify the perception that crime is implicitly associated with these communities. The war on drugs in Canada is an example. Gordon (2006: 74) argues that it is typically working class people and immigrants of colour who are the main targets in the "drug war" even though they are mostly small-time dealers and people in possession of cannabis. Furthermore, under the pretext of drug criminalization, the police have been able to intervene more broadly in these minority communities to maintain social order. Similarly, Silverstein's (2005) study of parole hearings found that the racial identity of inmates was a factor in the decision-making process for. Parole board members set out conditions using different standards depending on the inmate's racial background. Aboriginal inmates were required to have more community involvement in their rehabilitation compared to other inmates, while Hispanic and Asian inmates were required to demonstrate higher levels of shame for their crimes. These expectations, done in the name of protecting society, were often based on racial and ethnic stereotyping, and they raise many questions about fairness and due process in parole hearings (Silverstein 2005).

When crime rates rose during the 1990s in Canada, the government at the time implemented many tough-on-crime policies such as mandatory minimum sentences, longer maximum sentences, restricted access to parole and easier transfers for youths committing serious offences to adult courts. Public fear of crime and violence, and a perceived decline in public safety, created escalating anxiety amongst Canadians. These harsher policies and practices were not unusual, as the United States and the U.K. had enacted similar crime policies during this period. A number of high profiles cases also led the public to believe that the crime problem was caused by racialized offenders. For example, the 1994 Just Desserts case in Toronto, where Georgina Leimonis was shot and killed in the Just Desserts café by two men of Jamaican heritage, led to a moral panic where the public believed that there was a Jamaican crime wave in Toronto (D'Arcy 2007). Minority communities fought back against these claims, pointing out how only two years earlier, two police officers in the Toronto region were acquitted of killing Wade Lawson, a 17-year-old Black youth, and Raymond Lawrence, a 22-year-old Jamaican immigrant. Nonetheless, the report by the Commission on Systemic Racism in the Ontario Criminal Justice System (1995) found that in the minds of criminal justice managers, planners and workers, crime is strongly associated with particular racialized groups. Thus, the explosion of "get tough" measures aimed at assuaging public fears about crime had an implicit racial subtext.

Several decades later, the march towards increased punitiveness continues, despite falling crime rates and over-crowded prisons. In the fall of 2013, Stephen Harper's Conservative Government passed crime legislation that included the controversial provision of mandatory minimum sentences. Many critics argue that a tough-on-crime agenda is no longer appropriate, while one United Nations group has criticized the legislation for being "excessively punitive" on youth and expressed concern about the fact that Aboriginal and Black children are already dramatically overrepresented in the criminal justice system (Schrieber 2013; Canadian Press 2012). Critics add that successive studies have demonstrated that incarceration is ineffective and unsustainable and that draconian policies have had little influence on curbing undesirable behaviours (Schrieber 2013).

Further criticism from Howard Sapers, the Correctional Investigator of Canada, highlights the depth of the problem. In his annual report, he notes that federal correctional centers are currently over-crowded, dangerous and violent, all factors that could potentially result in riots (Correctional Investigator of Canada 2013). Sapers observes that "the growth in the custody population appears to be policy, not crime driven" (Correctional Investigator of Canada 2013). In other words, the drive towards punitive criminal justice treatment is not undertaken due to problems with high crime rates. Rather, it is a symbolic gesture by politicians seeking to demonstrate their ability to govern, and this relies on using racialized minorities as scapegoats. These "reforms" find their support in public opinion rather than criminal justice experts and professionals, and these reforms give priority to the interests of victims and victims' families (Garland 2000).

It has been suggested by scholars that current crime policies are a symbol for other social anxieties such as high unemployment and increasing poverty (Wacquant 2001). The "Blackening" of the carceral system is part of a larger risk management project to surveil and neutralize populations that are superfluous to the global economy and deemed a threat to social stability (Wacquant 2001).

This phenomenon is not only racialized, but it is also deeply gendered. For example, in Canada, the number of Black inmates, the majority of whom are men, has increased 75 percent in the last ten years (Correctional Investigator of Canada 2013), highlighting how these individuals have become collateral damage in the current neo-liberal economic regime, where secure, full-time work is no longer the norm. While women are being funneled into part-time, precarious employment, unemployed, racialized men are increasingly being managed by the penal system (Wacquant 2001). Government efforts to rehabilitate or retrain citizens have been displaced by strategies aimed at simply neutralizing and managing these populations. Thus, those who are unable to find a place for themselves in the labour market are penalized and criminalized, and this is more likely in racialized communities where there are higher levels of economic deprivation and poverty.

RACIAL PROFILING

The use of race as a proxy for dangerousness is best exemplified by the practice of racial profiling. Targeting individuals for law enforcement based on the colour of their skin demonstrates how race informs the contemporary understanding of who or what poses a risk to society. In Canada, the debate on racial profiling has mostly focused on whether or not police forces actual practice racial profiling. A series of articles on racial profiling in the *Toronto Star* in 2002 highlighted the use of racial profiling, such as stop and searches, by the Toronto police force, sparking an intense public debate. In a follow-up report, the African Canadian Coalition on Racial Profiling found that there is widespread evidence that racial profiling exists in the greater Toronto area, with Black people being the primary targets of police stop and searches (Brown 2004). There have been many subsequent reports confirming the use of racial profiling in other provinces.

Racial profiling in Canada is a controversial practice, and police forces have routinely denied that they racially profile, despite many complaints by racialized Canadians (Smith 2006). However, after September 11, racial profiling became more widely accepted as a necessary tool for combatting terrorism and maintaining national security. Bahdi (2003: 295) states that in the context of the war against terrorism, racial profiling debates focused on whether Canadian society can morally, legally or politically condone the practice. Arab and Muslim communities became key targets of law enforcement. Arabs and Muslims found themselves subjected to multiple layers of screening at Canada's borders, with pre-entry assessments, fingerprinting and interviews with security or border officials becoming a common routine for many who wished to travel. Stories of people being denied access onto a plane, removed from planes for praying, denied visas to other countries or questioned extensively about their Canadian identity played out in a context where public sympathy was in short supply and recourse to fair treatment was not a priority.

Several high profile cases of Arab and Muslim people being mistreated demonstrates how different life is for them compared to other Canadians. Maher Arar, a dual Canadian and Syrian citizen, was detained at JFK airport in New York while enroute home to Ottawa from a vacation. Arar was (falsely) accused by U.S. officials of being linked to al-Qaeda and was deported to Syria, where he was imprisoned for ten months, during which time he was beaten, tortured and forced to make a false confession (maherarar.net). A Commission of Inquiry into Arar's case found that he was cleared of all terrorism allegations. In a similar case, Abousfian Abdelrazik, a Black, Muslim Canadian citizen, was accused of being a supporter of al-Qaeda and a terrorist during a trip he took to Sudan to visit his sick mother in 2003 (Brown 2008). He was jailed and tortured for nine months but never charged. Abdelrazik was arrested again in November 2005 and released in July 2006 (Brown 2008). The Sudanese Government formally exonerated Abdelrazik in 2005, finding that there was no evidence of any links to al-Qaeda or terrorism (Koring 2011).

The consequences, both intended and unintended, suffered by Maher Arar and Abousfian Abdelrazik, and the many other racialized minorities in Canada, suggests that their suffering is not inconsequential. The lives of these two men have been shattered by Canada's national security agenda, which allows the terrorist label to be applied to citizens as easily as it is applied to non-citizens. Bahdi (2003) argues that while some people may argue that the harms endured are justified as the price to pay for fighting terrorism, the consequences, when viewed from a community perspective of systematic exclusion and marginalization, are not insignificant. Acts of discrimination fuel the belief that members of Muslim and Arab communities are dangerous internal foreigners despite their citizenship status (Dhamoon and Abu-Laban 2009). As Bahdi (2003: 317) states, "Those who turn to racial profiling as an anecdote for uncertainty will find neither solutions nor comfort. Racial profiling will produce only illusions of security while heightening the disempowerment and sense of vulnerability of racialized groups in Canada."

The association in the minds of many people between crime and racialized groups stems from crime legislation and from the activities of law enforcement agencies. It is also reinforced by the disproportionate media coverage of racialized individuals involved in crime. Numerous studies have found that racialized minorities are under-represented in positive roles and overrepresented in negative portrayals that link them to social disorder and criminal behavior (Larsen 2006). Furthermore, recurring images in the mainstream media of racialized people generally having undesirable, dangerous or inferior traits or behaviours reinforces biases about the guilt or innocence the defendant (Entman and Gross 2008). Thus, when news stories focus on violent crimes, racialized people are more likely to appear as the perpetrators rather than the victims (Entman and Gross 2008). When racialized people are criminally victimized, their experiences are either minimized or ignored altogether. For example, media coverage of the missing/murdered Aboriginal women in Canada highlights the value judgments made by media institutions in which white women are positively portrayed as legitimate, innocent and worthy victims — "the girl next door" — while Aboriginal women victims are largely ignored and rendered invisible (Jiwani and Young 2006). Amnesty International notes that this hierarchy of worthiness creates an underclass of victims that could increase the victimization of Aboriginal women since the message to the rest of society is that these women don't matter (Amnesty International 2009). Media stereotyping of racial groups exacerbates the mentality that Canadian society is composed of "us" and "them," making it much more difficult for racialized and marginalized groups and individuals to be heard and treated with dignity and respect.

Thinking about how crime is racialized allows us to interrogate the policies and practices in the criminal justice system that continue to subjugate racialized people by labelling and treating them as deviant and dangerous. Historically, the criminal justice system has been, and continues to be, a key institution used to control racialized populations. As the discussion in this section illustrates, racialized groups have been the targets of moral panics and continue to be stereotyped as the criminal other. As Angela Davis remarks, "The figure of the 'criminal' — the racialised figure of the criminal — has come to represent the most menacing enemy of 'American society'" (1998: 270). The legacy of institutional and systemic racism has brutalized many communities, leaving them socially excluded, economically impoverished and politically disenfranchised. The politicization of crime in Canada, evident in the most recent crime legislation by the Conservative Government, will do little to mend the problems of racial inequality in the justice system.

CRIMINALIZING RACIALIZED BODIES

Racialized communities are the target of law enforcement practices due in large part to how we define what is a crime and who are the criminals in our midst. However, these communities have also been constructed and identified by the state as problematic and in need of greater surveillance and control. The racialization of crime works in tandem with the criminalization of race, which refers to the ways that racialized groups and individuals are labelled and targeted by the state as undesirable, leading to their subsequent criminalization, illegalization, marginalization and exclusion. In this final section, I examine how different racial groups have been the objects of increased criminalization and how various state agencies have relied increasingly on criminal justice strategies to manage a broad range of social issues such as immigration and welfare services. As Simon (2007: 8) observes, we govern through crime when we see crime as "the problem through which we seek to know and act on the conduct of others." Crime provides the metaphors and narratives for those seeking to make claims on those who are being governed in a non-criminal context such as immigration, schools or the welfare system. Governments are then able to deploy the use of criminal law and its associated technologies and mentalities as crime becomes the dominant rationale for governance. Simon (2007) states that "governing through crime" is now the default response by many governments to social, political and economic problems, and this wider use of crime control strategies in non-criminal contexts has expanded the net of control and punishment in racialized communities.

Immigrants and Refugees as "Criminals"

Within the last decade, migrants and asylum seekers have increasingly become the objects of intense policing. As migration becomes synonymous with risk, many developed nations have securitized their borders as a strategy for managing contemporary anxieties and fears arising from the effects of globalization. A key strategy adopted by Canada and other Western states for preventing unwanted migrants and immigrants from entering their respective countries is to criminalize their activities. The increasing criminalization of immigration taking place across many Western nations is the result of immigration and criminal justice practices merging and unifying to fend off the "criminal alien" (Kanstroom 2005). Aas (2007) notes that the image of the "deviant immigrant" is not new and has been a recurring theme in social research. Foreigners were often depicted as possessing powerful criminal tendencies, and their appearance as a threat typically occurs in concert with global and national migratory movements (Aas 2007).

Current images of the "deviant immigrant" are a prominent feature in Canadian political and media discourse. For example, Jason Kenney, the previous minister for immigration, repeatedly referred to asylum seekers as "bogus" or "queue jumpers," suggesting that their need for state protection is not legitimate, particularly those who come from countries he claimed were "safe" (Levine-Rasky 2012). The mainstream media also routinely depicts refugees as the cause of chaos and disorder, suggesting that their troubled backgrounds and cultural differences make them unsuitable for Canada (Bradimore and Bauder 2011). The treatment of 492 Sri Lankan asylum seekers who came by cargo ship to the west coast of Canada in the summer of 2010 illustrates this process. They were portrayed and treated as deviant and criminal rather than given compassion and protection. All of the asylum seekers were detained for several months, including women and children, with most of them eventually being deported from Canada. The representation of the Sri Lankan asylum seekers as posing a very real threat, as being "different from us," underscores how poverty and racial difference, disguised as dangerousness, is mobilized to justify the violation of their human rights. The government's response in light of this event was to introduce legislation, the *Protecting Canada's Immigration System Act*, which would impose mandatory detention for those the government deems to be "irregular arrivals," by which they are primarily referring to large numbers of boat migrants. Not only would these migrants be automatically detained for up to one year, they would also have reduced access to health care and delayed access to permanent residency, family reunification and travel documents even if they were found to be "genuine" refugees (Alboim and Cohl 2012).

Immigrants who are not highly skilled and economically independent do not fit the government's image of immigrants who are worthy and desirable. Instead, these "undesirable" immigrants and migrants have been constructed as deviant for causing social problems or needing state protection. For example, the passage of a recent parliamentary bill (C-43 — *Faster Removal of Foreign Criminals Act*) seeking to expedite the process of removing "foreign criminals" has been criticized for suggesting that Canada is "overrun with foreign terrorists, escaped convicts, war criminals and the like" (*Huffington Post* 2012). Non-citizens who have been convicted of a crime and sentenced to six months imprisonment or more will be deported without access to the appeals process. Critics have described this bill as an American style, "one strike and you're out" policy (Godfrey 2012). One major criticism of this policy is the removal of long-time permanent residents who have lived in Canada since childhood but never applied for citizenship. Lorne Waldman (2013) contends that this law has nothing to do with "foreign criminals" — it is about stripping appeal rights from permanent residents.

Immigration enforcement has been given higher priority over issues such as refugee protection or humanitarian cases. Within the *Immigration and Refugee Protection Act* is a long list of preventative and deterrent measures that have been added or bolstered to control non-citizens and police the external borders. Expanded visa regimes (travelers who come from countries that require a visa to enter Canada), increased fines and penalties for airlines transporting foreign nationals without proper documentation, increased use of immigration detention and greater denial of access to appeals demonstrates how "undesirable" immigrants have been rebranded as security and criminality risks. Their treatment by the state reinforces and reproduces the boundaries between citizen and non-citizen, between those who belong to the nation, and those who do not, and, in the process, it offers us a very particular vision of national identity. Racial politics are deeply embedded in immigration policies, making it possible to routinely deny basic rights to racialized groups defined as outsiders.

As a result of growing suspicion and resentment towards immigrants and refugees, public support for all these harsh measures has been high. This is not a new phenomenon, as there have always been groups of immigrant and refugees that have been the targets of intolerance and hate. However, as more people migrant around the world due to wars, environmental disasters or economic turmoil, rather than providing support for migrants, Western governments have bolstered their exclusionary policies in order to demonstrate that they are in control of their borders. The current Canadian Government has incorporated many criminal law practices into immigration proceedings without providing procedural protections to immigrants and refugees. Immigrants and refugees who arrive in Canada without proper documentation, who seek asylum or who arrive through irregular channels such as using the help of smugglers to escape have all been rebranded as criminals. One of the harshest criticisms levelled at the Canadian Government is the use of prisons to detain immigrants, a practice that has been widely condemned by national and international organizations since many immigrants are detained for non-criminal offences and the mixing of non-criminals with criminals is seen as highly undesirable.

The criminalization of immigrants and refugees illustrates how the mythical figure of the "deviant immigrant" has come to embody the dangers, insecurities and perceived risks of a rapidly changing global environment (Melossi 2003). The connection between migration and crime has been reinforced by the construction and treatment of foreignness as a criminal threat, and it has paved the way for punitive and restrictive policies. Furthermore, when these policies and practices are based on the racially motivated stereotype of migrants as the cause of crime and disorder, it is much more difficult to challenge their legitimacy. As Bosworth (2011) observes, foreign offenders often have limited numbers of supporters, therefore governments seldom experience any qualms about disrupting social relationships or violating human rights.

Policing Non-White People

However, it is not just immigrants and refugees who are subjected to intrusive levels of surveillance and policing. Aboriginal communities have been particularly impacted by intensive policing practices and mistreatment. Black people in the greater Toronto region, for example, are grossly overrepresented in use of force statistics, especially in police shooting incidents (Wortley 2006). Not surprisingly, various studies conducted on minority views of the police have found that visible minorities have less confidence in the police (Cao 2011) and that Canadian-born minorities perceive the justice system to be more biased than people of colour born outside of Canada (Wortley and Owusu-Bempah 2009).

A number of high-profile incidents involving Aboriginal men point to the tense relationship between these communities and the criminal justice system. In 1998, Frank Paul was picked up by the police in Vancouver's downtown eastside for being drunk in a public place, placed in lockup, released, then taken into custody again where the sergeant in charge refused to accept him a second time. At the time of his second arrest, he could barely walk. Frank Paul was then left in an alleyway, where he was found dead of hypothermia a few hours later (Razack 2012: 909). Six Aboriginal men in Saskatchewan have also died as a result of mistreatment by the police. These men froze to death when they were given a "starlight tour" — the police picked up the intoxicated Aboriginal men, drove them to a remote area of town and then dropped them off, leaving them to find their way home (Comack 2012). In most cases of starlight tours, the men are only lightly dressed and not prepared for the cold weather. While Aboriginal leaders argued that the treatment of these men demonstrates the pervasive racism in the Saskatoon Police Service, the police force and its supporters denied any wrong-doing and claimed that the stories were myths (Comack 2012). Eventually, an inquiry was conducted into the death of one of the men, Neil Stonechild, with the conclusion that the police did not adequately investigate the case for fear that one of their own officers may have been involved his death (Cheema 2009: 91). A public inquiry was also held to investigate Paul's death, and although the report acknowledged how racism and colonialism contributed to Frank Paul's demise, in the end, no one was found criminally responsible for his death (Davies 2011). Finally, there is also the well-known case of Donald Marshall, a Mi'kmaq man from Halifax who was wrongly convicted of killing Sandy Seale in the 1970s. He spent eleven years in prison until he was finally released and an inquiry was held to investigate his wrongful conviction. The Commissioners for the Inquiry concluded that the criminal justice system had failed Donald Marshall (Hickman 1989). Not only did the courts accept perjured evidence, but also the Crown, the judge and even the defence lawyer for Marshall had made many errors in his case (Hickman 1989). It was only by coincidence that his innocence was finally established (Hickman 1989: 5).

While many of these well-known cases involved racialized men, racialized women's experiences of the criminal justice have not been significantly more positive. For example, their experiences of criminal victimization has often been minimized or dismissed by the justice system. It is not uncommon for police officers to view violence within racialized communities as normal or reasonable, and, therefore, when racialized women are victimized, they are often left with few options for seeking protection (Adelman et al. 2003). Furthermore, Aboriginal women's sexual victimization is often not believed in court trials and the harms they suffer are trivialized (Dylan, Regehr and Allaggia 2008). Racialized and indigenous women typically do not fit the role of the "ideal" or "authentic" victim of sexual assault because racial stereotypes depict them as more blameworthy and less deserving of protection (Randall 2010). Women in general are reluctant to report crimes of sexual assault or domestic violence, but racialized women, despite higher rates of victimization, are even less likely to seek legal redress through the justice system for fears of not being believed or being re-victimized by the system (Regehr et al. 2008).

Race and Poverty

Poor people, particularly poor, racialized women, are typically portrayed as individuals with moral or psychological deficiencies (Fraser and Gordon 1994). Despite years of significant cutbacks in state support, the assumption held by many is that poor people deserve their life situations because they fail to rise up to the challenges of the labour market. Constructions of their poverty emphasize their pathological lifestyles, such as the belief that women of colour are hypersexed and promiscuous and that they have children to obtain more welfare money (Abramovitz 2006). Many people thus assume that poor people, especially poor, racialized individuals, are receiving state support illegitimately and believe that punitive action is needed to control this population. Municipalities across Canada have passed bylaws and legislation criminalizing the activities of poor people. Panhandling, squeegeeing, sleeping in public and loitering are activities that have been reconstituted as disorderly and result in criminal sanctions (Hermer and Mosher 2002). Welfare policies have also been re-crafted with the presumption that recipients are "guilty until proven innocent," that their conduct needs to be carefully supervised and remedied by restrictive and coercive measures and that deterrence and stigma are necessary to modify behavior (Wacquant 2009: 79). This approach rejects racism and sexism, believing that anyone who really wants to work hard will succeed (Davis 2007). The convergence of penal and welfare practices illustrates how harsher treatment will be the default response to managing the problems of poverty.

MARGINALIZED AND CONDEMNED

The criminalization and marginalization of racialized communities has been made possible by depicting people of colour as less deserving of state protection or support and more likely to be in need of surveillance and control. For example, in 2005, concerns about gun violence by young Black men in Toronto led to explanations that the problem was one of family dysfunction, where many Black youths were growing up in households without a father figure (Lawson 2012). Media discourse at the time repeatedly highlighted how Black single mothers were failing to raise their children properly and how these Black youths were now becoming a dangerous class. Rarely was there acknowledgement of the structural barriers such as inadequate education or employment discrimination that shape and limit the possibilities of parenting in Black families. Even less talked about are the ways in which criminal justice practices, such as over-policing and racial profiling, destabilize Black families, which is seen most clearly in the high rates of incarceration for Black males and the high rates of Black, single-female parented families (Lawson 2012: 815–16) As a result, even as crime rates decline in the twenty-first century, the disproportionate representation of people of colour throughout Canada's justice system remains. Racialized patterns of crime and punishment are taking place in a context where public discourse about crime excludes and/or dismisses the problems of race and racism and, therefore, excludes any need to acknowledge or address issues of racial discrimination in the justice system. Yet, racism continues to shape the social and economic outcomes for many people, and while many social institutions may eschew racialized language in their polices, practices and discourse, the prevalence of racism's institutional entrenchment — most evident in the criminal justice system — is clear.

There is a deep reluctance in the justice system and, arguably, in Canadian society to address issues of racial discrimination and engage in meaningful discussions about the treatment of racialized Canadians. Even as criminal justice practices are now extending into other social institutions such as immigration and welfare services as a way to manage potential threats and security issues, and even though the co-optation of criminal justice policies and practices has a disproportionate effect on racialized communities, there is a "socially recurrent blindness to racism" present (Hesse 2011). Racism is no longer seen as a social problem, and discussions about race in the public sphere are taboo. As a result, practices of race privilege, racial discrimination and racial profiling are now denied public representation. There is a tendency to avoid any acknowledgement of racialization and state-racial arrangements, yet, under the threat of terror or crime, the state simultaneously enforces racial oppression through increased surveillance and policing. As the examples throughout this chapter highlight, there are many state policies and practices that disproportionately disadvantage racial groups but have been legitimated as necessary in order to protect Canadians. The discourse of risk and safety allows the state to police racialized people and communities, overriding equality laws. Thus commitments to address racial inequalities and to uphold the values of equality, due process and justice dissolve.

DISCUSSION QUESTIONS

1. In your opinion, should the government be collecting statistics on race and crime? Will it make a difference for racialized communities?

2. What criteria should be used to construct definitions of crime? Should definitions of crime focus on the behaviours of individuals or the identity of individuals?

2. Do you think it is possible for the police and other law enforcement agents to not racially profile?

4. How can we make the problem of racism more visible in Canada?

GLOSSARY

Criminalization: the social process of making something, such as people or behaviours, illegal.

Race Privilege: having access to advantages and opportunities because of one's membership in a particular racial group.

Racial Discrimination: an action or decision that treats a person or group negatively based on their race, culture or ethnicity.

Racial Profiling: any action that targets a sub-group of people for law enforcement based on racial stereotypes about race, culture or ethnicity.

Racial Stereotyping: simplistic and negative generalizations about a person or group based on their race, culture or ethnicity.

Racialization: the social process in which racial meanings are formed and re-formed in the creation of a racialized position. Racialization involves the act of racializing, which is the attribution of racial terms to social relations.

Racism: inequality of treatment based on assumptions, beliefs or behaviours about a person's race, culture or ethnicity.

SUGGESTED READINGS

C.J. Mosher, *Discrimination and Denial: Systemic Racism in Ontario's Legal and Criminal Justice Systems, 1892–1961*, Toronto, ON: University of Toronto Press (1998).

J. Covington, "Racial Classification in Criminology: The Reproduction of Racialized Crime," *Sociological Forum* 10, 4: 547–668 (1995).

F. Henry and C. Tator, *Racial Profiling in Canada*, Toronto: University of Toronto Press (2006).

W. Chan and D. Chunn, *Racialization, Crime and Criminal Justice in Canada*, Toronto: University of Toronto Press (2014).

L. Wacquant, *Punishing the Poor: The Neoliberal Government of Social Insecurity*, Durham: Duke University Press (2009).

SUGGESTED WEBSITES

Canadian Race Relations Foundation <http://www.crr.ca/>

African Canadian Legal Clinic <http://www.aclc.net/>

Race Matters (*Toronto Star*) <http://www.thestar.com/news/gta/raceandcrime.html>

Stop Racism and Hate Collective <http://www.stopracism.ca/content/canadian-anti-racism-education-and-research-society-caers>

National Anti-Racism Council of Canada <http://www.narcc.ca/index.html>

REFERENCES

Aas, F. 2007. *Globalization and Crime*. London: Sage Publications.

Abramovitz, M. 2006. "Welfare Reform in the United States: Gender, Race and Class Matter." *Critical Social Policy* 26, 2: 336–64.

Adelman, M., E. Erez and N. Shalhoub-Kevorkian. 2003. "Policing Violence Against Minority Women in Multicultural Societies: 'Community' and the Politics of Exclusion." *Police and Society* 7: 105–33.

Alboim, N., and K. Cohl. 2012. *Shaping the Future: Canada's Rapidly Changing Immigration Poli-*

cies. Toronto: Maytree Foundation.

Amnesty International. 2009. *No More Stolen Sisters.* London: Amnesty International Publications.

Anand, S. 2000. "The Sentencing of Aboriginal Offenders, Continued Confusion and Persisting Problems: A Comment on the Decision in *R. v. Gladue.*" *Canadian Journal of Criminology* 42: 412–20.

Bahdi, R. 2003. "No Exit: Racial Profiling and Canada's War Against Terrorism." *Osgoode Hall Law Journal* 41, 2&3: 293–317.

Bannerji, H. 1997 "Geography Lessons: On Being an Inside/Outsider to the Canadian Nation." In L. Roman and L. Eyre (eds.), *Dangerous Territories: Struggles for Differences and Equality.* New York: Routledge.

Bosworth, M. 2011. "Deportation, Detention and Foreign-National Prisoners in England and Wales." *Citizenship Studies* 15, 5: 583–95.

Bradimore, A., and H. Bauder. 2011. *Mystery Ships and Risky Boat People: Tamil Refugee Migration in the Newsprint Media.* Metropolis BC, Working Paper Series 11-02.

Brown, J. 2008. "Ottawa Refuses to Help Canadian in Sudan: Lawyer." *Toronto Star*, April 28.

Brown, M. 2004. *In Their Own Voices: African Canadians in the Greater Toronto Area Share Their Experiences of Police Profiling.* Toronto: African Canadian Community Coalition on Racial Profiling.

Brown, M.K., M. Carnoy, E. Currie, T. Duster, D. Oppenheimer, M. Schultz and D. Wellman. 2005. *White-Washing Race: The Myth of a Color-Blind Society.* Berkeley: University of California Press.

Canadian Press. 2012. "Canada's Tough-on-Crime Agenda 'Excessively Punitive.'" *Canadian Press*, October 9.

Cao, L. 2011. "Visible Minorities and Confidence in the Police." *Canadian Journal of Criminology & Criminal Justice* 53, 1: 1–26.

Cheema, M. 2009. "Missing Subjects: Aboriginal Deaths in Custody, Data Problems, and Racialized Policing." *Appeal* 14: 84–100.

Comack, E. 2012. *Racialized Policing: Aboriginal People's Encounters with the Police.* Black Point, NS: Fernwood Publishing.

Commission on Systemic Racism in the Ontario Criminal Justice System. 1995. *Final Report.* Toronto: Queens Printer.

Correctional Investigator of Canada. 2013. *Annual Report of the Office of the Correctional Investigator 2012–2013.* Ottawa: The Correctional Investigator of Canada.

Covington, J. 1995. "Racial Classification in Criminology: The Reproduction of Racialized Crime." *Sociological Forum* 10, 4: 547–68.

D'Arcy, S. 2007. "The 'Jamaican Criminal' in Toronto, 1994: A Critical Ontology." *Canadian Journal of Communications* 32: 241–259.

Davies, W.H. 2011. *Inquiry into the Death of Frank Paul. Final Report: Alone and Cold.* Victoria, BC: Ministry of the Attorney General, Criminal Justice Branch.

Davis, A. 1998. "Race and Criminalization: Black Americans and the Punishment Industry." In W. Lubiano (ed.), *The House That Race Built.* New York: Vintage Books.

Davis, D. 2007. "Narrating the Mute: Racializing and Racism in a Neoliberal Moment." *Souls* 9, 4: 346–60.

Decoste, R. 2013a. "Don't Ask, Don't Tell: Canada's Approach to Racism." *Huffington Post*, November 18.

___. 2013b. "When You Commit a Crime, Your Race Matters." *Huffington Post*, May 27.

Dhamoon, R., and Y. Abu-Laban. 2009. "Dangerous (Internal) Foreigners and Nation-Building: The Case of Canada." *International Political Science Review* 30, 2: 163–83.

Douglas, P., and L. Rosella. 2013. "Racism Is Prevalent, Persisting and Perpetually Growing, Experts Warn." *Mississauga.com*, November 25.

Dua, E., N. Razack and J. Warner. 2005. "Race, Racism, and Empire: Reflections on Canada." Social Justice 32, 4: 1–10.

Dylan, A., C. Regehr and R. Alaggia. 2008. "And Justice for All? Aboriginal Victims of Sexual Violence." *Violence Against Women* 14: 678–96.

Entman, R., and K. Gross. 2008. "Race to Judgment: Stereotyping Media and Criminal Defendants." *Law and Contemporary Problems* 71: 93–133.

Fraser, N., and L. Gordon. 1994. "A Genealogy of 'Dependency': Tracing a Keyword of the U.S. Welfare State." *Signs* 19, 2: 309–36.

Gabor, T. 1994. "The Suppression of Crime Statistics on Race and Ethnicity: The Price of Political Correctness." *Canadian Journal of Criminology* 36: 153–63.

Garland, D. 2000. "The Culture of High Crime Societies." *British Journal of Criminology* 40: 347–75.

Godfrey, T. 2012. "Proposed Deportation Law Under Fire." *Toronto Sun*, October 1.

Gordon, R., and J. Nelson. 1996. "Crime, Ethnicity and Immigration." In R. Silverman, J. Teevan and V. Sacco (eds.), *Crime in Canadian Society*, fifth edition. Toronto: Harcourt Brace.

Gordon, T. 2006. "Neoliberalism, Racism and the War on Drugs in Canada." *Social Justice* 33, 1: 59–78.

Hawkins, D. 1995. *Ethnicity, Race and Crime*. Albany: State University of New York Press.

Hermer, J., and J. Mosher. 2002. *Disorderly People: Law and the Politics of Exclusion in Ontario*. Halifax: Fernwood Publishing.

Hesse, B. 2011. "Self-Fulfilling Prophecy: The Postracial Horizon." *The South Atlantic Quarterly* 110, 1: 155–78.

Hickman, T.A. 1989. *Royal Commission on the Donald Marshall, Jr., Prosecution: Digest of Findings and Recommendations*. Halifax, N.S.

Huffington Post. 2012. "Canada: A Nation of Foreign Terrorists According to Bill C-43." October 23. At <http://www.huffingtonpost.ca/irwin-cotler/billc-43_b_2005209.html> accessed November 5, 2012.

Jiwani, Y., and M.L. Young. 2006. "Missing and Murdered Women: Reproducing Marginality in News Discourse." *Canadian Journal of Communication* 31, 4: 895–917.

Johnston, J.P. 1994. "Academic Approaches to Race-Crime Statistics Do Not Justify Their Collection." *Canadian Journal of Criminology* 36: 166–74.

Kanstroom, D. 2005. "Immigration Law as Social Control." In C. Mele and T. Miller (eds.), *Civil Penalties, Social Consequences*. New York: Routledge.

King, J. 1981. *The Biology of Race*. Berkeley: University of California Press.

Koring, P. 2011. "Canadian Abousfian Abdelrazik Taken off United Nations Terror List." *Globe and Mail*, November 30. At <http://www.theglobeandmail.com/news/world/canadian-abousfian-abdelrazik-taken-off-united-nations-terror-list/article4179856/> accessed November 13, 2012.

Larsen, S. 2006. *Media & Minorities: The Politics of Race in News and Entertainment*. Lanham, MD: Rowman and Littlefield.

Lawson, E. 2012. "Single Mothers, Absentee Fathers, and Fun Violence in Toronto: A Contextual Interpretation." *Women's Studies* 41: 805–28.

Levine-Rasky, C. 2012. "Who Are You Calling Bogus? Saying No to Roma Refugees." *Canadian Dimension*, September 25. At <http://canadiandimension.com/articles/4959/> accessed November 11, 2012.

Mann, C. 1993. *Unequal Justice: A Question of Color*. Bloomington: Indiana University Press.

Mason, D. 2000. *Race and Ethnicity in Modern Britain*. Oxford: Oxford University Press.

Melossi, D. 2003. "'In a Peaceful Life': Migration and the Crime of Modernity in Europe/Italy." *Punishment and Society* 5, 4: 371–97.

Miller, J. 1996. *Search and Destroy: African-American Males in the Criminal Justice System*. Cambridge: Cambridge University Press.

Monaghan, J. 2013. "Settler Governmentality and Racializing Surveillance in Canada's North-West." *Canadian Journal of Sociology* 38, 4: 487–508.

Mosher, C. 1996. "Minorities and Misdemeanours: The Treatment of Black Public Order Offenders in Ontario's Criminal Justice System, 1892–1930." *Canadian Journal of Criminology* 38: 413–38.

Nelson, J. 2011. "'Partners or Thieves': Racialized Knowledge and the Regulation of Africville." *Journal of Canadian Studies* 45, 1: 121–42.

O'Connell, A. 2010. "An Exploration of Redneck Whiteness in Multicultural Canada." *Social*

Politics 17, 4: 536–63.

Omi, M., and H. Winant. 1994. *Racial Formation in the United States From the 1960s to the 1990s*. Second edition. New York: Routledge.

Oriola, T., and C. Adeyanju. 2011. "Perceptions of the Canadian Criminal Justice System Among Nigerians: Evidence from a local Church in Winnipeg, Manitoba." *International Journal of Human Sciences* 8, 1: 635: 56.

Owusu-Bempah, A., and P. Millar. 2010. "Revisiting the Collection of Justice Statistics by Race in Canada." *Canadian Journal of Law and Society* 24, 1: 97–104.

___. 2011. "Whitewashing Criminal Justice in Canada: Preventing Research through Data Supression." *Canadian Journal of Law and Society* 26, 3: 653–61.

Phillips, C., and B. Bowling. 2003. "Racism, Ethnicity and Criminology: Developing Minority Perspectives." *British Journal of Criminology* 43: 269–90.

Randall, M. 2010. "Sexual Assault Law, Credibility, and 'Ideal Victims': Consent, Resistance, And Victim Blaming." *Canadian Journal of Women and the Law* 22: 397–433.

Rankin, J., and P. Winsa. 2013. "Toronto Police Propose Purging Carding Information from Database." *Toronto Star*, October 4.

Razack, S. 2012. "Memorializing Colonial Power: The Death of Frank Paul." *Law & Social Inquiry* 37, 4: 908–32.

Regehr, C., R. Alaggia, L. Lambert and M. Saini. 2008. "Victims of Sexual Violence in the Canadian Criminal Courts." *Victims & Offenders* 3, 1: 99–113.

Roach, K. 1996. "Systemic Racism and Criminal Justice Policy." *Windsor Yearbook of Access to Justice* 15: 236–49.

Roberts, J. 1994. "Crime and Race Statistics: Toward a Canadian Solution." *Canadian Journal of Criminology* 36: 175–85.

Roberts, J., and A. Doob. 1997. "Race, Ethnicity and Criminal Justice in Canada." *Crime and Justice* 21: 469–522.

Satzewich, V., and W. Shaffir. 2009. "Racism versus Professionalism: Claims and Counter-Claims about Racial Profiling." *Canadian Journal of Criminal and Criminal Justice* 51, 2: 199–226.

Satzewich, V. 2000. "Whiteness Limited: Racialization and the Social Construction of 'Peripheral Europeans." *Social History* 66: 271–90.

Schreiber, M. 2013. "Editorial: Harper Government's Tough-On-Crime Laws Are Outdated." *Toronto Star*, August 19.

Silverstein, M. 2005. "What's Race Got to Do with Justice: Responsibilization Strategies at Parole Hearings." *British Journal of Criminology* 45: 340–54.

Simon, J. 2007. *Governing Through Crime*. New York: Oxford University Press.

Smith, C. 2006. "Racial Profiling in Canada, the United States, and the United Kingdom." In F. Henry and C. Tator (eds.), *Racial Profiling in Canada*. Toronto: University of Toronto Press.

Tanovich, D. 2008. "The Charter of Whiteness: Twenty-Five Years of Maintaining Racial Injustice in the Canadian Criminal Justice System." *Supreme Court Law Review* 40: 655–86.

Trevethan, S., and C. Rastin. 2004. *A Profile of Visible Minority Offenders in the Federal Canadian Correctional System*. Ottawa: Correctional Service of Canada.

Wacquant, L. 2001. "Deadly Symbiosis: When Ghetto and Prison Meet and Mesh." *Punishment and Society* 3, 1: 95–134.

___. 2009. *Punishing the Poor: The Neoliberal Government of Social Insecurity*. Durham: Duke University Press.

Waldman, L. 2013. "Faster Deportations Come at the Cost of Compassion and Fairness." *Globe and Mail*, May 14.

Walsh, A., and I. Yun. 2011. "Race and Criminology in the Age of Genomic Science." *Social Science Quarterly* 92, 5: 1279–96.

Wood, D., and C. Griffths. 1996. "Patterns of Aboriginal Crime." In R. Silverman, J. Teevan and V. Sacco (eds.), *Crime in Canadian Society*, fifth edition. Toronto: Harcourt Brace.

Wortley, S. 1999. "A Northern Taboo: Research on Race, Crime and Criminal Justice in Canada." *Canadian Journal of Criminology* 41: 261–74.

___. 2006. *Police Use of Force in Ontario: An Examination of Data from the Special Investigations Unit. Final Report.* Toronto, ON.

Wortley, S., and A. Owusu-Bempah. 2009. "Unequal Before the Law: Immigrant and Racial Minority Perceptions of the Canadian Criminal Justice System." *Journal of International Migration and Integration* 10, 4: 447–73.

12

TERRORISM AS CRIME OR WAR?

Robert Diab

KEY FACTS

> From 2000 onward, Canada imprisoned five men for between two and ten years without charge on secret evidence; three of whom continue to be subject to terms of release that are among the most restrictive ever imposed by a Canadian court, including twenty-four-hour surveillance.

> In 2002, Canada's Supreme Court held that the government could deport a person facing a risk of torture in their country of origin without violating that person's right to "life, liberty, and security of the person" under the Canadian Charter of Rights and Freedoms.

> Since 2009, President Obama has ordered 353 drone strikes against terror suspects in Pakistan alone, killing between 400 and 900 civilians, including at least 168 children. He has also order hundreds of other strikes elsewhere in Asia and the Arabian Peninsula.

> The U.S. continues to imprison 140 detainees at Guantanamo, all but 6 of whom are held without charge; Obama has expressed the intention to detain 46 of them indefinitely.

> As recently as 2012, 65 percent of Americans surveyed believe it is likely that "another 9/11 will take place in America in the next 10 years"; 58 percent of Canadians surveyed in 2011 were "more concerned about a terrorist attack in Canada now than before 9/11."

Sources: Chung 2011; Rasmussen 2012; Bureau of Investigative Journalism 2013, 2014; Pilkington 2013; Human Rights Watch 2013.

In the period before the events of September 11, 2001, terrorism was not a distinct crime in most domestic North American law. It was a possible motive for crimes such as hostage taking, setting off a bomb or murder. In the wake of 9/11, Canada, the United States and other governments began to question the relationship between terrorism and crime, acknowledging that terrorism was a form of crime but doubting that it could be effectively addressed within the conventional limits of the criminal law. As a consequence, two approaches became prevalent. One was to add new terrorism offences to the criminal law, offences that were understood as exceptionally serious, calling for greater prosecutorial powers. The other approach has been to treat terrorism as a threat to public safety closer in nature to war than to crime.

By conceiving of terrorism as a kind of super-crime or as a threat tantamount to war, both Canada and the U.S. have come to entrench in law a number of extraordinary measures. These include indefinite detention without charge, mass surveillance, vastly expanded state secrecy and, in the United States, the targeted killing of U.S. citizens. Many of these measures are designed to circumvent the protections of the criminal law, and many have resulted in serious human rights violations that have had a disproportionate effect on racialized minorities. In ways to be explored in this chapter, members of Arab or Muslim communities have been subject to racial profiling, secret surveillance, lengthy detention without charge, wrongful arrest and torture. Yet, in many cases, government conduct has been shielded from transparency and accountability due to assertions of national security privilege or confidentiality. And many of the measures are still in use.

The political rationale and public support for these measures is premised in part on beliefs about the greater threat that terrorism has come to pose since 9/11. This chapter will explore the process by which these beliefs have been socially constructed and sustained in post-9/11 political and media discourse. It will also explore how these beliefs have shaped law and policy, often with serious consequences for the human rights of minority populations. Then, applying a form of critical criminology, the chapter will conclude with an examination of whether such beliefs can be sustained in light of skeptical evidence and opinion on the evolving nature of terrorism.

PERCEPTIONS OF TERRORISM AFTER 9/11

September 11 transformed our perceptions of terrorism due in part to the magnitude of the event in relation to the history of terrorism. Before 9/11, by many accounts, the largest terror attack in modern history in terms of casualties was the bombing of Air India flight 182 from Vancouver to Bombay in 1985, which claimed 329 lives (Mueller and Stewart 2011: 886; Global Terrorism Database: 2007, cited in Mueller and Stewart 2011: 884). With few exceptions, major terror attacks of the late twentieth century entailed far fewer casualties. By contrast, the attacks of September 11 claimed 2,997 lives (Global Terrorism Database). The attacks involved the hijacking of four large passenger aircraft by nineteen members of the Islamic extremist group al Qaeda. The group had acted at the direction of Osama bin Laden, a Saudi Arabian who had a history of plotting attacks on the U.S. throughout the 1990s. On the morning of September 11, two of the four hijacked planes were flown into the Twin Towers moments apart from one another, and each building collapsed roughly an hour later from the impact of the burning airplane fuel. The third plane was flown into the Pentagon moments after the second of the Twin Towers was hit, and the fourth plane crashed in a Pennsylvania field as passengers struggled to regain control of the cockpit (9/11 Commission 2004: Chapter 1).

One response to the events of 9/11 might have been to conclude that they were extremely anomalous and that an attack on that scale or greater in the near future was highly unlikely to occur. But the event had also altered perceptions of the danger that terrorists were capable of posing. Partly on the basis of this, for many figures in government and security, and for large portions of the population of Canada and the United States, 9/11 came to be seen as the harbinger of a new order of terror, with further attacks on the scale of 9/11 or greater likely to occur in the near future (Mueller 2002; Diab 2015).

The harbinger theory became central to both U.S. and Canadian counter-terror policy. Following 9/11, President Bush and other members of his administration began to invoke the prospect of large-scale terror, or terrorism involving weapons of mass destruction (WMD), in defence of a host of measures, including new terrorism offences in the USA PATRIOT Act (or the *Uniting and Strengthening America by Providing Appropriate Tools Required to Intercept and Obstruct Terrorism Act*) and indefinite detention without charge at Guantanamo (see, for example, Bush's State of the Union address, January 2002; Bush 2002a). Throughout his term in office, the President and other key administration officials continued to describe the threat in these terms. A 2006 White House policy paper asserted: "The security environment confronting the United States today is radically different from what we have faced before ... Terrorists, including those associated with the al-Qaeda network, continue to pursue WMD" (White House 2006). President Obama would take a similar approach, invoking the prospect of WMD terror in defence of targeted killing and other extreme measures (White House 2011: 8). Other administration officials have continued to invoke mass terror in relation to a range of security policies. For example, following revelations in June of 2013 of the National Security Agency's mass surveillance program, James Clapper, Director of National Intelligence, stated that the program had "significantly contributed to successful operations to impede the proliferation of weapons of mass destruction" (Clapper 2013: 3).

Canadian officials have made similar claims. Anne McLellan, Minister of Justice, speaking to Parliament in October of 2001 when the Anti-terrorism Act was being debated, sought to justify the need for law that extends the scope of state secrecy, provides authority for mass surveillance and adds new terrorism offences to the *Criminal Code.* Terrorism, she asserted, had come to pose "a special threat to our way of life. When dealing with groups that are willing to commit suicidal acts of mass destruction against innocent civilians, it is necessary to consider whether existing legislative tools are adequate to the challenge" (Canada 2001). Fellow cabinet minister Irwin Cotler was more explicit. Writing in November of 2001, he described 9/11 as a "juridical watershed." From this point forward, new law had to be passed "in the context of the existential threat of this terrorism, including the lethal face of terrorism as in the deliberate mass murder of civilians in public places [and] the potential use of weapons of mass destruction" (Cotler 2001: 114). A host of policy statements and reports over the course of the post-9/11 period, from the Ministry of Public Safety to the Canadian Security and Intelligence Service, have continued to invoke the prospect of large-scale terror, possibly involving WMD (see, for example, CSIS 2009; Canada 2012).

In support of such claims, many experts on WMD have offered similar apocalyptic prognoses. Graham Allison (2005: 15) warned that "a nuclear terrorist attack on America in the decade ahead is more likely than not." Many experts agreed for reasons that include poor security around nuclear sites in the countries of the former Soviet Union, open access to the knowledge of how to build a bomb and the fact that al Qaeda and other groups were known to harbour nuclear ambitions (Barnaby 2004; Ferguson and Potter 2005; Bunn 2010). A similar claim has often been made in relation to bioterrorism. Many of the most lethal toxins known to science can be cultivated from natural sources and readily produced in large quantities using knowledge and techniques available on the Internet and elsewhere in the public domain (Kellman 2007; Davis 2004). Radiological terror seems even more likely, experts argue, given the ready availability of unguarded, highly radioactive material in industrial and institutional sites such as hospitals, universities and factories (Levi and Kelly 2002).

Public opinion surveys throughout the post-9/11 period suggest that large portions of the North American public believe that a large-scale terror attack is likely in the near future. A 2006 Gallup poll asked Americans whether they believed it was "likely that terrorists will set off a bomb that contains nuclear or biological material in the U.S.

within the next five years?" Forty-seven percent of those surveyed believed that it was. A survey that same year of "100 of America's top foreign policy experts" by the journal *Foreign Policy* found that "more than 8 in 10 expect an attack on the scale of 9/11 within a decade" (July/Aug 2006). The level of fear has remained high. In 2012, when asked "How likely is it that another 9/11 will take place in America in the next 10 years?" 65 percent of Americans surveyed believed that it was likely, with 29 percent expressing a belief that it was "very likely" (Rasmussen 2012). Data on Canadian opinion is less specific about the nature of our beliefs, but suggests that a substantial number of Canadians fear terrorism. An Ipsos Reid survey of 2011 found that 58 percent of Canadians affirmed that "they are more concerned about a terrorist attack in Canada now than before 9/11" (Postmedia News 2011). A full 77 percent of respondents disagreed that "Canada and the U.S. can relax security measures now that there hasn't been an attack in 10 years."

North Americans also continue to support security policy in large numbers. In 2013, a poll by Quinnipiac University researchers asked Americans whether anti-terror policies "have gone too far in restricting the average person's civil liberties" or "have not gone far enough to adequately protect the country" (Quinnipiac 2013). Thirty-nine percent of those surveyed said "not far enough." An Ipsos poll conducted in July of 2013, in the wake of NSA mass surveillance revelations by whistleblower Edward Snowden, found that 64 percent of Canadians surveyed found it "acceptable in some circumstances" for "governments to monitor everyone's email and other online activities" in order to prevent further attacks (Ipsos 2013). Similarly, an Abacus Data poll that summer found that 62 percent of Canadians surveyed supported an intrusion on personal privacy to enable the federal government to investigate possible terrorist threats (Abacus 2013).

These opinions are both reflected in and shaped by the frequent depictions of large-scale terror plots that have been featured in popular media since 2001. Such plots have been central to television series such as "24" and "Homeland," films including *The Sum of All Fears*, *Antibody* and *Blast!*, and books such as Tom Clancy's *Splinter Cell*, Dan Brown's *Deception Point* and James Patterson's *London Bridges* (Lustic 2006: 25). Notably, each of the nine seasons of "24," except the first, which aired in September of 2001, featured terror plots that involved WMD. Also, in each of these seasons, as in other shows, films and books, the threat was seen to be effectively resolved through the use of torture or cruel and inhumane treatment. Such measures were often depicted, therefore, as effective and proportionate responses to terror.

These pervasive depictions of terrorism in extreme and catastrophic terms have helped to ground an argument about the need to embrace a more pre-emptive approach to security. Prominent advocates of this view have included such figures as Harvard Law professor Alan Dershowitz, John Yoo, who was a member of President Bush's Office of Legal Counsel, and Federal Court of Appeal judge Richard Posner. They argue that given the much greater threat that terrorism has come to pose, it can no longer be understood exclusively or primarily as a form of crime. Put otherwise, the damage that individuals are now capable of posing to society is so much greater that, in their view, basic assumptions of criminal law are no longer valid. Until recently, it might have been reasonable for liberal societies to insist that a criminal conviction rest on proof beyond a reasonable doubt and to allow ten guilty men or women to go free to avoid sending one innocent person to prison on the assumption that the danger those ten guilty men or women posed to society was relatively limited. But the calculus changes with the prospect of an act of nuclear or biological terror (Posner 2007: 175; Yoo 2006: 9; Dershowitz 2006: 8). From this perspective, it may be necessary to detain several innocent people without charge for a period, or to surveil a wide portion of the population, or even to carry out the targeted killing of terror suspects, rather than acquitting one nuclear terrorist.

This pre-emptive logic can be seen as forming the basis for a series of laws and policies aimed at extending the limits of the criminal law or circumventing them altogether.

TERRORISM AS WAR IN U.S. LAW

Roughly six weeks after 9/11, the U.S. Congress passed the USA PATRIOT Act. Although the Act has come to symbolize America's legal response to 9/11 and signifies various infringements of civil liberties, it did not alter criminal law protections significantly (Roach 2011: 181). Unlike comparable laws in Canada, Australia or the U.K., the Act did not introduce new terrorism offences. Nor did it curb procedural protections, such as the need for Miranda warnings for terror suspects (or warnings given upon arrest that a suspect has the right to remain silent and anything they say may be used against them in a court of law), or the right, once charged with an offence, to full disclosure of the evidence against them. It did not introduce preventive detention provisions, and it did not criminalize membership in a terrorist group. It did, however, significantly expand the scope of warrants for the search and seizure of records in terrorism investigations, including data relating to phone and Internet communications.

The U.S. Government sought instead to circumvent rather than transform the criminal law by framing its response to the events of 9/11 as a form of war, perpetrated by a foreign enemy. The primary legal instrument by which it did so was a joint resolution of Congress passed on September 14, 2001, entitled the *Authorization to Use Military Force* (AUMF). The AUMF functions as a formal declaration of war on al Qaeda. "The President," it declares, "is authorized to use *all necessary and appropriate force* against those nations, organizations, or persons he determines planned, authorized, committed or aided the terrorist attacks that occurred on September 11, 2001" (emphasis added). Offering a rationale for this, the preamble states: "On September 11, 2001, acts of treacherous violence were committed against the United States ... and such acts continue to pose an unusual and extraordinary threat to the national security and foreign policy of the United States." The threat was therefore unprecedented and on-going, giving rise to a war with no end in sight. The AUMF thus contains no time limit and is still in force over a dozen years later.

President Bush would explicitly rely upon the AUMF for the authority to detain some 800 alleged terror suspects in Pakistan and Afghanistan in late 2001 and early 2002 and to imprison them without charge at Guantanamo Bay, a U.S. Military base on the coast of Cuba. In early 2002, he issued an executive order declaring those held at Guantanamo to be "enemy combatants" and thus prisoners of war, but not prisoners entitled to the protections of the Geneva Conventions given that al Qaeda was not a signatory (Bush 2002b). Nor, in the President's view, were the combatants entitled to the protections of the U.S. Constitution, since they were not being held on American soil. The detainees thus occupied a legal black hole and could be held without review for as long as the war lasted. Contrary to the Geneva Conventions, the President also authorized "enhanced" interrogations involving waterboarding, noise and stress positions, or generally subjecting detainees, as one legal memo put it, to forms of pain short of "organ failure ... or even death" (Human Rights Watch 2011: 4; Gonzales 2002).

In addition to Guantanamo, Bush relied upon the AUMF for the practice of targeted killing. Targeted suspects were persons deemed to pose an imminent and serious threat to the United States but whose capture was not feasible without incurring undue risks to civilians or U.S. agents. The criteria by which targets were selected and strikes authorized were entirely secret and subject to no external oversight. Administration officials argued that the practice was lawful under the AUMF on the basis that these were enemy combatants on the field of battle, not suspects of an alleged crime (Kaplan 2006).

The war model also shaped counter-terror policy within the United States. In the fall of 2001, acting pursuant to the AUMF, Bush issued a secret order allowing the National Security Agency to intercept phone calls and emails of foreign terror suspects, including cases where one party was an American citizen in the U.S. (Roach 2011: 184). By the time the program was uncovered in the press in 2005, thousands of Americans had been surveilled without cause or warrant.

In October of 2001, Attorney General John Ashcroft announced a "zero tolerance" policy toward Muslim and Arab non-citizens violating immigration laws. The administration created a "Special Registration Program" under which 80,000 persons from mostly Arab and Muslim countries were required to register (Cole and Lobel 2009: 107). Eight thousand young Arab and Muslim men were interviewed by the FBI, and a further 5,000 were detained for immigration law infractions in the two years following 9/11. Yet, as Cole and Lobel note (107), "Not one stands convicted of a terrorist crime today ... the government's record is 0 for 93,000." Immigration laws could not, however, be used for the preventive detention of U.S. citizens. For this purpose, the government resorted to using material witness warrants to have terror suspects detained without charge pending testimony before a grand jury (Roach 2011: 188). The detention of U.S. citizen Osama Awadallah lasted eighty-three days, during which he was kept in "solitary confinement, shackled, strip searched, and interrogated at length" (ibid). As Kent Roach notes (2011: 189), this process was used in at least seventy cases, with one-third of them involving detentions of at least two months.

Both the courts and Congress were often supportive of the government's approach to terrorism as war. From roughly 2004 to 2008, a series of high-profile decisions in the U.S. Supreme Court (*Hamdi et al.* (2004), *Rasul* (2004), *Hamdan* (2006), and *Boumedienne* (2008)) assessed the rights of detainees at Guantanamo. The Court held that detainees did have standing under the U.S. Constitution and could challenge the validity of their detention under *habeas corpus*, which is a right under the U.S. Constitution that allows any imprisoned person to challenge the grounds of their detention in a court of law where they are not detained following a trial and a jail sentence. But the hearings could be held in military tribunals, rather than ordinary open courts, and in closed hearings that may involve secret evidence not disclosed to the detainee. The tribunal could also order that the person be detained indefinitely on reasonable suspicion that the detention is necessary for public safety, rather than the standard of "reasonable grounds to believe" this is necessary, as is common in criminal cases where a person's detention is sought pending trial. Finally, a detainee's appeal rights in U.S. courts could also be limited by restricting the scope of their appeal to one set of courts in Washington on a limited set of grounds of appeal. During this period, Congress also amended the *Foreign Intelligence Surveillance Act* to authorize many of the powers that Bush had exercised in the earlier secret NSA program. Under section 702 of the *FISA Amendment Act* of 2008, warrants are now issued in secret hearings before the Foreign Surveillance Intelligence Court, and these warrants allow for mass surveillance of all internet traffic — not only metadata, but also the content of messages — from any sites or providers in which investigators believe foreigners of interest may traffic (Kaufman 2013).

Despite early indications that he would take a different approach, President Obama's policies have been largely consistent with those of his predecessors. While he seeks to close Guantanamo, Obama has also expressed the intent to detain indefinitely forty-six of the remaining 140 prisoners without charge (Pilkington 2013). He has also significantly increased the use of drone strikes, ordering some 353 attacks in Pakistan alone, in contrast to roughly eighty under President Bush, with civilian casualties estimated between roughly 400 and 900, including as many as 200 children (Bureau of Investigative Journalism 2013, 2014; Singh 2013). Yet Obama has gone further in asserting the power to carry out drones strikes against American citizens without charge. The President insists that such killings are consistent with the Constitution's guarantee of due process; these killings deprive a citizen not of due process but of judicial process. In 2012, the President authorized a drone strike killing an American born New Mexican cleric, Anwar al-Awlaki, who apparently conspired with others to bomb two passenger planes bound for the U.S. (Kasinof et al., 2011). The attack also killed a second American, Samir Khan, a blogger and propagandist for violent jihad, followed weeks later by a drone strike that killed Awlaki's 16-year-old son while apparently targeting another suspect. In early 2013, a debate arose in Congress as to whether the President has the authority to carry out targeted killings of American citizens *in* the United States without being charged or convicted of an offence. Attorney General Eric Holder expressed the view that he did and that the President might need to use this power in another attack on the order of 9/11, possibly to shoot down a hijacked plane about to be used to strike a civilian target (Savage 2013).

In May of 2013, the President gave a speech on national security policy that signaled the possible end of the war on terror (Obama 2013). It marked the first occasion on which a U.S. president, since 2001, had explicitly abandoned the position that terrorism continues to pose the threat of an attack on the order 9/11 or greater. Instead, Obama suggested, the threat has now become more diffuse and smaller in scale. The core al Qaeda group has largely been defeated, leaving only a series of disparate groups with more local, less ambitious goals. The focus of security efforts has shifted to homegrown terror, which poses a more limited threat than that posed by the 9/11 attackers. On this basis, Obama proposed that the time has come to consider "revising or revoking" the AUMF, revisiting the goal of closing Guantanamo, subjecting decisions about targeted killing to greater oversight and accountability and beginning a serious debate about the use of mass surveillance.

Obama's attempt to foresee an end to the war on terror was laudable. But his vision contemplated the continuing use of a series of war-like measures. The AUMF might only be revised rather than revoked; Guantanamo might be closed, but many prisoners would still be detained indefinitely; targeted killing might be subject to some form of oversight, but would continue; and mass surveillance would likely remain in some form. Moreover, while Obama may have begun to describe the threat of terror in more moderate terms, he would soon retreat from this position.

The President and members of his administration continued to invoke the prospect of large-scale terror in response to developments involving Edward Snowden, a 29-year-old contractor who had worked with the National Security Agency (NSA). Snowden had revealed in June of 2013 that the NSA had for several years been carrying out mass secret surveillance of cell-phone metadata (time, location and duration of calls) of all Americans and of the content of Internet communications involving large numbers of foreigners visiting U.S. websites (Greenwald 2014: 92–118). As noted above, in a press release issued within days of the first Snowden revelations, Director of National Intelligence, James Clapper, claimed that the surveillance programs had helped to "impede the proliferation of weapons of mass destruction" (Clapper 2013: 3). In a speech of January 2014 in which President Obama set out his intention to continue employing many of the surveillance programs at issue, Obama made several references to the possibility of large-scale terror. This included the claim that "the men and women at the NSA know if another 9/11 or massive cyberattack occurs, they will be asked by Congress and the media why they failed to connect the dots" (Obama 2014).

CANADA'S RESPONSE TO 9/11

Canada's response to 9/11 has been distinct from that of its southern neighbour in many ways. But it has been similar in its effort to exceed the conventional limits of the criminal law. One facet of this response was Parliament's passage of the *Anti-terrorism Act* in December of 2001, a bill that gave the government new and unprecedented powers by amending a series of other laws, including the *Criminal Code.*

For criminal prosecutions, the Act defined terrorism, broadly speaking, as a violent or destructive act carried out for the purpose of influencing or intimidating a government or population. Law scholars were critical of its breadth, which captures not only direct harm to persons, but also property damage that endangers the life, safety or health of a person or segment of the population, including such damage caused by protests or strikes that meet these and other parts of the definition of terrorism (Roach 2011: 377). The Act also gave the government the power to deem an individual or group a "terrorist" or "terrorist entity," adding them to a kind of blacklist. Yet the person or group listed need not be given prior notice of the decision and have only a limited right of review. As a consequence of being listed, assets can be confiscated and financial and other dealings with a listed person or group can be criminalized. Thirty-eight groups have been listed and, mistakenly, one individual who had to wait six months for his name to be removed (Roach 2005: 516).

To assist with investigations, the Act also allows for a warrant to be issued to arrest and detain a person not charged with an offence and bring him or her before the court for "judicial interrogation" when there are grounds to believe that person has knowledge relating to a past or future terrorist offence. This entails a new and unprecedented role for judges in Canada. In normal court proceedings, judges play an impartial role. Lawyers question witnesses, and judges watch, listen and assess credibility. They might occasionally ask a witness a question directly, for clarification, but they do not interrogate witnesses so as to advance one party's position. By contrast, under the Act, the judge here would act as an arm of the prosecution, seeking to elicit facts of criminal involvement. Answers given may not be used to incriminate the person, but a court may detain the person if they refuse to cooperate, and the Crown may use information obtained here in the prosecution of another suspect. Further provisions allow for the "preventive detention" of up to three days for persons not yet charged with an offence. In this case, the Crown must establish that there are reasonable grounds to believe that a terrorist act may be carried out and reasonable suspicion to believe the detention is necessary to prevent it. (By contrast, the *Criminal Code* imposes a more onerous test for when a person accused of a crime can be detained before trial; namely, whether, on a balance of probabilities, the person's detention is necessary for public safety, including any evidence that they are substantially likely to reoffend.) Finally, a series of provisions allow for harsher punishments than would otherwise be imposed for a criminal offence where the offence is carried out for the benefit of, or in association with, a terrorist group. The act also allows for life sentences to be imposed for a host of terrorism offences and requires mandatory consecutive sentences for a person convicted of multiple counts of terrorism offences.

The *Anti-terrorism Act* also added new powers that vastly increase the potential scope of state secrecy — powers that could be used in both criminal and other kinds of cases. Before 2001, the *Canada Evidence Act* directed judges to uphold government assertions of privilege only in cases where the court found that the public interest in disclosure outweighed the public interest in non-disclosure. Under the new provisions, persons in possession of information "potentially injurious" to international relations or national security, including journalists, can be ordered not to disclose the information pending a court hearing. The court would then apply the older balancing test to decide whether the information should be disclosed. But if a court orders disclosure in this kind of case, or in any other case where national security privilege is raised, the Act gives the Crown the power to trump the decision of the court by issuing a "secrecy certificate." The certificate can be appealed only to a single judge of the Federal Court of Appeal on the limited ground of whether the decision to issue the certificate was "reasonable." These provisions have the practical effect of providing the Crown with something close to the last word as to whether information will remain secret (Stewart 2003: 255).

Other provisions have been added to Canadian law permitting forms of mass surveillance similar in nature to those allowed in the U.S. under the PATRIOT Act and the *Foreign Intelligence Surveillance Act*. Canada's *National Defence Act* allows the Minister of National Defence to issue a warrant permitting Canada's Communications Security Establishment to intercept private communications, including Internet data and phone metadata, involving foreign entities. But while the Act is intended for the surveillance of foreigners of interest, it permits forms of surveillance broad enough in many possible instances to capture Internet or phone communications of unsuspecting Canadians. Section 21 of the *Canadian Security Intelligence Service Act* permits CSIS to carry out secret surveillance by obtaining a court order, but in this case, so long as the investigation relates to a "threat to the security of Canada," the surveillance may be directed at Canadians. A concern with both Acts is that they authorize secret surveillance in cases where there are no grounds to believe that an individual being targeted has committed a crime (Geist 2013).

Among the most controversial aspects of Canada's counter-terror policy in the post-9/11 period has been the use of what are called "security certificates" under Canada's *Immigration and Refugee Protection Act*. These allow for the arrest and detention of non-citizens without charge, on secret evidence, pending their deportation. The Ministers of Public Safety and Immigration can issue a certificate where there is reason to believe a non-citizen is involved in a terror organization or poses "a danger to Canada." The certificates have existed since the late 1970s and have been used a number of times prior to 9/11. Yet in those cases, detentions were soon followed by deportations. In the post-9/11 period, the certificates were used to detain five Muslim men from between two and ten years without charge, due in part to concerns about them being tortured if they were deported. Upon release, three of the men have continued to be subject to some of the most onerous terms of conditional release known in Canadian law (including twenty-four-hour surveillance and house arrest) for several years.

Canadian courts have sided with lawmakers and a broader public in accepting that many of these measures are reasonable and necessary. They have confirmed the constitutional validity of the expanded scope of state secrecy under the *Canada Evidence Act* and the use of secret evidence in security certificate cases. Perhaps most notoriously, in 2002, Canada's Supreme Court also upheld the constitutionality of the government's discretion to deport a person to face a serious risk of torture, contrary to a host of international treaties and conventions (*Suresh v. Canada* 2002).

Relying on many of the powers surveyed above, Canada and the U.S. have been found to be responsible for, or complicit in, many serious human rights violations, mostly involving members of Arab and Muslim minorities. Yet both nations have tended to resist taking accountability or providing redress to innocent victims for reasons that point back to a larger belief in terrorism as a threat closer in nature to war than to crime.

HUMAN RIGHTS IN THE U.S. WAR ON TERROR

Since 9/11, 160 people are believed to have been the subject of kidnappings and detentions in secret "black sites" under the CIA's "extraordinary rendition" program (Cole and Lobel 2007: 25). Dating to at least the Reagan administration, but used with much greater frequency after 9/11, the CIA's practice of extraordinary rendition involves the secret capture of persons of interest to the CIA in a foreign country or the United States and their illegal transfer to a "black site" in another country (Roach 2011: 167). Black sites are secret prisons where the CIA has detained a suspect for extended periods and carried out interrogation involving torture or cruel treatment, either directly or through the assistance of agents of the host state. Various human rights groups have documented scores of abuses of detainees in U.S. custody since 2001, including torture and other acts of cruelty (Human Rights Watch 2006, 2011; International Committee of the Red Cross 2007; Amnesty International 2012).

In December of 2014, the U.S. Senate released to the public a 525 page summary of what may be the most authoritative and detailed investigation into CIA involvement in torture after 9/11; some six thousand pages remain confidential (U.S. Senate Select Committee on Intelligence 2014). Drawing on extensive documentation including emails, memos and other communications, the report confirms the use of torture or cruel and inhumane techniques of detention and interrogation involving 119 persons from 2001 to 2009 — 22 percent of whom were eventually found to be innocent (Bromwich 2015). As David Bromwich notes, at the time the summary was released, CIA Director John Brennan "offered no challenge to the facts" (Bromwich 2015). As Bromwich writes: "Some of the methods employed were atrocious in ways that are scarcely imaginable. One prisoner was subjected to forced 'rectal feeding.' Another was chained to a wall for 17 days. A third, subjected to sensory and sleep deprivation and chained to a concrete floor, died of hypothermia" (ibid).

Earlier reports suggest that the CIA's use of torture in this period was only a small part of a wider practice of cruelty and inhumanity on the part of U.S. forces. One report by Human Rights Watch (2006: 2) noted that some 600 U.S. personnel have been implicated in abuses of 460 prisoners at Guantanamo and in Iraq and Afghanistan. Yet, a later report, looking back on the progress of these cases, found that "few military personnel had been punished and not a single CIA official held accountable" (Human Rights Watch 2011: 6). In the wake of the Senate's report in late 2014, many have called for the indictment of key officials in the Bush administration and the CIA who exercised oversight or authority over torture, but the Obama Administration has thus far been reluctant to heed these calls.

The U.S. has also failed to provide accountability in some of the most egregious cases of rights violations, including those of Syrian-Canadian Maher Arar and German national Khalid el-Masri. In 2002, passing through JFK Airport in New York on his way back to Canada from a vacation in Tunisia, Arar was detained by U.S. officials who were acting on information the Royal Canadian Mounted Police (RCMP) had provided that tied Arar to a person of interest in Montreal. The RCMP did not consider Arar a suspect, and he was not a target of their investigations. They sought only to interview him about his connection to other persons. There was no indication that he was involved in criminal activity or posed a threat to national security. However, in the process of gathering information about him and later sharing it with U.S. officials, the RCMP had made various errors that would eventually portray him as a greater concern (Arar Inquiry 2006: 9). For example, the RCMP's report to U.S. agents indicated that the brother of Abdullah Almalki, a primary target of investigation, had stated that Arar had a business relationship with his brother. But in fact, the brother had told the RCMP that he "wasn't sure" whether Arar and his brother had a business relationship (ibid: 25). In addition to investigative errors, when passing information about Arar to U.S. officials, the RCMP had also failed to vet the material for relevance or reliability and placed no restrictions or caveats on its potential use, as was commonly done when information was shared in the past (Roach 2011: 374). On the basis of the information the RCMP had provided, U.S. officials held Arar for twelve days, during which time a regional director for U.S. Immigration issued an order declaring Arar to be a member of al Qaeda and required that he be sent not to Canada but to Syria (ibid: 27). There, he was tortured on numerous occasions and detained in a "tiny cell with no natural light" and in what the Arar Inquiry described as "disgusting sanitary conditions" for close to a year (ibid: 45). Arar was eventually released due in part to the efforts of Canadian consular officials and a direct appeal on the part of the Prime Minister to the Syrian President (ibid: 42). But to a significant extent, the momentum for these efforts was due, in turn, to the pressure on Ottawa and the public interest profile that Arar's wife Monia had maintained from the outset of the ordeal.

Another well-documented case of extraordinary rendition involves the abduction in 2003 of a German national, Khalid el-Masri, by Macedonian officials and his transfer to CIA custody. El-Masri was a victim of mistaken identity. Acting on the basis of information provided by U.S. officials, he was detained upon entry to Macedonia in the course of a brief vacation. He was held for some twenty days in a hotel room where he was continuously questioned about his involvement with al Qaeda and then flown to a black site in Afghanistan where he was beaten, tortured repeatedly and kept in a "small, dirty, dark concrete cell" with nothing but a blanket (*El-Masri v. Macedonia* 2012). Four months into his ordeal, the CIA conceded el-Masri's mistaken identity and decided to return him to Europe covertly (Cole and Lobel 2007: 23–26). He was given the clothing and luggage he was carrying upon his initial detention and then blindfolded, handcuffed and chained to the floor of a plane and flown to a secret location in Eastern Europe. Upon arrival, he was driven for several hours blindfolded and left in a field in Albania. Albanian officials flew him to Germany, where, upon his return, he weighted some eighteen kilograms less than when he left.

Arar, el-Masri and a host of other victims of American involvement in torture or rendition have attempted to sue the U.S. government in U.S. courts. The actions have consistently failed largely on the basis of the operation of the "state secrets" doctrine in U.S. common law. The doctrine precludes a lawsuit from being brought "where the very subject matter of the action … [is] a matter of state secret," or where the admission of evidence would reveal the "means, sources and methods of intelligence gathering" (*Totten v. United States*). But while the doctrine had been applied prior to 9/11 in cases involving personal injury, it had never been used persistently as a tool to shield state officials for liability for involvement in torture.

Litigation is, however, only one avenue of redress. Other avenues include inquiries, commissions or special legislation providing for compensation. Yet both the Bush and Obama administrations have consistently resisted calls for accountability for violations of human rights. Doing so would entail giving up some of the secrecy that shields executive decision making. It might also lead to restrictions on the power to conduct targeted killing or indefinite detention without charge. Such powers are believed to be necessary so long as the threat of terror continues to appear extraordinary or significant.

TERROR, SECURITY AND HUMAN RIGHTS IN CANADA

In some ways, Canada has demonstrated a greater willingness to accept responsibility for its involvement in serious rights violations. But in many ways, its conduct has been similar to that of the United States.

Parliament ordered two inquiries to examine the involvement of state agents in the torture of Canadians abroad. The Arar Inquiry in 2006 cleared Maher Arar of wrongdoing and found the RCMP directly responsible for providing U.S. officials with the faulty information that formed the basis of his rendition to Syria. With litigation and a substantial damage award likely to follow, Canada reached a settlement with Arar for $10.5 million. This was a laudable gesture of accountability. But the settlement also helped to avoid a larger measure transparency. In this sense, it was in keeping with one of the salient features of the Inquiry itself: the concealment of most of the conduct at issue from public scrutiny. Almost all of the RCMP and CSIS testimony at the Arar Inquiry was censored under the *Canada Evidence Act*, as were significant portions of the Inquiry's final report. By settling with Arar, the government avoided further exposure of state conduct through pre-trial discoveries, witness testimony and the controversial use of state privilege at trial.

A second major inquiry, headed by former Supreme Court Justice Frank Iacobucci, examined the involvement of Canadian officials in cases involving Canadian citizens Abdullah Almalki, Ahmad Abou-Elmaati and Muyyed Nureddin. The three were travelling independently through Syria (and in Elmaati's case, Syria and Egypt) in 2002 when they were arrested, detained and tortured (Elmaati in both countries). Justice Iacobucci found that while information that Canadian officials provided to these governments did not directly result in the imprisonment and torture of the three men, it "indirectly contributed" to this (Iacobucci Report 2008: 36–39). In the cases of Elmaati and Almalki, the Canadian Security Intelligence Service provided Syrian officials with questions to be put to each man in detention and provided Syria with Nureddin's travel itinerary as a means to detain him. While Elmaati was held in Egypt, Canadian intelligence conveyed to Egyptian officials concerns about his possible activities if released, causing a delay in his release — a delay that led to further mistreatment. The various communications were made with knowledge of the possibility of mistreatment or torture if the three men were held in custody. The Iacobucci Inquiry lasted some twenty-two months. All but four days of it were held in private. In response to a Parliamentary sub-committee's recommendations, a majority of the House of Commons voted to issue the three men an official apology and provide compensation. The minority Conservative Government of the time declined to do so. The assertion of state secrecy continues to hinder a lawsuit brought by Almalki, Abou-Elmaati and Nureddin in Federal Court.

A final case worth noting involves the ordeal of Sudanese Canadian Aboufsian Abdelrazik. A refugee to Canada in the mid-90s, Abdelrazik chose to return to Sudan in 2003 to visit his ailing mother. At this time, CSIS was investigating him for suspected ties to terrorism, given his acquaintance with persons of interest in Montreal. Both CSIS and the RCMP would eventually conclude that Abdelrazik had no involvement in any criminal activity. But prior to making this finding, CSIS agents gave the Sudanese Government information leading to Abdelrazik's arrest, and agents then travelled to Sudan to interrogate him in Sudanese custody. Abdelrazik alleges that, following these events, he was tortured, detained without charge for several months and eventually released, only to be arrested and detained for another nine months due once again to the involvement of Canadian officials. By the time of his release, Abdelrazik's passport had expired, but Canada refused to renew it, stranding him in Sudan for a further eighteen months. The Federal Court of Canada held that the decision to refuse Abdelrazik a new passport was contrary to his Charter right to return to Canada, and compelled the government to arrange his immediate return (*Abdelrazik v. Canada* 2009). Abdelrazik is now suing the Canadian Government for its complicity in his torture and detention in Sudan. The government has thus far vigorously opposed Abdelrazik's claims, despite an earlier court's finding of serious rights violations.

CHALLENGING TERRORISM AS WAR

Stepping back from this overview of post-9/11 law and policy, we return once again to the broader rationale for treating terrorism as a kind of super-crime or a form of war. For much of the post-9/11 period, governments have held the view that terrorism ought be understood as something more than conventional crime because it poses a much greater threat to public safety than most crime. Earlier parts of this chapter have surveyed examples of this argument in political and popular discourse, but a critical assessment of this reasoning is necessary.

Following the passage of the *Anti-terrorism Act* in 2001, Canada's *Criminal Code* has recognized the act of participating in or facilitating terrorism to be a distinct offence. Prior to this, terrorism cases were successfully prosecuted under older criminal offences that acts of terror might involve (for example, murder, hijacking or destruction of property). When sentencing a person for murder, attempted murder or some other offence that formed an act of terror, the offender's broader political motives were considered an aggravating circumstance that warranted a longer sentence. The need for new terrorism offences in the *Criminal Code* was therefore not clear. Nor was it clear that a host of new powers were necessary to prosecute terrorism offences, such as the use, in some cases, of secret evidence, preventive detention and mandatory consecutive sentences. Both of these issues point to the larger question of how we came to perceive terrorism as a special kind of crime — a super-crime — or almost as a form of war.

Part of the answer can be found in the Code's definition of terrorism, which uses similar language to the law adopted in many other Western nations after 9/11. The hallmark of terrorism, its essential feature, is the purpose for which a violent act is carried out. As the Code's definition states, an act of terror is carried out "for a political, religious or ideological purpose," and "with the intention of intimidating the public ... or compelling a person, a government [or an organization] to do or to refrain from doing any act." Thus, in one sense, adding terrorism as a distinct offence in our *Criminal Code*, with additional powers for its enforcement, reflects the notion that terrorism poses a threat not simply to individual victims or even groups, but to the sovereignty and power of the state itself. It thus differs from conventional forms of crime because it poses a threat closer in nature to the kind of threat posed by an enemy nation. Even if the capability of individual terrorists or groups falls far short of this, the quality of the threat they pose bears this basic similarity.

Put otherwise, in one sense, the *Criminal Code* conceives of terrorism offenders not simply as treasonous, but as enemy outsiders who no longer merit being recognized as members of our political community. Courts have expressed this view in their reluctance to place much emphasis on rehabilitation when dealing with terrorism offenders after 9/11, suggesting that society's need to separate and contain the threat posed by a radicalized individual should take absolute priority over any interest in their possible reintegration, regardless of their prospects for rehabilitation (Diab 2014). Parliament has taken this idea a step further, passing a bill that strips Canadian citizenship from those convicted of terrorism or those who are believed, on reasonable grounds, to have been involved in terrorism abroad but have not been convicted (*Strengthening Canadian Citizenship Act* 2014). The new law applies only to Canadians who are also citizens of another country, but this can include persons born in Canada. Removing citizenship is the ultimate expression of the idea that the terrorist is an outsider whom we seek to banish or exclude, rather than a criminal that we seek to punish and rehabilitate.

But the idea of terrorism as a kind of super-crime or a threat closer in nature to war has also drawn much of its persuasive force by drawing on two further assumptions. One is that terrorism involves individuals acting in coordination with large and elaborately structured transnational terrorist groups such as al Qaeda that are able to marshal considerable resources for their cause. The other assumption is that such groups are capable of carrying out acts of terror on a much greater scale than was believed possible before 9/11. If such a group could carry out an attack claiming some three thousand lives in 2001, and further attacks on that scale or greater are conceivable in the near future, it therefore makes sense to think of terrorism as a threat on a different order from most conventional crime.

A critical response to the idea of terrorism as a threat involving an enemy force rather than an individual criminal, or a group of them, might begin by recognizing how closely the terrorist as "enemy outsider" is based on the model of 9/11 itself. Put otherwise, we have come to assume that terrorism presents a threat that is both qualitatively and quantitatively different from other forms of crime largely on the basis of the belief that the future of terrorism will entail more activity by a large non-state actor such as al Qaeda and that such an actor will be capable of carrying out acts comparable in scale to 9/11 or greater. But if these beliefs can be challenged, it becomes more difficult to sustain the argument for terrorism as war or a kind of super-crime.

For roughly a decade after 9/11, politicians and security officials made a plausible case for the danger posed by al Qaeda on the basis of the assumption that the group remained large, well coordinated and capable of carrying out large-scale attacks. However, after extensive military efforts on the part of the U.S. and its allies in Afghanistan and Pakistan, the core al Qaeda group has diminished in strength, with the focus of concern shifting to smaller associated groups across North Africa and Central Asia (more on this below). Yet politicians have continued to assert that al Qaeda or its offshoots still pose a danger of carrying out a large-scale act of terror at some point in the near future. As noted above, President Obama invoked the prospect of "another 9/11" in the course of defending the NSA's mass surveillance programs. Similarly, in the lead up to the President's decision to bomb targets in the emerging Islamic State in Iraq and Syria (ISIS) in September of 2014, Director of Operations for the Joint Chiefs of Staff, William Mayville, told the media that the bombing was necessary to address the threat posed by the "Khorasan Group," a group of militants in Syria working under the direction of al Qaeda leader Ayman al-Zawahiri. Mayville asserted that the group was in the "final stages of plans to execute major attacks against Western targets and potentially the U.S. Homeland" (McCoy 2014). Other administration officials indicated the plot was said to involve a Yemeni bomb-maker working with the Khorasan Group on "new ways to slip explosives past airport security" so as to bomb multiple flights into the U.S. (Dilanian and Sullivan 2014).

As the earlier part of this chapter has demonstrated, the pattern of invoking the prospect of large-scale terror to justify extraordinary measures in national defence has been consistent from 9/11 onward. Yet a crucial, recurring feature of this pattern is that assertions on the part of politicians and security officials about the likelihood of 9/11-scale terror seldom involve a reliance on evidence or expert authority. Thus, when President Obama, Director of National Intelligence, James Clapper, and others have recently invoked the prospect of terrorism involving WMD or large-scale terror in the ways noted above, they offered no evidence in support of the claim. And while much of the expert literature does cite evidence in reliance on claims about the likelihood of mass terror, many authors have tended to present these claims as self-evident or beyond debate. For example, Graham Allison, Mathew Bunn and other experts on nuclear terrorism have argued that such an event is possible, if not likely, in the near term in a North American city partly on the basis of how easy it is to build and deploy a nuclear bomb if terrorists could manage to obtain enough fissile material (Allison 2005: 96; Bunn 2010: 16; Ferguson and Potter 2005: 131). But in the work of each of these experts, the claim is presented without reference to a considerable body of skeptical opinion on point. Contrary to their view, a number of experts have argued that building a nuclear bomb is much more challenging than is often assumed, for a host of reasons (explored below) (Levi 2009: 36–42; Wirz and Egger 2005). The tendency to present the danger of large-scale terror as a self-evident fact extends beyond the discourse of politicians and experts. In much of the public debate about national security since 9/11, discussion about the appropriate limits of rights and security have often taken as their point of departure the likelihood of further large-scale attacks rather than calling this fact into question.

What follows is only a brief overview of some of the arguments that have been made to challenge the view that future acts of terrorism in North America will involve large groups such as al Qaeda, carrying out terror on the scale of 9/11 or greater. In the absence of these assumptions, not only does it become harder to justify treating terrorism as a form of war or a kind of super-crime, but it also becomes harder to justify measures that circumvent the protections of the criminal law or violate core human rights.

Terrorism and WMD

Consider briefly the case of terror involving WMD and, in particular, nuclear terror. As noted earlier, many experts believe this to be likely on the basis of the abundance of poorly guarded fissile material, the simplicity of building and deploying a bomb and al Qaeda's ambitions in this regard. For example, in 2005, Charles Ferguson and William Potter asserted that the United States "has faced the threat of nuclear terrorism for many years, but this peril looms larger today than ever before" (2005: 1). Writing in 2009, Mathew Bunn claimed, "There remains a very real danger that terrorists could get and use a nuclear bomb, turning the heart of a major city into a smoldering radioactive ruin" (2009: 112). These and other experts bolster their case by citing frequent reports of theft, loss or illicit transfer of fissile material from sites in the former Soviet Union, among others, and the ease with which such material can be transported across borders (Allison 2005: 98; Ferguson and Potter 2005: 119; Bunn 2010: 6). In addition to arguments about the simplicity of building a bomb (noted above), the authors also cite known attempts on the part of al Qaeda to attain fissile material in the late 1990s and early 2000s (Allison 2005: 12–14; Bunn 2010: 13; Ferguson and Potter 2005: 116–17).

Yet a number of other experts have called these facts into question, suggesting nuclear terror to be a highly improbable event (Levi 2007; Younger 2008; Wirz and Eggerts 2005). In their view, throughout the various stages of acquiring or building and then deploying a bomb, terrorists would face a host of significant challenges. First, both nuclear terror alarmists and skeptics agree that the production of fissile material is beyond the capacity of most individuals, small groups and even larger, non-state groups. Yet acquiring a fully functional nuclear bomb, by theft or other means, is unlikely because most are stored disassembled or with elaborate codes closely guarded by a small few. And while there may be an abundance of fissile material, very little of it has been stolen. Even if fissile material of a sufficient quantity could be obtained — a significant hurdle in itself — non-state actors would confront several more challenges at the bomb-building stage. These include the task of shaping the material to be used in a bomb device and crafting the weapon itself. The material would be highly challenging to shape or mold, requiring special expertise, equipment and time. The tasks of crafting and transporting the bomb would furnish further opportunities for detection, accidents or failure. Given the challenge these tasks have posed to nations actively seeking the bomb, they would seem especially daunting for a group of non-state actors.

A number of experts have also advanced a skeptical view of the likelihood of biological terror (Leitenber 2007; Wenger 2007; Clark 2008). They concede that certain bio-toxins may be quite lethal, produced from natural materials (for example, anthrax spores) and widely dispersed to cause mass casualties. Yet at each stage, they argue, the practical challenges are extensive —in fact, no group has ever succeeded in causing mass casualties using biological weapons, despite considerable efforts in some cases, including the Japanese Aum Shinrikyo cult in the mid-1990s. This was a group led by Seiichi Endo, who possessed a doctorate in molecular biology and sought to inflict as many casualties as possible. In 1995, the group carried out seven attacks, four with anthrax and three with botulinum toxin, killing thirteen people — while still a significant number, it was far lower than Endo intended (Clark 2008: 164–69). As William Clark has noted, the group sought to act upon the ability to produce strains of highly dangerous biotoxins such as anthrax from natural sources or to obtain them illicitly from an industrial lab or other source (in this case, some of the material was believed to be stolen from a hospital). But the group could not overcome the problem of cultivating the material into sufficiently large quantities of biotoxins and stabilizing them in their lethal form (ibid: 169). The problem has proven exceedingly challenging to experts and military personnel in nations with the largest and most advanced militaries, including the U.S. and Russia (ibid). Moreover, as Clark and others have noted, the act of dispersing the material in an effective manner presents a greater challenge still, requiring considerable expertise in a range of fields, special equipment, sufficient personnel and space in which to work (Clark 2008; Leitenberg 2007: 49). All of this would increase the prospect of detection, logistical error,and the likelihood of the material destabilizing or spoiling. Indeed, the sole example of a non-state actor's effective use of a deadly biotoxin in world history was the 2001 congressional incident involving anthrax in letters addressed to Senators Tom Daschle and Patrick Leahy, which caused a total of five deaths (Leitenberg 2007: 65). The FBI concluded in 2010 that the likely source of the sample was a senior bioweapons researcher in the U.S. military (U.S. Department of Justice 2010).

Similar arguments have been made to call into question the likelihood of other forms of terror involving WMD (on radiological terror, see, for example, Wirz and Egger 2005; on chemical weapons, see Meselson 1991 and Gilmore Commission 1999). To be clear, the point here is not that such forms of terror are impossible, only that a significant body of evidence challenges the claim that they are likely to occur. How plausible, then, is another 9/11-scale attack at the hands of a group without special weaponry?

Terrorism and al Qaeda

John Mueller and Mark Stewart (2011) have drawn upon various sources to assess the current status of al Qaeda. They argue that what remains of the group is likely "a few dozen individuals," joined by "perhaps a hundred fighters left over from al Qaeda's golden days in Afghanistan in the 1990s." They note that every terror attack linked to al Qaeda since 2001 appears to have been carried out by a group only tenuously connected to the core group in the Afghanistan-Pakistan region. Much of the focus of concern about international terrorism has thus shifted to what are described as offshoots of al Qaeda elsewhere in Asia and Africa. Yet, as Mueller and Stewart argue (2011: 617), attacks from Morocco to Jakarta exhibit a similar tendency to involve groups whose primary grievance is with regional governments and events. This has remained true in the sense that the almost weekly bombings in Iraq and Afghanistan have stemmed primarily from conflict between local Sunni and Shia groups or linkages of these groups with foreign allies. And events such as the Jakarta bombing of 2009, the attack at a Nairobi shopping mall in 2013 or the suicide bombing in Nigeria in 2014 have all involved radical groups or individuals seeking to install in each nation a fundamentalist form of Islamic government. Moreover, while the emerging Islamic State in Iraq and Syria (ISIS) has carried out massacres of civilians and minority populations in the region, it has not sought to wage a war against the U.S. or other Western states by carrying out attacks in those nations (Rashid 2014).

Mueller and Stewart also contend that what remains of international terrorism has dwindled to "thousands of sympathizers and would-be jihadists spread around the globe who mainly connect in Internet chat rooms, engage in radicalizing conversations, and variously dare each other to actually do something" (2011: 698). Leon Panetta, Director of the U.S. Central Intelligence Agency, lent official recognition to this view when he asserted in 2010 that the "lone wolf" terrorist has become America's "main threat" (Mueller and Stewart 2011: 763). Future attacks in North America are therefore likely to involve, as Brian Jenkins has put it, "tiny conspiracies, lone gunmen, one-off attacks rather than sustained terrorist campaigns" (2010: 4, cited in Mueller and Stewart). Indeed, a survey of some fifty plots in the United States over the course of the post-9/11 period demonstrates a consistent tendency of domestic terrorism to be attempted by less sophisticated and/or poorly funded individuals or groups with much more limited goals and abilities than the 9/11 attackers (Mueller 2013).

The 2009 plot involving Najibullah Zazi is instructive in this regard. An Obama Administration official described the plot as the "most serious" in the U.S. since 9/11 and said it marked an attempt by al Qaeda to "carry out another mass-casualty attack in the United States," confirming the group continued to pose an "existential" threat to the U.S. (*New York Times* September 25, 2009, cited in Mueller and Stewart 2011: 785). Zazi was a high school dropout working in a donut shop in Manhattan. Having decided to set off a bomb in New York, he travelled to Pakistan and received training on bomb building from members of al Qaeda. He then spent a year in New York trying to build the bomb. However, using stolen credit cards to buy material, he set off various security and surveillance traps that helped authorities to foil the plot. He also never succeeded in building the bomb, despite several "frantic" attempts to communicate (on a tapped line) with sources in Pakistan (Mueller and Stewart 2011: 785).

The Boston bombing in April of 2013 and the killing of two Canadian soldiers in Ottawa in October of 2014 are consistent with this analysis. The Boston bombing was carried out by two young Chechen immigrants to the United States, Dzhokhar and Tamerlan Tsarnaev, who were inspired by extremist ideologies to build bombs and deployed a crude home-made explosive near the finish line of the Boston Marathon, which claimed 3 lives and injured 264 (Wines and Kovaleski 2014). In October of 2014, a Quebec man, Martin Couture-Rouleau, who had been inspired by the ideology espoused by members of the Islamic State of Syria and Iraq drove his truck into two soldiers in a Quebec parking lot, killing one of them, Warrant Officer Patrice Vincent (Payton 2014). Three days later, Michael Zehaf-Bibeau, also acting under the influence of Islamic extremism, used a rifle as his only weapon and shot another soldier, Corporal Nathan Cirillo, as he stood guard at the Ottawa war memorial. Zehaf-Bibeau then entered Parliament in an effort to claim more lives but was killed soon after entering the building (Gollom 2014).

All three events caused an enormous amount of fear and terror. But notably, none of the actors were affiliated with a larger domestic or international terrorist group. Each involved the use of primitive weaponry and caused a relatively small number of casualties. While these casualties are certainly significant and tragic, they are closer in magnitude to attacks prior to 9/11. The acts were also not prevented through the use of post-9/11 extraordinary measures, including mass secret surveillance or preventive arrests powers. And in the case of the Boston bombings, the culprits were quickly located using conventional methods of police investigation.

TERRORISM IS A CRIME

The Boston, Ottawa and Quebec attacks were clearly tragic and terrifying. The question is whether they present a threat to public order closer in nature to war than to crime. The argument here is that what occurred in each of these cases is consistent with a growing body of evidence suggesting that future acts of terror in North America will involve a degree of harm more in line with attacks that occurred prior to 9/11. This assertion is important to the question of whether terrorism is closer to war than to crime because the war theory is premised on the contrary. Without assuming that future acts are likely to involve larger transnational groups carrying out attacks that are much larger in scale or more frequent or both, it becomes more difficult (though not impossible) to argue that terrorism is best approached as a kind of super-crime or a form of war. The nature of the outstanding threat of terror is, of course, debatable. While it may not be possible to settle the issue decisively, the contrary evidence surely calls the issue into question.

This chapter has not addressed other important causes of public support for extraordinary measures to counter terrorism. A number of criminologists have argued that support for these measures mark the extension of a "culture of control" or of "securitization" that began some two or three decades before 9/11 (Lynch, McGarrity, and Williams 2010; Zedner 2009). As these authors point out, for many years prior to 2001, due process and other criminal law protections were often eclipsed or scaled back in favour of victims' rights or other laws designed to quell concerns about public safety. Examples of this trend include the expansion of powers to place individuals under probation-like conditions without being convicted of an offence (using what are called "control orders" in the United Kingdom or a "recognizance" under section 810 of Canada's *Criminal Code*). Other examples include the expansion of the grounds on which an accused may be detained pending trial. Prior to the 1970s, Canadian law generally allowed for a person to be held in jail prior to their trial on a criminal charge only where there were significant concerns about the person's likelihood to attend court (McLellan 2010: 56). A person may now be held in jail before their trial on a broader set of grounds including concerns about the likelihood of reoffending or the need to maintain the repute of the administration of justice, despite the presumption of innocence (section 515(10) of the *Criminal Code*). The scope of the criminal law has also been significantly expanded through the creation of sex-offender registries, DNA databases, dangerous offender designations and the proliferation mandatory minimum sentences. In light of these earlier developments, the expansion of security measures after 9/11 was at least in part an extension of an earlier trend toward the expansion of measures that are grounded in public safety concerns.

Scholars of immigration law and policy have also noted that for at least a decade before 9/11, fears of security around borders, and a suspicion of migrants, led to an increase in both military and criminal law measures, including administrative detention (Dauvergne 2009; Pratt 2005). A further group of scholars has characterized post-9/11 security policy as inextricably tied to a larger suspicion or animus toward Arab or Muslim minorities (Butler 2004; Razack 2008). For example, for Razak, the use of many extreme measures, along with the "war on terror" generally, derives support from the "ideological underpinning of a clash of civilizations: the dangerous Muslim man, the imperiled Muslim woman, and the civilized European" (Razack 2008: 5). Public perceptions of Islamic extremism are, on this view, closely tied to "a story about a family of white nations, a civilization, obliged to use force and terror to defend itself against a menacing cultural Other" (ibid). This story, as Razak argues, "Underwrites the expulsion of Muslims of political community, a casting out that takes the form of stigmatization, surveillance, incarceration, abandonment, torture, and bombs" (ibid). Support for extraordinary measures is therefore not simply a matter of rational calculations about terrorist capabilities.

Each of these approaches has important insights to offer. Yet the intent here was to highlight facets of law and policy unique to the post-9/11 period. Contrary to the securitization theorists, many extraordinary measures used and widely accepted after 9/11 (torture, targeted killing, rendition) were not inevitable or predictable extensions of an earlier culture of control or security. Also, fears and suspicions about migrants may have shaped immigration policy before 9/11, but official defences of counter-terror policy have involved a shift in focus. In ways explored throughout this chapter, when defending extraordinary measures, politicians have consistently relied on a set of claims about the greater magnitude that terrorism has come to pose after 9/11. Some or even much of this rhetoric may mask darker motives or racist or imperialist assumptions about the sources and nature of terrorism. But so long as politicians focus their arguments in favour of greater security on claims about the larger threat that terrorism has come to pose, the debate about whether to approach terrorism as a form of crime or war won't get very far without addressing these claims directly.

DISCUSSION QUESTIONS

1. What arguments have been made to support the claim that 9/11 was the harbinger of a new order of terrorism, with future attacks in North America likely to occur on the same or greater scale at some point in the near future?

2. In what ways have these claims been supported by evidence?

3. In what ways does U.S. or Canadian counter-terror law or policy circumvent or violate the conventional protections of persons investigated or accused of a crime?

4. Is the Boston Marathon attack of April 2013 best understood as a form of crime or war, and why?

5. Is mass secret surveillance in Canada justified on the basis that the information it allows officials to gather may help to prevent acts of terror comparable in scale to the 2013 attack in Boston?

GLOSSARY

The AUMF, or the Authorization to Use Military Force: a joint resolution of both chambers of the United States Congress, passed on September 14, 2001, serving as an official declaration of war against al Qaeda and any nations, groups or individuals that harboured or assisted them.

Black Site: a secret prison usually held in a country with a poor human rights record to which subjects of rendition (see definition below) are taken by agents of the Central Intelligence Agency of the United States for the purposes of secret interrogation and possibly torture.

Crime: conduct that is prohibited in a society's legal system on the basis of a belief in its inherently wrongful nature and is sanctioned or punished with a view to deterring, denouncing and rehabilitating.

Indefinite Detention: the context of counter-terror law, the practice of imprisoning non-citizens suspected of involvement in

terrorism pending deportation or (in the U.S.) the conclusion of the "war on terror."

Judicial Interrogation: a process under the terrorism provisions of Canada's *Criminal Code* by which a person may be arrested without charge and brought before a court for questioning by a judge where the person is believed to have knowledge of or be involved in terrorist activity.

Mass Surveillance: the practice of surveilling or intercepting the activity or communication of individuals who are not suspected of involvement in a specific crime.

Preventive Detention: the detention of a person under the *Criminal Code* for up to three days without charge in a case where there are grounds to believe a terrorist act will be carried out and a reasonable suspicion that the detention is necessary to prevent the act.

Rendition (also referred to as "extraordinary

rendition"): a practice the Central Intelligence Agency of the United States is known to carry out that involves the abduction of a terror suspect or person of interest from the U.S. or another country and their illegal, covert transfer to another country for secret interrogation and possibly torture.

Security Certificate: a document issued jointly by Canada's Minister of Immigration and Minister of Public Safety authorizing the arrest and detention of a non-citizen pending deportation, in a case in which he or she is suspected of involvement in terrorism or of posing a "danger to Canada."

Targeted Killing: the use of remote controlled, unmanned drone aircraft to locate and assassinate persons suspected of involvement in terrorism but without charge and without any form of judicial review.

Terrorism: defined in Canadian law as an act of violence against persons or property that claims lives or causes a serious risk to the health or safety of any person and is carried out for a political, ideological or religious purpose, with the intention of intimidating or compelling a person or government to do or refrain from doing something.

War: a state of conflict between two nation states, or significant portions of a population within a nation, in a struggle for sovereignty or control over a specific territory or resource.

SUGGESTED READINGS

K. Roach, *The 9/11 Effect: Comparative Counter-terrorism,* Cambridge: Cambridge University Press (2011).

I. Lustic, *Trapped in the War on Terror,* Philadelphia: University of Pennsylvania Press (2006).

D. Cole and J. Lobel, *Less Safe, Less Free: Why America Is Losing the War on Terror,* New York: New Press (2009).

R. Diab, *The Harbinger Theory: How the Post-9/11 Emergency Became Permanent and the Case for Reform,* New York: Oxford University Press (2015).

J. Mueller and M. Stewart, *Terror, Security and Money: Balancing the Risks, Benefits, and Costs of Homeland Security,* Oxford: Oxford University Press (2011).

SUGGESTED WEBSITES

Amnesty International Canada <http://www.amnesty.ca/>
Human Rights Watch <http://www.hrw.org/>
The American Civil Liberties Union <https://www.aclu.org/>
The Canadian Civil Liberties Association <http://ccla.org/>
The British Columbia Civil Liberties Association <http://bccla.org/>

REFERENCES

Abacus Data. 2013. "NSA and Snowden: Canadians, Terrorism and Online Privacy." At <http://abacusinsider.com/politics-public-affairs/nsa-snowden-canadians-terrorism-online-privacy/> accessed November 2014.

Allison, G. 2005. *Nuclear Terror: The Ultimate Preventable Catastrophe.* New York: Henry Holt.

Amnesty International. 2012. "Guantanamo: A Decade of Damage to Human Rights." January 11.

Barnaby, F. 2004. *How to Build a Nuclear Bomb and other Weapons of Mass Destruction.* London: Granta Books.

Bunn, M. 2009. "Reducing the Greatest Risks of Nuclear Theft and Terrorism." *Daedalus* 138: 4.

___. 2010. "Securing the Bomb 2010: Securing All Nuclear Materials in Four Years." Cambridge: Project on Managing the Atom, Belfer Center for Science and International Affairs, Harvard Kennedy School and Nuclear Threat Initiative.

Bureau of Investigative Journalism. 2013. "Covert Drone War." At <http://www.thebureauinvestigates.com/category/projects/drones/> accessed November 2014.

___. 2014. "November 2014 Update: U.S. covert actions in Pakistan, Yemen and Somalia." At <http://www.thebureauinvestigates.com/2014/12/01/november-2014-update-us-covert-actions-in-pakistan-yemen-and-somalia/> accessed November 2014.

Bush, George W. 2002a. "Text of President Bush's 2002 State of the Union Address." *Washington Post*, January 29. At <http://www. washingtonpost.com/wp-srv/onpolitics/transcripts/sou012902.htm>.

___. 2002b. Executive Order, February 7, 2002. At <http://www.lawofwar.org/Bush_memo_Genevas.htm>.

Butler, J. 2004. *Precarious Life: The Powers of Mourning and Violence*. London: Verso Press.

Canada. 2012. "Building Resilience Against Terrorism: Canada's Counter-Terrorism Strategy." Ministry of Public Safety.

Canada. Parliament. House of Commons. Standing Committee on Justice and Human Rights. Evidence. (Meeting No. 29, October 18, 2001) 37th Parliament, 1st session.

Canadian Security and Intelligence Service. 2009. "2008–2009 Public Report."

Chung, A. 2011. "Canadians' Fears of Terror Rose Post 9/11." Postmedia News, September 7.

Clark, William. 2008. *Bracing for Armageddon: The Science and Politics of Bioterrorism in America*. Oxford: Oxford University Press.

Clapper, J. 2013. "Facts on the Collection of Intelligence Pursuant to Section 702 of the Foreign Intelligence Surveillance Act." Office of the Director of National Intelligence June 8.

Cole, D., and J. Lobel. 2009. *Less Safe, Less Free: Why America Is Losing the War on Terror*. New York: the New Press.

Commission of Inquiry into the Actions of Canadian Officials in Relation to Maher Arar. 2006. "Report of the Events Relating to Maher Arar: Analysis and Recommendations." Ottawa: Public Works.

Cotler, I. 2001. "Thinking Outside the Box: Foundational Principles for a Counter-Terror Law and Policy." In Ronald Daniels, Patrick Macklem and Kent Roach (eds.), *The Security of Freedom: Canada's Anti-Terrorism Bill*. Toronto: University of Toronto Press.

Dauvergne, C. 2009. *Making People Illegal: What Globalization Means for Migration and Law*. Cambridge: Cambridge University Press.

Davis, J. 2004. "A Biological Warfare Wake-Up Call: Prevalent Myths and Likely Scenarios." In Jim A. Davis and Barry R. Schneider (eds.), *The Gathering Biological Warfare Storm*. Westport, CT: Praeger.

Department of Justice (United States). 2010 "Amerithrax Investigative Summary." At <http://www.justice.gov/archive/amerithrax/docs/amx-investigative-summary.pdf> accessed November 2014.

Dershowitz, A. 2006. *Preemption: A Knife that Cuts Both Ways*. New York: W.W. Norton.

Diab, R. 2014. "R. v. Khawaja and the Fraught Question of Rehabilitation in Terrorism Sentencing." *Queens Law Journal* 39: 2.

___. 2015. *The Harbinger Theory: How the Post-9/11 Emergency Became Permanent and the Case for Reform*. New York: Oxford University Press.

Dilanian, K., and E. Sullivan. 2014. "Syrian Extremists May Pose More Direct Threat to U.S. than Islamic State." Associated Press, September 13.

Ferguson, C., and W. Potter. 2005. *The Four Faces of Nuclear Terrorism*. London: Routledge.

Foreign Policy and the Centre for American Progress. 2006. "The Terrorism Index." *Foreign Polic.y* July–August.

Gallup. 2006. "Terrorism in the United States." At <http://www.gallup.com/poll/4909/Terrorism-United-States.aspx> accessed November 2014.

Geist, M. 2013. "Why Canadians Should Be Demanding Answers about Secret Surveillance Programs." Michael Geist's blog. At <http://www.michaelgeist.ca/content/view/6869/125/> accessed November 2014.

Gellman, B., and A. Soltani. 2013. "NSA Tracking Cellphone Locations Worldwide, Snowden Documents Show." *Washington Post*, December 4.

George W. Bush. 2002. "State of the Union Address." *Washington Post*, January 29.

___. 2002a. "Memorandum for the Vice President." White House. At <http://www.lawofwar.org/Bush_memo_Genevas.htm> accessed November 2014.

Gilmore Commission (Advisory Panel to Assess Domestic Response Capabilities for Terrorism Involving Weapons of Mass Destruction). 1999. "First Annual Report: Assessing the Threat." At <www.rand.org/nsrd/terrpanel> accessed November 2014.

Gollom, M. 2014. "Michael Zehaf-Bibeau and Martin Couture-Rouleau: Their Shared Traits." CBC News, October 27.

Gonzales, A. 2002. "Memo to the President, August 1, 2002." Office of Legal Counsel. At <http://www.nytimes.com/ref/international/24MEMO-GUIDE.html> accessed November 2014.

Greenwald, G. 2014. *No Place Left to Hide: Edward Snowden, the NSA, and the U.S. Surveillance State*. New York: Metropolitan Books.

Human Rights Watch. 2006. "By the Numbers: Findings of the Detainee Abuse and Accountability Project." New York: Human Rights Watch.

___. 2011. "Getting Away with Torture: The Bush Administration and Mistreatment of Detainees." New York: Human Rights Watch.

___. 2014. "Facts and Figures: Military Commissions v. Federal Courts." At <http://www.hrw.org/features/guantanamo-facts-figures> accessed November 2014.

Internal Inquiry into the Actions of Canadian Officials in Relation to Abdullah Almalki, Ahmad Abou-Elmaati and Muayyed Nureddin. 2008. "Final Report of the Iacobucci Inquiry." Ottawa Public Works.

International Committee of the Red Cross. 2007. "Report on the Treatment of Fourteen 'High Value' Detainees in CIA Custody." February. At <http://www.nybooks.com/media/doc/2010/04/22/icrc-report.pdf>.

Ipsos Inc. 2013. "Canadians Split on Whether It's Acceptable for Governments to Monitor Email and Online Activities in Some Circumstances." At <http://www.ipsos-na.com/news-polls/pressrelease.aspx?id=6233> accessed November 2014.

Johnston, D., and S. Shane. 2009. "Terror Case Is Called One of the Most Serious in Years." *New York Times*, September 25.

Kaplan, E. 2006. "Q&A: Targeted Killings." *New York Times*, January 25.

Kasinof, L., M. Mazzetti and A. Cowell. 2011. "U.S.-Born Qaida Leader Killed in Yemen." *New York Times*, September 30.

Kaufman, B. 2013. "A Guide to What We Now Know About the NSA's Dragnet Searches of Your Communications." American Civil Liberties Union. At <https://www.aclu.org/blog/national-security/guide-what-we-now-know-about-nsas-dragnet-searches-your-communications> accessed November 2014.

Kellman, B. 2007. *Bioviolence: Preventing Biological Terror and Crime*. Cambridge: Cambridge University Press.

Leitenberg, Milton. 2007. "Evolution of the Current Threat." In Andreas Wenger and Reto Wollenmann (eds.), *Bioterrorism: Confronting a Complex Threat*. Boulder, CO: Lynne Rienner Publishers.

Levi, M. 2009. *Nuclear Terrorism*. Cambridge: Harvard University Press.

Levi, M., and H. Kelly. 2002. "Weapons of Mass Disruption." *Scientific American* 77.

Lustic, I. 2006. *Trapped in the War on Terror*. Philadelphia: University of Pennsylvania Press.

Lynch, A., N. McGarrity and G. Williams (eds.). 2010. *Counter-Terrorism and Beyond: The Culture of Law and Justice After 9/11*. London: Routledge.

McLellan, M. 2010. "Bail and the Diminishing Presumption of Innocence." *Canadian Criminal Law Review* 15: 51.

Macleod, I., and A. Duffy. 2004. "A Question of Balance: Canada's Justice Minister Says New Anti-Terror Laws Protect Human Rights. Critics Beg to Differ." *Ottawa Citizen*, December 11.

McCoy, T. 2014. "Targeted by U.S. Airstrikes: The Secretive al Qaeda Cell Was Plotting an 'Imminent Attack." *Washington Post*, September 23.

Meselson, M. 1991. "The Myth of Chemical Superweapons." *Bulletin of the Atomic Scientists* April.

Mueller, J. 2002. "Harbinger or Aberation? A 9/11 Provocation." *The National Interest* Fall.

___. (ed.). 2013. "Terror Since 9/11: The American Cases." Mershon Centre, Ohio State University.

Mueller, J., and M. Stewart. 2011. *Terror, Security and Money: Balancing the Risks, Benefits, and Costs of Homeland Security*. London: Oxford University Press.

Obama, Barak. 2013. "Obama's Speech on Drone Policy." *New York Times*, May 23.

___. 2014. "Remarks by the President on Review of Signals Intelligence." Washington, DC: Department of Justice, Jan. 17.

Payton, L. 2014. "Martin Couture-Rouleau Case Underscores Passport Seizure Dilemma." CBC News, October 21.

Pilkington, E. 2013. "U.S. Government Identities Men on Guantanamo 'Indefinite Detainee' List." *The Guardian*, June 17.

Posner, R. 2007. *Countering Terrorism: Blurred Focus, Halting Steps*. Maryland: Rowman and Littlefield.

Pratt, A. 2005. *Security Borders: Detention and Deportation in Canada*. Vancouver: University of British Columbia Press.

Qunnipiac Univeristy Polling Institute. 2013. "U.S. Voters Say Snowden Is Whistle-Blower." Quinnipiac University, July 10. At <http://www.quinnipiac.edu/institutes-and-centers/polling-institute/national/release-detail?ReleaseID=1919> accessed November 2014.

Rasmussen Reports. 2012. "65% See Another 9/11 as Possible in Next 10 Years." At <http://www.rasmussenreports.com> accessed November 2014.

Razack, S. 2008. *Casting Out: Race and the Eviction of Muslims from Western Law and Politics*. Toronto: University of Toronto Press.

Roach, K. 2005. "Canada's Response to Terrorism." In V. Ramraj, M. Hor and K. Roach (eds.), *Global Anti-Terrorism Law and Policy*. Cambridge: Cambridge University Press.

___. 2011. *The 9/11 Effect: Comparative Counter-Terrorism*. Cambridge: Cambridge University Press.

Savage, C. 2013. "Senators Press Holder on Use of Military Force." *New York Times*, March 6.

Singh, R. 2013. "Drone Strikes Kill Innocent People. Why Is It So Hard to Know How Many?" *New Republic*, October 25.

Stewart, H. 2003. "Public Interest Immunity after Bill C-36." *Criminal Law Quarterly* 47.

Wenger, A. 2007. "Securing Society Against the Risk of Bioterrorism." In Andreas Wenger, and Reto Wollenmann (eds.), *Bioterrorism: Confronting a Complex Threat*. Boulder, CO: Lynne Rienner Publishers.

The White House. 2006. *The National Security Strategy of the United States of America*. September.

___. 2011. *National Strategy for Counterterrorism*. June.

Wines, M., and S. Kovaleski. 2014. "Marathon Bombing Suspect Waits in Isolation." *New York Times*, April 14.

Wirz, Christopher, and E. Egger. 2005. "Use of Nuclear and Radiological Weapons by Terrorists?" *International Review of the Red Cross* 87: 859, 497. At <https://www.icrc.org/eng/resources/documents/article/review/review-859-p497.htm>.

Yoo, J. 2006. *War by Other Means: An Insider's Account of the War on Terror*. New York: Atlantic Monthly Press.

Younger, Steven. 2008. *Endangered Species: How We Can Avoid Mass Destruction and Build a Lasting Peace*. New York: Harper Perennial.

Zedner, L. 2009. *Security*. London: Routledge.

Zimmerman, P., and C. Loeb. 2004. "Dirty Bombs: the Threat Revisited." *Defense Horizons* 1.

Canadian Case Law:
Abdelrazik v. Canada 2009 FC 580.
Suresh v. Canada 2002 SCC 1

U.S. Case Law:
Hamdi et al. v. Rumsfeld, Secretary of Defence, et al, 542 U.S. 507 (2004).
Rasul v. Bush, 542 U.S. 466 (2004).
Hamdan v. Rumsfeld, 548 U.S. 557 (2006).
Boumediene v. Bush 476 F. 3d. 981 (2008).
Totten v. United States, 92 U.S. 105, at 107 (1876)

European Case Law:
El-Masri v. the former Yugoslav Republic of Macedonia, Appl. No. 39630/09, ECtHR, 13 December 2012

Canadian Statutes:
Anti-terrorism Act, S.C. 2001, c. 41.
Canadian Security Intelligence Service Act, R.S.C., 1985, c. C-23.
Canada Evidence Act, R.S.C. 1985, c. C-5.
Criminal Code, R.S.C., 1985, c. C-46.
Immigration and Refugee Protection Act, S.C. 2001, c. 27.
National Defence Act, R.S.C., 1985, c. N-5.
Strengthening Canadian Citizenship Act, S.C. 2014, c. 22.

U.S. Statutes:
Authorization to Use Military Force, Public Law 107-40.
Uniting and Strengthening America By Providing Appropriate Tools Required To Intercept and Obstruct Terrorism (USA PATRIOT Act), H.R. 3162.
Foreign Surveillance Intelligence Act, Public Law 95-511.
Foreign Surveillance Act of 1978 Amendments Act of 2008, H.R. 6304.

PART IV

CRIME AND GENDER

The chapters in Part IV focus on gender as a central topic within criminology and criminal justice studies. As introduced in Chapter 5, gender is an established and central concern within criminology, and fundamental issues related to gender include different crime rates and crime involvement between genders as well as the treatment of men and women in the criminal justice system. Authors in this section draw on criminological and feminist theory to understand gendered factors linked to conflict with the law, media, public perceptions and punishment.

The existing current research on gender and crime generally shows that there is a gender gap in crime, with men more likely to be involved in crime and the criminal justice system than women. Many sources provide data that allow comparisons of offending patterns between the genders. Statistics Canada (2011, 2012), for example, shows us that men made up the majority (85 percent) of those admitted to correctional services in Canada (Perreault 2013), and in 2009, more males (776,000) versus females (233,000) were accused of having committed a *Criminal Code* offence (Mahoney 2011). Female involvement in the criminal justice system is more often through their victimization and less often through perpetrating crime. Explanations of the gender gap as well as variations in the gender gap depending on age, race, time and geographic location are widely researched and debated by criminologists.

There are also popular media myths that depict females who are involved in violence and who are confronted by the criminal justice system as particularly anomalous (and often demonized as non-female and masculinized), whereas male violence and involvement in crime is normalized and celebrated. Men's violence is arguably reinforced through media representations of "tough guys" in war, sport and prison. In contrast to the images of criminals in film and news stories, statistics on women and men's involvement with the criminal justice in Canada portray a quite different picture. As Carolyn Brooks details in this section, women in trouble with the law, for example, tend to be overwhelmingly young, poor and under-educated, with little or no work experience or vocational training. Further, such women are generally victims of physical, sexual and/or emotional abuse and racial discrimination. And, as Earle and Drake point out, men in prison are often very like the men we meet in school, at work and in our lives, in general. The problem is that whether men and women in prison are dangerous or not, media images may influence viscerally how the public thinks and feels about women and men's involvement in crime, and these perceptions are then reflected in public policy.

The first two chapters in this section provide insights into the origins of public misinformation about crime. They focus on the media and on official statistics, and they explore the politics of using information in a partial or biased way. They reveal that media accounts are biased constructions of crime and that official statistics count only those who get caught (people who are easily identifiable and easy to convict). They point to how, at times, politicians use crime policy to promote themselves in election battles.

In "The Social Construction of 'Dangerous' Girls and Women," Karlene Faith and Yasmin Jiwani explore the world of popular images of violent girls and women by investigating several high-profile cases that have captured the public's imagination. They look at the history of the condemnation of women and place this history in the context of the development of "scientific knowledge" about women and badness. Their historical review ends in the present with an overview of current studies of female violence, most of which draw on conventional (conservative) understandings of femininity and masculinity. They then investigate three high-profile cases: Leslie Van Houten, in California, Karla Homolka, in Ontario and Kelly Ellard, in British Columbia. These cases show how the media construct images of immoral girls and women that are consonant with the views of those in power. In the end, the authors discuss how the media draw on orthodox gender stereotypes to create powerful images of "bad women." The creation of such images is, in itself, an ideological or political act. Faith and Jiwani argue that the media, by condemning women for their "out of character" behaviour, reinforce a sexist normative and moral order.

In Chapter 14, "Reforming Prisons for Women?", Carolyn Brooks similarly reveals how the general public comes to see women's crime from a particular vantage point and how this often misinformed perception may influence criminal justice for women. Brooks questions the public construction of crime and shows how, in contrast to the news, women in actual conflict with the law are not hardcore violent women, but are generally overwhelmingly young, poor, uneducated mothers who are most often victims of violence and racial discrimination.

Brooks shows that most women in prison have experienced violence either personally or indirectly through poverty or substance abuse and that they have more in common with non-offending women than they do with male prisoners. She suggests that corrections facilities in Canada are not equipped to be a solution for women in conflict with the law and that women prisoners are faced with a system ill-equipped to deal with their personal problems. Her discussion of *Creating Choices,* and the reforms for women within federal penal institutions, shows that although such legislation was intended to create central facilities that would increase choices and empower federally sentenced women, many of the long-standing problems of female incarceration remain unsolved. Brooks engages the debate of whether feminist prisons are possible or even desirable. Her assessment of the reform of federal prison in Canada suggests that prison reform may risk expanding female incarceration to the detriment of addressing structural inequalities and issues of human rights.

Earle and Drake's chapter focuses on gender, especially masculinity as an idea that infects and shapes everyone, not only men. Similar to other chapters in this book, their work develops a critical and intersectional gaze that considers how class, race and ethnicity intersect with gender to all affect life possibilities. Their work challenges readers to consider why men are more involved in crime than women. They also investigate how men make sense of their lives in prisons, places that are defined and publicly accepted as "hypermasculine" places.

Just as Messerschmit has argued that "doing crime" is equivalent to "doing masculinity," Earle and Drake show how crime involvement helps males become men, especially when other masculine outlets (in, for example, sport, relationships or work) are less available to them. Drawing on their recent ethnographic work in English prisons, they detail how the men they have met inside prisons are just like the men and boys they know in school, life and work. Their chapter reminds readers of the importance of understanding biographies of real (as opposed to fictional) men and life experience. Prisons become places where men are controlled and punished and in many ways this reflects the brutality and masculine value system that governed them on the outside.

All of the chapters in this section demonstrate why gender cannot be ignored and the importance of providing a conceptual and theoretical tool kit as a framework for understanding how hierarchies of gender intersect with class, race and age.

13

THE SOCIAL CONSTRUCTION OF "DANGEROUS" GIRLS AND WOMEN

Karlene Faith and Yasmin Jiwani

KEY FACTS

> Women have been charged with approximately 10 to 15 percent of all violent crimes since the beginning of record keeping.

> While the media continued to falsely report a rising degree of violence by girls and women, the actual rates of violence, and rates of most other crimes (by both men and women), were on the decline through the 1990s and continue to decline.

> In 2000, about 18 percent of the 357 federally sentenced women incarcerated in Canada were classified as "maximum," and they were disproportionately Aboriginal women.

> Only two women in Canada, Marlene Moore and Lisa Neve, have been designated dangerous offenders. Critics observe that men require much more serious criminal histories, usually involving rape and/or murder, before being designated a dangerous offender.

> A study of sixty televised crime and legal dramas found that fictional stories on crime and homicide focus on individual and psychological episodes in characters lives. There is little effort made to examine social institutions or the nature of the society.

> Canadian newspaper industries are increasingly monopolized by major media corporations: CanWest Global, Shaw Communications, Rogers Media and Bell Canada own and control a significant portion of Canadian media. CanWest Global, for example, owns twenty-six daily Canadian newspapers (and the corresponding television stations in the same locations) and 50 percent of the National Post.

Sources: Reiman 2007; Fabianic 1997; Brownlee 2005.

Most criminalized women do not come from middle-class families. The crimes committed by women tend to be the result of poverty, privation and past experiences of abuse. When women kill, their victims are most often family members, particularly abusive spouses (Boritch 1997: 219–20), and these women cannot readily be characterized as "violent." Rather, these criminalized women are the "underclass," generally not the stuff of which big news is made.

Instead the news focuses on another class: the "dangerous" woman, a figure who appears regularly on our newspaper pages and television screens. Intensive media attention targets in particular women who commit crimes of fatal violence against strangers. Print and television journalists and traditionalist criminologists are mutually reinforcing in their attention to sensational, anomalous, violent offences by girls and women. Indeed, popular and academic theories of girls' and women's "dangerousness" in this regard abound. The general effect is to place disproportionate attention in the least representative cases of the women who come into contact with the criminal justice system — and to draw generalizing conclusions from those atypical cases. The dangerous, violent women become the ones whose media images extend in the public imagination to all "criminal" women. The result is the skewing of the public's perception of girls and women convicted of illegal behaviour.

The decontextualized nature of news reporting results in misrepresentations of social reality. A one-year study (1992–93) of Saturday news stories in five regional papers concerning crime by women found that more than 50 percent of the stories focused on the issue of women committing serious violence. Such crimes represent less than 0.5 percent of all charges laid against women for violent crimes (Boritch 1997: 16). (Most violence-related charges are for common assault.) The majority of the articles, aside from those that dealt with Karla Homolka, were stories about women who had killed their spouse or a child (Gordon, Faith and Currie 1995). This press coverage is a serious overrepresentation of violent crimes by women. There was not a single article in any of the papers on shoplifting, which is the predominant crime committed by both men and women. Ultimately, this phenomenon prompts fear, outcry, more aggressive prosecution of girls and women, harsher punishments for all women convicted of crime and a backlash against feminist and womanist movements.

Prison is a junction in which social inequities converge. In Canada, it is primarily Aboriginal people and Blacks who are overrepresented in jails and prisons, and this is because of structured racism. But media accounts of crimes by girls or women seldom acknowledge structural factors. Focusing on uncommon crimes of violence, the accounts individualize and pathologize the accused (see Appendix) with little or no reference to social context. The accounts tend not to stress another fact: that recidivism among women who have served sentences for murder is extremely rare (which is also the case for men).

In the following pages, serving as examples of media-saturated crimes involving girls or women, we discuss three cases: Leslie Van Houten, who was involved in one of the 1969 "Manson murders" in California; Karla Homolka, who in the early 1990s assisted Paul Bernardo in the sexual-torture killings of three young women, including her own sister, in Ontario; and Kelly Ellard, convicted of the brutal 1997 murder of classmate Reena Virk, in British Columbia. In each instance, the offender was a pretty, middle-class white girl, which not only distinguishes her from most criminalized women but also exacerbates the horror of the white majority — because, after all, "she's one of us." In other words, people seem to expect violent behaviour from people who are "not like themselves," people who are different. They do not expect it from themselves or their own. As it seems to go: when "we" (whoever "we" is) commit behaviour that shocks "our own kind," we are appalled, unlike when "they" misbehave, to which "we" respond with "Well, what can you expect?"

The three young women in our cases exuded danger because they broke gender codes in the most extreme ways possible. Their crimes are not comprehensible to the white middle class that bred them. Although the crimes seemed senseless, all three cases are indicative of power abuses — either because of having social power or reacting to others who have it.

The stigma of dangerousness, as applied selectively to individuals and to entire marginalized populations, is rooted in tradition. We begin, then, by setting the historical context in which the social divisions of "us" (good) and "them" (bad) became firmly entrenched in Western societies.

THE CONSTRUCTION OF "DANGEROUS CLASSES" IN WESTERN HISTORY

According to the Christian Bible, the first woman on Earth, Eve, committed the first human sin by eating an apple from the tree of knowledge, thus losing her innocence. She exacerbated her sin by seducing Adam; the snake signified the sexualized evil that now contaminated God's first human creatures. Women were by nature either evil or saints: whores or madonnas. It was about their sex. The dangers of women's sexuality is a recurrent theme in religion and in the history of theoretical criminology (Lombroso and Ferrero 1895; Pollak 1950). The theme reflects attitudes that feminists generally refer to as misogyny. The evil of women as sexual beings has also been a dominant theme in modern Western practices of criminal (in)justice.

The witch hunts of the fifteenth to eighteenth centuries are a conspicuous example of traditional fears of women and of the uses of the church, law and public hysteria to construct the idea of a dangerous woman (Klaits 1985; Marwick 1975; Trevor-Roper 1975; MacFarlane 1970; Parrinder 1963). The Bible declared that witches, as allies of Satan, were to be killed (Exodus 22: 18). The churches conducted the witch hunts, generating rumours, distrust, accusations and social panic. They turned suspects over to the state for trial in a court of law followed by execution (burned at the stake; drowned in boiling oil; hanged; beheaded). About 15 percent of the executed witches were men; often they had the choice of testifying against their wives or being themselves convicted of witchcraft (Wilson 1993).

Understanding that the best defence is a good offence, a woman afraid of being accused would lay blame on a neighbour for causing a misfortune: a miscarriage, illness or death, a cow drying up or a chicken that stopped laying, a storm damaging the barn, or some other calamity. The accused were charged with fornicating with the Devil, as his servant. Since witches committed havoc unseen by mortal eyes, no witnesses were necessary. Married women, rich as well as poor, and mothers together with their daughters were executed indiscriminately. Disproportionate numbers of single women and widows were executed — women without men, women who by choice or circumstance lived independently of men's supervision. If they kept small, domesticated animals as companions, as many did, they were de facto suspects. These were women who did not satisfy gender-role expectations, and they were thus perceived as dangerous women. As many as nine million women and girls may have been executed over three centuries, contributing to one of Europe's greatest holocausts (Ehrenreich and English 1973).

Women were censored and silenced in all realms of public life, and it was up to the men to keep their wives in line. For one thing, they would not tolerate abusive language (Sharpe 1984). In accordance with Blackstone's British legal commentaries in the eighteenth century, men had a responsibility to discipline women, with the caveat that the stick the man used to beat his wife should not be thicker than his own thumb (from whence tradition came the expression "rule of thumb"). When women scolded, both men and women were breaching gender codes. It was a crime for women to nag their husbands or harangue others in public. The punishment for this crime was public humiliation of both the woman and the man. The harshest punishments fell on women, who were often whipped, confined in a pillory in the town square, dunked in water or forced to wear a brank, also known as a "scold's bridle" — a helmet with a mouthpiece with small metal spikes inserted into the woman's mouth; if she attempted to speak, it would cut into her tongue (Underdown 1985: 123). Men were humiliated in noisy public rituals, subject to intensive ridicule for failing at manhood.

The formal tradition of criminology, the study of crime and punishment, commenced in nineteenth-century Europe in concert with the Industrial Revolution and the emergence of modern capitalism. In England, masses of people migrated to the newly urbanized centres, particularly London, where the lure of factory jobs supplanted agrarian culture (Thompson 1963). The promise of urban comforts, however, was not fulfilled for many of these unskilled migrants, and high unemployment produced rashes of what we now call street crime. These crimes, primarily related to the theft or destruction of property, were indicative of class divisions that separated the emerging capitalist class from people who were relegated to bare-survival wages or no paid work at all. The more affluent members of society, a distinct minority of the population, correctly perceived the antipathy of the unruly masses upon whose labour they depended for their affluence. Thus was born the political notion of "the dangerous classes."

The writings of Karl Marx were unequivocally focused on the work and social conditions of working-class men, whom he identified as the proletariat who would ultimately overthrow the capitalist class and establish a communal, profit-sharing, worker-owned industry (Marx 1970). He failed to recognize the significance of the chronically unemployed, the lowly riff-raff, whom he labelled the *lumpenproletariat*. In his estimation, they were social pariahs and parasites who contributed nothing to society. In his glib dismissal of the least resourceful victims of capitalism, Marx, in effect, was colluding with the bourgeois notion of the dangerous classes.

Women who failed to find legitimate employment, however dubious the benefits of such labour, often found themselves in brothels or working as street prostitutes and petty thieves. In Marx's terms, they, too, were relegated to the despised *lumpenproletariat*. More seriously, they were stigmatized as the dangerous carriers of sin and disease, which justified England's *Contagious Diseases Acts* (1860–83). This Act gave police the power to stop any woman on the street and send her off for an invasive medical examination. By the late nineteenth century, the nuclear family, with parents and children living as an insulated unit and the patriarchal father at the head, had replaced the extended family in which women had held more decision-making power. This familial arrangement was "naturalized" through social ritual and legal regulation, effectively domesticating middle-class Western women. Rather than being described by male authors as evil, they were now idealized as the heart of the family, virtue personified. Their "natural" compliance and nurturing ways would earn them the protection of their husbands and, by their example and adherence to Christian teachings, instill morality in their children. As Kathleen Kendall (1999: 111) puts it, "Convict women were perceived as either more morally corrupt than criminal men because they violated natural law, or as innocent victims of circumstance."

Canada's first separate jail for women, Toronto's Mercer Reformatory, which opened in 1880, was built on the premise that women and men require different approaches to confinement (Strange 1985–86). Incarcerated women were perceived as being more rowdy than the men, requiring strict discipline to develop good work habits, self-control over passions and a cessation of drunken or violent behaviours (Goff 1999: 165). With its emphasis on instruction in the domestic arts and religion, the reformation of imprisoned women in Canada was inspired by the work of Elizabeth Fry in England. Her goal was to reform women who, upon release, could attract a husband and manage a household and who would give up drinking, prostituting, gambling, yelling and cursing. With sufficient religious and domestic instruction, and with discipline and patience, she believed, these rebellious, ill-kempt, mean-tempered women would metamorphose into quiet, respectable homemakers.

Like women in jail, women at large required instruction in the arts of compliance and subordination — the need for which contradicted the ideology of women's natural submission to men (Faith 1993a). In European criminal courts, men could be held responsible for crimes committed by their wives, because women (notwithstanding their "natural" evil) were now thought to be "naturally" passive, and therefore incapable of conceiving and carrying out a crime. If a middle-class woman became unruly, that behaviour was blamed on the father or husband. These attitudes culminated in the Victorian age.

When ill-paid workers engaged in strikes and protests against those who exploited their labour, they were perceived not only as a threat to the smooth running of a profit-driven market economy but also as a danger to the safety and comfort of those upon whom they were dependent for their meagre livelihoods. Women were often active as "Luddites," weavers who smashed mechanical looms in protest against losing jobs to technology (Thompson 1963: 216–19). They protested food prices and scarcities and chased after the middleman, taking the grain from him and paying him a fair market price (Stevenson 1979). Women who aggressively and collectively protested on the streets and in the factories were de facto dangerous because they were behaving like men.

Cesare Lombroso (with his son-in-law, William Ferrero) was the first "scholar" to write about women who broke the law (1895). The "father of criminology," Lombroso formally established the myth that, when out of (men's) control, women at large were more vicious, dangerous and monstrous than any man. In 1950, criminologist Otto Pollak published a speculative essay on "female criminality" in which he asserted that women were more deceptive than men due to having both to hide their monthly period and to fake orgasm. Biology thus equips women with the skill of deception. He speculated that nurses and caretakers often kill the ill or elderly with poison, but get away with it.

Men have taken a great deal of effort over the centuries to teach women to stay in their place and to restrict their opportunities for immoral or illegal behaviour. In this postmodern age, gender-bending is commonplace and gendered hierarchies are legally challenged, often successfully, everywhere in the Western world. Women themselves are now in social-control positions as policy-makers, practitioners and professionals in every field. And yet, half a century later, Pollak's concerns with women's dangerousness, apparently based on the fear of women's sex, have by no means abated in society (Hudson 1989), despite and consistent with the preponderance of male sexual violence.

THE TWENTIETH CENTURY

The popularization of psychology in the mid-twentieth century caused a shift from generalizing women as inherently bad to seeing them as inherently mad. In the 1950s, new pharmaceutical industries promoted mood-changing and tranquilizing pills specifically targeted for depressed housewives and prisoners. Women were more likely to be sent to a mental hospital than to a prison. Because the numbers of women in the criminal justice system were so low, relative to men, and because men dominated the academic world, very little was published that shed any light on women in the system. When they weren't fictionalized as masculine and violent, they were seen, as by the Gluecks in the 1930s, as a pathetic but dangerous class who transmitted sexual diseases and bred inferior offspring (Glueck and Glueck 1934, 1965). "Bad seed" theories have proliferated in Western history, literature and entertainment: the simple idea that some people are born bad — supernaturally cursed or genetically unfortunate.

Beginning in the late 1960s, the interdisciplinary field of criminology came under the strong influence of critical sociologists and historians, some of whom were examining criminal justice systems as implicated in widespread social injustice and material disparity. Others, particularly feminist scholars, began to rectify the absence of women in the criminology literature (Heidensohn 1968; Bertrand 1969; Klein 1973). By the end of the 1970s, an abundance of new research had produced a rapidly growing literature in the areas of women, crime, and punishment. Two of the most prominent books, Freda Adler's *Sisters in Crime* (1975) and Carol Smart's *Women, Crime and Criminology: A Feminist Critique* (1976), were to have significant international influence on the direction of new scholarship. By the 1980s, gender was an exponentially expanding area in criminological research, as well as in every other discipline.

Adler's work stimulated a shift from thinking of criminalized women as monstrous, pathetic and/or pathological to thinking of women as independent agents, in a process of "gender convergence" with men in society as a consequence of the "freedoms" gained by the women's movement. These new freedoms, as Adler saw it, included women's increased opportunities to break the law. This "liberation thesis" was unsupportable, but the media were unrelenting in associating a fictional rise in violent crime by women with the women's movement. In fact, women have been charged with approximately 10–15 percent of all violent crimes since the beginning of record keeping, but to make their point the media offered skewed percentage increases. For example, if one jurisdiction had zero murders by women in 1974, but two murders by women the following year, the homicide rate for women would increase by 200 percent, as a blip. The press would headline the percentage increase but omit the low base numbers in their reports. When in the following year there were again zero murders by women, the press did not issue headlines declaring that women's homicide rate had decreased by 200 percent. Women killing people is far more titillating and newsworthy than women behaving themselves.

Adler (1975) was strenuously criticized for suggesting that women's liberation would result in increased crimes by women, and Smart (1976) demonstrated otherwise. Women's theft rates did go up in the late 1970s, but the robberies were not committed by women who had been influenced by women's liberation, nor were these women serious crooks. They were primarily the work of young single mothers who were experiencing the "feminization of poverty." They bore no resemblance to news reporters' fictionalized versions of wild, violent women running amok, as was propagated through the 1970s and again in the 1990s (Chesney-Lind 1997). At all periods of history, when women have organized for women's rights, they have met with fierce resistance from men and women who represent the status quo. In exploiting Adler's study, the media played directly into the hands of male supremacists. However, Adler's work as a sociologist also invited challenges from feminist scholars, and much research was catalyzed by her theory.

While the media continued to falsely report a rising degree of violence by girls and women, the actual rates of violence, and rates of most other crimes (by both men and women), were on the decline through the 1990s (CCJS 1999: 188–226), and they continue to decline (Alvi 2000: 56–57). Marge Reitsma-Street (1999) thoroughly examined the data, arguing that it conclusively proved that over the past twenty years charges for murder and attempted murder by girls had been constant and infrequent. The work of Walter DeKeseredy and his colleagues (1997) demonstrates that when girls and women are violent they are most commonly defending themselves or fighting back, with a man initiating the violence. Assault rates have gone up for girls in some locations, but this has less to do with more violence by girls than with social responses to those behaviours (DeKeseredy 2000: 45-46; Pate 1999: 39; Schramm 1998), including official reporting and prosecution. The kind of schoolyard bullying or scuffles with parents that would formerly have been resolved privately has now, with "zero tolerance," become a matter for criminal justice.

In 1998, the Canadian journalist Patricia Pearson revived and capitalized on the recurrent myth of women's dangerousness. Recycling an old theory, Pearson asserted that the feminist movement bears some responsibility in this (fictional) crime wave by violent women. Her basic argument, which is much like Pollak's earlier theory, is that our "politically correct" society is in denial about female aggression; in the feminist tradition of identifying girls' and women's victimizations and systemic powerlessness, feminists rob women of the need to accept responsibility and to be accountable for their actions, such as husband-beating (Pearson 1998: 30). Feminists, in Pearson's critique, have failed to recognize women as "rational" decision-makers with personal agency, who commit aggressive and/or violent crime as a calculated individual choice. The news media again, predictably, exploited the provocation that women's liberation was making excuses for violence by women.

Meda Chesney-Lind (1999: 114) points out, though, that feminists do not campaign for the right to be violent. She criticizes Pearson's "conflation of aggression and violence" and her false assertions of increases in women's serious crime. As Chesney-Lind (1999: 116) notes, "Troublesome facts rarely disrupt Pearson's flow." Given that men commit up to 90 percent of violent aggression, rather than vie for equality in this area, it would make more sense, as Chesney-Lind observes, to focus on theorizing about the "consistent, powerful sex difference" in men's and women's crime rates. Moreover, Pearson "minimizes and dismisses women's victimization and its clear connection to women's violence, and then argues that such violence should be punished without regard to gender" (Chesney-Lind 1999: 117–18).

Chesney-Lind (1997) uncovers how the media and the criminal justice system tend to label a group of girls a "gang" if they are not white. Bernard Schissel (1997: 51) refers to the exaggerated press coverage accorded to youth gangs as hate crimes perpetrated by the media. Journalists quote academics who haven't studied gangs but offer expert opinions (DeKeseredy 2000: 55). Media reports about gangs take on a tone of moral panic even though, as Sandra Bell (1999: 157–63) observes, most so-called youth gangs are involved neither in violent crime nor in claiming turf. In support, Bell cites Karen Joe and Chesney-Lind (1993), who found that girl gangs are primarily social support groups for marginalized girls.

Critical scholars recognize how the media skew reality by focusing on statistically insignificant but culturally sensational crimes, such as school shootings or a girl beating another girl to death. Contrived imagery of a rising tide of delinquency sets up destructive misrepresentations about young people and crime (Alvi 2000: 15–18; Bell

1999: 84–85; Schissel 1997). Shahid Alvi (2000: 18) reports that 94 percent of Toronto newspaper stories on youth crime involve violence, even though most crimes by youth, such as theft, are non-violent (Bell 1999: 80). Girls are rarely aggressors in these stories, and they more often appear as victims.

A study of girl violence in Western Canada (Artz 1998) was based on interviews with just six adolescent girls who were involved in assaultive behaviours. The media colluded with the author's emphasis of girl-on-girl violence as signifying a rising trend, with the attendant theme of family dysfunction. In a study of girl's "dope gangs" in Detroit (Taylor 1993), the author emphasizes the factor of violence as an element in the drug use, but does not suggest that girl gangs signify a trend. Certainly the evidence is lacking for establishing a trend of violent girl gangs in Canada, but the media insist on it with an explicit anti-feminist stance. For example, in *Alberta Report,* under the headline "Killer Girls," the author states: "The latest crop of teenage girls can be as violent, malicious and downright evil as the boys. In fact, they're leading the explosion in youth crime. It's an unexpected by-product of the feminist push for equality" (quoted in DeKeseredy 2000: 38). By contrast, the Detroit study includes an analysis of poverty, racism and criminal (in)justice and a discussion of a steady stream of resourceless Black girls who are processed through the system unheard and unseen, as if they were dangerous (Taylor 1993).

In establishing various levels of security, Correctional Services of Canada (CSC) classifies prisoners in the following ways: those who are not deemed a risk (for escape, or to cause harm to others) are classified minimum or medium security; maximum security is reserved for those perceived as a threat to the good order of the institution, whatever their crime. In 2000, about 18 percent of the 357 federally sentenced women incarcerated in Canada were classified as "maximum," and they were disproportionately Aboriginal women. Through the 1990s, women labelled "maximum" were sent to men's psychiatric prisons around Canada, where they were placed in solitary and drugged. In committing millions of dollars to new segregation buildings at four women's prisons, CSC is implying that these units are needed for the safety of the public (Hayman 2000). In fact, very few women are criminally "dangerous," or even perceived to be. The women so labelled would be more accurately generalized as "uncooperative" with the prison regime.

Even more restricted than prisoners labelled "maximum security" have been those officially declared by the court as a "dangerous offender." Following from the *Habitual Offenders Act* of 1947 and the *Criminal Sexual-Psychopath Act* of 1948, the dangerous offender designation was first proposed by the Ouimet Committee, a 1969 government commission for prison reform. The commission reasoned that the distinction, and tight control over those so labelled, would encourage communities to be more accepting of the vast majority of prisoners and those newly released, who pose no threat. The designation, which came into force in 1977, is based on these criteria:

- Pattern of unrestrained behaviour;
- Pattern of aggressive behaviour with indifference as to the consequences;
- Behaviour of such a brutal nature that ordinary standards of restraint won't control it. (Criminal Code, Part XXIV, Section 753)

Only two women in Canada, Marlene Moore and Lisa Neve, have been designated dangerous offenders. Critics observe that men require much more serious criminal histories, usually involving rape and/or murder, before being designated a dangerous offender, and that Moore and Neve were victims of a double standard. Neither of them had killed anyone, but the net-widening law permits use of the designation with just one violent offence, which can be assault, as in the case of both Neve and Moore. Both were chronically abused, in trouble from a young age, and in and out of prison from their teens. Marlene Moore robbed a woman on the street at knifepoint. Lisa Neve, who worked in the sex trade, assaulted a co-worker with a knife and issued threats. Moore, after spending much of her life in prison, committed suicide at the Prison for Women in 1988 at age twenty-eight (Kershaw and Lasovich 1991). After five years with the label, Neve's super-maximum dangerous offender classification was overturned in 1999, when she was twenty-six, and she was immediately released from prison. By all accounts, she has been "reformed."

FACING THE CONTRADICTIONS

For half a century, from *Caged* in 1950 to the prison-porn flicks of the 1990s, Hollywood movies set in women's prisons have consistently presented a pat set of stereotypes: evil, masculine women, both prisoners and matrons, presented as violent lesbians, often as women of colour; the sweet, innocent, blonde white girl who is imprisoned due to a mistake, often wrongly convicted for a crime committed by her boyfriend; the psychotic criminal who goes berserk; the super-sexy bad girls who cheerfully do the dirty work for a controlling, sadistic dominatrix. The most common stereotypes are devil women, lesbians as villains, teenage predators and super-bitch killer beauties (Faith 1993a, 1993b; Birch 1993).

The fictions of Hollywood rarely coincide with the truths of women's lives. It is neither monsters nor pathetic victims who get locked up. Rather, upon first entering a woman's prison, one is struck both by the diversity of the women, in terms of age, appearance and demeanour, and by their ordinariness and approachability. The same "types" of women one finds in prison would be found in an urban department store. They do not look dangerous, and indeed few are. Certainly women of colour are vastly overrepresented (Monture-Angus 2000a; Gilbert 1999; Neugebauer-Visano 1996), and the white women are not middle class. Race, class and gender are both distinct and conjoined, each dynamically influencing the other in criminal justice processes.

Women on death row are not usually conventionally feminine in appearance (Farr 2000). An exception was the softly appealing Karla Faye Tucker, who was executed in Texas in 2000 after winning the hearts of Christians throughout the United States through national television interviews. Tucker was not a feminine woman when she was sentenced; she was softened by her conversion to Christianity, following the crime. Women with masculine characteristics are not more likely to kill than feminine women. They are, however, perceived as more dangerous, and if convicted they are more likely than feminine women to receive the death penalty, especially if they are lesbians and most especially if they are women of colour (Farr 2000).

The closer a woman is to the ideals of femininity, the more shocking it is when she violently betrays her gender role. Because the offence defies "common sense," particularly when the victims are strangers, the accused are often dismissed as pathological (see Appendix). But pathology suggests that the crime is the outcome of a deranged mind, a sick individual detached from society at large.

The three very feminine women who make up our case studies are far from the stereotypical monsters of film, psychiatry or criminology, although the seriousness of their crimes rivals any of the monster stories. In addition to the headline murders in which they were implicated, they continue to attract media attention because they were young, attractive, white, middle-class women at the time of their crimes. All are currently in prison. We focus on these sensational cases even while critiquing sensationalism. We do not see these women as presented by the media, but as women whose life experiences prior to their crimes were not unlike those of other women of their cultures and generations. They are not aliens but rather signifiers of the times and places in which they lived.

Leslie Van Houten[1]

On August 9 and 10, 1969, in affluent neighbourhoods in Los Angeles County, two sets of murders were orchestrated by a cult guru who had spent most of his life in prison. Four men and three women were killed, and the name Charles Manson entered the lexicon of American popular culture, signifying an end to the idealism of the 1960s. Manson, in his mid-thirties, and three young women aged nineteen to twenty-one were arrested in late 1969. In July 1971, they were sentenced to death and transported to state prisons to await execution. The media were unrelenting in the attention given to the case until spring 1972, when the U.S. Supreme Court declared the death penalty unconstitutional and their sentences were amended to life in prison.

Manson had about twenty-five followers (aged thirteen to early twenties), any of whom would have been happy to have been selected for these murder missions. Most of these disciples had been extremely feminine young women when he met them — on streets, in parks, in hippie pads in San Francisco. Each of them, all white and most of them middle class, had been successfully socialized to be attractive, soft and feminine in appearance and demeanour. They were all skilled in the domestic arts, and they honoured men's hierarchical privilege in the social order. They excelled in submissiveness.

In the beginning, Manson presented himself as a gentle man with spiritual wisdom and no fear. Through the use of drugs, especially LSD, and intensive, unrelenting mind-control games, his followers became convinced that he had supernatural powers. They revered him as the reincarnation of Jesus Christ. At a time when millions of young people throughout North America were rebelling against the hypocrisies and barbarities of the establishment, and seeking enlightenment from Eastern religions, these young people were convinced of Manson's higher authority. He looked up to Aboriginal peoples, he opposed the war in Vietnam, he preached peace and love. He had magical qualities. He played his guitar and sang self-penned songs with social commentary. Wild animals weren't afraid of him. Even rattlesnakes let him pet them. He washed the feet of his disciples, just as Christ had done. His followers were ready to follow him anywhere, which turned out to be "Helter Skelter." This was Manson's vision of the world in chaos, with himself, a white man, at the helm of a new revolution that would give the power back to the Black man and rain terror on "Whitie" for centuries of abuse against transported, enslaved Africans and their descendants. Manson, an undisguised sexist, recruited young trophy women to serve him and his male friends in every respect. His plan to start a race war was patronizingly racist; and his selection of victims was based on straightforward class antagonism against materialist consumer "piggies."

On August 9, 1969, Manson selected four of his followers, "Tex" and three of "the girls," and sent them out to start the revolution. (On this first night he didn't send Leslie, who stayed home at the communal ranch to take care of the family's babies.) He targeted the former residence of a music producer who had failed to satisfy Manson's ambition for a rock 'n' roll career. Unbeknownst to Manson, the house had been leased to a film director who was then away. At home were his pregnant wife, an actor, and several of her friends. Five people were mercilessly killed, and messages taken from lyrics in Beatles songs were left in blood on the walls. Manson himself didn't attend the killing; he just told his followers what to do and they obeyed. He was the general, and they were his soldiers.

When the crew reported back to Manson, he was displeased with their "messy" job. On the following night, August 10, he went along with a somewhat changed crew to make sure things were properly set up. Again, Tex was chosen to commit the murders along with two girls, Pat and Leslie. Like most of the other girls, Leslie had a wholesome upbringing. She sang in the church choir as a teen and was a smart, popular, classic beauty, a homecoming princess, active in the community and just generally a well-admired middle-class Southern California girl. She had joined up with Manson in September 1968. In the spirit of the times, a period of great social upheaval and protest against universal injustices, Leslie was looking for answers to life's big questions, and she thought Manson had them. He promised to help her kill her ego. As his disciple, she gave up her name, her birthday and every facet of her former self. She was just nineteen.

This second night, Manson chose a house at random, though significantly in another affluent neighbourhood and next door to a house where he had once partied as an aspiring rock 'n' roller. He and Tex went in first and tied up the occupants, Leno and Rosemary LaBianca, parents and owners of successful retail businesses. Manson then left the house, telling Pat and Leslie to go in and do whatever Tex told them to do. Manson himself drove to what he mistakenly thought was a Black neighbourhood, where, in a gas station restroom, he left the wallet he'd stolen from Mr. LaBianca. He expected Black men would be blamed for the crime, and that Black men would then rise up in a race war. The "family" would live in a hole in the desert, staying young and healthy somehow, until the war ended and they would surface as the ally of the victorious Blacks. Anything he said sounded like prophecy to those who believed in him, and they were prepared to do his bidding at any cost. Yet, in the LaBianca home, Leslie was unable to perform as a good soldier. She recoiled at the prospect of killing and backed off into another room when the murders started. After Tex had already killed Leno Bianca, and had struck the fatal blow to Rosemary after Pat was unsuccessful, he then insisted that Leslie also come into the room and stab the by-now dead woman, which she did, fourteen to sixteen times in a brutal act of frenzy. She later described to a parole board that she both felt like a wild animal with its prey and was filled with fury at herself for having not lived up to Manson's faith in her.

As he was to later testify, and contrary to the women's boastful testimony at trial, later refuted, it was Tex Watson who dealt the death blow to all seven of the victims of Manson's forays into Helter Skelter. (Watson was tried separately, and continues to serve life in a California state prison.) All three of the women had proven inadequate to the task. Like any good girl would be, each was terrified at the murders. Each resisted, and each proved incompetent as murderers, even while trying to act the good soldier. As young women, they had no training for violence. It was not so much a matter of conscience that bothered Leslie afterward but rather frustration and disappointment at her inability to perform as instructed and her failure to meet their leader's expectations.

The press routinely demonizes people who have been criminalized, and with Manson this practice did not require much journalistic imagination. He presented himself as both a deity and Satan. (He was once booked in jail as Jesus Christ, Saviour and Lord.) As the mastermind conspirator, he was sentenced to death along with the three women who took credit for the killings on the two nights. During trial, on his instruction, they all shaved their heads, carved Xs into their foreheads and taunted the judge. The press characterized the women as pathologically evil, and they did appear to be serving Satan. Compounding the theatrics were the numerous "Manson girls" who lived on the sidewalk outside the L.A. court building for almost two years in solidarity. They too shaved their heads and wore long cloaks that reinforced the witchy impressions.

In 1972, when the death penalty was rescinded throughout the United States (until 1976), Leslie and the others were still housed on death row in the California women's state prison. They continued to live in their six-by-nine-foot cells for four more years, when they were gradually transferred to the main prison. By 1974, five years after the trial, Leslie had completely shed her attachment to Manson. She was racked with remorse, and she expressed her guilt with anorexia. In 1976, her case was separated from that of her co-defendants. Because she was not in her right mind at the time of the crime, had never killed anyone, had been the victim of cult conditioning and, most relevantly, had never had a proper defence (her lawyer had drowned on a camping trip during the trial), her previous sentence (death, converted to life in prison) was overturned and she was granted a new trial. In this 1977 trial the jury was deadlocked as to her guilt, so a third trial was scheduled.

For six months prior to and during the third trial, Leslie was permitted to leave the county jail on bail, having now served over eight years, much of it in solitary. While on bail she worked as a legal secretary when not in court, and she was able to reunite with family and old friends. She lived a normal life and the media was respectful of her privacy. Reporters were startled to discover the change in her, from the 1971 clone of Satan to the calm young woman of 1977 who showed humility, remorse, compassion, integrity and a grounded intelligence. This time she was convicted for robbery-murder (the wallet, some coins), rather than first-degree murder, and she was returned to state prison. She is still there, at the age of sixty-six.

The public first saw the rehabilitated Leslie in 1976 when she was interviewed on ABC television by Barbara Walters. She did not disclaim responsibility for the crimes, and she said she was as guilty as if she had taken the victims' lives. Her guilt was for following Manson, giving him her power. With that interview, the public began to see "the Manson girls" as individuals, not as robots who all used the same voice — saying the same words, using the same mannerisms — when they were under Manson's control. Subsequent interviews with Leslie by Larry King and Diane Sawyer further erased the monstrous images that had accompanied the first seven years of reportage on the case.

Over twenty-five years ago, while in her early twenties, Leslie returned to her self with help from therapists, family, friends, teachers, and sympathetic prison staff. She would have to live with the nightmare of the torment she helped cause and the enduring grief of the victims' family and her own. Permanently humbled, she lives as healthfully as anyone can while incarcerated, and she became a model prisoner who engages in service to her prison community and beyond. By day she works full time at prison jobs, which rotate every several years, in the hospital, school, administrative and chaplain's offices. In her spare time she reads onto tape for the blind, makes quilts for the homeless, teaches English to women for whom it isn't a first language and organizes talent for the annual AA dinner show. When she entered the prison, there were six hundred women there. Now there are two thousand. Younger women who come in learn from Leslie how to survive prison with grace. She's the old-timer who doesn't complain. The parole board has turned her down in fifteen hearings, often reluctantly, it seems; they encourage her to remain hopeful that "one day soon" she'll be released.

The death penalty may have been a less painful punishment than living out a life sentence with a deeply injured conscience and no hope for making restitution. Life sentences commonly do not exceed twenty-five years, especially for someone like Leslie with an unblemished prison record and who poses no threat of violence or escape. If she is soon released her nightmares will accompany her, and getting out after almost forty years would not be getting off easy.

Karla Homolka

Normally, in making a release decision, the Canadian National Parole Board conducts a risk assessment, considering the applicant's criminal history, alcohol or drug use, violence on record, psychological state, information from experts and, sometimes, victims of the crimes. Those convicted of first-degree murder must generally serve a minimum of twenty-five years. In the case of Karla Homolka, whom many consider dangerous, a deal was made in 1993 in which she was granted a maximum twelve-year sentence on manslaughter charges. In exchange she offered information about her husband, but without revealing the extent of her own role.

The story of Karla Homolka and Paul Bernardo erupted on the media landscape in February 1993 with Bernardo's arrest on charges of murder and sexual assault. The murder charges stemmed from the discovery of the cement-encased body parts of 14-year-old Leslie Mahaffy and the abused body of 15-year-old Kristen French. Both young women had been kidnapped, raped and tortured. Bernardo and Homolka were also implicated and subsequently charged with the murder of Homolka's younger sister, Tammy Lynn. It was subsequently discovered that Bernardo had routinely engaged in sexual assault between 1983 and 1993. He was charged with two counts of first-degree murder and forty-three counts of sexual assault. The extent to which Homolka was a willing accomplice in committing the murders was then a matter of conjecture. Bernardo's lawyers argued that she was actively involved, as "home movie" tapes later demonstrated. While the actions of both Bernardo and Homolka were equally brutal, the media spotlight and public attention were focused on and continue to dwell on Homolka.

The 1992–93 survey of print media on issues dealing with women and the criminal justice system yielded a preponderance of stories dealing with Homolka (Gordon, Faith, and Currie 1995). A total of 136 women and crime articles appeared in the Saturday editions of five urban Canadian newspapers. Twenty-one of these articles focused on Karla Homolka, all of them published between May and July. Eight articles, more than a third, were in the *Toronto Star*, given the provincial interest in the case, but for three months Homolka stories dominated the media nationwide.

Despite a court-ordered publication ban, there were more stories published on the Homolka and Bernardo case than on any other criminal case that year. The media tended to focus their initial coverage not on details of the crimes but rather on the freedom of the press and the public's right to know (Gordon, Faith and Currie 1995; McCormick 1995). The publication ban itself incited speculation and rumours about the case, as well as a proliferation of websites and Internet news discussion groups (Regan Shade 1994). The cloud of secrecy intensified speculation when Bernardo's own lawyer argued against the ban (Walker 1994). In 1995, Homolka again dominated the airwaves and print media with her testimony at Bernardo's trial.

Initially Homolka's media representation alternated between heartless killer and victim slave. As with most media coverage, the tendency was to confine the figure or issue in easily understandable binary oppositions (bad versus good; savage versus civilized) (Hartley 1982). Yet this binary framing tended to collapse from the sheer velocity of the vacillations between competing representations. The oppositions relayed in news accounts were so extreme that the story became an exceptionally bizarre case of inconsistencies. For instance, a *Globe and Mail* article begins with a description of Homolka's "Barbie" image, describing her as "a stunning 23-year-old veterinarian's assistant ... long blonde hair and blue eyes ... peaches and cream complexion ... wouldn't hurt a fly." The same article refers to Bernardo as "26 ... accountant ... tall ... charming ... handsome enough to melt a young girl's heart. But behind the Ken and Barbie masks lurked the face of grotesque evil" (quoted in its entirety in McCormick 1995: 186).

Crime reporting is also based on the element of sensationalism, and much depends on how far a story departs from conventional standards and encapsulates an extreme (McCormick 1995). Homolka's crimes were unusual in the extreme. They were committed by a woman. They were taken as being crimes against humanity because they involved the torture and murder of adolescent women, one of whom was her sister. The pleasant, clean-cut news-photo images of Homolka and Bernardo were incompatible with the standard idea of sex murderers. The cognitive dissonance created by the juxtaposition of the stories with the photographs served to draw in readers who would not normally seek out stories about sex and violence. The sensationalism was supported by the unusualness of having a woman challenged and convicted of pornographic murders and by the offenders' disarmingly wholesome profiles.

Each time she appeared in the public arena, the media scrutinized and communicated Homolka's behaviour to fit into a conception of her as either cold psychopath or battered woman. At no time did the media engage in a critical analysis of the many women who are battered, murdered, raped and mutilated throughout the world on any given day, or of the reality that most homicides are committed by men. Rather the media focus on the unusual event or situation, and especially one that becomes a "continuing story," with new developments day by day or from time to time (Connell 1980; Hartley 1982). In the case of Homolka, the continuity was ensured for a period of at least two years — until 1995, when she was called to testify at Bernardo's trial. Homolka's plea bargain, resulting in the twelve-year sentence on the lesser charge of manslaughter, generated intense and negative public reaction, which, in itself, became a media story. More than three hundred thousand signatures were collected on a petition opposing the Crown's settlement and the lenient sentence (Boritch 1997: 3).

This intense reaction can be explained in terms of the contradictory identification that Homolka evoked — as a daughter and sister, and as tormentor and killer. Not only did she symbolize the deepest betrayal of trust among women by killing those of her own kind, but she also offered a symbol of daughter, sister or wife. She epitomized the potentiality of an evil that society seeks to constrain through the rationale of law and order, which gains its legitimacy at least partially through the media.

An additional but highly critical factor underpinning the moral outrage ignited by this case sprang from the identities and representations of the victims. The young women who were tortured, raped and murdered were not "deserving" victims. They were not on the streets. They came from good homes. They were innocent, pretty, white schoolgirls whose parents were solid citizens. In contrast, Homolka and Bernardo represented the fractured identities of individuals who were not what they purported to be.

Crime reporting is incident-driven and decontextualized (Gordon, Faith and Currie 1995; Schissel 1997). It is the lack of an overall social context that gives news stories their poignancy and dramatic flavour; the stories reveal the extremes of human behaviour without placing those extremes in context. Over a time the repeated stories and their common themes communicate a sense that the issue — whatever it is — is pervasive and increasing in intensity. The prevailing "new filter" — the means by which some details get into stories and others are left out — becomes entrenched, suggesting that the issue has always been problematic (Hall et al. 1978; Hall 1990). The most common example of this kind of entrenchment can be seen in news coverage of ethno-racial groups that are often presented as problematic immigrant groups who will not assimilate (Jiwani 1993).

From the start of the Homolka-Bernardo case, the media drew on entrenched filters to make sense of the story. For example, in one of the early articles published by the *Globe and Mail* the reporter notes, "The striking blonde is the daughter of Czechoslovakian refugees" (Sept. 28, 1993: 24–25). That this bit of information was considered pertinent suggests the reporter's search for potential explanations that would resonate with the public imagination and make "common sense."

As the case unfolded in media reports, part of the "common sense" explanations included the rationale that Homolka was either devoid of a moral conscience or under Bernardo's power. During her trial, the coverage described her as "stone-faced" amidst the "gasps of horror" that greeted her testimony (*Globe and Mail* Sept. 28, 1993). She provided "chilling testimony" (Warwick 1995). Reporters who listened to the audio tracks of four Homolka-assisted rapes by Bernardo underlined the horror of the murder-rapes. As a means of conveying unprintable words, one reporter explained, "The words were the same as those uttered on most X-rated movies — expletives and crude instructions to perform sexual acts" (Galloway 1995). Reporters noted that "a stunned silence took over the courtroom" during the playing of an audiotape of a drug-induced rape. According to one reporter, "The scant dialogue was enough to send an eerie chill through the court-room. For several moments after the tape stopped, nobody said anything" (Legall 1995).

The press alternately depicted Homolka as the devil's accomplice and a battered woman, helping to justify her short sentence and ensure Bernardo's conviction (Blackwell 1995a). By her own testimony, Homolka said she acquiesced and did everything she could to please Bernardo until she left him on January 5, 1993. She testified, "He treated me like a princess, like I was the only girl in the world" (Brown 1995), but said she feared for her life. Headlines communicated the press's skepticism of the use of the battered woman's syndrome to describe Homolka's actions by using such terms as "robo-victim defence" (Verburg 1995), despite photographic evidence of severe physical abuse (Blackwell 1995a).

These competing points of view accelerated as her testimony continued from late May to July 14, 1995, in what was described as "one of the longest and most dramatic appearances to take place in a Canadian courtroom" (Makin 1995b). Reports described Homolka as an extremely cold, manipulative and possibly insane personality who has "a truly sick, twisted side" (Stepan 2000), and they used testimony from experts to legitimize this perspective. The media representation was bolstered by the very backlash it helped to foment. From most media perspectives, Karla Homolka personified evil — a kind of evil that the justice system cannot rehabilitate. The system is "soft" and thus allows for the likes of Karla Homolka to escape without retribution (Wente 1999).

On the victimization-criminalization continuum, where does Homolka stand on the level of guilt? The only agency permitted her is that of complicity in a series of heinous crimes with her apparently psychopathic husband/abuser. Neither of them were aberrant in their observed everyday behaviours. As presented by the media, Bernardo and Homolka were over socialized to the worst extremes of their respective gender possibilities.

It would seem that Homolka's femininity was her nemesis. Her feminine passivity and fear led to her inability to resist Bernardo's sex, violence and death games. Her external femininity also caused uneasiness, because her media-transmitted image of attractive, pleasant normality disrupts conventional notions of women who can be trusted not to hurt people. Paradoxically, her crimes were also consistent with her image: she was acting out the extreme end of the compliant femininity continuum — absolute obedience.

Once placed in the centre of the media spotlight, Homolka and Bernardo were mutually but separately challenged to recreate themselves through the lens of innocence; they had to be reconstructed, based on who they were — or who they appeared to be — before the violence. They appear to be inflicted with the "shallow personality syndrome," which is endemic to a materialistic, individualistic, image-obsessed society. They invite armchair psychologizing. In her demeanour, Homolka retains a superficial quality, that of a "material girl" gone berserk.

Given the limits on and biases in media coverage, the rest of us are backed up against the limits of the personal/political dialectic — the contradictions inherent in trying to understand crime at a societal level but believing that explanations for certain types of crime must come from within the individual — forced to retreat with the conservatives, from the search for internal logic to the paradigm of pathology. Given the conflicting details of the crimes, it would be difficult to formulate a reading of the case that goes beyond the boundaries of the mainstream print and television coverage, which vacillates so strongly between Karla the Monster and Karla the Victim. The relatively restrictive Canadian approach to criminal trials, even one as sensational as this, is a far cry from the circus of the simultaneous O.J. Simpson trial in Los Angeles. We can only speculate from our global knowledge of femicide, ritual rape, wife battering and sex slavery that there is much more to the story than the newspapers and television stations are telling us, or than what Homolka and Bernardo themselves know, but aren't telling us — yet.

In 2005, after serving twelve years in federal prison, Karla Homolka was released in accordance with the deal she made prior to the court's knowledge of the extent of her involvement in the rapes and murders. Her release was not renegotiated despite protest from the public and the legal community. As of 2006, Karla lives as anonymously as possible somewhere in the province of Quebec.

Kelly Marie Ellard

On November 14, 1997, seven girls (aged fourteen to sixteen years) and one sixteen-year-old boy brutally attacked Reena Virk, a young girl of South Asian origin, in a suburb of Victoria, B.C. As Reena left the scene of the beating to make her way home, she was followed by two members of the group — Kelly Ellard and Warren Glowatski. Kelly called out to her to ask if she was okay. Reena told them to leave her alone and staggered across the road. They followed her to the other side of a park, near a body of water. According to Glowatski's testimony, Kelly asked Reena to remove her jacket and shoes. Kelly then proceeded to beat her up again, smashing her head against a tree trunk to the point where Reena was rendered unconscious. Ellard and Glowatski dragged the unconscious body to the water, where Kelly hit Reena in the throat again and forcibly drowned her. According to Glowatski in his trial, Ellard stood in the water with her foot over Reena's head and smoked a cigarette. Neither Ellard, nor Glowatski, had met Virk until that night.

The discovery of Reena's body eight days later and the subsequent arrest of the teens involved in the initial attack resulted in intense media scrutiny and publicity. Both nationally and internationally, Reena Virk's murder came to symbolize the increasing violence of girls and young women, despite statistical evidence to the contrary.

The early media coverage advanced a "liberation thesis" to explain the murder, dwelling on the violence as an outcome of girls achieving gender equality. Reena, as a victim, was explained in terms of her inability to fit into her peer culture. She was described as being overweight, tall for her age and plain in her looks. The news media failed to mention her South Asian origin or reflect on how her racial difference contributed to not fitting into the school culture (Jiwani 1999). She was not exotic enough in her difference to fit, nor was she acceptable according to the dominant, normative standards of her peer group or her family.

In March 2000, Kelly Marie Ellard was tried for the murder of Reena Virk. Media speculation about Ellard's role in the murder had continued throughout the two-year period prior to her trial. From January to April 21, more than a hundred local and national radio and television newscasts and press articles focused on the Virk murder. This sustained and, at times, heavy coverage appeared to be motivated by a desire to advance explanations of the crime that made "common sense." That desire to make sense emanated from the same cognitive dissonance that had occurred in the cases of Karla Homolka and Leslie Van Houten. Like them, Ellard came from a middle-class, white family. Although her parents were divorced, she appeared to have a close relationship with her family, which motivated one judge to rule that she could stay at home rather than be incarcerated in a youth detention centre. Her appearance did not fit her crime. As one columnist opined, "How do you match the sweet-looking teenage girl who doesn't stand five feet in her platform shoes, who's a little heavy in the hips, who speaks tremulously on the stand, with the image of an accused killer?" (McMartin 2000).

From the beginning of the trial, the press presented Ellard as a normal looking teenager "with straight black hair cut just above the shoulders," wearing "a gray sweater and black pants" (Stonebanks 2000). However, these descriptions were juxtaposed with photographs that portrayed Ellard with a smug expression, downcast eyes and a hint of a smile. The pictures communicated an image of an individual cognizant of more than she was willing to reveal.

The coverage of the Ellard trial was influenced by a number of external factors. Reporters attending the trial had followed the story from its inception two years earlier. Hence they were privy to details revealed in the testimonies presented at the previous trial of Warren Glowatski, the co-accused, and the hearings of the other young women who were involved in the beating. It was not uncommon to see reporters gather outside the courtroom to verify what they had heard and identify common themes of relevancy for their particular articles and newscasts. Additionally, reporters were cautioned by the outcomes of a preceding event in which one newspaper was severely chastised by a particular judge for revealing details of a trial prior to the jury going out for deliberation. In the Ellard trial, the presiding judge, Madam Justice Morrison, had decreed that the jury would not be sequestered for the length of the trial. This meant that journalists could not report on anything other than what witnesses stated in their testimonies. The reportage was thus extremely factual and rarely included the same level of descriptive discourse that appeared in the Homolka case. Nonetheless, reporters used terms such as "chilling," "gang-murder," "savage," "cold-blooded killing" and "calculated" to describe both Ellard and the murder. They borrowed most of these words directly from testimony provided by witnesses.

From the testimonies, the media constructed an image of Ellard as a cold-blooded killer who had deliberately murdered Virk. They portrayed her as being the most aggressive and leading the assault. She was also described as having bragged about the murder to her friends. Throughout the trial, Ellard's composure, as reported, vacillated from being tearful to being calm, depending on who took the witness stand. Between the sessions in court, she was often seen, and captured on camera, laughing and joking with her family and defence counsel.

Some thirty witnesses were called to testify at the trial over a three-week period. The Crown maintained that Ellard had committed the crime to ensure that Reena would not "rat" on the members of the group who had beaten her up. The defence strategy was to portray Ellard as a helpless victim of a conspiracy organized by the co-accused, Warren Glowatski. Ellard and members of her family were the key witnesses for the defence. Together they wove a picture of middle-class normalcy and concern. Ellard was composed on the stand. She spoke softly and denied any involvement. She identified Glowatski and two other young women as having committed the murder. According to news reports, Ellard cried when asked to recount why she had delivered the first blow to Reena Virk. She replied, "I guess I was being like them, victimizing her" (Moore 2000a).

While the media coverage was contained and cautious throughout the trial, once the jury went into deliberation the press focused on the information presented in the *voir dires* — information not accepted as evidence by the judge or seen by the jury. The media pointed to the inconsistencies between Ellard's statements to the police and the testimonies presented by the various Crown witnesses. Despite this, the tenor of the articles was not as damning as the coverage that came after the verdict was announced. The jury's verdict was a conviction for second-degree murder. Justice Morrison set the eligibility for parole at five years.

The news media used stock theories to account for Ellard's criminal behaviour. In some instances they identified teen group loyalty as the main motive underpinning Ellard's actions, as well as those of Glowatski, who refused to testify as a Crown witness against Ellard (Teahen 2000). Other accounts drew on previous psychological assessments to demonstrate Ellard's pathological character, her inability to assume responsibility and her lack of internalized social values (Hall 2000; see Appendix). Other news items focused on the need for increased law and order to control the increasingly violent actions of teens. This last point was underscored by Crown counsel, who stated to reporters, "I hope it will spur parents particularly to do whatever they can to make sure they know where their children are so that a little more control can be taken of the situation" (*Canadian Press*, March 31, 2000). Some of the coverage utilized the previous frame of girl violence, alleging that most of the girls involved in the attack on Virk had criminal records (Moore 2000b).

These same theories appear in letters to the editors. In an anonymous letter (April 4, 2000) printed in the *Province* (Vancouver), the author addresses "Killer Kelly Ellard" stating, "Perhaps we don't want to know how an attractive young woman like yourself, 15 at the time, could murder a younger school mate with a cruelty we've always preferred to believe was reserved for the vilest of villains — nearly always adult males." The author ends the letter by stating, "We'll just write you off as a whacky weirdo with a rotten childhood whose hatred of herself and the world is etched in her eyes. What else can we do? Except keep our fingers crossed that if the social network should fail, the jury system will prevail."

Significantly absent in the range of explanations put forward by the media was Reena Virk's marginalized positioning vis-à-vis those who had beaten and killed her. The issue of race and racism was either absent from the media discourse or presented in terms of her inability to fit in. Rarely did the media question why she could not fit in and what she might have been attempting to fit into. Even though both Ellard and Glowatski are white, and both were convicted of killing a young South Asian girl, the issue of racism only surfaced when Justice Morrison stated in her sentencing, "Whatever the motive for this crime, it was not racism" (Ivens 2000). Justice Morrison went on to portray Ellard as someone who had shown remorse as well as the potential for rehabilitation. She spoke at length about Ellard's love for animals and the positive references she had seen in the twenty-nine letters she had received from Ellard's friends and family.

Although the media works in concert with other dominant/elite institutions in society to legitimize perspectives that are consonant with the views of those in power (Hall et al. 1978; Hall 1980; van Dijk 1993), the relationship between the media and dominant institutions is not a direct one. Rather, in putting forward competing explanations, the media favour the explanations that make "common sense," and "common sense" perspectives often work in support of the dominant ideology. In this particular case, Justice Morrison underlined Ellard's presumed innocence and thereby contributed to the media's more muted condemnation of the murder. The coverage is starkly different from that of the Homolka case. It colludes with dominant "common sense" definitions of racism as extremist behaviours confined to the actions of hate groups, or as overtly racial slurs and insults. Within the landscape of "multicultural" Canada, these dominant definitions do not include systemic and invisible forms of everyday racism.

If the crime were to be recast — if a South Asian girl murdered a white girl or, more dramatically, an Aboriginal boy murdered a white girl — the denial and erasure of racism in the Ellard case would become apparent. Public outrage would have been intense, and the crime would probably not have elicited the same light sentence of five years.[2] Given the omission of the factor of racism and, with it, a profound denial of the unequal and hierarchical nature of society, we can only see the media as being complicit in presenting an image of a democratic society in which all members are equally vulnerable to victimization and equally accountable in the eyes of the law.

MEDIA AND DANGEROUS GIRLS AND WOMEN

When they occurred, these three cases incited considerable media coverage and public scrutiny. At the root of the public fascination and extensive coverage was that all three cases ruptured stereotypical notions of appropriate gender behaviour.

In numerous respects, these three women and their crimes have distinct commonalities. All three were involved in uniquely horrific murders. These were exceptional crimes in that the victims were also girls/women and primarily strangers. Van Houten and Homolka, and perhaps Ellard as well, explicitly committed their crimes in seeking a man's approval. None of them was a feminist. In the aftermath, all of them seemed unaffected by the consequences of their crimes and the immense pain caused by their actions. They were all from balanced, middle-class homes, which sets them apart from the majority of criminalized women. (This did not benefit Van Houten, who was declassed through her association with the outcast Manson.) According to contemporary, white femininity standards, all are good-looking with likeable personalities, which may well have been factors in the lenient deal/sentencing of Homolka and Ellard. (It didn't help Van Houten, who was originally sentenced to death.) None of them suffered from disabilities or was in any way stigmatized as "other" prior to their crimes. They all "fit in." Thus their behaviours were regarded as radical aberrations of gender expectations. In short, they were marked as dangerous women.

Van Houten, along with twenty-five or so other young people, was a straightforward victim of brainwashing by a cult guru. Her decisive crime was in surrendering her power to him. Her reasons were of a spiritual nature; she was seeking truths and believed he had them. Although Homolka was similarly entranced by Bernardo, her motives weren't at all spiritual. Van Houten's crime occurred at the peak of a massive social movement that had disrupted traditional capitalist values. By contrast, Homolka's crimes, and Ellard's, occurred during a period of conformity, consumerism and materialism. Whereas Van Houten rejected the consumer society, Homolka embraced it. According to the accounts, she was interested in the surface appearance of things.

The perception of dangerousness in each of these cases was heightened and exaggerated by intense media coverage. The coverage served to re-entrench the proverbial notion that women are as dangerous as men and that an increasing proclivity to violence among women is a result of their liberation from patriarchal control. Certainly some women such as Homolka and/or Ellard can be readily perceived as dangerous, but men are ten times more likely to kill someone. The fear of "criminal women," as a generalized, stereotyped group, is irrational. However, the hardware invested in locking up women — the bars, fences, lasers, electronic locks, cameras, guards and walls — are all signals to the public that these unseen women are dangerous. In a prison, every real or contrived crisis or emergency that gathers media interest is a means for correctional workers to express to the public the dangers of their occupations, and to be granted better wages, working conditions and "danger pay."

Theories of female criminality and dangerousness have evolved from essentialist notions regarding women's innate nature. The dangerousness of women, after all, can be traced back to Biblical times and Eve. Notions of women's inherent dangerousness have also existed in other cultural milieus, in part as a result of colonization and the spread of the Judeo-Christian and Islamic traditions.[3] Contradictory representations in this historical tradition clearly cohere around the notions of women as virgins or vamps, madonnas or whores.

The placing of some women on a pedestal of purity and innocence (representing woman as virginal) often comes at the expense of non-white, sexualized women in low-income households. To be effective, one representation is contrasted with another that is its opposite. We know that not all women are pure, innocent or chaste. We do not understand quite as well how social class, race, age, sexuality and able-bodiedness influence a girl's or woman's vulnerability to violence as victim and/or perpetrator. The three cases demonstrate the need to complicate the analysis — to begin to consider interlocking forms of oppression (Razack 1998) and relations of power that have an impact upon and among women who are in different places in the social hierarchy. Media monopolies are gendered, race-based and class-based. They are controlled by white, upper-class men. Media explanations for women's criminality borrow from an andocentric historical tradition and reflect the views of those who control them. From this perspective, women's "inherent proclivity" to criminality tends to be confined to the sexualized, racialized and low-income classes. Women who break the mould are most newsworthy.

The three cases illustrate the media's strategic use of isolated examples of female criminals to establish a generalized female proclivity to crime. These cases were headlined simply because such cases are rare — that is what makes them sensational. The horrors of the crimes committed by Leslie Van Houten, Karla Homolka and Kelly Marie Ellard are used to underscore how women in general are capable of committing violent crimes and becoming "like men." By this logic, women do not deserve any special consideration on the grounds of gender inequality; their criminality becomes a result of their achieving gender-parity. The media's decontextualized and case-specific reportage lends itself well to this kind of explanation.

Pathology occurs at extreme ends of a continuum of social values and behaviours. We are socialized for pathological behaviours as surely as we are socialized for acceptable behaviours. In focusing on these women's transgressions, the media reinforce the normative social and moral order. They imply the rewards that accrue if women stay "in their place." However few and far between as these cases of horrific violence by girls and women are, their actions ignite the fears engendered by Adler's work in the 1970s and Pearson's book in the 1990s. Women who engage in "senseless violence" are demonized and, if they excite the media, permanently stigmatized. Their identities are lost to processing by the state: the literal replacement of a person's name with a number, and the social death and invisibility of living behind bars. Their identities are reduced to their crimes.

Gayle Horii, a woman who served a life sentence in Canada, writes of that experience:

> I realized that probably less than five minutes of my life dictated my punishment, but it need not wipe out the woman I was for forty-two years previous to my particular madness, nor dictate how I live the remainder of my life. Because of the crime I committed, it may be difficult to accept my assertions that I should be granted human rights and that I could still maintain decent values. It is a most abstract conundrum, to wrap one's mind around the fact that a killer and/ or prisoner could also be a good person. (Horii 2000: 104)

POSTSCRIPT

As of 2014, Leslie has been in prison forty-five years, her entire adulthood. Periodically, members of the California Board of Parole meet with her to discuss her application for parole. At some hearings, they raise her hopes for release; other times she is shamed and harangued for her association with Charles Manson and the heinous crimes he orchestrated in 1969.

Leslie has been a model prisoner for decades. She completed a Bachelor's degree with the support of a nearby university. At age 63 she completed a Master's degree, with a thesis on critical thinking. Over the years she has made blankets for the homeless, recorded tapes for the blind and assisted young women entering prison bewildered and afraid. She has been a respected role model in her community, admired by both prison staff and other prisoners. She has given wise counsel, provided tutoring services and worked as a teaching assistant to instructors who offer college classes to prisoners. She has demonstrated her commitment to atone for the rest of her life. The parole board is not attentive to Leslie's complete rehabilitation, which she achieved decades ago. Instead they focus on the seriousness of the crime, the stigma attached to it and the potential danger to "the public" as their reasons for denying her parole. However, as the parole board well knows, Leslie was released on bail in 1978 during her re-trial, and for six months she worked as a legal assistant when not in court. She was never recognized in public, and she in no way posed a threat to society. It is well understood that she is not a danger to anyone. It is also understood that, given the notoriety of the crime, it would take a politically courageous parole board to release any of those associated with it.

Karla Homolka, meanwhile, was released from prison in 2005, just twelve years from the time of her arrest. She changed her name, got married, gave birth to three children and, to escape the press and an angry nation, settled in the Caribbean.

DISCUSSION QUESTIONS

1. In what ways can the media be seen as an arm of the criminal justice system?

2. What are some of the social or policy effects of the media focus on murders by girls?

3. How do you explain the erasure of racism in the murder of Reena Virk and in the trial of the defendant Kelly Ellard?

4. Cite reasons why Leslie Van Houten should be released from prison or reasons why she should not be released. Include a discussion of whether there should be limits to punishment.

5. If Karla Homolka were to be retried, and you were the presiding judge, what would be your sentencing decision? (Consider options outside of conventional punishments.)

6. Explain the social construction of "dangerousness" as it affects women who are criminalized.

GLOSSARY

Backlash: a negative reaction that thwarts someone's intentions.

Biblical Constructions: ways of seeing the world that are formed from the traditions and lore of early Christianity as documented in the Bible, including patriarchal and hierarchical social relations.

Common Sense: also known as "conventional wisdom"; the unexamined cultural beliefs, attitudes and opinions held as truths by a majority of a specific group within a specific time period.

Criminalized Women: women who, through discriminatory social processes and law enforcement, are selected for the prosecution of illegal behaviours, convicted and imprisoned and thereafter labelled and stigmatized as members of the criminal class.

Dangerous Offender: a designation that came into effect in 1977, based on patterns of unrestrained behaviour, aggressive behaviour and behaviour deemed "brutal" in nature. Those designated as "dangerous offenders" are sentenced to indeterminate sentences that have no set warrant expiry date.

Dangerousness: a presumed propensity for causing physical harm to others.

Girl-on-Girl Violence: an occasion on which one girl assaults another, or a group of girls assaults one or more other girls.

Liberation Thesis: criminologists in the 1970s predicted wrongly that the women's liberation movement would cause women to commit a higher rate of violent crime.

Luddites: members of a nineteenth-century movement in Great Britain that protested the replacement of human labour with machines. The term Luddite comes from Ned Lud, a feeble-minded man who smashed two frames belonging to a Leicestershire employer, and was adopted by a group of workers in England who between 1811 and 1816 smashed new labour-saving textile machinery in protest against reduced wages and the unemployment attributed to that machinery's introduction.

Pop Psychology: commonplace formulations of "truths" about human behaviours, feelings and thoughts based on the superficialities of popular culture and commonly reflecting a disinterest in or lack of access to scholarly research. For example, over the last two decades there has been an increase in the publication of "psychology" books for laypeople to satisfy a growth in interest in understanding personal behaviour and the lives of those around them. These are the books you find in the psychology section in bookstores on issues such as multiple intelligence, personality typologies and emotional intelligence. Most materials of this nature are written by psychologists, adding at least a veneer of respectability.

SUGGESTED READINGS

Ellen Adelberg and Claudia Currie (eds.), *In Conflict with the Law: Women in the Canadian Justice System*, Vancouver: Press Gang. (1993).

The Honourable Louise Arbour, *Commission of Inquiry into Certain Events at the Prison for Women in Kingston*, Ottawa: Solicitor General of Canada (1996).

Cook, Sandy, and Susanne Davies (eds.), *Harsh Punishments: International Experiences of Women's Imprisonment*. Boston: Northeastern Press (1999).

Walter S. DeKeseredy, *Women, Crime and the Canadian Criminal Justice System*, Cincinnati, OH: Anderson Publishing Co. (2000).

Karlene Faith, *Unruly Women: The Politics of Confinement and Resistance*, Vancouver: Press Gang (1993).

Kelly Hannah-Moffat and Margaret Shaw (eds.), *An Ideal Prison? Critical Essays on Women's Imprisonment in Canada*, Halifax: Fernwood Publishing (2000).

Anne Kershaw and Mary Lasovitch, *Rock-a-Bye Baby: A Death Behind Bars*, Toronto: McClelland & Stewart (1991).

Rudy Weibe and Yvonne Johnson, *Stolen Life: The Journey of a Cree Woman*, Toronto: Alfred A. Knopf (1998).

NOTES

1. This section is culled from *The Long Prison Journey of Leslie Van Houten* (Faith 2001).
2. By spring 2002, Kelly Ellard's case had been appealed, and she was out of prison, living at home, pending a decision. Her second trial was aborted on a technicality. In her third trial, in the summer of 2005, Kelly was convicted of second-degree murder and she is now serving a life sentence in a federal prison.
3. This is not to suggest that these religions do not have their own feminist traditions, which have emerged in response to an androcentric interpretation of the respective faith and have resulted in a herstory that identifies the female aspects of a revered universal being.

APPENDIX

Summary of Psychopathology Checklist as developed by Dr. Robert D. Hare, *Without Conscience: The Disturbing World of the Psychopaths among Us* (New York: Pocket Books, 1993, pp. 3–34)

    1. Glib and superficial
    2. Egocentric and grandiose

3. Lack of remorse or guilt
4. Lack of empathy
5. Deceitful and manipulative
6. Shallow emotions
7. Impulsive
8. Poor behavioural controls
9. Need for excitement
10. Lack of responsibility
11. Early behavioural problems
12. Adult anti-social behaviours

Note: Everyone has some of the above characteristics. Others, the psychopaths, have strong constellations of many of these characteristics. Most of Hare's examples of psychopaths are men, which is consistent with the infrequency of women's crimes of violence.

REFERENCES

Adler, Freda. 1975. *Sisters in Crime: The Rise of the New Female Criminal.* New York: McGraw Hill.
Alvi, Shahid. 2000. *Youth and Canadian Criminal Justice System.* Cincinnati: Anderson.
Artz, Sibylle. 1998. *Sex, Power and the Violent School Girl.* Toronto: Trifolium.
Bell, Sandra J. 1999. *Young Offenders and Juvenile Justice.* Toronto: Nelson.
Bertrand, Marie-Andree. 1969. "Self-Image and Delinquency: A Contribution to the Study of Female Criminality and Woman's Image." *Acta Criminologica* 2.
Birch, Helen (ed.). 1993. *Moving Targets: Women, Murder and Representation.* London: Virago.
Boritch, Helen. 1997. *Fallen Women: Female Crime and Criminal Justice in Canada.* Scarborough, ON: ITP Nelson.
Brown, Barbara. 1995. "Homolka Says She Watched Killing of 2 Girls in Bedroom: 'Paul Strangled Them with a Black Electrical Cord,' Ex-Wife Tells Court." *Vancouver Sun*, June 20.
Brownlee, Jamie. 2005. *Ruling Canada: Corporate Cohesion and Democracy.* Black Point, NS: Fernwood Publishing.
Canadian Press. 2000. "Teen Girl Begins Life [sic] Sentence for Killing Reena Virk." March 31.
CCJS (Canadian Centre for Justice Statistics). 1999. *Canadian Crime Statistics: Annual Catalogue.* Ottawa: Statistics Canada.
Chesney-Lind, Meda. 1997. *The Female Offender: Girls, Women and Crime.* Thousand Oaks, CA: Sage.
___. 1999. "Review: P. Pearson, When She Was Bad." *Women & Criminal Justice* 10, 4: 113–18.
Connell, Ian. 1980. "Television News and the Social Contract." In Stuart Hall, Dorothy Hobson, Andrew Lowe and Paul Willis (eds.), *Culture, Media, Language.* London, UK: Hutchinson Press and the Centre for Contemporary Cultural Studies, University of Birmingham.
DeKeseredy, Walter S. 2000. *Women, Crime and the Canadian Criminal Justice System.* Cincinnati: Anderson.
DeKeseredy, W.S., D.G. Saunders, M.D. Schwartz and S. Alvi. 1997. "The Meanings and Motives for Women's Use of Violence in Canadian College Dating Relationships: Results from a National Survey." *Sociological Spectrum* 17.
Ehrenreich, Barbara, and Deirdre English. 1973. *Witches, Midwives, and Nurses: A History of Women Healers.* Old Westbury: Feminist Press.
Fabianic, David. 1997. "Television Dramas and Homicide Causation." *Journal of Criminal Justice* 25, 3.
Faith, Karlene. 1993a. *Unruly Women: The Politics of Confinement and Resistance.* Vancouver: Press Gang Publishers.
___. 1993b. "Media, Myths and Masculinization: Images of Women in Prison." In E. Adelberg and

C. Currie (eds.), *In Conflict with the Law: Women in the Canadian Justice System*. Vancouver: Press Gang.

___. 2001. *The Long Prison Journey of Leslie Van Houten, Life Beyond the Cult*. Boston: Northeastern University Press.

Farr, Kathryn Ann. 2000. "Defeminizing and Dehumanizing Female Murderers: Depictions of Lesbians on Death Row." *Women & Criminal Justice* 11, 1.

Galloway, Gloria. 1995. "Bernardo Jury Stoic as 'Disturbing' Videotape of Rape Played." *Vancouver Sun*, June 1.

Gilbert, Evelyn. 1999. "Crime, Sex, and Justice: African American Women in U.S. Prisons." In S. Cook and S. Davies (eds.), *Harsh Punishment: International Experiences of Women's Imprisonment*. Boston: Northeastern Press.

Glueck, Sheldon, and Eleanor Glueck. 1965 [1934]. *Five Hundred Delinquent Women*. New York: Kraus Reprint.

Goff, Colin. 1999. *Corrections in Canada*. Cincinnati: Anderson.

Gordon, Jody, Karlene Faith and Dawn Currie. 1995. "The Case of Karla Homolka: Crime, Media and Gender Politics." Unpublished data. President's Research Grant. School of Criminology, Simon Fraser University.

Hall, Neale. 2000. "Ellard's Nickname Was Killer Kelly, Court Told." *Vancouver Sun*, April 1.

Hall, Stuart. 1980. "Race, Articulation and Societies Structured in Dominance." In Stuart Hall, (ed.), *Sociological Theories: Race and Colonialism*. Paris: UNESCO.

___. 1990. "The Whites of Their Eyes." In M. Alvarado and J.O. Thompson (eds.), *The Media Reader*. London: British Film Institute.

Hall, Stuart, Chas Critcher, Tony Jefferson, John Clarke and Brian Roberts. 1978. *Policing the Crisis: Mugging, the State, and Law and Order*. London: Macmillan.

Hartley, John. 1982. *Understanding News*. London & New York: Methuen.

Hayman, Stephanie. 2000. "Prison Reform and Incorporation." In K. Hannah-Moffat and M. Shaw (eds.), *An Ideal Prison? Critical Essays on Women's Imprisonment in Canada*. Halifax: Fernwood Publishing.

Heidensohn, Frances. 1968. "The Deviance of Women: A Critique and an Enquiry." *British Journal of Sociology* 19, 2.

Horii, Gayle. 2000. "Processing Humans." In K. Hannah-Moffat and M. Shaw (eds.), *An Ideal Prison? Critical Essays on Women's Imprisonment in Canada*. Halifax: Fernwood Publishing.

Hudson, Annie. 1989. "'Troublesome Girls:' Towards Alternative Definitions and Policies." In Maureen Cain (ed.), *Growing Up Good: Policing the Behaviour of Girls in Europe*. London: Sage.

Ivens, Andy. 2000. "No Apology by Killer, She Got the Lightest Sentence Possible: Five Years Without Parole." *Vancouver Province*, April 21.

Jiwani, Yasmin. 1993. "By Omission and Commission: 'Race' and Representation in Canadian Television News." Unpublished doctoral dissertation, School of Communications, Simon Fraser University.

___. 1999. "Erasing Race: The Story of Reena Virk." *Canadian Woman Studies* 19, 3.

Joe, K., and M. Chesney-Lind. 1993. "Just Every Mother's Angel." Paper presented at meetings of the American Society of Criminology. Phoenix, Arizona, October.

Kendall, Kathleen. 1999. "Beyond Grace: Criminal Lunatic Women in Victorian Canada." *Canadian Woman Studies* 19, 1&2.

Kershaw, Anne, and Mary Lasovitch. 1991. *Rock-a-Bye-Baby: A Death Behind Bars*. Toronto: McClelland & Stewart.

Klaits, Joseph. 1985. *Servants of Satan: The Age of the Witch Hunts*. Bloomington: Indiana University Press.

Klein, Dorie. 1973. "The Etiology of Female Crime: A Review of the Literature." *Issues in Criminology* 8, 2.

Legall, Paul. 1995a. "Graphic Dialogue Sends Eerie Chill through Court: 200 Spectators Hear 6 Minutes of Drug-Induced Rape of Homolka Sister." *Vancouver Sun*, June 1.

___. 1995b. "Accused Killer Wails for his Wife: Court Hears Tape Recording of Pleas for Homolka to Return." *Vancouver Sun*, June 16.

Lombroso, Cesare, and William Ferrero. 1895. *The Female Offender*. New York: Philosophical Library.

MacFarlane, Alan. 1970. *Witchcraft in Tudor and Stuart England: A Regional and Comparative Study*. New York: Harper and Row.

Makin, Kirk. 1995b. "Homolka Ends Graphic Testimony." *Globe and Mail*, July 15

Marwick, Max (ed.). 1975. *Witchcraft and Sorcery*. Harmondsworth, Middlesex: Penguin.

Marx, Karl. 1970. *Das Kapital*. Moscow: Progress.

McCormick, Chris. 1995. *Constructing Danger: The Mis/Representation of Crime in the News*. Halifax: Fernwood Publishing.

McMartin, Pete. 2000. "Shock of Virk Trial Is Ordinary Appearance of Accused Teen — A Scared Little 17-year-old in Person Comes as a Surprise after Grisly Testimony and a Smug-Looking Photo." *Vancouver Sun*, March 23.

Monture-Angus, Patricia. 2000. "Aboriginal Overrepresentation in the Canadian Criminal Justice System." In David Long and Olive Patricia Dickason (eds.), *Visions of the Heart: Canadian Aboriginal Issues* 2nd edition. Toronto: Harcourt Canada.

Moore, Deme. 2000a. "Accused Teen Killer Says She Wasn't There when Virk Killed." *Canadian Press*, March 23.

___. 2000b. "Girls Who Beat Virk Had Long Histories of Violence." *Canadian Press*, April 1.

Neugebauer-Visano, Robynne. 1996. "Kids, Cops, and Colour: The Social Organization of Police-Minority Youth Relations." In G.M. O'Bireck (ed.), *Not a Kid Anymore: Canadian Youth, Crime, and Subcultures*. Toronto: Nelson.

Parrinder, Geoffrey. 1963. *Witchcraft: European and African*. London: Faber & Faber.

Pate, Kim. 1999. "Young Women and Violent Offences: Myths and Realities." *Canadian Woman Studies* 19, 1&2.

Pearson, Patricia. 1998. *When She Was Bad*. Toronto: Vintage.

Pollak, O. 1950. *The Criminality of Women*. Pennsylvania: University of Pennsylvania Press.

Razack, Sherene H. 1998. *Looking White People in the Eye: Gender, Race, and Culture in Courtrooms and Classrooms*. Toronto: University of Toronto Press.

Regan Shade, Leslie. 1994. "Desperately Seeking Karla: The Case of alt.fan.karla.homolka." Proceedings of the Canadian Association for Information Science, 22nd Annual Conference, May 25–27, McGill University, Montreal.

Reiman, Jeffrey. 2007. *The Rich Get Richer and the Poor Get Prison: Ideology, Class and Criminal Justice.* Boston: Allyn and Bacon.

Reitsma-Street, Marge. 1999. "Justice for Canadian Girls: A 1990s Update." *Canadian Journal of Criminology* 41, 3.

Schissel, Bernard. 1997. *Blaming Children: Youth Crime, Moral Panics and the Politics of Hate*. Halifax: Fernwood Publishing.

Schramm, Heather. 1998. *Young Women Who Use Violence: Myths and Facts*. Calgary: Elizabeth Fry Society of Calgary.

Sharpe. J.A. 1984. *Crime in Early Modern England, 1550–1750*. New York: Longman.

Smart, Carol. 1976. *Women, Crime and Criminology: A Feminist Critique*. London: Routledge & Kegan Paul.

Stepan, Cheryl. 2000. "Homolka Transcript Brings Tears to Court." *Calgary Herald*, April 28.

Stevenson, John. 1979. *Popular Disturbances in England, 1700–1870*. New York: Longman.

Stonebanks, Roger. 2000. "The Last Accused in Reena's Death: Families Gather to Witness Final Trial in Teen Tragedy." *Victoria Times Colonist*, March 7.

Strange, Carolyn. 1985–86. "'The Criminal and Fallen' of Their Sex: The Establishment of Canada's First Women's Prison, 1874–1901." *Canadian Journal of Women and the Law/Revue juridique "La femme et le droit"* 1, 1.

Taylor, Carl S. 1993. *Girls, Gangs, Women and Drugs*. East Lansing: Michigan State University Press.

Teahen, Kelley. 2000. "When Loyalty Turns Threatening." *London Free Press*, Opinion, April 4.

Thompson, E.P. 1963. *The Making of the English Working Class*. London: Penguin.

Trevor-Roper, H.R. 1975. "The European Witch-Craze." In M. Marwick (ed.), *Witchcraft and Sorcery*. Harmondsworth, Middlesex: Penguin.

Underdown, David E. 1985. "The Taming of the Scold: The Enforcement of Patriarchal Authority in Early Modern England." In A. Fletcher and J. Stevenson (eds.), *Order and Disorder in Early Modern England*. Cambridge: Cambridge University Press.

Van Dijk, Teun. 1993. *Elite Discourse and Racism*. California: Sage Publications.

Verburg, Peter. 1995. "'Battered Wife Syndrome' on Trial: Homolka's Complicity in the Bernardo Atrocities Dealt a Heavy Blow to the 'Robo-Victim' Defence." *Western Report* 10, 22 (June 26).

Walker, Robert. 1994. "Publication Ban Doing More Harm than Good, Lawyer Argues." *Montreal Gazette*, February 7.

Warwick, Liz. 1995. "Violent Women." *Ottawa Citizen*, August 1.

Wente, Margaret. 1999. "The New and Self-Improved Karla Homolka." *Globe and Mail*, November 6.

Wilson, Nanci Koser. 1993. "Taming Women and Nature: The Criminal Justice System and the Creation of Crime in Salem Village." In R. Muraskin and T. Alleman (eds.), *It's a Crime: Women and Justice*. Englewood Cliffs, NJ: Regents/Prentice Hall.

14

REFORMING PRISONS FOR WOMEN?

Carolyn Brooks

KEY FACTS

> The first prison for women in Canada, the Andrew Mercer Reformatory for Females, opened its doors in 1872 with the purpose of providing "maternal reform" to female inmates. Although it was designed with progressive approaches to treatment (including an all-female staff), the Mercer Reformatory was criticized for failing to address the true needs of female inmates.

> The 2012 Ashley Smith Inquiry made a series of recommendations regarding the mental health of criminalized women. The recommendations include immediate access to mental health professionals and services; mental health training for institutional staff; and arranging transfers to federally operated treatment facilities for those with serious mental health issues.

> In 1867, the police chief for the city of Hamilton, Ontario, noted that most of the women who were arrested (in the city) had committed trivial offences with the sole intention of incarceration. It was reasoned that the women were doing this because their "degraded state" had made it impossible for them to pay for food and shelter otherwise.

> A recent study of the type, quality and availability of occupational training for female inmates in provincial custody indicated that women had access to homemaking and crafts programs, but not to industry or occupation-related skills development.

Strange 1985; Correctional Service of Canada 2013; Findlay et al. 2013.

Another day I'm confined...
Inside of being confined,
Another day I am undefined...
With feelings of love and hate combined.
Another day I analyze...
I try to bend and compromise,
While fighting back tears from my eyes...
My faith dangles and my spirit dies...
— Summers 2011, Another day [in prison] series

Canada's treatment of women prisoners is said to "reveal a sad legacy of harsh, cruel, and discriminatory treatment" (Boritch 2002: 309). The media representations of women and crime contrasts sharply with the reality of women who have come into conflict with the law and how they have been treated in the criminal justice system. The treatment of federally sentenced women and the history of the Prison for Women in Kingston is one filled with harshness and cruelty. Both are also in sharp contrast to *Creating Choices: The Task Force Report for Federally Sentenced Women in Canada*, which is largely only symbolic of feminist engagement with the state. While we acknowledge the importance of documents such as *Creating Choices* as catalysts for broad-ranging transformations in federal corrections for women, and applaud the commitment and energy of those involved, we question the success of their implementation. Twenty-five years later, the realization of a new feminist-based prison system remains limited, both theoretically and practically.

MEDIA IMAGES VS. CRIME STATISTICS AND WOMEN'S STORIES

Media images often viscerally influence how we think and feel about women in trouble (Faith 2011, 1993; Schissel 2006). The resulting public perceptions influence public policy and criminal justice measures (Schissel 2006; Garland 2001). However, these perceptions rarely reflect reality.

Images in Film

The mid-twentieth century saw the rise of a genre of very crude prison films portraying incarcerated women as sexualized, demonized characters. Beginning with the infamous film *Caged* in 1950, the next four decades saw women presented as monsters and depicted as masculinized — often lesbian — predatory maniacs who are born criminals. Faith (1993, 2011) described this as an invention of women that bears no resemblance to real women actually locked inside prisons:

> The monster-criminal woman of fifties movies was the anonymous woman, the shadow woman, a killer so primitive as to lack an individual identity ... They and the psychotic lesbian matron are evil and terrifying, especially to the predictably white, pretty goody-goody who got there by mistake, the only character with whom the intended audience can identify. (1993: 258)

These demonized characters are starkly contrasted with women who are wrongly convicted; we are thus set up with images of good (innocent) and evil (guilty). Explicit, pornographic scenes add a component of Madonna (innocent) versus whore (guilty) as well as compliant versus dangerous.

I have shown part of the 1985 movie *Reform School Girls* in my classrooms and asked students what they see. Students talk about innocent young women corrupted by "wicked" "monster" "predators," routine physical damage amongst the women, disproportionate numbers of the women seen as lesbians, false images of lesbian women, brutal prison guards and staff and sexualized scenes. Many of the students in my classes throughout the years have pointed out that women in real prisons "likely don't wear lingerie or look like the women in the films."

These misrepresentations of incarcerated women create a misinformed ideological framework for understanding real women in trouble. The women in these films are shown punching each other in the face and raping and violating each other. These films exploit classism, racism and homophobia. Women with darker complexions or who are lesbians are depicted as being more dangerous, inviting hostility towards lesbian and racialized women (Faith 1993; Lawston 2011). Faith (2011, 1993) points out that few women prisoners are lesbians and few lesbian women are "sex-crazed." Such stereotypes reify dangerous and false images of women behind bars.

In the later 1980s and the 1990s, images in film shifted and introduced what Faith (2011, 1993) calls the "super-bitch killer beauties." These films had villains whose beauty was undermined by an evil nature. Faith describes the character of Alex Forest, played by Glenn Close in *Fatal Attraction* (1987), who rages against her loving and supposedly (except for the adultery) idyllic happy family:

> [Forest] is the image of the beautiful, solitary, ominous, male-identified, childless, pathologically obsessive woman, "liberated" in anti-feminist terms, who would take what she wants at any cost. (Faith 1993: 265)

Other examples include:

- *The Hand That Rocks the Cradle* (1991) — A deceptive, beautiful villain captures the heart of the family she is also seeking to destroy;
- *Single White Female* (1992), *Single White Female 2: The Psycho* (2005), *The Roommate* (2011) — These movies all portray beautiful young women trying to violently steal their roommate's life and soul; and
- *Basic Instinct* (1992), *Basic Instinct 2* (2006) — These homophobic dramas feature a deceptive and manipulative bisexual woman with stunning female lovers; the female characters violently destroy men's bodies and minds.

As Cecil (2007: 305–306) points out, "Because the correctional system is rarely depicted in the media ... images in "babes-behind-bars" films are detrimental in that they negate the issues surrounding women in prison." Although these characters are so far-fetched to be barely believable, they may influence how the public understands female crime (Cecil 2007; Clowers 2001). Faith (2011, 1993) argues that fear of the unruly women shown in many female prison films has helped justify maximum-security prison construction.

Images in the News

The news tends to focus on the most hard-core, violent women criminals. For example, Karla Homolka, Aileen Wuornos and Susan Smith all received extensive mass media coverage and all were labelled as "monsters" by the media. Karla Homolka is a Canadian serial killer who was convicted of manslaughter in the rape-murder cases of her own sister and two other teenage Ontario girls. Along with her husband, Paul Bernardo, Homolka was convicted of abduction and rape, but she was found guilty of manslaughter while Bernardo was found guilty of murder. This case dominated the news and one of the main stories was the prosecution's deal with Homolka to serve only a twelve year sentence if she testified against her husband. The news stories used two narratives of Karla Homolka as a morally depraved dangerous woman versus a passively innocent woman in danger of an abusive spouse (Banwell 2011). Aileen Wuornos was convicted of six counts of murder in the first degree and put to death by lethal injection in 2002. Susan Smith is an

American woman sentenced to life for murdering her four children.

Faith and Jiwani (in this volume) point out that women who commit fatal violence, especially against strangers, receive attention-grabbing and intense media coverage. As they note, in a study of newspaper stories about criminalized women in Saturday editions of five regional Canadian newspapers, 50 percent concerned serious violence; however, less than 0.5 percent of all criminal charges actually laid against women are for serious violence. No articles concerned shoplifting, despite it being most commonly committed crime by both genders.

Chesney-Lind and Eliason (2006: 29) argue that the attention on violence of women and girls in all forms of media lend legitimacy to female punishment and even execution through a "'masculinization' of certain girls and women." They write, "A review of the media fascination with 'bad girls' and crime provides clear evidence of the assumption that if women begin to question traditional femininity, they run the risk of becoming like men, that is more violent and sexually 'loose' (often conflated with interest and involvement in lesbian activities), particularly in prison settings" (2006: 31).

WOMEN AND CRIMINALITY

In contrast to the images of female criminals in film and news stories, women in actual conflict with the law in Canada are overwhelmingly young, poor, uneducated mothers with little or no work experience or vocational training, and they are generally victims of physical, sexual and/or emotional abuse and racial discrimination (Hannah-Moffat and Shaw 2000; Boritch 2002, 2008; Hotton-Mahony 2011; Barrett, Allenby and Taylor 2010).

Research consistently reveals that the lives of most women prisoners are characterized by disadvantages of every kind and reflect the prevailing subordinate status of women in society (Boritch 2002, 2008; Comack 1996, 2006; Barrett, Allenby and Taylor 2010). As a group, female inmates are socially and economically marginalized and have often been victimized by family members and intimates. The experiences of abuse, poverty and substance abuse are their most common pathways to crime (Boritch 2008). The Canadian Human Rights Commission (2003: 5) offered this visual snapshot of federally sentenced women:

- Disproportionately Aboriginal
- First-time offenders
- Under thirty-five years of age
- Survivors of physical and sexual abuse
- Single mothers with one or more children
- Significant substance abuse problems

Education and Work Experience

The majority of federal and provincial female offenders have only a high school education, and many have considerably less, particularly Aboriginal women (Delveaux, Blanchette and Wickett 2005: 27). Eighty-eight percent of Aboriginal women and 67 percent of non-Aboriginal women were unemployed at the time of their arrest. Twenty-eight percent of Aboriginal women and 13 percent of non-Aboriginal women had less than a grade eight education, and 87 percent of Aboriginal women had no high school diploma at the time of intake into the correctional system, compared to 35 percent of non-Aboriginal women. Aboriginal women scored lower than non-Aboriginal women with respect to all categories of employment needs. The work experience of sentenced women is generally characterized by low skill, low wage employment with little room for advancement (Boritch 2002, 2008).

Women Offenders Are Actually Non-Violent

An additional indication of women lawbreakers' impoverishment is the nature of their crimes. "Over 80 percent of all incarcerated women in Canada are in prison for poverty related offences" (Jackson 1999, cited in Comack 2006: 67). Although female crime generally and female crimes against the person are increasing, the majority of charges against women continue to be petty property offences. Crimes against the person are those that involve threatening of violence or the use of violence against another person. These include homicide, attempted murder, assault, sexual assault and robbery (Hotton-Mahony 2011). Property crimes, or offences/crimes against property, are acts considered unlawful that do not involve threat or violence but are done to gain property, including theft, fraud and break and enters. Petty property offences are those charged with theft under $5,000. Women have over time been shown to have a high percentage of theft-related charges. Historical data from Statistics Canada in 1993 and 1994 show that 66.8 percent of female crimes were property crimes and theft related (cited in Borich 2002). More recent data reflect the same trend:

> In 2009, approximately 233,000 females and 776,000 males (adult and youth) were accused by police of having committed a *Criminal Code* offence in Canada. Females accounted for more than one quarter (28 percent) of youth (under 18 years of age) accused by police and more than one fifth (22 percent) of adult accused. The most common offences for which females were accused were theft under $5,000, assault level 1, and administration of justice violations (e.g., failure to appear in court, breach of probation, etc.). (Hotton-Mahony 2011: 19)

Put simply, women have consistently comprised a very small proportion of adults charged with violent offences. Women account for only 16 percent of persons charged with violent crimes, with 62 percent of these charges being level one common assaults, the least serious form of violence.

Abuse

Crimes committed by women against the person — assaults, manslaughter, murder and sex offences — become more understandable in the context of the history of violence in these women's lives. Evidence of physical, sexual and/or emotional abuse prior to incarceration is overwhelming. The *Report Back to All Federal Women in the 1989 Survey of Your Views* indicates that 68 percent of women prisoners were physically abused and 53 percent were sexually abused; 89 percent of the entire female prison population indicated some experience of abuse. Comparing these numbers to the profile of federally sentenced women twenty years later, these figures have either remained the same or have worsened. In *A Profile Comparison of Federally Sentenced Women 1991–2010*, Barrett et al., state:

> In terms of victimization, the majority of women (86 percent) reported being physically abused at some point in their lives. As compared to the original survey this represents a significant increase as in 1991 68 percent of the women

> reported experiencing physical abuse. In general, a greater proportion of women
> were abused as adults. (2010: 2)

The numbers are even higher for Aboriginal female inmates, with 90 percent being victims of physical abuse and 61 percent disclosing sexual abuse. Helen Boritch summarizes the harsh realities of female offenders:

> These statistics paint a dismal portrait of the life experiences of most women
> prisoners, the stories of individual women prisoners tell us of women who have
> endured fractured childhoods of neglect, abandonment and abuse and gone
> on to struggle with often unimaginably painful and violent circumstances.
> (2002: 317)

There is no clear evidence of whether victimization of women is a direct predictor of criminality, but the prevalence of victims of violence, substance abuse and addiction and mental health issues among criminalized women cannot be ignored (Barrett et al. 2010). In addition, some women retaliate to violence against them by fighting back in kind, dealing with anger and aggression by using drugs and alcohol or through violence as a learned behavior. Evidence suggests a connection between the condition of women in society, and their exposure to violence and poverty, and criminal behavior. For example, in *Women in Trouble* (1996), Elizabeth Comack interviewed twenty-four incarcerated women and revealed experiential evidence of the interconnection between their imprisonment and their histories of violence and abuse. She suggests that these connections may be as direct as women imprisoned for manslaughter for resisting abuse against them. She tells the story of Janice, for example:

> I was at a party, and this guy, older guy, came, came on to me. He tried telling
> me, "Why don't you go to bed with me. I'm getting some money, you know."
> And I said, "no." And then he started hitting me. And then he raped me. And
> then [pause] I lost it. Like, I just, I went, I got very angry and I snapped. And I
> started hitting him. I threw a coffee table on top of his head and then I stabbed
> him. (cited in Comack 2006: 37)

Racism and Colonization

There is a notable intersection of race, class and gender in the lives of criminalized women as well as a connection between Aboriginal over-incarceration and the historical forces of colonization (Comack 2006). Boritch (2002: 316) states, "Among female prisoners, Aboriginal women are even more disadvantaged than non-Aboriginal women along virtually every conceivable dimension, because they have also endured the formidable burden of racism and oppression throughout their lives." Aboriginal women are subject to a lack of opportunities as well as more overt racism. As Monture-Angus writes, "Often, what [Aboriginal women] can experience in the city (from shoplifting to prostitution, drug abuse to violence) arising from their experiences of poverty and racism, leads to contact with the criminal justice system" (2000: 57). Aboriginal women are the fastest growing population in Canada's federal prisons, increasing over 80 percent in the previous decade; they represent 33.6 percent of all incarcerated women (Office of the Correctional Investigator 2013). High rates of incarceration are linked to the history of colonialism, systemic discrimination including racial prejudice, social and economic disadvantages, violence, trauma and intergenerational factors, all of which is documented in *R. v. Gladue* (1999) and *R. v. Ipeelee* (2012):

> Courts must take judicial notice of such matters as the history of colonialism, displacement, and residential schools and how that history continues to translate into lower educational attainment, lower incomes, higher unemployment, higher rates of substance abuse and suicide, and of course higher levels of incarceration for Aboriginal peoples. (Justice LeBel for the majority in *R. v. Ipeelee* 2012: cited in Office of the Correctional Investigator 2013).

The overt racism within the justice system has become prominent with the call for an inquiry into Canada's missing and murdered Aboriginal women. The Commissioner of the RCMP led a study of incidents on murdered and missing Aboriginal women in Canada and found that between 1980 and 2012 there have been 1017 police reported Aboriginal female homicides and an additional 164 missing Aboriginal women. Tragically, the disappearance and violence against Aboriginal women has not demonstrated significant formal interest. In comparing the dreadful occurrence of missing women from Vancouver's Downtown Eastside, where so many women disappeared and where there was comparably little formal attention, politicians and researchers are asking important questions, such as, "Do you think if 65 women went missing from Kerrisdale [and affluent Vancouver neighborhood] we'd have ignored it so long?" (cited in Hugill 2010: 10).

THEORETICAL CONSIDERATIONS

Traditional criminological theories and some feminist inquiries have attempted to explain "female criminality," but in doing so they have often contributed to stereotypical definitions of criminals by scientifically justifying harmful myths. Early theories of female criminality perpetuate delinquent behavior amongst women by justifying treatment that reinforces traditional gender stereotypes. Any theory of crime must begin with an understanding of the position of women — including racialized women — in the larger society.

Biology

The so-called classical work of Lombroso and Ferrero, *The Female Offender* (1895), represents the first "scientific" inquiry regarding women and crime. Using a biological determinist perspective, they define criminality as a pathology originating from the biological make up of individuals. Central to their thesis is the notion of "atavism," which they use to suggest that criminals are genetically deficient and evolutionarily regressive. Atavists are identifiable through certain physical features that symbolize genetic deficiency.

Lombroso began his work by defending the use of anthropemetry, measuring bodies and studying abnormalities. His analysis detected that "criminal women" had smaller cranial capacity than non-criminal women. The criminal woman was also said to have a heavier and masculine jaw. This work also identified physical abnormalities depending on the type of crime. Baez explains:

> Criminal women, particularly in murder, theft and prostitution, are close to or above the average female weight but are rarely of average height. For prostitutes, the proportion of arm span to height is smaller than other women ... prostitutes had disproportionately larger hands and shorter and narrower feet. (2010: 3–4)

The descriptions become quite bizarre and even included the color of hair, suggesting that criminal women are usually dark haired and go grey faster. Women who are involved in crime are also said to have vivid wrinkling and resemble images of witches.

According to Lombroso and Ferrero, some of these features are harder to distinguish among women criminals because women are in general "less evolved" than men. They argue that women's biologically determined nature is antithetical to crime but, because of the woman's lower form, she makes up for her lower crime rate in the cruelty and vileness of her crimes. Lombroso and Ferrero write:

> We also saw that women have many traits in common with children; that their mental sense is deficient; that they are revengeful, jealous, inclined to vengeance of a refined cruelty. In ordinary cases these defects are neutralized by piety, maternity, want of passion, sexual coldness, by weakness and an undeveloped intelligence. (Lombroso and Ferrero 1895: 151)

Although Lombroso and Ferrero's biological explanations have been largely discredited, parallels still exist in more recent works. *Delinquency in Girls* (Cowie, Cowie and Slater 1968) argues that female crime requires a biological explanation whereas delinquency in boys requires a socio-economic explanation. The authors include social and environmental causal factors as predisposing boys to delinquency. In contrast, biological factors are maintained as more important than environmental factors for young women:

> Pathological psychiatric deviations are much more common in delinquent girls than boys ... Delinquent girls more often than boys have other forms of impaired physical health; they are noticed to be oversized, lumpish, uncouth, and graceless, with a raised incidence of minor physical defects. (cited in Burns 2006: 123)

They also note that "pathological psychiatric deviations are much more common in delinquent girls than boys" (166).

Dalton (1978) and Pollack (1979) also provide biological explanations for female delinquency. In her study of imprisoned women, Dalton claims that a relationship exists between the criminality of women and women's menstrual cycles. Pollack similarly argues that women are more likely to commit crime during hormonal changes, especially during pregnancy and menopause (Pollack 1979). Dalton states:

> 3 women successfully pleaded diminished responsibility or mitigation due to premenstrual syndrome in crimes of manslaughter, arson, and assault. All had long histories of repeated misdemeanours, which continued while in prison. Police and prison records confirmed the diagnosis of premenstrual syndrome. The women were successfully treated with progesterone, and their behaviour returned to normal. (1978: abstract)

According to these theories, women pose a risk for committing crimes for approximately 75 percent of their lives.

Role Theory

Role theory moves away from solely biological explanations, offering the notion that individual pathologies are induced by society and can, therefore, be modified by society. Role theorists consider sociological factors such as inequality and utilize concepts such as "diverse socialization." Inadequate socialization becomes an individual pathology, which can be cured through re-socialization.

Hoffman-Bustamente (1975) argues that boys are encouraged to be aggressive while girls are encouraged to be passive and non-violent. Freda Adler, in *Sisters in Crime* (1975), suggests that the women's liberation movement allowed women to challenge traditional sex role stereotypes and to enter into fields that were once restricted to men. A problem in Adler's argument is that she attributes female crime to an increase in masculine qualities but fails to explain why males commit crime. Role theory in general does not discuss structural origins of differential roles in society (Smart 1976; Currie 1986). These theories reify and obscure the social and political processes underlying criminality (Currie 1986). It was feminists who insisted on digging deeper into the social and political inequality that is related to crime, criminality and criminal justice.

Feminist Theory

Early feminist criminological theories mainly critiqued prior attempts to include women in mainstream criminology, labelling such work as sexist and making efforts to revise it (Smart 1976). The mission to revise differential association theory, labelling theory, social control and conflict theory (all discussed in detail in Chapter 2) were criticized as an "add women and stir" approach (Schram and Tibbetts 2014). Critical feminist theories refute these explanations and argue that understanding women and crime must be located in a socio-economic, gendered and racialized context. Critical feminists (including standpoint feminist work, such as Comack 1996) introduced more qualitative research, attempting to provide women a voice, instead of male academics telling us about women's lives, in order to better understand their conflict with the law. The intention of this critical, empowering research was to place women at the center of the inquiry in order to learn from the voices of experience. Much of the research that foregrounded criminalized women's voices identified strong links between women's crimes and victimization, poverty, racialization and violence against them (Comack 2006).

Feminist criminology often cautions against quantitative approaches towards understanding female crime, favouring women-centered narrative approaches to research (see, e.g., Comack and Balfour 2006; Wattanaporn and Holtfreter 2014). Critical feminist theories identify the importance of including women's voices while recognizing that women's agency (their capacity for independent action) is shaped by — and also shapes — larger relations of power and social control. Feminist-based theories engage the question of the interaction between human agency and social structure — essential to understanding the different meaning of empowering women in conflict with the law and the impact their stories will have on the social forces that affect their lives.

Some critical feminist theories give primacy to certain social structures, such as patriarchy. Others give primacy to agency while acknowledging that women's lives are shaped by social structures such as colonialism, patriarchy and capitalism. Comack argues that feminist research studies the dynamics of class, race and gender and how these play out in the everyday lives of women, while still acknowledging that all of these categories are socially constructed. Comack (1996: 34), for example, emphasizes that what we know of the world is conditional upon one's social location:

> In taking the women's lives as my starting point, my aim has been to develop a
> way of knowing ... that is capable of shedding light on the factors and conditions

which brought them into conflict with the law. Central to the formulation of this standpoint is the attempt to situate their lives within the nexus of the class, race and gender relations of our society.

Critical feminist criminology also offers a critique of prisons, noting that they provide women few opportunities to either challenge or overcome racial, sexual or class barriers. As Carlen writes:

> In so far as prisons debilitate, women's prisons feed off their own product ... it is an indictment of society at the end of the twentieth century, and not of the penal system itself when women tell me that they will go out to a world that has even less to offer them than prison. (1988: 163)

From the critical feminist perspective, prison and its reform may be seen as a furthered mechanism of social regulation over women.

WOMEN IN PRISON

Women have often been deemed as "too few to count" (see Adelberg and Currie 1987) as they constitute such a small percentage of adult offenders in correctional systems in Canada. Women accounted for only 16 percent of criminal offences by adults in 1998 and 9 percent of admissions to provincial/territorial and federal prisons (Thomas 2000, cited in Boritch 2008). This number has only slightly increased over time from 10 percent in provincial and federal custody in 1999–2000 to 12 percent in 2008–09 (Hotton-Mahoney 2011).

Historically, only one prison held federally sentenced women in Canada compared to over forty federal facilities for men. Prior to the building of Prison for Women, women were housed in the Kingston penitentiary for men, where they wereconfined to a very small area in the attic above the mess table of the male inmates and moved frequently to serve the needs of the male offenders. Since its inception in 1934, the Prison for Women at Kingston (P4W) was criticized for being dark, foreboding and dysfunctional. More than a dozen government reports[1] denounced the P4W for a number of factors; all but one called for the closure of the prison. These examinations of women's prison(s) indicted its centralized location, the over-classification of inmates with respect to security risk, the lack of programming, the inadequate provisions for francophone and Aboriginal inmates and its insufficient recognition of the special needs of incarcerated women.

The single location of the P4W, in Kingston, Ontario, meant that pretty well all Canadian imprisoned women were removed from their communities and support systems. At the time *Creating Choices* was published, only 60 of the 130 women inside the P4W were from communities in Ontario (CSC 1990: 74). In addition, access to Kingston was very difficult for visitors, and the trip could be costly, leaving many families unable to visit. Morever, many of the imprisoned women remained geographically stranded upon their release (Boritch 2002, 2008).

The neglect of the needs of women was, in part, the result of the maximum security design of the P4W. Many historical documents note that tight security conditions are unsuitable for most women offenders. For example, the *Report of the Standing Committee on Justice and Solicitor General* reviewed sentencing, conditional release and related aspects of corrections, noting that "concern[s] that large numbers of women prisoners across the country are being detained in facilities which provide much higher security than most of them require and that most of them would be subjected to if they were men" (Canada 1977: 135).   The correctional programs offered at the P4W were highly lacking with respect to both quantity and quality. For example, the *Report to Parliament* (Canada 1977) disclosed the lack of recreation, adequate programs and space for an activity center. Counselling services were minimal, and, in the case of drug and alcohol rehabilitation, programs were developed based on a correctional philosophy for men. The *Report on Self-Injurious Behavior in the Kingston Prison for Women* (Heney 1990) revealed that 98 percent of the prison population and 93 percent of the correctional staff thought the counselling services at the P4W were inadequate. Many prisoners had suffered physical, sexual and emotional abuse in their lives, yet programs failed to address their immediate psychosocial or medical needs (Kendall 2000). Mental health services at the P4W were only available during regular hours, leaving segregation units as the alternative for after-hours crises. Moreover, the counselling available in the prison generally only addressed coping with confinement and the resulting emotional distress (Kendall 2000). Prison programming reflected the needs of prison management, and limited help was available for imprisoned women to deal with the root of their problems (Kendall 2000; Boritch 2002, 2008).

Specific services pertaining to Aboriginal and francophone women at the P4W were almost non-existent. Aboriginal women had access to mainstream psychological services but these were limited in cultural awareness and not readily available (Heney 1990). Similarly, the cultural needs of francophone women were ignored, especially in terms of the absence of French programs.

PAIN OF IMPRISONMENT FOR WOMEN

Compared to their male counterparts, women in prison are more strictly supervised and are charged for behavior that is less serious (Shaw 2000). In one woman's words, "You come in here as an adult and you leave as a child" (CSC 1990). Women prisoners reported feeling a lack of respect, favouritism regarding staff relations, discrimination and arbitrary rules, all contributing to a feeling of worthlessness and pain (McDonagh 1999). Yvonne Johnson, a prison activist who spent time in the P4W, wrote that "by law they must keep our bodies alive in here, but what will we be when we're released? The human need for kindness, grace — it's impossible in prison" (Wiebe and Johnson 1998: 326). Prison rules and regulations that limit inmate movements and interactions, especially the rules of solitary confinement, created a feeling that women have described as "powerlessness" (Heney 1990; Kendall 2000). The correctionalist alternative to counselling in the P4W was a policy of isolation for punishment and behaviour modification (Kendall 2000).

Incarcerated women's experiences differ from men's, especially when they are housed in a prison that is very far away from their families. Female inmates experience no greater pain of imprisonment than separation from their children, and they worry about losing their children to child welfare and about the placement of their children in foster care. In contrast, male inmates often have partners or family members to care for their children. P4W rules and policies created a situation in which it was often very difficult for the women inmates to see their children (Martin 1997).

Imprisoned women have greater emotional and mental health problems than male prisoners, which is manifested in suicide attempts and other self-injurious behavior

(Daigle et al. 1999). For women prisoners, cutting is a long-standing problem linked to both life situations of abuse and enduring the pain of imprisonment; it offers distraction from the tension and anger caused by conditions of imprisonment (Hoffman and Law 1995). In the words of one prisoner at the P4W, "Prison is frustration and anger so intense that cutting into the arteries of my own arm only alleviates some of the pain" (CSC 1990: 6, cited in Borich 2002: 320).

The suicides of four Aboriginal women — Marlene Moore, Lorna Claira Jones, Careen Daigneault and Sandy Sayer — are evidence of the personal pain experienced by female prisoners and the horrific conditions at the Prison for Women. These suicides were labelled by the news media as a "form of liberation" (*Star Phoenix*, March 23, 1991) and an "escape from the pain of imprisonment" (*Ottawa Citizen* 1991). These tragedies received national attention, and feminist reformers began using the law to demand better treatment for female prisoners. *R. v. Daniels* was a landmark decision in which the Supreme Court agreed that a federal prisoner's right to life and security would be violated under the *Canadian Charter of Rights and Freedoms* if she were sentenced to the P4W because of the high risk of suicide (Arbour 1996: 246).

CHANGING WOMEN'S PRISONS: CREATING CHOICES

The impetus for the Canadian Government to assess the needs of federally sentenced women came from a number of suicides of women at the P4W, a shifting mentality towards female prisoners as "high needs/low risk," the enactment of the *Canadian Charter of Rights and Freedoms* and an increased feminist voice relating to inequality, poverty, racism and violence against women (Shaw 1993; Kershaw and Lasovich 1991, cited in Boritch 2002). The result was the completion and implementation of *Creating Choices: The Task Force Report for Federally Sentenced Women in Canada* (1990).

The Task Force

With continued pressure by groups outside the government, the Correctional Service of Canada (CSC), in partnership with the Canadian Association of Elizabeth Fry Societies (CAEFS), appointed the Task Force on Federally Sentenced Women in March 1989. The mandate of the Task Force was "to examine the correctional management of federally sentenced women ... and to develop a plan which will guide and direct the process in a manner that is responsive to the unique and special needs of this group" (CSC 1990).

This Task Force was exceptional due to its composition: it included seventeen members from women's groups and voluntary organizations outside of the government as well as two federally sentenced women. In total thirty-eight of the forty-two members were women. The steering committee and the working group had more community representatives than government representatives. As Shaw observes:

> No previous government inquiry into women's imprisonment had included so many voluntary sector representatives, or Aboriginal or minority groups, and certainly no women who had personal experience of prisons. And many of those in the voluntary sector reflected the feminist perspectives. (1993: 53)

Notably, the Native Women's Association of Canada (NWAC) was initially not interested in becoming involved with the Task Force. The NWAC was reluctant in part because of its volunteer involvement in other grassroots issues and also because it disagreed with the differentiation being made between men and women. First Nations Elders convinced the NWAC that their voices were essential to the Task Force. Ultimately, five Aboriginal women were appointed to the steering committee and two to a working group. Two of these seven Aboriginal women were federally sentenced women who had served time in P4W. Patricia Monture, however, cautioned that the participation of Aboriginal women in the Task Force "must never be viewed as a recognition that the jurisdiction of the federal government of Canada … in the affairs of our Nations is valid" (CSC 1990: 17, cited in Hayman 2000: 46).

The participation of women with experience as prisoners at P4W was particularly unique, and the report gave these women (and those still at P4W) a voice:

> I and women like myself, who contribute to this chapter [of *Creating Choices*] are the flesh that has fed the need for this Task Force. Our pleas are drawn from our hearts and souls. We are witnesses to the human pain, the tears and the blood spilled within traditional prisons in the name of justice. (Prisoner at the Kingston Prison for Women) (CSC 1990: 13)

Shaw describes the committee as passionately dedicated to major changes for federally sentenced women and frustrated because of the "enormity of the task" (1993: 53). The Task Force members were particularly affected by suicides of two Aboriginal P4W inmates in 1989 and the suicides of four Aboriginal P4W inmates in 1990.

TASK FORCE RESEARCH AND CONCLUSIONS

Creating Choices was largely based on extensive interviews with federally sentenced women. This consultation and research was "groundbreaking" (Shaw 1993: 54), framing female offenders within their social context of inequality, dependency and discrimination. The report emphasized that the vast majority of women in prison were "low risk/high needs" — referring to the low risk of reoffending posed by federally sentenced women as well as the enormity of the physical, emotional and sexual abuse in these women's lives. Statistics demonstrated a clear link between socio-economic status and criminality of women, with federally sentenced women tending to be under-educated, poor, young, addicted to alcohol and/or drugs, victims of abuse and emotionally and financially dependent on abusive partners (CSC 1990). These conclusions have held steady through years of additional research. See, for example, Helen Boritch (2002); Elizabeth Comack (1996) Hannah-Moffat and Shaw (2000), Colleen Dell, Catherine Filmore and Jennifer Kitty (2009) and Ferrari (2011), to name but a few.

Considering the experiences of the federally incarcerated women, the Task Force members agreed that imprisonment had failed to provide the support female offenders needed to avoid recidivism. The Task Force concluded that fundamental changes within the women's correctional system were required, with the long-term goal of restorative justice options and an Aboriginal system of justice (CSC 1990: 95).

Reiterating the many problems cited in previous investigations — over-classification regarding security, ignoring women's special needs, geographic dislocation, inadequate services, ignoring needs of Aboriginal and francophone women — *Creating Choices* recommended that P4W be closed and replaced by a Healing Lodge for Aboriginal women (in Saskatchewan) and four regional correctional facilities (in Alberta, Ontario, Québec, and Nova Scotia).

GUIDING PRINCIPLES AND RECOMMENDATIONS

The overall statement of principle guiding *Creating Choices* was the following:

> The Correctional Service of Canada with the support of communities, has the responsibility to create an environment that empowers federally sentenced women to make meaningful and responsible choices in order that they may live with dignity and respect.

The women-centred philosophy of *Creating Choices* has been viewed as transformative for women's corrections in Canada. The Task Force critiqued the traditional male model, with its focus on assessing inmates as either high, medium or low security risk, pre-structured programming and the prioritizing of needs, and replaced it with a new model emphasizing the assessment of imprisoned women's needs and the holistic treatment of these needs. Five new guiding principles were stressed:

1. creating meaningful choice;
2. empowerment;
3. respect and dignity;
4. supportive environments; and
5. sharing responsibility (with community and corrections) for the incarcerated women's welfare.

The Task Force defined empowerment as a means to help the women raise their self-esteem and overcome inequalities brought about through poverty, racism and abuse. The recommended training and vocational facilities, for example, illustrated a move away from limited traditional gender roles. Education at all levels was to be offered, including adult education, university and other post-secondary education.   The Task Force emphasized the importance of incarcerated women gaining respect for others and to be given respect in return. The Task Force insisted that women could not fit into existing programs designed by correctional staff but should identify their own needs and subsequently have them fulfilled through physical space and programming. This became a "resources approach," in which programming responds to the "multifaceted, inner-related nature of women's experience" (CSC 1990: 103). The regional women's facilities and Healing Lodge were meant to emphasize individual healing and wellness and offer programming according to the needs of women, addressing such issues as addiction, childhood sexual, physical and emotional abuse, domestic abuse, spirituality, independent living, self-reliance and positive interaction. In support of self-determination and self-esteem, the Task Force maintained the emphasis of staffing shifts from traditional security to dynamic security and support. In the "Report of the Task Force on Security" (CSC 2008), it is recommended that "the term 'dynamic security' be defined and understood as 'those actions that contribute to the development of professional, positive relationships between staff members and offenders."

Discrimination against Aboriginal women led the Task Force to conclude that Aboriginal people should not be dealt with as add-ons inside corrections, but instead they must be handled through an Aboriginal-directed approach. A Healing Lodge in Maple Creek, Saskatchewan, was proposed — and implemented — with program offerings to include Aboriginal teachings and spiritual ceremonies, culturally sensitive counselling services and frequent contact with Elders and Aboriginal staff. The Task Force clearly stated that this had to be adopted by and developed by Aboriginal people for it to be most effective.

SHARING RESPONSIBILITY

The Community Release Strategy was an extremely important component within the Task Force plan. Increased facilities were intended to accommodate women upon their release from prison and provide treatment within communities. This included halfway houses, community-based residences, Aboriginal centres and home placements. Each woman was to have a personalized release strategy, developed in conjunction with correctional staff, the woman herself and community workers.

REGIONAL FACILITIES

The new regional facilities aimed to approximate norms of community, emphasize the development of self-sufficiency in daily living, provide holistic and sensitive programming including counselling and treatment for abuse and substance abuse problems, provide educational and vocational development, provide family visits, recognize spirituality and use the local communities for support and services. The new facilities were designed to promote wellness through natural light, space, privacy and colour. The facilities included cottage-style houses that could accommodate six to ten women as well as a family visiting facility for women and children to live together in, all situated on several acres of land.

IMPLEMENTATION OF CREATING CHOICES REPORT

> *Creating Choices* is probably one of the most powerful things that has ever been written by so many women, but it's still only a piece of paper. And sometimes I look at it and think it's not worth the paper it's written on. (Prisoner, Edmonton Institution for Women, cited in Gironella 1999: 35)

Creating Choices was published in April 1990. A few months later, the Solicitor General formally and publicly announced that P4W would close by 1994 and that 50 million dollars would be available to implement the Task Force recommendations, including the construction of the four new regional facilities and the Healing Lodge as well as improvements to and expansions of community services and halfway houses (Shaw 1993). By 1997, new prisons were opened in Joliette, Québec, Kitchener, Ontario, Edmonton, Alberta, and Burnaby, British Columbia, and a Healing Lodge for Aboriginal women was established on the Nekaneek Reserve in Saskatchewan. The Prison for Women was closed officially on July 6, 2000.

Safeguards were built in by the Task Force to ensure that the plan was enacted as intended. These included an implementation committee that would be externally based as well as an Aboriginal advisory committee, both of which were to oversee the implementation process (Shaw 1993). However, various events during and since the implementation of the Task Force Report suggest that it was modified beyond recognition (Hannah-Moffat and Shaw 2000; Boritch 2008; Dell et al. 2009). The implementation of *Creating Choices* is attributed largely to the efforts of a constellation of people acting when feminism had impacted the highest levels of government (Hayman 2000). When *Creating Choices* was submitted, the situation at P4W had become so severe that not acting would have been inimical to everyone, including the officials from corrections. Ole Ingstrup, the Commissioner of Corrections at the time, was prepared to give those outside of correctional institutions a voice. Specifically, he listened to the Canadian Association of the Elizabeth Fry Societies (CAEFS). Although CAEFS' relationship with the Correctional Service of Canada (CSC) was difficult, and their preference was not to be involved in creating new prisons for women,[2] Bonnie Diamond, the executive director of CAEFS at the time, recognized that Ingstrup was willing to hear alternative ideas and did not want to miss this window of opportunity for change.[3] CAEFS especially did not want to see any more federally sentenced women lose their lives through suicide.

Many criticisms of this Task Force implementation suggest that the feminist ideals were undermined by the Correctional Service of Canada in response to concerns of the public, false stereotypical perceptions of women in conflict with the law (Hayman 2000; Shaw 1993) and shifting strategies of managing risk and need (Hanna-Moffat 2000; Shaw 2000). Indeed, many problems identified with the federal Prison for Women remained unresolved (Boritch 2002, 2008; Monture-Angus 2000; Shaw 2000; Dell et al. 2009; Sapers 2008; Ferrari 2011). The commitment of the Healing Lodge Circle (Ke-kun-wem-kon-a-wuk) to manage the Healing Lodge, and to base the Healing Lodge on Aboriginal cultural principles, was also not upheld (Ferrari 2011).

While many of the main Task Force recommendations were accepted in principle, the recommendations concerning implementation were not. A number of problems with implementation are discussed more detail below.

The Choice of Sites

The Task Force stressed the importance of the establishment of a prison in a community with women's support services and good transport facilities. However, the choices of Truro, Nova Scotia, (a small rural community approximately ninety kilometers away from Halifax), Joliette, Quebec, and Kitchener, Ontario, were heavily criticized for lacking community resources for inmates and adequate travel facilities to prevent costly journeys for family and visitors. In response to the sites chosen, one federally sentenced woman said, "My spirit was engulfed in deep shame for having contributed to the work that was intended to assist in positive change for Federally Sentenced Women but was now politically sabotaged" (Joanne Mayhew, CAEFS Newsletter, Spring 1992).

Community Release Strategies

Another major concern of the Task Force and public sectors was that the government was building the new facilities with less attention towards the community release strategy and less money for development of community resources. The government announced that the money for community development was not intended to come from the 50 million dollar budget but must be found at the local level.

Failure to Address Needs of Violent and High Security Risk Women

Creating Choices portrayed women as victims of violence, but it is criticized for failing to address violent and high-security-risk women (Hannah-Moffat and Shaw 2000; Ferrari 2011; Dell et al. 2009). Correctional Services of Canada responded to difficulties in the new prisons with the prevailing view of women as dangerous and violent. For example, the Edmonton Institution, which opened on November 20, 1995, had difficulties from the outset. In February 1996, investigations began regarding several incidents of self-injurious behavior. On February 29, Denise Fayant, a twenty-one-year-old Saskatchewan woman, was found hanging in her cell, and another inmate was charged with her murder. More self-injuries and suicide attempts were documented in the following days, as well as assaults on staff and three escapes.

Problems with violence in the new regional facilities led correctional authorities to quickly fall back on punitive measures (Shaw 2000; Boritch 2002; Dell et al. 2009; Ferrari 2011). In Edmonton, Correctional Services of Canada responded to these concerns by redefining the women as dangerous, transferring the maximum and medium security women out of the facility and increasing their own security, including installing security cameras and an eight-foot perimeter fence with barbed wire. Unfortunately, the women heard the news of the transfers from the media rather than from prison officials. This resulted in two women slashing their own necks and the police riot squad using pepper spray to extract the women from their rooms (CAEFS 1999).

The failure of *Creating Choices* to deal with women labelled as maximum security was most acute with respect to the Healing Lodge. Aboriginal women were (and continue to be) disproportionately labelled high risk/maximum security, but because the Healing Lodge has been deemed a medium-security facility, many Aboriginal women were not offered the chance to benefit from the Healing Lodge (Monture-Angus 2000). Therefore, those most in need of reformed conditions are confined in men's institutions; they were also those left the longest in P4W prior to its closing in July 2000. As Monture-Angus (2000: 55) notes, "Unfortunately, many of the women that the Lodge was visioned around will never serve their sentences at the Lodge as the institution is now too full, and clearly, selection is based on the borrowed notion of security classification."

Principles of Law and Order

The issue is even more complicated when we consider the time frame of the opening of the first three regional prisons for women: the Healing Lodge, the Edmonton Institution for Women (EIFW) and the Nova Institution for Women in Truro. In the mid-1990s, an overall increased emphasis on law and order was emerging in politics and the media (Hayman 2000; White 2002). Media scrutiny and public concerns found their way to the EIFW, which witnessed severely hostile local community reactions to prison escapes, murder and self-mutilation. As a result, the EIFW was temporarily closed on May 1, 1996. This was followed by intense political pressure — especially from the Reform Party and the public — to address the fear that women who were potentially dangerous were escaping into the community. Not one woman who escaped from the prison committed an illegal offence while absent from the facility. The public believed the facility closed because the women were too violent to be held there (Hayman 2000). Moreover, the escapes from the EIFW affected more than just the inmates in Edmonton. All of the regional prisons — except the Healing Lodge — increased security measures, "signalling that all the imprisoned women were potentially dangerous ... every federally sentenced woman paid the price for the misbehaviour of the few" (Hayman, 2000: 44).

When the EIFW reopened on August 29, 1996, medium-security inmates were re-admitted. The CSC spent $289,000 at the Saskatchewan Penitentiary and $222,000 at the Regional Psychiatric Centre in Saskatoon, Saskatchewan, to accommodate the remaining maximum-security inmates who were not eligible for the regional facilities. As Hayman notes, "This happened despite the fact that *Creating Choices* envisaged that all federally sentenced women, regardless of their security level, would be housed in the new regional facilities" (2000: 44).

The Canadian Association of the Elizabeth Fry Societies (1999, 2000) affirmed that women in the regional prisons continued to be subjected to strip searches, excessive force and interventions of emergency response teams. Minimum-security women prisoners have been shackled when being escorted into the community. One regional prison used pepper spray and stripped a woman naked when she cut herself; she was subsequently left in handcuffs and shackles on a steel bed frame with no blanket for several hours (Boritch 2002). The consequences of incidents in Edmonton (among others) as well as the re-intro-duction of security classification schemes contributed to the expansion of physical security measures in many of the regional facilities as well as the holding of some female inmates in isolated units in prisons for men (Boritch 2002; Dell et al. 2009). In 2005, the deputy wardens of Canada's federal prisons for women recommended ceasing strip searches for women for two reasons: the searches traumatize women, conjuring up histories of sexual assault against them, and they yield little or no contraband from the women (Pate 2011).

Recent events have drawn additional attention to the increased use of security pri-orities and control in women's prisons and that the suicides, deaths and disturbances are still frequent. Segregation continues to be used in women's prisons to separate those who are disruptive or misbehaving and the practice is unable to address the psychologi-cal, behavioural and emotional needs of the women (Sapers 2008; Dell et al. 2009). The use of segregation in the Ashley Smith case was strongly challenged (Sapers 2008). It has been reported that Ashley Smith spent more than two thirds of her time in prison in segregation, which also means being excluded from participating in programming (Sapers 2008). It was clear that Ashley Smith required specialized care and that she had been in segregation for unthinkable time frames, which meant her treatment for her self-harming and mental health concerns were left unaddressed (Sapers 2008; Ferarri 2011).

Power Imbalances between Staff and Inmates

Programming in the regional prisons was designed to empower female inmates and of-fer choices that are meaningful in a supportive atmosphere. Yet Shaw (2000) argues that power imbalances between staff and prisoners in these new facilities made the aim to empower the women and increase their self-esteem unattainable. The women prison-ers have said the correctional workers were unable to apply the new women-centered approach, did not apply the rules inconsistently and often had very little knowledge of policy (Ferrari 2011). As one prisoner noted, "Person-to-person, staff to staff, shift change to shift change, everybody interprets the rules and regulations of this institution the way they want to, for whatever their purposes" (Gironella 1999: 58). Six women interviewed at the Edmonton regional facility all complained about the negative relationships with staff and said that, because of the unpredictability of outcomes, they would rather be at the Prison for Women in Kingston (Gironella 1999).

The women also complained that they did not have choices concerning the selection of the programming yet were penalized if they failed to meet rehabilitation expectations (Boritch 2002; Monture-Angus 2000). If a woman refused to participate in programs such as parenting, vocational, educational and substance abuse programming, she was labelled as a risk and assigned a higher security classification (Hannah-Moffat 1999). This again led to women being classified as un-reformable and moved into conditions that were more secure (including men's facilities). Thus, many federally incarcerated women have not benefitted from the women-centered model proposed in *Creating Choices*.

Correctional Strategies of Empowerment

Creating Choices was intended to promote a woman's power to make her own choices and to negate the traditional paternalistic and maternal correctionalist regimes (Hannah-Moffat 1999; Faith 2011, 1993). This included allowing women to regain control of their lives through the development of self-confidence, autonomy and an influence over social conditions in life. Yet, upon implementation of *Creating Choices*, the notion of empowerment was compromised by the penal culture (Dell et al. 2009; Ferarri 2011). *Creating Choices* in practice was criticized by feminists such as Hannah-Moffat as being reflective of a wider shift in governing "wherein governments and corporations with little or no interest in granting real power to dispossessed groups have merely adopted discourses of empowerment" (2000: 31).[4] This is a strong criticism linking the empowerment politics of *Creating Choices* to neo-liberal strategies, questioning whether empowerment is possible (Rose 1996, 2000).

More specifically, the Correctional Service of Canada defined empowerment as "the process through which women gain insight into their situation, identify their strengths, and are supported and challenged to take positive action to gain control of their lives" (csc 1994: 9, cited in Hannah-Moffat 2000). However, after the closure of P4W, women's choices within this model of empowerment continued to be limited to those deemed by prison administration as being responsible and meaningful. In other words, to escape and run to see their children was not a choice, yet the choice to participate in Alcoholics Anonymous was responsible. Critics argue that this interpretation of empowerment simply shifts the old management strategies onto the women inmates, in effect, to have them police themselves. As Simon (1994: 33) writes, "The new techniques [like empowerment] do not so much replace these traditional measures as embed them in a far more comprehensive web of monitoring and intervention" (cited in Hannah-Moffat 2000: 33).

STRATEGIES OF RISK MANAGEMENT

There is a recent trend towards standardized correctional practice through the classification of prisoners (developed through the new Offender Intake Assessment process) that is contradictory to *Creating Choices* and the differential treatment of women. Characteristics such as low self-esteem, poor education, foster care placement, residential placement, prostitution, suicide attempts, substance abuse and others now represent both risk *and* need. Correctional researchers have linked these characteristics to violent recidivism and argue that this constitutes risk; this is in direct contrast to feminist researchers who argue these are mental health concerns that constitute the need for treatment (Heney 1990).

Task Force members and others[5] claim that risk categories are not highly relevant for female prisoners. Hanna-Moffat suggests that the discussion to date about the needs of female inmates relies not on feminist interpretations of needs for women but rather "depends on correctional interpretations of women's needs as potential or modified risk factors that are central to efficient management of incarcerated women" (2000: 38). This points once again to a wide discrepancy between the intentions of *Creating Choices* and the current practice within correctional settings.

Gendered Risk

In theory, crime can be reduced through scientific determination of a prisoner's risk score and classification for security. However, this calculation has been criticized as gendered and racialized (Hannah-Moffat 2000). Boritch (2002) demonstrates how this calculation is gendered — the labelling of the risk level of offenders lowers the bar for women in the calculation of dangerousness. Evidence for this is found by examining the label of dangerous offender and the actions of the women who acquire this label versus the actions of men. For example, Lisa Neve was labelled a dangerous offender yet her most serious crime was aggravated assault; this fails to compare to the types of offences committed by men who are labelled as dangerous offenders, which are typically murder, serial sexual assault and pedophilia. The same discrepancy is noted with security risks and those deemed high security. In 1999, 31 percent of incarcerated women were deemed to be maximum security; only 22 percent of men shared this label despite men being sentenced for more violent crimes overall (Correctional Service of Canada 1999).

Racialized Risk

Ideas regarding risk are racialized, highlighted by the disproportionate labelling of Aboriginal women as maximum security. Risk-prediction scales, responsibility and need dimensions are problematic for Aboriginal offenders. Individualization of risk does not address colonial impacts and the oppression of Aboriginal women, and offender-based notions of responsibility are lopsided from an Aboriginal view.

Racism is also a key factor of discrimination in security classification and risk assessment. For example, the Case Needs Identification and Analysis protocol identifies need dimensions based on seven categories: "employment, marital/ family, associates, substance abuse, community functioning, personal/ emotional and attitude" (Motiuk 1997, cited in Monture-Angus 2000: 57). These dimensions are problematic because colonialism has led to Aboriginal communities that are not defined as healthy or functional, which leads to a failure to score well in this category as well.

The idea of responsibility embraced by correctional structures is lopsided from the Aboriginal point of view because it is solely based on the offender (Monture-Angus 2000: 55). Relationships are central in First Nations legal practices, whereby healing of individuals and healing of communities are co-constitutive. All of this has been eroded by concerns for security and standard correctional agendas (Monture-Angus 2000).

This concept of risk management adds to earlier explanations of why twenty women remained at P4W until it closed in July 2000. It also helps to explain why these so-called high-risk and high-need women are now housed in men's maximum-security institutions around Canada. Women who are resisting the new women-centered vision are demonized and pathologized; moreover, many of these women are Aboriginal and therefore not able to benefit from the regional cites.

SUMMARY

Rich and diverse feminist approaches attempt to assess the reform efforts of *Creating Choices* and the meaning of justice for women in trouble. Much of this discourse remains optimistic about the potential of *Creating Choices* even while acknowledging problems with its implementation (Hannah-Moffat 2000; Hayman 2000; Shaw 1993).

Other feminist authors question whether feminist prisons are possible or even desirable (Faith, 2011, 1993; Comack 1996; Boritch 2002; Shaw 2000). While *Creating Choices* is viewed as making fundamental changes in women's federal corrections, criticisms force a rethinking of the original vision.

The key criticisms of *Creating Choices* are that the voices of the federally sentenced women have not been heard and the report has not been not implemented as intended. This is evident in the definition of empowerment; the classification of risk versus need; forced participation in programming; the negative relationships with staff; the continued use of segregation, handcuffs, pepper spray and strip searches; and the ranking of commitments to correctional and cultural programming.

The critical position is that implementation strategies must therefore be revisited with attention to need versus risk, proper hiring and instruction of staff, women's voices and agency and the renouncement of harmful operations such as segregation, pepper spray and strip searches. Planning for the long-term sentences of the federally sentenced women at the Healing Lodge must be linked to the increased involvement of the Nekaneet Band, Elders and their teachings. The initial vision, which stated that the Healing Lodge "must [be] developed by and connected to Aboriginal communities" (CSC 1990: 122), should therefore be revisited. "Connected" here means more than just placing the facility on Aboriginal land, which simply becomes the "prisonization" of the Healing Lodge (Monture-Angus 2000: 54). Much more research is also necessary to uncover the needs of more violent women, especially given the abundance of stereotypical and false information in the news media (c.f., Faith 2011, 1993; Faith and Jiwani in this volume). New strategies are also needed to measure risk and responsibility. As DeKeseredy (2011) points out, women who are violent are most often reacting to violence against them.

There has also been a shift in how women offenders are perceived, which has affected their treatment since the closure of P4W. The idea that women are high need yet low risk has been replaced with the perception of women as high need and high risk. Characteristics of the women, such as their history of abuse and self injurious behaviour, are now used to justify higher security classifications rather than as reasons suporting the need for therapeutic intervention.

This chapter has examined the social control of criminalized women through the criminal justice system, media, education, violence and the law. The relationship between women's criminalization and social justice issues was explored in relation to race, gender and class. We have drawn attention to the contrast between the image of the "monster woman" in film and the news and the statistical reality of criminalized women whose crimes are generally not violent and who have often experienced economic marginalization, racism and violence. By focusing our attention on Canada's most violent and notorious women offenders — such as Karla Homolka — and creating false and hateful pornographic images of female prisoners, we forget how class, race and gender inequalities affect women's criminalization.

Themes of criminal responsibility and dangerous social groups are criticized in feminist literature as ideological tools that attempt to manage the most vulnerable people (Morris 2000; Shaw 2000). The criminal justice system and the media function as powerful hegemonic tools that convince the majority that the poor and marginalized must be feared as the most dangerous and criminal class (Collins 2014).

Critical feminist literature also provides an in-depth critique of the complex nature of law and order politics. These critical views also show ways that P4W and the new regional prisons have failed to reduce the incidence of female criminality because they fail to address problems such as violence against women and children, poverty, continued racism and inequality of opportunity. Prisons cannot address these broader structural, economic, social and political problems. This chapter suggests that we cannot limit our discussions to criminal justice or penal reform; rather, we have to also query the relationships between law, legislative reform and social regulation.

Critical feminist authors such as Karlene Faith (2011, 1993), Helen Boritch (2002, 2008) and Margaret Shaw (2000) argue that reform within the prison system risks expanding and justifying the use of incarceration for women. *Creating Choices* offers feminist reforms that may negate the offering of socially informed alternatives to imprisonment for women. The goal for feminist reformers must be to reduce reliance on imprisonment for women in trouble and to push for the implementation of non-carceral correctional approaches.

We cannot (in good conscience) conclude by arguing that *Creating Choices* has simply failed to achieve its vision upon implementation and is doomed. *Creating Choices* has improved some women's lives and may, with much continued effort, help (not hinder) reform-minded feminists in their efforts towards eventually de-institutionalizing women, using restorative and community initiatives and addressing structural inequalities and issues of human rights. Critical feminists attest that we must not abandon prison reform for women; however, more research and consciousness-raising must be done to demonstrate that female offenders are relatively low risk, that their lives are characterized by abuse, poverty and inequality and that ill-designed systems can be reformed. Considerations of the power of both the media and out-dated criminological theory in shaping public opinion must also be considered with respect to the social regulation of criminalized women.

Women in prison, academics and activists continue to call our attention to the voices of women in prison and the importance of protecting their real human rights:

> *Tears have long since been subdued*
> *My waters have run dry*
> *I just might come unglued*
> *As I start to cry.*
>
> *Time is suffocating*
> *My flow*
> *I'm tired of waitin*
> *I'm ready to go!*
> — *Summers 2011: Another Day [in prison] Series*

DISCUSSION QUESTIONS

1. Creating Choices has been viewed as a paradigm shift in federal corrections for women and an extended form of social regulation over criminalized women. Compare and assess these two different positions.

2. What are some of the factors that bring women into conflict with the law?

3. Locate a movie, reality television program or current newspaper story about female crime and discuss what ideological message it puts forth. Do you agree or disagree that this form of media may influence the public perception of female criminality? Explain your position.

4. Discuss the history of the treatment of federally sentenced women in Canada and the problems at the Prison for Women in Kingston (P4W) that led to its demise.

5. Compare Lombroso and Ferrero's biological explanation for female criminality to Freda Adler's role theory. Include a discussion of the key criticisms of both types of theories.

GLOSSARY

Prison for Women (P4W): historically, only one prison held federally sentenced women in Canada, compared to over forty federal facilities for men. Since its inception in 1934, the Prison for Women at Kingston (P4W) was criticized for being dark, foreboding and dysfunctional. More than a dozen government reports denounced P4W for a number of factors; all but one called for the closure of the prison.

Creating Choices: a report of the Task Force on federally sentenced women that has been viewed as transformative for women's corrections in Canada. Based on researching the needs of federally sentenced women and their experience in prison in Canada, *Creating Choices* critiqued the traditional male model of imprisonment and replaced it with a new model that emphasized the assessment of imprisoned women's needs and the holistic treatment of these needs. Five new guiding principles were stressed: creating meaningful choices, empowering women, respect and dignity and support and sharing responsibility with communities.

Canadian Association of Elizabeth Fry Society (CAEFS): works with women and girls that are involved in the justice system, especially those who are criminalized and/or imprisoned. The association works towards equity in services for women and promotes research, education, program delivery, scholarship and administrative reform.

Property Crimes: offences/crimes against property are acts that do not involve violence and are done to gain property, including theft, fraud and break and enters.

Crimes Against the Person: Crimes against the person are those that involve threatening of violence or the use of violence against another person. These include homicide, attempted murder, assault, sexual assault and robbery.

Biological Theory: defines criminality as a pathology originating from the biological make up of individuals.

Role Theory: offers the notion that individual pathologies are induced by society and can, therefore, be modified by society. Role theory considers sociological factors to explain behavior such as diverse socialization.

Feminist Criminology: feminist-based theories of crime insist women's criminalization is worthy of academic inquiry and have contributed to understandings of victimization, criminalization and the criminal justice system. Feminist criminologists engage the question of the interaction between human agency and social structure (including gender, class, age, race, sexuality) and bring forward voices of those in conflict with the law.

SUGGESTED READINGS

Gillian Balfour and Elizabeth Comack (eds.), *Criminalizing Women: Gender and (In)justice in Neo-Liberal Times,* Halifax: Fernwood Publications (2014).

Karlene Faith, *Unruly Women: The Politics of Confinement and Resistance,* New York: Seven Stories Press (2011).

Gillian Balfour and Elizabeth Comack, *The Power to Criminalize: Violence, Inequality, and the Law,* Halifax: Fernwood Publishing (2004). <http://www.fernwoodpublishing.ca/The-Power-to-Criminalize-Gillian-Balfour-Elizabeth-Comack/>.

Jane Barker (ed.), *Women and the Criminal Justice System: A Canadian Perspective,* Toronto: Emond Montgomery (2009).

Karlene Faith with Anne Near (eds.), *13 Women: Parables from Prison,* Vancouver: Douglas and McIntyre (2006).

SUGGESTED WEBSITES

Canadian Association of Elizabeth Fry Society (caefs), "Fact Sheets and Newsletters," 2014. <caefs.ca/resources/fact-sheets-in-pdf/>.

Statistics Canada, "Women and the Criminal Justice System," 2011. <statcan.gc.ca/pub/89-503-x/2010002/article/11416-eng.htm#a3>.

SUGGESTED FILMS

Christine Welsh, *Finding Dawn,* National Film Board of Canada (2006).

Sarah Zammit, *Life Inside Out,* National Film Board of Canada (2005).

Peter Cohn, *Power and Control: Domestic Violence in America,* New Day Films (2010).

"Behind the Wall: A Closer Look at the Death of Ashley Smith," *The Fifth Estate.* <http://www.cbc.ca/fifth/2010-2011/behindthewall/> accessed February 2012.

NOTES

1. Canadian Corrections Association, Brief on the Woman Offender (Canada 1968); Report of the Canadian Committee on Corrections (Canada 1969); Report of the Royal Commission on the Status of Women (Canada 1970); Ministry of the Solicitor General, Report of the National Advisory Committee on the Female offender (Canada 1976); Report to Parliament by the Sub-Committee on the Penitentiary System in Canada (Canada 1977b); Canadian Association of Elizabeth Fry Societies, "Brief on the Female Offender" (1978); Brief to the Solicitor General (Canada 1978); Ministry of the Solicitor General, Report on the National Planning Committee on the Female Offender (Canada 1978); Ten Years Later (Canada 1979); Women for Justice, "Brief to the Canadian Human Rights Commission" (Canada 1980).
2. caefs philosophy supports the eventual abolition of prisons for women.
3. Ole Ingstrup had been commissioner for six months, with the average term being three years.
4. Governing has moved from the regulation of an individual's behaviour in the more coercive institution, towards strategies of empowerment which rely on self-governing and creates prudent subjects who are responsiblized (who take responsibility for their own behaviour) (Rose 1996, 2000).
5. See also, for example, the Arbour Commission, Public Hearings 1995.

REFERENCES

Adelberg, E., and C. Currie. 1987. *Too Few to Count: Canadian Women in Conflict with the Law.* Vancouver: Press Gang.

Adler, Freda. 1975. *Sisters in Crime: The Rise of the New Female Criminal.* New York: McGraw-Hill.

Arbour, Honourable Louise. 1996. "Commission of Inquiry into Certain Events at the Prison for Women in Kingston." *Ottawa: Public Works and Government Services Canada.*

Baez, H. 2010. "Lombroso, Cesare: The Female offender." In F. Cullen and P. Wilcox (eds.), *Encyclopedia of Criminological Theory.* Thousand Oaks, CA: Sage Publications.

Banwell, Stacey. 2011. "Women, Violence and the Gray Zones: Resolving the Paradox of the Female Victim-Perpetrator." *Internet Journal of Criminology ISSN 2045-6793.* At <internetjournalof-criminology.com/banwell_women_violence_and_gray_zones_ijc_september_2011>.

Barrett, Meridith Robeson, Kim Allenby and Kelly Taylor. 2010. "Twenty Years Later: Revisiting the Task Force on Federally Sentenced Women." *Correctional Service Canada* July. At <csc-scc. gc.ca/005/008/092/005008-0222-01-eng.pdf>.

Boritch, Helen. 2002. "Women in Prison in Canada." In B. Schissel and C. Brooks (eds.)., *Marginality and Condemnation: An Introduction to Critical Criminology.* Halifax and Winnipeg: Fernwood Publications.

___. 2008. "Women in Prison in Canada." In C. Brooks and B. Schissel (eds.), *Marginality and Condemnation: An Introduction to Criminology* (second edition). Halifax and Winnipeg: Fernwood Publications.

Burns, Jan. 2006. "Mad or Just Plain Bad? Gender and the Work of Forensic Clinical Psychologists." In Jane M. Ussher and Paula Nicolson (eds.), *Gender Issues in Clinical Psychology.* New York: Routledge.

CAEFS (Canadian Association of Elizabeth Fry Society archives). 2014. "Fact Sheets and Newsletters." At <caefs.ca/resources/fact-sheets-in-pdf/>.

Canada. 1977a. *Report on the Standing Committee on Justice and Solicitor General on its Review of Sentencing, Conditional Release and Related Aspects of Corrections.*

___. 1977b. *Report to Parliament by the Sub-Committee on the Penitentiary System in Canada.* Ottawa: Supply and Services. 1977.

Canada: Correctional Service Canada. 1990. *Creating Choices: The Report of the Task Force on Federally Sentenced Women.* Ottawa, Canada: Correctional Services Canada, April.

Canadian Human Rights Commission. 2003. "Protecting Their Rights: A Systemic Review of Human Rights in Correctional Services for Federally Sentenced Women." *Canadian Human Rights Commission,* December. At <caefs.ca/wp-content/uploads/2013/05/fswen.pdf>.

Carlen, P. 1988. *Women, Crime, and Poverty.* Milton Keynes, Philadelphia: Open University Press.

Cecil, Dawn K. 2007. "Looking Beyond Caged Heat: Media Images of Women in Prison." *Feminist Criminology* 2: 304–26.

Chesney-Lind, Meda, and Michele Eliason. 2006. "From Invisible to Incorrigible: The Demonization of Marginalized Women and Girls." *Crime, Media and Culture* 2: 29–47.

Clowers, M. 2001. "Dykes, Gangs, and Danger: Debunking Popular Myths about Maximum-Security Life." *Journal of Criminal Justice and Popular Culture* 9, 1: 22–30.

Collins. Racheal. 2014. "'Meet the Devil... He'll Chill You to the Bone' Fear, Marginalization, and the Colour of Crime: A Thirty-Year Analysis of Four Canadian Newspapers." At <ecommons. usask.ca/handle/10388/ETD-2014-03-1491>.

Comack, Elizabeth. 1996. *Women in Trouble.* Halifax: Fernwood Publishing.

___. 2006. "The Feminist Engagement with Criminology." In Gillian Balfour and Elizabeth Comack (eds.), *Criminalizing Women: Gender and (In)Justice in Neo-Liberal Times.* Halifax: Fernwood.

Correctional Service of Canada. 1999. "Profile of Incarcerated Women Offenders: September, 1999." At <www.csc-scc.gc.caa/text/releases00-07-06e.shtm>.

___. 2008. "Report of the Task Force on Security." At <www.csc-scc.gc.ca/text/pblct/security/toc-eng.shtml>.

Correctional Services of Canada. 2013. *Coroner's inquest touching the death of Ashley Smith.* At:

csc-scc.gc.ca/publications/005007-9009-eng.shtml>.

Cowie, John, Valerie A. Cowie and Eliot Slater. 1968. *Delinquency in Girls.* New York: Humanities Press.

Currie, Dawn. 1986. "Female Criminality: A Crisis in Feminist Theory." In B. MacLean (ed.), *The Political Economy of Crime.* Scarborough: Prentice-Hall.

Daigle, Marc, Mylene Alaire and Patrick Lefebvre. 1999. "The Problem of Suicide Among Female Prisoners." *Forum on Corrections Research* 11, 3.

Dalton, Katharina. 1978. *Cyclical Criminal Acts in Premenstrual Syndrome.* Elsevier.

Dekeseredy, Walter. 2011. *Violence Against Women: Myths, Facts and Controversies.* Toronto: University of Toronto Press.

Dell, Colleen Anne, Catherine J. Fillmore and Jennifer M. Kilty. 2009. "Looking Back 10 Years After the Arbour Inquiry: Ideology, Policy, Practice, and the Federal Female Prisoner." *The Prison Journal* 89, 3: 286–308.

Delveaux, K., K. Blanchette and J. Wickett. 2005. *Employment Needs, Interests, and Programming for Women Offenders.* Ottawa: Correctional Service of Canada.

Faith, Karlene. 1993. *Unruly Women: The Politics of Confinement & Resistance.* Vancouver, BC: Press Gang Publishers.

___. 2011. *Unruly Women: The Politics of Confinement & Resistance.* New York: Seven Stories Press.

Ferrari, J. 2011. "Federal Female Incarceration in Canada: What Happened to Empowerment?" At <qspace.library.queensu.ca/bitstream/1974/6352/3/Ferrari_Jacqueline_201104_MA.pdf>.

Findlay, Isabel, James Popham, Patrick Ince and Sarah Takahashi. 2013. *Through the Eyes of Women: What a Co-operative Can Mean in Supporting Women During Confinement and Integration.* Saskatoon: Centre for the Study of Co-operatives, University of Saskatchewan.

Garland, E. 2001. *The Culture of Control: Crime and Social Order in Contemporary Society.* Chicago: Oxford University Press.

Gironella, Fiona D. 1999. "Creating Choices or Redefining Control? Prisoners from the Edmonton Institution for Women Share Their Standpoint." Edmonton: University of Alberta.

Hannah-Moffat, K. 1999. "Moral Agent or Actuarial Subject: Risk and Canadian Women's Imprisonment." *Theoretical Criminology* 3, 1: 71–94. Reprinted 2006 by the International Library of Essays in Law and Society, in P. O'Malley (ed.), *Governing Risks.* Ashgate Publishing Ltd. <tcr.sagepub.com/content/3/1/71.abstract>.

Hannah-Moffat, K., and M. Shaw. 2000. "Gender, Diversity and Risk Assessment in Canadian Corrections." *Probation Journal.* 47, 3: 172. <prb.sagepub.com/content/47/3/163.abstract>.

Hayman, Stephanie. 2000. "Prison Reform and Incorporation: Lessons From Britain and Canada." In Kelly Hannah-Moffat and Margaret Shaw (eds.), *An Ideal Prison? Critical Essays on Women's Imprisonment in Canada.* Halifax: Fernwood Publishing.

Heney, J.H. 1990. *Report on Self-Injurious Behaviour in the Kingston Prison for Women.* June (revised). Submitted to the Correctional Service of Canada.

Hoffman-Bustamente, D. 1973. "The Nature of Female Criminality." *Issues in Criminology* 2.

Hoffman, L.E., and M.A. Law. 1995. "Federally Sentenced Women on Conditional Release: Survey of Community Supervisors." Ottawa: Federally Sentenced Women Program, Correctional Service of Canada.

Hotton-Mahony, Tina. 2011. "Women and the Criminal Justice System." Statistics Canada Catalogue no 89-503-X. *Women in Canada: A Gender-Based Statistical Report.* April. <statcan.gc.ca/pub/89-503-x/2010001/article/11416-eng.pdf>.

Hugill, David. 2010. *Missing Women, Missing News: Covering Crisis in Vancouver's Downtown Eastside.* Halifax and Winnipeg: Fernwood Publishing.

Kendall, K. 2000. "Psy-Ence Fiction: Inventing the Mentally-Disordered Female Prisoner." In Kelly Hannah-Moffat and Margaret Shaw (eds.), *An Ideal Prison? Critical Essays on Women's Imprisonment in Canada.* Halifax: Fernwood Publishing.

Labrecque. R. 1995. *Study of the Mother-Child Program.* Ottawa: Federally Sentenced Women Program, Correctional Services of Canada.

Kershaw, Anne, and Mary Lasovich. 1991. *Rock-a-Bye Baby: A Death Behind Bars.* Toronto: McClelland and Stewart.

Lawston, Jodie. 2011. "From Representations to Resistance: How the Razor Wire Binds Us." In Jodie Lawton and Ashley Lucas (eds.). *Razor Wire Women: Prisoners, Activists, Scholars and Artists.* Albany: State University of New York Press.

Lombroso, Cesare, and Guglielmo Ferroer. 1895. *The Female Offender.* New York: D. Appleton and Company.

Martin, M. 1997. "Connected Mothers: A Follow-Up Study of Incarcerated Women and Their Children." *Women and Criminal Justice* 8, 1.

McDonagh, Donna. 1999. "Maximum Security Women: 'Not Letting the Time Do You.'" *Forum on Corrections Research* 11, 3.

Monture-Angus, Patricia. 2000. "Aboriginal Overrepresentation in Canadian Criminal Justice." In David Long and Olive Patricia Dickason (eds.), *Visions of the Heart: Canadian Aboriginal Issues,* second edition. Toronto: Harcourt Canada.

Morris, Ruth. 2000. *Stories of Transformative Justice.* Toronto: Canadian Scholars' Press.

Office of the Correctional Investigator. 2013. "Aboriginal Offenders – A Critical Situation." At <oci-bec.gc.ca/cnt/rpt/oth-aut/oth-aut20121022info-eng.aspx>.

Pate, Kim. 2011. "When Strip Searches Are Sexual Assaults." At <http://www.caefs.ca/wp-content/uploads/2013/05/October_2011_Kim_Pate_When_strip_searches_are_sexual_assaults.pdf> accessed June 2014.

Pollack, O. 1979. "The Masked Character of Female Crime." In Adler and Simon (eds.), *The Criminality of Deviant Women.* Boston: Houghton Millin.

Rose, N. 1996. "Governing Advanced Liberal Democracies." In A. Barry, T. Osborne and N. Rose (eds.), *Foucault and Political Reason: Liberalism, Neo-Liberalism, and Rationalities of Government.* Chicago: University of Chicago Press.

___. 2000. *Government and Control.* Oxford and New York: Oxford University Press.

Sapers, Howard. 2008. "A Preventable Death: Correctional Investigation into the Death of Ashley Smith." Canada: Office of the Correctional Investigator.

Schissel, Bernard. 2006. *Still Blaming Children: Youth Conduct and the Politics of Child Hating.* Black Point, NS: Fernwood Publishing.

Schram, Pamela, and Stephen Tibbetts. 2014. *Introduction to Criminology: Why Do They Do It?* Thousand Oaks, CA: Sage Publication.

Shaw, Margaret. 1993. "Reforming Federal Women's Imprisonment." In Ellen Adelberg and Claudia Currie (eds.), *In Conflict with the Law: Women and the Canadian Justice System.* Vancouver: Press Gang.

___. 2000. "Women, Violence and Disorder in Prisons." In Kelly Hannah-Moffat and Margaret Shaw (eds.), *An Ideal Prison? Critical Essays on Women's Imprisonment in Canada.* Halifax: Fernwood Publishing.

Smart, Carol. 1976. *Women, Crime and Criminology: A Feminist Critique.* London: Routledge and Kegan Paul.

Star Phoenix. 1991. "Dying to Get Out of P4W: In Kingston's Prison for Women Some Natives Find Death a Form for Liberation." March 23.

Strange, C. 1985. "The Criminal and Fallen of Their Sex: The Establishment of Canada's First Women's Prison, 1874–1901," *Canadian Journal of Women and the Law* 79.

Summers, Tammica L. 2011. "Stories So Strong They Crumble Concrete." *Another Day Series.* At <womenandprison.org/poetry/view/another_day_series/>.

Thomas, Jennifer. 2000. "Adult Correctional Services in Canada, 1998–99." *Juristat* 20, 3. Canadian Center for Justice Studies.

Wattanaportn, Katelyn A., and Kristy Holtfreter. 2014. "The Impact of Feminist Pathways Research on Gender-Responsive Policy and Practice." *Feminist Criminology* 9: 191–207.

White, R. 2002. "Restorative Justice and Social Inequality." In B. Schissel and C. Brooks (eds.), *Marginality and Condemnation: An Introduction to Critical Criminology.* Halifax: Fernwood Publishing.

Wiebe, Rudy, and Yvonne Johnson. 1998. *Stolen Life: The Journey of a Creee Woman.* Toronto: Alfred A. Knopf Canada.

15

MEN, MASCULINITY AND CRIME

Rod Earle and Deborah H. Drake

KEY FACTS

> Across different countries, and over any time scale, and in all forms of measurement, men outnumber women in crime statistics by a ratio of up to 10:1.

> Gender theorists suggest that adolescents become familiar with the gender-based expectations of the dominant culture, which compels them to conform to identities emphasizing strength, toughness and aggression. Similarly, researchers link street level gang activity to hyper-masculine practices encouraging youth to conform with conceptions of acting like a "real man."

> Assumptions that male prisoners are hyper-violent and embody a dangerous masculinity has a profound negative effect on the running of prisons and the interactions of prisoners and staff in correctional centres. The idea of prisoners' dangerous masculinity simplifies men's actual biographies.

> The devastating occurrence of murder-suicide has been explained by Oliffe et al. (2014) as an end product of "failed manhood" within families, school and work places.

Sources: Newburn and Stanko 1994; Henry 2013; Curtis 2014; Oliffe et al. 2014.

In May 2011 one of the most powerful white men in the world, Dominic Strauss-Khan, was arrested in New York and taken to the city's notorious Rikers Island prison. The world's media focused on his detention because he was the Managing Director of the International Monetary Fund and a prospective candidate for the French presidency. He was detained under suspicion that he had raped the black woman whose job it was to clean his hotel room. He was released after a few days and the charges were dropped.

In June of the same year, serious rioting broke out in several English cities following the shooting death of a black man by police officers on the edges of a London housing estate where he was suspected of leading gangs and drug dealing. Amidst widespread looting and arson over several days, five people were killed. In the following weeks and months thousands of young men were arrested and charged with a variety of criminal offences. Many were jailed.[1] Women were also involved in the riots, although official figures based on arrest data indicate only 10 percent of those taking part were women. Some young women were jailed as a result but the riots prompted two widely respected feminist sociologists (Cockburn and Oakley 2011) to comment on the relationship between violence, crime and cultures of masculinity:

Today is the International Day for the Elimination of Violence Against Women. The phrase "violence against women" calls for comment. It names the victims but not the perpetrators. The fact that men are mainly responsible for violent and health-harming behaviours, not only against women and children but also against each other, is so taken for granted that it slips beneath the radar of commentators and policymakers.

The two events, the arrest for rape in the U.S. of Dominic Strauss-Khan and the English Riots, are completely unconnected if you think questions of gender, race, class and power should be excluded from attempts to understand what crime is and how it is controlled.

RE-INTEGRATIVE NAMING? BRINGING MASCULINITY BACK IN

Concern about crime as a problematic feature of social life rose dramatically in the second half of the twentieth century in most Western countries (Garland 2001). As crime rates started to peak in the late 1980s and early 1990s, some feminist scholars and activists (Heidenshon 1987) began to characterize the problem of crime in gender terms. They challenged the discipline of criminology to account for the "facts of crime" that consistently revealed men's pre-eminent position. Across different countries, and over any time scale, and in all forms of measurement, men outnumber women in crime statistics by a ratio of up to 10:1 (Newburn and Stanko 1995).

In Britain, after a series of urban disorders and moral panics in the early 1990s, the feminist journalist and activist Bea Campbell (1993: 319) suggested that "the great unspoken in the crime angst of the 80s and 90s was that it is a phenomenon of masculinity." In her analysis of urban disorder, Campbell identified aspects of masculine, working-class culture that were, according to her viewpoint, inextricably linked with their subjugated position within the economic system and thus their social status. Men found in criminal activity, she argued, the social status they were denied by their social positioning. Moreover, with respect to the problem of crime, Campbell suggested that "crime and coercion are sustained by men. Solidarity and self-help are sustained by women. It is as stark as that." Though she was subsequently accused of over simplification and further fuelling the accelerating demonization of the working class in general, and working class men in particular, her more careful qualifications were frequently overlooked:

> This is not to say that boys and men are bad and girls and women are good, it is simply to repeat the obvious, *that men and women do something dramatically different with their troubles*." (ibid. 1993: 319, emphasis added)

Examining the actions of men and women and their troubles as arising from the social processes of gender relations, rather than the innate characteristics of men and women, has been, and continues to be, the exception rather than the norm, both in everyday understandings of social life (as expressed between people as well as in media and popular culture) and in many areas of academic study.

The hostile critical reaction to Campbell's analysis reveals a common and continuing difficulty in discussing men's involvements and investments in crime and crime control. In policy making, criminal justice practice and academic criminology, there is a tendency to disassociate the concept of masculinity from that of gender. Additionally, in societies that are heavily divided along class lines, such as Britain, there is often a corresponding but ironic insensitivity and blindness to the enduring and embedded nature of class hierarchies among those most privileged by it. As is the case with white people and the dynamics of racialization, those with the most power are least likely to recognize its privileging effects. So it is with gender.

When talking about masculinity we are not talking simply "about men" as such. Far from being just about men, the idea of masculinity engages, inflects and shapes everyone (Sedgwick 1985). It works across hierarchies of class, gender relations, race and ethnicity. Naming men as gender players, as agents of gendered power, need not efface or overshadow the ways in which these other features of social and personal interaction structure the possibilities of life. However, in this chapter, we argue that it is helpful for gender to be brought firmly within what might be called a critical, intersectional gaze.

An intersectional perspective insists on the indivisibility of the interactive constituents of class, race and gender in social life at the same time as recognizing their distinctive features (see Anthias 2013). An analogy might be made in the way that knowing water is composed of two hydrogen atoms to every oxygen atom allows for a certain kind of knowledge, but identifying the chemical composition of water does little to appreciate its wetness. In order to provide a detailed and textured understanding of the interaction between men, masculinity and crime, we build on Comack's analysis of gender in Chapter Two by turning our attentions to examining how criminology first emerged in nineteenth century Italy as a science fascinated by gender and difference. We then go on to look at how twentieth century theorists of crime in the U.S. also noted the particularity of men's behaviours, but abandoned any account of the significance of gender or masculinity because they lacked the conceptual tools, and insights, to integrate either systematically into their analysis.

Our analyses then cross the Atlantic to consider the way studies of working class young men preoccupied British subcultural theorists in the 1970s and 1980s. Having laid this ground work, we go on to investigate the emergence of critical masculinity perspectives within criminology at the end of the twentieth century by engaging with the contributions of James Messerschmidt and Tony Jefferson, among others. We then conclude the chapter with a short vignette that considers a kind of "paradigmatic prison masculinity" to illuminate the personal tragedies and sociological conundrums they so frequently embody.

CESARE LOMBROSO AND THE NEW SCHOOL BOYS: THE ORIGIN OF THE SPECIES

Conventional accounts of the origins of criminology identify the emergence of two perspectives associated with the European Enlightenment: classicism and positivism (Young 1981). The distinction between the two is neatly expressed by Hamel (1906: 265, cited in Young 1981): "The Classical School exhorts men to study justice; the Positive School exhorts justice to study men." It is only with the privilege of hindsight and the theoretical insights of feminism that we may recognize the unintended gender dimensions of Hamel's remark. Taken as a gender specific observation, it neatly encapsulates the challenges that continue to confront contemporary criminology.

Positivism in criminology is most powerfully associated with the nineteenth century work of Cesare Lombroso. Lombroso's work was widely read and popularized across Europe. His studies proposed that criminals were a different class of human, a throwback to more primitive types of "early human", almost a separate species of sub-human. This remains a powerful, if sometimes implicit, theme of some strands of criminology and forensic psychology.

According to Lombroso (and, to be fair to him, the dominant currents of thought at the time), the fit and healthy white male represented the apex of evolution, while women and criminals were closer to their "primitive origins."

Lombroso is sometimes referred to as "the father of modern criminology" (Newburn 2007: 122). His symbolic influence can be gauged by the fact that David Garland's (2001) revision of the intellectual trajectory of criminology over two centuries identifies the current resurgence of the discipline in the convergence of its two dominant streams of thought: "the governmental project" (effectively, if loosely, classicism) and "the Lombrosian project" (broadly, positivism). The Lombrosian project, according to Garland, is all about establishing categorical differences between "criminal-types" and "non-criminal-types."

Lombroso's interests were enthusiastically developed by his Italian contemporaries, Enrico Ferri and Raffaele Garofalo, who together became known as The Italian School after Ferri's 1901 book *The Positive School of Criminology*. Their influence in establishing the idea of a "criminal type of man" is a lasting one, as Garland suggests, and although it is tempting to dismiss the cruder notions of biological gender difference they deploy, it reminds us of the importance of situating social and scientific theories in their cultural and historical contexts (Valier 2001). Lombroso and his contemporaries in the Positive School had no effective social theory of gender and sought to explain difference in the powerful slipstream of the intellectual revolution of Darwinism because it offered such radically new perspectives on humanity's place in the world. It might appear crude and deterministic now, but at the time it was the height of theoretical sophistication and the cutting edge of innovation. Many of the Italian positivists were social radicals, associated with the socialist and communist movements in Italy and abroad. Though we might not wish to rescue Lombroso's theories, it is just as important to avoid what the historian E.P. Thompson (1963) calls "the enormous condescension of posterity" when reviewing earlier efforts to make sense of the social world and shape its destiny.

BORN IN THE USA: DELINQUENT BOYS, TYPICAL GIRLS

In the United States, the search for a more sociological, less biologically deterministic, explanation of crime was spurred on by Robert Merton's (1938) creative adaptation of Durkheim's theory of anomie. Merton was inspired by the effects of the American Dream as a form of capitalist development, and its first major crisis in the 1929 Crash and subsequent Depression years of the 1930s. Merton's theory of deviance is credited as being "the single most influential formulation in the sociology of deviance" (Clinard 1964: 10). His assertion that "a cardinal American virtue, ambition, promotes a cardinal American vice, deviant behaviour" (1949: 137) addressed the booming rates of crime that accompanied the explosive growth of American cities, most famously and most paradigmatically, Chicago.

The frustrations and adaptations Merton identified in the early twentieth century were not explicitly gendered but resonated most forcefully in the construction of working-class masculinities. Operating at the leading edge of capitalist development in the West, male employment and the breadwinner wage were central to these aspirational, industrial, U.S. masculinities. Structural unemployment in the 1930s challenged the much-idealized stability of the male breadwinner role and threatened the secure occupational identities around which conventional definitions of male self-esteem were increasingly gathered (Connell 1987 1995).

The significance of the masculine life-course, and specifically the strains Merton identified, became central to what has come to be celebrated as The Chicago School of American sociology. Wide in scope, and profound in influence, Chicago School sociology was heavily pre-occupied with men and fascinated by deviance. Albert Cohen's (1955) study of young men in New York, "Delinquent Boys," set both the tone and much of the agenda:

> The delinquent is the rogue male. His conduct may be viewed ... positively ... as the exploitation of modes of behaviour which are traditionally symbolic of untrammeled masculinity ... which are not without a certain aura of glamour and romance. (ibid: 140)

There is more than a hint of an echo of Lombrosian atavism in Cohen's reference to "untrammeled masculinity," as if masculinity was intrinsically wild, but his debt to Merton is clearer. He finds that the subculture among New York's marginalized young men was a solution to "problems of adjustment" which were "primarily problems of the male role." Developing into the male role included, first, overcoming the dependency of childhood and then becoming established within an appropriate work identity. With respect to middle-class boys, Cohen argued that there was a more prolonged dependence upon parental support that had to be confronted:

> Not only must the middle-class boy overcome an early feminine identification and prove his maleness, even the opportunities to assume the legitimate signs of maleness are likely to be denied him. (ibid.: 166)

Within this analysis, the "breadwinner role", it was argued, established the basis (if only in principle and fantasy) for a lasting domestic symmetry with a steadfast, stay-at-home wife providing unwaged domestic labour (cooking, laundry, household maintenance and childcare), emotional comfort and sexual gratification. However, working class boys' earlier departure from the feminized home and entry into the (masculinizing) job market, by contrast, provided a distinctive dividend — they were able to accrue masculine (and often muscular) capital sooner.

Cohen's work is clearly sensitive to gender but shackled to the limitations of what is known as "sex-role theory." Cohen attributes middle-class male delinquency to "an attempt to cope with a basic anxiety in the area of sex-role identification; it has the primary function of giving reassurance to one's essential masculinity." Sex-role theory, as Connell (1987) argues, always tends to reinforce, rather than challenge, naturalized gender categories. The working class male, according to Cohen, is more likely to be secure in his masculine identity through his earlier transition from the feminizing influence of the domestic space of home to the male-dominated spheres of work. His troubles, specifically his delinquency, arise from the difficulties of "adjustment in the area of ego-involved status differences in a status system defined by the norms of respectable middle class society" (ibid.: 168). In other words, his masculine aspirations for power do not correspond with his class opportunities.

Albert Cohen can be credited with putting masculinity in the criminological picture, but he is hampered by the prevailing assumptions of biologically determined natural differences between men and women that took the form of complementary breadwinning and domestic roles. As such they were regarded as peripheral to the more determining forces of class stratification.

An unintended gender perspective comes across strongly in a section of Cohen's "Delinquent Boys" headed "What About Sex Differences?" that candidly reveals Cohen's personal reading of his own natural, "representative" masculinity:

> My skin has nothing of the quality of down or silk; there is nothing limpid or flute-like about my voice. I am a total loss with needle and thread. My posture and carriage are wholly lacking in grace. These imperfections cause me no distress — if anything they are gratifying — because I conceive myself to be a man and want people to recognise me as a fully-fledged representative of my sex. (ibid: 138)

Albert Cohen's revealing, reflexive meditations and his sensitivity to the empirical realities of gender differences are a welcome exception to the more conventionally and casually gender-blind approach of a lot of mainstream criminology, both then and now.

An emerging concern about the significance of gender relations is also evident in Richard Cloward and Lloyd Ohlin's (1961) work, *Delinquency and Opportunity: A Theory of Delinquent Gangs*. With hindsight it is easy to see the constraints imposed on them by the sex-role paradigm, as it was with Cohen's work. The tension between a cultural faith in the notion of fixed gender identities despite empirical evidence of their fluidity, variation and instability is a consistent feature of any historical study of masculinities (Harvey and Shepard 2005). Responding to such empirical realities and theoretical difficulties, Cloward and Ohlin (ibid: 51) record their doubts about "the distribution of the masculine-identity crisis" and indicate that "there is no firm agreement among theorists as to where in the social structure this problem occurs most frequently or in most acute forms". It is illuminating to note Cloward and Ohlin's early engagement with this tension and the popular belief that the "wayward" behavior of some men, and any empirical evidence of such behavior, denoted an alarming crisis in masculinity. Equally, despite these persistent misgivings about masculinity, it tended to remain under researched, and the structures of masculine authority were left relatively untouched.

The lack of theoretical consensus around the relationship between men, masculinity, deviance and crime, or the contours of various crises facing men, sociology or capitalism, was not confined to the U.S. in the 1960s. On the other side of the Atlantic, broadly similar men in similar academic institutions studied corresponding cohorts of men a little younger than themselves in British cities and they began to generate further theoretical innovations (Dorn and South 1982).

NEVER MIND THE CHICAGO SCHOOL, HERE'S THE U.K. SUBCULTURALISTS

London and Birmingham, rather than Chicago, provided the backdrop for the development of the new subcultural studies that emerged in the U.K. David Downes (1966) adapted and inverted the conventions of his U.S. contemporaries by asserting that conformity to norms, rather than rejection and rebellion, was the hallmark of British working class masculine subcultures. Pride in, and possession of, working class values, such as solidarity and group identity, provided the young men Downes studied with positive resources rather than a sense of deficit, a solution to predicaments imposed on them by the deeply embedded class hierarchy of British society.

Subcultural sociologists like Phil Cohen (1972) and Paul Willis (1977) found inspiration in the vitality and diversity of working-class young men's cultures in a country moving across the cusp of the post-war gloom through to the 1960s boom and subsequently into the crash of the OPEC high oil price–induced recession of the 1970s (Hobsbawn 1995). In a country whose labour movement prided itself not only on its post-war achievements in establishing the world's first welfare state, but also its traditions as the first industrial proletariat, the forward march of labour was halted in its tracks (Hobsbawm 1978). The Cold War stand-off between the capitalist West and the Rest (i.e., the Soviet Union, the developing countries of the global south and China) was eventually lost to a triumphant neo-liberal order. Its threatening shadow chilled the hopes and aspirations of the post-war generation, stilling the tide of progressive liberalization after 1945 that rode on the back of the economic consensus delivered by Keynesianism in Britain. The Cold War ground out the contours of the reaction to come in the late 1980s as the Berlin Wall fell and Soviet power financialized itself in the image of Chicago's finest criminal icons and free-market gurus.

British popular culture in the 1960s and 1970s expressed an appetite for young white men in black leather jackets on motorbikes (rockers), or khaki parkas and Lambretta scooters (mods). Skinheads were perhaps the most aggressively masculine, assertively white and working class of these subcultures. As skinheads, young men reduced their dress code and self-presentation to a simple, masculine, no-frills essence: tight denim jeans, high Doc Marten boots, cropped or shaved heads and a T-shirt. Their neo-brutal minimalist fashion aesthetic co-existed with a paradoxical affection for the sensuous rhythms of Jamaican ska and reggae that was crossing the Atlantic in the 1960s with the Caribbean immigrants brought over to the British Isles during the post-war era, when the British welfare state was being built.

Although the distinctive aspects of white men's working class cultures in Britain, and those of its emerging black and minority ethnic groups, propelled correspondingly distinctive theoretical development from those in the U.S. (see Hall et al. 1978; Gilroy 1987), the analysis of gender remained much closer to Albert Cohen's, rather than offering new and distinctive insights. Hall and Jefferson (1975: 60), for example, re-state Cohen's thesis that "middle class youth remains longer than their working class peers 'in the transitional stage,'" living in the shelter of their (feminizing) families while working-class young men depart earlier to the masculinizing culture of work.

Paul Willis's *Learning to Labour* is considered the landmark ethnographic study of this generation in Britain, the sub-title "How Working Class Kids Get Working Class Jobs" providing a succinct account of the narrative, while obscuring the fact that it is almost exclusively a story about boys and young men. His account is a compelling one. Willis vividly describes a process of class differentiation occurring in the second or third year of secondary school (i.e., ages 14–15), prior to which all the boys who would become "lads" (loosely, delinquents) could be described as "ear 'oles" (loosely, conformists because an "ear hole" was British slang for someone who listens). The lads accomplish their differentiation by a conscious process of identification with clothes, smoking, drinking, fighting and sex, which Willis insightfully collects under the young men's own collective term of "having a laff." Willis artfully presents the "'boys' secret and delicious joy in defying authority, celebrating their own values, and most important, confirming both, getting away with it" (Willis 1975: 6).

The tragic irony Willis apprehends is that the means of transcending school through their triumph over boredom, and their investment in time-wasting leavened with heavy and physical humour, only accelerates the young men's incorporation into dead-end jobs. These jobs are themselves recognized as such by the lads as mere instruments to the maintenance of an independent working class culture that pits (masculine) authenticity, subterfuge and humour against the duplicity of a meritocratic (i.e., middle class) work ethic, a kind of avowedly working class consciousness but one that is more passive-aggressive than revolutionary.

Willis's work is innovative for including an explicit analysis of the articulation of capitalism with patriarchy but, according to Connell (1983), it is constrained by its orientation to an inflexible structuralist Marxism. In other words, in Willis's analysis, class is privileged at a fundamental, functional and structural level. The modes of production, and the complex particularities of the young men's relation to physical and mental labour are so cleverly revealed in Willis's meticulous ethnography that they are inevitably reduced to a homogenous class experience. As Connell points out:

> The fieldwork doesn't react on the conceptions of the social structure. Indeed, in the gradual elaboration of an analysis of patriarchy, we can see the structuralist approach taking over the new material as it arrives. The eventual result is an abstract theory of social reproduction, not a theory of what the field material so beautifully demonstrates, sexual power structure. (ibid: 225)

Willis is eloquent in his appreciation of the injuries of class, hidden, self-inflicted or otherwise, but relatively silent about the boys' casual misogyny, fear of domesticity and horror of effeminacy. Angela McRobbie (1980) shares Connell's critique of Willis's attempt at theoretical synthesis, concluding that, unfortunately, as with Albert Cohen, masculinity in this and other subcultural accounts rarely achieves any theoretical purchase on the young men's presence in the narrative. However, both note and welcome the way masculinity registers positively, if only at the level of description. For McRobbie the rich qualitative traditions of ethnographic research to be found in subcultural studies on both sides of the Atlantic should not now be dismissed for its gender blinkers, but revisited "so that questions hitherto ignored or waved aside in embarrassment become central" (1991: 17). Recognition of the need to bring a stronger theoretical grip to the study of masculinity and crime to prevent it slipping below the analytical radar or out of the story-line altogether has since become a major preoccupation for some critical criminologists.

THEORIZING CRIME AND MASCULINITY

In the history of criminology, it sometimes seems as if masculinity takes the position that the French novelist Gustav Flaubert recommended for the "authorial voice" in a novel — that is, to be everywhere present but nowhere fully identifiable. Feminist scholars' insistence throughout the 1970s and 1980s on the salience of gender across all the social sciences has forced the pace of change and Frances Heidensohn indicates its emerging effect in criminology:

> Gender is no longer ignored ... but it is consigned to an outhouse, beyond the main structure of the work and is almost invariably conflated with women; males are not seen as having gender; or if their masculinity does become an issue, it is taken-for-granted and not treated as problematic. (1987: 23)

Until relatively recently in criminology, there has been little enthusiasm for explicitly studying masculinity, but there are signs this is changing. (For a critical account, see Collier 1998.) Bringing masculinity into the story at a more coherent theoretical level has been significantly advanced by Raewyn Connell's account of gender and power. For Connell (1983, 1987, 2002), appreciating the emergence of a historical consciousness of gender is critically important. She suggests that gender is a structure of social relations, is open to social reform and has been slower to emerge than the same corresponding knowledge of class. However, now that gender has emerged, it cannot be placed back in the box of biology from whence it came. That hitherto reliable alibi for inequality and privilege has been blown, just as it has for race (Hall 1992). Connell argues that we have passed "a horizon of historicity" in relation to gender, and although it crossed this horizon by focusing on the subordinate position of women, it now includes men and masculinity, in particular.

For Tony Jefferson (1993: 73; 1994, 1996, 1997), the task facing criminology is to account for "the near perfect fit between the mortice of masculinity and the tenon of crime", to understand why crime is overwhelmingly a male pursuit. In Canada, 95 percent of those admitted to federal custody are men, with very similar proportions sentenced in provincial and territorial courts. Likewise, 80 percent of the young people who are processed through youth courts are young men (Comack 2008). In the U.K., where detailed crime data is routinely collected through both self-report surveys and police generated data, men persistently account for eight out of every ten people cautioned by the police (representing those people diverted away from formal prosecution but who nevertheless accept they have committed a crime, albeit usually a relatively minor one). Nearly nine out of ten people found guilty for indictable (relatively serious) offences are men. Men are responsible for 92 percent of violent crimes against the person and 97 percent of burglaries. In prisons, 96 percent of the population is made up of men, mostly young men. The modal ages of the male prison population are twenty-five and twenty-six (Newburn 2007). Despite some fluctuations in recorded crimes committed by adult or young women in some countries, the empirical data across most jurisdictions suggests that those most it is adult or young men who are most frequently convicted of criminal activity.

These figures inevitably tend to reflect the traditional selective concerns of criminal justice system agencies, such as the police, and government priorities on public order and private property. They neglect the less thoroughly policed sections of the social hierarchy, occupied by figures like Dominic Strauss Khan, but it seems highly likely that if they were, a range of harmful and criminalisable activities could be identified. A theoretical toolkit has begun to take shape that helps to understand these enduring gender dimensions of the crime equation, tools that can analyze the hitherto invisible "joint" Jefferson describes.

As Comack (2008 and Chapter Two of this volume) argues, such a toolkit is necessary to "bring masculinity into view." Significantly for the study of masculinity in relation to crime, Raewyn Connell's work provides a vocabulary and conceptual map that offers a framework for systematically examining and understanding masculinities. Connell identifies how the vast constellations of the different ways of being a man secure a distinctive pattern of social relations. This pattern is dynamic and contested within certain defining limits, prompting Connell to use the term "hegemony." Hegemony denotes a dominant and dominating pattern of social relations secured by a combination of consent, habit and the exclusion of alternatives. For Connell, it captures the way multiple masculinities operate around certain organizing principles of masculinity that privilege some ways of being a man over others, while maintaining an overall pattern of domination over women (Connell 1987, 1995, 2002, 2005, 2008).

A recurring theme of hegemonic masculinity is that it is heterosexual and closely connected, at least symbolically, if not always in practice, to the institution of marriage. The changing balance of forces in gender relations is closely mapped through patterns of family form, childcare and wage-labour relations. Despite significant legislative reform in many Western democracies, male homosexuality remains the kind of masculinity most antithetical to hegemonic form. Subordinated masculinities are those forms of masculinity, such as homosexuality, that are most discredited or oppressed in the culture, and are commonly marked as feminine.

Connell identifies the notion of "protest masculinities" to capture the pressures hegemonic masculinity exerts on men to conform to its organizational and experiential principles and some of the more resistant masculinities that develop as a result. These are often the ill-fitting masculinities associated, in the West, with adolescence as young men feel the attractions of their potential for power, status hierarchies and the benefits available to them in the conventions of the gender order (Connell 2005). Connell stresses the fluid and contested nature of this order as a historical composition, always in process, always unfinished but dynamically reproducing itself as a pattern of gender relations that tends toward the privileging of men and the subordination of women. By using the term hegemony, Connell reminds us that gender is a struggle, not a fact of nature. Masculinity is a form of politics rather than of biology. The persistent historical recurrence of concerns about "crisis" in relation to men's identities, of masculinity in crisis, underlines this dynamic feature of the gender order (see Tosh and Roper 1991; Tosh 1999, 2005).

The contemporary problematics of masculinity are profiled in the crime statistics that became so prominent and public in many Western societies in the closing quarter of the twentieth century. Complex varieties of empirical evidence back up what the English social reformer Barbara Wootton observed in 1959: "If men behaved like women, the courts would be idle and the prisons empty (Wootton 1959: 32). At the start of the twenty-first century, criminal courts are busier than ever and prisons are full, multiplying and expanding in size. Even though the rate of women's imprisonment is accelerating faster than it is for men, the gender gap remains a compelling, under-theorized and overlooked feature of crime and criminal justice systems. We urgently need new answers to the question of why "men and women do something dramatically different with their troubles."

DOING GENDER AND DOING CRIME — JAMES MESSERSCHMIDT

James Messerschmidt (1993, 1997, 2005) has been at the forefront of efforts to account for the masculinity of crime, and has collaborated with Connell (2005) to consolidate a theoretical framework that can account for men's pre-eminent position in the gender dimensions of crime.

Messerschmidt concentrates on the way in which men position themselves in relation to hegemonic masculinity and how their identities are framed in a broader social context. Messerschmidt suggests that men's social and emotional investments in crime can be better understood by examining more closely the situations and masculine dynamics in which they are involved. That is, for Messerschmidt, "doing crime" becomes an equivalent to "doing masculinity." Men's accomplishment of various diverse criminalized activities provides them with masculine resources and status, which may be as much emotional as material. As Comack's (2008) work with young men in Canadian prisons shows, the struggle of young men to align themselves with tough guys, sports, school (in) discipline, hardness, gang activity and drugs forms part of a series of activities that help make them feel they are men or becoming a man. As Comack's interviews so poignantly demonstrate, their crimes often feed a hunger for authentic masculine "truths" that are almost impossible to satisfy and that they are poorly resourced to pursue. More commonly, their aspirations for achieving a particular version of masculinity propels them, instead, into descending spirals of destructive (often self-destructive) and harmful actions. Nevertheless, the way these activities make men feel like they are men, in a social and personal context, is central to their attraction.

Messerschmidt borrows from Robert Merton's strain perspectives (see Chapter Two), arguing that the social structures of capitalism block legitimate opportunities for working-class men to secure many of the privileges associated with conventional hegemonic masculinities and, furthermore, that these blockages are compounded by racism. Black, minority and Aboriginal men are thus more highly represented in the crime statistics because they are more likely to have to draw from a narrower and less highly valourized repertoire of masculine opportunity. They don't, won't or can't talk the talk of the powerful white men at the top of the social hierarchy any more than they walk the walk of their corporate boardrooms. Unlike men at the top of the social hierarchy, men like Dominic Strauss-Khan, mentioned at the start of this chapter, their struggles to establish a viable trajectory to their life are ringed ever closer with criminal justice and welfare agencies that increasingly monitor and track every wayward impulse. Likewise, returning to the other vignette that we started this chapter with, many of the men who looted shops, attacked police and created mayhem on the streets of England in 2011 were quickly arrested and thousands were prosecuted with the full force of the criminal law. Many ended up in prison, serving long sentences and will now carry the burden of criminal convictions that will weigh down any further effort to move beyond their positions at the social and economic margins of society once they are eventually released.

Messerschmidt uses a series of detailed case studies to argue that the general patterns of masculine practice that constitute hegemonic masculinity, such as competitiveness, physical toughness, emotional hardness and heterosexuality, are always personally configured according to circumstance and the structured opportunities of particular men. These features of masculine practice, these ways of being a man, are recognizable throughout the social hierarchy, but the contexts in which they occur for any one man, the opportunities that each man can capitalize on and generate, are structurally constrained by their class position and experiences of racialization. Masculinity is always lived in the plural as these variable combinations take shape and are shaped in each man's life and relationships. There are many masculinities, but they do not randomly occur in haphazard combinations.

According to Messerschmidt (1993: 84), "Particular types of crime can provide an alternative resource for accomplishing gender, and therefore, affirming a particular type of masculinity". Street crime, corporate crime, sexual harassment, domestic violence and rape are thus conceived as both the accomplishment and fulfillment of various types of masculinity that collectively collaborate in securing men's structural power over women. As with other masculinity scholars, Messerschmidt does not confine the problematics of male power to crime and criminalized activity because, as he points out in a series of detailed case studies, they are as equally evident in activities as diverse as the decisions that led to the disastrous launch of the Challenger space shuttle in 1986 and the lynching of Black men by white men in the nineteenth century. In the former case, masculine pride in risk-taking behavior and the desire for prestige resulted in the neglect of evidence that launch safety systems were radically compromised, leading to the catastrophic and fatal explosion of Challenger. According to Messerschmidt's analysis, key technicians in the Challenger team were so heavily invested in "doing masculinity," asserting their virility and masculine prowess, that they were prepared to abandon the safety of the flight crew. Similarly, in the nineteenth century, white men's conflicted investments in their own virility was counter-posed by their fear of Black men's sexual potency. They combined to sanction the savagery of lynching because it provided both a collective affirmation of their insecure desires and a cathartic release for the emotional blockage their fear generated.

The problematics of male power that we opened this chapter with and which link the arrest in New York of a middle-aged white man of the cosmopolitan elite to the Black and white men living precariously in the urban margins of north London (Standing 2011) are not reducible to crime, but, if we care to examine them, the dynamics involved can tell us a lot about crime, men, gender and power. What keeps one kind of man out of prison and throws many of another kind of man into prison — that deepest recess of the criminal justice system — should be at the forefront of criminological enquiry. The stark racialized patterning of the prison population is one starting point, and so too are its gender dynamics. Prison is a particularly revealing place to pursue these enquiries. Although, as Don Sabo (2001) remarks, "Prison is a hyper-masculine place where no-one speaks about masculinity."

PRISON LIFE, PRISON MASCULINITIES?

The academic study of men's prison life in the United States was first embarked upon by Donald Clemmer in 1940. Since then a number of in-depth studies of men's prisons have been undertaken in a variety of penal settings (for example, *inter alia* Sykes 1958; Irwin 1970; Morris and Morris 1963; Jacobs 1977; Sparks, Bottoms and Hay 1996; Liebling and Arnold 2004; Drake 2012). The main theoretical models that aim to explain and understand prison social life include a deprivation model, an importation model and those that integrate aspects of the two. In the deprivation model, it is argued that prison life is shaped by the coercive nature of the prison environment. The purest branch of this model argues that any differences in the organization of prison establishments are irrelevant because the experience of total institutions is so coercive that it homogenizes prisoner responses to their environment (see Goffman 1961; Sykes 1958). By contrast, a more situational model argues that prisoners' responses to prison life are situationally dependent on institutional characteristics (Grusky 1959; Wilson 1968). Broadly speaking, these perspectives are deprivation models because they seek to explain prison life and prisoners' adaptations to it as responses to the pains of imprisonment and the deprivations associated with the loss of liberty.

In response, and in contrast to, these explanations, an importation model to understanding prison life emerged. Importation models argue that the social environment of prison life is shaped by the imported characteristics of the prisoner group and that these originate in the subcultures to which prisoners belong prior to their entry into prison (Irwin 1970; Irwin and Cressey 1962). Further studies of prison life have proposed slight deviations from these models (e.g., Dilulio 1987; Useem and Kimball 1989). However, much contemporary prison literature tends to present integrated versions of prison social life that draw on aspects of both importation and deprivation models (Toch and Adams 1989; Liebling and Arnold 2004; Harvey 2007; Crewe 2009).

Despite the recognition amongst prison researchers that men's prison life is best understood by examining both the characteristics men bring with them into the prison environment and the peculiarities of the total institutions in which they are confined, there has been relatively little attention given to the way these experiences are gendered *as masculine*. Although numerous studies of women's imprisonment expose the specific dynamics of gender (Carlen 1983) that result in differential and differentiating experiences of prison, little corresponding work has been done with men that acknowledges their gender specificities. For example, men's specific relations to liberty and movement, to public and private space, to time structured by the labour process, and so on, remain largely unexamined through the gender lens that is routinely brought to bear on women in prison.

For all too many men, the journey from the harsh economic margins of society to prison is a cumulative and sometimes tragically terminal experience. It can be the result of patterns of behaviour or exceptional ruptures in established ones, as well as differential and discriminatory policing. Attending to how men make sense of their life in an institution that deprives them of so much that is conventionally central to masculine status, such as heterosexual relations and work, is strangely underdeveloped within criminology. Why are these "emasculations" regarded as so central to the process of punishment when masculinity is so thinly theorized in the critical literature? Men's prisons are, as Sabo observes, hyper-masculine places where cultures of machismo may flourish, and be taken for granted, among staff cultures and prisoners alike, but the cliché of the macho-man does little to shed light on the complex ways in which men make sense of themselves and their lives in prison. Men are complex and diverse, even as prison forces them into its narrow correctional molds.

UNPACKING MEN IN CRIMINOLOGY — A VIGNETTE, A MAN

Drawing from recent work in English prisons, we present below a short composite case study that seeks to capture some of the issues at stake in men's imprisonment. Recent psycho-social approaches to criminology (Gadd and Jefferson 2007; Maruna and Matravers 2007) have pioneered a more personal and biographical approach to the study of crime. It is an approach that counters the tendencies of crude categorization and aggregation that criminology can be prone to.

Both crimes and prisons succeed in generating the driest of data and the most numbing forms of analysis, whilst also remaining utterly compelling to the imagination. The reasons for this are undoubtedly complex, but one of the most unsettling features that both authors of this chapter have encountered in our prison research is how ordinary most of the men there are. Far from being beasts or monsters, men in prison are very much like the men or boys we have met at school, or at work, or in the streets where we live. It is another cliché to say they are all different, and each have their own story to tell, but it seems these stories are rarely told, barely register in popular consciousness and are relentlessly outshone by the dazzling fictions of films, television series and novels. Either that or they are erased by statistical and scientific reports oblivious to their detail. The vignette below is not intended to be representative, or even deeply illustrative. It is little more than a thumbnail sketch designed to convey some basic features of a man's life in crime. Drawn from research experiences in English prisons, it functions as a device to insist that we take crime personally, to recall the person into the picture and to deal with people, not criminals. Finding a way of taking masculinity seriously can involve engaging, as Gadd and Jefferson suggest, more thoroughly with the details of men's biographies rather than their categorical characteristics.

John: A Criminalized Man

John is a middle aged white man who grew up in a social housing block in the English midlands where unemployment was high, where there were few opportunities for young people to make the transition from school to work and where there were high levels of crime and vandalism. His parents divorced when he was twelve, and he went to live with his father, who worked full time in a factory and was not around for much of the day or the evenings. He was good at sports and enjoyed the time he spent with other boys and the sports coaches. When he was thirteen he met a girl who introduced him to cannabis and to other boys who were beginning to get into dealing drugs. Soon his involvement with drugs and the new-found independence he got from low-level drug dealing began to pull him away from sports and school. By the time he was fifteen, John was a physically big lad and had a developing reputation as someone who people could rely on to supply drugs (mostly cannabis) and who other (more powerful) drug dealers could call on to ensure that people paid up what they owed. His intimidating stature ensured that people would not mess with him. Due to John's increasingly late nights and chaotic lifestyle, his dad threw him out of the house when he was sixteen, and John turned to 'the lads' he knew from the street. John's life became a mixture of drug dealing, acting as an enforcer for drug debts owed to other dealers and the occasional mugging or robbery to maintain his own growing drug dependency. These activities and the friends he was associating with, however, provided John with opportunities to gain a reputation and a status that felt meaningful to him. He felt he was working hard to achieve notoriety amongst his peer group, and by the time he was nineteen, few people were willing to challenge or stand against him. When John was twenty-two, he and one of his mates went to collect on a debt owed to them by another drug dealer. They knew going into the confrontation that they would be evenly matched and so they each brought along a knife. Perhaps they suspected the other man would be armed with one, perhaps they thought they could be useful for intimidation. The usual reasons men give for carrying weapons are "defensive," in both senses. A fight ensued, and the man they wanted to overpower was stronger than either of them anticipated. The fight ended, however, when John and his mate drew their knives and killed the person they went to collect their money from.

Both John and his mate were given mandatory life sentences for murder, each with a minimum term of eighteen years.

John's entry into the prison world was not a difficult one. His reputation preceded him to some extent, and he found he could slot in well to prison social life and the prisoner hierarchy. He found similar value systems on the inside to those he had encountered and subscribed to on the outside. Moreover, prison life afforded John some of the basic needs he had had difficulty securing on the outside, such as a roof over his head, regular meals and overcoming his addiction to drugs.

John's relationships with women were tangled in his unstable domestic circumstances. He may have fathered children, but if so, he had no sense of himself as a father. His relationships with women tended to be brief. He kept in touch with his mother only intermittently. His father refused to see him.

Whilst the punishing aspects of prison were difficult to endure, at times, John learned to cope with the rules and deprivations of prison, and, as a "lifer," John was able to maintain his reputation and status as a "hard man." It was not until John had served the majority of his minimum term and began to face the prospect of possible release that he began to realize he had no idea how he would fit in on the outside. He was now getting close to forty and nearly half of his life had been spent in prison. He recognized that although being a lifer had placed him at the top of the prisoner hierarchy, once he was released, as an ex-prisoner who had a murder conviction on his record, his status would completely reverse and he would enter a world where he was a social outcast, an ex-prisoner who would have to continue to live for the rest of his life under licence conditions. One false move and he could wind up straight back inside prison. At the same time, John realized he would likely have significant difficulties finding a place to live, finding a job, finding a partner or making new friends. John was unable to see any way he might fit in to society again and he realized he had never really fit into it in the first place. Six months prior to his release, after seventeen years in prison, John took his own life.

John's story illustrates a relatively common set of circumstances for men who find themselves in prison. The "prisoner society" and the constitution of prisons as places of power, control and punishment, in many ways, replicate the hierarchical, status-oriented and, often brutal, life that many men experience before they enter prison. Moreover, prisoner society is often replete with the same *sub rosa* economies and masculine value systems that governed men's lives on the outside — as Sim (1994) notes, "To speak in terms of normal and abnormal men ... is to miss the fundamental point, namely that normal life in male prisons is highly problematic — it reproduces normal men".

On both sides of the prison walls there is a valourization of strength and fearless-ness, an impossible identification with masculine invulnerability. One has only to think of the bizarre character traits played out to cartoon proportions by Hollywood heroes from John Wayne (Rio Bravo) to Sylvester Stallone (Rambo), Bruce Willis (Die Hard) to Robert Downey Jr. (Iron Man) to recognize how durable, pervasive and profitable this identification is (Pfiel 1995). In this value system, men award other men status and respect according to their willingness and capacity to exploit vulnerability and inflict harm rather than extend empathy and consideration toward each other. The omnipotent hero is the singular individual, a culturally iconic form of masculinity, no less influential than the calculating risk-taking individual (man) of conventional liberal economics. Men inside and outside prison adhere to negotiated codes on how to earn and maintain respect (Bourgois 1995), how to be a man in a man's world, but they are no more born to do it than they are doomed to it.

For John, above, the accomplishment of his masculinity and the absence or neglect of viable alternatives that might displace his continuing investments in narrowing social and economic prospects proved ultimately as fatal to him as it did to his victim. The irony and the paradox is that having made himself a successful prisoner in the homo-social, ultra-masculine prison world, he cannot face the journey back into a more complex, unstable and gender-variegated world. It's a man's world in prison, but that was no longer so much the case beyond its walls. It makes the journey back all the more challenging for men and the journey back into prison more likely.

Studying the inner life of prisons brings to light a stark picture of the pernicious and deeply ingrained structures of men's social and personal lives and their orientations to domesticity, intimacy and care. It tells us something of what men do with their troubles and what becomes of troubled men. Violence features as prominently in the "solutions" as the problems. Examining the connections between this penal inner life and the inner life of men can tell us more about the relationships between men, masculinity and crime. It forges the connections suggested in Oakley's observation:

> Criminality and masculinity are linked because the sort of acts associated with each have much in common. The demonstration of physical strength, a certain kind of aggressiveness, visible and external proof of achievement, whether legal or illegal – these are facets of the ideal male personality and also much of criminal behaviour. Both male and criminal are valued by their peers for these qualities. Thus, the dividing line between what is masculine and what is criminal may at times be a thin one. (1972: 64, revisited in 2011 with Cockburn)

As the French filmmaker and feminist activist Virginie Despentes commented in reaction to the media focus on Dominic Strauss Kahn's predicament, and its neglected contexts:

> *If anything is as disgusting and incomprehensible as rape, it's prison: this rape by the state, this abject useless destruction of humanity. What does prison create? It is no solution, just the face of inhumanity, the dirty mirror reflecting how poorly we live together, how we only know how to respond to violence by unleashing more violence ... Whether it is called rape or jail, we need to ask ourselves how we developed the sordid habit of considering either one as part of the landscape, or as tolerable.*— Despentes, The Guardian, 23 May 2011

DISCUSSION QUESTIONS

1. Why are prisons full of men rather than women?

2. Criminology has always been about men. Discuss

3. Do young men grow out of crime?

GLOSSARY

Gender: the pattern of social relations that cluster around sexual difference.

Hegemonic Masculinity: the historical and cultural ascendancy of men over women in complex patterns of fluctuating and multiple social relations. It is not the identity characteristic of any single person, but a combination of social arrangements.

Intersectionality: the way distinctive experiences of race, class, gender and a variety of other socially determining forces combine in people's lives and interactions. Rather than identifying hierarchies of precedence, intersectionality examines the interplay of such social forces.

Sex-Role Theory: the common assumption that men and women are pre-destined to perform particular social functions.

Strain Theory: based on the U.S. experience of capitalist development in which the possibility of infinite reward for everyone is confronted by structural denial for the majority of the people. The resulting "strain" generates the frustration and creation of alternative and sometimes illegal forms of achieving rewards.

Sub-Cultures: the analysis of cultural groupings in society that are generally subordinate to the dominant cultures. Such analysis frequently focuses on young people, minority sexualities and ethnicities.

SUGGESTED READINGS

Tim Newburn and Elizabeth Stanko (ed.), *Just Boys Doing Business: Men, Masculinities and Crime*, London: Routledge and Kegan Paul (1993).

Mairtin Mac an Ghaill (ed.), *Understanding Masculinities*, Philadelphia, Open University Press (1996).

Don Sabo, *Prison Masculinities*, Philadelphia: Temple University Press (2001).

SUGGESTED WEBSITES

The From Boys to Men Project <http://www.boystomenproject.com/> is funded by the Economic and Social Research Council (ESRC) to explore why some boys become domestic abuse perpetrators when others do not. The aim of the research is to establish what more can be done to reduce the number of young men who become perpetrators.

Raewyn Connell is the most significant theorist of masculinities and has been involved in the development of both theory and research. Her own account of this, and links to many academic papers and research reports on masculinity can be found on <http://www.raewynconnell.net/p/masculinities_20.html>

The two sociologists cited in the article, Ann Oakley and Cynthia Cockburn have updated (March 2013) their analysis on the harms of masculine crime: <http://www.opendemocracy.net/5050/ann-oakley-cynthia-cockburn/cost-of-masculine-crime>.

Bea Campbell, also cited in the article discusses (Jan. 2014) her analysis of neo-liberal neo-patriarchy with Cynthia Cockburn. It includes discussion of recent urban disorders: <http://www.opendemocracy.net/5050/beatrix-campbell/neoliberal-neopatriarchy-case-for-gender-revolution>.

NOTE

1. For a full account, see <http://www.theguardian.com/uk/series/reading-the-riots>.

REFERENCES

Anthias, F. 2013. "Moving Beyond the Janus Face of Integration and Diversity Discourses: Towards an Intersectional Framing." *The Sociological Review* 61: 323–43.

Bourgeois, P. 1995. *In Search of Respect: Selling Crack in El Barrio*. Cambridge: Cambridge University Press.

Campbell, B. 1993. *Goliath: Britain's Dangerous Places*. London: Methuen.

Carlen, P. 1983. *Women's Imprisonment*. London: Routledge & Kegan Paul.

Clemmer, D. 1940. *The Prison Community*. New York: Holt, Rinehart and Winston.

Clinard, M. 1964. "The Theoretical Implications of Anomie and Deviant Behaviour." In M. Clinard (ed.), *Anomie and Deviant Behaviour*. New York: Free Press.

Cloward, R.A., and L.E. Ohlin. 1961. *Delinquency and Opportunity: A Theory of Delinquent Gangs*. London: Routledge:

Cockburn, C., and A. Oakley. 2011. "The Culture of Masculinity Costs All Too Much to Ignore." *Guardian*, 25 November. At <http://www.guardian.co.uk/commentisfree/2011/nov/25/dangerous-masculinty-everyone-risk> accessed January 2012.

Cohen, A.K. 1955. *Delinquent Boys*. New York: Free Press.

Cohen, P. 1972. "Sub-Cultural Conflict and Working Class Community." Working Papers in Cultural Studies 2: 5–52. Centre for Cultural Studies, University of Birmingham.

Collier, R. 1998. *Masculinities, Crime and Criminology*. London: Sage.

Comack, E. 2008. *Out There: In Here – Masculinity, Violence and Prisoning*. Winnipeg: Fernwood Publishing.

Connell, R.W. 1983 *Which Way Is Up – Essays on Sex, Class and Culture*. Sydney: Allen & Unwin.

___. 1987. *Gender and Power: Society, the Person and Sexual Politics*. Cambridge: Polity Press.

___. 1995. *Masculinities*. Cambridge: Polity Press.

___. 2002. *Gender*. Cambridge: Polity Press.

___. 2005. "Growing Up Masculine: Rethinking the Significance of Adolescence in the Making of Masculinities." *Irish Journal of Sociology* 14, 2: 11–28.

___. 2008. "A Thousand Miles from Kind: Men, Masculinities and Modern Institutions." *Journal of Men's Studies: A Scholarly Journal about Men and Masculinities* 16, 3: 237–52.

Crewe, B. 2009. *The Prisoner Society: Power, Adaptation and Social Life in an English Prison*. Oxford: Clarendon Press.

Curtis, Anna. 2014. "'You Have to Cut It off at the Knee': Dangerous Masculinity and Security Inside a Men's Prison". *Men and Masculinities* 17, 2.

Despentes, V. 2011. "A Game Only One Side Plays." *Guardian*, 23 May: 17.

DiIulio, J. 1987. *Governing Prisons: A Comparative Study of Correctional Management*. London: Collier Macmillan.

Dorn, N., and N. South. 1982. "Of Males and Markets: A Critical Review of 'Youth Culture' Theory." Research Paper 1, Centre for Occupational and Community Research. London: Middlesex Polytechnic

Downes, D. 1966. *The Delinquent Solution: A Study in Subcultural Theory*. London: Routledge, Kegan and Paul.

Drake, D.H. 2012. *Prisons, Punishment and the Pursuit of Security*. Basingstoke: Palgrave Macmillan.

Gadd, D., and T. Jefferson. 2007. *Psychosocial Criminology: An Introduction*. London. Sage.

Garland, D. 2001. *The Culture of Control: Crime and Social Order in Contemporary Society*. Oxford: Clarendon.

Gilroy, P. 1987. *There Ain't No Black in the Union Jack*. London: Routledge.

Goffman, E. 1961. "On the Characteristics of Total Institutions." In D. Cressey (ed.), *The Prison: Studies in Institutional Organization and Change*. New York: Holt, Rinehart and Winston.

Grusky, O. 1959. "Organizational Goals and the Behavior of Informal Leaders." *American Journal of Sociology* 65 (July): 59–67.

Hall, S. 1992. "New Ethnicities." In J. Donald and A. Rattansi (eds.), *"Race," Culture and Difference*. London: Sage.

Hall, S., C. Critcher, T. Jefferson, J. Clarke and B. Roberts. 1978. *Policing the Crisis: Mugging, the State and Law and Order*. London: Macmillan.

Hall, S., and T. Jefferson (eds.). 1975. *Resistance through Rituals: Youth Subcultures in Post-War Britain*. New York: Holmes and Meier.

Harvey, J. 2007. *Young Men in Prison: Surviving and Adapting to Life Inside*. Cullompton: Willan.

Harvey, K., and A. Shepard. 2005. "What Have Historians Done With Masculinitiy? Reflections on Five Centuries of British History, Circa 1500–1950." (Editorial Introduction.) Special Issue on History and Masculinity, *Journal of British Studies* 44: 274–80.

Heidensohn, F. 1987. "Women and Crime: Questions for Criminology." In P. Carlen and A. Worrall (eds.), *Gender, Crime and Justice*. Milton Keynes, Open University Press.

Henry, R. 2013. "Social Spaces of Maleness: The Role of Street Gangs in Practicing Indigenous Masculinities." In K. Anderson and R. Innes (eds.), *Indigenous Masculinities in a Global Context*. Winnipeg, MB: University of Manitoba Press.

Hobsbawm, E. 1978. "The Forward March of Labour Halted?" *Marxism Today* (Sept.) CPGB.

Irwin, J. 1970. *The Felon*. Englewood Cliffs, NJ: Prentice-Hall.

Irwin, J., and D. Cressey. 1962. "Thieves, Convicts and the Inmate Culture." *Social Problems* 10: 145–47.

Jacobs, J.B. 1977. *Stateville: The Penitentiary in Mass Society.* Chicago: University of Chicago Press.

Jefferson, T. 1993. "Crime, Criminology, Masculinity and Young Men." In A. Coote (ed.), *Families, Children and Crime.* London: IPPR.

___. 1994. "Theorising Masculine Subjectivity." In T. Newburn and E. Stanko (eds.), *Just Boys Doing Business.* London: Routledge.

___. 1996. "Introduction to British Journal of Criminology Special Issue on Masculinities, Social Relations and Crime." *British Journal of Criminology* 36, 3: 337–47.

___. 1997. "Masculinities and Crimes." In M. Maguire et al., *The Oxford Handbook of Criminology.* Oxford: Clarendon.

Liebling, A. (assisted by H. Arnold). 2004. *Prisons and Their Moral Performance.* Oxford: Clarendon.

Maruna, S., and A. Matravers. 2007. "N=1: Criminology and the Person." *Theoretical Criminology* 11, 4: 427–42.

McRobbie, A. 1980. "Settling Accounts with Subcultures: A Feminist Critique." *Screen Education* 39.

___. 1991. *Feminism and Youth Culture: From Jackie to Just Seventeen.* London: Macmillan.

Merton, R.K. 1938. Social Structure and Anomie. *American Sociological Review* 3: 672–82.

___. 1949. "Social Structure and Anomie: Revisions and Extensions." In R. Anshen (ed.), *The Family.* New York: Harper Brothers.

Messerschmidt, J. 1993. *Masculinities and Crime: Critique and Reconceptualisation of Theory.* Maryland: Rowman & Littlefield.

___. 1997. *Crime as Structured Action: Gender, Race, Class and Crime in the Making.* Los Angeles, CA: Sage.

___. 2005. "Men, Masculinities and Crime." In M. Kimmel, J. Hearn and R.W. Connell (eds.), *Handbook of Studies on Men and Masculinities.* London: Sage.

Morris, T., and P. Morris. 1963. *Pentonville.* London: Routledge and Kegan Paul.

Newburn, T. 2007. *Criminology.* Cullompton: Willan

Newburn, T., and E. Stanko. 1995. *Just Boys Doing Business.* Abingdon: Routledge.

Oakely, A. 1972. *Sex, Gender and Society.* London: Temple-Smith.

Oliffe, J., C. Han, M. Drumand, E. Maria, J. Bottorff and G. Creighton. 2014. "Men, Masculinities, and Murder-Suicide." *American Journal of Men's Health* 1,13.

Pfiel, F. 1995. *White Guys – Studies in Postmodern Domination and Difference.* London: Verso.

Sabo, D., T. Kupers and W. London (eds.). 2001. *Prison Masculinities.* Philadelphia: Temple University Press.

Sedgwick, E.K. 1985. *Between Men: English Literature and Male Homosocial Desire.* New York: Columbia University Press.

Sim, J. 1994. "Tougher than the Rest: Men in Prison." In T. Newburn and E. Stanko (eds.), *Just Boys Doing Business.* Abingdon: Routledge.

Sparks, R., A.E. Bottoms and W. Hay. 1996. *Prisons and the Problem of Order.* Oxford: Clarendon Press.

Standing, G. 2011. *The Precariat: The New Dangerous Class.* London: Bloomsbury.

Sykes, G. 1958. *The Society of Captives: A Study of a Maximum-Security Prison.* Princeton: Princeton University Press.

Thompson, E.P. 1963. *The Making of the English Working Class.* London: Penguin.

Tosh, J. 1999. *A Man's Place: Masculinity and the Middle-Class Home in Victorian England.* New Haven, CT: Yale University Press.

___. 2005. "Masculinities in an Industrialising Society, 1800–1914." *Journal of British Studies* 44: 330–42.

Toch, H., and K. Adams. 1989. *Coping: Maladaptation in Prisons.* Piscataway: Transaction Publishers.

Tosh, J., and M. Roper (eds.). 1991. *Manful Assertions: Masculinities in Britain Since 1800.* Abingdon: Routledge.

Useem, B., and P. Kimball. 1989. *States of Siege: US Prison Riots, 1971–1986.* Oxford: Oxford University Press.

Valier, C. 2001. *Theories of Crime and Punishment.* Oxford: Longman.

Willis, P. 1977. *Learning to Labour – How Working Class Kids Get Working Class Jobs*. Farnborough: Saxon House.

Wilson, T.P. 1968. "Patterns of Management and Adaptations to Organizational Roles: A Study of Prison Inmates." *American Journal of Sociology* 74: 146–57.

Wootton, B.F. 1959. *Contemporary Trends in Crime and Its Treatment*. London: Clarke Hall.

Young, J. 1981. "Thinking Seriously About Crime – Some Models of Criminology." In M. Fitzgerald et al. (eds.), *Crime and Society: Readings in History and Theory*. London: Routledge & Kegan Paul/The Open University Press.

PART V

CRIME AND YOUNG PEOPLE

Understanding crime is not easy, and we suggest that it is even more difficult when it is in regards to children and youth. The construction of responses to crime and anti-social behaviour can be even more perplexing, to the point where it seems that nothing works. Yet we remain optimistic, and critical criminology, in its ability to situate crime and justice within our stratified political economy, is the source of our optimism. In this final section, we focus on youth crime, Canadian youth justice policy and youth violence; we put forward ways of understanding and addressing the "youth crime problem" that are alternative to conventional ways or established ways

In 2010, 153,000 youth were accused of a *Criminal Code* offence and over 40 percent of these cases were considered less than serious offences, including property-related crimes. Research on youth consistently indicates that there is a fine line between vic-timization and perpetration of crimes. Neglect, abuse, poverty, discrimination, labelling, addiction, poor housing, unhealthy environments, failure of the child welfare system and exploitation all interact with criminality and involvement in street life.

The diversity of solutions to crime — for youth as well as adults, as seen throughout the chapters in this book — is striking, ranging from a rise in retributive vigilantism (the so-called "get tough" approach to crime) to a growing movement for treatment, rehabilitation and restorative measures. A new era of juvenile justice began in 2002 with the development of the *Youth Criminal Justice Act* (YCJA). Formally implemented on April 1, 2003, the YCJA introduced a bifurcated model of justice: harsher punishments for youth accused of violent crimes and lesser custody and extrajudicial measures for crimes considered non-violent.

Canada, a country that relies on deterrence, has been criticized for its over-incar-ceration of youth. In fact, until the implementation of the *Youth Criminal Justice Act*, the rate of incarceration of youth in Canada surpassed the rate in the United States. And, although there is currently a declining rate of youth crime, the Conservative Government is swinging back towards increased retribution and away from a more rehabilitative model. Hogeveen and Minaker point out that while violent youth crime rates are declining, in 2012 the Federal Government put into effect the "violent and repeat young offender" segment of the *Safe Streets and Communities Act* (SSCA) (Canada 2012), which cracks down on young people.

Supporters of the movement towards restorative, extrajudicial and transformative measures criticize the youth criminal justice system on the basis that it ignores the social context in which youth crime occurs. This position puts forward the argument that those youth involved in violence have also experienced violence against them. The authors in this final section ask how we can understand violence void of its social context.

The diversity in youth justice, from restorative, extrajudicial programs to get-tough measures, is, in part, a reflection of the various streams of criminological theory, which provide advice for the creation of policy at the same time that they provide abstract explanations of criminal and anti-social behaviour. The policy debates within criminology centre on at least three key questions: what are the "new" responses to youth-crime, and what potential do these measures have to deal with the crime problem? What policy responses best address the problems of youth crime within our communities? Can criminal justice responses address issues of social injustice? The readings here elaborate on critical criminological approaches that run counter to the injustices and inadequacies of the discourse and practice of conservative, consensus-based justice and punishment, with a focus on young people.

As we have seen, consensus theories, in general, define crime as a violation of the law or the norms within society, and the policies for dealing with crime focus on punishment, rehabilitation or treatment for individual offenders. Consensus theories that are based on deterrence advocate punishment that "fits the crime" — an approach that supports traditional criminal justice systems, relying heavily on individual punishments in the form of incarceration, fines and fine options.

Ironically, these conservative law and order approaches are criticized by other consensus theories, in part, because most serious analysis has always shown that imprisonment is ineffective at reducing crime and especially youth crime. In response to this finding, certain consensus theory adherents advocate policies that increase social bonding and other restorative initiatives to decrease crime. Interventions here include individual and family counselling and extrajudicial measures that develop social unity and the sense of right and wrong in youth. Consensus approaches, such as the social control approach, may also support education and work projects designed to foster conformity through involvement in conventional activities, exemplified by community outreach vans that supply food, warmth, counselling and caring for street youth (who may be working in the sex trade and/or involved in drugs and drug-related activities, or youth who have run away from home or migrated from rural areas to the city). The outreach vans and workers, for example, work to develop bonds with the street-involved youth, helping them to eventually discover more self-worth and a connection to safe and nurturing lifestyles.

Even interactionist theories, which generally tend to de-emphasize the punitive responses of most other consensus theories, blame the least powerful for social ills such as crime. The premise of interactionist theories is that people come to define themselves — who they are, what kind of person they are — in interaction with others. For crime policy, this understanding implies that youth offenders need to be placed in contexts that will enhance their self-image and power. From an interactionist perspective, the traditional criminal justice system works to disintegrate and rebuild the young person through the process of negative labelling and social control.

John Braithwaite offers, in this conceptual context, the idea of re-integrative shaming, which he argues can be self-empowering: youth offenders are given the opportunity to make amends within their communities. Sentencing circles and family group conferences are, similarly, strategies aimed at giving offenders an interpersonal context in which they can take responsibility for their actions and restore the damage they have done. They are both personally empowering activities. Unfortunately, such policies still rest upon the orthodox assumption that young people who do bad things are solely responsible for their deviance.

As we have learned throughout the book, the consensus approaches in criminology

— as well as the more liberal interactionist approaches — rarely question what is defined as "criminal." They persist in locating the problem of crime — rather than the problem of justice — within the individual rather than in the structure of inequality in society. They are based on the philosophical assumption that individuals have free will and freedom of choice to be rich or poor or to commit crimes.

All consensus approaches, even those advocating less punitive responses such as reintegrative shaming, see the solution to crime in the transformation of individual youth behaviour. All such theories, then, accept, rather categorically, that economic opportunity and morality are personal matters, and as such not linked to social structure. They advocate, as a consequence, policies such as individual access to education, community outreach services, and counselling. They do not advocate the transformation of the prevailing social structure, and without that crucial step, the crimes of inequality — the exploitation of labour by capital, discrimination against minorities, subjugation of women — will persist.

Critical criminology shares the optimism of non- punitive crime policies yet critiques their adoption, arguing that they choose to ignore the existence of crime and deviance as social definitions created in the interests of elite groups and ruling classes. What gets defined as "crime" and who gets processed through the criminal justice system are the results of social and political acts. As witnessed in the earlier sections, this critical perspective demonstrates that many actions deemed criminal (typically, actions of the marginalized) are relatively less socially and economically damaging than many of the actions of the elite and corporations, which are often less regulated or, if regulated, more lightly punished for an offence. Therefore, a critical approach to crime and youth crime in particular argues for diverse proposals that advocate social change as well as non-punitive responses to the problems of crime and (in)justice. All of the critical criminological perspectives reject "tougher" laws and incarceration and advocate instead for structural and cultural changes: abolishing prisons in favour of restorative justice; structural transformations; redefining what we define as "crime"; and challenging institutions, such as the media and law, that frame public understandings of crime.

The policy implications of critical criminological approaches for youth are by no means simple and straightforward. Such approaches argue for non-punitive measures to deal with the problem of crime, but they fear that support for these measures may perpetuate the conventional definitions of crime as the actions of mainly the poor and racial minorities. Critical criminologists also fear that proposed reforms will only reinforce the notion that crime is about individual youths doing bad things and that the only solutions rest with changing the individual, not the social structure. For example, the approaches of peacemaking, abolitionism, left realism, and postmodernism all advocate for reducing or eliminating imprisonment, as a means of empowering the disadvantaged and rebuilding communities. Prison reduction is to be accompanied by restorative measures such as sentencing circles and family group conferencing, along with a call for the eventual elimination of structural inequalities. Some critical criminological discourse (often found in the structuralist or instrumentalist Marxist research) argues that restorative measures are only a band-aid solution and do nothing to redress inequality. More importantly, critical criminologists often argue that solutions such as restorative justice continue to focus on working-class crime and crimes related to marginalized people and, consequently, reinforce the ideology that the "poor are more criminal."

Upon examination of the 2009 Report Card on Child Poverty, we find that more than one million Canadian children live below the poverty line—one in ten children live in poverty. In addition, one in four First Nations children suffer from poverty. Because of such disturbing realities, critical theories' response to youth crime is generally: to attack the get-touch agenda and argue for a redistribution of wealth, argue for the provision of opportunities for poor families to escape poverty, and lobby to ensure that problems for youth in education, of employment, of homelessness and of victimization and are priorities. This goes beyond restorative and criminal justice initiatives; the focus is the redressing of inequality.

The chapters in this final section demonstrate that youth criminality—like adult criminality —is not an individual, but a social problem. The criminal justice system is often used as the only response; the chapters herein argue that it should be the last one.

In chapter 16, Shahid Alvi focuses on the historical transformation of youth crime, policing, and justice in Canada. The emphasis is on how, both historically and currently, Canadians have tended to condemn children and youth, and how our collective enmity towards children and youth is associated with historically specific socio-political and socio-economic circumstances— especially with the criminal justice system.

Alvi focuses on the historical transformation of youth, crime, policing and justice in Canada. The critical criminological framework that he presents reveals the connections between the development of different forms of youth justice and the place of children and youth in the political economy of Canada. His descriptions of the three major historical changes in youth justice in Canada show how, in large part, the official condemnation of "bad" children and youth alters with changes in the importance of young people to the demands of capitalism. In effect, Alvi's chapter reveals how the systems of justice and punishment, past and present, have contributed to the further condemnation of certain groups of people who are already disadvantaged and oppressed by society.

Chapter 17, by Joanne Minaker and Bryan Hogeveen, is a new addition to this book and addresses the multi-faceted problem of youth violence and the importance of care. The authors begin by reminding readers that all children and youth must have a right to care and love: to grow in a safe world. They then present the number of ways violence is a part of the everyday lives of children and youth. Minaker and Hogeven point out that 360,000 Canadian children are exposed to violence within their homes and that such violence has an impact on how they make life choices and on their own potential diposition to violence. Yet they remind readers that violence, whether real or virtual, is an everyday part of life for all youth-especially those involved in brutalities within sports, video games, television, and movies. And while policy makers and the general public focus so much energy on youth who are violent, they neglect to understand or admit that violence against children and youth (often within a culture of violence) is the precursor to acts of violence perpetrated by youth. Importantly and ironically, part of the culture of violence results from the draconian measures applied to criminalized youth. Incarceration is, in the end, an act of violence.

Minaker and Hogeveen humanize the actions of youth by helping readers to understand the lived realities of children and youth. Their chapter challenges readers to re-conceptualize how we come to understand violence and the impact of punitive responses on children and youth. In the end, this chapter discusses the importance of creating inclusive spaces of "care and community" for youth.

We conclude the book with Kearney Healy's chapter, "Letter from Saskatoon Youth Court," which is is both emotive and practical, informed as it is by his many years in youth court as a legal aid lawyer. Healy maintains that we could eradicate youth crime by applying the principles of restorative justice and offering what youth in conflict with the law actually need and want — not to lose hope, and to control their lives and become respected community members. This may be, he adds, as simple as education and the support of a tutor, a little money, and some love. He argues that we know too well that the youth who fill our detention centres are uneducated and have often been victimized by families, schools, and communities; yet our response is to further victimize them through the criminal justice system. Imprisoning these kids — which we do at an alarming rate — is not just unethical but also impractical. It is an expensive form of ensuring that those who have been hurt and abused and who have suffered poverty will lose even more hope. The promise lies instead in how communities treat the poorest and the weakest among us.

The chapters in this final section provide a concluding sense of passion and optimism with the reminder of the role that all of us play in the continuing struggle to realize social and criminal justice by embodying models of caring.

16

YOUNG PEOPLE AND THE
YOUTH CRIMINAL JUSTICE ACT

Shahid Alvi

KEY FACTS

> A 2008 survey of over 7000 Canadian adults (over the age of eighteen) showed that fully 78 percent believed that youth crime overall had increased in the past five years (Latimer and Dejardins 2008: 9–10). Youth crime rates, have, in fact, decreased or remained stable.

> Under the Juvenile Delinquents Act, it was assumed that if parents could not control and properly socialize their children, the state would have to intervene as a "kindly parent" in order to protect the best interests of the child — a principle known as parens patriae.

> According to a 2006 study by the Department of Justice, judges believed that more than half of cases coming before them could have been dealt with appropriately outside of the formal youth court system.

> Child poverty, which is an important correlate of health and developmental problems, behavioural conditions, social exclusion and diminished capacity to learn, now stands at 15 percent in Canada.

> The central ideas of neo-liberal policies are that democracy is about profit, deregulation, privatization, transfers of wealth to a small proportion of the population, commercialization, "punishment creep," individualism, responsibilization and the notion that "the market" is a template for values.

> An important positive aspect of the YCJA is that it recognizes the diminished moral blameworthiness of young persons.

> Although they represented only 6 percent of the general population in 2006, Aboriginal youth represented 27 percent of youth remanded in custody, 36 percent of youth admitted to sentenced custody and 24 percent of youth admitted to probation.

Sources: Latimer and Dejardins 2008; Conference Board of Canada n.d.; Canada, Department of Justice. 2006a; National Crime Prevention Centre 2012.

> *[Many] people will continue to be convinced that juvenile crime is exceptionally high, that it was not a problem in the "good old days," and that it would not be a serious problem today if we only had the proper justice policies in effect.*
> — *Thomas J. Bernard (1991: 39)*

A little over a decade has passed since the law governing youth justice (*The Youth Criminal Justice Act* or YCJA) came into force. So it would seem appropriate to look back not only at the history of youth justice in Canada, but also at what we know about its latest incarnation in the YCJA ten years after its implementation. While there have been some interesting if preliminary observations regarding the impact of the legislation, the story of the YCJA remains unfinished. In many ways, it would seem that not much has changed. When it was passed, the Act was heralded by some commentators as a progressive development in a long trajectory of attempts to address youth justice issues. It attempts to focus on a series of important and intertwined concerns, including long-term protection of public safety, due process for youth, addressing the causes of youth crime and meaningful consequences for youth offenders. Yet, as I argue in this chapter, there has been a disturbing trend away from a real analysis of and commitment to tackling the causes of youth crime and an associated trend towards punishment, control and a just-desserts philosophy, which, to be fully understood, must be contextualized within recent neo-liberal political and economic developments in Canada.

Writing over forty years ago about the importance of understanding the role of social context in conditioning social responses to deviant behaviour, Stan Cohen (1972) argued that societies periodically demonize people who are considered threats to dominant social values and interests. Writing about British youth culture, he contended that one of the most frequently demonized groups, subject to such "moral panics," has been young people. Moreover, he asserted that the categorization of young people as "folk devils" was due primarily to the influence of the media, whose role in modern societies had increasingly become that of shaping and defining events for the public.

Moral panics are not unique to Britain. Driven by a largely unsophisticated and often irresponsible media, Canadians have willingly participated in similar moral panics over youth crime, particularly over the past few decades. Indeed, during the era of the *Young Offenders Act* (YOA), which preceded the YCJA, and prior to the enactment of the current law governing youth crime — the *Youth Criminal Justice Act* or YCJA which came into force in April of 2003 — many Canadians believed that youth-court sentences were too lenient, that it should be easier to try young people as adults, that sentencing should be harshe and that disciplinary initiatives akin to those of a boot camp should prevail (Sprott 1996). As of 2008, approximately four in ten Canadians lacked confidence in the youth justice system, a sentiment mostly due to the perceptions that the correctional system is failing in efforts to rehabilitate youth after sentencing, and that courts are unable to pass what the public consider to be appropriate sentences (Latimer and Desjardins 2008). More recently, politically conservative voices have been particularly strident, with some calling for a return to the death penalty, transfers of young offenders to adult court and prison sentences for parents of youth offenders (Hartnagel 2004). While these are certainly harsh proposals, there are also more subtle yet disturbing trends at work. In Quebec, for instance, convenience store owners have tested devices that produce high frequency noise that only people under the age of twenty-five can hear, thereby preventing them from loitering (White et al. 2011). A 2008 survey of over 7000 Canadian adults (over the age of eighteen) provides further cause for concern around the "responsibilization" and "individualization" of youth crime. In that study, 88 percent of respondents indicated that parents bore a "high degree of responsibility" for preventing youth crime, while 77 percent pointed to "youth themselves" as having such responsibility, and fully 78 percent believed that youth crime overall had increased in the past five years (Latimer and Dejardins, 2008: 9-10). These data suggest that despite the fact that youth crime has decreased since the 1990s, and in spite of growing evidence regarding the "lack of moral culpability" of youth (discussed below), governments and the general public continue to blame youth and families for their mistakes while ignoring the complexities (and facts) associated with youth crime.

On the legal front, the new act has been hailed as a significant improvement over the YOA (Tustin and Lutes 2015). As Hartnagel (2004) suggests, the YCJA came into force as a result of the then Liberal Government's stated commitment to "protect the public" while focusing on rehabilitation and reintegration of the offender, meaningful consequences and alternatives to incarceration. However, it is also clear that the new act was a response to public dissatisfaction with the YOA, particularly in relation to perceived leniency in sentencing, and the need to "get tough" on offenders, all sentiments that were fuelled by the media's sensationalized accounts of brutal (but rare) homicides committed by youth (Varma and Marinos 2000; Doob and Cesaroni 2004).

Indeed, the recent history of youth criminal justice legislation (in the era of the YOA) can be characterized as punitive, where activities once considered minor and dealt with outside the justice system became increasingly criminalized. During the period between the *Juvenile Delinquents Act* and its successor, the YOA, more youth were placed in custody and the system favoured punishment and deterrence over leniency and rehabilitation. This "punishment ethos" is even more paradoxical given that since the mid-1990s the number of both violent and property crimes committed by youth in Canada decreased (Gannon 2006). Since the passage of the YCJA, youth court caseloads have dropped approximately 26 percent, reflecting a decline in police charges (Tustin and Lutes 2015: 7). Youth crime rates continue to decline, and the severity of crime committed by young people has also dropped (National Crime Prevention Centre 2012). The most recent data of which I am aware points to a decrease in youth accused of a crime of 40 percent since 2003 and a decrease in the severity of crimes committed by youth (as measured by the Crime Severity Index)[6] of 39 percent since 2003 (Boyce et al.). These data stand in sharp contrast to previous trends under the YOA. Until passage of the YCJA, the rate of incarceration for young offenders had increased by 26 percent since 1987 (Canadian Centre for Justice Statistics 1997), which gave Canada the questionable distinction of having a youth incarceration rate four times higher than those for adults, twice that of the United States and more than ten times higher than many countries in Europe (as cited in Bala and Anand 2004). In 2003, however, the number of youth beginning custodial sentences in secure custody decreased by 65.5 percent, and although there have been some years where decreases are not the case, overall, youth incarceration has continued to drop to the present day (Statistics Canada 2014). On the face of things, these data seem to suggest that the current Act is "working," though we must be careful in implying that the shifts in legislation were the only potential causes of changes in youth crime rates and sentencing trends. As good social scientists, we must be wary of attributing outcomes (crime rates) to shifts in legislation, particularly since there are so many other factors that may be playing a role in the trends we have observed over the past thirty years. Rather, we must take account of broader social forces and, in particular, the ideology underpinning youth justice legislation.

At the heart of the fixation on the discipline and control of youth is the assumption that young people's problems can be understood by focusing attention on the offenders' traits and the failure to make "good choices." Like the bulk of public perceptions, mainstream criminological accounts (defined and discussed below) tend to downplay or altogether ignore the social basis and context of crime. By decontextualizing youth crime, these mainstream approaches to youth justice in Canada have selectively ignored decades of criminological research pointing to the critical role of the social environment in the etiology of youth crime. What I would argue is that shifting historical perceptions of "youth" in Canada, particularly notions of the role and status of Canadian youth in relation to the economy, have been, and continue to be, crucially related to criminal justice responses to their transgressions.

Most Canadians would probably agree with the idea that childhood is, and always has been, a sacred time during which children are nourished, cared for and socialized to take their place in society. As an extension of this romantic assumption, it might also seem logical to assume that throughout history Canadian laws have consistently reflected concern for the well-being of young people, while balancing that concern with the rights of society. To the contrary, I would argue that laws addressing the wrongdoings of young offenders in Canada represent a broader problem of integrating youth into the dominant economic and social norms governing society at any given time and that various forces have accomplished this goal by demonizing those youth who are unable or "unwilling" to measure up. In the remainder of this chapter, I will outline a critical criminology framework that will be used as the theoretical lens through which developments in youth justice legislation can be viewed. I also provide, from a critical point of view, a preliminary assessment of the extent to which the new legislation can be viewed as an improvement over previous legislation and some cautionary observations related to very recent amendments to the YCJA.

A CRITICAL CRIMINOLOGY FRAMEWORK

Although there are many variants of critical criminology (see Chapter 2), they possess in common an emphasis on the analysis of crime in its social and economic context, with particular concentration not only on the experiences of the underprivileged and weak but also on a commitment to transforming social structures (Schwartz 1991). During the 1970s, a handful of scholars (see Taylor et al. 1973; Taylor et al. 1975) began to demonstrate that there were serious empirical and theoretical flaws in mainstream arguments, resulting in negative consequences for the criminal justice system. Their research demonstrated clearly that deterrence simply did not work. Many scholars within the mainstream traditions countered that rising crime rates in that era were clearly the product of misguided and "soft" policies, underpinned by the notion that "behaviour is controlled by its consequences" (Wilson and Herrnstein 1985: 49). They maintained that the problem with crime of all sorts was that we simply were not getting tough enough with offenders, and that the solution to crime was to be more punitive because offenders had "chosen" to do the crime and therefore needed to "do the time." They simply felt that the criminal justice system was not harsh enough to be effective. In contrast, critical criminology recognized that while individuals make decisions and to an extent choose their own behaviours, they do not necessarily make such decisions in circumstances chosen by and for themselves. In short, the social, political and economic environment sets limits upon, and conditions, human behaviour.

Crime, from a critical criminological perspective, is not an event, or a social fact, but rather has a dynamic history. This basic framework stands in opposition to the more commonly held view of crime as simply anything that people do or don't do that is against the law — a "legalistic" perspective that fails to recognize that laws and people possess a social history. Laws do not appear "out of thin air," nor do they necessarily reflect the consensus of the general public, as mainstream explanations of law would suggest. Mainstream perspectives assume that laws are a product of people's shared values, are impartial and are generated and managed by a "neutral" state committed to helping people resolve conflicts (Lynch and Groves 1989). A critical perspective, in contrast, recognizes that law reflects the continuing and historical concerns of those with power in society, such as lawmakers, economic elites and the media. As Walter DeKeseredy and Martin Schwartz (1996) point out, a critical perspective on law highlights how, rather than emphasizing "justice for all," ours is more of a system that acts to maintain the interests and advantages of the wealthy and powerful in a society characterized by conflict rather than consensus.

Thus, if we are to understand the official legal response to youth crime in Canada, we need to examine the roles played by young people in our society, not just today but also historically. Additionally, we must pay attention to dominant expectations for young people and to how laws have changed to reflect these different roles and perceptions.

Critical criminology also attempts to examine how systems of production and consumption influence the construction of people's roles and aspirations, as well as their capacities to attain those aspirations. To examine the relationship between the Canadian criminal justice system and young people, we will assess the links between young people's material position in society, changes in the laws concerning them and the ideological motivations buttressing these laws.

Although very few in-depth accounts of youth in the criminal justice system exist in Canada, we do have enough information to paint a general picture of the transformation of youth justice policies (Smandych 2001). The essence of this criminal justice history is that perceptions of Canadian children have varied between, on the one hand, the notion that youth are both dependent on adults and different from adults physically and cognitively, and, on the other, the idea that youth are independent and essentially similar to adults when it comes to rights and responsibilities. What is missing from purely historical accounts, however, is the connection between these perceptions and the conditioning effects of the socio-economic milieu.

THE PRE-LEGAL ERA: CANADIAN CHILDREN IN THE NINETEENTH CENTURY

The children of the early Canadian pioneers were treasured and valued by their parents and the community, and even indulged. Indeed, although the relatively unrestrained period of the fur trade provided ample opportunities for offending, commentators often cited parental overindulgence as one of the primary causes of children's wrongdoings (Bell 1999).

As far as we can tell, the majority of youth in the nineteenth century were relatively law abiding. In the pioneer days of Canada, youth crime consisted of a wide range of behaviours, from what we would today consider relatively minor offences — violations of local ordinances, nuisance offences, vandalism, brawling, swearing or petty theft — to what were considered to be more serious violations of "moral" laws such as adultery, bigamy, rape, indecent behaviour and prostitution (Carrigan 1998). Most of these offences would now be considered "status offences" (transgressions that did not apply to adults).

Most of the offences committed by children and youth were, then, relatively minor and inconsequential. Still, at that time, like today, the level of sanctions for committing offences seems to have depended greatly on the social characteristics of the offender.

The minor quality of offences did not preclude harsh adjudication and penalties. Indeed, youth who did commit crimes and were caught by authorities were often punished severely. It was not unusual for youngsters caught violating a range of laws (including minor infractions) to be whipped, incarcerated in workhouses, detained in jail indefinitely, held in custody until their parents paid a fine or even hanged (Carrigan 1998). In addition, children could be punished even if the authorities found only the potential for committing a crime (Schissel 1993). The justice meted out to young people in this era tended to be harsh, lacking in any semblance of due process and applied inconsistently across jurisdictions.

The range of punishments adopted indicates a basic disorganization in the justice system, which operated very much according to the whims of individual judges. But the early history of juvenile crime and punishment in Canada also suggests that children were viewed as little more than miniature adults. Except for the children of the upper classes, who had access to schooling and other privileges, young people were not seen as having special needs and were expected to toil alongside adults in menial, hard-labour jobs (Bala 1997). Children were assumed to have the same levels of understanding of right and wrong as adults. They were tried according to the principles of law existing in the adult courts, and they were frequently incarcerated with adults. Although the offenders came from diverse backgrounds, and all of them experienced parental neglect, the delinquents who committed the most serious offences tended to come from unemployed families, were indentured servants or lived in slum neighbourhoods (Carrigan 1998). For the most part they were not the children of the wealthy.

The gradual influx of immigrant European children around the mid-nineteenth century exacerbated problems. These often-parentless children came to fulfil the function of serving the rich. providing cheap labour as fieldworkers, or satisfying the needs of an emerging class of industrializing entrepreneurs, for instance. Many of the young newcomers were also considered to be "homeless waifs" or "street urchins," products of questionable backgrounds. Many youth wandered aimlessly around with no adult supervision, suffering from malnutrition, with "drunken and dissolute parents," a lack of education and mental or emotional problems (Carrigan 1998). These poor and neglected youth, who were viewed as "problem children" (Currie 1986), tended to be blamed for the incidences of youth deviance (Schissel 1993; West 1984). Within urban centres especially, they received the bulk of attention from the criminal justice system.

While those in authority saw the behaviour of young people in conflict with the law as emanating from the failures of parents and families, not many of them would have linked family troubles to the pressures of a rapidly transforming society. As in other nations during this era, families in Canada were attempting to adapt to urbanization and industrialization. Children had to take their place in a society that was no longer agricultural and rural and in which close kinship ties were eroding. The family became smaller, more mobile and, according to some scholars, internally mirrored the exploitative relationships characterizing capitalist economies (Alvi 1986, 2000; Barrett and McIntosh 1982; Currie 1986). On moral grounds, most people began to see family life as central to the socialization and control of children. But on practical grounds, as the economy increasingly required trained and skilled labourers, compulsory schooling came to be seen as a major player in the "proper" development of children.

Adolescence gradually became seen as a period of "innocence" in which, ostensibly, the child would delay entrance into the labour market by receiving compulsory education in the context of a nurturing family environment (Currie 1986). In the context of social reformism, which presumed the value of rehabilitation, a "child-saving movement" composed largely of middle-class women argued that the justice system of the past could not preserve this state of innocence, because that system assumed that children's and adults' behaviours were essentially the same. Only children under seven were considered to be incapable of understanding right from wrong, and while those between the ages of seven and fourteen could sometimes raise a defence of *doli incapax* (incapacity to do wrong), criminal liability essentially began at the age of seven (Bala 1997).

Developments in criminology, psychiatry and psychology also played a part in transforming the approach to young offenders. Positivist criminology, which emphasized the role of factors beyond the control of the individual in causing crime, began to be preferred over the arguments previously advanced in the field of classical criminology. Thus, while classical criminology saw crime as a consequence of "bad decision-making," positivist criminologists argued that factors "outside" the individual were to blame.

Accordingly, people came to believe that if a child committed a crime, responsibility for that child's condition should be laid on institutions, especially the family (and, more specifically, mothers) and the school. Again, many critics believed that it was the "lower-class" family that tended to fail, and thus any reform of the justice system for children should provide alternatives that fit more closely with an emerging "middle-class" ideal of the family, one that emphasized proper care and nurturing, love, discipline and appropriate education so that family members could rise above their lower-class situation. Essentially, the idea was that youth were vulnerable, in a stage of "innocence," and should be accorded special treatment under the general rubric of a model emphasizing the needs and welfare of the child. Those concerned began to argue that the country needed legislation to deal with these new perspectives on the role and nature of youth.

The first legislation enacted to address the new perspective on youth, *An Act for the More Speedy Trial and Punishment of Juvenile Offenders* (1857), was intended to accelerate the trial process for juvenile delinquents and to reduce the probability of a lengthy spell in jail before trial. The Act defined a juvenile delinquent as a person under the age of sixteen who had committed an offence. Sentencing consisted of imprisonment in a common jail or confinement in a correctional house, either with or without hard labour, and for no longer than three months, or a fine not to exceed five pounds. The accused could also be ordered to restore any stolen property or pay the equivalent compensation (Gagnon 1984: 21–22).

Quebec was the first province to add, in 1869, a sentencing provision reflecting a newfound emphasis on correction through proper schooling. While maintaining the three-month sentence, Quebec changed its legislation to abolish hard labour while including a mandatory two- to five-year term in a certified reformatory school after the jail sentence had been served.

By 1894, some basic principles regarding juvenile delinquents had become entrenched:

- Juvenile offenders were to be separated from adult offenders at all stages of the criminal justice process;
- Instead of imprisonment, juvenile delinquents were to be sent to certified industrial schools, a Children's Aid Society, or a home for neglected children, where they could be "taught to lead useful lives" (Gagnon 1984).

Approaches to youth crime in the pre-formal legal stage, then, reflected a new perception of youth as being marginally different from adults in their cognitive abilities and responsibilities. In addition, the approaches reflected the shifting economic and political realities of a nascent Canadian society. Young people now represented an important source of labour, servicing the developing Canadian economy, which entailed transforming uneducated, indigent children into educated, docile workers. At the same time, these changes created another potential future of formal discipline, punishment and control for those children who did not assimilate into the new order required by an emerging industrial capitalism.

While the burden of controlling young people's behaviour fell to families, and gradually widened to include schools, one other major social institution, the law, was in need of reform to reflect the changing role of Canadian youth.

THE JUVENILE DELINQUENTS ACT

By 1908, the passage of the *Act Respecting Juvenile Delinquents*, which later became the *Juvenile Delinquents Act* (JDA), represented a solidified philosophy of aid and protection for juvenile delinquents that located the causes of delinquency in the child's environment and maintained that the solution to youth crime was to have the state take the place of the (incompetent) parent. In effect, the system assumed that if parents could not do the job of controlling and properly socializing their children, the state would have to intervene as a "kindly parent" in order to protect the best interests of the child — a principle known as *parens patriae*. The policy structure for this act was based on a welfare model, which assumed that certain people needed to be cared for in society and that their care could be administered by and through government assistance.

The outcome of this philosophy was that judges were directed to treat children not as criminals but as "misdirected and misguided" children requiring "aid, encouragement, help and assistance" (*Juvenile Delinquents Act*, section 38). The Act contained a number of key principles:

(1) A juvenile delinquent was defined as "any child who violates a provision of the Criminal Code, federal or provincial statute, municipal ordinance or by-law, or who is guilty of 'sexual immorality' or of similar vice, or who is liable for any other reason to be committed to an industrial school or reformatory" (section 21);

(2) Judges were counselled to balance a courtroom approach to the juvenile delinquent that was informal, but still take seriously appropriate procedures and due process (section 17.1);

(3) A child adjudged to be a juvenile delinquent would be subject to one or more dispositions, such as a suspension of the disposition, a fine not to exceed $25, probation, placement in a suitable foster home, commitment to the care of a Children's Aid Society or industrial school, or any other conditions the court deemed advisable (section 20); and

(4) The legislation was based on a commitment to the therapeutic treatment of the juvenile delinquent with such treatment provided by professional social workers who were to aid families perceived to be lacking in supervisory skills (Alvi 2000).

In many ways, the JDA represented a fundamental shift away from the earliest approaches to juvenile justice, which tended to view youth and adult behaviour as being more or less the same. But although there was now a more formal Act in place to address the uniqueness of the young person, much of its humanitarian potential was undermined by vague language, minimal guarantees of due process, the inclusion of a wide range of "status" offences and the almost random discretion of judges to invoke a range of dispositions (West 1984).

More specifically, as Nicholas Bala (1997) points out, one of the major problems with the *Juvenile Delinquents Act* was in its erratic and often biased application. Criminal justice officials such as police and judges had broad powers to interpret the child's best interests, so there was little consistency in application across the country. Due process, such as the right to legal representation, tended to be inconsistently applied in different jurisdictions. The minimum age that defined a juvenile ranged from seven to fourteen, depending on the province. The application of the Act also saw considerable gender and class bias. For instance, female adolescents, but not males, tended to be arrested for the vague offence of "sexual immorality," and typically these girls came from socially disadvantaged backgrounds. Similarly, middle-class children were more likely to be released to their parents or subject to diversion, whereas immigrant and working-class children tended to receive more severe punishments, such as custodial sentences (see Sangster 2002).

A growing body of legal scholars, lawyers and judges identified several other problems. For one thing (as discovered in the 1980s), many children were abused while inmates in reformatory schools. Another problem was the fundamental question of whether the best interests of the child and the accompanying notion of rehabilitation should be the only principle governing youth crime, or whether the system ought to be based on the principles of punishment and deterrence. Given claims that rehabilitation programs had failed, the principles of punishment and deterrence appeared to be of particular importance.

The provisions of the JDA were clear improvements over the random and disorganized system of the pre-legal era. But, tacitly, the principles of the Act supported the medicalization of deviant behaviour and an expansion and deepening of the net of social control over children to regulate them towards "normal" behaviour. The medicalization of deviance meant transforming problems with social causes and correlates into problems in which the causes of deviant behaviour were thought to lie in personal pathologies or individual traits that presumably could be "cured" through medical interventions such as drugs or therapy. In this framework, because delinquency is considered more of a disease than a social problem, the social and structural environment in which young people live becomes less important than the individual's supposed lack of ability to control personal actions. The JDA thus emphasized "therapeutic treatment," the important role of industrial schools and reformatories, and the expanding role of professional social-control agents such as probation officers and social workers. As Bala's summary of criticisms of the Act illustrates, too often it was the disadvantaged and poor who were singled out for these "treatments."

During the first half of the twentieth century, then, the *Juvenile Delinquents Act* provided the legal framework for youth in conflict with the law. By the 1960s, enough questions and issues had arisen to warrant reconsideration of the legislation (Hylton 1994). Eventually the dissatisfaction resulted in the development and implementation of new legislation, the *Young Offenders Act*.

THE YOUNG OFFENDERS ACT

While the central principle of the JDA was rehabilitation of the individual in the context of a welfare model, the *Young Offenders Act* (YOA) that replaced it represented a shift towards accountability within a "justice" framework — a set of ideas and practices emphasizing the rights of society, victims, due process and efficiency coupled with a philosophy of punishment rather than rehabilitation. Central to this perspective is the idea that crime is a matter of lack of personal accountability for actions, a view that once again, pays little, if any, attention to the reality that the social environment plays a critical role in conditioning people's choices.

That the *Juvenile Delinquents Act* came under major scrutiny in the 1960s is not surprising given that decade's reputation as a time of unprecedented economic, social and cultural change. Although it is difficult to say that such large-scale changes were solely responsible for shifting attitudes and policies towards young offenders, it would be careless to dismiss their influence (Corrada and Markwart 1992). If we were to try and capture the tenor of the times in one word, we would probably be safe in calling this a modern "enlightenment" era. The heightened attention paid to the Vietnam War, for example, increased awareness of the problematic nature of foreign policy and the ulti-mately destructive nature of war. The second wave of the women's movement challenged male hegemony, and civil rights leaders such as Martin Luther King Jr. led the movement for greater racial equality. Bob Dylan, John Lennon and other folk and rock and roll musicians sang songs about peace, love and achieving higher consciousness through the use of drugs such as LSD, mescaline and marijuana. An attitude of "free love" seemed to be sweeping sexual consciousness, as many young people attempted to break free from traditional social norms and customs. Many people sought new freedoms, experimented with alternative lifestyles and started taking problems of social inequality seriously.

The 1960s spawned new concerns about the importance of equality and emancipation in all facets of life, including the law. The decade also provided people with a framework that would permit them to re-examine notions such as "immorality," "class" and "race." While many people were calling "traditional" social values into question, it was young people who seemed to be yelling the loudest. Indeed, some commentators, such as Bala (1997), have argued that the YOA was the expression of "anti-youth sentiment" and that today's youth are less likely to respect adult conventions of dress, taste, style and atti-tudes, are more individualistic and are less likely to show respect for authority. Then, as now, there also appears to have been a longing for a return to "basic values," entrenched in romantic notions of the "good old days" and an impetus towards conformity, in the context of a world that seemed more than ever to be fractured, unstable, fast-moving and pluralistic. It did not help that youth crime was starting to increase and that the media increasingly exploited the discourse of "bad kids" or "violent youth out of control."

Economic change also played a part in creating the conditions for the transformation of juvenile justice. The 1960s was a prosperous decade, with many people enjoying greater comforts and job security, conditions which prompted a willingness to consider the plight of those less fortunate than themselves. In Canada, these changing attitudes manifested themselves in several major social policy changes. For instance, a system of socialized health care, or Medicare, was initiated in the early 1960s and became a national program by the early 1970s. The federal *Unemployment Insurance Act* was reformed in 1955 and 1971, and the *Canada Pension Plan Act* was introduced in 1966. The ideas underpin-ning each of these important programs had to do with a philosophy of equality and help for those who had "fallen through the cracks" of an economic system whose fruits most people enjoyed. The approach was buttressed by the economic ideology of Keynesism, which seemed to be functioning well in prolonging prosperous times.[1] In the end, these developments provided the backdrop for a focus on "rights and responsibilities," which was later solidified in law via the realization of the *Charter of Rights and Freedoms.*

The *Charter*, implemented in 1982, provided a new framework for interpreting the rights and responsibilities of Canadians. Among other freedoms, it guaranteed a host of legal rights including equal treatment under the law, the right to legal counsel and the right not to be subjected to cruel and unusual punishment. Given these new rights, the JDA would most likely not have been able to withstand legal challenges under the *Charter* (Hylton 1994), but it was much earlier, within the context of an emerging "liberal" ideology and shifting economic conditions, that Canadian policy-makers began to question the Act's efficacy.

After much debate, the federal Committee on Juvenile Delinquency in Canada concluded in 1965 that the legislation had to be changed. Three separate bills followed the decision to replace the JDA, and in 1984 the *Young Offenders Act* became law.

Essentially, the YOA was a "hybrid" of the JDA and a new set of principles emphasizing the rights of society to protection from crime, the rights of accused young persons to fair, equitable and consistent justice and the notion that young people should be held accountable for their actions, but not in the same way as adults. Furthermore, and in keeping with the later *Charter* provisions, young people were guaranteed the same due process rights and freedoms as adults, including the opportunity to retain legal counsel paid for by the state if they were unable to afford a lawyer, the right to remain silent and the right to consult with a parent or lawyer and to have them present when making a statement to police. In keeping with the Act's emphasis on the efficient and equitable administration of justice, Maureen McGuire (1997: 4) reminds us, "The *Young Offenders Act* provides instruction for criminal procedure and administration of dispositions relating to young persons. It is an offender management tool, not a crime prevention tool."

The Act stresses that a young person in conflict with the law is a criminal (albeit a "special kind" of criminal) and not a misguided child (note, for instance, the different connotations of the term "juvenile delinquent" versus "young offender"). As well as the focus on the efficient and egalitarian administration of justice, the Act includes an important section that allows individuals in conflict with the law to avoid the stigmatizing and potentially harmful effects of processing in the criminal justice system. Section 4, "Alternative Measures," maintains that whenever possible young offenders should be diverted from the criminal justice system, as long as such diversion is consistent with the protection of society. Youth participating in diversion programs might engage in a variety of activities such as reconciliation and restitution to the victim, performing services for the victim and making an apology or providing service to the community. As well, the provinces varied in their approaches to the types of offences considered to be eligible for alternative measures, with some considering all offences and others excluding the more serious crimes such as murder and manslaughter.

The assumption behind alternative measures was that when young people go through arrest, detention, court and sentencing, the very act of being labelled a "young offender" greatly contributes to those individuals seeing themselves as young offenders and potentially taking on a self-proclaimed identity as young offenders. Thus, alternative measures exist to divert "suitable" individuals (those who are very young or who have committed minor offences) away from the criminal justice system so that they do not identify themselves as criminals and thus "become" criminals. In principle, alternative measures would have reduced incarceration rates and reduced the stigma of being labelled a "young offender." The real question, however, was whether all young people had equal opportunities to participate in alternative measures programs, and while there is little good empirical data addressing this question, many critics suspect that equality of opportunity in this regard did not prevail (Alvi 2000). Indeed, a Royal Commission study examining the experiences of Aboriginal youth offenders between the years of 1986 and 1989 found that only 11.1 percent were referred to the alternative measures program, compared with 33 percent of non-Aboriginal offenders (Pleasant-Jette 1993). In practice, alternative measure programs were poorly realized, leaving criminal justice officials little choice but to apply formal legal sanctions to young offenders (Schissel 1997) despite the fact that 54 percent of judges, according to one study, believed that more than half of cases coming before them could have been dealt with appropriately outside of the formal youth court system (Department of Justice Canada 2006a). According to a 1995 report summarizing cross-Canada consultations on youth justice with policy-makers, front-line workers and young people, many communities experienced cuts in funds to the pool of available programs designed to reintegrate young people. These stakeholders also complained that young people had inadequate access to counselling, training or treatment programs because those programs were rarely seen as legitimate components of alternative measures. Conversely, alternative measures approaches often seemed to be restricted to a narrow range of options such as essay or apology writing, which did not adequately "address the unique needs and realities of many young people and which do little to address the harm done or to reintegrate the young person into the community" (National Crime Prevention Council 1995).

A key dimension of alternative measures is their emphasis on community delivery of programs (Wardell 1986). While it has been suggested that this strategy is designed to have community members more involved with their children, it could also be argued that alternative measures represent the inclusion of "the community" into an ever-widening array of social-control mechanisms aimed at young people (Matthews 1979). Furthermore, while the emphasis on community involvement places the burden on the public to deal with the transgressions of youth, an important shortcoming of the alternative measures section was that it relied on broad definitions of "the community" to determine the level and kind of restitution that a young person should offer. A further question is what happens if communities are asked to use their resources to make suitable dispositions when these communities do not have access to such resources? As Wardell (1986) suggests, the real reason behind government commitment to the principle of "non-intervention" may be cost control through devolution of responsibility to communities.

In spirit, the YOA recognized the special status and needs of wayward youth and the importance of due process, and it sought to balance these principles with the rights of victims and society at large. In practice, though, the era of the YOA witnessed a slide towards a law and order mentality, because deeper, structural problems in Canada, such as inequality, racism, sexism and poverty, remained (and as I will argue, continue to remain) unexamined in relation to youth crime. Instead, the system favoured a strategy that paid lip service to the possibilities inherent in alternative measures, overemphasized individual responsibilities and traits and, consequently, witnessed the steady entrenchment of punishment and incarceration. The Act also reflected the social reconstruction of youth in conflict with the law as "young criminals" in a social environment characterized by fear of youth crime and mistaken public perceptions about the nature and level of youth criminality (Hogeveen and Smandych 2001). Moreover, via alternative measures, the Act implicitly constructed two categories of offenders: those who have temporarily stepped off the "up escalator," and those seen as "bad, dangerous, super-predators." Rather than providing a framework for critically examining the social forces that cause crime in the first place, and by distancing itself from the welfare approach, the YOA reflected a readiness to ignore and thereby tacitly reproduce those forces.

As noted earlier, in the late 1990s Canadians began to discuss the ramifications of a reform and partial reconceptualization of young offenders and the law. The legislation, the *Youth Criminal Justice Act* (YCJA), which went into effect in April of 2003, represents a cementing of strategies such as the cost-effective management of "risky children," a continued expansion in the age range that defines an "adult" and a focus on creating a justice system that provides "meaningful consequences" for youth. In theory, then, the new Act signifies a concern for the welfare of young people, coupled with the crystallization in law of a crime-control ideology.

MANAGING THE "RISKY CHILD": THE YOUTH CRIMINAL JUSTICE ACT

Some years ago during a general election campaign, British citizens were confronted with a crime-control slogan promoted by then Prime Minister Tony Blair. In an attempt to be all things to all voters, Blair argued that his new policy reflected a philosophy of "getting tough on crime, [but also] getting tough on the causes of crime." Shortly thereafter, then Home Secretary Jack Straw, the person responsible for law and order in Britain, argued that the country's increases in violent crime were attributable to wayward youth who have "never had it so good." In effect, he attributed the causes of crime to wealth instead of poverty and inequality (Assinder 2000).

Canadian politicians have taken similar steps to distract the public from the realities and social precursors of youth crime. Proponents of the new law maintained that the YOA was not "tough enough" on young offenders and that we should instead create a legal framework reflecting current social values, one that "commands respect, fosters values such as accountability and responsibility ... makes it clear that criminal behaviour will lead to meaningful consequences, [and that reflects the need for a] broader, more comprehensive approach to youth justice that looks beyond the justice system for solutions to youth crime" (Canada, Department of Justice 2001). In effect, like developments in the U.K., the new YCJA is an attempt to be "all things to all people" (Barber and Doob 2004).

Central to this development is a growing reliance on the "criminology of the dangerous other" in which youth (as well as women, the poor and particular racial/ethnic groups) are singled out as the category considered most risky and in need of control (Garland 2001).

In Ontario, for instance, Conservative Premier Mike Harris began his tenure in 1995 by waging a campaign to discipline particular categories of youth, most notably "squeegee kids," whose only "crime" appeared to be that of attempting to make a living in an economy that has consistently denied them legitimate opportunities.[2] Moreover, in the two decades prior to Harris's term in office, youth unemployment rates in Canada rose from 14 percent in 1980 to 18 percent in 1995 for those completing high school, and more and more youth were working part-time in low-paying, service-sector jobs with little chance of advancement, minimal training for more advanced jobs and reduced or non-existent benefits (Health Canada 1999). Today, in the wake of the recession of 2008, inequalities and insecurity have intensified in Canada. While many pundits refer to the current generation as the "millennials," it may be more accurate to refer to them as the "zero generation" due to the lack of employment and self-fulfillment prospects afforded them now and for the foreseeable future. For instance, child poverty, which is implicated in health and developmental problems, behavioural conditions, social exclusion and diminished capacity to learn, now stands at 15 percent in Canada (one in seven children) (Conference Board of Canada 2014). Youth aged fifteen to twenty-four have the highest self-reported use of illicit substances in the past year compared to other age groups in Canada (Canadian Centre on Substance Abuse 2013). Unemployment among youth aged fifteen to twenty-four reached 14 percent in January of 2014, while nearly half of all employed youth were working in contingent, part-time jobs that offered little if any security, no benefits and few prospects for permanence or advancement (Statistics Canada 2014). As well, youth make up 20 percent of the homeless population in Canada (Gaetz and Hub 2013), and nearly one-third of the people using food banks in Canada were children (Food Banks Canada 2013). According to the Canadian Mental Health Association, the number of twelve- to nineteen-year-olds in Canada at risk of developing depression is 3.2 million. Relatedly, although I am not aware of any large scale Canadian studies of psychiatric disorders among incarcerated youth in Canada, one small study found that 30.4 percent of incarcerated youth in the sample were currently depressed, compared to 4.1 percent of the non-incarcerated youth comparison group (as reported in Odgers et al. 2005). Moreover, recent studies in the United States indicate that more than 70 percent of incarcerated youth suffer from at least one mental disorder, with 20 percent suffering from a "serious" mental health problem. There is no reason to believe that incarcerated Canadian youth are any different in this regard from their U.S. counterparts, and while the YCJA acknowledges the need to provide intensive rehabilitation for such youth, only empirical evaluation of this claim in the near future will help us to determine whether this has indeed been the case (Odgers, Burnette, Chauhan, Moretti, and Reppucci 2005).

These conditions occur in the context of transformations in our market-based society that paradoxically rely on youth to consume goods and services but at the same time systematically exclude large segments of them from participation in worthwhile, remunerative work. Indeed, today's youth are increasingly forced into a "prolonged state of social marginality" (Petersen and Mortimer 1994), given the rapid decline of decent work opportunities for young people — and in particular for those who come from poor or dispossessed backgrounds. At the same time, and perhaps more than ever, young people are subjected to a market orientation in which consumption is depicted as "an end in itself and as a measure of social status and human value" (Caston 1998). Further, "this culture of consumption is pervasive, fed by advertising campaigns and intense media coverage of affluent lifestyles, and feeds the alienation of youth" (McMurtry and Curling 2008: 21). Consider that trillions of dollars are now spent on advertising to young people every year so that they can "brand" themselves with goods they generally can only afford to purchase on their parent's bloated credit lines. In 2005, Canadian youth spent nearly three billion dollars of their own money (double that of 1995) and influenced the spending patterns of their parents by over $20 billion (Canadian Teachers' Federation 2006). Advertising has become, along with families and schools, one of the most important socialization agents in our society.

Accordingly, we are now in an era in which more and more youth are experiencing relative deprivation,[3] coupled with fewer opportunities to attain the "glittering prizes" of capitalism through legitimate means (Young 1999).

Many contemporary Canadian youth live in a context in which the state is attempting to control the activities of a new youthful *lumpenproletariat*[4] (Taylor 1999), while simultaneously trying to cope with difficult social circumstances as the brief examples noted above suggest. What is more, recent socio-political developments in Canada do not bode well for any potentially progressive movement on the problem of youth crime as contained in the original declaration of principle of the YCJA.

The current Conservative Government has reverted to a "law and order" mentality in the context of global economic and political shifts that most progressive scholars are labelling neo-liberalism, and these scholars are calling attention to an attendant "punitive turn" (Garland 2001; Muncie 2008; Giroux 2009). Neo-liberalism has been defined as a system of governance based on the principles of the (so-called) free market. As Giroux (2004) defines it, the central claims of neo-liberal policies are that democracy is about profit, requiring deregulation, privatization, transfers of wealth to a small proportion of the population, commercialization, "punishment creep," individualism, responsibilization and the credo that the market should shape and guide values.

With respect to youth justice, and as we have seen earlier, the original idea of the YCJA was to balance the protection of society while tackling the underlying causes of youth criminality. With the rise of neo-liberal political culture, this balance is now being tipped in favour of law, order and the protection of society.

On October 23, 2012, the Government of Canada passed an omnibus crime bill entitled the *Safe Streets and Communities Act* (Bill C-10, previously Bill C-4) which has major implications for the *Youth Criminal Justice Act*. Briefly, some of the key amendments to the YCJA's general principles (Canada 2012) are as follows:

- The emphasis is now on protection of the public (not the *long term* protection of the public) by holding young offenders accountable. The Canadian Bar Association (CBA) has serious reservations on the omission of the words "long term" in relation to protection of the public in the original version of the Act (section 3(1)a), since this revision opens the door to longer sentences, thereby precluding the goal of rehabilitation and reintegration.
- The Act recognizes diminished moral blameworthiness or culpability of young persons. This has generally been seen as one positive outcome of the amendments. (See the Supreme Court of Canada case, *R. vs. DB*.)
- Serious offences now include offences that *might* endanger the public. What might endanger the public is open to discretion and individual interpretation and is therefore imprecise.
- The Act now includes specific deterrence (invoking sentences that prevent an offender from harming the public, e.g., incarceration) and denunciation as principles. Drawing on decades of social science research, the CBA argues that deterrence simply does not work:

  > Putting young people in jail is a waste of human potential. Unless incarceration is actually required for a valid social purpose, it is also a terrible waste of tax dollars that could be spent on positive steps aimed at reducing poverty and crime, like schools and social housing. If simply addressing misconceptions about youth crime being out of control, the government might focus efforts on correcting that misconception. In our view, unnecessary incarceration of young people is a mistake that Canada cannot afford. (Canadian Bar Association 2010: 8)

- The definition of a "violent offence" now includes offences that *could* endanger the life or safety of another person by creating a substantial likelihood of causing bodily harm. This may create variation in what is considered to be "substantial likelihood" across jurisdictions.

- The YCJA now allows the court to consider "extrajudicial sanctions" in addition to "findings of guilt" in determining whether a young person could be eligible for a custodial sentence due to a pattern of criminal activity.

- The YCJA now requires that the Crown consider seeking an adult sentence for youth aged fourteen and older who are charged with murder, attempted murder, manslaughter or aggravated sexual assault.

- In cases of sentences for violent offences, judges now have discretion to lift publication bans. The CBA has voiced unease that publication bans have been lifted given the expanded definition of "violent" offences, and given our knowledge that publication bans help to diminish stigma and labelling, which in turn enhances the effectiveness of rehabilitation. (See the Supreme Court of Canada case, *R. vs. Williams.*)

- Police are now required to keep records when they impose extrajudicial measures. This would mean extra work for officers and a review by judges of previous encounters with the police in potential subsequent sentencing decisions for a youth.

- No young person under the age of eighteen can serve a sentence in an adult prison or penitentiary regardless of whether they are given an adult or youth sentence. This is another potentially positive outcome of the amendments, but it leaves open the question of where these youth will serve their sentence. While incarceration has decreased, this amendment leaves open the question as to whether any currently empty cells will eventually be filled.

It is important that under the clause of extrajudicial measures (formerly known as alternative measures under the YOA) those convicted of lesser crimes such as petty theft or vandalism should be afforded sanctions other than jail (such as no further action, warnings, cautions or referrals to special programs). Extrajudicial sanctions (Section 4. 10.) can be seen as an extension of extrajudicial measures in that they can be applied if the young person is alleged to have committed an offence that cannot be adequately dealt with by a warning, caution or referral. The youth must consent to extrajudicial sanctions, has the right to counsel, must accept responsibility for the act or omission and there must also be sufficient evidence for the Crown to proceed with prosecution. The real question, which can only be answered empirically, is what individual characteristics or circumstances might influence the levying of extrajudicial measures? As we noted earlier with respect to section 4 of the *Young Offenders Act*, there remains a potential for bias to creep into the decision making process regarding diversion from the system. One recent study determined that three factors — having no prior convictions, being charged with a property offence and having fewer current and outstanding charges — were statistically significant predictors of being diverted from the formal criminal justice system (Moyer and Basic 2004). We also know that Aboriginal youth, while representing just 6 percent of the general population in 2006, represented 27 percent of youth remanded in custody, 36 percent of youth admitted to sentenced custody, and 24 percent of youth admitted to probation (National Crime Prevention Centre 2012: 11).

One of the stated goals of the YCJA was to reduce the use of incarceration for youth in conflict with the law. On this subject, we know that while there were initial decreases in the use of remand Canada wide of 11.1 percent in 2002–3, these changes have remained relatively stable from year to year and seem to have slowed in 2011–12.[5] Still, we have no good data on the nature of the decision-making processes that underpin the choice, by police, of diversion for Aboriginal youth, let alone youth of colour or females. This lack of data leaves open the question of whether the implementation of extrajudicial measures may well result in a process of judicial triage for young offenders, with some individuals ("our" children) deemed suitable for diversion from the juvenile justice system and others ("other people's" children) sent straight to youth or adult court (Bell 1999; Feld 1999).

There is some degree of optimism, as of this writing, that extrajudicial measures are in fact being used (Carrington and Schulenberg 2005). As the Department of Justice (2006b) states:

- There has been an increase in the use of extrajudicial measures by police, and, preliminary indications are that they appear to be using the full range of measures set out in section 6.
- In jurisdictions that have crown caution programs or pre-charge screening, crown prosecutors appear to be using cautions and encouraging the use of extrajudicial measures by police.

However, the same Department of Justice report notes that there are less encouraging signs and some issues that will warrant further investigation in coming years:

- Net widening can be defined as the use of interventions outside the criminal justice system that "may result in more, not less, intervention than would have occurred in the past. For example, police may be inclined to use formal cautions and referrals with youths with whom, in the past, police would have taken no further action" (Barnhorst 2004). While national figures reported by the Canadian Centre for Justice Statistics for 2003 do not indicate any significant increase in the number of youth being brought into the youth justice system, there have been instances where net widening appears to have occurred in the use of extrajudicial measures programs.
- There is not sufficient data yet available to determine the extent to which the use of extrajudicial measures, particularly extrajudicial sanctions, is proportionate to the seriousness of the offence.
- There is evidence that conditions are being attached to the use of some police referrals that are not consistent with the objectives of reform at the front end of the process.

Further, given that under the YCJA, police are now mandated to consider extrajudicial measures before starting judicial proceedings, it will be important to determine if communities have the necessary resources to address the needs of youth who should be diverted from the criminal justice system.

A paper drafted in 1999 to justify the introduction of the new Act discussed the role of "community-based crime prevention" and the need to address "the social conditions associated with the root causes of delinquency" (Canada 1999). The document makes clear, though, that most serious offenders come from troubled homes characterized by violence, physical and sexual abuse, poverty, substance abuse, attachment disorders, poor housing and the difficulties associated with neighbourhood disorganization — factors that critical criminologists have been calling attention to for decades. It is surely false piety to acknowledge the crucial role of social inequality in fostering youth crime in a society that continues lurching towards a "dystopia of exclusion" (Young 1999). An "ideal" or "utopian" society would possess several characteristics including low rates of crime, social advancement on the basis of merit, truly representative democracy, full and worthwhile employment and a celebration of diversity. In contrast, as Jock Young (1999) argues, in the "dystopia of exclusion" many people are being ever more excluded from participating in "the good life" because of poverty, inequalities, insecurity and other unfairness, and they are also increasingly demonized as being unworthy.

The truth is that as of yet, no government has seriously committed itself to programs and strategies that might begin to foster greater equality, such as increasing government support for at-risk families, creating a nationally funded childcare system or providing real work opportunities, because such policies would entail a fundamental rethinking of the socio-economic system and a dismantling of neo-liberalism and the advantages that this system confers on the wealthy and powerful in our society, including their children. Instead, the legislation proposes the need for more stringent punishment but better reintegration after custody via periods of community supervision and vague notions of "meaningful consequences" aimed at rehabilitation in "communities" that have little resources and remain ambiguously defined (for a broader discussion of this last issue, see McMurtry and Curling 2008).

Taken together, recent "reforms" of the laws governing youth crime in Canada reflect a heightened sense of the danger that disenfranchised youth represent to the social order because these children underscore our failure as a society to deal with widening social and economic disparities. More fundamentally, the law and order mentality reflected in the legislation is a reflection of the attitude that such individuals can, and should, be thrown away or "quarantined" in prison, or controlled in other ways (Garland 2001); they are merely part of the wounded debris characterizing the "new economy." If the data over the past decade indicates that we are reducing our reliance on incarceration, the question still remains: what are we to do with youth still growing up in risky, unstable circumstances who may well run afoul of the law during adolescence?

The Act also reflects a concern with cost-effectiveness, efficiency and the management of offending risk, rather than disquiet with the structural conditions that encourage youth to offend. In a culture of risk management, the emphasis is no longer on the nature of the processes and conditions that generate criminal opportunities and behaviours. Rather, risk management approaches assume that offenders simply exist, that they have "chosen" their behaviours (without recognition of the context in which these choices are made) and that the real task is to manage away their existence and the potential harm they might cause through strategies such as "target hardening," a crime-reduction strategy aimed at reducing opportunities for offending (for example, by increasing lighting, shuttering windows or placing padlocks on property). As well, the Act focuses on making the system as cost effective as possible through the use of tools such as sentencing grids (frameworks used to determine the length and nature of an offender's sentence based on prior records and the seriousness of the offence) and risk assessment tools (designed to "predict" future offending or manage case dispositions or treatments).

And yet, as Pate points out:

> Correctional authorities in many provinces and territories are utilizing actuarial risk assessment procedures with criminalized adults and youth within their jurisdictions. Although there are some incredibly problematic philosophical issues and extremely challenging practical problems that have been created by attempts to adapt imperfect models of risk assessment(s) designed for adults

to the circumstances of youth, there is virtually no research regarding the appropriateness of applying such approaches to youth. This is especially the case when one considers the circumstances of some of our most marginalized young people. (2006: 1)

In effect, Canadian society has increased its commitment to managing the risk of dangerous/criminal youth while paying selective inattention to the social, political and economic factors that create youth at risk. By itself, a risk-management strategy does nothing to address why offenders are motivated to commit offences in the first place. The attitude seems to be that it is much easier to lock up or in some way, shape or form "process" those who break the law rather than to deal with the social and economic conditions that foster crime.

CONCLUSION

Although youth who have "failed" to integrate into society have to some extent always been demonized in Canada, never have our attitudes been so narrow, unsympathetic and controlling as they are today. Concomitant with these attitudes, the current legislation reflects a return to the narrow individualism and decontextualized framework of classical, administrative criminology, with its emphasis on "rational choice" and crime control and its use of the rhetoric, but not the content of notions of social justice and reform.

Our legal orientation towards youth has been greatly influenced by perceptions of their role in the broader context of the socio-economic system. Prior to the rise of capitalism in Canada, the law, such as it was, reflected a blasé and ad hoc attitude towards children. As capitalism developed through the late nineteenth and early twentieth centuries, formal social control strategies reflected the need for a well-socialized, compliant labour force at a time when jobs were relatively plentiful. Gradually, as the nature and availability of work changed in the context of an increasingly polarizing society, it became seemingly less practical to talk about rehabilitating and integrating young offenders and much more politically expedient to address real, but misplaced, public demands to "get tough on crime."

More recently, in the midst of deepening social inequality and fewer opportunities for youth, Canadian young offenders law reflects a further retreat from any realistic commitment to rehabilitation and significant social transformation. Contemporary Canadian youth justice policy is based on the erroneous assumption that punishment works, and that "shot in the arm" treatment programs are available, accessible, and effective. Its bankruptcy is also exposed by the system's willingness to continue to scapegoat and criminalize "dangerous" children to deflect attention from economic, political and social crises in Canada and the fundamentally inequitable nature of Canadian society. We must begin to develop adequate and sustainable solutions to the structural contradictions of Canadian society if we are to truly advance youth justice and justice for youth.

DISCUSSION QUESTIONS

1. What are some of the key differences between mainstream and critical accounts of the history of youth justice in Canada?

2. What are some similarities and differences between alternative measures and extrajudicial measures as laid out in the YCJA?

3. Why do some young people become marginalized in our society? Who do these people tend to be, and why are their social characteristics important?

4. Given the arguments presented in this chapter, should Canada have strengthened the YOA, rather than creating an entire new Act? Why or why not?

5. What are some elements of modern youth culture in your community? In what ways are these elements "criminalized" or at least seen to be expressions of deviant behaviour?

GLOSSARY

Administrative Criminology: a criminological approach that focuses on traditional, individualistic explanations of crime and emphasizes already existing approaches to crime control rooted in "counting" crime, assessing risk and penality.

Dystopia of Exclusion: an "ideal" or "utopian" society would possess several characteristics, including low rates of crime, social advancement on the basis of merit, truly representative democracy, full and meaningful employment, celebration of diversity, and so on. In contrast, as Young (1999) argues, modern societies like Canada are tending toward a "dystopia of exclusion" in which many people are ever more excluded from participating in "the good life" because of poverty, inequalities, insecurity and other unfairness, and they are also increasingly demonized as being unworthy.

Etiology: the study of causation.

Extrajudicial Measures: police charging practices that divert the young person away from the formal criminal justice system. It is a set of informal actions designed to

decrease the number of minor infractions that might otherwise appear in court.

Extrajudicial Sanctions: similar to "Alternative Measures (section 4) of the *Young Offenders Act*, extrajudicial sanctions are imposed when informal measures (such as warnings, cautions or referrals as per extrajudicial measures) are not appropriate. What is "appropriate" is decided on the basis of the seriousness of the offence, prior record, or mitigating circumstances.

Justice Framework: a set of ideas and practices emphasizing the rights of society, victims, due process and efficiency coupled with a philosophy of punishment rather than rehabilitation. Central to this perspective is the idea that crime is a matter of lack of personal accountability for actions — a view that pays little, if any, attention to the reality that the social environment plays a critical role in conditioning people's choices.

Keynesianism: maintains that governments should actively intervene in the economy to create demand for products when capitalist economies are in a slump. Thus, by spending money on policies that put money in people's hands (like welfare, tax cuts, or unemployment insurance), consumers are able to continue spending, which in turn helps the private sector through the economic slump.

Lumpenproletariat: what Marx called the "refuse of all classes." Today the term refers to the idea that in situations of economic and social crisis in capitalist society, large numbers of impoverished masses tend to become disconnected from their class and also tend to be susceptible to reactionary ideas.

Parens patriae: the notion of the "state as parent."

Relative Deprivation: the notion that people perceive their position in society relative to others. Thus, those who are poor might not view themselves as worse off than others if *everyone* around them is poor, but when such people live in a society where inequality is blatantly evident, and when they feel that such inequality is unfair, they are said to experience relative deprivation.

Remand: people in remand are facing charges but have yet to be tried. They are kept in custody for two central reasons, there is a high risk they will commit another offence, or there is a risk that they will not appear in court for a hearing.

Responsibilization: an approach that encourages people to encounter the consequences of their actions and accept personal responsibility for those actions. Importantly, this idea assumes that children and youth have the same capacity as adults to assess the consequences of their actions.

SUGGESTED READINGS

N. Bala, *Young Offenders Law,* Concord, ON: Irwin Law (1997).

E. Currie, *The Road to Whatever: Middle-Class Culture and the Crisis of Adolescence,* Metropolitan Books (2004).

A.N. Doob and C. Cesaroni, *Responding to Youth Crime in Canada,* Toronto: University of Toronto Press (2004).

B. Schissel, *Blaming Children: Youth Crime, Moral Panics and the Politics of Hate,* Halifax: Fernwood Publishing (1997).

R. Smandych, *Youth Justice: History, Legislation, and Reform,* Toronto: Harcourt Brace (2001).

Ian Taylor, *Crime in Context: A Critical Criminology of Market Societies,* Boulder, CO: Westview Press (1999).

NOTES

1. Keynesianism maintains that governments should actively intervene in the economy to create demand for products when capitalist economies are in a slump. Thus, by spending money on policies that put money in people's hands (such as welfare or unemployment insurance), the government allows consumers to continue spending, which in turn helps the private sector through the economic slump.
2. The *Ontario Safe Streets Act* (2000) makes it a crime, punishable by a $1,000 fine or six months in jail, for people to approach a vehicle with intent to provide services, and also outlaws "aggressive panhandling."
3. Relative deprivation is the notion that people perceive their position in society relative to others. Thus, those who are poor might not view themselves as being worse off than others if everyone else around them is poor, but when such people live an a society in which inequality

is blatantly evident and when they feel that such inequality is unfair, they are said to experience relative deprivation.

4. Marx called the *lumpenproletariat* the "refuse of all classes." Today, however, the term refers to the idea that in situations of economic and social crisis in capitalist society, large numbers of impoverished masses tend not only to become disconnected from their class but also to be susceptible to reactionary ideas.

5. These data should also be interpreted with caution, as data for Ontario, which has almost half of young persons in remand in Canada, is not available prior to 2003.

6. The Crime Severity Index measures both the volume and seriousness of crimes for youth who have been accused.

REFERENCES

Alvi, Shahid. 1986. "Realistic Crime Prevention Strategies Through Alternative Measures for Youth." In D. Currie and B.D. MacLean (eds.), *The Administration of Justice.* Saskatoon: Social Research Unit, Department of Sociology, University of Saskatchewan.

___. 2000. *Youth and the Canadian Criminal Justice System.* Cincinnati: Anderson Press.

Assinder, N. 2000. "Crime Statistics Deal New Blow to Blair." *BBC News Online.* At <http://news. bbc.co.uk/2/hi/uk_news/politics/838195.stm>.

Bala, N. 1997. *Young Offenders Law.* Concord, Ontario: Irwin Law.

Bala, N., and S. Anand. 2004. "The First Months under the Youth Criminal Justice Act: A Survey and Analysis of Case Law." *Canadian Journal of Criminology and Criminal Justice* 46: 251–71.

Barber, J., and A.N. Doob. 2004. "An Analysis of Public Support for Severity and Proportionality in the Sentencing of Youthful Offenders." *Canadian Journal of Criminology and Criminal Justice* 46: 327–28.

Barnhorst, R. 2004. "The Youth Criminal Justice Act: New Directions and Implementation Issues." *Canadian Journal of Criminology and Criminal Justice* 46: 231–50.

Barrett, M., and M. McIntosh. 1982. *The Anti-Social Family.* London: Verso.

Bell, S. 1999. *Young Offenders and Juvenile Justice: A Century After the Fact.* Toronto: ITP Nelson.

Bernard, T. 1991. *The Cycle of Juvenile Justice.* New York: Oxford University Press.

Boyce, J., A. Cotter and S. Perreault. "Police-Reported Crime Statistics in Canada, 2013." *Juristat.* Canadian Centre for Justice Statistics.

Canada, Department of Justice. 1999. "A Strategy for the Renewal of Youth Justice." Ottawa: Department of Justice.

___. 2001. "Canada's Youth Criminal Justice Act: A New Law — A New Approach." At <http:// canada.justice.gc.ca/Orientations/jeunes/penale/youth_en.html>.

___. 2012. "Recent Changes to Canada's Youth Justice System." At <www.justice.gc.ca/eng/cj-jp/ yj-jj/ycja-lsjpa/sheets-feuillets/amend-modif.html>.

Canadian Bar Association. 2010. "Bill C-4 — Youth Criminal Justice Act Amendments." National Criminal Justice Section: Canadian Bar Association, Ottawa.

Canadian Centre for Justice Statistics. 1997. "Justice Data Fact Finder." *Juristat* 16, 9.

Canadian Centre on Substance Abuse. 2013. "Trends in Drug Use Among Youth." Canadian Centre on Substance Abuse

Canadian Teachers' Federation. 2006. "Commercialism in Canadian Schools: Who's Calling the Shots." Canadian Teachers' Federation, Canadian Centre for Policy Alternatives. At <www. policyalternatives.ca/publications/reports/commercialism-canadian-schools>.

Carrigan, D.O. 1998. *Juvenile Delinquency in Canada: A History.* Concord: Irwin.

Carrington, P.J., and J.L. Schulenberg. 2005. *The Impact of the Youth Criminal Justice Act on Police Charging Practices with Young Persons: A Preliminary Statistical Assessment.* Department of Justice Canada.

Caston, R.J. 1998. *Life in a Business-Oriented Society: A Sociological Perspective.* Boston: Allyn and Bacon.

Cohen, S. 1972. *Folk Devils and Moral Panics*. London: MacGibbon and Kee.

Conference Board of Canada. 2013. "Child Poverty." At <http://www.conferenceboard.ca/hcp/details/society/child-poverty.aspx> accessed July 2014.

___. n.d. *How Canada Performs: Child Poverty*. At: <conferenceboard.ca/hcp/details/society/child-poverty.aspx>.

Corrado, R., and A.E. Markwart. 1992. "The Evaluation and Implementation of a New Era of Juvenile Justice in Canada." In R. Corrado, N. Bala, R. Linden and M. Leblanc (eds.), *Juvenile justice in Canada*. Toronto: Butterworths.

Currie, D. 1986. "The Transformation of Juvenile Justice in Canada." In B.D. MacLean (ed.), *The Political Economy of Crime*. Toronto: Prentice-Hall.

DeKeseredy, W.S., and M.D. Schwartz. 1996. *Contemporary Criminology*. Belmont, CA: Wadsworth.

Department of Justice Canada. 2006a. "The Youth Criminal Justice Act: Summary and Background." At <http://www.justice.gc.ca/eng/cj-jp/yj-jj/ycja-lsjpa/back-hist.html>.

___. 2006b. Youth Criminal Justice Act 2005 Annual Statement: Executive Summary." Ottawa: Department of Justice Canada. At <http://www.justice.gc.ca/eng/pi/yj-jj/ycja-lsjpa/stat-declar/sum-som.html>.

Doob, A.N., and C. Cesaroni. 2004. *Responding to Youth Crime in Canada.* Toronto: University of Toronto Press.

Feld, B.C. 1999. *Bad Kids: Race and the Transformation of the Juvenile Court*. New York: Oxford University Press.

Food Banks Canada. 2013. Hungercount 2013. At <http://www.foodbankscanada.ca/getmedia/b2aecaa6-dfdd-4bb2-97a4-abd0a7b9c432/HungerCount2013.pdf.aspx?ext=.pdf>.

Gaetz, S.A., J. Donaldson, T. Richter and T. Gulliver. 2013. "The State of Homelessness in Canada 2013." Homeless Hub. At <www.homelesshub.ca/SOHC2013>

Gagnon, D. 1984. "History of the Law for Juvenile Delinquents." Ministry of the Solicitor General of Canada, Government Working Paper No. 1984-56.

Gannon, M. 2006. *Crime Statistics in Canada, 2005.* (Rep. No. 85-002-XIE, vol. 26, no. 4). Ottawa: Canadian Centre for Justice Statistics.

Garland, D. 2001. *The Culture of Control*. New York: Oxford University Press.

Giroux, H.A. 2004. *The Terror of Neoliberalism: Authoritarianism and the Eclipse of Democracy*. Hemdon, VA: Paradigm Publishers.

___. 2009. *Youth in a Suspect Society: Democracy or Disposability?* Palgrave Macmillan.

Hartnagel, T. 2004. "The Rhetoric of Youth Justice in Canada." *Criminal Justice* 4: 355–74.

Health Canada. 1999. "Healthy Development of Children and Youth: The Role of the Determinants of Health." Ottawa: Minister of Health.

Hogeveen, B., and R. Smandych. 2001 "Origins of the Newly Proposed Canadian Youth Criminal Justice Act: Political Discourse and the Perceived Crisis in Youth Crime in the 1990s." In R. Smandych (ed.), *Youth Justice: History, Legislation and Reform*. Toronto: Harcourt Canada.

Hylton, J.H. 1994. "Get Tough or Get Smart? Options for Canada's Youth Justice System in the Twenty-First Century." *Canadian Journal of Criminology* 36, 3.

Latimer, J., and N. Desjardins. 2008. *The 2008 National Justice Survey: Tackling Crime and Public Confidence*. Department of Justice Canada.

Lynch, M.J., and W.B. Groves. 1989. *A Primer in Radical Criminology*. New York: Harrow and Heston.

Matthews, R. 1979. "Decarceration and the Fiscal Crisis." In B. Fine (ed.), *Capitalism and the Rule of Law*. London: Hutchinson.

McGuire, M. 1997. "C.19: An Act to Amend the Young Offenders Act and the Criminal Code — Getting Tougher?" Canadian Journal of Criminology 39, 2.

McMurtry, R., and A. Curling. 2008. A Review of the Roots of Youth Violence: Community Perspectives Report. 3. Service Ontario.

Moyer, S., and M. Basic. 2004. *Crown Decision-Making under the Youth Criminal Justice Act*. Ottawa: Youth Justice Policy, Research and Statistics Division.

Muncie, J. 2008. "The 'Punitive Turn' in Juvenile Justice: Cultures of Control and Rights Compliance in Western Europe and the USA." *Youth Justice* 8, 2: 107–21.

National Crime Prevention Council. 1995. *Mobilizing Political Will and Community Responsibility to Prevent Youth Crime: A Summary Report of 30 Consultation Meetings to Explore Effective Community Responses to Youth Crime*. Ottawa, Government of Canada.

___. 2012. *A Statistical Snapshot of Youth at Risk and Youth Offending in Canada*. PS4-126/2012E-PDF. National Crime Prevention Centre.

Odgers, C., M. Burnette, P. Chauhan, M. Moretti and N.D. Reppucci. 2005. "Misdiagnosing the Problem: Mental Health Profiles of Incarcerated Juveniles." *The Canadian Child and Adolescent Psychiatry Review* 14: 26–29.

Pate, K. 2006. *The Risky Business of Risk Assessment* Ottawa: Canadian Association of Elizabeth Fry Societies.

Petersen, A.C., and J.T. Mortimer. 1994. *Youth, Unemployment and Society*. Cambridge: Cambridge University Press.

Pleasant-Jette, Corinne Mount. 1993. *Creating a Climate of Confidence: Providing Services Within Aboriginal Communities*. National Round Table on Economic Issues and Resources (Royal Commission on Aboriginal Issues).

R. v. D.B. 2008. 2 S.C.R. 3, 2008 SCC 25

Sangster, J. 2002. *Girl Trouble: Female Delinquency in English Canada*. Toronto: Between the Lines.

Schissel, Bernard. 1993. *Social Dimensions of Canadian Youth Justice*. Toronto: Oxford University Press.

___. 1997. *Blaming Children: Youth Crime, Moral Panics and the Politics of Hate*. Halifax: Fernwood Publishing.

Schwartz, M.D. 1991. "The Future of Critical Criminology." In B.D. MacLean and D. Milovanovic (eds.), *New Directions in Critical Criminology*. Vancouver: Collective Press.

Smandych, R. 2001. "Accounting for Changes in Canadian Youth Justice: From the Invention to the Disappearance of Childhood." In R. Smandych (ed.), *Youth Justice: History, Legislation, and Reform*. Toronto: Harcourt Canada.

Sprott, J. 1996. "Understanding Public Views of Youth Crime and the Youth Justice System." *Canadian Journal of Criminology* 38, 5.

Statistics Canada. 2014. Table 251-0009: Youth Custody and Community Services (YCCS), Young Persons Commencing Correctional Services, by Initial Entry Status (Percentage Change (year-to-year), CANSIM (database). Accessed: 2014-07-19.

Taylor, I. 1999. *Crime in Context: A Critical Criminology of Market Societies*. Boulder, CO: Westview.

Taylor, I., P. Walton and J. Young. 1973. *The New Criminology*. London: Routledge and Kegan Paul.

___. 1975. *Critical Criminology*. London: Routledge and Keegan Paul.

Tustin, L., and R.E. Lutes. 2015. *A Guide to the Youth Criminal Justice Act*. Markham: LexisNexis.

Varma, K.N., and V. Marinos. 2000. "How Do We Best Respond to the Problem of Youth Crime?" In J. Roberts (ed.), *Criminal Justice in Canada: A Reader*. Toronto: Harcourt Brace.

Wardell, B. 1986. "The Young Offenders Act: A Report Card 1984–1986." In D. Currie and B.D. MacLean (eds.), *The Administration of Justice*. Saskatoon: Social Research Unit, University of Saskatchewan.

West, W.G. 1984. *Young Offenders and the State: A Canadian Perspective on Delinquency*. Toronto: Butterworths.

White, R.D., J. Wyn and P. Albanese. 2011. *Youth and Society: Exploring the Social Dynamics of Youth Experience*. Oxford University Press.

Wilson, J.Q., and R. Herrnstein. 1985. *Crime and Human Nature: The Definitive Study of the Causes of Crime*. New York: Simon and Schuster.

Young, J. 1999. *The Exclusive Society*. London: Sage.

17

YOUTH VIOLENCE

Joanne Minaker and Bryan Hogeveen

KEY FACTS

> Violence is much more widespread and omnipresent than most people believe.

> Humans hold contradictory views of and have complex relationships with violence.

> Violent youth crime rates in Canada are declining.

> Structural inequalities (such as male dominance, racism and poverty) impact situational violence, as illustrated by the cases of girls and violence and Aboriginal youth and violence.

> Bullying in North America has become socially constructed as an act of violence and can be a pathway to violence. Bullying involves deliberate acts of aggression, sustained over a period of time and reflects power differences.

> Despite declining violent youth crime rates, the Federal Government recently enacted the 'violent and repeat young offender' segment of the Safe Streets and Communities Act.

> We learn violence through the experience of it as much as we learn how to care through caring relationships.

> Practices of care have potential to challenge violence and produce more caring citizens.

> To unlearn violence, kids must learn to care.

> An alternative to anti-violence campaigns are frameworks of caring.

Sources: Statistics Canada 2014; Minaker 2013; Minaker and Hogeveen 2009; Bloom 2008.

Even a serious matter like violence is not a simple fact which speaks loudly for itself. — Colin Sumner (1997: 1)

The practice of violence, like all action, changes the world, but the most probable change is to a more violent world. — Hannah Arendt (1969: 177)

Cared for people care for people. — Joanne Minaker (2013)

Violence is everywhere, but so is care. Human beings practise care and inflict pain in our homes, schools, workplaces, sporting arenas and communities. Canadian youth see and participate in a culture that paradoxically teaches and trains them both toward and against violent ideas and actions. North American society socializes children to learn contradictory lessons about what is acceptable, appropriate and available to them as ways of being or means to make their way in the world. The goal of this chapter is to encourage critical reflection about violence and meaningful social engagements with caring social relations.

All children and youth deserve to live in spaces where they can experience love, care and safety and where they can play, create, learn and grow. Nevertheless, an estimated 360,000 children in Canada are exposed to violence in their homes (UNICEF et al. 2006). Witnessing domestic violence is often a significant factor in street youth's decisions to engage in violence (Baron and Hartnagel 1999). For many youth, especially marginalized young people, like one of our research participants, Damon, violence is a very useful tool to secure desired ends. Damon's story, as you will see, highlights the relationship between being violent and not being cared for. Damon experienced his childhood as a poor, Aboriginal boy, immersed within a social environment where violent interaction was normalized. He witnessed, experienced, inflicted and came to understand his world *through* violence. Yet, it is not only the most socially excluded or marginalized who encounter violence. Young people's lives are touched by violence in different ways. Almost all Canadian children, whether we want to admit it or not, are impacted in one way or another by violence.

Consider the sports boys and girls play. On the surface these games are intended to teach respect and provide physical activity. Canadian sport is an excellent way for our children to learn about themselves, develop self-confidence and healthy body images, understand why exercise matters and receive instruction in the importance of teamwork. This becomes possible only to the extent that kids can negotiate the ugly underbelly of these games. A quick search of YouTube provides abundant examples of the nastiness of sport. A father in Winnipeg, Manitoba, threatens to cave in another parent's glasses, all the while holding a toddler. Why? This was his response to another dad referring to his child in derogatory terms. In 2012, in Vancouver, B.C., a hockey coach, one who we entrust to teach our children the positive values listed above, tripped a 13-year-old player from the opposing team during the post-game handshake. He was arrested and pled guilty to assault and was handed fifteen days in jail. Does this signal social disapproval?

Are many of these games not themselves violent in their design and in the brutality they occasion? Punishing bodychecks in hockey, smashing bodies in football and slashes with sticks across forearms and shoulders in lacrosse are all "part of the game" in many of the sports Canadian youth play. Consider what would happen if you were to bodycheck a fellow passenger on a plane as she exited her seat. Sporting physicality can spill over into intensified brutality and fighting. In Stonewall, Manitoba, a young hockey player from Lake Manitoba took exception to the officiating and blasted the puck at the referees. In Belleville, Ontario, parents' brawled in the stands as verbal assaults escalated into physical violence. It is not clear, nor is there evidence to suggest, whether violence in the sports children play has escalated in recent years or if the ease and pervasiveness of video recording has brought their brutality to the forefront of public discourse. Nevertheless, assaults of officials, confrontations between parents, coaches blindsiding players and fistfights between players constitute the landscape of contemporary sporting culture.

Violence infuses everyday life in Canada. Although we used sport as an example, violence can be linked to many other settings. It is a dominant theme in video games, television programs and movies. Even some children's programming is seemingly centered on violence. Take Pokémon, The X-Men, Teenage Mutant Ninja Turtles, Scooby Do, SpongeBob SquarePants, Star Wars or classic Bugs Bunny cartoons as illustrations of primarily male, powerful characters solving conflict with physical violence and verbal acts of aggression. Researchers, parents and teachers hold differing views on the extent these images and messages (i.e., depicted, fantasy or animated violence) affect kids' play or negatively impact children. Viewers may become desensitized by violence in screen-based media, which may affect empathy (Strasburger and Wilson 2002).

Although public alarm has increasingly been drawn to these forms of violence, nothing seems to raise the public ire as violence in Canadian streets. Fears about youth violence, in particular, are enduring even though in 2013 the overall rate of youth accused of violent crime decreased by 13 percent (Statistics Canada 2014). A different kind of game is at play here too: politicians and newspaper reporters, throughout the Western world especially, are players in a game of enthusiastically condemning *some* forms of human action as "violent," while others continue to exist unremarked, acceptable or even praised (e.g., the not-so "rule of law" killing of Osama bin Laden). The harms done against and toward youth are oftentimes overshadowed by the harms they are accused of causing against others. Put another way, youth victimization from violence receives far less attention in popular and media discourse than does youth violent offending (Minaker and Hogeveen 2009).

Few other platforms are so successful in obtaining votes for politicians than promises to crack down on and get tough on violence (Hogeveen 2005). For example, in 2012, the Canadian Government put into effect the "violent and repeat young offender" segment of the *Safe Streets and Communities Act* (SSCA) (Canada 2012). Aimed at violent offenders, the legislation promised to shore up what the government called holes in the *Youth Criminal Justice Act*. Specifically, arguing for the government in the debates about SSCA, Senator Boisvenu complained, "All too often, the justice system was powerless to keep violent or repeat young offenders in custody even when they posed a danger to society" (Canada, Department of Justice 2012). "From now on," he continued, "violent or repeat young offenders will be held fully accountable for their actions and the safety and security of law-abiding Canadians will be given full consideration at sentencing." It is important to point out that the SSCA was enacted at a time of declining violent youth crime rates (Canada 2013).

Neglected from this rhetoric and vitriol is how young people's lives are acutely affected by violence. Children are much more often the victims of crime than the perpetrators of violence (Statistics Canada 2013). While considering this claim, it is important to keep in mind that the categories of offender and victim frequently overlap and are rarely distinct. Marginalized young people who are often the tragic and silenced victims of violence get obfuscated in debates about "best practices" or "crack downs" against their violence. Instead, politicians and other anti-youth crusaders are often more concerned with whetting the public's appetite for increasingly draconian measures to be applied to young people who traverse the bounds of law, without, at the same time, acknowledging their abuse. Violent crime does not occur in a vacuum, but is rather conditioned by societal structures that shape and contour young lives in deleterious directions.

A common framing of the discussion about youth violence locates the issue as one of how we (should or could) respond to violent conflicts and ways to control violent youth. What if we looked at the relationship between youth and violence through the lens of care? More specifically, imagine thinking about how to create and foster caring encounters between human beings? What about developing ways to heal the suffering occasioned by violence among and against youth? In this chapter we approach the study of violence by humanizing the people involved and locating violent encounters in the social settings in which they occur. This enables us to appreciate the complexities involved in understanding social harms and what we ought to do about them. We begin by considering the meanings associated with violence. That is, if we are going to attend to violence, we better begin by attempting to grasp its meaning. This effort is much more complicated than it first appears and this work is much more important than it might initially seem. Next, we provide a "grammar," a repertoire, or language, that can help decipher the kind of narratives (e.g., media stories) that fuel public fear and the call for something (read: a punitive response) to be done about youth violence. Our discussion about the relationship between marginalization, victimization and offending explores the underlying conditions that produce suffering and explores the fundamental importance of human caring.

WHAT IS VIOLENCE?

We all know what is and what is not violence, right? Ask yourself: How would I define violence? Take a second before reading more to jot down a few ideas. Did you find this an easy task? Philosophers, criminologists, politicians, judges and sociologists have struggled for decades to arrive at an agreed upon definition. This task has not proven particularly definitive. You might say, "I know violence when I see it." In our experience, "murder" is a common response students give to the question. However, murder is not violence. It is an effect or an outcome of violence. Violence is something other. Violence is an abstraction. While it may reflect the vision of the beholder, something is being seen and must be present for the name and intonation of violence to be applied. That is, defining violence need not be concerned with its ends. Rather, we attempt to say something about its essence (if there is such a thing).

We invite you to consider the following scenarios and ask yourself in each case: Is this an example of violence? Why? These are all real situations that we have witnessed and/or experienced:

- At a gymnasium in San Diego a man flashes me an aggressive stare and charges. Sensing his approach, I ducked to the side, grabbed his leg and tossed him to the ground. Many people who had gathered around to watch the spectacle burst into spontaneous applause.
- Waiting for a bus on a Vancouver street a car whizzes past me at a blazing speed.
- While walking in a forest a girl tugs forcefully to pull a leaf off of a tree.
- Emerging from my local Starbucks I witnessed a professionally dressed woman holding a Venti Caramel Macchiato accost an Aboriginal man calling him "homeless" and accusing him of being "lazy."
- Two grade school boys argue with each other in the locker room. Rudely, one says: "You're gay," and the other retorts: "No, you're gay!"
- A woman scratches my arm, hits my knee, pushes me to the floor and leaves me bleeding with a sore neck.

Which, if any, of the above did you characterize as violent? What would make any of these scenarios examples of violence? We can find support and rejection for each one of the above as "violent" in philosophical, legal, social or ethical discourse (yes, even the leaf pulling). Indeed, of all of these examples, the first seems to be the most clear cut example of violence, doesn't it? Perhaps we can agree that throwing someone to the ground is a quintessential violent act. However, what if I were to tell you that this situation occurred at a Brazilian jiu-jitsu tournament? Does it matter that the opponent fell to a soft mat and that no physical damage was sustained? When it comes to violence, context matters. What about the case of the boys talking to each other and the insults against the man in the street? Words and the meaning behind them can cause harm and be interpreted as forms of violence. When it comes to violence, motivation and intention matter. What about the impact of social actions? When it comes to violence, consequences matter. The final example occurred during a self-defence class (a course designed for women to teach skills and instill confidence for defending against violent attacks) between two willing participants. The scratch occurred accidentally while practising a technique and both parties hit each other's knees as part of a warm-up exercise, as per the instructions.

What *is* violence? The answer, as you can begin to see, is not simple or straightforward. Etiological, actuarial, statistical and common engagements with violence tend to gloss over the term, assuming meaning is evident. Despite the claim "we know violence when we see it," the essence of violence is patently unproblematic, and it is extremely difficult to offer a universal definition that is internally valid with itself. Despite projects aimed at reducing and eliminating violence from our society, can we ever be sure exactly what we are attempting to eliminate? There's more complexity if we recognize that efforts to curb, stop or prevent violence appear alongside facilitation and celebration. Simply, "[violence] cannot be readily objectified and quantified so that a 'check list' can be drawn up with positive criteria for defining any particular act as violent or not" (Litke 1992: 171).

Can actions against property be deemed violent? Is it possible to do violence to oneself? Rates of self-harm among youth are on the rise in Canada, especially among girls. According to the Canadian Institute for Health Information (2014), in 2013–14, 500 hospitalizations among youth between the ages of ten and seventeen were the result of intentional self-harm, which amounts to one in four injury-related hospital stays. Eighty percent of the patients were girls. Is this human suffering and pain a form of violence? Or, can violence only be done to another person, an interpersonal conflict such as assault and/or bullying? What about a violent sneeze? What of a violent storm? A violent stomach? A violent skin reaction? Although these latter examples may be conceptually related, they are clearly not of the same order, magnitude or intensity. Equating bodily functions or weather patterns to physical interpersonal harm is telling of how taken-for-granted our use of violence has become. Defining violence has much to do with our subjective sensitivity. Let us push this a little further and consider what constitutes violence. When we say that a storm is violent, at what point does it become so? What is the limit? What linguistic, social or other element may a "violent sneeze" share in common with aggravated assault as described in the Canadian *Criminal Code* (if anything)? This partial unpacking of how violence is employed in the English language provides some insight into the conceptual quicksand intrinsic to understanding violence.

Coming to grips with violence has traditionally meant situating its statistical oddity. If we were to follow this line of thinking to its logical conclusion, it would mean that occasions of violence would shake up our normative being in the world. Is this really the case? Boxing spectators are certainly not surprised by the violence they witness, rather it is the very reason for their attendance (i.e., boxers are expected to punch each other with jabs and undercuts). Despite assurances by politicians and newspaper reporters that violence is some*thing* other, it surrounds us and is seemingly everywhere. Sergio Cotta reminds us:

> The subject of violence has already made its way into the daily conversations of our times; it leads to reflections and inquiries, is at the center of politicians' preoccupations and the worries of private citizens, given inspiration for novels and films. That is not surprising, for violence is so widespread and frightening in all aspects and at all levels of today's life that press, radio, and television never stop reminding us of it. (1985: 1)

Litke (1992: 173) maintains that "violence is intriguing. It is universally condemned, yet to be found everywhere." Most of us are both fascinated and horrified by it. It is a fundamental ingredient of how we entertain ourselves (children's stories, world literature, the movie industry, sports and music) and an essential feature of many of our social institutions. In most parts of the world, violence is notoriously common in family life, religious affairs and political history. Human revulsion of and desire for violence are further evidence of the labyrinth that constitutes the essence of violence. Human relationships to and with violence are not as clear as they might outwardly appear. There are evidently countless meanings when it comes to defining and making sense of violence.

Debate and discourse on and about violence is essential. Difficulties defining violence should not be taken as evidence that we have become bogged down at some epistemological cul-de-sac or that the effort to understand it should be abandoned. It profoundly matters how and what we define as violence. Further, how and under what conditions we employ the term has intense implications in law, politics, interpersonal relations and our psyches (Hogeveen 2007). To avoid the ontological baggage commonly associated with attempts to define violence, we maintain that it ought to be more soberly defined and without hyperbole. If everything (i.e., pulling a leaf from a tree) is violent, it follows that nothing *is* simply violent because the possible term of comparison (in relation to which violence acquires distinct definition as a specific behavior identifiable in itself) is lacking (or, better, obliterated) (Cotta 1985: 50). Toward deepening our understanding of violence and how it has implications for our being in the world we turn out attention to violence as rhetoric.

VIOLENCE AS RHETORIC

Why does it matter how we define violence? There are two very important reasons to take this question seriously. First, violence is an emotionally packed signifier. Because of our visceral reaction to violence, the term has dramatic implications for how lawmakers, educators, health professionals, parents and especially the courts think about and govern youth. Nevertheless, when thinking about violence, citizens often hold a very narrow view based on a public discourse that decontextualizes youth and violence. Like our students, when asked to think about violence, many people immediately recall the criminal variety. This so-called commonsensical way of thinking tends to overlook other more insidious (state violence, corporate crime) and less outwardly appalling (sporting, comedic, accidental, fantasy) forms. Second, under the *Youth Criminal Justice Act* (YCJA) violence is employed as a sentencing criterion. In Canada, the YCJA governs youthful offenders between the ages of twelve and seventeen years. Thus, if we use violence as a benchmark for how and under what circumstances young people are punished for their actions, it becomes paramount to know what exactly constitutes violence.

Committing a violent crime under the YCJA is one of the primary judicial justifications for sentencing young people to custody. Section 39 (1) states, "A youth justice court shall not commit a young person to custody under section 42 (youth sentences) unless (a) the young person has committed a violent offence." Those who framed the YCJA were intent on reducing the numbers of young peoples in Canada's youth detention centres. They aspired to a system of justice whereby only the most serious and repeat offenders would be incarcerated. This was a clear and decisive shift away from the widespread practice of detaining young people for property and administrative offences that was characteristic of how justice was administered under the *Young Offenders Act.* In effect, legal reform led to impressive reductions in custodial sentences across Canada.

If "violent offence" is set down in law as a sentencing criterion, it follows that the court must operate with a clear and concise understanding of violence. A definition of violence was lacking in the first iteration of the Act and the *Criminal Code* of Canada provided no further guidance. Nevertheless, lacking an explicit definition of violent offence, judges, politicians and lawyers were uncertain as to what exactly constituted a violent crime. Would a strictly legal definition be sufficient or do broader, social definitions matter as well? What about the role of judicial discretion?

Two cases came before the Supreme Court of Canada in 2005 asking the Court to clarify the meaning of violent offence under the YCJA. The first involved a young person (C.D.) who approached another young person at a party while ominously holding a table leg over his head. C.D., however, never struck the other individual involved. The second case involved C.D.K., who stole a vehicle and became involved in a high-speed police chase where he ran two red lights and drove his car at almost twice the posted speed limit. He was subsequently found guilty of dangerous driving and possession of stolen property. Are these examples of violent crime? What criteria did you employ to arrive at this determination? For their part, the Supreme Court ruled that "no argument was made that the requirements of one of the other gateways to custody set out in s. 39(1) of the YCJA were satisfied" (*R. v. C.D.* 2005 *R. vs. C.D.K.*).

In the wake of *R. v. C.D.* and *R. v. C.D.K*, it is significant that the YCJA has been amended. Section 2(1) now more explicitly sets out the criteria the court should employ: "'violent offence' means a) an offence committed by a young person that includes as an element the causing of bodily harm b) an attempt or a threat to commit an offence referred to in paragraph a); or c) an offence in the commission of which a young person endangers the life or safety of another person by creating a substantial likelihood of causing bodily harm" (Safe Streets and Communities Act). Under the YCJA, corporeal harm and threats thereof are paramount to violent crime. Nonetheless, as we have already seen, this hardly exhausts the meaning of violence. Other challenges are conceivably on the horizon.

When depriving a young person of his/her liberty, it is incumbent upon justice officials and the courts to be operating with a precise understanding of what is meant by the phrase "violent crime." As Elizabeth Comack and Gillian Balfour (2004: 9) explain: "extracting the legally relevant facts of a case from the messiness of people's lives involves a deciphering or translation. It also involves making judgments on the legal subjects themselves, in terms not only of what they have done, but also of who they are, and on the social settings or spaces in which they move." We found in our study of youth professionals and criminalized youth in Alberta that "the extent that a young person's personal characteristics and social background become part of the judgments made by different players at various levels of the YCJA, gender, class, and race *matter*" (Minaker and Hogeveen 2009: 109).

Violence elicits strong emotions. When these cases came to the public's attention, some reporters were quick to point out the inadequacies built into the legislation. Critics claimed that the YCJA was incapable of protecting the public and holding young people like C.D. and C.D.K. accountable. For example, Joe Thompson (2007), from the *Vancouver Province*, lamented "The law's flaw — a matter of great concern in legal circles — is that jail is an option only for youth convicted of a violent offence. And the legislation drafters didn't intend 'violent' to also mean 'dangerous,' the Supreme Court of Canada concluded in nixing C.D.'s and C.D.K.'s six-month custodial terms."

This brings us to another key reason why we must come to grips with the core of violence. Violence has an intense effect on us and has been effectively deployed to great effect in election campaigns and to sell newspapers. Charner Perry maintains that rhetoric is fundamental to, and built into, violence. He explains that because it elicits strong emotions, "violence has great rewards for the propagandist":

> The most obvious propaganda procedure is *to emphasize the physical, visible aspects of action*. Visible physical damage easily triggers emotion and distracts attention from less immediate or visible damage, which may be much more serious and lasting. When the propagandist can keep attention focused on physical actions involving injury, bloodshed or death, he may so influence ethical assumptions that the audience will see violence where [s]he points. (1970: 14)

This tactic has been employed to great effect by scores of politicians, perhaps (constructing and/or) manipulating the fears of the voting public. Despite stable or declining violent crime rates, many politicians continue to clamour for more robust and austere punishments for youth who run afoul of the law (Statistics Canada 2013).

IMPLICATIONS OF VIOLENCE

Violence takes many different shapes within the context of the social, economic and technological world. New ways of harming and maiming others appear at regular intervals. Aided by technological advancements, states, for example, can now deploy novel weapons (such as tasers, drones and "smart" bombs) that more efficiently inflict pain on its, and other, citizens. Marcuse (1968: 90) argues: "Drawing public attention to particular socio-legal and interpersonal manifestations of violence obscures other, perhaps more insidious and harmful, forms. State violence, through police action or war and war crimes, and corporate forms of harm go relatively unremarked as violence."

How a problem is defined holds tremendous significance for how it is governed (Hogeveen 2005). In Western societies, violent crime receives the lion's share of attention. Typical and commonplace crimes such as shoplifting or mischief do not make headlines. Who might pay for a newspaper that runs a headline about a young person who stole a T-shirt from the Gap? Would advertisers plop their money down for such a paper? Is there an audience for the mundane goings-on of adolescence? Visible, spectacular and atypical violence by young people, by contrast, engages the public interest. The mundane and everyday washes over us while the sensational grabs our attention and raises our indignation (Debord 1970; Schissel 2006). Consider, for example, this headline that ran on the front page of the *Toronto Star*, which read: "Kid-glove treatment for young offenders" (Bruser 2011). "We need go only a little further to grasp the author's point. According to the author, young people are being punishing far too leniently for their violent criminality. Delving more deeply into the article confirms our suspicions. We see case after case of a young person getting away with what the reporter deems a light sentence. A four-month study of the Toronto Youth Court concluded that "kids who committed serious crimes got little or no jail time; repeat offenders whom the court failed to rehabilitate; and youth charged with serious, violent crimes granted bail too easily and released to the street" (Bruser 2011: A1).

Criminology classes, like the one you are taking, that encourage critical thinking about crime and society are not the typical way people obtain knowledge about violence. Since most of us receive our information and develop our understanding about the criminal justice system and violent crime rates from the news media, stories such as the one penned by Bruser have predictable results. Citizens are not hearing stories about young offenders who stay out of the YCJS, or the ones who are repeatedly victimized by violence. They may instead receive the message that the youth justice system is not protecting them from the most notorious offenders and that it might in fact be making matters worse. Presenting the anomalous as the norm has dramatic consequences. Fear of crime is often amplified out of proportion to relative risk of victimization (Sprott and Doob 1997). Such discourse furnishes negative evaluations of the system, which becomes coupled with a distrust of youth justice officials and demands for more intrusive and corrective punishments.

In such an ethos, "facts" of crime and to what extent crime rates are increasing or decreasing seem irrelevant. A manufactured perception that crime is escalating provides sufficient justification for ratcheting up more and stronger punitive youth justice interventions. When violent crime regularly appears in newspapers and political debate, the public typically wants something (read: deliver more pain to offenders) to be done. In the interest of garnering political favour, federal officials are delighted to oblige such calls to employ the criminal justice arm of the state. We saw this with Bill C-10, now the *Safe Streets and Communities Act* (2012), which implemented stronger measures against youthful offenders. However, when we speak in popular discourse, the face of the other who is on the receiving end of these policies is obscured. Those who are victimized by violence are often silenced.

Youth are active agents in constructing and creating their worlds in a context they did not design, one rife with systemic inequalities and race, class and gender hierarchies. This backdrop forms the environment in which young men and women make choices and create identities. While every youth makes his or her own choices about how they operate in their world, the control s/he has over structural-level circumstances during childhood and into adolescence is limited. These pathways — toward violence or non-violence — dramatically influence possibilities, constraints and life chances. In what follows, we place the spotlight on circumstances of structural inequality and situational violence in an effort to humanize the young people most directly impacted.

STRUCTURAL INEQUALITY AND SITUATIONAL VIOLENCE I: GIRLS AND VIOLENCE

Who experiences the most personal victimization? Does it surprise you that among all age groups, females between fifteen and nineteen have the highest victimization rates in

Canada (McClelland 2003)? The United Nations has declared violence against women one of the most egregious forms of discrimination and abuse of human rights. Men are overwhelmingly the perpetrators of violence against women. According to the United Nations, females also suffer consequences on sexual and reproductive health, including forced and unwanted pregnancies, unsafe abortions and resulting deaths, traumatic fistula and higher risks of sexually transmitted infections (STIs) and HIV (UNFPA 2012: 7).

Every minute of every day, a Canadian woman or child is sexually assaulted (Canadian Research Institute for the Advancement of Women 1998). Canada's only national Violence Against Women Survey (VAWS) found that half of Canadian women (51 percent) have experienced at least one incident of physical or sexual violence since the age of sixteen (Statistics Canada 1993).[1] VAWS also found that 16 percent of women had experienced physical or sexual violence in a dating relationship since the age of sixteen. Among college students, physical and sexual coercion rates are even higher, ranging from 20 percent to 30 percent. Adolescent females had rates of dating violence that were almost ten times higher (38 per 100,000 people) than for adolescent males (4 per 100,000 people).

Women and adolescent girls worldwide are the primary targets of gender-based violence (GBV). Bloom argues that GBV refers to violence that results from normative role expectations associated with the male and female gender that are fueled by unequal power relations between men and women (2008: 14). For example, spousal violence in Canada resulted in the largest number of convictions involving violent offences between 1997 and 2002. Men were responsible in 90 percent of these cases (Statistics Canada 2006). This trend continues. Women and girls suffer exacerbated consequences of violence (compared to what men endure), given gender discrimination, women's lower socio-economic status and the fact that as a group, women have fewer options and resources that enable them to avoid, escape or redress abusive situations. Women are three times more likely than men to be physically injured by spousal violence, five times more likely to require medical attention and five times more likely to fear for their lives (Statistics Canada 2005). In another study, the severity of this violence, or the threats experienced by women, is so serious that 38 percent of women feared for their lives compared with 7 percent of men (Statistics Canada 2000).

Violence against girls and women reflects, reinforces and reproduces the sexual double standard. The sexual double standard operates as a process of "tacitly encouraging male sexual exploration and promiscuity and punishing female sexuality" (Minaker and Hogeveen 2009: 131). A longstanding dichotomy for females functions more insidiously and invariably than for males. The good girl/bad girl dichotomy operates when individuals and institutions interact with females on the socially constructed basis of "what kind of girl" they are presumed to be. In *Youth, Crime and Society* we argue the following:

> [The]pervasiveness of sex-typing in textbooks, on television, in magazines, and in video games (among other places [on-line, for example]), the persistence of tired ideologies (from "good daughterhood to good motherhood"), and the accompanying gendered practices (employment hierarchies, wage differentials, etc.,) all suggest that gender stratification is being reproduced in the next generation of adolescents. (Minaker and Hogeveen 2009: 126)

Currie and Kelly identify a central contradiction that girls today are forced to endure. Young women navigate the boundaries between the demands that girls "must be pretty" but not "self absorbed"; they must be attractive to boys but not seen as "slutty";

they must be popular among the "right people" but not a social "snob"; independent but not a "loner," and so on (2006: 4). Their study found the widely popular dictum that "girls can be anything" butted up against their acute awareness "that girls, unlike boys, are judged by their looks, are emotionally rather than physically expressive, and not physically adept, and can be 'ruined' by sexually demeaning labels." Girls' character is questioned when they go too far toward either pole of the Madonna/whore dichotomy: "Girls who are too overtly sexual are labeled 'sluts.' Indeed, girls' subculture is rife with examples of punishing females for being 'bad girls'" (Minaker and Hogeveen 2009: 131).

Understanding girls *as girls* and boys *as boys* means locating their lives, experiences and behaviour in a socio-cultural, political and historical context. This violence is not only gendered but also situated in racialized and class-based terms. Among the most socially excluded and victimized in Canada are the thousands of Indigenous girls and young women who have been murdered or are still missing from Vancouver's Downtown Eastside, Highway 16 (known as the "Highway of Tears") and across the prairies since the 1970s.

Yet, the physical and sexual victimization of girls and women is frequently masked by public unease about violence done by females and efforts to demonize girls as being as mean and malicious as boys/men. In the 2014 collection *Faces of Violence*, Canadian feminist scholars and activists examined the subtle and explicit forms of violence young women and girls encounter in their lives. The essays demonstrate the complex and insidious ways that violence profoundly affects different groups of girls (e.g., Aboriginal girls, racialized newcomer girls, gay/lesbian/bisexual/transgendered girls) and shapes their experiences of girlhood. South of the border, in *Fighting for Girls*, Meda Chesney-Lind and Nikki Jones (2010) also challenge the widely accepted notion that girls are becoming increasingly more violent and contest the media "girls gone wild" panic. They present evidence of shifts in institutional responses to girls' actions and demonstrate how poor girls of colour face the most punitive consequences of the twenty-first century crackdown against girl violence. Chesney-Lind and Jones assert that our analyses of girls' violence must be contextualized in the social settings that shape girls' use of violence in response to the (potential) threat of violence and their experiences of victimization. They maintain that changes in the policing of girlhood and in girls' structural and situational circumstances explain the increase in their charges for assaults in the United States.

The most common pathway toward girls' criminalization is their victimization, which is most often at the hands of men and dominant institutions (Minaker and Hogeveen 2009). Focusing on the context of social and economic marginalization and histories of trauma reveals the unique problems that girls may be confronting when they engage in interpersonal violence. Past trauma includes high levels of violence in families, neighbourhoods and schools, settings that Chesney-Lind and Katherine Irwin (2008) argue produce girls who use violence.

The sexual double standard remains one key variable in girls' criminalization as well as their victimization. Societal agencies of care and/or control (family, school, workplaces, criminal justice system, etc.) routinely reinforce boys' dominance and girls' subordination. They do so by re-inscribing power, strength and control as masculine while reifying femininity as compliant, courteous and caring. Artz, Nicholson and Rodriquez (2005: 305) situate girls' involvement in crime in a complexity of psycho-social processes "that seem to draw in most of those who are marginalized and especially those who suffer from sexual abuse." Artz (1997) found that the girls most at risk for engaging in same-sex peer violence lacked self-confidence and did not perceive that their own sexual desires were valued. Instead, they saw that their sexual value was solely prized in relation to how well they satisfied males and measured up to idealized standards of femininity. Artz (1997) concludes that girls often strike out at other girls when they feel threatened in their relationships with valued males. The horizontal use of violence by girls against girls is telling of the cultural strength of patriarchy, normalizing violence against women.

A Violent Masculinity?

We cannot look at youth violence nor violence in North American society without centering a violent masculine culture. Stop for a minute to consider the following: In what ways is being male bound up with violence and physical aggression? What are the implications? Much of the anti-social and violent acts in which boys engage can be linked to attempts to express, attain, show and/or prove dominance and control over others. Dominance is a core prerogative of hegemonic masculinity (Connell 1995, 2002; Messerschmidt 2000, 2004).

Ubiquitous cultural messages across the globe not only emphasize gender *difference*, but also sustain gender *inequality*. Gender stratification and socially constructed gender differences impact and affect all youth in complex, and at times contradictory, ways. Minaker and Hogeveen (2009: 125) argue that a "gender-sensitive analysis is not simply about recognizing distinct gender identity (masculinity or femininity) or pointing to different gender roles (socialization)." This approach situates young people's lives within a structural context stratified by gender. Overt and subtle forms of patriarchy or male dominance — its institutional and interpersonal manifestations and psychological dimensions — are at work in youth violence. A case in point: gay and lesbian youth are more likely to be victims of violence than heterosexual youth (Wells 2009). We can make a link between homophobic harassment of men and boys and violence against women. Ask yourself: Why would fear of not being (perceived as) a "real man" influence a young man's choice to verbally and/or physically abuse other youth — males or females — to prove himself as powerful and gain respect? Sexism and violence is bred through cultural discourse that purports being male is antithetical to being female. Think about the worst insults used to put down boys and men. Are some of these words not euphemisms for "a woman?" What does this say about the status of women relative to men in contemporary society?

While normative expectations for behaviour and identities among youth have become more fluid and dynamic in the last several decades, research continues to demonstrate powerful gender codes that dictate appropriate conduct for boys and girls. While not all men become violent themselves, all boys in Canada are exposed to a dominant narrative that reminds them continually that being a man is defined in opposition to being (viewed as) feminine (read: inferior) and that a "real man" is tough, strong and invulnerable. Prevalent experiences of violence (e.g., homophobia, criminal violence, violence in sports) function to normalize and sustain the ideas that employing violence is part of being a real man, that women and girls are legitimate targets or that violence is an acceptable way to resolve conflict. While boys may be called upon and punished for going too far with aggression and violence, the underlying assumption that boys will and do engage in violence remains intact. What's at stake if a boy shows his vulnerability or displays a caring, loving and nurturing version of manhood? What may be at stake if more boys and men don't learn more empathetic and kinder forms of masculinity?

STRUCTURAL INEQUALITY AND SITUATIONAL VIOLENCE II: ABORIGINAL YOUTH

Young, marginalized and structurally disadvantaged populations, such as Aboriginal youth in Canada, are the most likely to be on the receiving end of punitive interventions. The same group is at the same time more likely to experience victimization from violence. Yet, political discourse, media portrayal and public paranoia about this group tends to focus on the need to control and punish over young people's needs for care and support.

Canada's history of colonization, institutional violence and racism and ongoing mistreatment of Aboriginal youth make injurious marks on many Aboriginal communities. Aboriginal youth, for their part, are overrepresented at almost all levels of the criminal, child welfare and youth justice systems. According to Carrington et al. (2004), young Aboriginal people are more likely to be denied bail, to spend more time in pre-trial detention and to be charged with multiple offences. Former judge Ted Hughes aptly summarized the enormity of the situation for Indigenous children in care:

> Of the more than 9,700 children in the care of child welfare agencies in Manitoba, more than 80 per cent are aboriginal, and the numbers have been increasing since 1997 ... In Winnipeg, 83 per cent of the 5,291 children in care in 2012 were aboriginal. (cited in Meissner 2014)

It is paramount that we stop to consider frightful cuts to social welfare spending in recent years. It would appear that any and all programs that do not purport to deliver pain are expendable to governments intent on solidifying their economic standing and attracting foreign investors. In Alberta, at a time when numbers of homeless peoples are swelling in the major centres of population, the affluent province has continued to cut funding for social programs intended to ameliorate social suffering. The 1990s saw substantial spending cuts in all ministries, including health and education. Social assistance rates were reduced by nearly 20 percent over three years (Milke 2012).

These funds have not been recovered. In April 2014, the Provincial Government decided to axe the only probation positions intended to aid Aboriginal youth. The Director reports: "The program has run extremely well, there's been no issues with the program ... Without any notice, justification, explanation, the money was just cut." A social worker lamented: "I honestly believe it's the difference between success and failure for some of these [Aboriginal] kids" (CBC 2014).

In Canada, the face of the marginalized other is indigenous children and youth. The marginalized other is usually voiceless, powerless, and a member of a group that is most vulnerable to social circumstances, which limits or excludes them from meaningful participation in social life. Policing is one of the primary and most heavily funded resources in Canada for dealing with marginalized youth and others who are systematically excluded. Services and institutions that exact surveillance and inflict control over marginalized youth always seem to be available. Sam, who is a director of a large inner-city agency, relays his frustration over how his organization lacks the necessary funding to do effective, helpful work and to provide his staff with much-needed health benefits:

> Our staff doesn't get shit and they have no benefits ... We don't have any fucking money. Our budget is like 300,000 dollars, Buddy. The police of Edmonton get a budget of 120 million dollars last year; that is escalating every year by 10 percent. And more cops are being hired. (Hogeveen 2010)

Understandably, he is irritated by what he considers an egregious oversight. While count-less dollars are increasingly being pumped into police and correctional budgets to bolster coercive interventions, we are witnessing social services and non-profit agencies being forced to locate alternate funding sources. What are the implications of this trend for a young person's capacity to care for her/himself?

Perhaps more troubling, and again lost in most of the public discourse, is the fact that Aboriginal youth are also overrepresented as victims of violence (Brzozowski et al. 2006). All too often kids' care needs are not met. As a group, Aboriginal youth experience an increased vulnerability to physical and sexual abuse (harm by others) as well as suicide attempts, poor health, drug and alcohol abuse (self-harms) (Minaker and Hogeveen 2009: 153). "Before killing oneself or harming others, disenfranchised youth experience feelings that no one cares, loves them, or is there to help" (Minaker and Hogeveen 2009: 161). We are careful here not to paint a portrait of Aboriginal families as violent places. The systemic and historical context of expressions of violence within Aboriginal com-munities is eclipsed by individualized depictions of "bad parenting" in media and public discourse. We learn violence through the experience of it as much as we learn how to care through caring relationships.

Let's reflect on the following illustration of the kind of violence one Aboriginal boy was forced to endure. At the time of our interview, Damon was thirty-two, struggling to cut ties with his former gang and with the violence that enveloped his life. Damon was frequently forced to hear his mother being sexually assaulted. "I remember times where him and my mom would be in the bed. My mom would be sleeping and he would rape her while she was passed out. I didn't say anything 'cause I was just young, right? You know, I had to sit there and listen to it because I was too scared to get up." Such occasions psychologically scarred Damon. These events had another effect — they taught him lessons not only in violence, but in being a man. He learned that conflicts could be easily settled through violence. At the time, for him, women who did not comply could be beaten into submission. Damon came to understand how power, control and intimidation could all be won through violence. Violence became a tool used upon him and one he used.

Damon also came to understand violence as a resource for accomplishing mascu-linity, a *violent* masculinity (Messerschmidt 2005). Damon's mother was not alone in suffering violence at the hands of the men in her life. Aboriginal women are not only three times more likely than their non-indigenous counterparts to experience domestic violence, but 90 percent of federally sentenced Aboriginal women have been sexually abused (Brennan 2009; Canadian Association of Elizabeth Fry Societies 2013; Amnesty International 2004). What's more, Aboriginal women between the ages of twenty-five and forty-four are five times more likely than non-Indigenous women to die as a result of violence (White Ribbon Campaign 2006).

Aboriginal children are not immune from the sexual violence experienced by their mothers. Damon, for his part, was sexually abused by several of the suitors that his mom brought to their home. One night, his mother left her current boyfriend to babysit while she went drinking at the local pub. Shortly after she had departed Damon reports that the man started "doing shit." He was deeply scarred by sexual abuse and other incidents he describes as horrific violence. Damon's story is not much different from other young victims/perpetrators of violence in that systemic forces beyond his control conditioned and contoured his life chances. For non-Indigenous youth, the root of violence may lie in poverty and/or gender inequality.

Why are Aboriginal peoples overrepresented as victims of violence and in Canada's detention centres? What happened to condition such a tragic state of affairs and experiences like Damon's? Put most simply, colonialism, and the interrelationships of poverty, gendered violence and racism. During centuries of Euro-Canadian occupation, the Indigenous peoples of Canada have been ravaged by invading armies, had their spiritual beliefs and religious systems disrupted and devalued by missionaries, been forcibly removed from land they inhabited for millennia and had their languages obfuscated by cultural imperialists (Paul 2006). Residential schools, the reserve system and intrusive state interventions are at the heart of the issue (Miller 1996; Hogeveen, 1999, 2010). The Aboriginal Healing Foundation concluded that colonialism, specifically the residential school system, bears much responsibility for the contemporary conditions. In their report on domestic violence, they maintain:

> The legacy of the residential school experience has been well documented and is clearly linked to symptoms of post traumatic-stress disorder, as well as to a wide range of social problems, including addiction and physical and sexual abuse. This body of research, theories and models all point to the same general conclusion — family violence and abuse in Aboriginal communities has its roots, at least in part, in historical trauma and in the social realities created by those historical processes. (2003: 22)

For many decades, Indian Affairs agents in collaboration with residential schools and religious officials uprooted Aboriginal children in order to inculcate Euro-Canadian ideals. Removed from their communities and obliged to renounce their former selves in favour of alien values and symbols, residential school survivors never fully recovered (Knockwood 1992). Torn from their parents and elders and forced to live at some distance from their traditional lands, their manner of being in the world was almost completely shaped by residential school officials who were notoriously physically violent and sexually abusive. In place of traditional Aboriginal values, young Indigenous peoples were taught lessons in violence and abuse. It is little wonder, then, why many Aboriginal youth inhabit a cruel and violent ethos.

Systemic inequalities of race, class and gender, and other injustices, continue while politicians, media officials and some conservative academics who engage in victim-blaming may pass violence off as simply being the result of bad individual choices made in isolated situations. Rather than making a simple *choice* of whether to employ violence — to be or not to be violent — many, but not all, Aboriginal youth are shaped almost from infancy by an immersion in a regrettably violent milieu (Minaker and Hogeveen 2009, Blackstock, Brown and Bennett 2007). Far too many Aboriginal young people struggle to find their way in the world only to be thwarted by poverty, racism, alcohol and drug abuse, misogyny and intergenerational violence, which are the current material and experiential realities of the colonial encounter (Comack et al. 2013). Damon, as we will see later in the chapter, did not become another casualty of colonialization.

PATHWAYS TO/FROM VIOLENCE: SCHOOL VIOLENCE AND BULLYING

There are many tragic brands of exclusion that happen every day all over the world in the place where children and youth spend the majority of their days — school. As we argued earlier, when it comes to understanding violence, the context, consequences and conditions under which it is exercised are important considerations. School-based violence takes many different forms, such as peer aggression and fighting, shootings and emotional abuse. In recent decades, the problem of "bullying" has caught the attention of teachers, students and parents, to varying degrees. In your mind, what meaning and strength lies behind the word "bullying" today?

In Alberta, for instance, youth report bullying as one of the most significant problems they face today. Bullying has many different connotations, meanings and reactions. Here we are referring to something more harmful than peer conflicts, which are inevitable. Bullying in North America has become socially constructed as an act of violence. Bullying involves deliberate acts of aggression, sustained over a period of time and reflects power differences. While the experience of bullying takes specific forms, according to Alberta Education (2005), schools using character education programs can employ a checklist that includes four key indicators to determine whether a behaviour is, or is not, an act of bullying: a power imbalance, an intent to harm, feelings of distress by the student who is being bullied and repetition over time.

A recent Alberta study found that over 47 percent of parents reported their child was a victim of bullying, yet one in three surveyed saw bullying as a normal part of growing up. That obviously means that two others believed the experience of being on the receiving end of aggression from peers is not normative. The Society for Safe and Caring Schools and Communities (sscs) promotes works to refocus attention and efforts on reducing bullying indirectly by helping children and youth feel safe and cared for. Dada Alice Mwemera and Ben Tsang, Youth Engagement Coordinators at sscs, explain:

> In the past, I have personally shared my concerns about bullying with an adult and their reply would often be "it will get better," "it is part of growing up," or "sometimes you just don't get along with everyone." This response made me feel powerless, as though I was being overly emotional and needed to just accept the situation.

Dada did not feel safe. Research from a multitude of social science and health disciplines tells us how important feeling safe is for a child's well-being (Shanker 2012). Attention to the social problem called bullying could be an opening for Canadians to seriously consider what we mean by safe, caring, supportive communities. When we engage children and youth in a discussion about how violence affects them we can listen to their struggles and stories of trauma.

Given what we have already said about violence, you should not be surprised to learn that bullying is gendered, and lesbian, gay, bisexual, or transgender (LGBT) youth, or LGBTQI (lesbian, gay, bisexual, transgender, questioning, intersexed), and those perceived as LGBT/LGBTQI have an increased risk of being bullied. Health Canada (2005) found sexual minorities among the most frequently targeted victims of hate-motivated violence in Canada. However, the relationship between gender, sexuality and bullying is much more complex than researchers once believed. Early scholars argued that boys were more likely to be the perpetrators and victims of direct bullying; that is, with immediate violent physicality and/or derogatory words and gestures. Girls, on the other hand, were seen as both less likely to offend and be victimized. When females were implicated in bullying behaviour, their actions were typically thought to be less physical and more indirect (e.g., spreading rumors) (Olweus 1993; Harris and Isernhagen 2003). Wendy Craig and Debra Pepler (2007), for example, assert that boys' bullying takes both direct and indirect forms, and girls' participation is not limited to relational aggression and non-physical harms.

Like their male counterparts, girls may earn status or at least "save face" through their fighting prowess. Leitz (2003), for example, found that some girls who perceived themselves as negatively "marked" by minority racial and socio-economic identity maintained their status in school by not backing down when confronted by peers and/or when they were angry with teachers. Girls may also fight out of a sense of hopelessness. Molnar, Browne, Cerda and Buka (2005), in their study of adolescent girls in Chicago, found that girls who were previously victimized, who lived in neighborhoods with a high concentration of poverty, or in places with high homicide rates, were more likely to perpetrate violence and engage in bullying behaviour.

In the wake of the tragic death of Amanda Todd in 2012, and other young girls' whose suicides have been linked to online exploitation, the devastating effects of cyber-bullying are now visible. Todd, a British Columbia teen, took her life after years of verbal abuse, bullying and online harassment. Rehtaeh Parsons' cyber-bullying suicide also made headlines across the nation. At 17, Parsons was tormented after a digital photo of her allegedly being sexually assaulted went viral. Two teens were eventually charged in the case with creating and distributing child pornography.

Cyber-bullying is a relatively newer form of bullying that has received much media and social media attention in recent years. Cyber-bullying involves using information and communication technology (email, cell phones, text messages, websites and social media) for the purpose of taunting, threatening, shaming or otherwise humiliating the intended target. New languages are emerging to describe different types of aggressive relational strategies, such as "text wars" (e.g., many people email or text a victim with negative messages). From threatening text messages to circulating private photos, many different harmful tactics are being referred to as cyber-bullying. Like bullying that takes place offline, the perpetrator intends to humiliate, ridicule, shame or otherwise cause pain. Responding to youth violence and violence against youth involves unraveling the complex meanings of violence and transforming the conditions that foster violent ways of being.

TOWARDS TRANSFORMATIVE CHANGE

Changing the landscape of violence and its dimensions of gender, race and class becomes possible when young men and women, girls and boys, are actively engaged in the process. A key component of this involves the empowerment of girls and women as well as reclaiming a safe space in which to reconstruct masculinity and dismantle privilege. While support and intervention has been directed toward women for decades, efforts aimed at prevention, awareness and education for men and boys are in their infancy. Given that the vast majority of those who perpetrate violence are males, attending to and addressing violent masculinity is paramount.

Men and boys must play a role in reducing violence and shifting cultural consciousness around masculinity (Katz 1995; Kaufman 2001). For their part, the World Health Organization and Instituto Promundo, a Brazilian non-governmental organization, has conducted the first comprehensive assessment of gender equality programs for boys and men. United around the cause of gender equality, through Instituto Promundo, Brazilian young men and women activists are speaking out against family and community violence. They analyzed evaluation data from fifty-eight projects around the world and across a wide spectrum of initiatives (e.g., gender-based violence prevention, sexual and reproductive rights). The study identified three different kinds of programming: (1) gender neutral, (2) gender sensitive and (3) gender transformative. Among these, which do you think had the highest rate of effectiveness? Gender transformative programs sought to promote equitable relationships and change gender norms and cultural expectations. These programs had a greater impact to reduce violence than programming that did not distinguish between the needs of men and women (gender neutral) or programs that recognized gender norms but did little to make change. The Mentors in Violence Prevention (MVP) in the United States was classified as both gender sensitive and transformative. MVP, created by a team led by Jonathan Katz, is a school-based violence prevention program that uses a "bystander" approach and trained mentors in secondary and post-secondary schools. MVP was rated as promising for overall effectiveness (MVP 2001). The only Canadian program that made the list was Caring Dads, a group education program aimed at urban, "high-risk fathers," men at risk of neglecting and abusing their children. Overall, the program's effectiveness was rated unclear. Although it was aimed at gender transformation, its outcomes were limited (Scott et al. 2004). If Canadians are truly serious about reducing or even eliminating violence and providing children and youth with the care and support they need to develop and grow, much more needs to be done.

Knowledge mobilization is another strategy. For example, Promoting Relationships and Eliminating Violence Network (PREVNet) is aimed at addressing children's aggression, bullying, and victimization and is led by psychologists Wendy Craig and Debra Pepler. PREVNet is a collaborative and interdisciplinary initiative, bringing together researchers from Canadian universities and national organizations.

The extent to which young people are empowered to confront bullying depends on a variety of factors, and many initiatives are being developed across North America to address it. Many projects follow anti-bullying strategies like Bullying Ends Here <www.bullyingendsshere.ca>. Others are community-based and are often situated where emphasis is placed on fostering a pro-social and positive school climate. Integrated approaches to prevent, address and/or reduce bullying tend to be focused on developing strategies and partnerships with schools, parents, police and community members (i.e., <www.erasebullying.ca>. Still other initiatives are grassroots and emerge ad hoc in response to local adversity, such as what happened at a Nova Scotia school.

In 2007, a grade nine student named Charles McNeill dared to arrive for the first day of school at Central Kings Rural High School in Berwick, Nova Scotia, in a pink T-shirt. He was publicly ridiculed and bullied for his audacity. McNeill was singled out, hurt and harmed. In response, his friends David Shepherd and Travis Price organized a protest where they distributed pink tank tops to everyone who would wear one. On this day, a sea of pink happy faces welcomed McNeill to school. The emphasis on standing united together builds community and can help reinforce what is acceptable school conduct. The pink shirt has come to symbolize citizens taking a stand against bullying in Canada. Price has since co-founded the Pink Shirt Movement <www.pinkday.ca>, which is spreading with teens across the country. On February 26, 2014, Pink Shirt Day, the Edmonton Oilers wore pink jerseys in support of anti-bullying initiatives and in support of the Nova Scotian teen. Pink could also be seen scattered throughout the halls and classrooms of Edmonton's schools. Nevertheless, a school that participates in Pink Shirt Day but fails to educate students about the problem or does little to reinforce values of caring, respect and unity is simply inadequate and disingenuous.

Mainstream interventions in the area of youth violence can be characterized as anti-violence strategies. These initiatives are aimed at stopping or minimizing the problem. For example, in January 2014 the Canadian government launched a national campaign to stop cyber-bullying. Phase one, called Stop Hating Online, features television and online ads showing how cyber-bullying often crosses the line into criminal activity. This dominant approach emphasizes the violent offender and the need to change his/her problematic behaviour, usually through punishment and/or other community-based options. A case in point is the Conservative Government's Bill C-13, colloquially known as the cyber-bullying bill. The *Protecting Canadians from Online Crime Act* or "cyber-bullying bill," which was tabled in 2013, would make it illegal to send "intimate images" without consent. (Note: the Act's first incarnation was Bill C-30, the *Protecting Children from Internet Predators Act*.) That *something* is being done to address the violence youth experience is encouraging. However, more innovative (and non-state) programs are required to attack this form of systemic violence. A criminal justice–oriented focus on controlling violence is a tactic with limited potential to realize meaningful change because it does not address the root conditions of violence. Punitive sanctions against perpetrators will not necessarily make victims feel safer or more cared for, nor will it help them to heal. There is much more transformative potential outside of criminal law and punitive extra-legal consequences that emphasize the value of human caring, interdependence and community.

AMELIORATION, CARE AND SOCIAL JUSTICE

To ameliorate means to make something better. Youth, parents, teachers, social workers, politicians, policy-makers, practitioners and academics have all taken on the challenge to make the problems associated with violence for youth better. There are few points of convergence about *how* to accomplish this task and on exactly what we mean by "better." As this chapter has shown, the relationships between youth, violence and society are complex, significant and contradictory. All violence (emotional, psychological, physical and institutional) causes pain (Minaker and Hogeveen 2009: 288). Towards ameliorating the conditions that produce and reinforce violence — the social aspects discussed above, which involve (but are not limited to) race, gender, class and age inequalities — we need to challenge our assumptions about violence and imagine how different kinds of social relations are possible. Doing so involves ongoing work with youth to develop meaning-ful, creative and inclusive strategies. These interventions, we argue, are not exclusively based on responding to violence or directed against "violent youth," but rather are aimed at fostering caring relations and building social systems that offer support, compassion, direction and guidance for all children and youth.

An alternative question to "What we are trying to stop?" is "What we are trying to start?" Or, "What do youth need?" Together, what can we cultivate in order to build safer, more livable communities for children to grow and youth to thrive in? The for-mer approach is *against* violence, while the alternative one is *for* care. Put another way, rather than working to eliminate something, there is a potential for social justice in our efforts toward that which we hope to see. Namely, to cultivate care is a way of thinking (discourse) and way of being (practice).

Conceptualizing Care: A Discourse and Practice

The discourse of care has a long history with children and youth in conflict with the law and those who are marginalized by social institutions. Care is a complex set of practices, including all that humans do to "maintain, continue and repair our world so that we can live in it as well as possible ... Caring can be seen as a process of four intertwining phases: caring about, taking care of, caregiving, and care-receiving" (Fisher and Tronto 1990). In essence, care is human sustenance (Minaker 2013). Philosophically, an ethic of care in feminist writings has its roots in the work of Carol Gilligan (1982). Central to her work was a focus on our connections with (and responsibility to) others, especially for females. An ethics of care, especially feminist care ethics, has been incorporated into the ways many scholars of crime and social justice make sense of approaching violence (Noddings 1984, 2002; Ruddick 1989; Gilligan 1982; Tong 1998; Tronto 1993, 2006; Held 1995; Sevenhuijsen 2003). Pause for a moment and name some of the ways to practise care in your own community.

In approaching the problems intrinsic to and surrounding violence that we have identified in this chapter, an orientation that values care for the other is not only required but also urgently needed. A care lens provides an alternative opening for understanding and action in the area of youth violence intervention. According to Virginia Held (1995: 131), "Within a network of caring, we can and should demand justice, but justice should not then push care to the margins, imagining justice's political embodiment as the model of morality, which is, I think, what has been done." We take up Held's (1995) call for "frameworks of caring about and for one another as human beings." A framework of caring opens up critical questions such as:

- What would more just and humane environments for children and youth to learn, grow and develop look like?
- What might social engagement with the world from an ethic of care look like?
- What impact does valuing and practising care more systematically have on children and youth?

The issue for social engagement becomes how does it become possible to create more caring relations and construct new practices that offer care without conditions? We need to give special consideration to the experiences of marginalized communities, such as Indigenous youth, criminalized and victimized young women and LGBT or LGBTIQ youth. We could ask young people what these spaces and places of care (would) *feel* like. All youth are engaged in a process of becoming, yet their journeys are personal and diverse. *Feeling with* youth by recognizing their struggles with violence, supporting them as they heal from trauma, building resiliency and showing respect in our encounters with young people is how we can create caring spaces for youth to thrive. In schools, for example, pro-caring strategies are aimed at cultivating non-violent conflict resolution and creating safe learning environments. In the wider community, this work involves fostering respect, creating kinder systems and encouraging more humane ways of being with others. A care-based approach aims to humanize, heal human suffering and offer hope to victims. Just Listen to Me: Youth Voices on Violence (2004), a collaborative project based on eighty young Ontario citizens between the ages of thirteen and twenty-four, is an innovative youth-centred, experiential-based approach that recognizes the importance of listening to young people (Minaker and Hogeveen 2009: 272). In short, the youths asked to be heard. Among the main themes to emerge from their project, such as increasing involvement and engagement with young people, the one that stands out for us is the need to create a system that cares. Stephanie Ma explains:

> We need to be involved and included within the institutional hierarchy: we can help make the system more caring, respectful and humane ... youth stigmatize adults as being uncaring and "out to get them." This reciprocal treatment only helps to perpetuate negative stereotypes, creating an atmosphere of general mistrust, anxiety, and anger. (2004: 15–16)

Care-based engagements could include, but are not limited to, the following interventions:

- integrating gender issues and human rights into school policies and practices;
- creating cultures of care;
- mobilizing individuals through social media campaigns;
- providing care and counselling support and empowering youth to access such services;
- fostering a culture of non-violence;
- institutionalizing sensitization on violence against women and gender issues; and
- building partnerships and encouraging collaboration across different organizations (faith-based, community-based, school-based, non-profit, government, corporate).

Think about the work being done in your own community. Can you identify examples of any of the above interventions? For any approach to bring about meaningful change in the lives of youth, respect is crucial. Working toward a more caring and just future for youth involves creating spaces of care and community. Youth empowerment, voices and engagement are all approaches that progressive groups and organizations are employing to bring into being the value of youth inclusion. An example of an agency working with youth to bring about meaningful change is YOUCAN Youth Society in Edmonton, Alberta, and Ottawa, Ontario <http://youcan.ca/>. Youth who feel disconnected from their communities (many of whom have histories of gang involvement, child welfare and street involvement) come to YOUCAN and find — sometimes for the first time — caring adults willing to meet them where they are at. Together they work on building transformative relationships and engaging youth to make amends, take responsibility and learn positive ways to cope with stress and anger. Another illustration is the work of LOVE, or Leave Out Violence <http://www.leaveoutviolence.org/>. LOVE aims to reduce violence in young people's lives by building a team who communicate a message of non-violence. This has involved over seventeen years of work, hundreds of community safety programs in five cities, a youth-run blog, videos, leadership camps and other creative projects. Investing into these kinds of organizations and programs that aim to instill kindness and cultivate care (rather than control or inculcate against violence) would go a long way toward building safer communities. Is there public and political will to collectively organize and build more inclusive spaces for young people?

All youth have "the fundamental right to feel safe, cared for, and included in their school environments ... [and] we must support these students to move from simply trying to survive in their school, family, and community environments to a place where they can begin to thrive" (Wells 2009: 27). One way to create a caring school environment is by establishing supporting school-based gay-straight student alliances (GSAs) (Griffin et al. 2004; Lee 2002; Wells 2006). Gay-straight student alliances are relatively new to North American schools, and they originate from 1989 in Concord, Massachusetts. GSAs are "student-run and teacher-supported school-based groups that work to create safe, caring and inclusive spaces for LGBTQ students and their allies in schools" (Wells 2006: 11).

GSAs are intended to create a safe space for students to connect and support each other and communicate their feelings and experiences on sexual orientation and gender identity issues. GSAs are a relatively new phenomenon in North American schools. The first known Canadian GSA started in 1998 at Pinetree Secondary School in Coquitlam, B.C. According to Kristopher Wells, author of the Government of Alberta's new resources on homophobic and transphobic bullying and GSAs, they are "More accurately understood as one vital part of a systematic approach to reducing bullying and improving student safety and acceptance of differences" (2006: 15). These creative approaches are important, especially as children and youth have at their disposal (with technological change) new ways of engaging in violence and methods to threaten, degrade and harm. Seen differently, however, communication technologies could offer a tool for engaging in violence reduction and remediation. Like a kid can send/receive a hurtful text, s/he can also use the power of digital connection to reach out for help and/or offer support.

Violence is everywhere, but so is care. Challenging boys' dominance and girls' subordination by inscribing power evenly and socializing children to come to understand care as a human habit is central to promoting care in society. To unlearn violence, kids must learn to care. There is more work to be done to understand how best to cultivate caring relationships built on trust and respect in the lives of the most marginalized youth, like Damon, whose experiences of childhood are fraught with instability, insecurity and violence. Addressing the root conditions that reflect and reinforce a violent way of being and make violence a readily available tool is a complex undertaking. It requires fostering and learning alternative coping strategies for resolving conflict and dealing with fear and anger. While, some argue, violence is deeply embedded in our culture, our society and our psyche, others believe in the human capacity for empathy and kindness and in the power of care (Krznaric 2014). Damon was a child desperately in need of love, support and unconditional caring. While in his formative years, he learned violence as a way to survive, during his early adulthood, Damon's life began to transform as he benefitted from caring relationships. Ultimately, Damon learned how to give and receive care and became a contributing citizen and a committed advocate for young people. He deeply cares. Youth need champions of care, diversity, equity and human rights in their schools, communities and homes.

Kanawayhitowin is a Cree word that means "taking care of each other's spirit." On November 25, 2014, the Ontario Federation of Indigenous Friendship Centres (OFIFC) launched a public awareness campaign called Kanawayhitowin – Honour Life, End Violence <www.kanawayhitowin.ca>. This initiative, funded by the Ontario Women's Directorate, comes out of the Ontario Government's strategic plan to end violence against Aboriginal women and girls. The website home page welcomes you to "find out how we're taking care of our youth," and "find out how we take care to stop violence and how you can help." The material that will be used in the public awareness program outlines similar themes as we have identified in this chapter, including cyber-bullying, LGBT individuals, Aboriginal culture, men at risk and women at risk. The campaign was youth oriented and was based on input from the OFIFC Aboriginal Youth Council. The program is intended to compliment Kizhaay Anishaabe Niin: I Am A Kind Man, which works with men on developing positive, cultural ways of being and altering the cycle of violence. Both of these programs honour traditional teachings based on principles of peace, respect, love, kindness and caring.

We are social beings who hurt, harm, heal and show compassion for another's suffering. As we look to a future of what *could be,* we encourage you to examine your own relationships to violence, to care and with one other. Damon's story reminds us that there is hope.

> *Our Children are Gifts*
>
> *Do not let our children suffer from such violent ways. Creator's gifts are many and we each have been given a spirit to guide and to share as it is an honour for Creator to bestow this gift to you. We have spoken and we continue to watch over you, we are your helps from the other world, listen and we speak through others, our words will come. We as people, we as strong, strong people, will get together and look violence in the eye as we have not the hear but the strength to change our ways. As the wind blows in many directions, so do the voices of our ancestors. Let us open our hearts and souls and listen, for these voices are clear. Our ancestors speak." — Jake Thomas <http://www.kanawayhitowin.ca/>*

DISCUSSION QUESTIONS

1. Why does it matter how violence is defined and/or conceptualized?

2. How are care and violence related?

3. Why are politicians and the public preoccupied with violent youth crime despite declining rates?

4. Explain Western culture's paradoxical relationship to violence. Discuss examples of how Canadians promote and loathe violence at the same time.

5. In what ways could an orientation around human caring offer meaningful ways to address violence among youth?

GLOSSARY

Bullying: acts of aggression and violence usually between peers that involve a power imbalance, intent to harm, feelings of distress by the student who is being bullied and repetition over time.

Care: care is a human sustenance and is conceptualized broadly. It is a complex set of practices, including all that humans "do to maintain, continue and repair our world so that we can live in it as well as possible. Caring can be seen as a process of four intertwining phases: caring about, taking care of, caregiving, and care-receiving" (Fisher and Tronto 1990: 40).

Colonialism: centuries-old patterns of exclusion and intrusion into the lives of Canada's Aboriginal peoples. State and religious officials employed various tactics and strategies to disempower and inculcate Euro-Canadian cultural values and institutions into the lives of Aboriginal peoples. The lingering and continuing effects of colonialism continue to haunt all Aboriginal peoples.

Gender-Based Biolence (GBV): violence that results from normative role expectations associated with the male and female gender (e.g., women are passive and compliant, men are strong and dominant) and is fueled by unequal power relations between men and women.

Marginalization: the exclusion of racialized and impoverished groups from key segments of the social world. These groups experience inequalities that might contribute to their criminal involvement.

Marginalized Other: refers to groups and/or individuals that are subject to othering or practices of social exclusion. Young people are marginalized as the other when they are silenced and abused. The voiceless, or the powerless in society are vulnerable to social circumstances (such as gendered violence, racism, poverty), which limits or excludes them from meaningful participation in social life.

Systemic Problems/Issues: problems embedded in the social, legal, political and economic milieu of Canadian society. Poverty, racism, sexism and colonialism are examples. These problems/issues negatively

structure life chances for marginalized and othered populations.

Violence: acts of violence involve practices used to injure, harm and inflict pain, as well as the misuse of power over another, which violates his/her rights. To understand violence, we can examine violence as rhetoric and the implications of violence.

Violent Masculinity: being "tough" is a critical component of the cultural script for boys and men in Canadian society. A "real man" is compelled to respond to violence or threats thereof with violence.

Youth: a social definition of youth extends beyond the 12–17 age range legal definition in *Youth Criminal Justice Act*. Youth includes young people in their teen years and into their mid-twenties.

SUGGESTED READINGS

Sergio Cotta, *Why Violence? A Philosophical Interpretation*, Gainsville, FL: University of Florida Press (1985).

Fran Fearnley (ed.), *I wrote on All Four Walls: Teens Speak Out on Violence*, Toronto, Canada: Annick (2004).

James Messerschmidt, *Nine Lives: Adolescent Masculinities, The Body and Violence*, Boulder, CO: Westview Press (2000).

Kevin Young, *Sport, Violence and Society*, New York: Routledge (2012).

SUGGESTED WEBSITES/VIDEOS/ACTIVIST RESOURCES

iHuman Youth Society <http://ihumanyouthsociety.org/>

YOUCAN Youth Society <http://youcan.ca/>

Jackson Katz – 10 Things Men Can Do to Prevent Gender Violence <http://www.jacksonkatz.com/wmcd.html>

Just Care, TEDx Garneau Women <http://tedxtalks.ted.com/video/Just-care-Joanne-Minaker-at-TED>.

Canadian Women's Foundation <http://www.cdnwomen.org>

Promoting Relationships and Eliminating Violence Network <http://www.prevnet.ca/>

Truth and Reconciliation Commission of Canada <http://www.trc.ca/>

National Aboriginal Circle Against Family Violence <http://www.nacafv.ca>

Justice for Girls <http://www.justiceforgirls.org/>

Sisters in Spirit <http://www.sistersinspirit.ca/>

L.O.V.E. Leave Out Violence <http://www.leaveoutviolence.org/>

NOTE

1. *The Violence Against Women Survey*, Statistics Canada, 1993. Although more up-to-date data would be preferable, no future Statistics Canada survey asked women about their life-time experience of violence. At <http://www23.statcan.gc.ca/imdb/p2SV.pl?Function=getSurvey&SDDS=3896&Item_Id=1712>.

REFERENCES

Aboriginal Healing Foundation. 2003. *Aboriginal Domestic Violence in Canada*. Ottawa: Aboriginal Healing Foundation. At <http://www.ahf.ca/downloads/domestic-violence.pdf>.

Alberta Education. 2005. *The Heart of the Matter: Character and Citizenship Education in Alberta Schools*. Alberta Education. Learning and Teaching Resources Branch. At <http://ednet.edc.gov.ab.ca/charactered/PDF/intro.pdf>.

Amnesty International. 2004. *Stolen Sisters: Discrimination and Violence Against Indigenous Women in Canada*. Amnesty International.

___. 2014. "Violence Against Indigenous Women and Girls in Canada." At <www.amnesty.ca/sites/default/files/iwfa_submission_amnesty_international_february_2014_-_final.pdf>.

Anishinabek. 2014. "Ending Violence Against Aboriginal Women and Girls Campaign Launched." November 25. At <http://anishinabeknews.ca/2014/11/25/ending-violence-against-aboriginal-women-and-girls-campaign-launched/>.

Arendt, Hannah. 1969. *On Violence*. New York: Harcourt Brace.

Artz, S. 1997. "On Becoming an Object." *Journal of Child and Youth Care* 11, 2:17–37.

Artz, S., D. Nicholson and C. Rodriguez. 2005. "Girl Delinquency in Canada." In K. Campbell (ed.), *Understanding Youth Justice in Canada*. Toronto: Pearson Education Canada.

Baron, Stephen, and Timothy Hartnagel. 1998. "Street Youth and Criminal Violence." *Journal of Research in Crime and Delinquency* 35, 2 (May): 166–92.

Berman, Helene, and Yasmin Jiwani. 2014. *Faces of Violence in the Lives of Girls*. London, ON: Althouse Press.

Blackstock, Cindy, Ivan Brown and Marlyn Bennett. 2007. "Reconciliation: Rebuilding the Canadian Child Welfare System to Better Serve Aboriginal Children and Youth." In I. Brown, F. Chaze, D. Fuchs, J. Lafrance, S. McKay and S. Thomas Prokop (eds.). *Putting a Human Face on Child Welfare: Voices from the Prairie*. Prairie Child Welfare Consortium/Centre of Excellence for Child Welfare.

Bloom, Shelah. 2008. "Violence Against Women and Girls: A Compendium of Monitoring and Evaluation Indicators." Washington, DC: USAID.

Brennan, Shannon. 2009. "Violent Victimization of Aboriginal Women in the Canadian Provinces, 2009." At <http://www.statcan.gc.ca/pub/85-002-x/2011001/article/11439-eng.htm>.

Bruser, David. 2011. "The Kids of 311 Jarvis: Kid-Glove Treatment for Young Offenders: Ontario Courts Deliver Light Sentences for Serious Crimes." *Toronto Star*, A1.

Brzozowski, Jodi-Anne, Andrea Taylor-Butts and Sara Johnson. 2006. *Victimization and Offending among the Aboriginal Population in Canada*. Ottawa: Canadian Centre for Justice Statistics.

Canada. 2012. *Safe Streets and Communities Act*. S.C. 2012, c.1 At <http://laws-lois.justice.gc.ca/eng/annualstatutes/2012_1/>.

Canada. Department of Justice. 2012. "Government of Canada Announces Coming into Force of the Violent and Repeat Young Offenders Segment of the *Safe Streets and Communities Act*." <http://www.justice.gc.ca/eng/news-nouv/nr-cp/2012/doc_32801.html>.

Canada. Statistics Canada. 2013. *Police Reported Crime Statistics in 2012*. At <http://www.statcan.gc.ca/pub/85-002-x/2013001/article/11854-eng.htm?fpv=269303#a7>.

Canada. Supreme Court. 2005. R. v. C.D.; R. v. C.D.K. At <http://scc-csc.lexum.com/scc-csc/scc-csc/en/item/2261/index.do>.

Canadian Association of Elizabeth Fry Societies. 2013. *Aboriginal Women*. At <http://www.caefs.

ca/wp-content/uploads/2013/04/Aboriginal-Women.pdf>.

Canadian Institute for Health Information. 2014. *Self-Harm and Assault: A Closer Look at Children and Youth.* At <http://www.cihi.ca/web/resource/en/pub_sum_child_injury_en.pdf>.

Canadian Research Institute for the Advancement of Women, 1998. "Fact Sheet." Extrapolated from Ontario Women's Directorate, *Dispelling the Myths about Sexual Assault.* Fact sheet, Queen's Printer for Ontario.

Carrington, Peter, Jennifer Schulenberg, A. Brunette, J. Jacob and I. Pickles. 2004. *Police Discretion with Young Offenders.* Ottawa: Department of Justice.

CBC. 2014. "Alberta Axes Probation Position Aiding Aboriginal Youth Position Eliminated to Save $80,000." At <http://www.cbc.ca/news/canada/edmonton/alberta-axes-probation-position-aiding-aboriginal-youth-1.2578349>.

Chesney- Lind, Meda, and Katherine Irwin. 2008. *Beyond Bad Girls: Gender, Violence and Hype.* New York: Routledge.

Chesney-Lind, Meda, and Nikki Jones (eds.). 2010. *Fighting for Girls: New Perspectives on Gender and Violence.* New York: SUNY Press.

Collin-Vézina, Delphine, Jacinthe Dion and Nico Trocmé. 2009. Sexual Abuse in Canadian Aboriginal Communities: A Broad Review of Conflicting Evidence. *Pimatisiwin: A Journal of Aboriginal and Indigenous Community Health* 7: 27–48.

Comack, Elizabeth, and Gillian Balfour. 2004. *The Power to Criminalize*: *Violence, Inequality and the Law.* Halifax and Winnipeg: Fernwood.

Comack, Elizabeth, Lawrence Deane, Larry Morrissette and Jim Silver. 2013. *Indians Wear Red.* Halifax and Winnipeg: Fernwood.

Connell. R.W. 1995. *Masculinities.* Cambridge, UK: Polity Press.

___. 2002. *Gender.* Cambridge, UK: Polity Press.

Cotta, Sergio 1985. *Why Violence? A Philosophical Interpretation.* Gainsville, FL: University of Florida Press.

___. 1991. "The Nihlistic Significance of Violence." In James Brady and Newton Garver (eds.), *Justice, Law and Violence.* Philadelphia, PA: Temple University Press.

Craig, W.M., and D.J. Pepler. 2007. Understanding Bullying: From Research to Policy. *Canadian Psychology* 48: 86–93.

CTV News. 2014. "Timeline: Amanda Todd Investigation." April 18. At <http://www.ctvnews.ca/canada/timeline-amanda-todd-investigation-1.1782168>.

Currie, D.H., and D.M. Kelly. 2006. "I'm Going to Crush You Like a Bug': Understanding Girls' Agency and Empowerment." In Y. Jiwani, C. Steenbergen and C. Mitchell (eds.), *Girlhood: Redefining the Limit.* Montreal: Black Rose Press.

Debord, Guy. 1970. *Society of the Spectacle.* Detroit, MI: Black and Red.

Fisher, B., and J. Tronto. 1990. "Toward a Feminist Theory of Caring." In Emily K. Abel and Margaret K. Nelson (eds.), *Circles of Care: Work and Identity in Women's Lives.* Albany: State University of New York.

Gilligan, Carol. 1982. *In a Different Voice: Psychological Theory and Women's Development.* Cambridge, MA: Harvard University Press.

Griffin, P., C. Lee, J. Waugh and C. Beyer. 2004. "Describing Roles that Gay–Straight Alliances Play in Schools: From Individual Support to School Change." *Journal of Gay & Lesbian Issues in Education* 1, 3: 7–22.

Harris, S., and J. Isernhagen. 2003. "Keeping Bullies at Bay: Ten Ways to Keep Your Students and Schools Safe." *American School Board Journal* 190: 43–45.

Health Canada. 2005. "National Clearinghouse on Family Violence: Defining Youth and Violence." At <www.hc-sc.gc.ca/hppb/familyviolence/html/nfntsyjviolence_e.html> accessed March 3, 2005.

Held, Virginia. 1995. "The Meshing of Care and Justice." *Hypatia* 10, 2: 128–34.

Hogeveen, Bryan. 1999. "An Intrusive and Corrective Government: Political Rationalities and the Governance of the Plains Aboriginals, 1870–1890." In R. Smandych (ed.), *Governable Places: Readings on Governmentality and Crime Control.* Aldershot: Dartmouth Publishing.

___. 2005. "If We Are Tough on Crime, if We Punish Crime, then People Get the Message':

Constructing and Governing the Punishable Young Offender in Canada During the Late 1990s." *Punishment and Society* 7, 1: 73–89.

___. 2007. "Youth and Violence." *Sociology Compass* 1, 2: 463–85.

___. 2010. "Finding Light in So Much Darkness": Violence, Youth and (Masculine) Subjectivities." *Juventudes, Subjetivações e Violências* 2, 1.

Indian and Northern Affairs. 2001. "A Profile from the 1996 Census." Ottawa.

Katz, Jackson. 1995. "Reconstructing Masculinity in the Locker Room: The Mentors in Violence Prevention Project." *Harvard Educational Review* 65, 2 (Summer): 163–74.

Kaufman, Michael. 2001. "Violence Against Women and the Culture of Masculinity." September. pp. 9–14.

Knockwood, Isabella. 1992. *Out of the Depths: The Experiences of Mi-kmaw Children at the Indian Residential School at Shubenacadie*. Lockeport, NS: Roseway Publishing.

Krznaric, Roman. 2014. *Empathy: Why It Matters, and How to Get It*. New York: Penguin Random House.

Lee, C. 2002. "The Impact of Belonging to a High School Gay/Straight Alliance." *High School Journal* 85, 3: 13–27.

Leitz, L. 2003. "Girl Fights: Exploring Females' Resistance to Educational Structures." *International Journal of Sociology and Social Policy* 23, 11: 15–43.

Litke, Robert. 1992. "Violence and Power." *International Social Science Journal* 132: 173–83.

Ma, Stephanie. 2004. *Just Listen to Me: Youth Voices on Violence*. Toronto, ON: Office of Child and Family Services.

Mahony, Tina Hotton. 2008. *Police-Reported Dating Violence in Canada*. Statistics Canada.

Marcuse, Herbert. 1968. "Student Protest Is Non-Violent Next to Society Itself." *New York Times magazine*, 27 October.

McClelland, S. 2003. "Sugar and Spice No More." *McLeans*, July 21.

Meissner, Dirk. 2014. "Canada Must Tackle Serious Aboriginal Child Welfare Problem: Former Judge." *CTV News*. At <http://www.ctvnews.ca/canada/canada-must-tackle-serious-aboriginal-child-welfare-problem-former-judge-1.1855709#ixzz34Ax6gVF1>.

Messerschmidt, J.W. 1995. "Men, Masculinities, and Crime." In M. Kimmel, J. Hearn, and R.W. Connell (eds.), *The Handbook of Studies on Men and Masculinities*. Thousand Oaks, CA: Sage.

___. 2000. *Nine Lives: Adolescent Masculinities, the Body and Violence*. Boulder: Westview.

___. 2004. *Flesh and Blood: Adolescent Gender Diversity and Violence*. Lanham, MD: Rowman and Littlefield.

___. 2005. "Men, Masculinities and Crime." In M. Kimmel, J. Hearn and R.W. Connell (eds.), *The Handbook of Studies on Men and Masculinities*. Thousand Oaks, CA: Sage.

Milke, Mark. 2012. "Ralph Klein's Real Record." *Calgary Herald*. At <http://www.fraserinstitute.org/research-news/news/commentaries/Ralph-Klein-s-real-record/>.

Miller, J.R. 1996. *Shingwauk's Vision: A History of Native Residential Schools*. Toronto: University of Toronto Press.

Minaker, Joanne. 2013. "Just Care." TEDxGarneau Women. December 5. At <http://tedxtalks.ted.com/video/Just-care-Joanne-Minaker-at-TEDx>.

Minaker, Joanne, and Bryan Hogeveen. 2009. *Youth, Crime and Society: Issues of Power and Justice*. Toronto: Pearson.

Molnar, B.E., A. Browne, M. Cerda and S.L. Buka. 2005. "Violent Behavior by Girls Reporting Violent Victimization." *Archives of Pediatric and Adolescent Medicine* 159: 731–39.

MVP Program. 2001. *Mentors in Violence Prevention*. Boston, Northeastern University Center for the Study of Sport in Society.

Noddings, Nel. 1984. *Caring: A Feminine Approach to Ethics and Moral Education*. Berkeley, CA: University of California Press.

___. 2002. *Starting at Home: Caring and Social Policy*. Berkeley: University of California Press.

O'Donnell, Vivian, and Susan Wallace. 2011. "Women in Canada: A Gender-Based Statistical Report: First Nations, Inuit and Métis Women. Statistics Canada." At <www.statcan.gc.ca/pub/89-503-x/2010001/article/11442-eng.pdf>.

Olweus, D. 1993. *Bullying at School: What We Know and What We Can Do.* Oxford: Blackwell.

Paul, Daniel. N. 2006. *We Were Not the Savages: Collision between European and Native American Civilizations.* Halifax: Fernwood.

Perreault, Samuel. 2012. "Police-Reported Crime Statistics in Canada, 2012." Statistics Canada. At <http://www.statcan.gc.ca/pub/85-002-x/2013001/article/11854-eng.htm?fpv=269303>.

Perry, Charner. 1970. "Violence: Visible and Invisible." *Ethics* 81, 1: 1–21.

R. v. C.D. 2005.

R. v. C.D.K 2005 3 SCR 558 (Supreme Court of Canada. At <http://scc-csc.lexum.com/scc-csc/scc-csc/en/item/2261/index.do>.

RCMP (Royal Canadian Mounted Police). 2014. "Missing and Murdered Aboriginal Women: A National Operational Overview." At <http://www.rcmp-grc.gc.ca/pubs/mmaw-faapd-eng.htm>.

Roach, Kent. 2014. "Missing Aboriginal Women: More Imprisonment Is Not the Solution." *Globe and Mail*, May 27.

Ruddick, Sara. 1989. *Maternal Thinking: Toward a Politics of Peace.* Boston: Beacon Press.

Saskatchewan Provincial Partnership Committee on Missing Persons. 2007. "Final Report of the Provincial Partnership Committee on Missing Persons." At <http://www.justice.gov.sk.ca/adx/aspx/adxGetMedia.aspx?DocID=3025,104,81,1,Documents&MediaID=1615&Filename=missing-persons-final.pdf>.

Schissel, Bernard. 2006. *Still Blaming Children: Youth Conduct and the Politics of Child Hating.* Halifax and Winnipeg: Fernwood Press.

Scott, K., et al. 2004. *Caring Dads: Helping Fathers Value Their Children.* Toronto, University of Toronto.

Sevenhuijsen, Selma. 2003. "The Place of Care: The Relevance of the Feminist Ethic of Care for Social Policy." *Feminist Theory* 4, 2:179–97.

Shanker, S.G. 2012. *Calm, Alert and Learning: Classroom Strategies for Self-Regulation.* Toronto: Pearson.

Sprott, Jane, and Anthony Doob. 1996. "Understanding Public Views of Youth Crime and the Youth Justice System." *Canadian Journal of Criminology* 38, 3: 271–90.

___. 1997. "Fear, Victimization, and Attitudes to Sentencing, the Courts and Police." *Canadian Journal of Criminology* 39, 3: 275–91.

Statistics Canada, 1993. "Violence Against Women Survey."

___. 2000. "Family Violence in Canada: A Statistical Profile."

___. 2005. "Children and Youth as Victims of Violent Crime. Family Violence in Canada: A Statistical Profile." Canada: Canadian Centre for Justice Statistics.

___. 2006. "Persons Charged by Type of Offence." Canada: Statistics Canada.

___. 2011. "Family Violence in Canada."

___. 2013. "Children and Youth as Victims of Violent Crime." At <http://www.victimsweek.gc.ca/res/r56.html>.

___. 2014. "Police Reported Crime Statistics 2013." At <http://www.statcan.gc.ca/daily-quotidien/140723/dq140723b-eng.pdf>.

Strasburger, V.C., and B.J. Wilson. 2002. *Children, Adolescents, and the Media.* Thousand Oaks, CA: Sage.

Sumner, Colin. 1997. "Introduction: The Violence of Censure and the Censure of Violence." In C. Sumner (ed.), *Violence, Culture and Censure.* UK: Taylor & Francis.

Thompson, Joe. 2007. "Why Dangerous Deeds Earn Kids No Prison Time." *Vancouver Province*, May 4. At <http://www.canada.com/story_print.html?id=17f0e98d-6211-4615-8c1c-6f35a3c0160c&sponsor>.

Tong, Rosemary. 1998. *Feminist Thought: A More Comprehensive Introduction.* Boulder, CO: Westview Press.

Tronto, Joan. 1993. *Moral Boundaries: A Political Argument for an Ethic of Care.* New York: Routledge.

___. 2006. "Vicious Circles of Privatized Caring." In Maurice Hamington and Dorothy C. Miller (eds.), *Socializing Care.* Maryland: Rowman and Littlefield.

UNFPA Strategy and Framework for Action to Addressing Gender-based Violence 2008–2011. 2012. At <http://www.unfpa.org/webdav/site/global/shared/documents/publications/2009/2009_add_gen_vio.pdf>.

UNICEF 2006. *World Report on Violence Against Children*. At <http://www.unicef.org/violencestudy/I.%20World%20Report%20on%20Violence%20against%20Children.pdf>.

Wells, C. 2009. "Research Exploring the Health, Wellness, and Safety Concerns of Sexual Minority Youth." *The Canadian Journal of Human Sexuality* 18, 4: 221–29. At <http://www.sieccan.org/pdf/wellsfinal7dec24.pdf>.

Wells, K. 2006. "Gay–Straight Student Alliances in Alberta Schools, A GUIDE FOR TEACHERS." Edmonton: The Alberta Teachers' Association and Kristopher Wells.

Wells, L., L. Lorenzetti, H. Carol, T. Dinner, C. Jones, T. Minerson and E. Esina. 2013. *Engaging Men and Boys in Domestic Violence Prevention: Opportunities and Promising Approaches*. Calgary, AB: The University of Calgary, Shift: The Project to End Domestic Violence.

White Ribbon Campaign. 2006. Kizhaay Anishnaabe Niin, Community Action Kit. Ontario Federation of Indian Friendship Centres.

World Health Organization 2007. *Engaging Men and Boys in Changing Gender-Based Inequity in Health: Evidence from Programme Interventions*. Geneva.

Zahn, Margaret A., Susan Brumbaugh, Darrell Steffensmeier, Barry C. Feld, Merry Morash, Meda Chesney-Lind, Jody Miller, Allison Ann Payne, Denise C. Gottfredson and Candace Kruttschnitt. 2008. *Violence by Teenage Girls: Trends and Context*. U.S. Department of Justice Office of Justice Programs Office of Juvenile Justice and Delinquency Prevention. May.

18

LETTER FROM SASKATOON YOUTH COURT

Kearney Healy

KEY FACTS

> Unemployment among youth worldwide is rising and at an all time high.

> Regina Police Chief Cal Johnson stated that the living conditions of Aboriginal people in Regina (poverty, substance abuse, unemployment and dysfunction within families) are directly connected to Regina's position as the leader for break and enter offences.

> Seventy-five percent of youth in prison have some form of disability.

> Chief Judge Barry Stuart of the Yukon Territorial Court states that at least half of the youth in custody are mentally challenged from fetal alcohol effects and early life trauma and that the dangers of incarcerating these youth "cannot be overstated."

> Massachusetts Department of Youth Services closed down maximum-security facilities for youth inmates in 1969 and introduced community homes, prevention programs and education and work opportunities. The recidivism rates for youth dropped dramatically.

> Family Group Conferencing was introduced in New Zealand in 1989 in response to high incarceration rates. Between 1989 and 1995 the number of youth incarcerated dropped by 80 percent, with no rise in detected youth offending.

> Youth offenders who are steered away from custody and complete conditions within restorative circles are "rarely seen by the justice system again."

Sources: Schissel 2006; Green and Healy 2003; Mallea 1999.

Dear fellow students of our society:

I am writing this letter, after many years of daily observation, to tell you that in Saskatoon it seems the Emperor is naked. Punishment does not end youth crime. It may actually increase it.

Maybe these things are only true of Saskatoon, and other communities are different. Perhaps in other communities punishment diminishes crime. Let me tell you about youth in Saskatoon, and you judge if this applies to your community.

We all know that virtually everyone commits crimes at some point in their lives. As I write this I'm in youth court. Perhaps I'm using a pen provided by my employer, and if I'm using it outside my employment without permission, that would be theft under Canada's

Criminal Code. If I am doing that and it can be proved beyond a reasonable doubt, I can be found guilty. If I am guilty and you are careless about my guilt, perhaps you are guilty of possession of stolen property, because without the ink I can't argue these ideas.

So what is the difference between ourselves (those who think about our civilization and seek out others who are serious about understanding our civilization) and those who are punished for their crimes? Generally, the ordinary person in Saskatoon, when presented with this question, will try to describe crime either in terms of someone like themselves ("When I was young," or "when we were young, my father would...") or someone very unlike themselves ("I don't understand how a person could get to that point where they could..."). These seem like reasonable starting points, so perhaps we could look at youth crime and our response from these two perspectives.

Let's look at ourselves. Since we have all committed at least one crime in the past, let's, for the moment, call ourselves criminals. While no doubt a few among us might have been charged and convicted of a criminal offence, most of us weren't caught. Surely, as thinkers who are serious about our civilization, and as honest, fearless students, we can see there is essentially no difference between us in this regard. (Unless, of course, we still believe that punishment for crime improves us, which means we must admit that those of us who were caught and punished for our crimes are better people than we who were not caught.)

So the question becomes the difference between us and those in prison, and there is no doubt that there are important differences. Average Saskatoonians would object that the crimes they committed were minor, related to specific circumstances and youthful excesses, and in any case, they never (or rarely) break the law anymore because they don't like to hurt people, or they value our community, or for some other moral reason. Many theorists would argue with all these points, but could we, for the sake of our exploration, accept that the average Saskatoonian is mostly right, and let the theorists, who need to leave us at this point, go?

The average Saskatoonian would argue that if there were no chance of getting caught, well, then they would commit many more crimes. There's a difference, of course, between being caught and being punished, but the essence of the objection should be examined, at least, to understand ourselves. I assume that you are like me: I object to the notion that all that stops me from crime is that I'll be punished. In fact, I constantly try to change my behaviour so that my eccentricities are less painful for others, and so that whatever I have to offer others is made available to them, whether it's pounding nails to help house those without a home or going to meetings to try to develop a community strategy to end homelessness. These are parts of the same reason we don't commit crimes that would injure our community. You too probably feel this way, or I suspect you wouldn't be reading this far.

Let's assume we are different from the average Saskatoonian because our interests are in this field as opposed to, say, curling, or snowmobiling, or gardening, whatever. Ah, but that's the problem, you may say. Just because you can gather together a group of people who are driven, for whatever personal reasons, to consider society and crime, and just because generally people like us do like to modify our behaviours so that our relationships, from familial to social, constantly move forward to greater harmony, doesn't mean that everyone else feels that way. Well, I don't know about your community, but in Saskatoon, volunteerism is a way of life across all cultural barriers. Charities are very alive and well. The spirit of cooperation is strong. Curlers, snowmobilers and gardeners also work towards a more peaceful community.

So, once again, why don't we commit more crimes? Surely punishment is more likely to be the deterrent than the reliance on something so ephemeral and uncertain as … as … alms-giving? But is punishment the disincentive? I know it's our habit to think so, and I rely on habits to organize my life. My biggest victories are creating more effective habits. I would guess that you do that too. I read detective fiction, which has as its implicit belief that criminals will always get caught (Wile E. Coyote never gets the Road Runner, Tom never catches Jerry) because the criminals are not very smart (like Wile E. Coyote, like Tom, they never learn from their mistakes). Youth crime in Saskatoon fits into the Wile E. Coyote category. It's amazing how poorly thought out it is.

But let us ask ourselves, does this describe us? Are we unable to learn from our mistakes? Is the average Saskatoonian able to learn from his or her mistakes? Surely that does not describe us. Surely we would be quite capable of committing crimes to our benefit, safe in the knowledge that it's as likely that we would be struck by lightning as that we would be caught. Crime is such a broad category that perhaps some of us are still committing crimes now, and we feel quite safe. If we examine the closed-custody facilities and the jails of Saskatoon and find mainly the poorly educated and almost never the reasonably well-educated, resourceful, well-adjusted, thinking person, then we know that some force other than punishment keeps us criminals at bay. Since we could out-think and out-plan those who would catch us (and some of us possibly still do), then there must be something else that determines our actions. Crime can include my use of this pen, but we are quite capable of stretching our tale.

Just a minute, you might say — what force? Could we hold that question until we look at the second half of the average Saskatoonian's defence of the theorists who may have already put this down? The average Saskatoonian said, "I don't understand how someone could do something so terrible." Note the need to underscore the difference that implies a divide, a gap, in social or moral understanding. Let us criminals take a walk down to the closed-custody facility for youth in Saskatoon, called Kilburn Hall. We won't be staying long, not overnight, probably not even for a meal. That's the first thing we should notice. We're not going to live there. In Saskatoon, the next thing you'd notice is that all those who have to stay are very young (this is a youth facility) and that they are almost all of Aboriginal descent. Some days, many days, they all are of Aboriginal descent.

Many people in Saskatoon, nurses in hospitals, for example, will tell you that they can predict the children who will have trouble in school and are likely to end up in youth facilities. Others, like schoolteachers of the early grades will tell you that they have similar powers. They probably do. When you speak to these children about their early child-hoods, or when you speak to those involved in their early lives, you are struck by the trauma you'll find. You'll hear of children alone, children abused, children huddled while violence rages around them, constant moving, constant racism, constant failing in school.

Indeed, if you speak to the guards either here at the facility or in the lock-up behind youth court, many of them will say it's the parents who belong in jail, not these kids. That, of course, is the age-old chicken-and-egg problem, not the least of which is the 14-year-old in closed custody who is pregnant and wants to keep her baby. That this is true is no revelation; other pages in this book speak eloquently of these facts. The purpose of this letter is to say that in Saskatoon, in this closed facility, in Kilburn, the Emperor Punishment has no clothes.

So I'm noticing that you are looking a little shaken by these kids. That's okay. Everyone feels bad. What's that? You say if they quit committing crimes their lives could get bet-ter. The person next to you argues that this place is *better* for a lot of these kids. Maybe you're both sort of right, maybe a little wrong. Let's stop for a moment and ask why our community picks this place, jail, as an answer to crime. But, someone says, don't crime and punishment go together? Everybody says so. Why, just the other day Saskatoon's newspaper quoted Osama bin Laden; he wanted the Danish cartoonists turned over to him for "trial and punishment." Clearly most people agree that crime and punishment belong together. Who needs to look behind that formula? Wouldn't we be better off without trials and lawyers so that punishment became more automatic? Maybe we could have mandatory sentences to make sure criminals got enough punishment.

Enough punishment to do what? Well, the theory is that people are kind of like bookkeepers, a person who sits in their office or some quiet place and calculates something like this. If I commit such-and-such a crime, the chances of getting caught are x, the benefit to me of committing a crime is y and the benefit of getting caught is z, so clearly x plus z is less than y, so I benefit in doing crime. Solution? Make x, your chance of being caught, and more importantly, make z, the cost of crime, more expensive (i.e., harsher punishment). And what's the gold standard in punishment? Jail, of course. It is sometimes called the economic model of crime response. All you do is make crime too painful (i.e., expensive) for there to be any benefit.

So you know the theory, but you still feel bad for these kids. You wonder why: I think it is because you have a good heart and you suspect that these kids don't have such a clear balance sheet. They've already experienced so much pain from babyhood on. Maybe, you think, it's time to work on the happy, successful side of the balance sheet. Well you're not alone in thinking like that.

This facility's workers, over a period of time, took a bold step. They questioned every youth in the facility as to his or her position in school. They discovered that not one child in Saskatoon's closed-custody facility had been in school when they were arrested. Furthermore, they discovered that before being arrested, these children, or youth, if you will, had not been in school for an average of two years. The average age was approximately fifteen.

You'll notice that the conversations among the young people will often veer to their family's failures (a good disclosure, think the guards and therapists), the bad teachers, bad neighbours, strangers, abusive common-law partners to their mothers. They're encouraged to get it out. Alone they come to the obvious conclusion: they can only rely on each other day after day. And who is to say they're wrong?

We can leave youth jail now — oh, just a minute! Here's a worker who is doing a risk assessment on these youth. Risk assessments, in Saskatchewan, are examinations of such things as a kids' contact with police, their school experience, their family, how they spend their leisure time, who their friends are and what contact their friends have with criminal justice, whether they have an alcohol or drug problem and whether their attitudes and opinions are consistent with those of people who commit crimes. Some of you may think that marginalized kids would do badly on these scores, partly because of lack of money and a stable residence. I agree, but the worker explains to us that research shows that the children of the very rich seem to commit as many crimes per capita as do the children of the very poor but that their tests don't reflect poverty and racism. You have a question. How many children of the very rich are here in this youth jail? None. When was the last time such a youth was here? No one can remember. How many of these youth are children of the very poor? Almost all. Would it be fair to guess that maybe the worst criminals, the children of the very rich, are dealt with in a different way? A way that involves improving their life circumstances? Not in a financial way, perhaps, but in the sense that they are taught how to see the connection between their personal success and their community's success?

So what does this mean? Remember the average Saskatoonian said, "I don't know how someone could do something like that." And clearly many Saskatoonians, and you too, no doubt see a direction here and that an objection — or better yet, an observation — is in order. It is correct to say that there are children who grow up in similar circumstances who don't commit terrible and hurtful acts, and, therefore, can this background ever be an excuse? I suppose it's possible, but after twenty years I can't say that any situation comes to mind. So it's rarely an excuse. The average Saskatoonian comes to my aid and says that they can see, though, that this helps to explain what's going on: a fair comment, so let's follow down that path and see where it takes us.

One wonders why these children/youth are not in school (or why they don't show great educational improvement when they graduate to the adult criminal justice system; jails and prisons are notorious for the low educational levels of their inmates). Isn't a necessary function of our society to educate? If all our children (or even many of our children) decided not to go to school anymore, ever, wouldn't that be a crisis? Is it not true that my responsibility to my children, to my city, to my civilization, ends with making education available for my 14-year-old child? I work with my partner to make sure my child goes to school. Given the opportunity to miss school on any given day, how many of our children would opt out? And if given the opportunity day after day, how long would it take before they would start to fall behind? Then what? Stay home? I am not talking about the failures of some parents here. I'm saying as a civilization, as a citizen of Saskatoon, we have the responsibility to see to this education; it's in our best interests to do so.

So why are these youth in Kilburn not in school? And what does that have to do with punishment for crimes (or the price of tea in China, for that matter)? Remember that we've been asked, "How could someone get like that?" How could someone get to the point where at fifteen years of age they've given up on entering the job market? Hands up all of you who think that in the twenty-first century, Grade seven, eight, nine or ten is enough education to ensure a reasonable and comfortable living. And guess what? Not one hand went up in Kilburn Hall. Not one guard, not one youth, raised their hand.

In Saskatoon I'm asked by teachers to speak to their children about the YCJA. I ask: "How many of you can imagine yourselves at, say, thirty years old, deciding that you'd like to buy a new car. I know it's better that you walk, or rollerblade, or skateboard, bike, or bus it, but you decide, for whatever reason, that you'd like to buy a new car. You've decided you'll get a job, if you don't already have one, or if you already have a job you'll be careful with spending and you'll try and save at least a down payment. You then go to the car lot, pick one out, get a loan for the rest and drive away when you're finished. Right?" In middle-class classrooms, everyone says yes. The kids in Kilburn, they all say no.

We're talking about why punishment doesn't work here. We're talking about why it may, and probably does, make it worse. You see, the children/youth in Kilburn don't believe that they have a future in the mainstream society; their only future is with each other. And they don't want to be a Wile E. Coyote or a Tom, oh no, and so their future depends on ever more effective criminality. And so, you see, the difference between us criminals and those criminals is that they are marginalized and have no hope of ending their marginalization. While we, lucky people that we are, are becoming, on the whole, ever less marginalized and as time passes ever more effective at looking after ourselves within our community.

I know all that, says the average Saskatoonian, and I must say it took you a long time to get there, but so what? Crimes must be punished, or else there'll be more. We can't reward criminal behaviour; that'll only encourage more. We must discourage it. Ah yes, but what discourages crime? Is it the fear of punishment that keeps us from staying awake all night with a gun, waiting for the graffiti artist who painted our building or who painted some other building, you know, just to scare him or her? Really, the chance of getting caught can be extremely small.

No, it's many reasons. Moral reasons are very important, but for a moment let's look at another reason. Who really wants to change their life that much? In this extreme example you have to get a gun and bullets so that it can't be traced back to you. Even the research in how to do such a thing can't be traced back to you.

Let's recap — everyone commits crimes, so we can't divide ourselves simply on that basis. We aren't deterred from crime because of punishment alone, because we are quite capable of committing crimes and never being caught. We don't commit crimes because we want to live a better life tomorrow than today, if at all possible. Youth who are in custody for their crimes are different from the rest of us in that not only do they normally come from terrible circumstances, but they've also given up on their future, as evidenced by not going to school. So what are the punishment fans not telling us?

I would suggest, then, to my ordinary Saskatoon friend that the answer seems clear. I would say that each young person who is in custody for her or his crimes is there because of a path, so to speak, that they are on. That path is one of growing discouragement; the people there are losing hope. They are losing hope that they will be able to control their lives and get the benefits of being a well-accepted member of our society. The answer, then, I would suggest, includes, as a basic, giving whatever attention is necessary to show these young people how to succeed at being respected members of our community on terms acceptable to the youth.

That's utopian, and it's not clear, my friend says. It's expensive, it's impossible, and it takes criminals and rewards them, for crying out loud. Besides, it's likely to cause more crime because it treats criminals too well.

Let's look at the last objection first. As a parent, when I struggle with my children I use the technique of catching them when they're good. That is, I try to keep separate their mistakes (bad behaviour, if you will) and their successes. The youth who hurt others need to know that they have hurt others. They need to be encouraged to react in a positive way to the harm they have caused. It is always the moral position to correct the harms we inflict. It is meant to be an expression of dignity to acknowledge mistakes and to attempt to correct them. The tailors who persuaded the Emperor to try these fine new clothes have tried to convince us that the acceptance of guilt is to allow ourselves to be degraded. "You must sentence me to the maximum possible sentence," said Mahatma Gandhi to his judge, "because I am unrepentant and I believe in an independent India." In effect, Gandhi reversed the process. Unless they could recognize their mistake (in denying India its freedom) and correct it, they must degrade him, but Gandhi turned their attempt at degradation into a moral victory. These kids need moral victories: look at their histories.

The response to crime is one thing; the response to marginalized youth is another. The response to crime, while it must be a separate process, must never allow itself to interfere with the process of persuading people, in this case marginalized youth, not to hurt others — or to prevent crime — if you wish to put it that way. The presence of almost exclusively marginalized youth in Kilburn Hall tells us we have failed. We accepted the tailors' arguments; we responded to the crime; we did not care to use our enormous intellectual, financial and community resources to reduce further harmful behaviour. In effect, we put these youth into an environment where hopelessness becomes more real. We created more crime.

Taking youth out of hopelessness and to a state of enthusiasm for their future reduces crime. Many would say, though, that post-industrial capitalism requires a constant supply of inexpensive labour and that unemployment is a part of its structure. With the decline in the power of states as a result of the globalization of market economies, arguably, the marginalization of significant portions of the workforce is inevitable. That in some regions unemployment is coincidental with race is unfortunate and certainly not an intended result. Wow. How can someone in Saskatoon keep all that in mind?

In Saskatoon we estimate that there are about 1000 children from Grade one to Grade eleven, inclusive, who aren't in school. They've given up. We've tried to estimate what the costs are of these youth remaining out of school and with minimal chances of employment. Let's start with a couple of crimes — home break-ins and car thefts. Now, as luck would have it, my office does the defence work for almost all those charged with these offences (the police solve about 10 to 11 percent of all the break-and-enters in Saskatoon residences). We studied the relationship between school, and B&Es and car theft. We found that virtually every one of these crimes was committed by groups of youth, and these groups were either dominated by or consisted entirely of children who had lost their connection to school.

Of the 1000 children out of school in Saskatoon, there are some in a smaller group who do B&Es and car thefts; estimates vary from as few as fifty or eighty to as many as three hundred. A conversation with the appropriate people in the insurance industry reveals that it costs city insurance offices about $5 million to cover B&Es and car thefts committed by this small number of youths. The custody facilities (remember they're mainly for youth who haven't been in school for two years) cost about $4 million per year in Saskatoon, or $4,000 for every youth out of school.

The Provincial Government gives grants to the school boards of $5,000 per youth in school. If you have 1000 youths not in school, that equals $5 million not sent by the province of Saskatchewan to my city of Saskatoon. These youths, not being in school, will soon be adults not working and/or in need of social assistance. Assuming social assistance costs of over $800 per month, or about $10,000 per year for each person, and multiplying that by 1000 — it's about $10 million per year the province spends by the time these youths become adults and parents.

Youth not in school become adults not working, which means adults not purchasing from local businesses, not paying taxes and not making Saskatoon an attractive place to do business. In Saskatoon, for example, if we were to achieve a level of employment incomes for Aboriginal people that were equal to non-Aboriginal Saskatoonian incomes, the benefit would be around $250 million per year. But as the Linn Commission on Aboriginal Justice noted, an Aboriginal male youth is more likely to go to jail than to graduate from high school.

We could also look at the health costs, the value of housing, the tourism potential, whatever — the value of ending marginalization would be enormous. All that's assuming a completely amoral attitude.

Of course things can get better or they can get worse. In this case, youth in custody, we the people, us, we can make it better or worse. To take again my home city and province for example, consider this: the marginalized youth in my city and province are mostly Aboriginal youth, and most Aboriginal youth are marginalized. And on some days, sadly, virtually all the youth in our local custody facility are Aboriginal. Now think about this: 90 billion dollars.

In 2011, professor Eric Howe, an economist (he taught the present-day Premier of this province) estimated the benefit to this province of having Aboriginal people achieve educational levels equivalent to the majority of the people in this province: 90 billion dollars. That number was widely publicized, the Premier acknowledged it, not seriously contested it, and this has led to little action. Earlier, using 1990s estimates, I said that for my city of Saskatoon, the benefit would be about $250 million per year (professor Howe's $90 billion was a lifetime benefit amount, not an annual amount). Saskatoon's population is almost one-quarter of the province's population (i.e., there is about 230,000 people in Saskatoon and about 1,100,000 in Saskatchewan). The situation seems to be getting worse, as a benefit of over $80,000 to every child, senior and adult in Saskatchewan is not a matter of cash, it is a matter of will.

Sure, sure, says my gentle Saskatoonian opponent, but before we try it here shouldn't we look elsewhere? It is being tried elsewhere, and it is succeeding. Great Britain, for example, embarked on an experiment in September 1999. The country provided special funds to each family of a child disconnected from school to figure out unique ways of ensuring reconnection. A few months later, in March 2000, it cancelled the experiment. It was clear the initiative worked, and so the British Government made it permanent, expanded it and cited crime reduction as one of the benefits.

The Ford Foundation Quantum Opportunities Project enlisted, at random, twenty-five children from high-crime neighbourhoods in five different U.S. cities. The foundation provided them with caring, compassionate and consistent tutors and paid them to do community work at the rate of $1 per hour (later raised to $2 per hour) from 1989 to 1994. In addition to all the other benefits that a society can expect from better-educated youths, the arrest rate for these youths was 70 percent less than it was for others in their neighbourhood.

In Regina, a brief but brilliant experiment, the most difficult of all, involved the most marginalized youth. The youths had to go to school every day from Monday to Thursday. On Friday they became a part of a job co-op. They had a contract to valet government cars to places where the vehicles could be washed, vacuumed, given an oil change, and so on. The youth had among them amassed some five thousand convictions before they entered the experiment (indeed, most of them had an "escape lawful custody" included in their convictions). During the life of the experiment, the youth committed six new offences. Somehow, the dreamer who began it, Denis Losie, persuaded the youths to begin a pension plan. Then the program ended. We could walk around Saskatoon. I could show you these same kids working on art, or on computers, or on their drama skills, or on repairing bicycles, or on their paddling strokes and their wilderness skills, or on their bank accounts, in schools, in homes, in groups — youth who have a community of growth, hope and dignity are abandoning crime shamelessly.

So what I want to tell you is that we're working too hard, we're running too fast. What it is is that we're running on a barrel — you know, the faster we run, the faster the barrel spins. What's really happening is we're taking frustrated, isolated youth with little hope and treating them to more isolation, more frustration, and giving them reasons for hopelessness. What if traditional justice and restorative justice, if punishment and rehabilitation, if shame and reintegration, if crime control and due process were all only parts of the puzzle? What if our youth criminal justice system has a basic structural flaw? Like a building or bridge that looks just great but once every couple of decades, the wrong combination of weather events, the wrong storm, comes along and the building or bridge collapses.

In Saskatoon, and in Saskatchewan, we incarcerate more youth (mostly Aboriginal youth) per capita than anywhere else in North America. This should be enough to cause us to re-examine our assumptions. But our demographic future is that our population will increasingly be young and Aboriginal. More and more of our population will be made up of marginalized youth (as well as adults who were marginalized as youth and are still marginalized). Remember Judge Linn's note that an Aboriginal male youth in Saskatchewan had statistically a better chance of going to jail than graduating from high school.

What if the structural defect in our thinking is trying to divide the well-being of marginalized youth charged with a crime and our social well-being? What if the structural defect is in the habit of thinking that being tough on crime means being tough on those charged? What if, with marginalized youth, being tough on them is encouraging crime? What if equality before the law is a fraud, because with marginalized youth it controverts (in the interest of being hard on offenders) their right to equality within our society? What if the addition of the concept that leading youth out of marginalization is the most effective tool for crime reduction? The price of maintaining our small slice of paradise is how we treat the weakest and poorest among us.

Not likely in my community, you say. All right, in Saskatoon we have youth committing robberies. They steal hats, sweaters and other clothes. We have thefts, often children stealing clothes, maybe junk food snacks, sometimes fruit. Forget cars: youths are wearing other people's clothes. In Saskatoon youths are dying at an alarming rate, at least my clients are. They're sick — sometimes almost every other client has kidney disease, liver disease, Hep C, HIV or diabetes.

Every indicator we have to measure happiness — such as health, an okay place to live, friends and family doing well, having the possessions you need, having enough money to look after yourself and, most importantly, having some sense that your life can be better — these young people we call criminals don't have it.

The study of crime has been taken over by the Emperor's sycophants. They ask us to examine details, pieces of the puzzle. They say don't look up. They say don't ask why, after hundreds of years of crime and punishment, we haven't moved forward. Why must we get into our most pretentious clothes, hold ourselves a little more tensely and pontificate that it's more complicated than connecting youth with caring, compassionate and consistent tutors who are dedicated to making their lives better? How dare we dodge the question by saying that this is too complicated, that it requires too great a reorientation of too many government agencies, too many businesses, that it is too big a change for lawyers, police and judges? How dare we take refuge in hopelessness and then condemn those who live in hopelessness?

So thank you for hearing me out. I know that you're a busy person who is worried about much more than just youth crime and what it means. I hope this letter finds you in good health and that all your families, friends and loved ones are all happy and healthy. I hope that you enjoy your studies and that you have great success. I am sure that people who know you expect great things from you and, while you'll be your own person, that they will have great pride in your accomplishments. Someday you'll look back and you'll see that you made contributions to our community that gave you a sense of real accomplishment. I hope your children, if you have any, grow strong and full of hope for their futures. But most of all I hope that one day we'll meet and we can laugh about the darker days, when the Emperor had no clothes.

Sincerely,

Kearney Healy

DISCUSSION QUESTIONS

1. If you were to set out to create a society, what role would you give to criminal law?

2. If a society is structured so that almost all people born to a certain race (or races) or a certain class will never be able to enjoy the full benefits of that society, can the criminal law be based on equality?

3. Assume that one of the primary purposes of criminal law is the prevention of serious harm. However, not all cases of serious harm or even death are considered to be criminal. This is true even when the deaths and injuries are caused by human interaction, and even when a decision is made knowing that it could well result in deaths. How would you decide when an act is criminal and when it must be permitted?

4. In your life, do you find that the threat of punishment governs your ordinary choices? Do you think businesses should use punishment more often with their employees and customers?

5. When Erik Nielsen was the deputy prime minister (to Brian Mulroney), he was asked to examine the federal civil service to find ways of making it more efficient. He reported that, with business, the least effective method of changing behaviour in a positive way was punishment. If that is true for business, do you think that punishment is more effective with children who are poor, subjected to racism or who come from broken homes?

GLOSSARY

YOA/YCJA: in Canada, youth between twelve and eighteen years old are charged as youth in the YOA. In April 2003, the *Young Offenders Act* {YOA} was replaced by the *Youth Criminal Justice Act* (YCJA). One of the goals of the YCJA is to reduce "the over reliance on incarceration for non-violent young persons" (from the Preamble to the YCJA).

SUGGESTED READINGS

"The Effects of Punishment on Recidivism," Public Safety and Emergency Preparedness Canada (2002), at <http://publicsafety.gc.ca/res/cor/sum/cprs200205_1-en.asp> accessed July 2007.

Thomas Gabor, *Everybody Does It!* Toronto: University of Toronto Press.

Barry Holman and Jason Ziedenberg, "Dangers of Detention: The Impact of Incarcerating Youth in Detention and Other Secure Facilities," Justice Policy Institute Report, at <http://www.justice-policy.org/reports_jl/11-28-06_dangers/dangers_of_detention_report.pdf> accessed July 2007.

REFERENCES

Green, R.G., and K. Healy. 2003. *Tough on Kids: Rethinking Approaches to Youth Justice.* Saskatoon: Purich Publishing.

Mallea, Paula. 1999. *Getting Tough on Kids: Young Offenders and the "Law and Order Agenda."* Winnipeg: Canadian Centre for Policy Alternatives-Manitoba.

Schissel, Bernard. 2006. *Still Blaming Children: Youth Conduct and the Politics of Child Hating.* Halifax: Fernwood Publishing.

INDEX